OCA: Oracle Application Server 10*g* Administration I Study Guide

Exam # 1Z0-311

D1807744

OBJECTIVE	CHAPTER
Oracle Application Server Key Components and Features	
Describe the solution areas addressed by Oracle Application Server	1
Describe the key components of Oracle Application Server	1
Analyzing Oracle Application Server Architecture	
Explain the different installation options for Oracle Application Server	1
Explain the installation dependencies of Oracle Application Server components	1
Installing OracleAS Infrastructure	
Define the installation requirements for OracleAS Infrastructure	2
Describe OracleAS Infrastructure installation types	2
Install OracleAS Infrastructure	2
Start and stop OracleAS Infrastructure	2
Installing OracleAS Middle Tier	
Describe the Oracle Application Server 10*g* Middle Tier installation types and their requirements	2
Perform preinstallation tasks	2
Install the middle tier with Portal and Wireless installation type	2
Verify completion of the installation	2
Access the installed OracleAS middle-tier components	2
Using Oracle Application Server Management Tools	
Start and stop Application Server Control	3
Access OracleAS Component pages of the Application Server Control	3
Start and stop an OracleAS instance or a component using Application Server Control and Oracle Process Monitoring and Notification interface (opmnctl)	3
Use dcmctl utility to obtain configuration information	3
Managing the Oracle Internet Directory	
Explain Directory and LDAP concepts	9
Describe Oracle Internet Directory (OID)	9
Explain Oracle Internet Directory architecture	9

Sybex®
An Imprint of

WILEY

OBJECTIVE	CHAPTER
Start and stop Oracle Internet Directory processes	9
Identify various OID command-line tools	9
Connect to and disconnect from the Directory by using Oracle Directory Manager	9
Managing and Configuring Oracle HTTP Server	
Explain the Oracle HTTP Server processing model	4
Describe the Oracle HTTP Server modules	4
Specify the server and file locations for Oracle HTTP Server (OHS)	4
Control the number of processes and connections, manage network connection for OHS	4
Configure and use OHS log files	4
Configuring Directives and Virtual Hosts	
Describe the configuration directories and their scope	4
Describe the process of merging containers and contents	4
Configure directories and enable directory indexes	4
Describe the process of setting up virtual hosts	4
Use configuration directives such as Option, Alias, and Script Alias	4
Managing and Configuring OracleAS Web Cache	
Start, stop, and restart OracleAS Web Cache	5
Change passwords for administrative users and listener ports	5
Specify site-to-server mappings	5
Create and configure caching rules	5
Set up basic invalidation mechanism	5
Set up expiration rules	5
Configure access and event logs	5
Obtain basic performance statistics	5
Managing and Configuring OC4J	
Create OC4J instances	7
Start and stop OC4J instances	7
Enable or disable application startup	7
Configure OC4J Instance Properties	7
Configure web site and JSP properties	7
Edit OC4J configuration files	7

Exam objectives are subject to change at any time without prior notice and at Oracle's sole discretion. Please visit Oracle's website (`www.oracle.com`) for the most current listing of exam objectives.

OBJECTIVE	CHAPTER
Managing the OracleAS Portal	
Describe OracleAS Portal Administrative Services	6
Describe tools to monitor the OracleAS Portal instance	6
Manage OracleAS Portal users, groups, and schemas	6
Administer the portlet repository	6
Perform export and import of portal content	6
Configuring OracleAS Portal	
Describe OracleAS Portal configuration tasks	6
Configure the Self-Registration feature to enable users to create their own portal accounts	6
Configure OracleAS Portal for WebDAV	6
List the configuration modes of the Oracle Portal Configuration Assistance (OPCA)	6
Configure Language support	6
Configure the OracleAS Portal instance dependencies by using the Portal Dependency Setting file	6
Deploying J2EE Applications	
Deploy Web applications to Oracle Application Server	7
Configure data sources to be used with OC4J	7
Provide necessary mappings for an Oracle database	7
Deploy J2EE applications	7
Deploy and register web providers	7
Configuring Oracle Application Server Components in OID	
Describe identity management	9
Explain the default Identity Realm	9
Describe the OracleAS Administration Model	9
Explain application-specific access control	9
Manage users and groups	9
Describe the relationship between OracleAS Portal and Oracle Internet Directory	9
Identify OracleAS Portal entries in the directory	9
Configure OID settings in OracleAS Portal	9
Managing Access Using Delegated Administration Service	
Explain the DAS Architecture	10
Describe how DAS works	10

Sybex®
An Imprint of

OBJECTIVE	CHAPTER
Start and stop DAS	10
Access DAS home page	10
Use OID Self Service Console	10
Manage user entries using DAS	10
Manage group entries using DAS	10
Create Identity Management Realm	10
Access DAS from OracleAS Portal	10
Administering the OracleAS Single Sign-On Server	
Describe OracleAS Single Sign-On server components	10
Explain OracleAS Sign-On server authentication flow	10
Manage and configure OracleAS Single Sign-On server	10
Administer partner and external applications	10
Monitor OracleAS Single Sign-On Server	10
Access OracleAS Single Sign-On server from OracleAS Portal	10
Securing OracleAS Components Using SSL	
Explain Oracle wallet manager functionality	8
Manage wallets	8
Upload and download wallets	8
Manage user certificates	8
Manage trusted certificates	8
Enable Oracle HTTP Server, SSO, Web Cache, and Portal to Use SSL	8
Managing and Configuring OracleAS Certificate Authority	
Explain Public Key Infrastructure	8
Describe Oracle Public Key Infrastructure Management Tools	8
Describe OracleAS Certificate Authority	8
Explain OracleAS Certificate Authority Architecture	8
Access OCA Administration Pages	8
Access OCA User Pages	8

Exam objectives are subject to change at any time without prior notice and at Oracle's sole discretion. Please visit Oracle's website (`www.oracle.com`) for the most current listing of exam objectives.

OCA

Oracle® Application Server 10*g* Administration I

Study Guide

OCA
Oracle® Application Server 10*g* Administration I
Study Guide

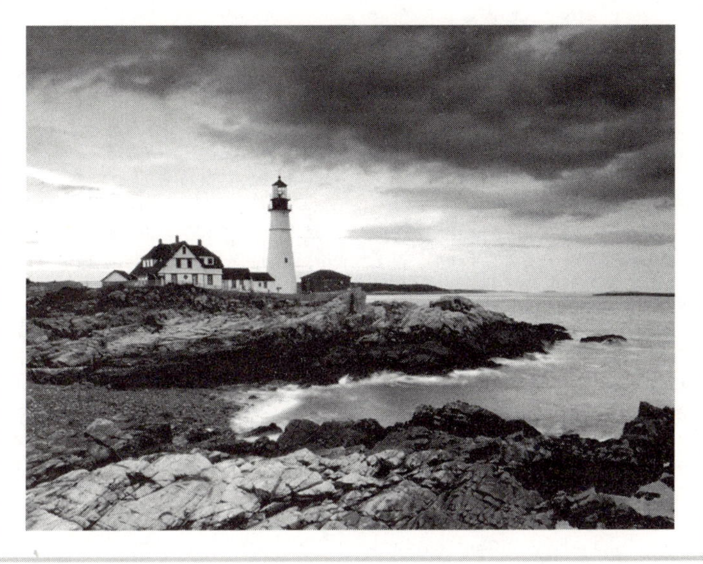

Bob Bryla

April Wells

Wiley Publishing, Inc.

Acquisitions Editor: Jeff Kellum
Development Editor: Toni Zuccarini Ackley
Technical Editor: Joe Johnson
Production Editor: Tim Tate
Copy Editor: Judy Flynn
Production Manager: Tim Tate
Vice President and Executive Group Publisher: Richard Swadley
Vice President and Executive Publisher: Joseph B. Wikert
Vice President and Publisher: Neil Edde
Media Development Specialist: Kit Malone
Book Designers: Judy Fung and Bill Gibson
Compositor: Craig Woods, Happenstance Type-O-Rama
Proofreader: Ian Golder
Indexer: Ted Laux
Cover Designer: Ryan Sneed

Copyright © 2006 by Wiley Publishing, Inc., Indianapolis, Indiana

Published simultaneously in Canada

ISBN-13: 978-0-471-78757-0
ISBN-10: 0-471-78757-4

No part of this publication may be reproduced, stored in a retrieval system or transmitted in any form or by any means, electronic, mechanical, photocopying, recording, scanning or otherwise, except as permitted under Sections 107 or 108 of the 1976 United States Copyright Act, without either the prior written permission of the Publisher, or authorization through payment of the appropriate per-copy fee to the Copyright Clearance Center, 222 Rosewood Drive, Danvers, MA 01923, (978) 750-8400, fax (978) 646-8600. Requests to the Publisher for permission should be addressed to the Legal Department, Wiley Publishing, Inc., 10475 Crosspoint Blvd., Indianapolis, IN 46256, (317) 572-3447, fax (317) 572-4355, or online at http://www.wiley.com/go/permissions.

Limit of Liability/Disclaimer of Warranty: The publisher and the author make no representations or warranties with respect to the accuracy or completeness of the contents of this work and specifically disclaim all warranties, including without limitation warranties of fitness for a particular purpose. No warranty may be created or extended by sales or promotional materials. The advice and strategies contained herein may not be suitable for every situation. This work is sold with the understanding that the publisher is not engaged in rendering legal, accounting, or other professional services. If professional assistance is required, the services of a competent professional person should be sought. Neither the publisher nor the author shall be liable for damages arising herefrom. The fact that an organization or Website is referred to in this work as a citation and/or a potential source of further information does not mean that the author or the publisher endorses the information the organization or Website may provide or recommendations it may make. Further, readers should be aware that Internet Websites listed in this work may have changed or disappeared between when this work was written and when it is read.

For general information on our other products and services or to obtain technical support, please contact our Customer Care Department within the U.S. at (800) 762-2974, outside the U.S. at (317) 572-3993 or fax (317) 572-4002.

Wiley also publishes its books in a variety of electronic formats. Some content that appears in print may not be available in electronic books.

Library of Congress Cataloging-in-Publication Data is available from the publisher.

TRADEMARKS: Wiley, the Wiley logo, and the Sybex logo are trademarks or registered trademarks of John Wiley & Sons, Inc. and/or its affiliates, in the United States and other countries, and may not be used without written permission. Oracle is a registered trademark of Oracle Corporation and/or its affiliates. All other trademarks are the property of their respective owners. Wiley Publishing, Inc., is not associated with any product or vendor mentioned in this book.

10 9 8 7 6 5 4 3 2 1

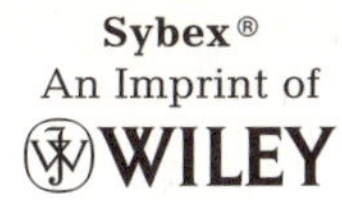

To Our Valued Readers:

Thank you for looking to Sybex for your Oracle Application Server 10*g* Administration I exam prep needs. We at Sybex are proud of our reputation for providing certification candidates with the practical knowledge and skills needed to succeed in the highly competitive IT marketplace. Certification candidates have come to rely on Sybex for accurate and accessible instruction on today's crucial technologies and business skills.

Just as Oracle is committed to establishing measurable standards for certifying Oracle Certified Associates (OCAs) and Oracle Certified Professionals (OCPs) by means of the Oracle Application Server 10g Administration I certification, Sybex is committed to providing those individuals with the knowledge needed to meet those standards.

The authors and editors have worked hard to ensure that this edition of the *OCA: Oracle Application Server 10*g *Administration I Study Guide* you hold in your hands is comprehensive, in-depth, and pedagogically sound. We're confident that this book will exceed the demanding standards of the certification marketplace and help you, the OCA and OCP certification candidate, succeed in your endeavors.

As always, your feedback is important to us. If you believe you've identified an error in the book, please send a detailed email to `support@wiley.com`. And if you have general comments or suggestions, feel free to drop me a line directly at `nedde@wiley.com`. At Sybex we're continually striving to meet the needs of individuals preparing for certification exams.

Good luck in pursuit of your Oracle Application Server 10*g* Administration certification!

Neil Edde
Vice President & Publisher
Wiley Publishing, Inc.

To Ems, Cully, and my Honey
—Bob Bryla

To my husband, Larry; my totally odd son, Adam; and my very hip daughter, Amandya.
—April Wells

Acknowledgments

I would like to thank all the folks at Wiley who made this a most enjoyable and rewarding experience, including Jeff Kellum, who reinforced my attention to detail. Thanks go to April for not letting me write too many of these chapters myself. Thanks also to Toni Ackley, who filled in the gaps from my college writing courses, and to Joe Johnson for his insightful comments and suggestions.

This book wouldn't be possible without the love and support from my family throughout the long nights and weekends when I still managed to find time to help the kids with the homework and continue the two-week-long Monopoly game. I loved every minute of it.

Thanks also to my professional colleagues, both past and present, who provided me with inspiration, support, and guidance and pushed me a little further to take a little risk now and then, starting with that math teacher in high school, whose name eludes me at the moment, who introduced me to computers on a DEC PDP-8 with a teletype and a paper tape reader.

—Bob Bryla

I would like to thank my agent, Carole McClendon, for being there to support me and for helping me to help Bob. It has been an adventure. Thanks, too, to Bob for helping me through the rough spots and for being king of the screen shots. I don't know what I would have done without your help. To all of the people at Wiley, thank you for letting me be a part of this and for being such a supportive team.

To my family: Larry, you are always supportive and my biggest cheering section. Without you I would not have had the confidence to get this far. Adam and Amandya, we have had to get creative in our pursuit of the elusive Renaissance Faires and in finding time to spend just being together. But in the end, I hope that you will remember not only that I kept my nose to the keyboard, but that I was able to show you that dreams can come true if you want them badly enough.

To the people at Corporate Systems who allowed me to cut my teeth on the installation we did, a big thanks to you. Without that adventure, this one would not likely be possible.

—April Wells

Contents at a Glance

Contents

Introduction

There is high demand for professionals in the information technology (IT) industry, and Oracle certifications are the hottest credentials in the database world. You have made the right decision to pursue an application server certification because obtaining and keeping your Oracle certification current will give you a distinct advantage in this highly competitive market.

Most readers should already be familiar with Oracle and do not need an introduction to the Oracle database world and, more recent, the Oracle application server world, of which the database is just one of many components. For those who aren't familiar with the company, Oracle, founded in 1977, sold the first commercial relational database and is now the world's leading database company and second-largest independent software company, with revenues of more than $10 billion and serving more than 145 countries.

Oracle databases and middleware are the de facto standard for large Internet sites, and Oracle advertisers are boastful but honest when they proclaim, "The Internet Runs on Oracle." Almost all big Internet sites run Oracle databases and some component of Oracle Application Server. Oracle's penetration of the database market runs deep and is not limited to dot-com implementations. Enterprise resource planning (ERP) application suites, data warehouses, and custom applications at many companies rely on Oracle. The demand for Database Administrators (DBAs) and Application Server administrators remains higher than ever, even during weak economic times.

This book is intended to help you obtain your Oracle Application Server 10*g* Administrator Certified Associate certification, clearing the way for you to pursue an Oracle Application Server 10*g* Administrator Certified Professional certification. Using this book and a practice Application Server environment, you can learn about the most important and most used components of Oracle 10*g* Application Server and pass the 1Z0-311 Oracle Application Server 10*g*: Administration I exam.

Why Become an Oracle Certified Associate?

The number one reason to become an Oracle Certified Associate (OCA) or to maintain an OCA certification is to gain more visibility and greater access to the industry's most challenging opportunities. Oracle certification is the best way to demonstrate your knowledge and skills in Oracle Application Server environments. The certification tests are scenario based and multiple choice, which is the most effective way to assess your factual knowledge, hands-on expertise, and critical problem-solving skills.

Certification is proof of your knowledge and shows that you have the skills required to support Oracle core Application Server products. The Oracle certification program can help a company to identify proven performers who have demonstrated their skills and who can support the company's investment in Oracle technology. It demonstrates that you have a solid understanding of your job role and the Oracle products used in that role.

OCAs and Oracle Certified Professionals (OCPs) are among the best paid employees in the IT industry. Salary surveys consistently show the OCA and OCP certifications to yield higher salaries than other certifications, including Microsoft, Novell, IBM, and Cisco.

So, if you have a solid practical background as an application server administrator and you're ready to get your Oracle 10*g* Application Server Certified Associate certification, this book is for you!

Oracle Certifications

Oracle Application Server certifications follow a track that is oriented toward a job role. There are database administration, application developer, and web application server administrator tracks. Within each track, Oracle has a three-tiered certification program:

- The first tier is the Oracle Certified Associate (OCA). OCA certification typically requires you to complete one exam in a proctored environment.
- The next tier is the Oracle Certified Professional (OCP), which builds upon and requires an OCA certification. The additional requirements for OCP certification are an additional proctored exam and a hands-on classroom course.
- The third and highest tier is the Oracle Certified Master (OCM). OCM certification builds upon and requires OCP certification. To achieve OCM certification, you must attend two advanced Oracle Education classroom courses (from a specific list of qualifying courses) and complete a two-day practicum exam.

In addition to this three-tier approach, Oracle provides upgrade paths from previous versions of Oracle as well as special accreditations that you can attach to your OCP certification.

The material in this book will address only the Oracle 10*g* Application Server certified associate track and the exam 1Z0-311 Oracle Application Server 10*g*: Administration I. Other Sybex books at `www.sybex.com` can help students new to the DBA world prepare for the database-related exams: OCA exam 1Z0-042 Oracle Database 10*g*: Administration I and OCP exam 1Z0-043 Oracle Database 10*g*: Administration II. See the Oracle website at `www.oracle.com/education/certification` for the latest information on all of Oracle's certification paths along with Oracle's training resources.

Oracle Application Server 10*g* Administrator Certified Associate

The role of the application server administrator has become a key to success in today's highly complex application server environments. The best administrators work behind the scenes but are in the spotlight when critical issues arise. They plan, create, and maintain the application server environment and ensure that it is available for the business. They are always watching each application server component for performance issues and to prevent unscheduled downtime. The administrator's job requires broad understanding of the architecture of Oracle Application Server and expertise in solving problems.

The Oracle Application Server 10*g* Administrator Certified Associate certification is a streamlined, entry-level certification for the application server administration track and is required to advance toward the more senior certification tiers. This certification requires you to pass one exam that demonstrates your knowledge of Oracle basics:

- 1Z0-311 Oracle Application Server 10*g*: Administration I

This exam is offered at a Sylvan Prometric facility.

Oracle Application Server 10*g* Administrator Certified Professional

The OCP tier of the application server administration track challenges you to demonstrate your continuing experience and knowledge of Oracle technologies. The Oracle Application Server 10*g* Administrator Certified Professional certification requires achievement of the Administrator Certified Associate tier, as well as passing the following exam at a Sylvan Prometric facility:

- 1Z0-312 Oracle Application Server 10*g*: Administration II

In addition, the OCP candidate must take one instructor-led in-class course from the following list:

- Oracle Application Server 10*g*: Administration I
- Oracle Application Server 10*g*: Administration II
- Oracle Application Server 10*g*: New Features for Administrators
- OracleAS ProcessConnect 10*g*: Integrate Applications

Oracle Application Server Certified Master

The Oracle Application Server 10*g* Administration Certified Master is the highest level of certification that Oracle offers. To become a certified master, you must first achieve both Certified Associate and Certified Professional status, then complete two advanced instructor-led classes at an Oracle education facility, and finally pass a hands-on, two-day exam at Oracle Education. The classes and practicum exam are offered only at an Oracle Education facility and may require travel. More details on the required coursework will be available in late 2006.

Oracle Exam Requirements

The Oracle Application Server 10*g*: Administration I exam covers a number of core subject areas. As with many typical multiple choice exams, there are a number of tips that you can follow to maximize your score on the exam.

Skills Required for the Oracle Application Server 10*g*: Administration I Exam

To pass the Oracle Application Server 10*g*: Administration I exam, you need to master the following subject areas in Oracle Application Server 10*g*:

- Understanding the Architecture, Components, and Features of Oracle Application Server
- Installing the Oracle Application Server Infrastructure
- Installing the Oracle Application Server Middle Tier
- Using Oracle Application Server Management Tools
- Managing the Oracle Internet Directory
- Managing and Configuring Oracle HTTP Server
- Configuring Directives and Virtual Hosts

- Managing and Configuring Oracle Application Server Web Cache
- Managing and Configuring OC4J
- Managing and Configuring the OracleAS Portal
- Deploying PL/SQL, J2EE, and CGI Applications
- Configuring Oracle Application Server Components with OID
- Managing Access Using Delegated Administration Services
- Administering the OracleAS Single Sign-On Server
- Securing OracleAS Components Using SSL
- Managing and Configuring OracleAS Certificate Authority

Tips for Taking the OCA Exam

Use the following tips to help you prepare for and pass the exam.

- The OCA exam contains about 55 to 80 questions that must be completed in 90 minutes. Answer the questions you know first so that you do not run out of time.
- Many questions on the exam have answer choices that at first glance look identical. Read the questions carefully. Do not just jump to conclusions. Make sure that you clearly understand exactly what each question asks.
- Most of the test questions are scenario based. Some of the scenarios contain nonessential information and exhibits. You need to be able to identify what's important and what's not important.
- Do not leave any questions unanswered. There is no negative scoring. After selecting an answer, you can mark a difficult question or one that you're unsure of and come back to it later.
- When answering questions that you are not sure about, use a process of elimination to get rid of the obviously incorrect answers first. Doing this greatly improves your odds if you need to make an educated guess.
- If you're not sure of your answer, mark it for review and then look for other questions that may help you eliminate any incorrect answers. At the end of the test, you can go back and review the questions that you marked.

Passing Scores

The 1Z0-311 Oracle Application Server 10*g*: Administration I exam is a single set of questions with two different question types—basic and mastery. As we are writing this book, the passing score for the basic section is approximately 70 percent, and for the mastery section, it is 55 percent. Please download and read the Oracle 10*g* certification candidate guide before taking the exam. The basic section covers the fundamental concepts and the mastery section covers more difficult questions, mostly based on practice and experience. You must pass both sections to pass the exam. The objectives, test scoring, number of questions, and so forth are listed at `www.oracle.com/education/certification`.

Where Do You Take the Administrator I Exam?

The 1Z0-311 Oracle Application Server 10*g*: Administration I exam is available at any of the more than 900 Sylvan Prometric Authorized Testing Centers around the world. For the location of a testing center near you, call 1-800-891-3926 or go to `www.prometric.com`. Outside the United States and Canada, contact your local Sylvan Prometric Registration Center.

Here are some things to keep in mind when registering for a proctored Oracle Certified Associate exam at a Sylvan Prometric test center:

- Determine the number of the exam you want to take; for the Administration I exam, it is 1Z0-311.
- Register with Sylvan Prometric online at `www.prometric.com` or in North America, by calling 1-800-891-EXAM (1-800-891-3926). At this point, you will be asked to pay in advance for the exam. At the time of this writing, the exams are $125 each and must be taken within one year of payment.
- When you schedule the exam, you'll get instructions regarding all appointment and cancellation procedures, the ID requirements, and information about the testing-center location.

You can schedule exams up to six weeks in advance or as soon as one working day before the day you wish to take it. If something comes up and you need to cancel or reschedule your exam appointment, contact Sylvan Prometric at least 24 hours or 1 business day in advance.

What Does This Book Cover?

This book covers everything you need to pass the Oracle Application Server 10*g*: Administration I exam. Each chapter begins with a list of exam objectives.

Chapter 1 Discusses the architecture of Oracle Application Server 10*g* along with an introduction to several different installation options.

Chapter 2 Shows in detail the installation steps for an infrastructure and middle-tier installation, as well as the requisite postinstallation tasks. We also provide an overview of how to use Oracle Application Server Control to maintain and monitor all components.

Chapter 3 Discusses the various management tools you use to maintain, monitor, and configure all Application Server components. The management tools fall into two broad categories: Oracle Application Server Control tools and command-line tools.

Chapter 4 Shows you how to manage the various components of Oracle HTTP Server and gain an understanding of the contents of the configuration files, as well as learn how to manage client connections and use the server logs. In addition, we will provide a detailed discussion of HTTP server directives and how to create a virtual host.

Chapter 5 Explains the OracleAS Web Cache architecture and how to administer Web Cache. We will also show you how to configure listening ports, configure site definitions, create caching rules, and analyze event logs.

Chapter 6 Discusses OracleAS Portal configuration and management. We show you how to manage OracleAS Portal using AS Control and Administrative Portlets and how to manage Portal users and groups. Also included are the configuration tasks you need to perform on a daily or periodic basis.

Chapter 7 Shows you how to deploy and configure several types of applications, including PL/SQL applications, CGI applications, J2EE applications, and others. In addition, we show you how to create, enable, and configure OC4J instances.

Chapter 8 Focuses on application server security. In the first half of the chapter, we review the configuration tasks for OracleAS Certificate Authority (OCA), including how to create, manage, and revoke certificates. In the second half of the chapter, we discuss SSL concepts and how SSL is used in OracleAS.

Chapter 9 Discusses the Oracle Identity Management architecture and how to enable Oracle Internet Directory (OID) synchronization within the OracleAS Portal component. Finally, we discuss the LDAP components within OID and how to manage them using both AS Control and command-line tools.

Chapter 10 Covers two separate security components of OracleAS: Single Sign-On Server (SSO) and Delegated Administration Services (DAS). We review the SSO administrative tasks, including how to create and administer both partner and external applications. Using DAS, we also show you how to delegate some of your administrative tasks to other administrators and even to the users themselves.

Each chapter ends with review questions that are specifically designed to help you retain the knowledge presented. To really nail down your skills, read and answer each question carefully.

Appendix A In this appendix, we'll show you how to configure `mod_rewrite` to allow you to redirect your site's URLs without changing the URLs your customers or clients use to access your web site. Since `mod_rewrite` uses Unix regular expressions extensively, you must understand how regular expressions work; therefore, we'll first give you an introduction to regular expressions with plenty of examples.

Appendix B If you're familiar with previous releases of Oracle Application Server, this appendix will give you a good overview of what has changed between Release 1 and Release 2, primarily in the area of database infrastructure.

Appendix C To make your entire Oracle Application Server environment even more robust and available, you should move your infrastructure's database to a RAC environment. This appendix will show you how to create an OracleAS Metadata Repository in a new database.

Appendix D Another key to high availability in your Oracle Application Server environment is making sure your environment is backed up on a regular basis. Appendix D will give you the basics of backing up and restoring your OracleAS environment with examples of each.

How to Use This Book

This book can provide a solid foundation for the serious effort of preparing for the Oracle Application Server 10*g* OCA exam. To best benefit from this book, use the following study method:

1. Take the assessment test immediately following this introduction. (The answers are at the end of the test.) Carefully read over the explanations for any questions you get wrong, and note which chapters the material comes from. This information should help you plan your study strategy.
2. Study each chapter carefully, making sure that you fully understand the information and the test objectives listed at the beginning of each chapter. Pay extra close attention to any chapter related to questions you missed in the assessment test.
3. Complete all hands-on exercises in the chapter, referring to the chapter so that you understand the reason for each step you take. If you do not have an OracleAS installation available, be sure to study the examples carefully. Answer the review questions related to that chapter. (The answers appear at the end of each chapter, after the review questions.)
4. Note the topics of the questions that confuse or trick you, and review the sections of the book that cover those topics.
5. Try your hand at the bonus practice exam that is included on the CD that comes with this book. The questions on this exam appear only on the CD. This will give you a complete overview of what you can expect to see on the real test.
6. Remember to use the other products on the CD included with this book. The electronic flashcards and the Sybex Test Engine have been specifically designed to help you study for and pass your exam. The electronic flashcards can be used on your Windows computer or on your Palm device.

To learn all the material covered in this book, you'll need to apply yourself regularly and with discipline. Try to set aside the same time period every day to study, and select a comfortable and quiet place to do so. If you work hard, you will be surprised at how quickly you learn this material. All the best!

What's on the CD?

We have worked hard to provide some really great tools to help you with your certification process. All of the following tools should be loaded on your workstation when you're studying for the test.

The Sybex Test Engine for Oracle Application Server 10*g* Certified Associate Preparation

The Sybex Test Engine prepares you to pass the 1Z0-311 Oracle Application Server 10*g*: Administration I exam. In this test, you will find all of the questions from the book, plus two additional bonus exams that appear exclusively on the CD. You can take the assessment test, test yourself by chapter, take the practice exams that appear in the book or on the CD, or take an exam randomly generated from all of the questions.

Electronic Flashcards for PC and Palm Devices

After you read the *Oracle Application Server 10*g *Administration I Study Guide*, read the review questions at the end of each chapter and study the practice exams included in the book and on the CD. But wait, there's more! Test yourself with the flashcards included on the CD. If you can get through these difficult questions and understand the answers, you'll know that you're ready for the exam.

The flashcards include hundreds of questions specifically written to hit you hard and make sure you are ready for the exam. Between the review questions, practice exams, and flashcards, you should be more than prepared for the exam.

*Oracle Application Server 10*g *Administration I Study Guide* in PDF

Sybex is now offering the Oracle certification books on CD so you can read the book on your PC or laptop. It is in Adobe Acrobat format. Acrobat Reader 7 is also included on the CD. This will be extremely helpful to readers who fly or commute on a bus or train and don't want to carry a book, as well as to readers who find it more comfortable reading from their computer.

How to Contact the Authors

To contact Bob Bryla, you can email him at `rjbryla@centurytel.net`. To contact April Wells, you can email her at `awellsdba@gmail.com`.

About the Authors

Bob Bryla is an Oracle 8, 8*i*, 9*i*, and 10*g* Certified Professional with more than 15 years of experience in database design, database application development, training, database administration, and application server management. He is an Internet database analyst and Oracle DBA at Lands' End, Inc., in Dodgeville, Wisconsin.

April Wells is an Oracle Certified Professional (OCP) with over 12 years of database experience as a programmer, developer, designer, DBA, and Apps DBA. She has written numerous books on Oracle. April is currently an Apps DBA and support analyst working in Round Rock, Texas.

Assessment Test

1. At which tier do you not typically see clustering in an OracleAS environment?

   A. Database tier

   B. Web tier

   C. Middleware tier

   D. Client tier

2. The OracleAS __________________ component requires __________________ authentication to sign on to all applications.

   A. Single Sign-On, two-way

   B. Private Key Infrastructure, strong

   C. Single Sign-On, strong

   D. Directory, password

3. Which of the following components in an OracleAS deployment are not required for a user requesting a report from the database?

   A. OID

   B. BI Discoverer Viewer

   C. Oracle Database

   D. SSO

   E. Web Cache

   F. HTTP Server

   G. All of the above are required.

4. OracleAS Reports Services can build and publish reports from which of the following sources? (Choose the best answer.)

   A. Queries against an Oracle database

   B. Text files on the client PC or on a shared directory

   C. Spreadsheets

   D. Web Server log files

   E. All of the above

5. Access to which account is required to run the `root.sh` script during an OracleAS Infrastructure or OracleAS Middle-Tier installation?

   A. `oracle`

   B. `root`

   C. `oinstall`

   D. `dba`

6. What is the purpose of the TMP environment variable during an Oracle Application Server Middle-Tier installation?

   A. The TMP environment variable temporarily points to the workstation where OUI displays the installation screens.

   B. TMP points to a temporary file-based repository if no OracleAS Infrastructure exists yet.

   C. OUI writes temporary installation files to the directory specified in the TMP environment variable.

   D. OUI uses the directory specified in the TMP environment variable for swap space.

7. What does the operating system file `/etc/sysctl.conf` contain?

   A. Startup information for every Oracle instance on the host

   B. The location of OUI installer information on the host

   C. Configuration for privileged operating system users

   D. Changes to kernel parameters to support Oracle Application Server resource requirements

8. A Middle-Tier installation includes all but which one of the following components?

   A. Portal

   B. Wireless

   C. OracleAS Certificate Authority

   D. Web Cache

   E. OC4J

9. Which of the following is not a control console in an Oracle environment?

   A. Application Server Control

   B. Database Control

   C. Grid Control

   D. Middleware Control

10. The ______________ button on the Host home page initiates a text-based terminal session with the host.

    A. csh

    B. ssh

    C. Telnet

    D. ksh

    E. Host Session

11. Which of the following components are not managed by the Database Control console? (Choose all that apply.)

    A. Database

    B. ASM Disks

    C. RAC databases

    D. Host targets

    E. Log Repository

    F. All of the above are controlled by Database Control.

12. Which of the following is not an Oracle Application Server command-line tool?

    A. `emctl`

    B. `orapwd`

    C. `dcmctl`

    D. `opmnctl`

13. The core Apache HTTP server's executable code provides all of the following functionality except for which one?

    A. Directory filtering

    B. CGI processing

    C. Connection management

    D. Error logging

14. By default, what is the name of the directory that contains HTML scripts intended for web browser clients?

    A. `bin`

    B. `php`

    C. `htdocs`

    D. `Include`

15. Which of the following is not a valid parameter for the `Options` directive?

    A. `MultiViews`

    B. `All`

    C. `ExecCGI`

    D. `ServerName`

    E. `FollowSymLinks`

    F. `Indexes`

    G. `Includes`

    H. `IncludesNOEXEC`

    I. `SymLinksIfOwnerMatch`

    J. `None`

16. You can turn on or off the `Expires` header in a web document by using which of the following directives?

    A. `ExpireHeader`

    B. `ExpiresByType`

    C. `ExpiresActive`

    D. `ExpiresDefault`

17. You can administer Web Cache with all of the following tools except for which one?

    A. AS Control

    B. DB Control

    C. OracleAS Web Cache Manager

    D. The `opmnctl` command-line tool

    E. Grid Control

18. Which of the following is the name of the tag in the `webcache.xml` file that contains both the `administrator` and `invalidator` encrypted passwords?

    A. `PASSWORDHASH`

    B. `SECURITY_CONFIG`

    C. `SECURITY`

    D. `CONFIG`

19. By default, what IP addresses are allowed to access the Web Cache administrative functions?

    A. No IP addresses; at least one must be configured during installation.

    B. Only the IP address of the server running Web Cache.

    C. All IP addresses behind the firewall.

    D. All IP addresses.

20. Which of the following statistics are not on the Web Cache Performance page?

    A. Cache Hits

    B. Cache Misses

    C. Compression by File Type

    D. Compression by Size

    E. Compression by Requests

    F. Cache Errors

21. For a portal repository whose version is 10.1.4, from where must you get `ptllang.sh`?

    A. From the Metadata Repository Upgrade Assistant CD-ROM

    B. From the command line

    C. From the OracleAS Administration interface

    D. From the portal configuration interface

22. ____________________ is the configuration file that houses the portal dependencies.

   A. `dads.conf`

   B. `iasconfig.xml`

   C. `ptlconfig.xml`

   D. `oradav.conf`

23. On what maintenance interface can you find the Parallel Page Engine Service settings?

   A. Portal Configuration Page

   B. Application Server Metadata Repository

   C. Parallel Page Engine Service configuration page

   D. Application Server Portal instance home page

24. What management interface is installed automatically every time you install Oracle Application Server 10*g*?

   A. Application Server Control

   B. LDAP Server Control

   C. Portal Server Control

   D. SSL Control

   E. SSO Control

25. What two files are used for security in an OC4J instance?

   A. `server.xml`

   B. `security.xml`

   C. `jazn.xml`

   D. `jazn-data.xml`

   E. `jazn-security.xml`

26. Where can you alter the properties associated with the currently selected OC4J container?

   A. `container.xml`

   B. The Server Properties page, accessed from the OC4J Administration page

   C. The Container page, accessed from the OC4J Administration Page

   D. `dcmctl`

27. In what kind of a file is a J2EE application defined?

   A. JAR

   B. EAR

   C. WAR

   D. PLS

   E. CGI

28. With what command-line utility can you deploy J2EE applications?

 A. No command line utilities can accomplish this task.

 B. `dcmctl deployApplication`

 C. `deployApplication`

 D. `J2EEdeploy`

29. What role does OID play in managing certificates? (Choose all that apply.)

 A. Publishing issued certificates

 B. Granting certificates

 C. Revoking certificates

 D. Creating certificates

30. The ________________ server requires ________________ to provide a secure means of authenticating users uniquely to the application.

 A. Single Sign-On, certificates

 B. Private key infrastructure, certificates

 C. Private key infrastructure, Single Sign-On

 D. Private key infrastructure, LDAP

31. Through which of these components can a certificate be requested? (Choose all that apply.)

 A. OID

 B. OWM

 C. Oracle Database

 D. SSO

 E. Web Cache

 F. OCA

 G. All of the above are required.

32. Of what use is Single Sign-On to users?

 A. It provides a single point of entry into multiple applications, allowing users to remember fewer passwords.

 B. It provides users with a single place to store all of their certificates.

 C. It allows users to sign on to a single system and have all of their applications delivered to them through that single interface.

 D. All of the above.

33. What should you do before you stop an OID server instance?

 A. Make sure the OID server instance is running.

 B. Make sure you have read the manual.

 C. Make sure the OID Monitor process is running.

 D. Make sure you have a valid backup.

34. __________________ is the command that starts the OID server.

  A. `srvstrt sysadmin`

  B. `opmnctl startproc`

  C. `oractl oidctl`

  D. `oidctl oractl`

35. You should always make sure that __________________ is running before you stop the OID server instance.

  A. The OID Monitor process

  B. The server instance

  C. The Oracle database

  D. SSO

  E. LDAP

36. Whenever you install OID, what does Oracle Universal Installer install for you?

  A. All of OracleAS

  B. LDAP server

  C. Default information tree

  D. SSL

  E. SSO

37. What does the acronym DAD stands for?

  A. Database administration descriptor

  B. Database access descriptor

  C. Distributed access domain

  D. Database access domain

38. What is the main difference between a partner application and an external application?

  A. An external application does not store a cookie on the client.

  B. An external application uses SSO to authenticate the client; a partner application does not.

  C. A partner application uses SSO to authenticate the client; an external application does not.

  D. The only difference is that external applications exist on the extranet.

39. When you create a new realm, what information is not entered on the Create Identity Management Realm page?

  A. Realm description

  B. Realm contact information

  C. Realm name

  D. Product logo

  E. Realm logo

40. Which of the following statistics are not on the Single Sign-On:orasso page?

A. SSO server start time

B. Successful logins

C. Application Server version

D. Compression by size

E. Database version

F. Login failures

Answers to Assessment Test

1. D. Clustering is available for all components of an OracleAS installation, but the client web application is typically not clustered. For more information, see Chapter 1.

2. C. OracleAS Single Sign-On permits a user to authenticate explicitly once and automatically on successive connections to other data or applications granted to the user in OID. For more information, see Chapter 1.

3. G. All of the components are accessed. You send the request for the report using the BI Discoverer Viewer web client to the HTTP server, the user is authenticated and authorized using SSO and OID, and the report is generated using information from an Oracle database. If the report is not already present in the Web Cache, it is placed there for other users who need the same report. For more information, see Chapter 1.

4. B. OracleAS Reports Services can access data from nearly any source, including database queries, spreadsheets, or text files. Clients using OracleAS Reports Services have access to the same reporting capabilities as an Oracle Reports client. For more information, see Chapter 1.

5. B. The privileged account `root` is required to run scripts during an installation. The `oracle` account is the owner of the Oracle Application Server executables and configuration files; `oinstall` and `dba` are groups, not users. For more information, see Chapter 2.

6. C. OUI writes temporary installation files to the directory specified by the `TMP` environment variable and must have at least 400MB free. If the `TMP` environment variable is not set, OUI uses the `/tmp` directory. For more information, see Chapter 2.

7. D. The values in `/etc/sysctl.conf` override the default kernel parameters compiled into the operating system. The changes in `/etc/sysctl.conf` take effect at the next reboot or immediately when you run the `/sbin/sysctl -p` command. For more information, see Chapter 2.

8. C. OracleAS Certificate Authority is a component of an OracleAS Infrastructure installation only; Portal and Wireless are only part of a Middle-Tier installation. You install OC4J and Web Cache for both an Infrastructure and Middle-Tier installation. For more information, see Chapter 2.

9. D. There is no control console named Middleware Control. For more information, see Chapter 3.

10. C. The Telnet button on the Host home page initiates a terminal session to the host if the `telnet` command is available on the server. For more information, see Chapter 3.

11. F. Database Control manages all of the components listed, including the Log Repository, which is the database where Log Loader saves the components' log file entries. For more information, see Chapter 3.

12. B. You use the `orapwd` tool to create an Oracle Database password file. For more information, see Chapter 3.

13. B. CGI processing is provided by the Apache core module `mod_cgi`. For more information, see Chapter 4.

14. C. The directory `$ORACLE_HOME/Apache/Apache/htdocs` contains HTML scripts and any other web content for public consumption. For more information, see Chapter 4.

15. D. `ServerName` is a configuration directive, not a valid parameter for the `Options` directive. For more information, see Chapter 4.

16. C. The `ExpiresActive` directive turns the `Expires` header on or off in a web document. `ExpiresByType` controls expiry time by file type. `ExpiresDefault` sets a default expiry time. There is no such directive as `ExpireHeader`. For more information, see Chapter 4.

17. B. You use DB control only for database-related tasks. For more information, see Chapter 5.

18. C. The SECURITY tag contains the encrypted passwords for both the `administrator` and `invalidator` accounts in addition to the IP addresses of the hosts that are allowed to connect as one of these two accounts. For more information, see Chapter 5.

19. D. By default, the administration functions accept connections from any IP addresses.

20. C. The Performance page does not track compression statistics by file type.

21. A. A portal repository with version 10.1.4 requires `ptllang` to be run from the Metadata Repository Upgrade Assistant CD-ROM. For more information, see Chapter 6.

22. B. The `iasconfig.xml` file houses the portal dependencies. For more information, see Chapter 6.

23. C. You can find the Parallel Page Engine Service on the Application Server Portal instance home page. For more information, see Chapter 6.

24. A. The Application Server Control is a management interface that is automatically installed every time you install Oracle Application Server 10*g*. For more information, see Chapter 6.

25. C , D. `jazn.xml` and `jazn-data.xml` deal with security surrounding Java Authentication and Authorization Service (JAAS). For more information, see Chapter 7.

26. B. From the OC4J Administration page, you can access the Server Properties page, where you can alter the properties associated with the currently selected OC4J container. For more information, see Chapter 7.

27. B. Each J2EE application is defined in an Enterprise Archive (EAR) file. For more information, see Chapter 7.

28. B. `dcmctl deployApplication` is the command you use to deploy a J2EE application. For more information, see Chapter 7.

29. B, C. OID is responsible for publishing issued certificates and deleting revoked certificates. For more information, see Chapter 8.

30. B. Private key infrastructure requires the use of certificates as a means to uniquely identify a user in the system. For more information, see Chapter 8.

31. B, F. Oracle Certificate Authority (OCA) and Wallet Manager (OWM) are two locations through which a user can request a certificate. For more information, see Chapter 8.

32. A. Password security is often one of the most difficult security pieces to administer. Single Sign-On provides users with a single user ID and password to use for multiple applications. For more information, see Chapter 8.

33. C. You should always make sure that you have an OID Monitor process running before you stop the OID server instance. For more information, see Chapter 9.

34. B. `opmnctl startproc` is the command used to start the OID server. For more information, see Chapter 9.

35. A. You should always make sure that the OID Monitor process is running before you stop the OID server instance. For more information, see Chapter 9.

36. C. Whenever you install OID, the OUI installs the default information tree (DIT) so you can start using Oracle Components. For more information, see Chapter 9.

37. B. The database access descriptor is a set of values, including the hostname and port number, that specify how an application connects to an Oracle database to satisfy an HTTP request. For more information, see Chapter 10.

38. C. Partner applications use SSO to authenticate the client, and external applications store the user's credentials in OID, which passes them on to the external application when the client requests a connection to an external application. For more information, see Chapter 10.

39. D. You specify the image for the realm logo on this form and enable it, but you enable only the product logo. For more information, see Chapter 10.

40. C. The version of Application Server is not on this page. For more information, see Chapter 10.

Introducing Oracle Application Server 10*g* and Components

ORACLE APPLICATION SERVER 10*g* ADMINISTRATION I EXAM OBJECTIVES COVERED IN THIS CHAPTER:

✓ **Oracle Application Server Key Components and Features**

- Describe the solution areas addressed by Oracle Application Server
- Describe the key components of Oracle Application Server

✓ **Analyzing Oracle Application Server Architecture**

- Explain the different installation options for Oracle Application Server
- Explain the installation dependencies of Oracle Application Server components

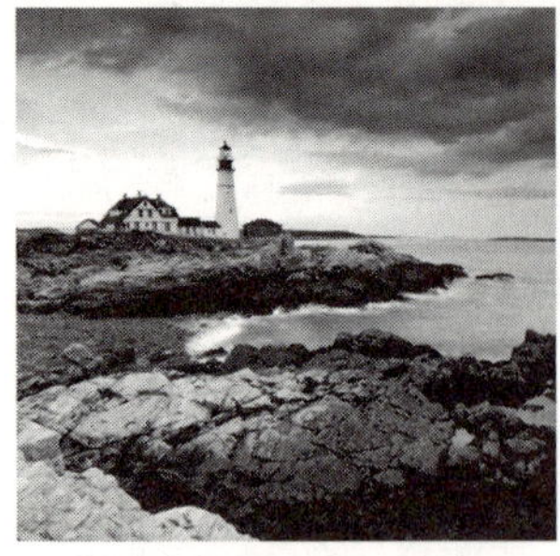

Oracle Application Server 10*g* (OracleAS) can be overwhelming at first glance; each version of OracleAS brings more functionality at every tier of an enterprise's computing infrastructure. Once you break it down into its components and how each component benefits your e-business, it becomes easier to manage and use.

In this chapter we'll cover two broad topics: understanding the key components of OracleAS and understanding how each of the components of OracleAS is installed and how they fit together in a number of common scenarios.

In the first half of this chapter, we'll start by introducing some of the terminology that you will use throughout this book to understand the architecture and components of OracleAS. We'll then present an overview of each component and its functionality. This includes one of the key management features that glues the components together in a common management interface: Oracle Enterprise Manager Application Server Control.

In the second half of the chapter, we will delve more deeply into the OracleAS architecture and give a brief overview of the different installation types; we will present the complete installation walkthrough in Chapter 2, "Performing Installation Tasks." At the end of the chapter, you will see an example of a common four-tier OracleAS deployment.

Understanding Oracle Application Server Key Components and Features

It's just as important to understand the terminology used in an OracleAS environment as it is to know each of the components available in the environment. We will present both of these topics in the following sections.

First, we'll go over some of the terms that are important in a discussion of application server components. Make sure you understand and memorize each of these terms because we will use them throughout the book.

Next, we'll review the two major OracleAS component groups, OracleAS Infrastructure components and OracleAS Middle-Tier components, and show you how the Infrastructure components provide the framework and glue that holds the Middle-Tier components together.

Finally, we'll present a high-level introduction to Oracle Enterprise Manager Application Server Control, the web-based management application that gives you complete visibility and control over your entire application server environment.

Oracle Application Server Terminology

Understanding the terminology surrounding the OracleAS components is half the battle in understanding how the components work and what each component does. In the following sections, we will present the key terms that we will use in the rest of this chapter and throughout the book.

OracleAS Installation

An *OracleAS installation* is the set of executables and configuration files you create when you install one or more OracleAS components. One physical server will host the Infrastructure components plus one or more of the other components, such as the Oracle HTTP Server, Oracle Portal, or Web Cache; because the installation process occurs twice in this scenario, you consider it two OracleAS installations.

OracleAS Instance

An *OracleAS instance* is an operational OracleAS installation that runs one or more of the OracleAS components at any tier. For example, an installation of Web Cache and HTTP Server on a single server is one OracleAS instance.

While the terms *instance* and *installation* are often used interchangeably, it is important to note that an installation is the set of files installed into an Oracle home, whereas the instance is the set of processes associated with those files.

Metadata Repository

A *metadata repository* is an Oracle database, created during the Infrastructure installation, that contains the persistent metadata required by various OracleAS instances. While some components of OracleAS can use a flat file for storing metadata, it is strongly recommended that you use an Oracle database to ensure reliability, scalability, and recoverability of the metadata.

Directory Server

A *directory server* is an OracleAS component that defines a hierarchical view of organizational data such as employees, resources, and applications. Directory servers can facilitate protection of components in the hierarchy by limiting access to particular branches in the hierarchy. Oracle's LDAP-compatible directory service is called Oracle Internet Directory, or OID.

Single Sign-On Server

An OracleAS *Single Sign-On server* (SSO server) is an OracleAS component that allows a user to authenticate explicitly one time and transparently on successive connections to other data or applications. Strong authentication is always used along with a single password to authenticate with other applications.

OracleAS Infrastructure

The OracleAS *Infrastructure* is a combination of middle-tier applications such as the Metadata Repository, Oracle Internet Directory, and Single Sign-On. The OracleAS Infrastructure components support other middle-tier applications.

OracleAS Farm

An OracleAS *farm* is a collection of OracleAS instances that share the same configuration data; this configuration can be stored in an operating system file or in the OracleAS Metadata Repository. Every farm has one and only one metadata repository.

OracleAS Cluster

An OracleAS *cluster* is a collection of application server instances within a farm that have identical configuration and application deployment. The cluster appears as a single unit to client requests and facilitates load balancing and fault tolerance. Conceptually, a clustered OracleAS component functions similarly to two or more database instances within a Real Application Clusters (RAC) environment.

Oracle Enterprise Manager 10*g* Application Server Control

Oracle Enterprise Manager 10*g* Application Server Control (OEM 10*g* AS Control) is a web application that manages individual OracleAS instances, an OracleAS farm of application server instances, or an OracleAS cluster.

Oracle Enterprise Manager 10*g* Grid Control

Oracle Enterprise Manager 10*g* Grid Control manages all network, application, and database servers in the enterprise.

OracleAS Infrastructure Components

The primary purpose of the OracleAS Infrastructure is to support middle-tier applications. It facilitates the deployment of SSO, OID, and AS clusters using Oracle Database 10g, either stand-alone or in a RAC configuration.

Whether your Infrastructure installation contains one component or all Infrastructure components, you consider the installation to be one of your managed OracleAS instances, controllable via Oracle Enterprise Manager Application Server Control.

In the following sections, I'll give a brief overview of the following OracleAS Infrastructure components:

- Oracle Internet Directory
- OracleAS Single Sign-On
- OracleAS Delegated Administration Services
- OracleAS Certificate Authority
- Oracle Database 10*g*

Oracle Internet Directory, OracleAS Single Sign-On, OracleAS Delegated Administration Services, and OracleAS Certificate Authority are the identity management components of the OracleAS distributed security solution, Oracle Identity Management.

Oracle Internet Directory

Oracle Internet Directory, or OID, is an LDAP version 3 directory service that enables retrieval of information about users, services, and applications. The directory entries are stored in an Oracle database. OID is part of Oracle's distributed security solution, *Oracle Identity Management*. OID implements three levels of user authentication:

- Anonymous
- Password based
- Certificate based using SSL to provide both authenticated access and encrypted communication

OracleAS Single Sign-On

Oracle Single Sign-On Server, or SSO, is another component of Oracle Identity Management that validates a user's credentials against OID. Once a user validates their credentials using OID, they do not have to reenter a username and password for any authorized applications.

OracleAS Certificate Authority

OracleAS Certificate Authority (OCA) generates and publishes public key infrastructure (PKI) certificates to support strong authentication between OracleAS applications and clients. OCA publishes its certificates in OID and automatically removes revoked certificates as well as certificates that have expired.

OracleAS Delegated Administration Services

OracleAS Delegated Administration Services, or DAS, enables you to store all of your user, group, service, and application data in OID while at the same time distributing the administration of that data to other administrators and even end users, depending on their job roles and capabilities.

Oracle Database

Although some components don't need a place to store metadata, and other components can store configuration information in one or more files, it is advantageous to use an Oracle database to store your OracleAS metadata. The scalability and failover capabilities of Oracle RAC mesh nicely with the scalability and failover capabilities in every other tier of an OracleAS deployment.

OracleAS Middle-Tier Components

Other Oracle middleware components outside of the Infrastructure components can be assigned to eight broad categories:

- Oracle HTTP Server
- OracleAS Containers for J2EE
- J2EE and Internet applications
- Portal

- Wireless
- Business Intelligence
- Web Cache
- E-business integration

In the following sections, I'll break down each component with a high-level overview and into bite-size pieces if necessary. In addition, I'll stress the relationship and interoperability of each component.

Oracle HTTP Server

Oracle HTTP Server (OHS) is the underlying deployment platform for all application types and services within OracleAS. It not only provides the framework for hosting static and dynamic pages, it also acts as a front end by listening for requests for OC4J applications, described in the next section. OHS is based on the open-source Apache HTTP server and supports many of the common platform-independent *modules*, also known as *mods*, such as `mod_php` and `mod_perl`. In addition, OracleAS provides a number of modules specific to OracleAS such as `mod_oc4j` and `mod_osso`. Here is a list of the most commonly used OHS modules:

`mod_php` Supports the open-source scripting language PHP (PHP: Hypertext Preprocessor) to support the dynamic generation of HTML pages

`mod_security` Protects web applications from both known and unknown attacks

`mod_fastcgi` Provides an optimized environment for persisting and running C, C++, and Java Common Gateway Interface (CGI) applications

`mod_perl` Routes requests containing Perl code to the Perl interpreter

`mod_plsql` Routes requests for PL/SQL (Procedural Language/Structured Query Language) stored procedures to one of the database servers

`mod_oc4j` Provides communication with OracleAS Containers for J2EE (OC4J), as well as providing basic load-balancing tasks for clustered OC4J instances

`mod_oradav` Supports file and database distributed authoring and versioning on the Web (Web-based Distributed Authoring and Versioning, or WebDAV)

`mod_ossl` Provides support for certificate sharing and Secure Sockets Layer (SSL) protocol, ensuring secure communications using strong encryption

`mod_osso` Forwards requests to OracleAS Single Sign-On (SSO)

The secure version of HTTP, the HTTPS OSI model Application layer protocol, uses the SSL protocol at the OSI model Transport layer to ensure security during a web session.

SSL, or Secure Sockets Layer, is a protocol developed by Netscape Corporation to transmit private documents over the Internet. The main components of SSL are a public key and a private key: everyone who will send a document knows the public key, and only the recipient of the document knows the private key.

OracleAS Containers for J2EE

OracleAS Containers for J2EE (OC4J) is a fully compliant Java 2 Platform, Enterprise Edition (J2EE) 1.3 certified server written in Java that runs on a standard Java Virtual Machine (JVM). The HTTP server module `mod_oc4j` calls one of many J2EE virtual machines that may contain one or many Enterprise Java Beans (EJB), Java Server Pages (JSPs), servlets, and database connections.

A J2EE application is an application written in Java using the J2EE application programming interfaces (APIs) and is deployed on a J2EE-compatible server. In addition, a J2EE application may span multiple tiers over several hosts.

For example, a J2EE application in an OC4J container may receive requests from a client via an HTTP request to send and receive their e-mail using the JavaMail API, display the mail message using the JSP API, and archive their e-mail to a database using the Java Database Connectivity (JDBC) API.

Do not confuse the commonly used term OC4J instances with OracleAS instances. An OracleAS instance can contain several OC4J instances. Therefore, throughout this book we will use the term *OC4J container* to refer to an OC4J instance.

For a refresher and tutorial on J2EE terminology and the latest version, see `http://java.sun.com/j2ee/1.4/docs/tutorial/doc/`.

J2EE and Internet Applications

OracleAS provides a number of toolkits and environments to make development, testing, and deployment of Internet applications easier than ever. In addition, support for integration of existing legacy PL/SQL applications into the OracleAS framework leverages existing skill sets and facilitates existing code reuse.

Here are the J2EE and Internet applications that an OracleAS developer is likely to use during the application development cycle:

- OracleAS TopLink
- Oracle JDeveloper
- Oracle Application Development Framework
- OracleAS Web Services
- Oracle XML Developer Kit
- Oracle PL/SQL Server Pages
- Oracle Content Management SDK
- OracleAS MapViewer

OracleAS TopLink

In a nutshell, OracleAS TopLink provides a framework to manage object-to-relational data persistence. Even though modern databases such as Oracle Database 10*g* can store objects natively, the current database design may be not be taking advantage of these features. Therefore, a product such as TopLink can help bridge the gap when there is a disparity in design principles, skill sets, and technologies.

In addition to object-to-relational mapping features, TopLink facilitates advanced object caching to minimize database access. Also included in the TopLink developer framework is a number of different dynamic query languages such as query by example (QBE), Java expression-based queries, Enterprise Java Bean Query Language (EJB QL), and Structured Query Language (SQL).

Oracle JDeveloper

As its name implies, JDeveloper is a J2EE development environment for business applications and web services. It includes everything that a traditional IDE has, supporting the entire development life cycle of design, edit, develop, test, debug, deploy, and optimize. It is designed to create all standard J2EE components such as applets, JavaBeans, JSPs, servlets, and EJB. It is certified for every major operating system platform, including Windows and Unix versions such as Solaris and Linux.

As are many of the OracleAS tools, JDeveloper is written entirely in Java. Unlike many other Java-based IDEs, it contains full support for Oracle SQL, PL/SQL, and Extensible Markup Language (XML). It can access the database directly and enables you to view, create, modify, and delete database objects such as tables, indexes, views, triggers, and so forth.

Oracle Application Development Framework

Oracle Application Development Framework, or Oracle ADF, is the runtime framework included with Oracle JDeveloper. It eases the partitioning of a J2EE application into the presentation tier, business tier, and integration tier.

OracleAS Web Services

OracleAS Web Services runs as servlets in an OC4J container. A *servlet* is a small Java program that runs on the web server (as opposed to the client browser) and takes client requests from the browser, generates dynamic content, and sends the response back to the browser.

OracleAS Web Services provides development and runtime support for web applications, such as generating J2EE `.ear` files and providing common functionality to other web applications using a standard interface.

Oracle XML Developer Kit

OracleAS includes the Oracle XML Developer Kit (XDK) to provide the libraries and utilities to create, store, and maintain XML-formatted data in a database or to exchange data between heterogeneous platforms and programming languages using a common format.

Oracle PL/SQL Server Pages

To leverage the existing expertise of PL/SQL programmers, OracleAS includes two tools: Oracle PL/SQL Server Pages and the Oracle PL/SQL Web Toolkit. Both tools rely on the HTTP server module called `mod_plsql` that maps client browser requests into PL/SQL stored procedures, which in turn retrieve data from one or more databases and generate HTTP responses (such as HTML pages built on-the-fly) to display in a web browser.

Oracle Content Management SDK

The Oracle Content Management SDK (CM SDK) contains all the pieces you need to quickly develop a content management system: a content and metadata repository, protocol servers, and class libraries. As expected, the CM SDK integrates easily with other Oracle products such as Oracle Text, Oracle Workflow, and Oracle *inter*Media. Also, this SDK is managed along with all other J2EE and Internet applications in OEM AS Control.

OracleAS MapViewer

OracleAS MapViewer is a customizable tool for rendering maps using spatial data (coordinates) managed by Oracle Spatial or Oracle Locator. MapViewer uses base maps, mapping metadata, themes, and styles to return a map image or a URL image.

In a MapViewer application, the client application requests a map with a center location and other parameters and the MapViewer returns the map image enhanced with data plotted on top of the map, such as a street location or nearby hotels and restaurants.

On one of the Oracle websites, a web application using MapViewer accepts a street address, city, state, and zip code and returns a map with a star indicating the location, as you can see in Figure 1.1.

FIGURE 1.1 MapViewer application sample page

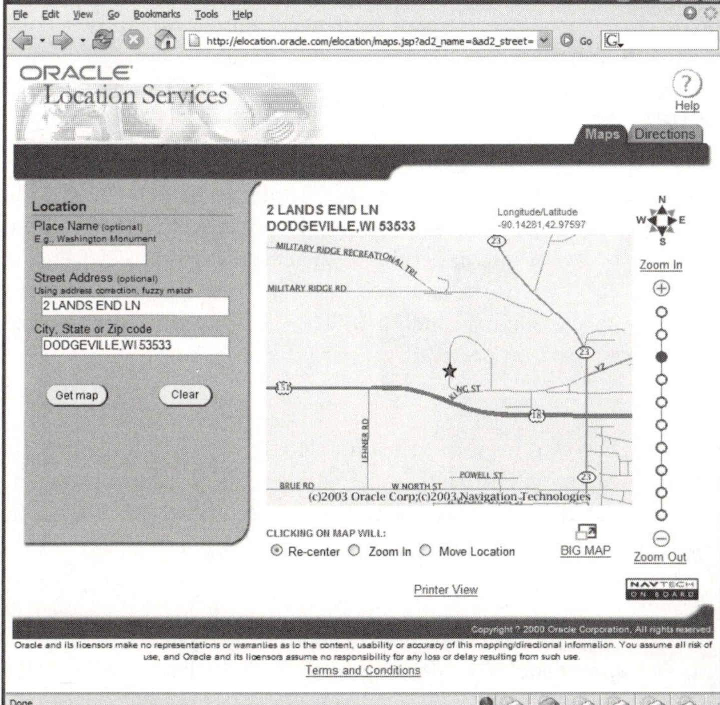

Portal

A *portal* is a website that provides a single access point to many different web applications and data sources, in many cases by using a single authentication method. To use an analogy, a portal is a customized web desktop with access to many different applications and data sources just as a Windows or Linux desktop is personalized for the user with access to many different local applications. A *portlet* is a component of a portal page; essentially, a portal comprises one or more portlets.

OracleAS Portal includes a Portal Developer Kit for developing portal applications as well as integration with Oracle Ultra Search to perform advanced search queries against all information managed by the portal. As a result, you can automatically use Ultra Search features such as near matches, soundex matches, and fuzzy matches.

Wireless

Oracle Wireless is the infrastructure that scales down the content of a portal to fit on a wireless device. Only the subset of portlets that generate OracleAS Wireless XML content is available to the wireless device.

In addition, Oracle Wireless supports advanced messaging techniques such as voice messaging, Short Message Service (SMS), and wireless e-mail.

The wireless capabilities of Oracle Wireless extend to wireless sensor technology in Oracle Sensor Edge Server: Oracle Sensor Edge Server easily integrates information from sensor technology into your business applications. For example, placing Radio Frequency Identification (RFID) sensors on all SKUs and instantaneously collecting location information for each SKU as it moves from manufacturer to warehouse to retail store to consumer can allow a company to react more quickly to inventory changes and trends.

Business Intelligence

The Business Intelligence (BI) components of OracleAS provide functionality and benefits via a web interface for employees in the enterprise as well as customers who buy the products or services provided by the enterprise. OracleAS Discoverer and Reports Services provide varying levels of reports depending on the needs and expertise of the end user; OracleAS Forms Services provides a robust data entry platform in a web interface that was previously only available via thick client applications. To drive incremental sales, OracleAS Personalization tailors the customer's experience based on previous visits to the website.

OracleAS BI Discoverer

OracleAS Business Intelligence Discoverer is the anchor for Oracle's application server BI solution. Using BI Discoverer, you can give your users immediate access to information via predefined or ad-hoc queries against data marts, data warehouses, and On-Line Transaction Processing (OLTP) systems.

OracleAS Reports Services

OracleAS Reports Services gives you the ability to build and publish reports from a variety of sources, whether it is text files, spreadsheets, or databases. You access Reports Services using a web browser and HTTP to an OC4J report services container, which in turn queries the Reports server. Alternatively, a full Oracle Reports client accesses the same Reports server directly and can retrieve the same reports.

OracleAS Forms Services

OracleAS Forms Services makes web-based data entry forms work much like data entry forms on desktop applications: immediate and strong validation as well as automatic completion. OracleAS Forms Services runs as a Java applet in the client browser. An *applet* is a Java program that runs from an applet viewer or is embedded in a web page.

OracleAS Personalization

OracleAS Personalization collects and stores customer data such as shopping preferences and purchase history in an Oracle database. Using this historical data, Oracle AS Personalization builds predictive models to recommend future purchases on return visits to the e-commerce site.

Web Cache

OracleAS Web Cache is a web caching solution that caches both static and dynamically generated web content. It is highly scalable and can even cache content for non-Oracle application servers. As with many other components of OracleAS, Web Cache can be clustered to prevent a single point of failure and to ease configuration and management of multiple cache servers. Conversely, you can configure Web Cache to cache content for more than one application server instance.

E-Business Integration

Not only is it important to integrate your applications and data sources for maximum usability and minimum redundancy, it's also important to make sure your integrated environment is scalable and manageable. OracleAS Integration Services gives you these features plus seamless query and transactional access to Oracle and non-Oracle data sources alike.

The three components of OracleAS—OracleAS InterConnect, OracleAS Integration B2B, and OracleAS BPEL Process Manager—help you achieve these goals.

OracleAS InterConnect

OracleAS InterConnect integrates your Oracle applications with any third-party applications or third-party middleware and makes it appear as though the third-party applications are running under OracleAS. The integration can occur within the enterprise or outside of the enterprise to locations accessible via the Internet.

OracleAS Integration B2B

OracleAS Integration B2B targets the business-to-business (B2B) exchange of services, information, and products; it connects to external trading partners using a variety of process, document, and exchange protocols. It can connect to the enterprise's e-business suite via an XML gateway and integrate into enterprise applications using OracleAS Interconnect.

OracleAS BPEL Process Manager

OracleAS BPEL Process Manager helps you to model and deploy business processes based on the Business Process Execution Language (BPEL). The BPEL Designer provides a graphical interface for building BPEL processes and how you send XML messages to and from remote services.

Oracle Application Server Management

Oracle Enterprise Manager Application Server Control, or OEM Application Server Control, is the functional counterpart to OEM Database Control for Oracle 10*g* Database; it is the "glue" that helps you manage all components of Application Server from a centralized web console.

In Figure 1.2, you can see how OEM Application Server Control centralizes the management of the application server's components as well as provides information about the host server itself.

FIGURE 1.2 OEM Application Server Control home page

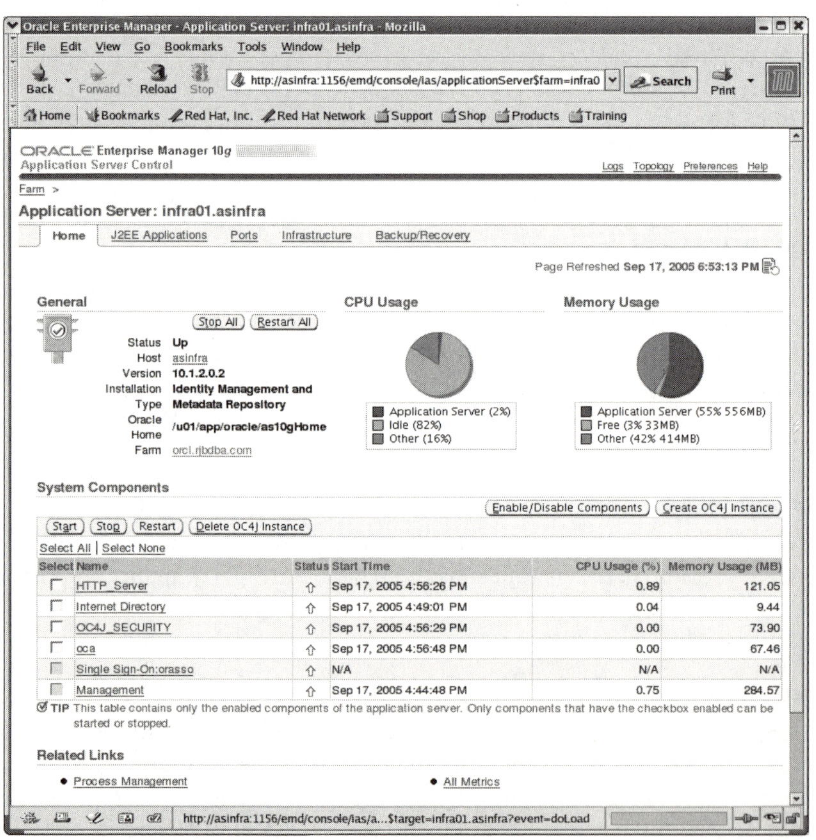

As with many, if not all, of Oracle's graphical toolsets, there is a set of equivalent command-line utilities that perform all of the tasks available via the web interface when a web interface may not be available or when the only connection to your server outside of the firewall is a terminal server connection. The following list includes the command-line utilities you will commonly use to manage and configure your server:

dcmctl The Distributed Configuration Management (DCM) tool manages the AS configuration and maintains the configuration repository.

opmnctl The Oracle Process Management and Notification Server command monitors all AS processes and restarts them when needed.

ocactl The Oracle Certificate Administration tool creates, manages, and expires secure certificates.

emctl The Enterprise Manager tool starts, stops, and manages security for Oracle Enterprise Manager 10*g*.

oidctl The Oracle Internet Directory tool starts and stops Oracle Internet Directory.

webcachectl The Oracle Web Cache tool administers OracleAS Web Cache in a standalone environment.

Analyzing the Oracle Application Server Architecture

Now that you have a good understanding of the terminology and the functionality of OracleAS components, it's time to put some of the pieces together by assigning them to tiers. A *tier* is a hardware layer consisting of one or more servers that implement a particular class of OracleAS components. In a nonclustered environment, most deployments of OracleAS use as few as two servers and up to four servers to implement these tiers:

Client tier Web browsers for end users

Web tier Oracle HTTP Server, Web Cache, and load balancing

Application server tier OracleAS Infrastructure, management, Portal, Wireless, Reports, developer tools

Database tier Oracle Database 10*g* to store OracleAS metadata, application data, and other persistent data, such as OID entries

In the following sections, we'll put the individual pieces of OracleAS into their respective tiers by presenting a typical four-tier deployment; in addition, we'll give you a head start on Chapter 2 and explain some of the installation dependencies.

Oracle Application Server Products and Installation Types

All installation types for OracleAS are accessible from the initial Oracle Universal Installer (OUI) window, as you can see in Figure 1.3. From this window, you can proceed to install the Middle-Tier components, the Infrastructure components, or the developer kits.

FIGURE 1.3 OracleAS OUI product window

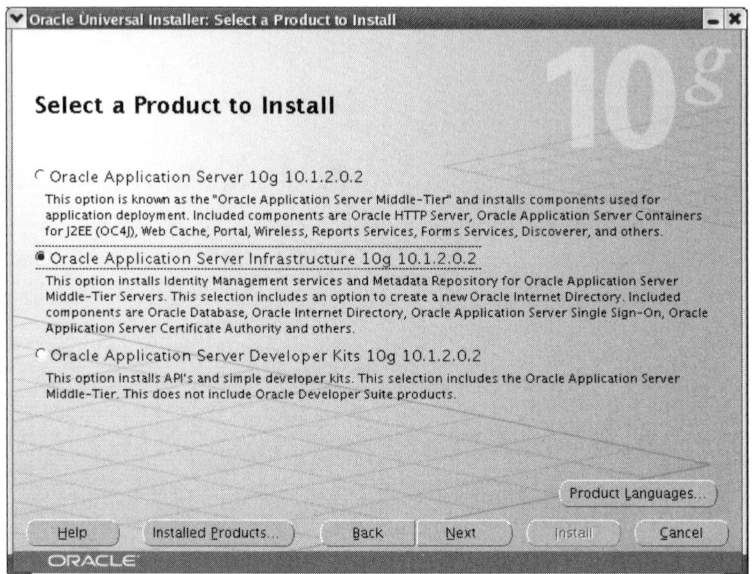

Oracle Universal Installer installs Application Server Control for any installation type, whether it is the Application Server components or the Infrastructure components.

OracleAS Middle-Tier Installation Types

The OracleAS middleware components fall into three categories: J2EE and Web Cache, Portal and Wireless, and Business Intelligence and Forms. You do not need to install the J2EE and Web Cache components separately if you install either Portal and Wireless or Business Intelligence and Forms; these two options install J2EE and Web Cache automatically. Figure 1.4 shows the middleware installation types.

All Application Server 10*g* installations except for J2EE and Web Cache require access to an Infrastructure instance.

FIGURE 1.4 OUI middleware installation types

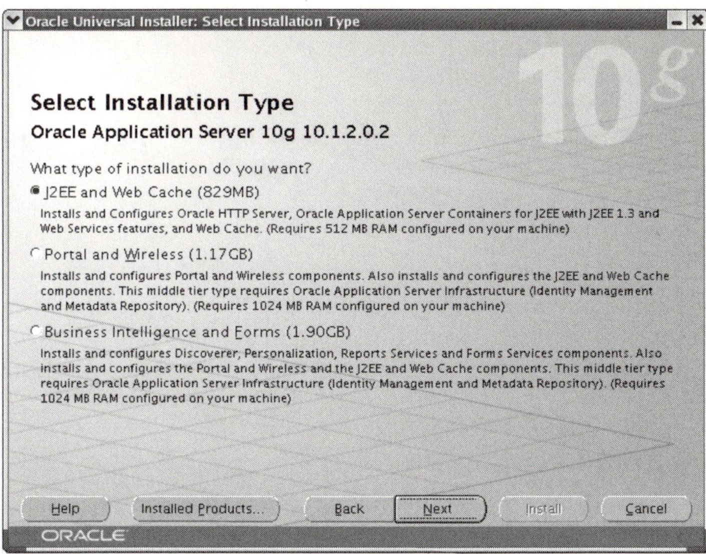

OracleAS Infrastructure Installation Types

The OracleAS Infrastructure components fall into two categories: OracleAS Identity Management components and OracleAS Metadata Repository components. If you want to install both groups on the same server, the installer provides a single option, as you can see in Figure 1.5.

FIGURE 1.5 OUI Infrastructure installation types

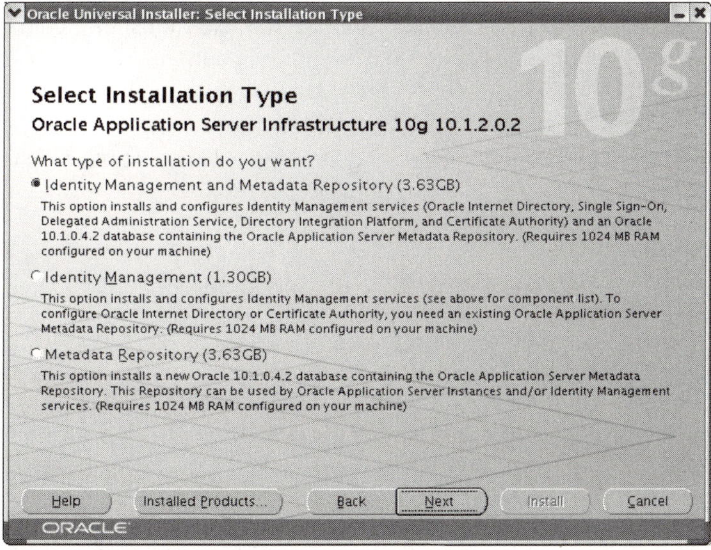

You will find a thorough discussion of component installation and a list of all installation tasks in Chapter 2. If you do not install both components in the same installation step, install the metadata repository first, then identity management. If you choose both, the installer chooses the correct order for installation.

If you want to use an existing database for the OracleAS Metadata Repository, you can use the Repository Creation Utility, a separate installation CD.

Installation Prerequisites

Certain Middle-Tier products require an Infrastructure installation: specifically, Portal and Wireless and Business Intelligence and Forms. If you install only the J2EE and Web Cache products, you still need an Infrastructure installation if you want to create AS clusters or you want to support single sign-on.

Metadata Repository Components

The Oracle Metadata Repository contains three subsets of metadata: product metadata, identity management data, and configuration management data. The identity management components discussed earlier in this chapter—Oracle Internet Directory (OID), Single-Sign On (SSO), and OracleAS Certificate Authority (OCA)—all use all three types of metadata; Delegated Administration Services (DAS) uses only the identity management and configuration management components.

The three services that support the three types of metadata are as follows:

Product Metadata Service Schemas for Portal and Wireless components

Identity Management Service Security metadata containing all administration and user privileges

Configuration Management Service Schemas containing OracleAS instance configuration

OracleAS Developer Kits

The third middleware installation option, OracleAS Developer Kits, installs APIs to support the following application types:

- OracleAS Portal
- OracleAS Wireless
- XML
- LDAP (OID)

This installation type does not include an integrated development environment (IDE); if you need an IDE, you can install Oracle JDeveloper as part of the Oracle Developer Suite or OracleAS Java Edition.

Introducing a Typical OracleAS Deployment

In this section, we'll create a hypothetical enterprise application server topology with components at all four tiers: the client tier, web tier, middle tier, and database tier. The client tier consists of many types of devices, including PCs with web browsers, cell phones, and wireless PDAs. We need three hosts to respond to HTTP requests and cache the results. Because we will have a lot of traffic for both J2EE applications and Business Intelligence Discoverer requests, we have two middleware hosts. Finally, the Infrastructure metadata and user data resides on a three-node RAC database.

Figure 1.6 shows the OracleAS components in the appropriate tier.

As you can see in Figure 1.6, two OracleAS instances are sharing the same metadata repository, but this may cause performance problems as the number of users or the number of middle-tier instances increases.

FIGURE 1.6 OracleAS components by tier

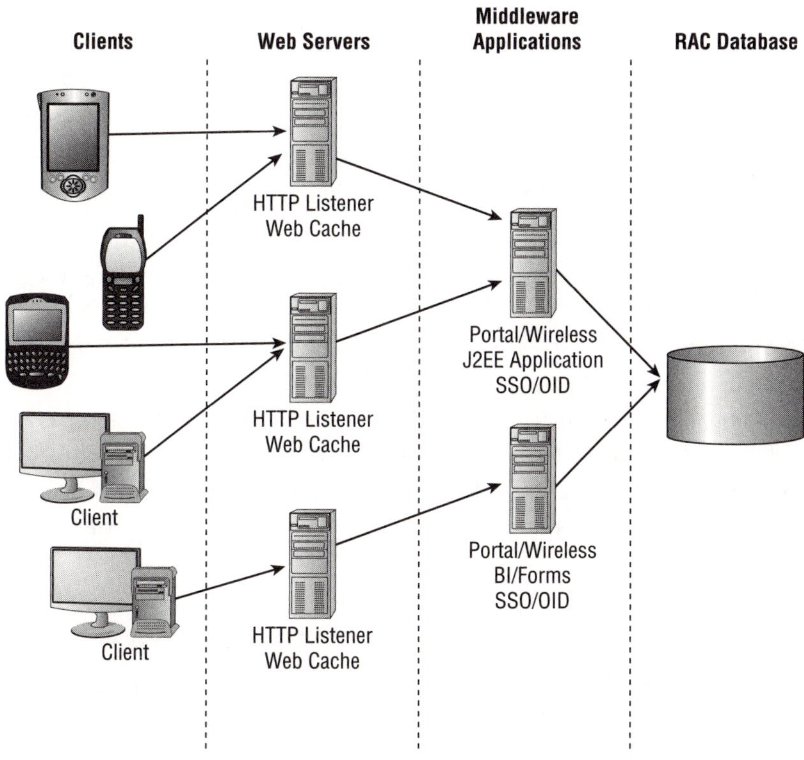

Summary

Oracle Application Server is a complex framework that has components at every tier of an enterprise, from the client to the backend database. In the first part of this chapter, we reviewed the application server terminology and provided a brief description of the main components of OracleAS to give you a foothold for understanding how the pieces fit together.

You can place the components of OracleAS into two broad categories: Infrastructure components and Middle-Tier components. The Infrastructure components control many of the backend processes, such as authorization, caching, and metadata management. The Middle-Tier components, in contrast, are generally more application specific, such as OracleAS Reports Services, OracleAS Portal, and any applications that use OracleAS Containers for J2EE (OC4J).

Next, we presented the dependencies and components you need to understand when you perform an installation of OracleAS. Specifically, during an Infrastructure installation, you must install the OracleAS Metadata Repository components before installing the identity management components. In addition, a metadata repository installation is required for all middleware installations except for J2EE and Web Cache.

Finally, we presented a sample deployment of OracleAS using a variety of client devices in a four-tier model with high availability and failover capabilities at the web server and database level.

Exam Essentials

Understand the OracleAS terminology. Be able to define the key terms you use to describe the function of the components in an OracleAS environment, such as *OracleAS installation*, *OracleAS instance*, *infrastructure*, *repository*, *server*, *farm*, and *cluster*.

Describe the components that make up an Infrastructure instance installation. Understand how the Infrastructure components store metadata for an OracleAS deployment. Be able to explain the dependencies between the Infrastructure components.

Describe the components that make up a middle-tier instance installation. Understand the functionality of each middle-tier component. Be able to identify the tools used to develop middle-tier applications.

List the primary command-line tools that provide equivalent functionality to OEM AS Control. Describe the function of each command-line tool and when you should use it.

Identify the OracleAS installation types. Understand the dependencies between different OracleAS installation types. Identify the Infrastructure and Middle-Tier components that each type of installation comprises.

Be able to place OracleAS components into a logical topology. Understand how each tier functions in an *n*-tier environment and be able to place each OracleAS component into the appropriate tier using a topology diagram.

Review Questions

1. Which of the following components are not parts of the OracleAS Infrastructure? (Choose all that apply.)

   A. Metadata Repository

   B. Business Intelligence Discoverer

   C. Single Sign-On

   D. Oracle Internet Directory

   E. Oracle Containers for J2EE

2. You install the OracleAS Infrastructure and the OracleAS Portal and Wireless option on the same server in two installation sessions and into two different Oracle home directories. How many installations and instances do you have?

   A. One installation and two instances

   B. Two installations and one instance

   C. Two installations and two instances plus the number of instances configured for the Oracle Database 10*g* component

   D. Two installations and two instances

3. An OracleAS instance can contain how many OC4J instances?

   A. As many as will fit into the server's memory.

   B. Zero, because there is no correlation between OracleAS instances and OC4J instances.

   C. Exactly one. OracleAS instances are functionally the same as OC4J instances.

   D. Up to four.

4. The metadata repository is created during which installation type?

   A. During every OracleAS installation

   B. During the Infrastructure installation

   C. During the Developer Kits installation

   D. During the Portal and Wireless or Business Intelligence and Forms installation

5. Which of the following characteristics does not apply to an OracleAS cluster?

   A. All instances within the cluster are part of the same farm.

   B. The cluster appears as a single unit to client requests.

   C. Clusters automatically provide load balancing and fault tolerance.

   D. An Oracle RAC database is an example of a cluster.

   E. All of the above.

6. Which of the following components is not a part of Oracle Identity Management?
   - A. Oracle Internet Directory
   - B. Oracle Database
   - C. OracleAS Certificate Authority
   - D. OracleAS Delegated Administration Services
   - E. OracleAS Single Sign-On
7. What is the primary function of Oracle Internet Directory?
   - A. Generates and publishes PKI certificates
   - B. Validates a user's credentials against OID
   - C. Stores metadata for most components of OracleAS
   - D. Maintains authentication and authorization information in an LDAP 3 directory
   - E. Assigns administrative duties to non-administrators
8. What is the primary function of OracleAS Single Sign-On?
   - A. Generates and publishes PKI certificates
   - B. Validates a user's credentials against OID
   - C. Stores metadata for most components of OracleAS
   - D. Maintains authentication and authorization information in an LDAP 3 directory
   - E. Assigns administrative duties to non-administrators
9. What is the primary function of OracleAS Certificate Authority?
   - A. Generates and publishes PKI certificates
   - B. Validates a user's credentials against OID
   - C. Stores metadata for most components of OracleAS
   - D. Maintains authentication and authorization information in an LDAP 3 directory
   - E. Assigns administrative duties to non-administrators
10. What is the primary function of Oracle Database?
    - A. Generates and publishes PKI certificates
    - B. Validates a user's credentials against OID
    - C. Stores metadata for most components of OracleAS
    - D. Maintains authentication and authorization information in an LDAP 3 directory
    - E. Assigns administrative duties to non-administrators

11. What is the primary function of Delegated Administration Services?

A. Generates and publishes PKI certificates

B. Validates a user's credentials against OID

C. Stores metadata for most components of OracleAS

D. Maintains authentication and authorization information in an LDAP 3 directory

E. Assigns administrative duties to non-administrators

12. The components ______________ reside in the web tier, whereas the components ______________ reside in the middleware tier.

A. Web Cache and HTTP Server, OC4J Containers and BI Discoverer

B. OC4J and BI Discoverer, Web Cache and HTTP Server

C. OC4J and Web Cache, BI Discoverer and HTTP Server

D. BI Discoverer and Web Cache, OC4J and HTTP Server

13. Which of the following components are middleware installation components of OracleAS? (Choose all that apply.)

A. Oracle HTTP Server

B. Oracle Internet Directory

C. Web Cache

D. Portal

E. Wireless

F. BI Discoverer

14. Which of the following components are not Infrastructure components of OracleAS? (Choose all that apply.)

A. Web Cache

B. Oracle HTTP Server

C. Business Intelligence and Forms

D. Oracle Internet Directory

E. Single Sign-On

15. Which of the following is not a module supported by the HTTP server?

A. `mod_php`

B. `mod_fastcgi`

C. `mod_plsql`

D. `mod_j2ee`

E. `mod_osso`

16. Identify the HTTP module that optimizes the execution of C++, C, and Java CGI applications.

A. `mod_fastcgi`

B. `mod_perl`

C. `mod_cpp`

D. `mod_cgi`

17. OracleAS Containers for J2EE (OC4J) can contain all but which one of the following Java components?

A. Enterprise Java Beans (EJB)

B. Java Server Pages (JSPs)

C. Servlets

D. Applets

E. Database connections

18. Your database was designed years ago using traditional relational design principles, but your new application development team is using pure object-oriented techniques with Java. Which of the following OracleAS development tools will facilitate object-to-relational mappings without redesigning the backend database using Oracle Database objects?

A. Oracle JDeveloper

B. Oracle XML Developer Kit

C. Oracle PL/SQL Server Pages

D. OracleAS TopLink

19. Identify the component of OracleAS Business Intelligence that collects and stores customer preferences and shopping data.

A. Customer Relationship Management (CRM)

B. Preference Manager

C. Recommendation Engine

D. Personalization

20. Identify the two types of components that can be installed during an OracleAS Infrastructure installation.

A. Identity Management and Web Cache

B. Identity Management and Metadata Repository

C. Web Cache and Metadata Repository

D. Metadata Repository and HTTP Server

E. Metadata Repository and OracleAS Developer Kits

Answers to Review Questions

1. B, E. The OracleAS BI Discoverer is part of the middleware tier. Oracle Containers for J2EE, or OC4J, is used to deploy applications in the middleware tier.

2. D. An installation is the set of executables and configuration files installed in a single Oracle home to support a set of OracleAS components. One of your installations creates an Infrastructure instance and the other installation creates a Portal and Wireless instance. Therefore, there are two installations and two instances.

3. A. An OracleAS instance can support as many OC4J instances as will fit into memory on the server. To avoid confusion, you should refer to an OC4J instance as an OC4J container.

4. B. The metadata repository is created during the Infrastructure installation and is required for most components of OracleAS except for the J2EE and Web Cache installation type.

5. E. A cluster is a collection of application server instances within a farm that have identical configuration and application deployment; the cluster appears as a single unit or target to a client application or user. Since an Oracle RAC database can be part of an OracleAS installation, it is a clustered component of OracleAS.

6. B. While Oracle Database stores the metadata for many components of OracleAS, including OID, it is not considered a part of Oracle Identity Management.

7. D. Oracle Internet Directory is an LDAP version 3 directory service that enables retrieval of information about users, services, applications, and which users can access the services and applications.

8. B. One of several components of OID, Single Sign-On validates a user's credentials against OID and allows transparent access to other applications without reauthenticating.

9. A. OracleAS Certificate Authority (OCA) generates and publishes public key infrastructure (PKI) certificates to support strong authentication between OracleAS and clients.

10. C. Oracle Database stores metadata and directory data for most components of OracleAS.

11. E. OracleAS Delegated Administration Services permits the distribution of administrative duties throughout the enterprise.

12. A. The web tier contains only the Web Cache and HTTP components. The middleware tier contains all other components except for the client browser and the database repository.

13. A, C, D, E, F. The only component in the list that is not one of the middleware components is Oracle Internet Directory, which is part of an Infrastructure installation.

14. C. The only component in the list that is not one of the Infrastructure components is Business Intelligence and Forms, which is part of a middleware installation.

15. D. There is no module called `mod_j2ee`. However, the module `mod_oc4j` provides communication with OracleAS Containers for J2EE as well as basic load balancing for clustered OC4J instances.

16. A. mod_fastcgi provides an optimized environment for running C, C++, and Java CGI applications. There are no modules called mod_cpp and mod_cgi. mod_perl routes only Perl code to the Perl interpreter.

17. D. OC4J containers can contain one or many EJB, JSPs, servlets, and database connections, but not applets. Applets run only within the client browser.

18. D. The OracleAS TopLink component provides a framework to manage object-to-relational data persistence in a relational database.

19. D. There are no components named Recommendation Engine, Preference Manager, and Customer Relationship Management in the OracleAS suite.

20. B. The only two Infrastructure installation types are Identity Management and Metadata Repository.

Performing Installation Tasks

ORACLE APPLICATION SERVER 10*g* ADMINISTRATION I EXAM OBJECTIVES COVERED IN THIS CHAPTER:

✓ **Installing OracleAS Infrastructure**

- Define the installation requirements for OracleAS Infrastructure
- Describe OracleAS Infrastructure installation types
- Install OracleAS Infrastructure
- Start and stop OracleAS Infrastructure

✓ **Installing OracleAS Middle Tier**

- Describe the Oracle Application Server 10*g* Middle-Tier installation types and their requirements
- Perform preinstallation tasks
- Install the middle-tier with Portal and Wireless installation type
- Verify completion of the installation
- Access the installed OracleAS middle-tier components

Installing Oracle Application Server (OracleAS) 10*g* can be overwhelming and frustrating if you do not lay the groundwork by understanding the software and hardware requirements, the operating system kernel parameter requirements, and the prerequisites for each of the components you want to install. In this chapter, we will help make this process more manageable by breaking it down into two broad topics: installing the OracleAS Infrastructure components on a dedicated host and installing the OracleAS Middle-Tier components on a second dedicated host.

In the first half of this chapter, we will help you to confirm the hardware and software requirements for an OracleAS Infrastructure installation on a dedicated host. In addition, we will show you how to view and change the operating system's kernel parameter values to those required by an OracleAS Infrastructure installation.

Next, you will step through the installation windows for an OracleAS Infrastructure installation that includes Oracle Identity Management components such as Oracle Internet Directory (OID) and Single Sign-On (SSO). In addition, you will install a single instance of Oracle Database 10*g* to hold the metadata for the OracleAS Infrastructure components as well as any application data required by middleware applications.

At the end of the first half of the chapter, we will present a high-level view of the OracleAS Infrastructure web interface as well as show you how to start and stop the OracleAS Infrastructure components.

In the second half of the chapter, we will step through the requirements for a OracleAS Middle-Tier installation that includes the Portal and Wireless components. This installation will be part of the same Oracle Application Server farm as the OracleAS Infrastructure installation, even though it is on a separate physical host.

At the end of the second half of the chapter, we will show you the web interface for accessing the Oracle HTTP Server, the Portal home page, and other OracleAS Middle-Tier components.

Overview of Infrastructure and Middle-Tier Installations

This chapter presents two sample installation sessions that include most, if not all, components of the Oracle Application Server Infrastructure components and the Oracle Application Server Middle-Tier components. We will step you through the installation screens in both scenarios and note the similarities and differences between the two types of installations.

In the examples in this chapter and throughout the rest of this book, we will use two physical hosts, not only to show how you can install Oracle Application Server components on multiple servers, but also to help differentiate the purpose and function of the components in each tier. Table 2.1 shows you the characteristics of the two hosts.

TABLE 2.1 Example Server Characteristics

Server Name	IP Address	Installation Name	Instance Name	Home Directory
`asinfra`	192.168.2.82	`as10g_infra`	`infra01`	`/u01/app/oracle/as10gHome`
`asmw`	192.168.2.81	`as10g_mw`	`mw01`	`/u01/app/oracle/as10gHome`
`oc1`	192.168.2.101	`db10gHome`	`rac1`	`/u01/app/oracle/DB10gHome`
`oc2`	192.168.2.102	`db10gHome`	`rac2`	`/u01/app/oracle/DB10gHome`
`oc3`	192.168.2.103	`db10gHome`	`rac3`	`/u01/app/oracle/DB10gHome`

The other three servers in the table, `oc1`, `oc2`, and `oc3`, are members of a three-node Real Application Clusters (RAC) database; initially, we will install a single-instance database on the first node, `asinfra`, for the OracleAS Metadata Repository. In Appendix C, we will show you how to move your metadata repository to the RAC database to enhance the performance, scalability, and reliability of your Oracle Application Server environment.

As we present the installation steps in this chapter, many of the terms we introduced in Chapter 1, "Introducing Oracle Application Server 10*g* and Components," will become clearer. For example, we will create an Oracle Application Server farm comprising the `infra01` and `mw01` instances.

Many of the requirements for both an Infrastructure and a Middle-Tier installation are the same; in the next few sections, we will show you the hardware, software, and configuration requirements for either type of installation. The Oracle Universal Installer (OUI) performs many of these checks at installation time, but knowing your target environment ahead of time will save time and frustration later.

Verifying Common Software and Hardware Requirements

OUI checks for these minimum requirements, except for disk space:

- CPU: 32-bit Intel or AMD at 450MHz
- Disk space: component dependent
  - OracleAS Infrastructure: 2.6GB
  - OracleAS J2EE and Web Cache: 0.5GB
  - OracleAS Portal and Wireless: 1.1GB

- Memory: component dependent
  - OracleAS Infrastructure (all): 1024MB
  - OracleAS Identity Management only: 512MB
  - OracleAS Metadata Repository only: 750MB
  - OracleAS J2EE and Web Cache only: 512MB
  - OracleAS Portal and Wireless: 1024MB
- Temporary disk space: 400MB
- Swap disk space: 1.5GB available at install time
- Monitor: 256 color
- Operating System: RHAS 2.1, RHEL 3.0, RHEL 4.0, SuSE Server 8 or 9

Since OUI does not know in advance which disk you will use to install the components, it does not perform a disk space check. Therefore, make sure that the disk you use for the installation has the required amount of free space.

To obtain the CPU speed, OS release, kernel version, free memory, free swap space, and free disk space, you can use the Linux commands in this example on the host `asinfra.` The file `/proc/cpuinfo` shows what kind of processor you have on your host; in this case, it's an AMD Athlon 64 dual core processor::

```
[root@asinfra root]# cat /proc/cpuinfo | grep 'model name'
model name      : AMD Athlon(tm) 64 X2 Dual Core Processor 4600+
```

On all Linux distributions, `/etc/issue` contains the Linux distribution type and version. The Oracle Universal Installer checks this file to make sure you are installing the software on a supported version of the operating system:

```
[root@asinfra root]# cat /etc/issue
Red Hat Enterprise Linux WS release 3 (Taroon Update 5)
```

The Linux `uname` command provides information about the operating system kernel version:

```
[root@asinfra root]# uname -srv
Linux 2.4.21-32.0.1.EL #1 Tue May 17 17:55:54 EDT 2005
```

The Linux `free` command provides general memory statistics, including the amount of physical memory and the amount of swap file disk space:

```
[root@asinfra root]# free
         total       used       free     shared    buffers     cached
Mem:   1027508    1003848      23660          0     104752     459612
-/+ buffers/cache:     439484     588024
Swap:      2048276     390604    1657672
```

You can use the `df -m` command to check the amount of disk space on each raw device:

```
[root@asinfra root]# df -m
Filesystem           1M-blocks      Used Available Use% Mounted on
/dev/hda3                12902      7692      4555  63% /
/dev/hda1                  244        14       217   7% /boot
none                       502         0       502   0% /dev/shm
[root@asinfra root]#
```

On this target server, we have 1GB of memory, 2GB of swap space (with more than 1.5GB free), and almost 13GB of free disk space. As a result, the disk space, swap file disk space, and physical memory is sufficient for the Application Server installation.

Other Prerequisites

To install any Oracle Application Server product, either you will need access to the *superuser account* (`root`) or you must have an administrator available to run scripts with administrator privileges during the installation. Setting up the initial user accounts and directories also requires an administrator with superuser privileges, as you will see in the next section.

In addition, read the Oracle Application Server Installation Guide and the latest release notes available at `www.oracle.com/technology/documentation/index.html`.

Setting Up the Environment

Before you can begin the installation, you must perform a number of specific tasks at the operating system level, as follows:

- Setting up the `oracle` account user and the `oinstall` and `dba` groups
- Creating the necessary software directories
- Setting environment variables
- Configuring kernel parameters
- Configuring user limits
- Adding entries to the `/etc/hosts` file
- Verifying the availability of listener ports

We will provide the details for each of these tasks in the following sections.

Creating User and Group Accounts

Other than the `root` account, the only other account you need on your Oracle server is the `oracle` account; in addition to creating the `oracle` account, you need to create two groups: `oinstall` and dba. In the following example, you create the groups and the `oracle` account and change the password for the `oracle` account:

```
[root@asinfra root]# /usr/sbin/groupadd oinstall
[root@asinfra root]# /usr/sbin/groupadd dba
[root@asinfra root]# /usr/sbin/useradd -g oinstall -G dba oracle
[root@asinfra root]# passwd oracle
Changing password for user oracle.
New UNIX password:________
Retype new UNIX password:________
passwd: all authentication tokens updated successfully.
[root@asinfra root]#
```

Creating Software Directories

You need to create one directory as the destination for the Oracle AS Infrastructure installation. Ensure that the file system for this directory has enough disk space per the disk space requirements provided earlier in this chapter. In the following example, you will create the directory `/u01/app/oracle` and apply the appropriate permissions. OUI and the root scripts it generates will apply any required subsequent permissions to this and other directories in the file system:

```
[root@asinfra root]# mkdir -p /u01/app/oracle
[root@asinfra root]# chown -R oracle:oinstall /u01/app/oracle
[root@asinfra root]# chmod -R 775 /u01/app/oracle
```

Setting and Unsetting Environment Variables

For the installation to complete successfully, you must set some environment variables as well as make sure some environment variables are not set. An *environment variable* is a variable that is assigned either during a user's login or during the session and containing values that you reference by the environment variable name later in the session.

TMP The directory used by OUI for temporary installation files. This directory must be writeable by the `oracle` user and must have at least 400MB of free disk space. If this variable is not set, OUI uses the directory `/tmp`.

DISPLAY The system name and display identifier of the location where OUI displays the installer pages and collects the installer responses. The client you use to install the software must have an X Windows server available.

ORACLE_HOME and ORACLE_SID If you already defined these variables for another Oracle product on the server, you should comment these out until the installation is completed.

Here is an excerpt of the login script for the `oracle` user that defines the environment variables properly:

```
TMP=/usr/tmp
DISPLAY=dba_ws01:0.0
```

```
ORACLE_BASE=/u01/app/oracle
# ORACLE_HOME=$ORACLE_BASE/db_10.2.0/DB10gHome
# ORACLE_SID=rac2
PATH=$ORACLE_HOME/bin:$PATH
export TMP ORACLE_BASE ORACLE_HOME ORACLE_SID
export DISPLAY PATH
```

In this example, the workstation dba_ws01 will display the installer pages on the first monitor of the first video card connected to dba_ws01. Before you start the installer, be sure to use the xhost command to allow a connection from the server running OUI; for example, if you install the Oracle products on server asinfra, then your xhost command looks like this:

```
[root@dba_ws01 root]# xhost asinfra
```

Once you are done with your installer session, you can set or reset ORACLE_HOME and ORACLE_SID appropriately.

You must install OracleAS Infrastructure in its own ORACLE_HOME, preferably on a host that does not have any other Oracle Application Server installations.

Configuring Kernel Parameters

Oracle Database 10*g* and OracleAS require adjustments to some operating system kernel parameters; Table 2.2 contains the list of kernel parameters that you may need to adjust. Non-default kernel parameters are stored in the Linux operating system file /etc/sysctl.conf.

TABLE 2.2 Required Kernel Parameters in /etc/sysctl.conf

Kernel Parameter	New Value
net.ipv4.ip_local_port_range	1024 65000
kernel.sem	256 32000 100 142
kernel.shmmax	2147483648
net.core.rmem_default	262144
net.core.rmem_max	262144
net.core.wmem_default	262144
net.core.wmem_max	262144

TABLE 2.2 Required Kernel Parameters in `/etc/sysctl.conf` *(continued)*

Kernel Parameter	New Value
`fs.file-max`	131072
`kernel.msgmnb`	65535
`kernel.msgmni`	2878

To make these changes permanent, add the following lines to your `/etc/sysctl.conf` file:

```
#
# Kernel requirements for both 10g DB R2
# and 10g AS R2
#

net.ipv4.ip_local_port_range = 1024 65000

kernel.sem = 256 32000 100 142
kernel.shmmax = 2147483648

net.core.rmem_default = 262144
net.core.rmem_max = 262144
net.core.wmem_default = 262144
net.core.wmem_max = 262144

#
# more requirements for Oracle AS 10g R2
#

fs.file-max = 131072
kernel.msgmnb = 65535
kernel.msgmni = 2878
```

Rebooting your server will set these parameters to the new values; if you do not want to reboot the server, you can use the `sysctl` command to read the file `/etc/sysctl.conf` and set the new values immediately, as in this example:

```
[root@asinfra root]# /sbin/sysctl -p
net.ipv4.ip_forward = 0
net.ipv4.conf.default.rp_filter = 1
net.ipv4.conf.default.accept_source_route = 0
```

```
kernel.sysrq = 0
kernel.core_uses_pid = 1
net.ipv4.ip_local_port_range = 1024 65000
kernel.shmmax = 2147483648
net.core.rmem_default = 262144
net.core.rmem_max = 262144
net.core.wmem_default = 262144
net.core.wmem_max = 262144
fs.file-max = 131072
kernel.msgmnb = 65535
kernel.msgmni = 2878
kernel.sem = 256 32000 100 142
[root@asinfra root]#
```

Configuring User Limits

To ensure that there are enough resources available for the Oracle Application Server modules, the `oracle` user requires higher values for the number of open files and number of concurrent processes. To set these values, add the following two lines to the file `/etc/security/limits.conf` and log in as the `oracle` user again:

```
oracle      hard  nofile 65536
oracle      hard  nproc  16384
```

Editing the */etc/hosts* File

Edit the `/etc/hosts` file to add an entry other than `localhost` for the host that will run Oracle Application Server as well as any other hosts that contain Oracle Application Server components in this farm. Provide both the fully qualified name and the alias as in this example:

```
192.168.2.82   asinfra.rjbdba.com   asinfra
192.168.2.81   asmw.rjbdba.com      asmw
```

Verifying Listener Ports

By default, the Oracle database listener installed with OracleAS Infrastructure uses port 1521 to listen for database requests. Before you start the installation, make sure that the following `grep` command does not find an existing service that uses port 1521:

```
[root@asinfra root]# grep 1521 /etc/services
[root@asinfra root]#
```

If the port is already in use, you can create a file called `staticports.ini` that OUI will use during installation to assign an unused port for the database listener. During the installation process, you have the option to accept the default port assignments or to specify the file system location of the `staticports.ini` file.

Installing the OracleAS Infrastructure

In the following sections, we will first review the prerequisites required to successfully install the OracleAS Infrastructure components. The prerequisites include ensuring that you have enough memory and disk space as well as verifying that you have the correct settings for specific operating system parameters. We presented the requirements for the Infrastructure and Middle-Tier installations earlier in this chapter.

Next, we will show you all of the installation screens from the *Oracle Universal Installer (OUI)* along with a detailed explanation of the parameters required in each of the screens. The Oracle Universal Installer, as the name implies, is the common application framework used by all Oracle products to install, uninstall, and configure Oracle application files.

Once you install the Infrastructure components, you must perform a few postinstallation tasks and verify that all of the components were installed and configured correctly. We will show you how to access the Oracle Enterprise Manager Application Server Control page as well as the Oracle Enterprise Manager 10*g* Database Control page; in addition, you will verify that Oracle Internet Directory (OID) components such as the Single Sign-On (SSO) server are accessible. We will present other Infrastructure components accessible via the Oracle Enterprise Manager Application Server Control home page in Chapter 3, "Understanding Application Server Management Tools."

Finally, you will need to know how to start and stop the Infrastructure components. We will present some scripts you can use to start and stop some or all of the Infrastructure components; you can run these scripts manually or you can incorporate them into the operating system's automatic startup and shutdown procedures.

Infrastructure Installation Overview

As you remember from Chapter 1, the OracleAS Infrastructure components fall into two categories: Identity Management components and Metadata Repository components.

Here are the components included in an Identity Management installation:

- Oracle Internet Directory
- OracleAS Single Sign-On
- Oracle Delegated Administration Services
- Oracle Directory Integration and Provisioning
- OracleAS Certificate Authority

A Metadata Repository installation creates a collection of schemas in a new or existing Oracle Database 10*g* to support other Oracle Application Server components, including the Infrastructure components previously listed. The schemas created fall into one of four categories:

- Product metadata
- Identity Management metadata
- Configuration Management metadata
- Application data

Regardless of which installation you choose, the Oracle HTTP Server (OHS), OracleAS Containers for J2EE (OC4J), and Application Server Control are always installed. You are not required to install the Metadata Repository in one scenario: when you install the OC4J and OracleAS Web Cache components without any clustering or Identity Management components.

OUI can install Identity Management and Metadata Repository components separately; this is especially useful when you want to put the Identity Management components on one server and the Metadata Repository components on another server. In any case, you must install the Metadata Repository components first because many of the Identity Management components require the Metadata Repository for, as you might surmise, its metadata! If you choose both sets of components during installation, OUI automatically installs them in the right order.

Infrastructure Installation Tasks

In this section, we will step through the installation pages for a complete OracleAS Infrastructure installation: in other words, an installation that includes both the Metadata Repository components and the Identity Management components.

Mount the first installation CD (out of a total of four) in the CD-ROM drive, and run the `runInstaller` script to start OUI. The installer performs a few basic installation checks, such as checking the operating system version, available disk space, and the number of display colors. An additional product-specific prerequisite check occurs later in the installation.

The first installation page gives you the opportunity to view existing products on this server as well as deinstall them. You can see the Welcome screen in Figure 2.1.

FIGURE 2.1 Infrastructure installation Welcome page

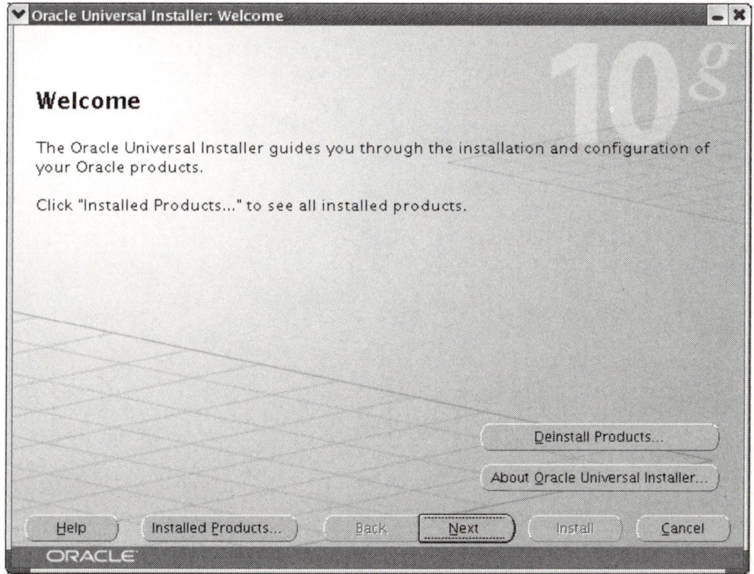

If this is the first installation of Oracle products on this server, you see the page in Figure 2.2. The `oraInventory` directory holds a list, in separate subdirectories, of all products installed on this server. This directory must be writeable by the user performing the installation.

After you click the Next button in the screen in Figure 2.2, you must run a script as the `root` user, as you can see in Figure 2.3. This script sets write permissions for the `oinstall` group on the inventory directory. In addition, the script creates the file `/etc/oraInst.loc` so that future installations of Oracle products can locate the inventory directory.

FIGURE 2.2 Infrastructure installation Specify Inventory Directory and Credentials page

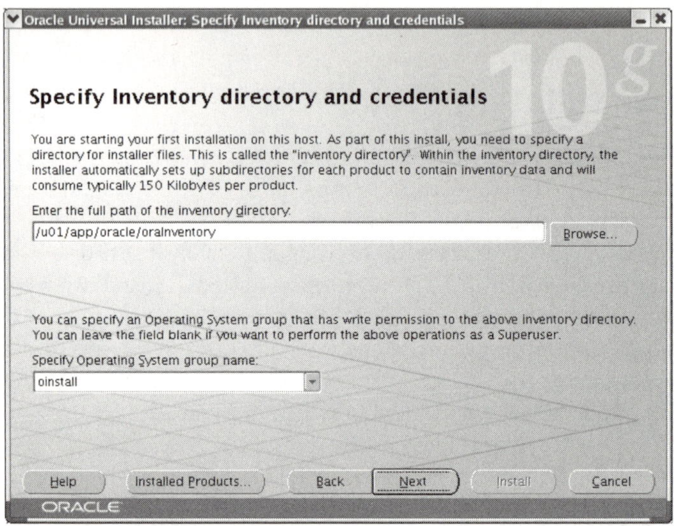

FIGURE 2.3 Infrastructure installation root actions page

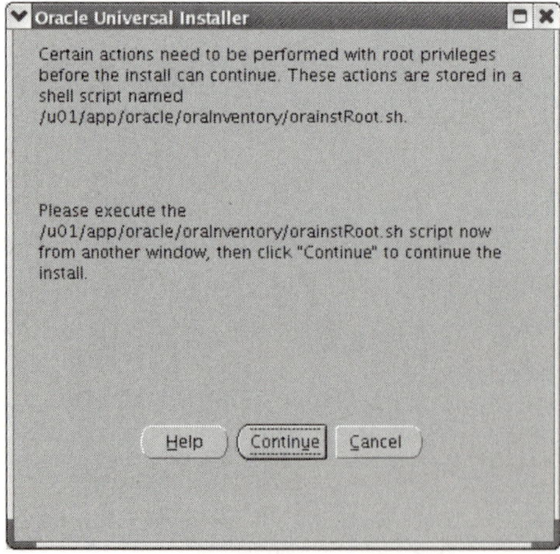

After you run the script, click the Continue button. The next screen, as you can see in Figure 2.4, asks for the location of the installation CD, the installation name, and where you want to install the files. In this example, a disk image is used instead of an actual CD that resides on a remote file system.

The name you provide for the installation in the Name field can be any string as long as it is 16 or fewer characters, and it cannot have any embedded spaces. You use this name to identify the installation in the inventory directory. In this example, the installation name is `as10g_infra`.

The directory name you provide in the Path field is the destination directory for the installation's executables and configuration files. You will assign this directory name to the `ORACLE_HOME` environment variable after you complete the installation. If this directory does not exist, the installer will create it.

On the page shown in Figure 2.5, you choose to install one or more Oracle Application Server Infrastructure components. In the second half of this chapter, you will install the Oracle Application Server Middle-Tier components on a different server. Click the Oracle Application Server Infrastructure 10*g* radio button, and then click the Next button to continue.

The next installer page (Figure 2.6) asks you which Infrastructure components you want to install. In this example, you will install both the Metadata Repository and the Identity Management components. OUI installs the Metadata Repository components before it installs the Identity Management components because the Identity Management components require the Metadata Repository.

FIGURE 2.4 Infrastructure installation Specify File Locations page

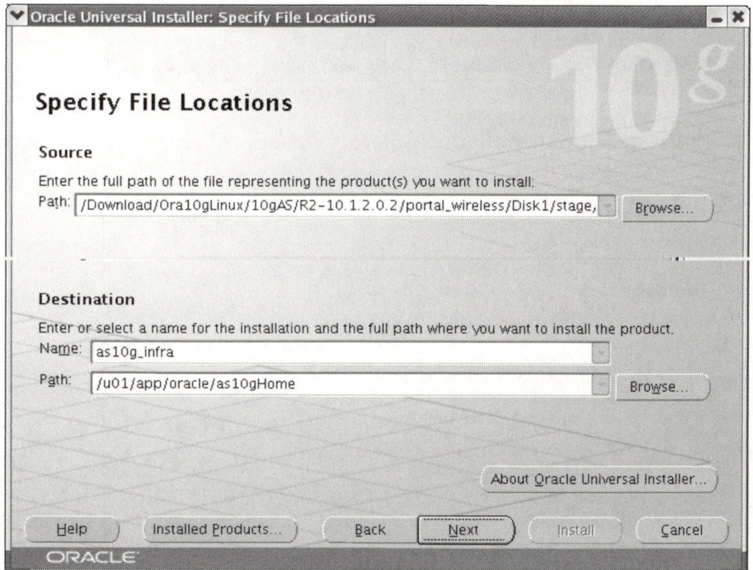

If you want to install the Metadata Repository into an existing Oracle database, you must use the OracleAS Metadata Repository Creation Assistant, available on a separate installation CD.

FIGURE 2.5 Infrastructure installation Select a Product to Install page

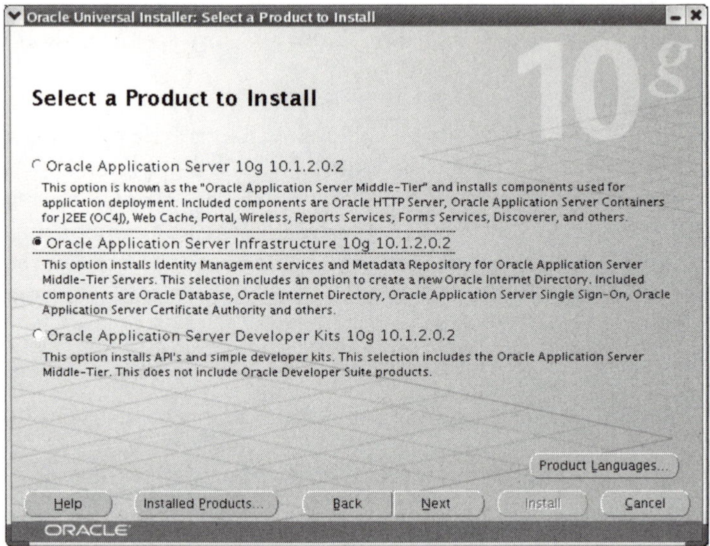

FIGURE 2.6 Infrastructure installation Select Installation Type page

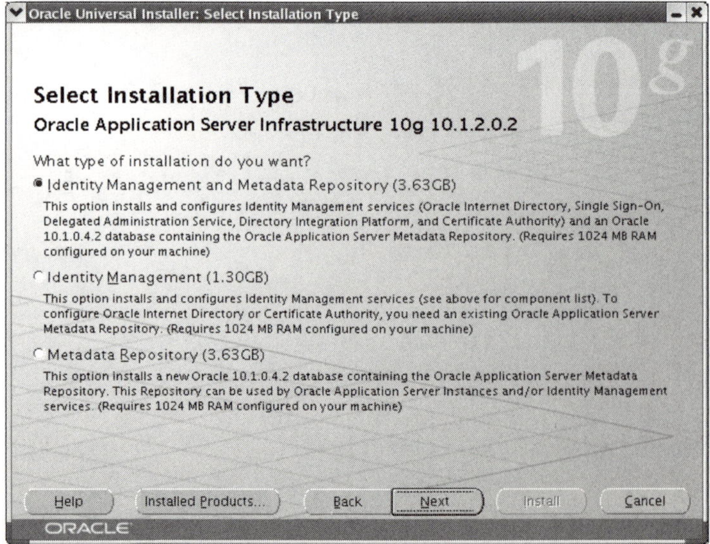

As you can see in Figure 2.7, OUI performs many additional prerequisite checks, some of which it has already performed, such as checking for the operating system version. In this installation, one of the required packages, `openmotif21`, appears to be missing. A quick check of the packages installed shows you why this discrepancy exists:

```
[oracle@asinfra oracle]$ rpm -q openmotif
openmotif-2.2.3-5.RHEL3.2
[oracle@asinfra oracle]$
```

The installer was looking for the Open Motif package name with a slightly different format; Open Motif 2.2.3-5 is already installed on the server, which is a newer version than 2.1. In this case, you can manually click the Warning box to verify the requirement. Click the Next button to continue to the next page.

FIGURE 2.7 Infrastructure installation Product-Specific Prerequisite Checks page

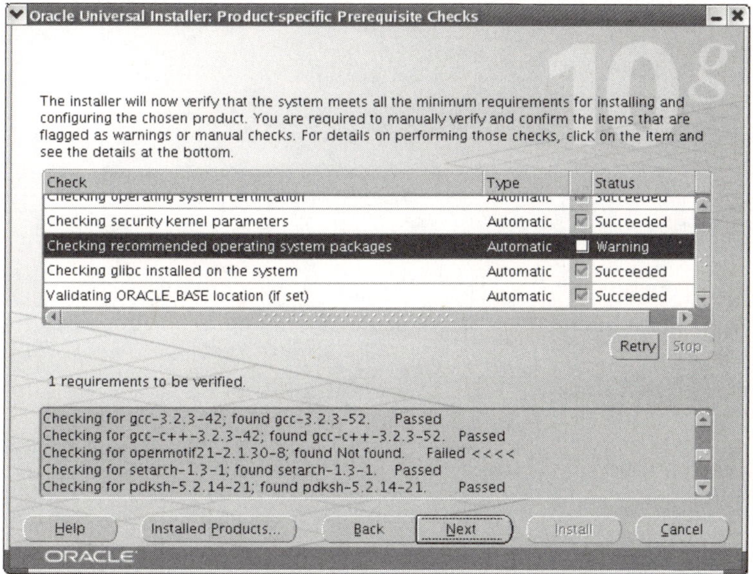

The final confirmation page, shown in Figure 2.8, confirms that you have `root` access on this server. If you do not have this access, subsequent installation steps may fail or some components of OracleAS Infrastructure will not run correctly. Confirm that you have `root` access, check the box, and click the Next button.

On the Select Configuration Options page (Figure 2.9), you have the option to automatically configure and start some of the Infrastructure components after installation is complete. In this example, you select all components. In all cases, you always configure and start the Metadata Repository, Oracle HTTP Server, and OracleAS Containers for J2EE after installation is complete. Regardless of whether you will configure a product or not, you still install it now; you can configure and start it later using the Application Server Control console. In this example, check every box except for High Availability and Replication. Configuring and using High Availability and Replication is beyond the scope of this book.

FIGURE 2.8 Infrastructure installation Confirm Pre-Installation Requirements page

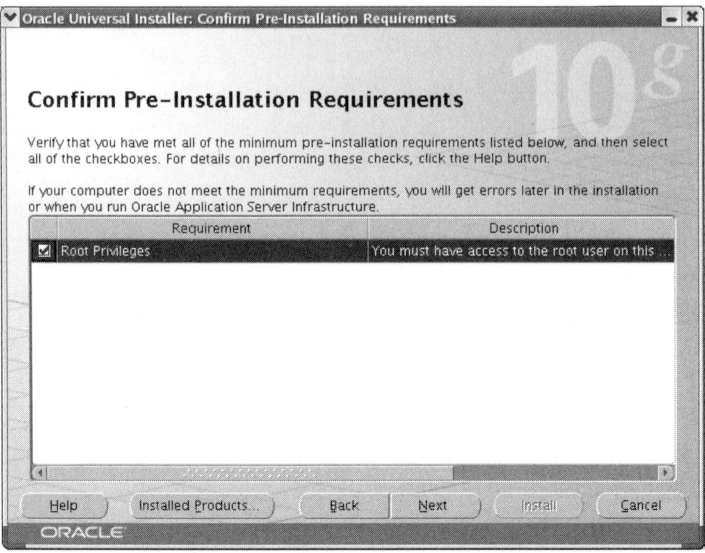

FIGURE 2.9 Infrastructure installation Select Configuration Options page

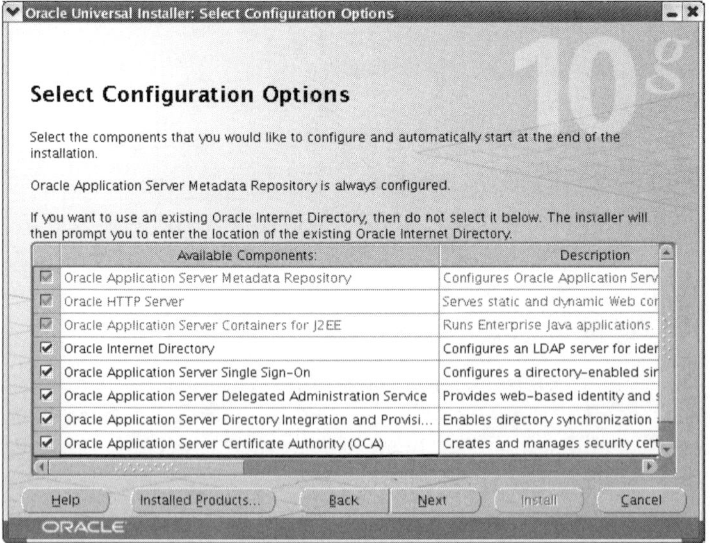

OUI can automatically configure the ports you use for each of the Infrastructure components, such as Oracle HTTP Server and OEM AS Control. If you have other Oracle products that already use the default ports, or if you want to use a specific set of ports for this installation, create a file containing the new port assignments. The default name for this file is `staticports.ini`, but it can have any name. Here are some sample entries from the Oracle-provided `staticports.ini`:

```
# J2EE and Web Cache
Oracle HTTP Server port = 8080
Oracle HTTP Server Listen port = 7778
Oracle HTTP Server Diagnostic port = 7201
# Infrastructure
Oracle Internet Directory port = 13061
Oracle Internet Directory (SSL) port = 13131
```

Figure 2.10 shows you the OUI page where you accept the default: automatic port configuration. Click the Next button to continue.

On the page in Figure 2.11, you define the *namespace*, or Identity Management *realm*, for your Infrastructure installation. An Identity Management Realm contains all the management policies for all users and groups in the Oracle Internet Directory. The installer uses the default domain name of the host server to build a unique LDAP directory tree, where `dc` stands for, logically enough, `domainComponent`.

FIGURE 2.10 Infrastructure installation Specify Port Configuration Options page

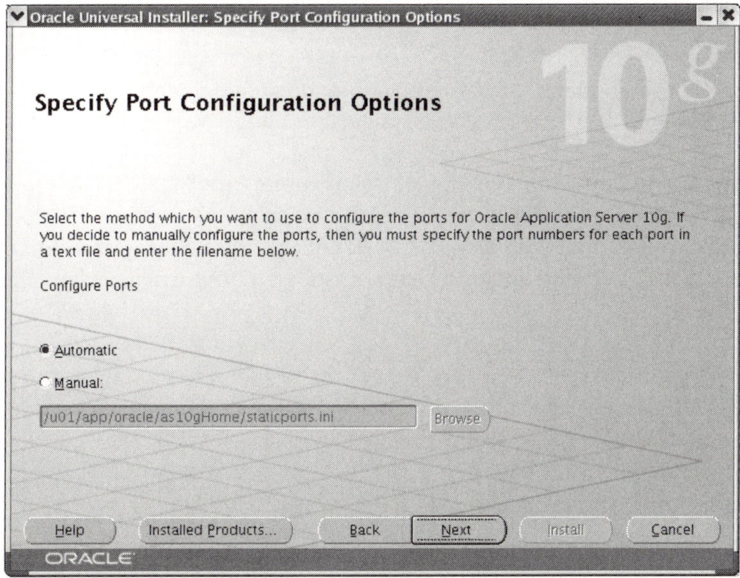

FIGURE 2.11 Infrastructure installation Specify Namespace In Internet Directory page

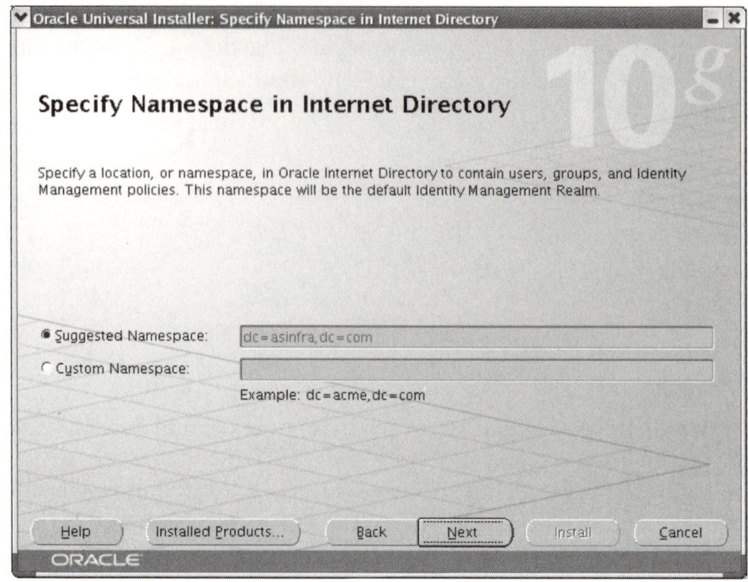

The OUI also creates two subcontainers for users and groups using directory entries `cn=users` and `cn=groups`, along with a default set of policies for the realm. Once OID is running, you can edit these policies using OEM AS Control.

In this example, you accept the default namespace and click the Next button.

You can find more information on understanding and configuring OID in Chapter 3, "Understanding Application Server Management Tools."

To issue digital certificates using OracleAS Certificate Authority (OCA), you must specify a unique distinguished name (DN) consisting of a common name (CN), organizational unit (OU), organization (O), and country (C). OUI places these entries into OID. On the page in Figure 2.12, you enter information that is unique for your organization and click the Next button.

On the Specify OCA Key Length page (Figure 2.13), you enter the key length, in bits, for the signature on each digital certificate. The longer the key length, the higher the security of the certificate, but a longer key length will take longer to generate. Oracle recommends a key length of at least 2,048 bits.

FIGURE 2.12 Infrastructure installation Specify OCA Distinguished Name page

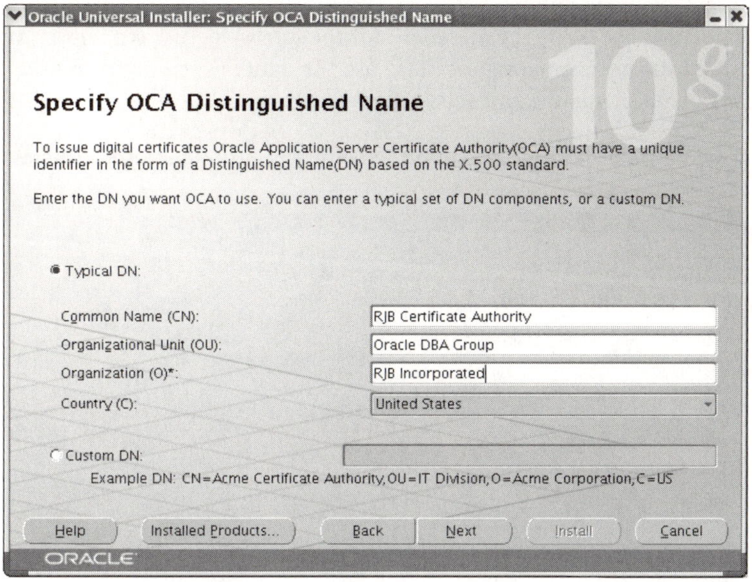

Oracle Universal Installer: Specify OCA Distinguished Name
Specify OCA Distinguished Name
To issue digital certificates Oracle Application Server Certificate Authority(OCA) must have a unique identifier in the form of a Distinguished Name(DN) based on the X.500 standard.
Enter the DN you want OCA to use. You can enter a typical set of DN components, or a custom DN.
Typical DN:
Common Name (CN):
RJB Certificate Authority
Organizational Unit (OU):
Oracle DBA Group
Organization (O)*:
RJB Incorporated
Country (C):
United States
Custom DN:
Example DN: CN=Acme Certificate Authority,OU=IT Division,O=Acme Corporation,C=US
Help
Installed Products...
Back
Next
Install
Cancel
ORACLE

FIGURE 2.13 Infrastructure installation Specify OCA Key Length page

Oracle Universal Installer: Specify OCA Key Length
Specify OCA Key Length
Oracle Application Server Certificate Authority uses a key to sign digital certificates. Longer key lengths provide stronger security, but require more time to issue each new certificate. Select the desired key length. Oracle recommends that you use at least a 2048-bit key length.
Key Length (bits):
2048
Help
Installed Products...
Back
Next
Install
Cancel
ORACLE

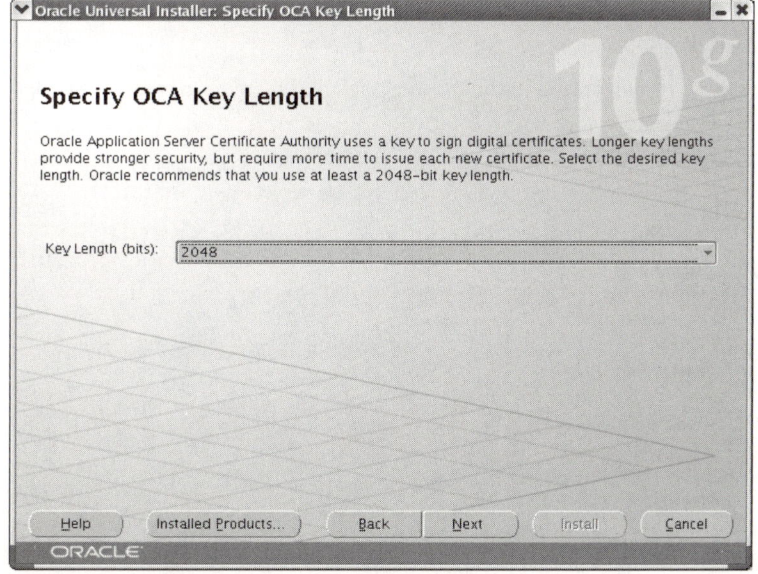

You control security for the OCA with its own password. On the page in Figure 2.14, you specify a password for the OCA administrator.

Figure 2.15 shows the page on which you specify the basic parameters to create an Oracle 10*g* Database. This database holds the metadata for the Infrastructure repository and, optionally, application data for user applications. You use the database name from other Oracle Application Server components to connect to the repository.

FIGURE 2.14 Infrastructure installation Specify OCA Administrator's Password page

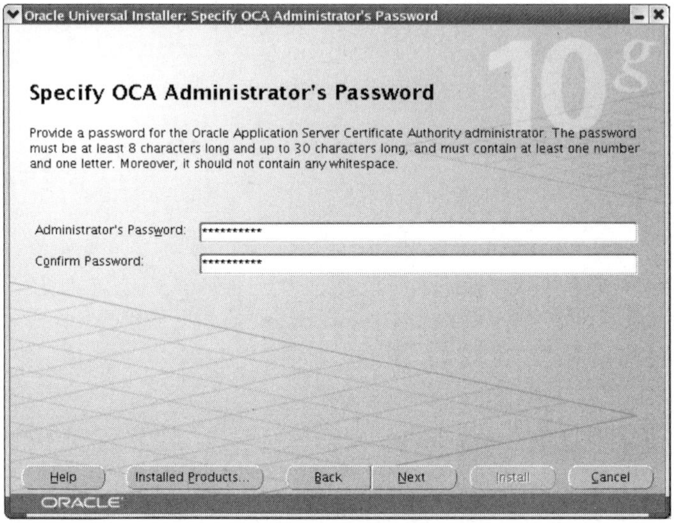

FIGURE 2.15 Infrastructure installation Specify Database Configuration Options page

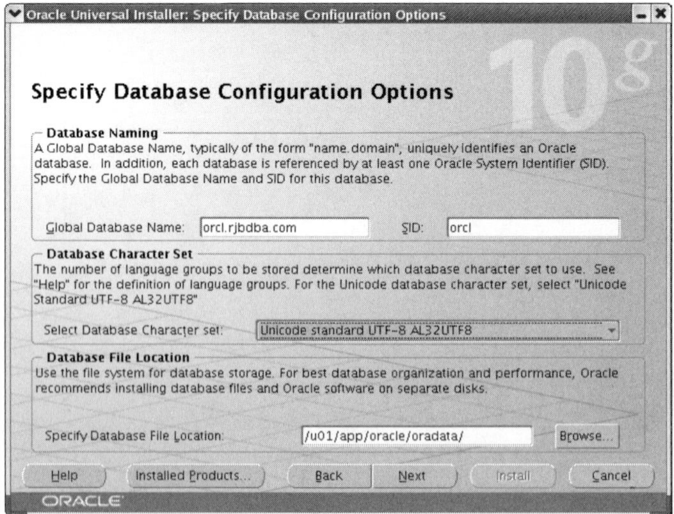

When you specify the global database name, make sure it is unique across your network. It is convenient but not required to construct the global database name using the domain name of your server.

Depending on which character sets you need to support in your applications, choose the appropriate database character set. In this example, choose the default character set, Unicode Standard UTF-8/AL32UTF8.

By default, the location for the database files is on the same file system as the Oracle Application Server software. To improve performance, Oracle recommends that you specify a location on a different file system. In this example, however, choose the default location, `/u01/app/oracle/oradata`. Under this directory, OUI creates one subdirectory for each Oracle instance configured on this server. In this example, OUI will create the directory `/u01/app/oracle/oradata/orcl` to hold the database files for the repository. Click the Next button to continue.

On the Specify Database Schema Passwords page (Figure 2.16), you have the option to specify the same password for all database accounts or separate passwords for individual database accounts. In this example, you enter the same password for all database accounts.

On the page in Figure 2.17, you specify the password for the Infrastructure instance as well as an instance name. Each instance on a host must have a unique name; in this example, you name the instance `infra01`. The fully qualified name for the instance comprises the instance name, hostname, and domain name; in this example, the fully qualified instance name is `infra01.asinfra.rjbdba.com`.

FIGURE 2.16 Infrastructure installation Specify Database Schema Passwords page

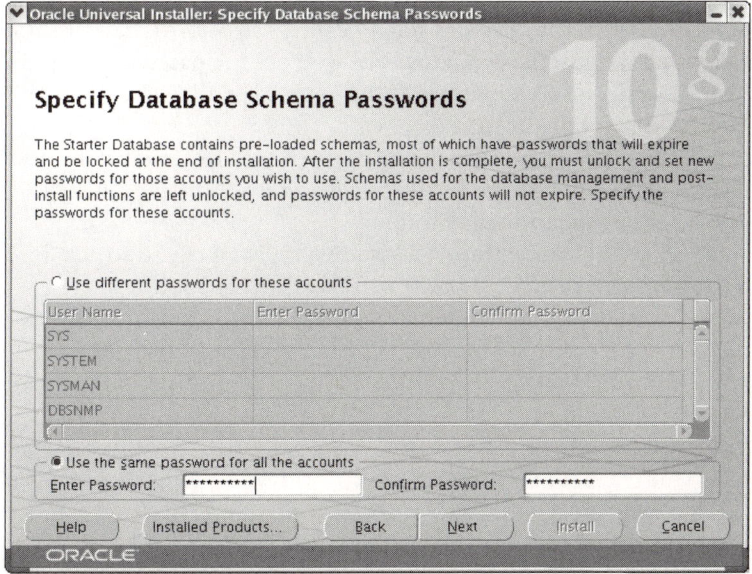

FIGURE 2.17 Infrastructure installation Specify Instance Name and ias_admin Password page

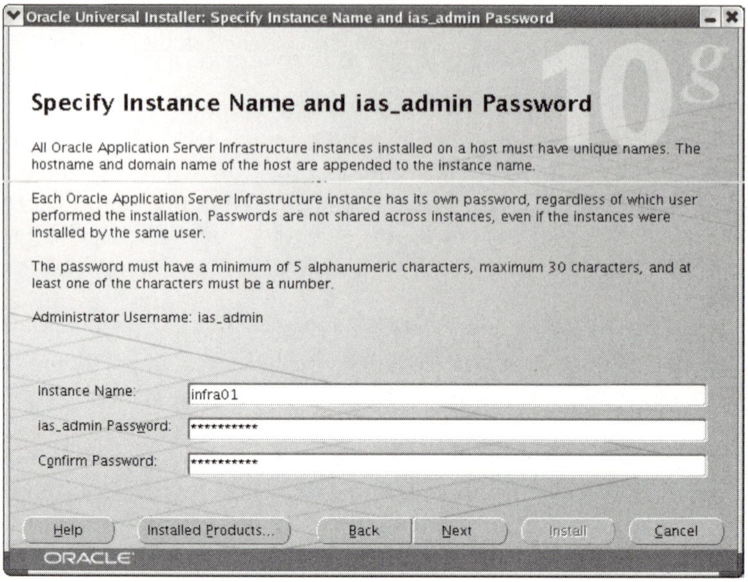

You use the password for the ias_admin account only for this instance; if you perform another Oracle Application Server installation on this host, even if it is an Infrastructure installation, you will have another administrator account called ias_admin that does not share the same password with the first installation. However, you use the password you enter on this page as the initial password within this instance for the portal administrator account (portal) and the OID administrator (orcladmin).

The summary page that follows gives you one more chance to review your installation options before OUI copies the files to the destination directory. After you click Next, OUI copies the product files to the destination directories.

Before OUI runs any of the configuration assistants, it prompts you to run another script as root before you can proceed. The output from this script is as follows:

```
[root@asinfra root]# /u01/app/oracle/as10gHome/root.sh
Running Oracle10 root.sh script...
\nThe following environment variables are set as:
    ORACLE_OWNER= oracle
    ORACLE_HOME=  /u01/app/oracle/as10gHome

Enter the full pathname of the local bin directory: [/usr/local/bin]:
   Copying dbhome to /usr/local/bin ...
   Copying oraenv to /usr/local/bin ...
   Copying coraenv to /usr/local/bin ...
```

```
\nCreating /etc/oratab file...
Adding entry to /etc/oratab file...
Entries will be added to the /etc/oratab file as needed by
Database Configuration Assistant when a database is created
Finished running generic part of root.sh script.
Now product-specific root actions will be performed.
/etc/oracle does not exist. Creating it now.

Entering Oracle Internet Directory Root Installation Section

OID Server Installation
Checking LDAP binary file protections
Setting oidmon file protections
Setting oidldapd file protections
Setting oidrepld file protections
Setting oidpasswd file protections
Setting oidemdpasswd file protections
Setting oidstats.sh file protections
Setting remtool file protections
Setting oiddiag file protections
FSetting oiddt file protections
Leaving Oracle Internet Directory Root Installation Section
[root@asinfra root]#
```

In summary, the script output provides the values you should use for your environment variables in the `oracle` user's login script; in addition, it copies some shell scripts to a common local directory. It also creates the */etc/oratab* file if it does not already exist; you use this file to automatically start one or all database instances on this host:

```
#
# This file is used by ORACLE utilities.  It is created by root.sh
# and updated by the Database Configuration Assistant when creating
# a database.
# A colon, ':', is used as the field terminator.  A new line terminates
# the entry.  Lines beginning with a pound sign, '#', are comments.
#
# Entries are of the form:
#   $ORACLE_SID:$ORACLE_HOME:<N|Y>:
#
# The first and second fields are the system identifier and home
# directory of the database respectively.  The third filed indicates
```

```
# to the dbstart utility that the database should , "Y", or should not,
# "N", be brought up at system boot time.
#
# Multiple entries with the same $ORACLE_SID are not allowed.
#
#
*:/u01/app/oracle/as10gHome:N
```

By default, all instances on this host are not automatically started because there is an *N* as the startup indicator and the * wildcard character represents all instances within the specified ORACLE_HOME. If you want to start a particular instance automatically, you add a new line to this file with the instance name to start and a *Y* for the automatic startup indicator. Here is an example:

```
orcl:/u01/app/oracle/as10gHome:Y
```

After you click the OK button on the Setup Privileges page, OUI launches the Configuration Assistants page, which you can see in Figure 2.18, and configures and starts all installed products that you selected for configuration earlier on the Select Configuration Options page (Figure 2.9).

One of the configuration assistants shown in Figure 2.18, the Database Configuration Assistant (DBCA), launches its own page (Figure 2.19). This is the same screen you see when you install a stand-alone Oracle Database 10*g* instance.

FIGURE 2.18 Infrastructure installation Configuration Assistants page

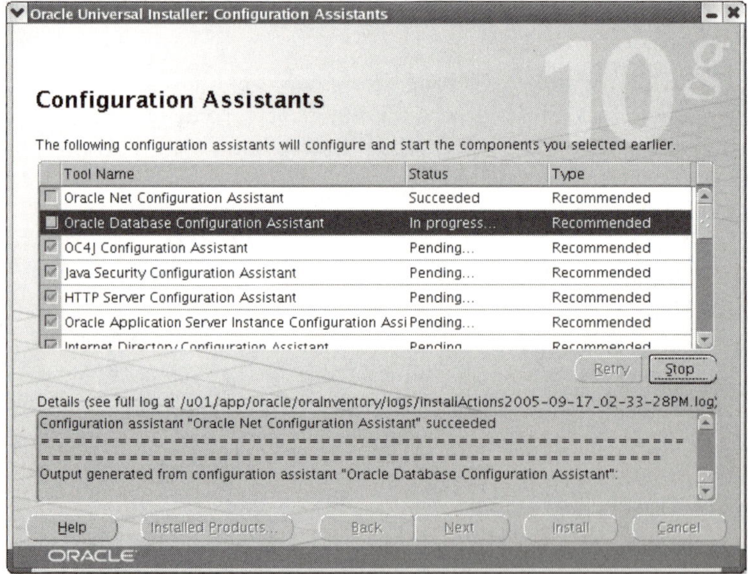

After the successful completion of all configuration assistants, you see the End of Installation page shown in Figure 2.20.

FIGURE 2.19 The Database Configuration Assistant page

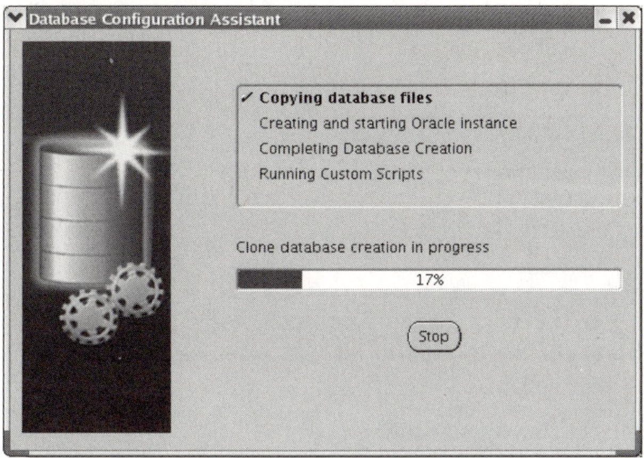

FIGURE 2.20 Infrastructure installation End of Installation page

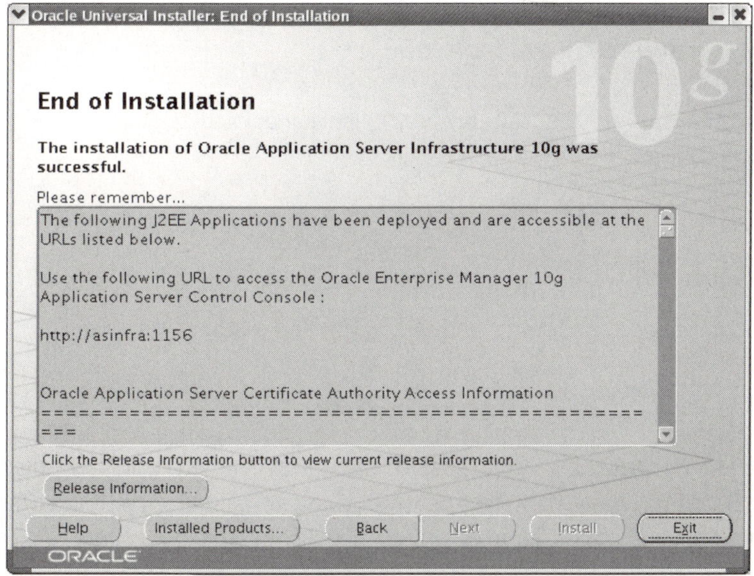

The information on the scrolling window within the page contains a number of URLs for accessing the installed Infrastructure components, as you can see in Listing 2.1.

Listing 2.1: Infrastructure Installation Log

```
The following J2EE Applications have been deployed and
➥are accessible at the URLs listed below.


Use the following URL to access the Oracle Enterprise
➥Manager 10g Application Server Control Console :

http://asinfra:1156

Oracle Application Server Certificate Authority Access Information
==================================================================


OCA User Page: https://asinfra:6600/oca/user
OCA Admin Page: https://asinfra:6600/oca/admin

This information is also available through Oracle
➥Application Server main website under the port information link.
The following information is available in:
/u01/app/oracle/as10gHome/install/setupinfo.txt

Oracle Application Server 10g (10.1.2.0.2) Usernames and Default
  password information:

Please refer to Oracle Application Server 10g Administrator Guide for
  more information.

Install Type: Identity Management and Metadata Repository

Configured Components: Oracle Application Server Metadata Repository |
  Oracle HTTP Server | Oracle Application Server Containers for J2EE |
  Oracle Internet Directory | Oracle Application Server Single Sign-On
  | Oracle Application Server Delegated Administration Service | Oracle
  Application Server Directory Integration and Provisioning | Oracle
  Application Server Certificate Authority (OCA) |

-----------------------------------------
```

```
New Database created with these properties:
Database File Location: /u01/app/oracle/oradata/
Database Global Name: orcl.rjbdba.com
Database SID:orcl
Database Name:orcl
Character Set:  -characterset AL32UTF8

http://asinfra:5500/em

-----------------------------------------

Use the following URL to access the Oracle HTTP Server and the Welcome
  Page:

http://asinfra:7777

-----------------------------------------
Use the following URL to access the Oracle Enterprise Manager
  Application Server Control:

http://asinfra:1156

Instance Name: infra01.asinfra

Installation of Oracle Application Server Infrastructure is Complete.
  Please note that any URLs created in this install may not be
  functional immediately.
```

In addition to providing a summary of the relevant URLs that you will use on a day-to-day basis, this log also provides a summary of the installation tasks and the database repository information.

Infrastructure Postinstallation Tasks

Once the installation is complete, you must verify that all components are available and that the database listener is ready to receive requests. In addition, you must modify your login script to facilitate access to the Infrastructure's database instance.

In the following sections, we will show you the changes to your login script that are required; in addition, we will show you how to verify the status of the database listener as well as the web-based interface to Oracle Enterprise Manager Database Control, Oracle Enterprise Manager Application Server Control, Oracle HTTP Server, the OID server, and the SSO server. Finally, we will show you how to verify the ports your installation uses to listen for each of these application interfaces.

Updating the Login Script

To access the Infrastructure's database, add the environment variables ORACLE_HOME and ORACLE_SID to your login script; on Linux using *Bash* (Bourne Again Shell), your .bash_profile login script contains lines that look like this:

```
ORACLE_BASE=/u01/app/oracle
ORACLE_HOME=$ORACLE_BASE/as10gHome
ORACLE_SID=orcl
PATH=$ORACLE_HOME/bin:$ORACLE_HOME/opmn/bin:$ORACLE_HOME/dcm/bin:$PATH
export ORACLE_BASE ORACLE_HOME ORACLE_SID PATH
```

In addition, you add $ORACLE_HOME/bin, $ORACLE_HOME/dcm/bin, and $ORACLE_HOME/opmn/bin to your path so you can access all Oracle utilities without knowing the full pathname. $ORACLE_HOME/opmn/bin contains utilities that start, stop, and check the status of the Oracle Application Server processes, such as opmnctl.

Verifying the Status of the Database Listener

To verify that the database listener is operational, use the lsnrctl command as in this example:

```
[oracle@asinfra oracle]$ lsnrctl status | grep "orcl.*status"
  Instance "orcl", status READY, has 3 handler(s) for this service...
[oracle@asinfra oracle]$
```

Since this listener may be listening for requests to other database instances, you specify orcl in the grep command.

Using Application Server Control for Infrastructure Components

You access the home page for Oracle Enterprise Manager Application Server Control using this URL:

```
http://<hostname>:<ASControlPort>
```

Looking at the Infrastructure Installation Log, the URL for the Oracle Enterprise Manager Application Server Control home page is http://asinfra:1156. Using this URL in a browser shows the farm's home page, as you can see in Figure 2.21. When you first launch this page, you must specify ias_admin for the username; you use the password you supplied on the OUI page shown in Figure 2.17.

FIGURE 2.21 Oracle Enterprise Manager Application Server Control Farm page

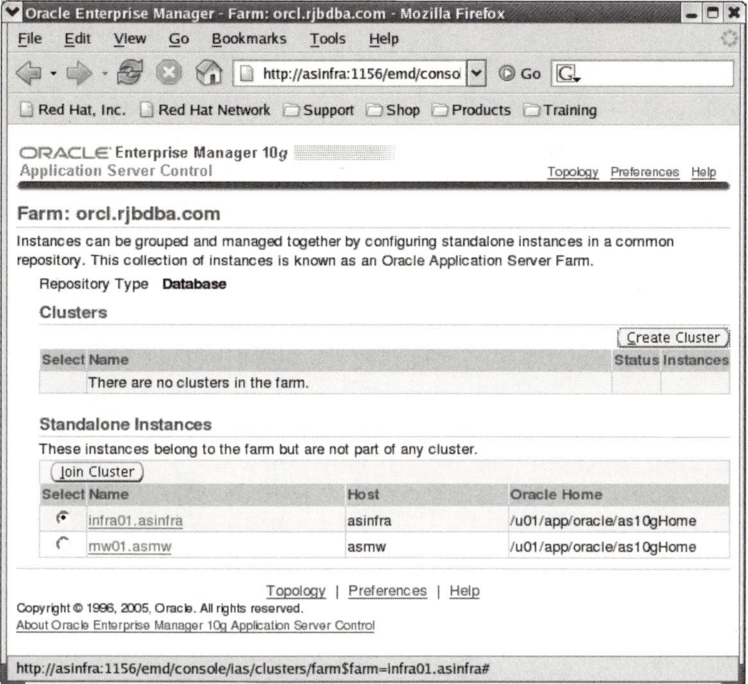

As you remember from Chapter 1, an Oracle Application Server farm is a group of Oracle Application Server instances that share a common metadata repository. In this case, the instances `infra01.asinfra` and `mw01.asmw` share the metadata repository created during the Infrastructure installation earlier in this chapter. We will show you how to install the Middle-Tier instance `mw01.asmw` in the second half of this chapter and how you connect it to the metadata repository you just created.

Clicking on the `infra01.asinfra` link on the farm's home page (Figure 2.21) opens the instance's home page, which you can see in Figure 2.22.

On this page, you see the status of many aspects of the Infrastructure instance, including CPU and memory usage on the host and the status of each component included in the installation.

FIGURE 2.22 Oracle Enterprise Manager Application Server Control instance home page

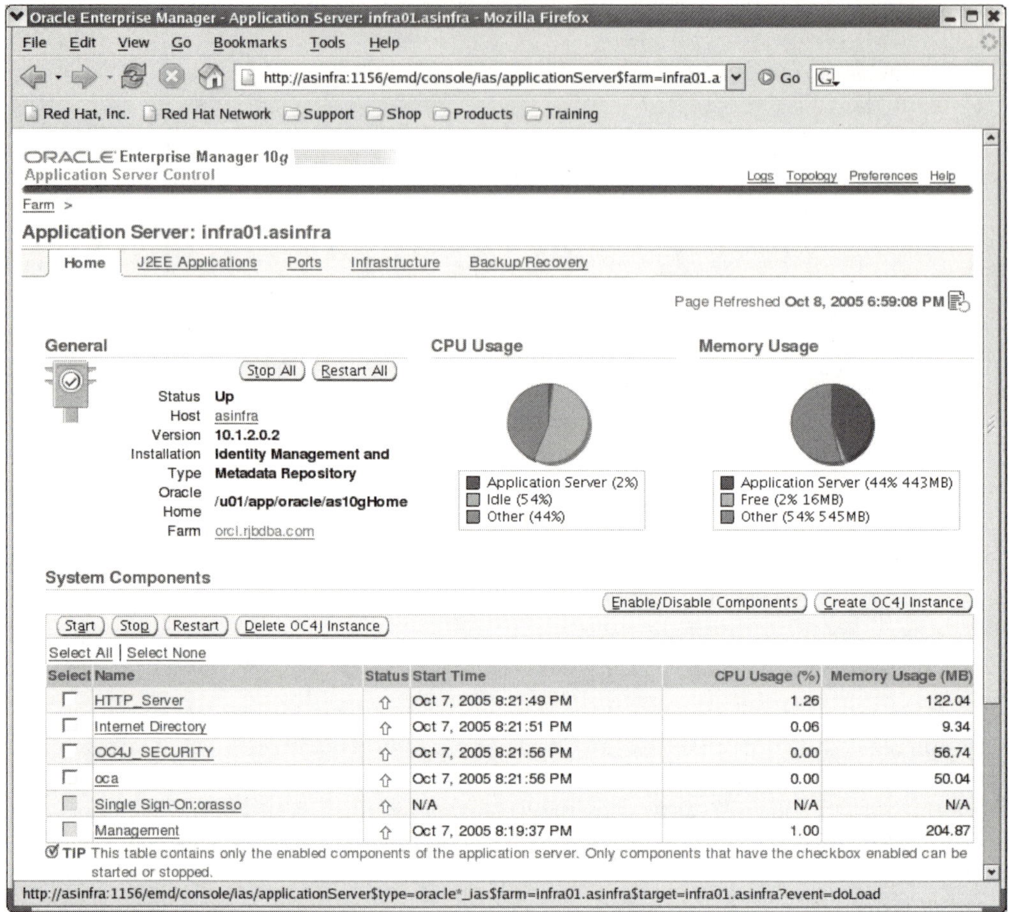

Reviewing the Oracle Application Server Port List

Keeping track of the list of ports your installation uses can be frustrating, especially if you have existing applications (including existing previously installed Oracle applications) using any of the default ports for an Infrastructure installation. The list of ports that OUI uses for the Infrastructure installation resides in the file `$ORACLE_HOME/install/portlist.ini`; for our Infrastructure installation, it looks like this:

```
;OracleAS Components reserve the following ports at install time.
;As a post-installation step, you can reconfigure a component to use a
  different port.
;Those changes will not be visible in this file.
[System]
Host Name = asinfra
[Ports]
Oracle HTTP Server port =  7777
Oracle HTTP Server Listen port = 7777
Oracle HTTP Server SSL port = 4443
Oracle HTTP Server Listen (SSL) port = 4443
Oracle HTTP Server Diagnostic port = 7200
Oracle Notification Server Request port = 6003
Oracle Notification Server Local port = 6101
Oracle Notification Server Remote port = 6200
ASG port = 7890
Log Loader port = 44000
Java Object Cache port = 7000
DCM Discovery port = 7100
Oracle Management Agent Port = 1157
Application Server Control RMI port = 1850
Application Server Control port = 1156
Oracle Internet Directory port = 389
Oracle Internet Directory (SSL) port = 636
Oracle Certificate Authority SSL Server Authentication port = 6600
Oracle Certificate Authority SSL Mutual Authentication port = 6601
Enterprise Manager Console HTTP Port (orcl) = 5500
Enterprise Manager Agent Port (orcl) = 1830
```

However, if you make any changes to your port assignments later, this list becomes obsolete. You can review and change the ports assigned to each component by clicking the Ports tab on the Oracle Enterprise Manager Application Server Control Instance home page (Figure 2.22). You can see the Ports page in Figure 2.23.

So as long as you can get to your instance's home page, you can get to all of your other components! From this page, you can also change component port assignments.

FIGURE 2.23 Oracle Application Server Ports page

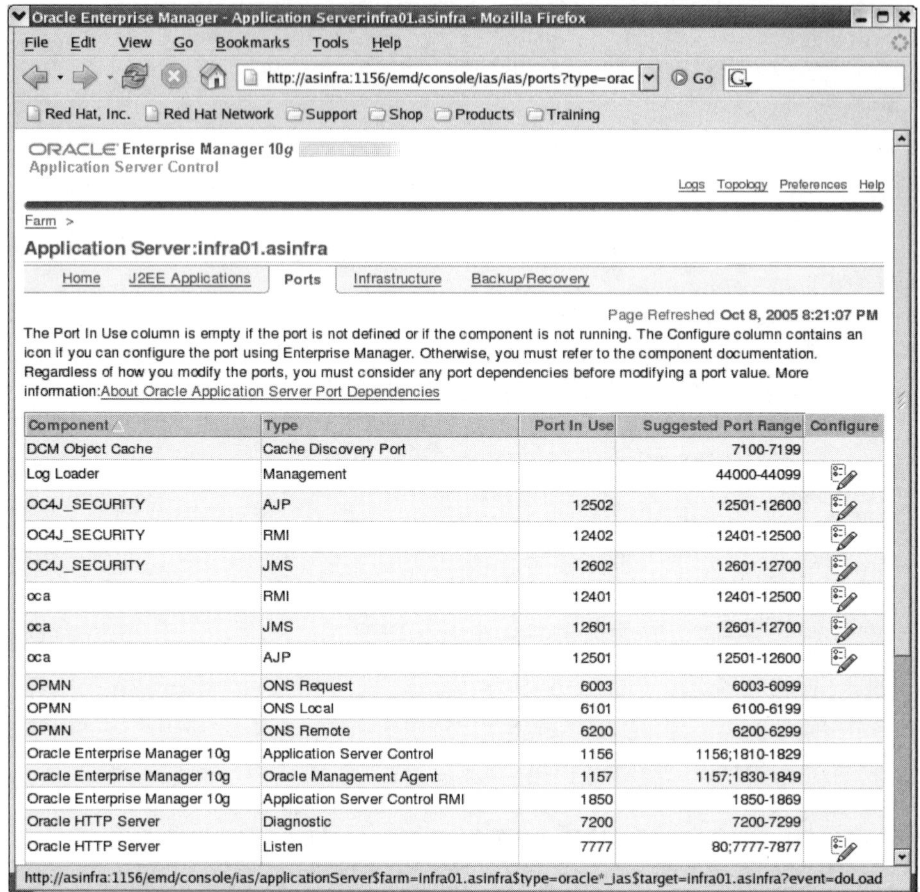

Connecting to the HTTP Server Home Page

By default, Oracle HTTP Server (OHS) is accessible via port 7777 of your host; in this case, `http://asinfra:7777`. You can see the OHS Welcome page in Figure 2.24.

You will most likely not access this page very often after installation. It contains links to release notes and new features, as well as a link to the Oracle Enterprise Manager Application Server Control home page.

FIGURE 2.24 OracleAS HTTP Server Welcome page

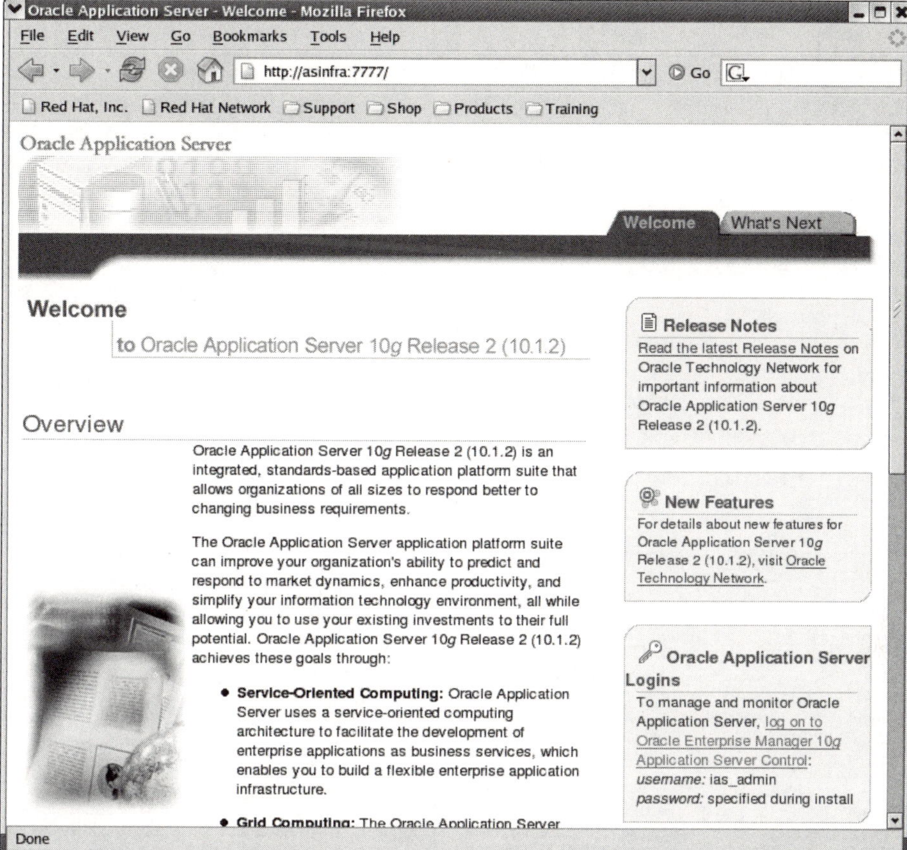

Using Enterprise Manager 10*g* Database Control

To access the database instance containing the metadata and application data for your Oracle Application Server instance, use this URL:

```
http://<hostname>:5500/em
```

In our sample Infrastructure installation, this URL is `http://asinfra:5500/em`. After entering the username SYS or SYSTEM and the password you provided during the Infrastructure installation on the Specify Database Schema Passwords page in Figure 2.16, and agreeing to the Oracle license, you see the Oracle Enterprise Manager Database Control home page in Figure 2.25.

FIGURE 2.25 OEM DB Control home page

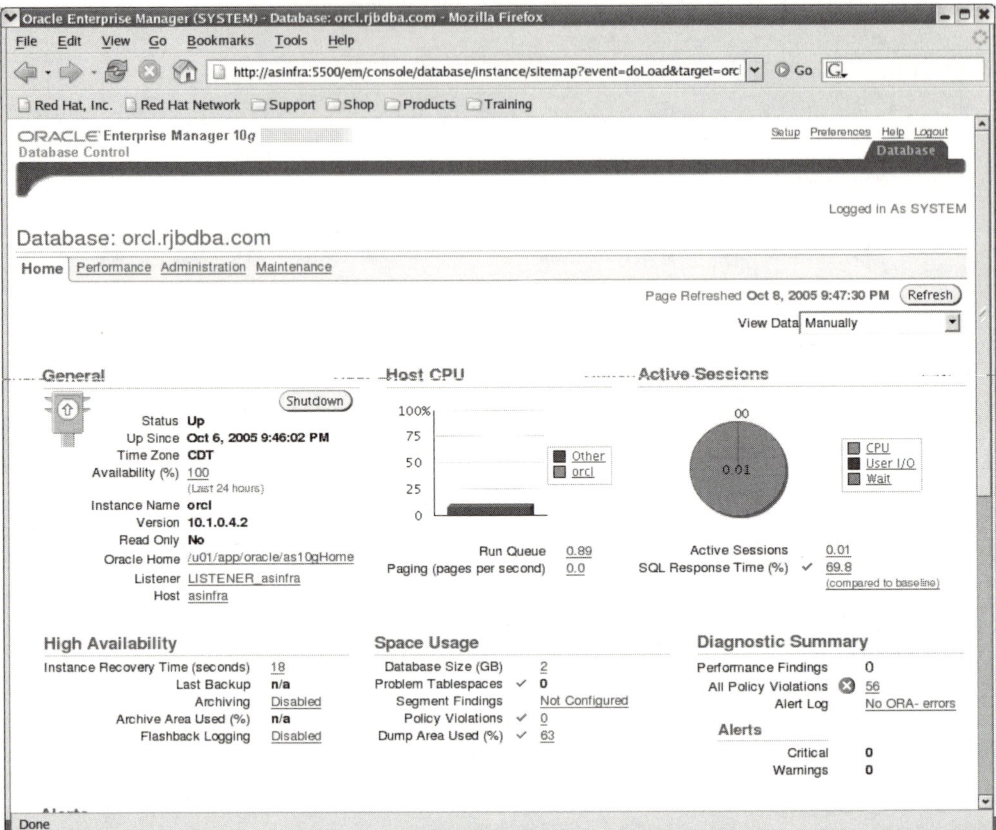

From this home page, you can control all aspects of the OracleAS Infrastructure's database.

Accessing the OID Server

To confirm that the Oracle Internet Directory (OID) server is active, navigate to the OID server home page from the OEM Application Server Control instance home page (Figure 2.22) by clicking the Internet Directory link in the list of system components. You will see the status of the OID server in the page shown in Figure 2.26.

This page contains the port number for OID; you will need this port number for any subsequent Middle-Tier installations that will use this OID server.

If you have other OID instances that are members of the same farm, you will see those instances on this page as well.

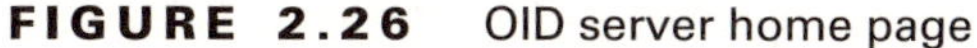

FIGURE 2.26 OID server home page

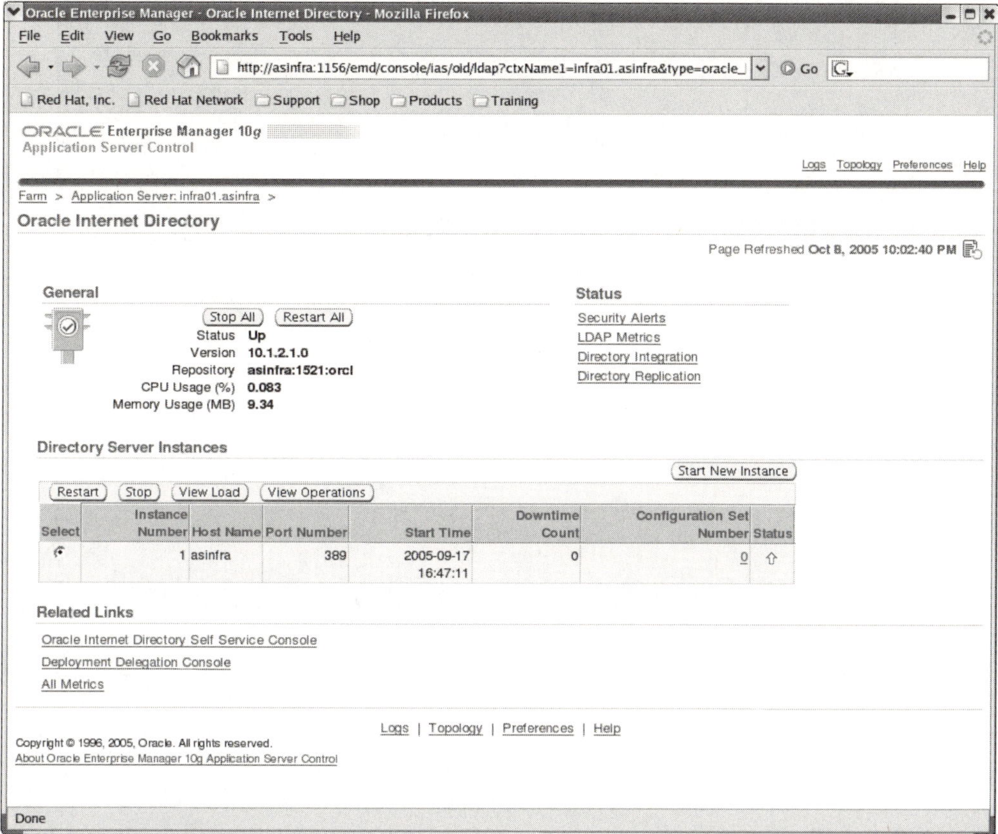

Accessing the SSO Server

To verify the status of the Single Sign-On (SSO) server, click the Single Sign-On:orasso link in the list of components on the OEM Application Server Control instance home page (Figure 2.22). On the Single Sign-On:orasso page, you can see whether the SSO server is up or down as well as some general login statistics. Next, click the Administer via Single Sign-On Web Application link, which brings you to the page in Figure 2.27. You may see more or fewer links on your page depending on whether you already have a Middle-Tier installation in your farm.

FIGURE 2.27 Oracle SSO Partner Applications page

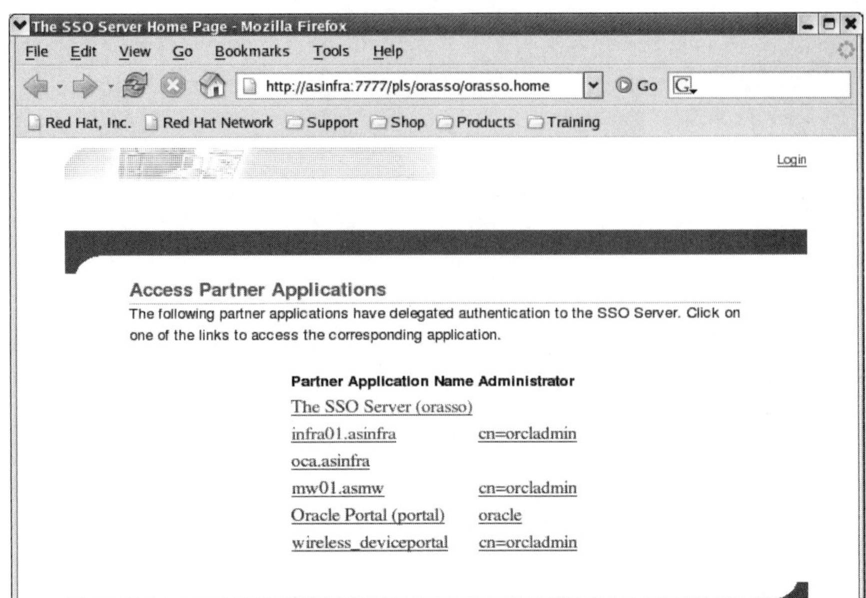

Click the Login link in the upper-right corner of this page. Use the user name `orcladmin` with the password you specified for the `ias_admin` account in the Specify Instance Name and `ias_admin` Password page (Figure 2.17); the Oracle SSO Partner Application page now has an SSO Server Administration page link. Clicking this link shows you the SSO Server Administration page; clicking the Administer Partner Applications link opens the page in Figure 2.28; on this page, you can edit the configuration of all partner applications. You add or configure external applications from a similar page. A *partner application* is an application that delegates authentication to the SSO server; an *external application* requires its own web-based authentication page. Although external applications do their own authentication, the SSO server will automatically log in to these applications for the user. As the name SSO implies, the user only has to authenticate once and the SSO server handles all subsequent authentications.

Starting and Stopping Infrastructure Components

To start up the Infrastructure components, after you either boot the host server or make changes to Infrastructure components, you should bring up the components in the following order:

- Database listener
- Metadata Repository database

- Enterprise Manager Database Control
- OracleAS Infrastructure instance processes
- Enterprise Manager Application Server Control

FIGURE 2.28 SSO Server Administration page

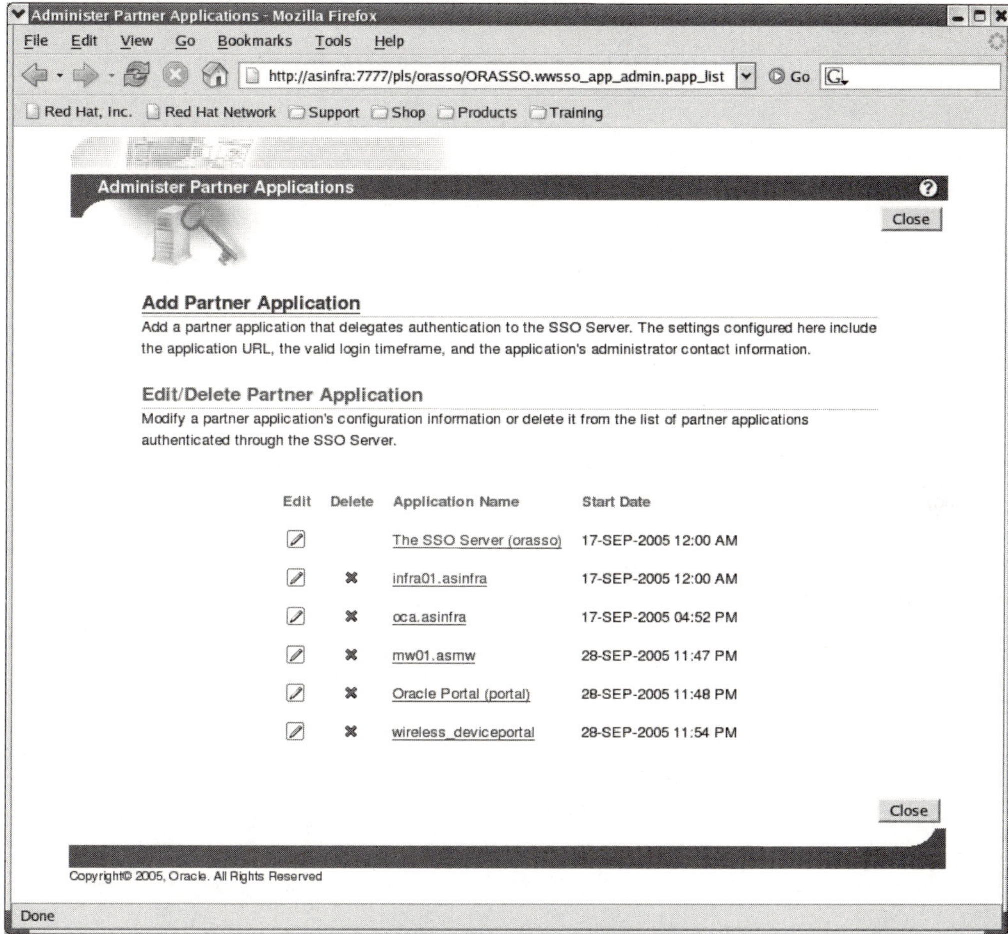

A custom startup script to perform these steps looks like this:

```
# start database listener
lsnrctl start
# start metadata repository database
dbstart
# start database console
emctl start dbconsole
```

```
# start infrastructure instance processes
opmnctl startall
# start AS console
emctl start iasconsole
```

The dbstart command is a shell script installed with Oracle Database 10*g* to start all databases configured with Y in the file /etc/oratab, discussed earlier in this chapter.

The output from these startup commands looks like this:

```
LSNRCTL for Linux: Version 10.1.0.4.2 -
           Production on 08-OCT-2005 23:14:04

Copyright (c) 1991, 2004, Oracle.  All rights reserved.

Starting /u01/app/oracle/as10gHome/bin/tnslsnr: please wait...

TNSLSNR for Linux: Version 10.1.0.4.2 - Production
System parameter file is
   /u01/app/oracle/as10gHome/network/admin/listener.ora
Log messages written to
   /u01/app/oracle/as10gHome/network/log/listener.log
Listening on:
  (DESCRIPTION=(ADDRESS=(PROTOCOL=tcp)(HOST=asinfra)(PORT=1521)))
Listening on: (DESCRIPTION=(ADDRESS=(PROTOCOL=ipc)(KEY=EXTPROC)))

Connecting to
  (DESCRIPTION=(ADDRESS=(PROTOCOL=TCP)(HOST=asinfra)(PORT=1521)))
STATUS of the LISTENER
------------------------
Alias                     LISTENER
Version                   TNSLSNR for Linux:
                            Version 10.1.0.4.2 - Production
Start Date                08-OCT-2005 23:14:04
Uptime                    0 days 0 hr. 0 min. 0 sec
Trace Level               off
Security                  ON: Local OS Authentication
SNMP                      OFF
Listener Parameter File
  /u01/app/oracle/as10gHome/network/admin/listener.ora
Listener Log File
  /u01/app/oracle/as10gHome/network/log/listener.log
```

```
Listening Endpoints Summary...
  (DESCRIPTION=(ADDRESS=(PROTOCOL=tcp)(HOST=asinfra)(PORT=1521)))
  (DESCRIPTION=(ADDRESS=(PROTOCOL=ipc)(KEY=EXTPROC)))
Services Summary...
Service "PLSExtProc" has 1 instance(s).
  Instance "PLSExtProc", status UNKNOWN, has 1 handler(s) for this
   service...
The command completed successfully

SQL*Plus: Release 10.1.0.4.2 - Production on Sat Oct 8 23:14:04 2005

Copyright (c) 1982, 2005, Oracle.  All rights reserved.

SQL> Connected to an idle instance.
SQL> ORACLE instance started.

Total System Global Area  281018368 bytes
Fixed Size                   778968 bytes
Variable Size             229645608 bytes
Database Buffers           50331648 bytes
Redo Buffers                 262144 bytes
Database mounted.
Database opened.
SQL> Disconnected from Oracle Database 10g Enterprise Edition
     Release 10.1.0.4.2 - Production
     With the Partitioning, OLAP and Data Mining options

Database "orcl" warm started.
TZ set to US/Central
Oracle Enterprise Manager 10g Database Control Release 10.1.0.3.0
Copyright (c) 1996, 2005 Oracle Corporation.  All rights reserved.
http://asinfra:5500/em/console/aboutApplication
Starting Oracle Enterprise Manager 10g Database Control ...... started.
------------------------------------------------------------------
Logs are generated in directory
  /u01/app/oracle/as10gHome/asinfra_orcl/sysman/log
opmnctl: starting opmn and all managed processes...
TZ set to US/Central
Oracle Enterprise Manager 10g Application Server Control Release
  10.1.2.0.2
Copyright (c) 1996, 2005 Oracle Corporation.  All rights reserved.
```

```
http://asinfra:1156/emd/console/aboutApplication
Starting Oracle Enterprise Manager 10g Application Server Control .....
  started successfully.
[oracle@asinfra oracle]$
```

Conversely, when you want to stop all components, do it in the reverse order. Therefore, your shutdown script looks like this:

```
# stop AS console
emctl stop iasconsole
# stop infrastructure instance processes
opmnctl stopall
# stop database console
emctl stop dbconsole
# stop metadata repository database
dbshut
# stop database listener
lsnrctl stop
```

No pathname is required for these commands as long as you include `$ORACLE_HOME/bin` and `$ORACLE_HOME/opmn/bin` in your `PATH` environment variable.

Installing the OracleAS Middle-Tier

The Oracle Application Server Middle-Tier component installation types fall into three categories: the J2EE and Web Cache installation, the Portal and Wireless installation, and the Business Intelligence and Forms installation. Regardless of which installation type you choose, Oracle HTTP Server (OHS), OracleAS Containers for J2EE (OC4J), and Oracle Enterprise Manager Application Server Control are always installed. You do not require the Metadata Repository installed earlier in this chapter in one scenario: when you install the OC4J and OracleAS Web Cache components without any clustering or Identity Management components.

For a Middle-Tier installation, you will follow the same pattern as we did earlier in this chapter for the Infrastructure installation:

- Present an overview of the installation
- Perform any product-specific preinstallation tasks
- Perform the installation of the Portal and Wireless components
- Perform product-specific postinstallation tasks
- Confirm access to the Middle-Tier components
- Create scripts to stop and start the Middle-Tier components

The hardware and software requirements presented earlier in this chapter in the section "Verifying Common Software and Hardware Requirements" apply to Middle-Tier installations as well. To emphasize the scalability and distributed nature of Oracle Application Server, we will walk you through the steps to install the Middle-Tier components on a different host, `asmw`, listed in Table 2.1. Perform the preinstallation tasks detailed earlier in this chapter on the second host.

You will install the Portal and Wireless components, which include the J2EE and Web Cache components. Since a Portal and Wireless installation requires an OracleAS Infrastructure, we will connect this installation to the Infrastructure installation performed on the server `asinfra` earlier in this chapter.

In addition, you will perform many of the same postinstallation tasks from the Infrastructure installation, such as updating the login script and ensuring that you are able to access each component home page. Finally, we will provide custom-built startup and shutdown scripts for the Middle-Tier components.

Middle-Tier Installation Tasks

In this section, we will step through the installation pages for a complete Portal and Wireless installation.

Mount the first installation CD (out of a total of four) in the CD-ROM drive, and run the `runInstaller` script to start OUI, just as you did with the Infrastructure installation. The installer performs a few basic installation checks, such as checking the operating system version, available disk space, and the number of display colors. An additional product-specific prerequisite check occurs later in the installation.

The first installation page gives you the opportunity to view existing products on this server as well as deinstall those products. You will see the same Welcome screen you saw with the Infrastructure installation (Figure 2.1). Since you are installing on a new host server, there are no existing products. After you click the Next button, you see the Specify Inventory Directory and Credentials screen that was shown in Figure 2.2; many of the pages in a Middle-Tier installation are identical to those from an Infrastructure installation. Accept the defaults and click the Next button to continue.

As you did in the Infrastructure installation, run the script identified in Figure 2.3 as the `root` user and click Continue.

On the Specify File Locations page (Figure 2.29), name the installation `as10g_mw` so it is easy to identify this installation in Oracle Enterprise Manager Application Server Control. The path name for the Oracle home is the same as on the Infrastructure installation: `/u01/app/oracle/as10gHome`. Click on the Next button to continue.

On the Select a Product to Install page in Figure 2.30, select Oracle Application Server 10*g* 10.1.2.0.2. This selection installs the middle-tier components. After you click the Next button, select the Portal and Wireless option on the page shown in Figure 2.31; this includes the J2EE and Web Cache components as well as the Portal and Wireless components; as mentioned earlier in this chapter, unless you are installing only J2EE and Web Cache, an OracleAS Infrastructure instance is required to store the metadata and configuration information for Portal and Wireless. Click the Next button.

FIGURE 2.29 Middle-tier installation Specify File Locations page

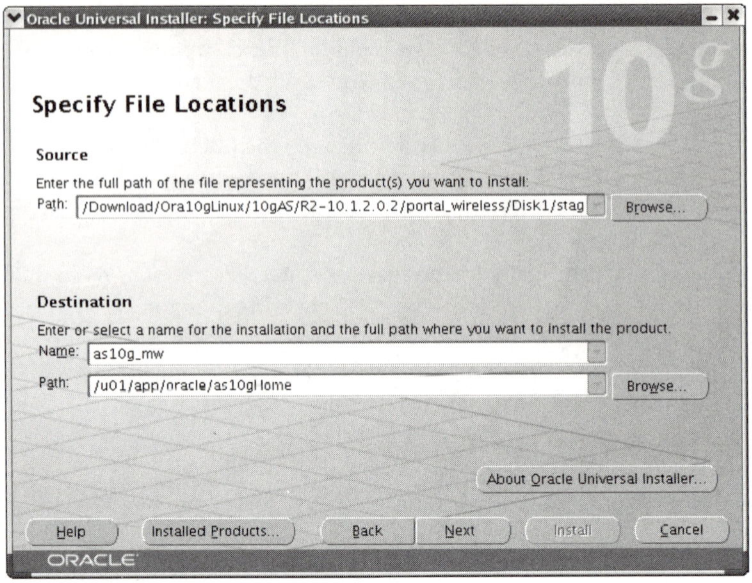

Oracle Universal Installer: Specify File Locations

Specify File Locations

Source

Enter the full path of the file representing the product(s) you want to install:

Path: /Download/Ora10gLinux/10gAS/R2-10.1.2.0.2/portal_wireless/Disk1/stag Browse...

Destination

Enter or select a name for the installation and the full path where you want to install the product.

Name: as10g_mw

Path: /u01/app/oracle/as10gHome Browse...

About Oracle Universal Installer...

Help Installed Products... Back Next Install Cancel

ORACLE

FIGURE 2.30 Middle-tier installation Select a Product to Install page

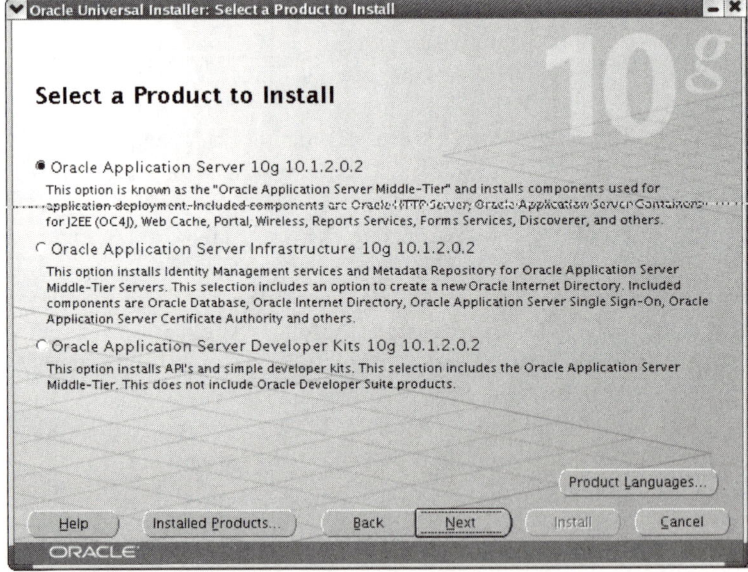

As shown on the page in Figure 2.32, OUI performs the same preinstallation checks that you see during an Infrastructure installation. Resolve any errors or warnings, click the Retry button, and once all checks pass, click the Next button. On the screen in Figure 2.33, you confirm that you have `root` access on this host and click the Next button.

FIGURE 2.31 Middle-tier installation Select Installation Type page

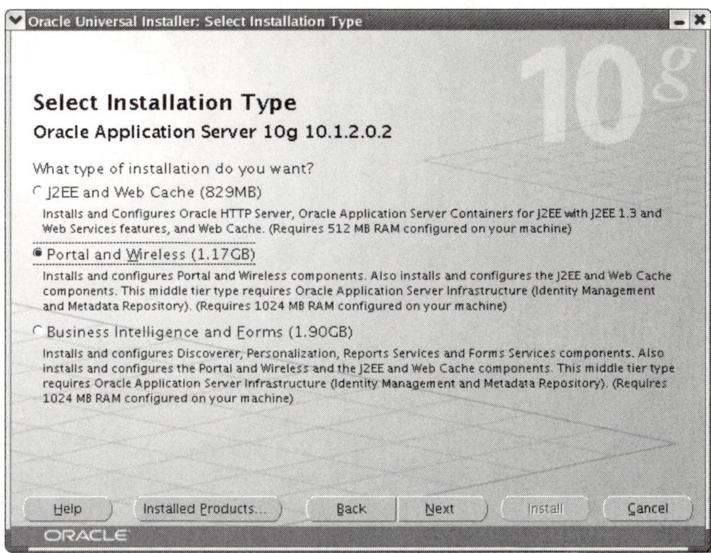

FIGURE 2.32 Middle-tier installation Product-Specific Prerequisite Checks page

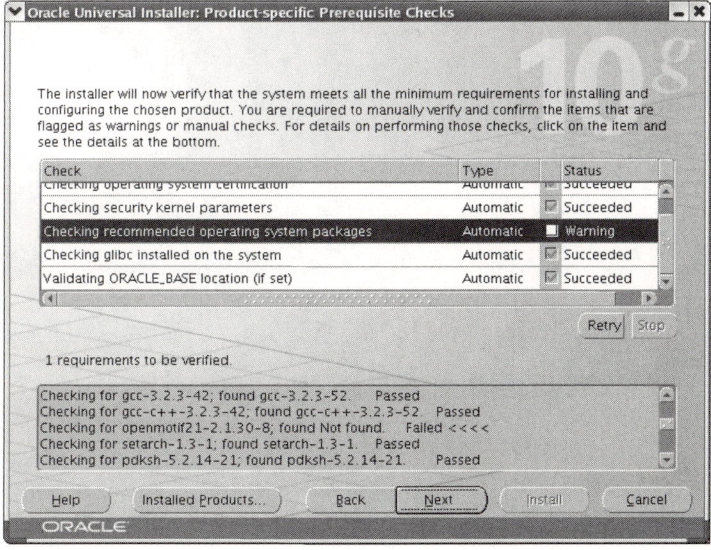

On the Select Configuration Options page (Figure 2.34), you select the components you want to configure once you complete the installation process. Any products you do not select are still installed; you can configure these components later. In this example, select both Portal and Wireless and click the Next button.

FIGURE 2.33 Middle-tier installation Confirm Pre-Installation Requirements page

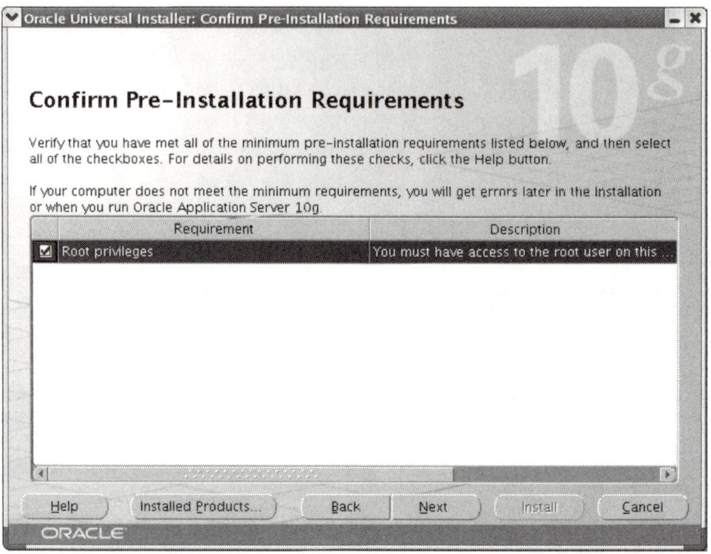

FIGURE 2.34 Middle-tier installation Select Configuration Options page

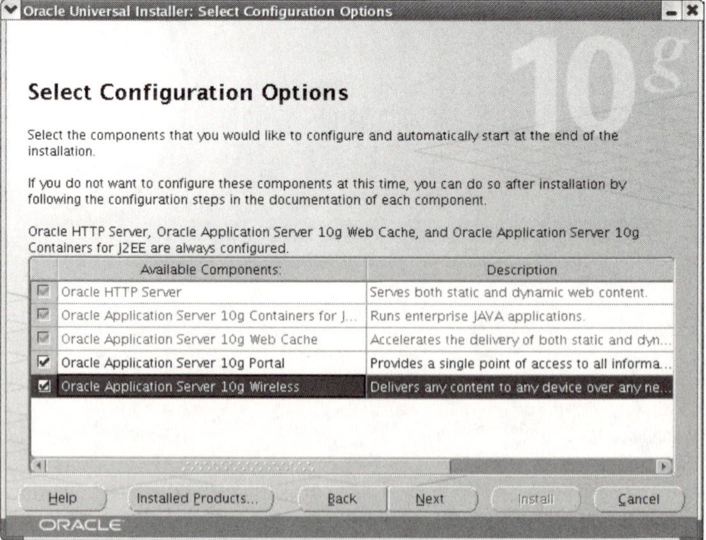

Since you do not have any other Oracle products or other applications installed on this host, you do not have to change the default port configuration; accept the Automatic port configuration option (Figure 2.35) and click the Next button.

Since you do not have an Infrastructure installation on this host, you must specify an Infrastructure installation on another host to support the metadata and directory requirements for the Portal and Wireless installation. From the Ports tab (Figure 2.23) on the Oracle Enterprise Manager Application Server Control instance home page, scroll down to reveal the SSL port used for OID on the host `asinfra`, as you can see in Figure 2.36.

You specify port 636 on the Register with Oracle Internet Directory page (Figure 2.37); since this is the SSL port, select the Use Only SSL Connections with This Oracle Internet Directory box to enhance the security of the connections between Oracle Application Server hosts. You installed the Infrastructure components on the host `asinfra`; put this hostname in the Host text box and click Next to continue.

FIGURE 2.35 Middle-tier installation Specify Port Configuration Options page

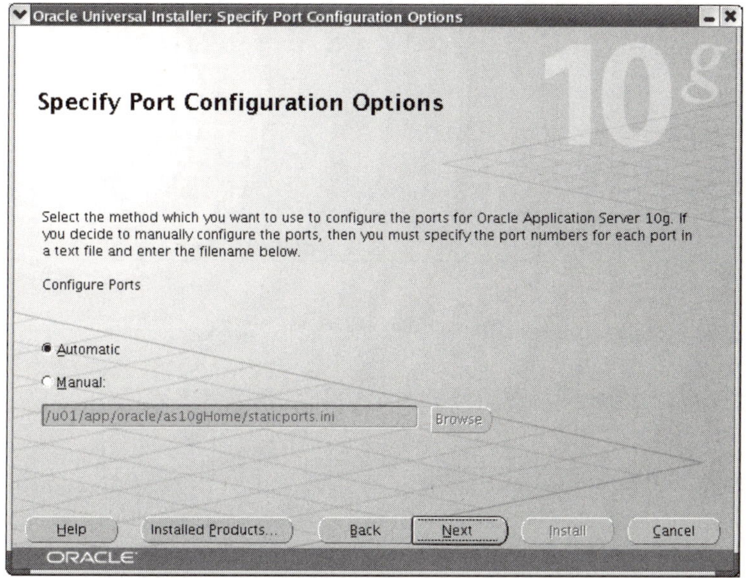

FIGURE 2.36 OID port assignment on asinfra

Oracle HTTP Server	Diagnostic	7200	7200-7299
Oracle HTTP Server	Listen	7777	80;7777-7877
Oracle HTTP Server	Listen (SSL)		443;4443-4543
Oracle Internet Directory	Non SSL Port	389	13060-13129
Oracle Internet Directory	SSL Port	636	13130-13199

Home J2EE Applications **Ports** Infrastructure Backup/Recovery

To use OID on `asinfra`, you specify the administrator username and password for `asinfra` on the page in Figure 2.38 as `cn=orcladmin` (where `cn=` stands for *common name* in LDAP terminology) along with the password you specified for `ias_admin` in the Infrastructure installation. Click the Next button to establish the connection to the OID server on `asinfra`.

FIGURE 2.37 Middle-tier installation Register with Oracle Internet Directory page

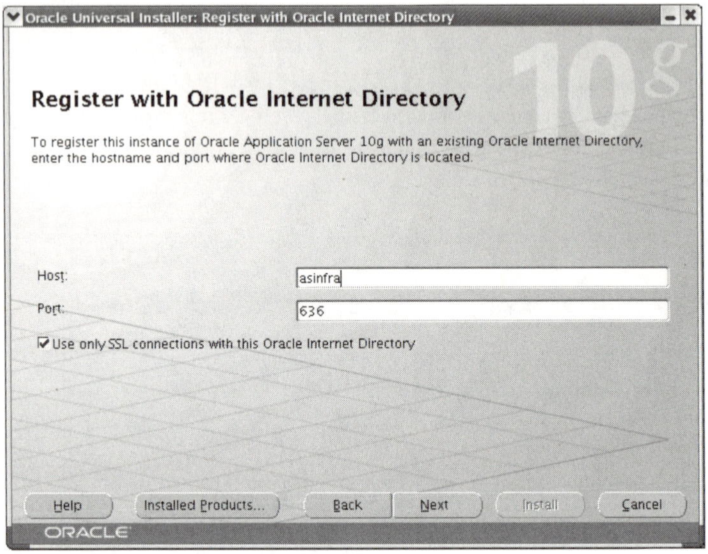

Oracle Universal Installer: Register with Oracle Internet Directory

Register with Oracle Internet Directory

To register this instance of Oracle Application Server 10g with an existing Oracle Internet Directory, enter the hostname and port where Oracle Internet Directory is located.

Host: asinfra

Port: 636

☑ Use only SSL connections with this Oracle Internet Directory

Help | Installed Products... | Back | Next | Install | Cancel

ORACLE

FIGURE 2.38 Middle-tier installation Specify OID Login page

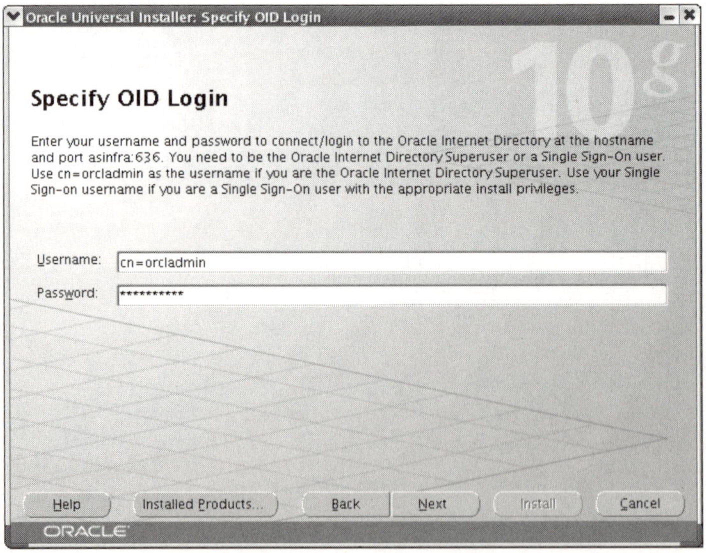

Oracle Universal Installer: Specify OID Login

Specify OID Login

Enter your username and password to connect/login to the Oracle Internet Directory at the hostname and port asinfra:636. You need to be the Oracle Internet Directory Superuser or a Single Sign-On user. Use cn=orcladmin as the username if you are the Oracle Internet Directory Superuser. Use your Single Sign-on username if you are a Single Sign-On user with the appropriate install privileges.

Username: cn=orcladmin

Password: ***********

Help | Installed Products... | Back | Next | Install | Cancel

ORACLE

To use the metadata repository created during the Infrastructure installation, specify the connection string for the Oracle 10*g* database on `asinfra`. The format of the connection string is as follows:

```
<hostname> : <port_number> : <global_database_name> : <service_name>
```

The default port number for an Infrastructure database is 1521, and in a non-RAC environment, the *`service_name`* is the same as the *`global_database_name`*; therefore, enter the following for the database connect string (Figure 2.39) and click the Next button:

```
asinfra:1521:orcl.rjbdba.com:orcl.rjbdba.com
```

FIGURE 2.39 Middle-tier installation Select Oracle Application Server 10g Metadata Repository page

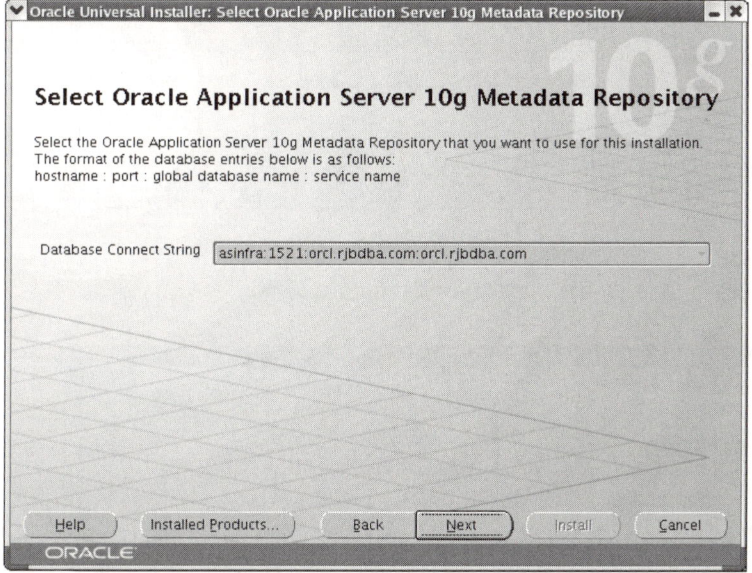

On the next page (Figure 2.40), provide an instance name and password for this Middle-Tier instance. Since you may soon have many middle-tier installations in this farm, specify `mw01` as the instance name and specify a password for the `ias_admin` account that is different from the password for the Infrastructure installation. Click the Next button.

The OUI Summary page shown in Figure 2.41 gives you one more chance to review your installation options before starting the installation. Click Install to proceed with the installation. Figure 2.42 shows the installer in action.

FIGURE 2.40 Middle-tier installation Specify Instance Name and ias_admin Password page

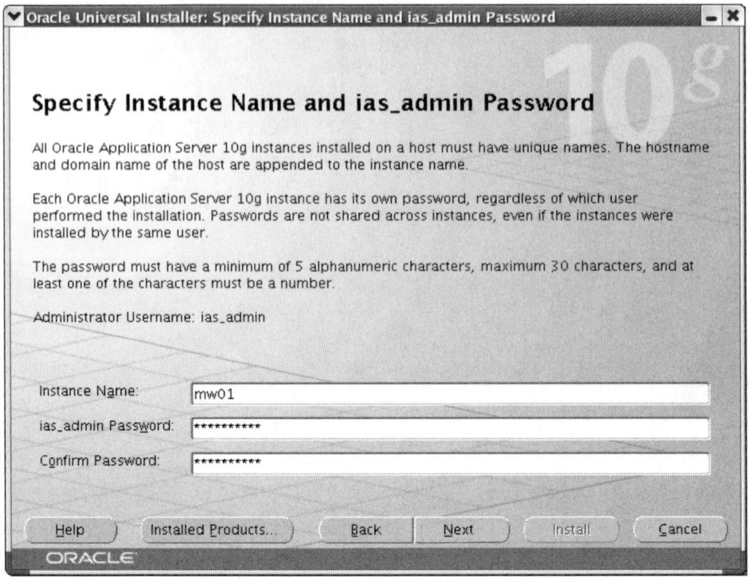

Oracle Universal Installer: Specify Instance Name and ias_admin Password
Specify Instance Name and ias_admin Password
All Oracle Application Server 10g instances installed on a host must have unique names. The hostname and domain name of the host are appended to the instance name.
Each Oracle Application Server 10g instance has its own password, regardless of which user performed the installation. Passwords are not shared across instances, even if the instances were installed by the same user.
The password must have a minimum of 5 alphanumeric characters, maximum 30 characters, and at least one of the characters must be a number.
Administrator Username: ias_admin
Instance Name:
mw01
ias_admin Password:
Confirm Password:
Help
Installed Products...
Back
Next
Install
Cancel
ORACLE

FIGURE 2.41 Middle-tier installation Summary page

Oracle Universal Installer: Summary
Summary
Oracle Application Server 10g 10.1.2.0.2
Global Settings
Source: /Download/Ora10gLinux/10gAS/R2-10.1.2.0.2/portal_wireless/Disk1/stage/product
Oracle Home: /u01/app/oracle/as10gHome (as10g_mw)
Installation Type: Portal and Wireless
Product Languages
English
Space Requirements
/ Required 1.13GB (includes 85MB temporary) : Available 8.21GB
New Installations (225 products)
ADF Business Components Config Assistant 10.1.2.0.2
ADF Business Components Config Assistant for agent 10.1.2.0.2
ADF Business Components Runtime Library 10.1.2.0.2
ADF Business Components Runtime for OracleAS 10.1.2.0.2
Help
Installed Products...
Back
Next
Install
Cancel
ORACLE

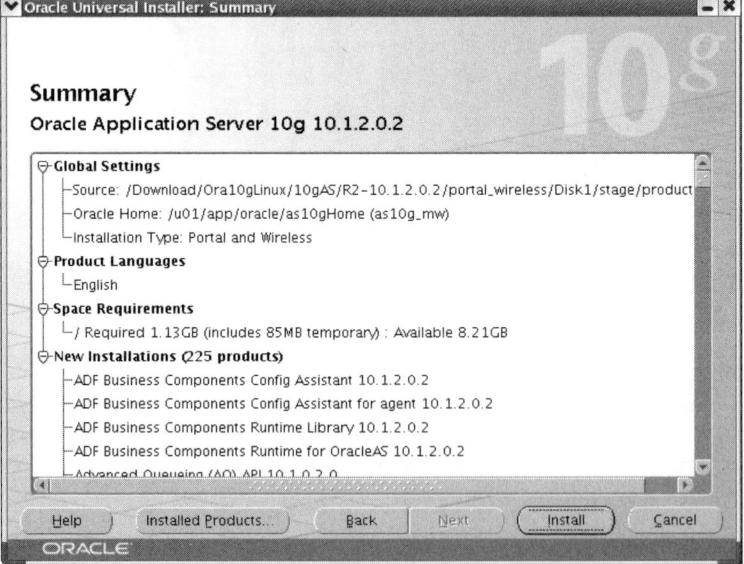

FIGURE 2.42 Middle-tier installation Install page

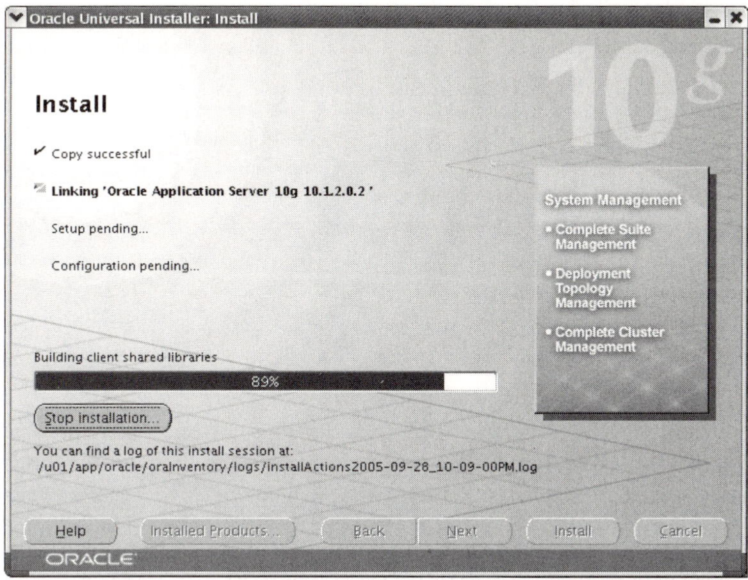

On the page shown in Figure 2.43, OUI prompts you to run a postinstallation script as the `root` user, similar to the postinstallation script you ran for the Infrastructure installation. The output from this script is as follows:

```
[root@asmw root]# /u01/app/oracle/as10gHome/root.sh
Running Oracle10 root.sh script...
\nThe following environment variables are set as:
    ORACLE_OWNER= oracle
    ORACLE_HOME=  /u01/app/oracle/as10gHome

Enter the full pathname of the local bin directory: [/usr/local/bin]:
   Copying dbhome to /usr/local/bin ...
   Copying oraenv to /usr/local/bin ...
   Copying coraenv to /usr/local/bin ...

\nCreating /etc/oratab file...
Adding entry to /etc/oratab file...
Entries will be added to the /etc/oratab file as needed by
```

```
Database Configuration Assistant when a database is created
Finished running generic part of root.sh script.
Now product-specific root actions will be performed.
```

FIGURE 2.43 Middle-tier installation Setup Privileges page

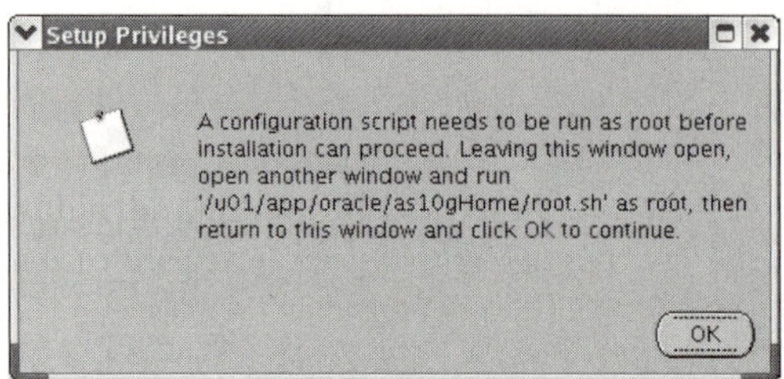

After this script has completed successfully, click the OK button to continue.

You see the configuration assistants for each installed component configure and start each component on the Configuration Assistants page (Figure 2.44).

When the installation completes, you see the End of Installation screen in Figure 2.45.

FIGURE 2.44 Middle-tier installation Configuration Assistants page

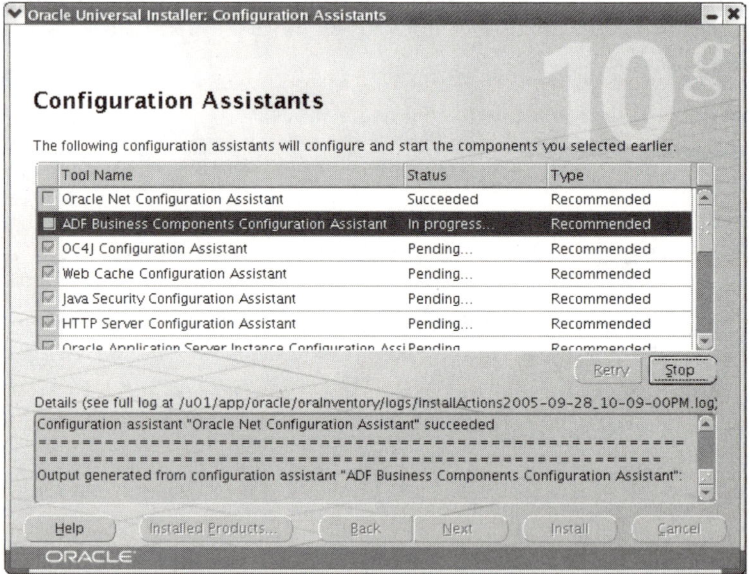

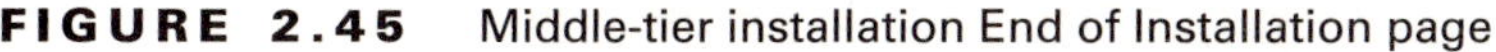

FIGURE 2.45 Middle-tier installation End of Installation page

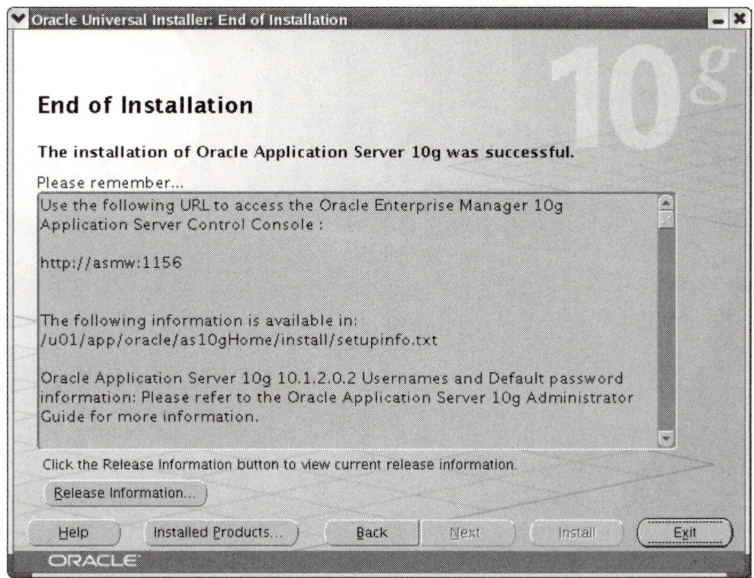

The End of Installation screen contains the URLs you need to access the various Middle-Tier components; here is the full text from Figure 2.47:

```
Use the following URL to access the Oracle Enterprise Manager 10g
  Application Server Control Console :

http://asmw:1156

The following information is available in:
/u01/app/oracle/as10gHome/install/setupinfo.txt

Oracle Application Server 10g 10.1.2.0.2 Usernames and Default password
  information: Please refer to the Oracle Application Server 10g
  Administrator Guide for more information.

Install Type: Portal and Wireless Services

Configured Components: Oracle HTTP Server, Oracle Application Server
  10g Containers for J2EE, Oracle Application Server 10g Web Cache,
  Oracle Application Server 10g Portal, Oracle Application Server 10g
  Wireless,
```

```
Registered with Oracle Internet Directory: asinfra:636

Use only SSL connections with this Oracle Internet Directory:Yes

Database Connection String:
  asinfra:1521:orcl.rjbdba.com:orcl.rjbdba.com
Use the following URL to access the Oracle HTTP Server and the Welcome
  Page:

http://asmw:7777

-----------------------------------------
Use the following URL to access the Oracle Enterprise Manager
  Application Server Control:

http://asmw:1156
Instance Name: mw01.asmw
```

Middle-Tier Postinstallation Tasks

The postinstallation tasks for an OracleAS Middle-Tier installation are similar to the OracleAS Infrastructure postinstallation tasks; accessing the Middle-Tier pages is identical in many respects to accessing the Infrastructure pages because the Middle-Tier installation and the Infrastructure installation share many of the same components. In the following sections, we will provide a high-level review of the components in the Middle-Tier installation that do not appear in the Infrastructure installation or have significant differences from their Infrastructure counterparts.

Updating the Login Script

Update the `oracle` user's login script to include new environment variables as you did for the Infrastructure installation in the section "Updating the Login Script."

Accessing the Middle-Tier Home Page

Since you install the Oracle Enterprise Manager Application Server Control console with each Oracle Application Server installation and both the Infrastructure and Middle-Tier installations share the same metadata repository, the URL `http://asmw:1156` shows you the same page you saw in Figure 2.21, the only difference being in the URL itself. The console application prompts for a username and password; specify the username `ias_admin` and the password you provided on the page shown in Figure 2.40.

When you click the `mw01.asmw` link, you see the Middle-Tier home page in Figure 2.46; it looks very similar to the Infrastructure home page since they both include the Oracle HTTP Server, Web Cache, and OC4J components. In addition, this installation includes the Portal and Wireless components.

FIGURE 2.46 Middle-tier home page

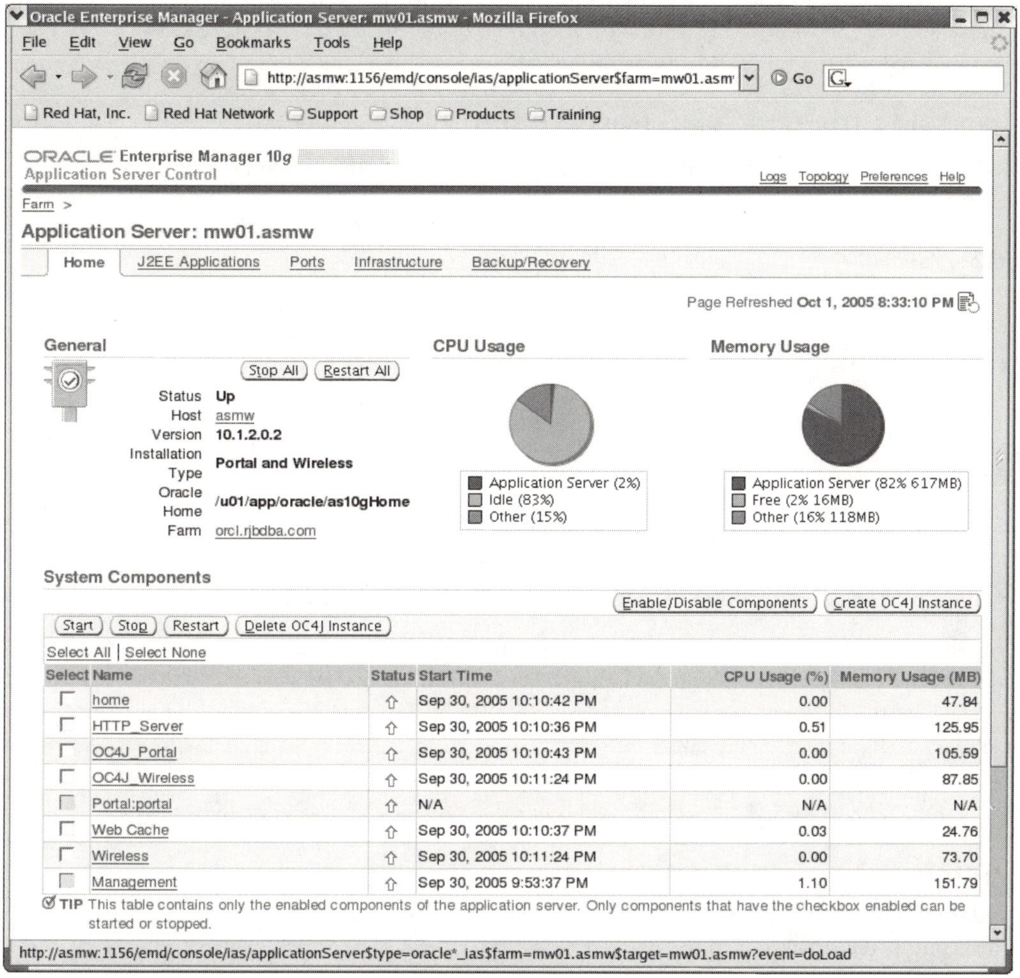

Accessing the Oracle Application Server Ports Page

The location for the initial port list for Middle-Tier components is the same as it is for an Infrastructure installation: `$ORACLE_HOME/install/portlist.ini`. From the Middle-Tier home page, the current port assignments are available by clicking the Ports tab; the port assignments listed in `$ORACLE_HOME/install/portlist.ini` are not updated later when you make changes to port assignments you make on the Ports tab.

Accessing the Oracle Application Server Welcome Page

The Oracle Application Server Welcome page is at the same location as it is for an Infrastructure installation; for the Middle-Tier installation on host `asmw`, the URL is `http://asmw:7777`. The main difference is the link to the Portal home page.

Accessing the OracleAS Portal Page

As an alternative to accessing the OracleAS Portal Welcome page from the Middle-Tier welcome page, you can use the following URL:

```
http://<hostname>:<port_number>/pls/portal
```

For the host `asmw`, this is the URL:

```
http://asmw:7777/pls/portal
```

When you navigate to this URL, you see the Portal home page in Figure 2.47. You log in to the portal management page with a username of `portal` and the password for the `ias_admin` account you created during the Middle-Tier installation.

FIGURE 2.47 Portal home page

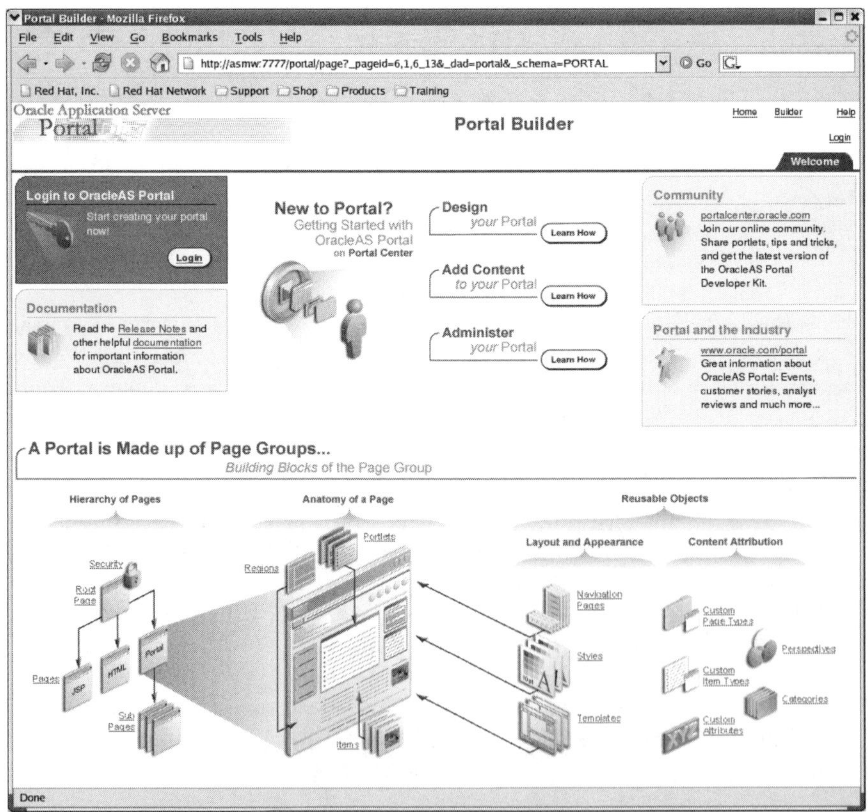

Starting and Stopping Middle-Tier Components

To start up the Middle-Tier components, after you either boot the host server or make changes to Middle-Tier components, you should bring up the components in the following order:

- Oracle Application Server Middle-Tier instance processes
- Oracle Enterprise Manager Application Server Control

The startup script to perform these steps looks like this:

```
# start middleware instance processes
opmnctl startall
# start AS console
emctl start iasconsole
```

Conversely, when you want to stop all components, do it in the reverse order. Therefore, your shutdown script looks like this:

```
# stop AS console
emctl stop iasconsole
# stop middleware instance processes
opmnctl stopall
```

No pathname is required for these commands as long as you include `$ORACLE_HOME/bin` and `$ORACLE_HOME/opmn/bin` in your `PATH` environment variable.

Not surprisingly, the startup and shutdown scripts are very similar to those you use for the Infrastructure installation except that the Middle-Tier installation does not have a database listener, a database instance, or a database console application.

Summary

You can easily install Oracle Application Server components with the Oracle Universal Installer (OUI). However, before you mount the first CD-ROM, you must verify that your host meets the minimum requirements for operating system, disk space, and memory: a typical Portal and Wireless installation requires 1024MB of RAM and at least 1.1GB of disk space.

In addition, your environment must be fine-tuned before an installation may begin. All Oracle Application Server products require specific user accounts, software directories, and environment variables. Just as important are the correct settings for operating system kernel parameters, such as the maximum number of processes and maximum number of open files. Without these limits increased, the installed components of Oracle Application Server may fail as the load on the host and the Oracle Application Server applications increases.

In the first half of this chapter, we presented a thorough walk-through of an OracleAS Infrastructure installation including both the Identity Management components and the Metadata Repository components. We also explained how a Metadata Repository installation is a prerequisite for nearly every other type of Oracle Application Server installation, except for a J2EE and Web Cache installation.

In the second half of this chapter, you installed the Portal and Wireless components on a second host, using the first host's Metadata Infrastructure and Oracle Internet Directory; as a result, you created an Oracle Application Server farm with two installations.

For both types of installations, it is important to automate your installation component startup and shutdown; we provided you with scripts for both an Infrastructure installation and a Middle-Tier installation that start up and shut down each component in the correct order.

Finally, we showed you how to access the Oracle Enterprise Manager Application Server Control and Oracle Enterprise Manager Database Control home pages as well as the configuration pages for the Oracle HTTP Server, the OID server, the SSO server, and the Portal server.

Exam Essentials

Understand the common software and hardware requirements for either an Infrastructure or Middle-Tier installation. Be able to determine the operating system version, memory, and disk space on your host using common operating system utilities. Based on these results, identify which Oracle Application Server products are installable on the host.

Describe the operating system requirements for both an Infrastructure and a Middle-Tier installation. Understand the operating system users and groups required for installation: the `oracle` user and the `oinstall` group. Become proficient in editing login scripts to set and unset required environment variables both during and after the installation. Adjust the kernel parameters to ensure that the Oracle Application Server processes will have enough resources to run efficiently and without error.

Identify the steps required to start and complete an Infrastructure installation. Be able to mount the CD-ROM or disk image containing the Oracle software and start the Infrastructure installation. Understand the two subcomponents of an Infrastructure installation: Identity Management and Metadata Repository. Understand the dependencies between these two subcomponents. Be able to update the appropriate environment variables after the installation is complete.

Identify the steps required to start and complete a Middle-Tier installation. Be able to mount the CD-ROM or disk image containing the Oracle software and start the Portal and Wireless Middle-Tier installation. Understand the dependencies between Middle-Tier components and OracleAS Infrastructure components and how to connect the Middle-Tier components to both the OID and Metadata Repository components of the Infrastructure. Be able to update the appropriate environment variables after the installation is complete.

Be able to create scripts to gracefully start and stop the processes for an Infrastructure or Middle-Tier installation. Understand the order in which you must start and stop the Oracle Application Server components as well as which startup and shutdown commands apply only to an Infrastructure installation.

Understand how to access each component's home page. Be able to access the Oracle Application Server home page from each host in a farm. Know the URL for each component, as well as where to look for the current port numbers assigned to each component on each host.

Review Questions

1. Which Oracle Application Server component requires the largest amount of disk space?
   - A. J2EE and Web Cache.
   - B. OracleAS Portal and Wireless.
   - C. OracleAS Infrastructure.
   - D. All components of Oracle Application Server require about the same amount of disk space.
2. How much swap space is required for any Oracle Application Server installation?
   - A. No swap space is required.
   - B. 0.5GB available at install time.
   - C. 1.0GB available at install time.
   - D. 1.5GB available at install time.
3. Which of the following is not a preinstallation task for a Middle-Tier installation?
   - A. Add entries to `/etc/hosts`
   - B. Create directories for Oracle software
   - C. Configure kernel parameters
   - D. Specify a metadata repository database connect string
   - E. Create user and group accounts
4. Given the four key environment variables `TMP`, `DISPLAY`, `ORACLE_HOME`, and `ORACLE_SID`, which of these variables must be set or not set during an OracleAS Infrastructure installation?
   - A. `TMP` and `DISPLAY` are not set; `ORACLE_HOME` and `ORACLE_SID` are set.
   - B. `TMP` and `DISPLAY` are set; `ORACLE_HOME` and `ORACLE_SID` are not set.
   - C. `TMP` and `ORACLE_HOME` are set; `DISPLAY` and `ORACLE_SID` are not set.
   - D. `TMP` and `ORACLE_SID` are not set; `DISPLAY` and `ORACLE_HOME` are set.
   - E. All four of these variables must not be set during an OracleAS Infrastructure installation.
5. If the `TMP` environment variable is not set during an Infrastructure installation, what happens?
   - A. OUI uses the `/tmp` directory to hold temporary files.
   - B. OUI will not start.
   - C. OUI uses swap space instead of temporary files.
   - D. OUI uses available RAM for temporary files.
6. For the `oracle` user, what is the minimum value for the `nofile` user limit?
   - A. 4096
   - B. 16384
   - C. 128
   - D. 65536

7. Which of the following locations does not have any information about ports used by the installed Oracle Application Server components?

   A. `/etc/services`

   B. `staticports.ini`

   C. The Ports tab on the Oracle Enterprise Manager Application Server Control home page

   D. `dynamicports.ini`

8. Which of the following Identity Management components has an administrator account with a password different from the `ias_admin` account password?

   A. Oracle Internet Directory

   B. OracleAS Single Sign-On

   C. Oracle Delegated Administration Services

   D. Oracle Directory Integration and Provisioning

   E. OracleAS Certificate Authority

9. Which of the following Identity Management components requires the OracleAS Metadata Repository? (Choose the best answer.)

   A. Oracle Internet Directory

   B. OracleAS Single Sign-On

   C. Oracle Delegated Administration Services

   D. Oracle Directory Integration and Provisioning

   E. OracleAS Certificate Authority

   F. All of the above

   G. None of the above

10. What is the primary function of the file `/etc/oraInst.loc`?

    A. Contains a pointer to Oracle Application Server installations on other hosts

    B. Determines which Oracle databases on this host should start automatically

    C. Stores the name of the directory where the OUI stores information about each installation performed on this host

    D. Contains the default list of ports used by each component in an Oracle Application Server installation

11. What are the two default subcontainers created, with a default set of policies, when OID is configured?

    A. `cn=users` and `cn=groups`

    B. `cn=users` and `cn=administrators`

    C. `cn=administrators` and `cn=ias_admin`

    D. `cn=users` and `cn=ias_admin`

12. For a Middle-Tier installation on a host without any existing Oracle products installed, what functions does the `orainstRoot.sh` script perform? (Choose all that apply.)

    A. Creates the scripts `dbhome`, `oraenv`, and `coraenv` in `/usr/local/bin`

    B. Creates the `/etc/oratab` file

    C. Grants permissions on the inventory directory to all users in the oinstall group

    D. Creates `/etc/oraInst.loc` to point to the inventory directory

    E. Creates the `/etc/oracle` directory

13. For a Middle-Tier installation on a host without any existing Oracle products installed, what functions does the `root.sh` script perform? (Choose all that apply.)

    A. Creates the scripts `dbhome`, `oraenv`, and `coraenv` in `/usr/local/bin`

    B. Creates the `/etc/oratab` file

    C. Grants permissions on the inventory directory to all users in the oinstall group

    D. Creates `/etc/oraInst.loc` to point to the inventory directory

    E. Creates the `/etc/oracle` directory

14. Which of the following components do you install in a Middle-Tier installation of Oracle Application Server? (Choose all that apply.)

    A. Web Cache

    B. Oracle HTTP Server

    C. Portal and Wireless

    D. Oracle Internet Directory

    E. Single Sign-On

15. Which of the following accounts do you use to administer Portal applications?

    A. `ias_admin`

    B. `orcladmin`

    C. `SYS`

    D. `portal`

    E. `SYSTEM`

16. You are installing a Middle-Tier instance and you need to specify the location of the OracleAS Metadata Repository; the host for the Metadata Repository is `oc12.rjbdba.com`, the port number for the listener on host `oc12` is 1522, and the global database name is `orcl2.rjbinc.com`. The service name is `orcl1.rjbinc.com`. Which of the following connection strings will connect you to this repository?

    A. `oc12.rjbdba.com:1522:orcl2.rjbinc.com:orcl1.rjbinc.com`

    B. `oc12.rjbdba.com:1522:orcl1.rjbinc.com:orcl2.rjbinc.com`

    C. `oc12.rjbdba.com:orcl1.rjbinc.com:1522:orcl2.rjbinc.com`

    D. `orcl2.rjbinc.com:1522:oc12.rjbdba.com:orcl1.rjbinc.com`

17. If you do not want to accept the default port assignments during an Infrastructure or Middle-Tier installation, you may manually specify component port assignments in a file named ___________ that resides in the directory ___________.

A. `portlist.ini`, `$ORACLE_BASE`

B. `staticports.ini`, `$ORACLE_BASE`

C. `portlist.ini`, `$ORACLE_HOME`

D. `staticports.ini`, `$ORACLE_HOME`

E. The file can have any name and reside in any directory.

F. You cannot override the port assignments until the installation is complete.

18. Access to which account is required to run the `root.sh` script during an Infrastructure or Middle-Tier installation?

A. `oracle`

B. `dba`

C. `oinstall`

D. `root`

19. Which Oracle Application Server component requires the smallest amount of disk space?

A. J2EE and Web Cache components.

B. OracleAS Portal and Wireless components.

C. OracleAS Infrastructure components.

D. All components of Oracle Application Server require about the same amount of disk space.

20. Which of the following components do you install in an Infrastructure installation of Oracle Application Server? (Choose all that apply.)

A. Web Cache

B. Oracle HTTP Server

C. Portal and Wireless

D. Oracle Internet Directory

E. Single Sign-On

Answers to Review Questions

1. C. The OracleAS Infrastructure installation requires the most disk space, 2.6GB.

2. D. For any Oracle Application Server installation, there must be 1.5GB of free swap space available; the total swap space may be more but currently used by other applications.

3. D. Specifying a connection to a metadata repository database occurs during a Middle-Tier installation and is not a preinstallation task. Other preinstallation tasks include setting environment variables, configuring user limits, and verifying the availability of listener ports.

4. B. `TMP` and `DISPLAY` must be set during the installation; `ORACLE_HOME` and `ORACLE_SID` must not be set. Once the installation is complete, you can set `ORACLE_HOME` and `ORACLE_SID` in the `oracle` user's login script.

5. A. OUI uses the `/tmp` directory if the `TMP` environment variable is not set. Regardless of the location, at least 400MB of temporary disk space must be available for temporary installation files.

6. D. In the operating system file `/etc/security/limits.conf`, the value for `nofile` must be at least 65536. In other words, the number of simultaneous open files for Oracle Application Server processes may be up to 65536.

7. D. There is no file named `dynamicports.ini`.

8. E. During an Infrastructure installation that includes Identity Management, you are prompted for an OCA password.

9. F. All of the listed components require a metadata repository.

10. C. The first installation performed by OUI creates this file; it contains the name of the inventory directory so that future installations can put inventory information in the same directory.

11. A. OUI creates two subcontainers, one for users and one for groups, with a default set of policies within the realm created during OID configuration.

12. C, D. For a Middle-Tier installation on a host without any existing Oracle products installed, the `orainstRoot.sh` script grants permissions on the inventory directory and creates the file `/etc/oraInst.loc` to point to the inventory location.

13. A, B, E. For a Middle-Tier installation on a host without any existing Oracle products installed, the `root.sh` script creates scripts in `/usr/local/bin`, creates `/etc/oratab` to contain database startup information, and creates `/etc/oracle` to hold information about Oracle cluster software on this host.

14. A, B, C. Web Cache and Oracle HTTP Server are parts of either installation type; Portal and Wireless components are installed only in a Middle-Tier installation.

15. D. The `portal` account is the administrator account for the Oracle Portal page; its password is the same as the password for `ias_admin`.

16. A. The following format is used for the connection string to a database repository:

    ```
    <hostname>: <port_number> : <global_database_name> : <service_name>
    ```

17. E. You may use any text file in any directory for overriding port assignments as long as the directory and file are accessible to the OUI process.

18. D. The privileged account `root` is required to run all scripts during an installation except for the script that starts the installation, `runInstaller`. The `oracle` account is the owner of the Oracle Application Server executables and configuration files; `oinstall` and `dba` are groups, not users.

19. A. The OracleAS J2EE and Web Cache installation requires the least amount of disk space, 0.5GB.

20. A, B, D, E. Web Cache and Oracle HTTP Server are parts of either installation type, Portal and Wireless components are installed only in a Middle-Tier installation, and Oracle Internet Directory and Single Sign-On are only included in an Infrastructure installation.

Understanding Application Server Management Tools

ORACLE APPLICATION SERVER 10*g* ADMINISTRATION I EXAM OBJECTIVES COVERED IN THIS CHAPTER:

✓ **Using Oracle Application Server Management Tools**

- Start and stop Application Server Control
- Access OracleAS Component pages of the Application Server Control
- Start and stop an OracleAS instance or a component using Application Server Control and Oracle Process Monitoring and Notification interface (`opmnctl`)
- Use `dcmctl` utility to obtain configuration information

No matter how good an application server product is, it must have the support tools to make it easy for you, the application server system administrator, to maintain the server. The application server tools should be web based for day-to-day usage and must have command-line equivalents for situations in which a web browser is not available. In addition, the tools must be highly scalable to manage your entire farm of application servers from a single point of entry. Oracle Application Server 10*g*'s (OracleAS's) suite of tools fulfills all of these requirements.

At the highest level of the tool hierarchy is Oracle Enterprise Manager (OEM) 10*g* Grid Control (Grid Control), incorporating most of the features of OEM 10*g* Database Control (Database Control) and OEM 10*g* Application Server Control (Application Server Control or AS Control) along with collaborative management and historical performance monitoring features.

This chapter will cover two broad topics: understanding and comparing the web-based management tools and using the equivalent command-line tools. We showed you some of these tools at a very high level in Chapter 1, "Introducing Oracle Application Server 10*g* and Components." In this chapter, we will drill down much more deeply into the understanding and usage of these tools.

In the first half of this chapter, we will explore the basic functionality of Grid Control and compare its characteristics and capabilities to the more focused Database Control and Application Server Control.

Next, we will focus on key pages within Application Server Control, including the home page, the Farm page, and the instance page, and review the components accessible from each of these pages. On the instance page, you can monitor the status of each component within the instance as well as start, stop, or restart any component.

Another important and useful feature of AS Control that will be discussed in the first part of this chapter is the Topology Viewer. Using this tool, you can not only visually assess the architecture of your application server components, but also drill down into each component to reveal its health and status.

Logging the events in the application server environment is another key function that Oracle Application Server handles automatically. OracleAS records log events in operating system files and optionally in the database repository; if you use a database repository, all events for all instances in a farm reside in the same database repository location. This feature also will be addressed in the first part of this chapter.

In the second half of the chapter, we will delve more deeply into the OracleAS command line tools `emctl`, `opmnctl`, and `dcmctl`. For example, the `emctl` command not only starts and stops Database Control and Application Server Control, but also secures the communications for Application Server Control connections using Secure Sockets Layer (SSL) to maximize security in your environment. We will also review how `dcmctl` can manage and deploy components in your environment as well as how to use `opmnctl` to start and stop instances and components.

Understanding Oracle Enterprise Manager 10*g* Application Server Control

The focus of this chapter is on OEM 10*g* Application Server Control; however, we will cover many aspects of both OEM 10*g* Grid Control and OEM 10*g* Database Control, and how they compare to Application Server Control. Your infrastructure may consist of only a handful of hosts with a few AS installations. Once you start adding other database servers or start clustering your application servers, the benefits of Grid Control may offset the resources needed to support a Grid Control installation.

In the following sections, we will review the Grid Control architecture before we dive right in and revisit some of the AS Control pages in more depth. We will also show you how to use these pages to start and stop an entire instance or an individual component of an instance.

Another important component of AS Control is the *Topology Viewer*: a graphical viewer, available as either an HTML-based or a Java-based application that shows the relationships between installations and components along with statistics for each installation or component. You can retrieve even more details of each component by clicking on an icon and drilling down into the details for the component.

Application Server Control also makes it easy to analyze the performance of your infrastructure. From an AS Control page, you can monitor application server performance in real-time and obtain tips on how to adjust application server parameters and resolve performance problems. Component performance over a longer period is available on a historical basis; you can monitor historical performance at the component level.

Finally, we will review the logging options available in Oracle Application Server and how to ease maintenance by recording log entries from multiple AS instances in a database repository.

Comparing Management Tools

Each Oracle product you install comes with its own management console; if you have a small shop, this may be sufficient for your needs. However, as the number of managed targets increases, installing Grid Control can centralize your management tasks from a single console. A *managed target* is an Oracle installation controlled by a Grid Control installation.

In the next three sections, we will compare and contrast Database Control, Application Server Control, and Grid Control.

Oracle Enterprise Manager 10*g* Database Control

The OEM 10*g* Database Control console manages these components:

- Database
- Database listeners
- Automatic Storage Management (ASM) disks
- Host *targets* (physical servers hosting the Oracle Application Server installation)

If you have only one or two stand-alone database instances or a single Real Application Clusters database to manage, Database Control is sufficient to monitor those targets and the host. Once you increase the number of managed targets, however, Grid Control becomes a more efficient way to manage multiple databases and their hosts.

Oracle Enterprise Manager 10*g* Application Server Control

The OEM 10*g* Application Server Control console manages these components:

- Application Server farm
- Clustered components with the farm
- Application server processes
- OracleAS Web Cache
- Oracle HTTP Server (OHS)
- OracleAS Containers for J2EE (OC4J)
- OracleAS Single Sign-On (SSO)
- Oracle Portal
- Wireless
- Business Intelligence
- Host targets

Application Server Control provides real-time monitoring for its target installation, and is required for configuration changes of an installation. In addition, AS Control provides a graphical view of the farm's components via the Topology Viewer; I will provide an in-depth review of the capabilities of Topology Viewer later in this chapter. Here is a complete list of Oracle Application Server Control's capabilities that are not directly available within Grid Control:

- Manage and configure Application Server components, individually or as a farm, including starting and stopping each component
- Monitor Application Server performance
- Access a graphical view of an application server farm's components
- Deploy and monitor J2EE applications
- Manage port values for components within an Application Server installation
- View and analyze application server logs

Oracle Enterprise Manager 10*g* Grid Control

OEM 10*g* Grid Control combines all the functions of Database Control and Application Server Control into a single console; when you install Grid Control you no longer need to use the standalone Database Control console. Grid Control has links to Application Server Control to make configuration changes to a particular application server instance's port numbers, for example. Grid Control also manages other Oracle products such as Oracle Collaboration Suite.

Above and beyond the features of either Database Control or Application Server Control, Grid Control provides other features such as role-based delegation of management tasks for multiple administrators. Grid Control also provides automatic monitoring for all targets as well as real-time and historical performance data collection.

In addition, Grid Control monitors and maintains hardware and software configurations for all members of the grid, and automatically deploys patches and upgrades to keep configurations consistent throughout the enterprise.

Understanding Oracle Enterprise Manager 10*g* Grid Control Features

OEM 10*g* Grid Control helps to centralize your management tasks and as a result saves you time and makes your job easier. Grid Control continuously collects statistics from all managed targets and warns the appropriate administrator when specific resource usage levels reach their respective thresholds. Even though Grid Control is not the focus of this chapter, we will present an overview of the grid architecture along with some examples of Grid Control in action to prepare you for the day in the future when your infrastructure is big enough to benefit from Grid Control.

Grid Control Architecture

The Grid Control architecture comprises three components in addition to the managed target: one or more Oracle Management Agents (OMAs), one or more Oracle Management Services (OMSs), and a single Oracle Management Repository (OMR). Figure 3.1 shows an example of an environment with three hosts, four managed targets, two OMS instances, and an OMR.

FIGURE 3.1 A sample OEM 10*g* Grid Control environment

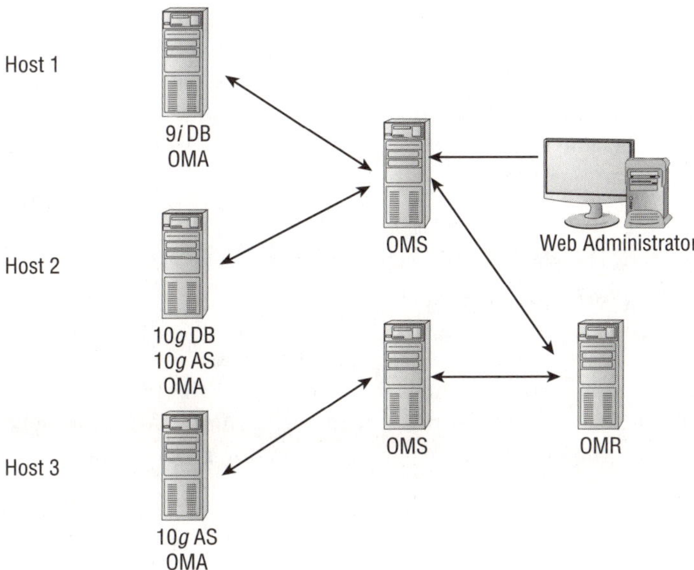

Grid Control manages all supported versions of Oracle Database, Oracle Application Server 9*i* Release 2, and Oracle Application Server 10*g* Release 1 and 2 as well as custom targets whose management agents are built with a custom Oracle-supplied application programming interface (API).

Oracle Management Agent

Each managed host requires one *Oracle Management Agent*, or *OMA*. An OMA collects information about performance, configuration, and availability for all targets on the host and passes that information to an Oracle Management Service. In the Grid Control environment in Figure 3.1, OMA is running on all three target hosts.

Oracle Management Services

An *Oracle Management Service*, or *OMS*, collects information from one or more OMAs and makes that information available to one or more administrators via a web interface or in the case of an alert, a pager message or an e-mail message. Conversely, an OMS passes on requests from an administrator to an OMA servicing one or more targets. In Figure 3.1, OMS runs on two servers; one of them collects statistics from Host 1 and Host 2, and the other collects statistics from Host 2 only.

Oracle Management Repository

Each OMS stores its data and metadata in an *Oracle Management Repository*, or *OMR*. An OMR is a schema in a new dedicated or existing database that stores the availability, configuration, and performance information from one or more OMS instances for later retrieval and analysis. An OMR can service more than one OMS, but an OMS stores its data in only one OMR. In Figure 3.1, one server manages the database containing the OMR database.

Using Grid Control

You access Grid Control using a URL and port number assigned when you install it. Figure 3.2 shows a Grid Control home page on the server `gridctl` listening on port 7777. We will not install Grid Control in this chapter; installing Grid Control is beyond the scope of this book.

In Figure 3.2, the Grid Control installation manages 39 targets, all of which are up. Of the 39 targets, 12 of them are database installations ranging from Oracle Database 8*i* to Oracle Database 10*g*. In Figure 3.3, you can see the Targets tab; you can easily filter by target type by selecting the target type in one of the sub-tabs.

Oracle Enterprise Manager 10*g* Application Server Control Architecture

In the following sections, we will present an overview of the OEM 10*g* Application Server Control architecture. This architecture includes the console, Distributed Configuration Management, Oracle Process Manager and Notification Server, Dynamic Monitoring Service, the Oracle Management Agent, the Oracle Management Watchdog process, and the Log Loader.

FIGURE 3.2 Grid Control home page

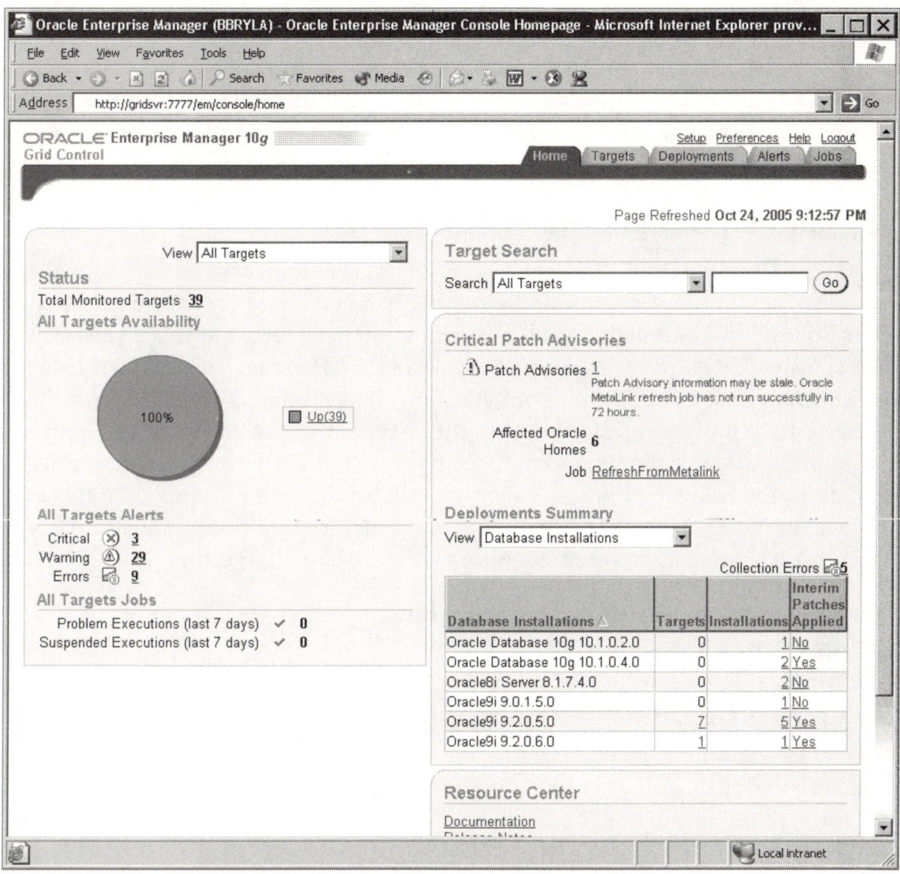

FIGURE 3.3 Grid Control Targets tab

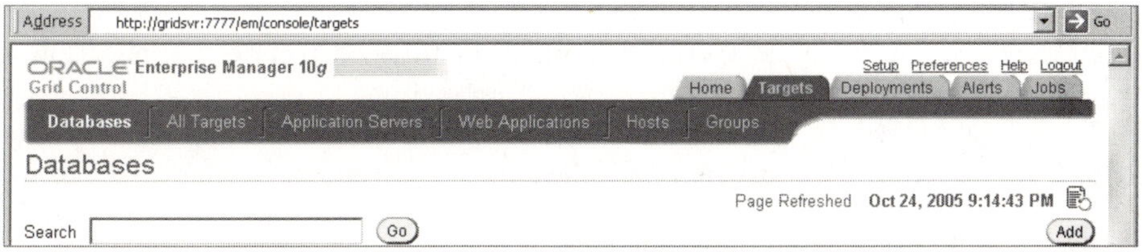

Address http://gridsvr:7777/em/console/targets Go

ORACLE Enterprise Manager 10g
Grid Control

Setup Preferences Help Logout

Home Targets Deployments Alerts Jobs

Databases All Targets Application Servers Web Applications Hosts Groups

Databases

Page Refreshed Oct 24, 2005 9:14:43 PM

Search Go Add

Application Server Control Console

Each installation of OracleAS includes an *Application Server Control console*, whether it is a minimal OracleAS Web Cache and OC4J installation, an Infrastructure installation, or a Portal and Wireless installation. An Application Server Control console provides you with a web-based user interface to monitor and administer every component within the installation.

Later in this chapter, we will review the most important Application Server Control pages and how to navigate them efficiently.

Distributed Configuration Management

Distributed Configuration Management, or *DCM*, enables you to create and manage multiple Oracle Application Server instances as a single instance. DCM synchronizes the configuration across all instances and maintains this information in either a file-based repository or a database repository. Regardless of the repository type, each instance maintains a local copy of the configuration; when you make a configuration change using DCM, it records the changes in the metadata repository and propagates the changes to all instances in the farm or cluster.

You use the `dcmctl` command to make changes to the DCM configuration. As with most commands, the equivalent functionality is available through the Application Server Control interface. In this example, you are on the infrastructure host and you want to know whether this instance is using a database repository or a file-based repository:

```
[oracle@asinfra oracle]$ dcmctl whichfarm
Farm Name: orcl.rjbdba.com
Host Instance: infra01.asinfra
Host Name: asinfra
Repository Type: Database (host)
[oracle@asinfra oracle]$
```

We will cover the `dcmctl` command in more detail later in this chapter.

Oracle Process Manager and Notification Server

Oracle Process Manager and Notification Server, or *OPMN*, is responsible for starting and stopping components within an application server instance. OPMN also collects status information from instances and instance components and makes the status information available to other processes. In addition, OPMN can automatically detect dead application server processes and restart them automatically.

Because OPMN starts, stops, and manages all application server components, it should be the first process started after the host is up and the last one to terminate before you shut down the host.

Dynamic Monitoring Service

In contrast to OPMN, which collects status information from application server components, *Dynamic Monitoring Service*, or *DMS*, collects performance data from application server components.

The `dmstool` command displays one or more performance metrics for an application server instance or instance component.

Oracle Management Agent

Application Server Control uses its own local version of Oracle Management Agent to monitor the instance's components. As you remember from earlier in the chapter, OEM 10*g* Grid Control uses an OMA to communicate with Grid Control's OMR.

Oracle Management Watchdog Process

The *Oracle Management Watchdog* process monitors the local OMA and the Application Server console itself to make sure that both of these components are up and running continuously. If OMA terminates unexpectedly, the watchdog process automatically restarts OMA.

Log Loader

The *Log Loader process* monitors instance components and updates a *log repository*; a log repository stores diagnostic and informational messages from multiple application server components that share a common Oracle home. The log repository is also known as the diagnostic message database repository.

In all cases, application server instances store local, text-based versions of log information. The Log Loader periodically scans these local log files and stores them in a common location, either in the Infrastructure database or in a single operating system directory to facilitate searching from Application Server Control. An Infrastructure database can store entries from multiple instances that belong to the same farm.

We will investigate the capabilities of the Log Viewer in more detail later in this chapter.

Oracle Enterprise Manager 10*g* Application Server Control Pages

As mentioned previously in this chapter, each installation of Oracle Application Server includes its own Application Server Control. Before you can use Application Server Control, however, you must start it using the `emctl` command as follows, as you saw in Chapter 2, "Performing Installation Tasks":

```
[oracle@asinfra]# emctl start iasconsole
```

To access an installation's Application Server Control with a web browser once you start the console process, you specify the host's name and the port assigned to Application Server Control. If you have not changed the default port number for Application Server Control, you can find it in the file `$ORACLE_HOME/install/setupinfo.txt`. In this example, you access Application Server Control on port 1156 of host `asinfra`:

```
http://asinfra:1156
```

The first time you access this page, use the username `ias_admin` and the password you specified during the Infrastructure installation. In the following sections, we will start with the highest-level Application Server Control page, the Farm page, then move on to the host computer home page, and finally drill down further into individual instance home pages and their respective component home pages.

Farm Page

If you install any component that requires OracleAS Infrastructure, the Farm page is the first page you will see when you connect to Application Server Control with the server name and the port number assigned to the instance. This page will show all instances sharing the same file-based or database-based repository. Figure 3.4 shows the Farm page accessed from the host `asinfra`. This farm comprises the two instances you installed in Chapter 2, the Infrastructure instance `infra01` on host `asinfra` and the middleware instance `mw01` on host `asmw`.

FIGURE 3.4 OEM 10*g* Application Server Control Farm page

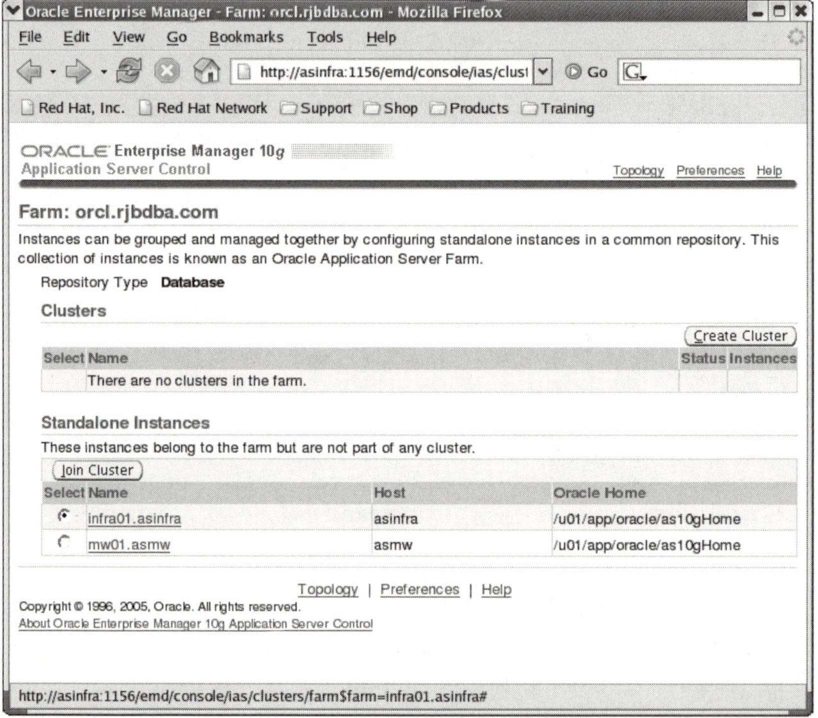

Accessing the Farm page from host `asmw` will produce the same results; both instances share the same metadata repository. Since both instances include Application Server Control and their own listener, all instances and clusters in the farm are available from either host.

The other major function of the Oracle Application Server Farm page is to create and manage Oracle Application Server clusters; in other words, you can combine two or more identical instances and treat the combined instances as a single instance to increase reliability and performance.

Instance Home Page

You can monitor and configure a single Oracle Application Server instance from an instance home page; selecting the `infra01.asinfra` link in Figure 3.4 shows you the instance home page for `infra01` in Figure 3.5. The home page has five tabs: Home, J2EE Applications, Ports, Infrastructure, and Backup/Recovery.

FIGURE 3.5 Application Server Control instance home page

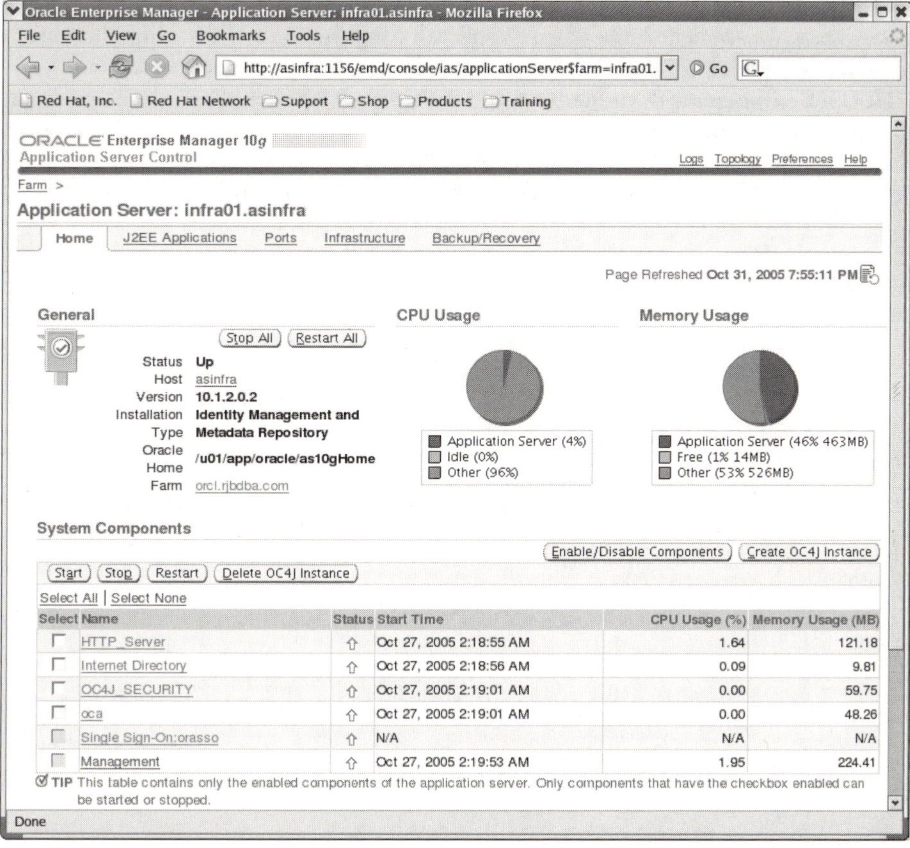

You can see all system components of this instance on the instance Home tab along with status information including host CPU and memory usage.

General

The General area of the Home tab includes an icon indicating whether the instance is up or down as well as the hostname, installation type, Oracle Home, and farm name, if applicable. It also includes buttons to stop or restart all components in the instance. If you want to start, stop, or restart an individual component, you use the System Components area.

CPU Usage

The CPU Usage area of the Home tab shows a pie chart of CPU usage on the host and the current percentage of CPU time used by the application server.

Memory Usage

The Memory Usage area of the Home tab shows a pie chart of memory usage on the host and the current percentage of memory used by the application server.

System Components

The System Components area of the Home tab contains a table providing the status of all configured and enabled components in the instance. In addition, you can select one or more check boxes next to the enabled components and delete, start, stop, or restart the checked components.

You can configure and monitor one of the instance's components by clicking one of the component links on the instance home page in Figure 3.5. Clicking the `HTTP_Server` link in Figure 3.5 sends you to, not surprisingly, the HTTP_Server home page for the instance, as you can see in Figure 3.6.

FIGURE 3.6 Oracle Application Server HTTP_Server home page

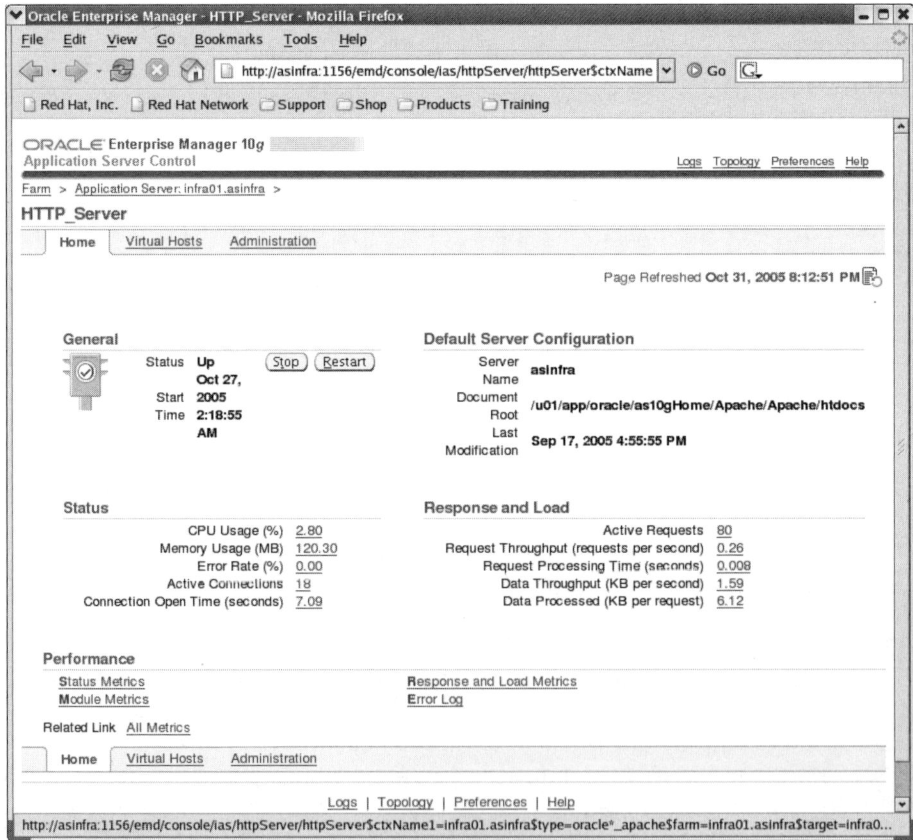

Host Computer Home Page

When you click on the name of the host computer in the General section of the instance home page, you can review more detailed information about the host. The Host home page contains a number of sections, including the General region, the Load region, the Targets list, Real-Time Metrics information, and the Telnet button.

General

The General region contains information about the host, such as how long the system has been up, the operating system type and version, IP address, memory capacity, total disk space, and total swap space.

Load

The Load region contains a CPU usage chart; this chart is similar to the chart on the instance home page except that it breaks down CPU usage by idle time, wait time, system mode time, and user mode time. It also summarizes the number of processes, memory and swap space utilization, and other statistics. Figure 3.7 shows the General and Load regions of a Host home page.

FIGURE 3.7 Host home page status information

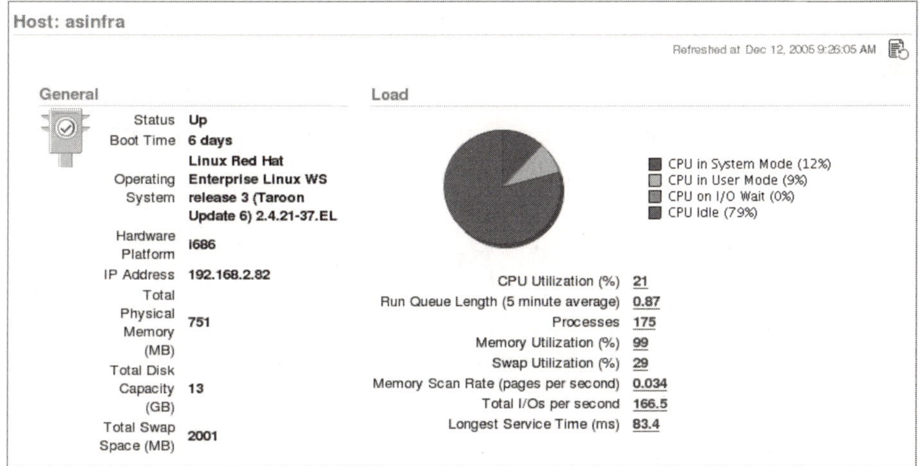

Targets

The Targets list shows the currently installed components on this host. If you have more than one instance on a host, this list shows the components from all installed instances. Clicking on one of the components in the Targets list directs you to the home page for the component; the link in the Targets list is the same as the corresponding link with the same name you see on the instance home page in the System Components region.

Real-Time Metrics

The Real-Time Metrics information includes currently logged on operating system users, top processes (by both CPU and memory usage), CPU usage, process paging statistics, disk I/O, and disk usage broken down by file system. *Metrics* are units of measurement used to report the health and performance level of an instance or its components. We will show you how to review historical metrics later in this chapter.

Telnet

Clicking the Telnet button opens a Telnet session on the host computer to run any command using a Unix command-line interface.

Some distributions of Linux do not install a Telnet server by default; in this case, the Telnet button will not work. The Telnet protocol is inherently insecure compared to more recent command-line tools such as ssh.

Component Home Pages

Each instance component has its own home page similar to the home page in Figure 3.6 for the HTTP_Server component. Each component home page has the following common elements:

- An icon indicating the up or down status of the components along with buttons to start, stop, or restart the component
- Status information including CPU usage, memory usage, and number of active connections
- Point-in-time performance information, such as response time and throughput
- Links to status and administrative functions relevant to the component

Starting, Stopping, and Restarting Components Using the Home Page

You can start, stop, or restart any component of an instance by using the System Components page of the instance home page, the component's home page, the component's icon in Topology Viewer, and a command-line tool. We will discuss the Topology Viewer's features and the command line tools later in this chapter.

To start, stop, or restart a component on the instance home page, scroll down to the System Components area. You can see the System Components area in the bottom third of Figure 3.5. To stop a component, click the check box next to the component and then click the Stop button at the top of the component list. The Status column will change to reflect the new status of the component.

You can also start, stop, or restart a component on the component's home page. If you click the `HTTP_Server` link in Figure 3.5, you see the HTTP_Server home page in Figure 3.6. In the General section of the page, you can click the Start/Stop or Restart button to start, stop, or restart the HTTP server. If you click the Stop button and return to the instance home page, you will see the new status of the HTTP server, as shown in Figure 3.8.

FIGURE 3.8 HTTP Server component status change

System Components

(Start) (Stop) (Restart) (Delete OC4J Instance)

Select All | Select None

Select	Name	Status	Start Time
☐	HTTP_Server	⇩	Unavailable
☐	Internet Directory	⇧	Dec 5, 2005 11:45:19 AM
☐	OC4J_SECURITY	⇧	Dec 5, 2005 11:45:29 AM
☐	oca	⇧	Dec 5, 2005 11:45:29 AM
☐	Single Sign-On:orasso	⇩	N/A
☐	Management	⇧	Dec 5, 2005 11:42:29 AM

Reviewing Performance Metrics

To detect performance problems, you need to know what components are having performance issues by reviewing the instantaneous component metrics and the component metrics over a recent period. You can see a complete list of all instantaneous and historical performance metrics for a particular component by clicking one of the metrics links on the component's home page. In Figure 3.6, on the `HTTP_Server` home page, the `All Metrics` link is at the bottom of the Home tab. Note that you can see some of the instantaneous metrics on the Home page; to retrieve historical metrics, you must click the `All Metrics` link. When you click that link, you see the list of available historical performance metrics in Figure 3.9.

FIGURE 3.9 HTTP Server Metrics links

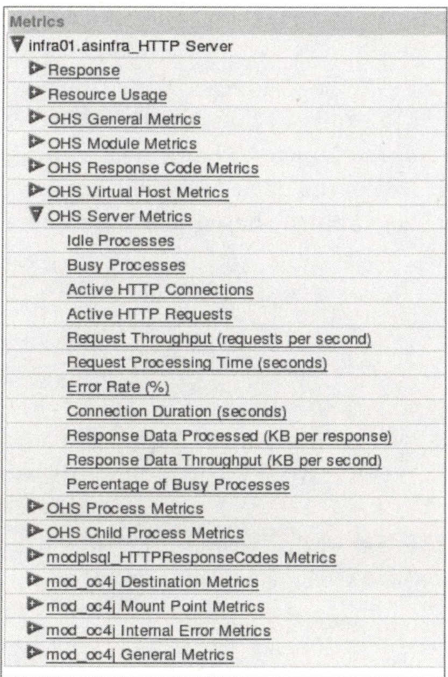

Clicking one of the links in Figure 3.9 displays a time graph that you can refresh manually or at an interval.

Using the Topology Viewer

The OracleAS Topology Viewer is a graphical tool that provides a real-time view and monitoring capability for all application server processes controlled by the OPMN server. All Oracle Application Server installations include a Topology Viewer; a new Oracle Application Server installation that uses the same Infrastructure automatically registers its components with the existing farm's Topology Viewer.

In the following sections, we will explain in detail the benefits of using the Topology Viewer; in addition, we will show you how to access and navigate the Topology Viewer.

Understanding the Features of Topology Viewer

Topology Viewer provides a clear visual representation of your application server environment with drill-down capabilities for each node or component. Each icon on the Topology Viewer represents either an application server or a component of an application server; alongside the icon is the status of the application server or component, either up or down. You can also start, stop, or restart application server processes by right-clicking on any farm, instance, or component in the Topology Viewer display.

Because Topology Viewer relies on status information from OPMN, nodes or components in an installation where the OPMN process is not running do not appear in Topology Viewer.

Topology Viewer is available in an HTML version or a Java applet version. The version you use depends on your browsers and whether you install the Java Plug-in version 1.4 or later for your browser; one advantage of using the applet version is that you can customize the colors used for the topology's components.

Configuring Topology Viewer

To change the preferred viewing format from HTML-only to Java applet, or vice versa, click the `Preferences` link in the upper-right corner of the OracleAS Farm or instance page, and then click the `Topology Viewer` link on the left side of the page. Select the preferred viewing format, either HTML only or Java applet, and click Apply. The setting takes effect the next time you launch Topology Viewer.

The viewing preference is stored in a persistent browser cookie; in other words, the browser cookie is available even after you close and reopen the browser.

Accessing Topology Viewer

To access the Topology Viewer, click the `Topology` link in either the upper-right corner or the bottom of any Application Server Control screen; you can see the Topology Viewer page in Figure 3.10.

In Figure 3.10, you can see the icon for the `HTTP_Server` process for the `infra01.asinfra` Infrastructure instance; underneath the icon are the start time for the process and the elapsed CPU time and memory in use by the process.

FIGURE 3.10 Topology Viewer page

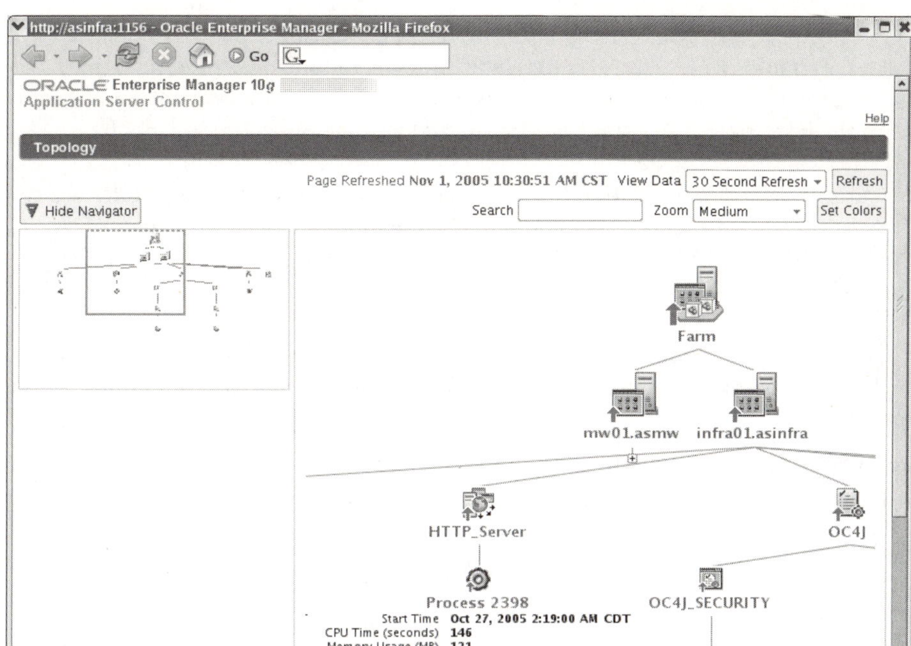

Navigating Topology Viewer

The Topology Viewer page comprises three areas: the configuration and search area, the navigator pane, and the topology pane.

Configuration and Search Area

The configuration and search area controls the refresh rate and zoom level for the topology pane; in addition, you can find a particular component and automatically center the component in the topology pane using the search box. If you are using the Java applet version of Topology Viewer, you have a Set Colors button to change the text, nodes, connecting links, and background color in the topology pane.

In Figure 3.10, the refresh level is set at 30 seconds with a Medium zoom level.

Navigator Pane

The navigator pane provides a quick way to change the viewing area for the topology pane; clicking anywhere within the navigator pane centers the topology pane viewing area at the point you clicked.

You can hide or unhide the navigator pane to provide more area for the topology pane by clicking the Hide Navigator/Show Navigator button.

Topology Pane

The topology pane contains one icon for each component or instance in the farm. For each component that has one or more subcomponents, you can expand or collapse the node to make the topology pane more readable or to focus on one area of your farm. A + appears underneath a node if that node is collapsed. In Figure 3.10, the entire component tree underneath the instance `mw01.asmw` is collapsed and you see only components from the instance `infra01.asinfra`, such as the `HTTP_Server` process. When you start Topology Viewer, only the current instance's node tree is fully expanded; all other instances' nodes are collapsed.

If the node is a process node, you see a number of statistics about the process, such as the start time, elapsed CPU time, and current memory usage. In Figure 3.10, the `HTTP_Server` process has used 146 seconds of CPU time since October 27, 2005, at 2:19AM and is currently using 121MB of memory on the host.

To perform an action on a node, click on the node in the Java version or on the arrow in the HTML version and a pop-up appears. The pop-up menu for each node depends on the node type. If you click on a node representing a process, you see these actions:

Go to Home Page Go to the home page that controls the configuration and monitoring of this process. For the HTML version, clicking anywhere on the node except for the arrow navigates automatically to the component's home page. In the Java version this option appears on the same menu with the other options below.

Start Start this process if it is not running.

Stop Stop this process if it is running.

Restart Restart this process if it is running.

If you click on any other parent node in the hierarchy above a process node, you see these additional actions:

Collapse Node Collapse the node display if it is expanded.

Expand Node Expand the node and all subnodes if it is collapsed.

Expand All Show all nodes under this node.

If you use the HTML version of Topology Viewer, you click on one of the four arrows on the border of the topology pane to change the viewing area. In the Java applet version, you click and hold on any part of the viewing area and drag the mouse to change the contents of the topology pane.

Using the Log Viewer

Each component of Oracle Application Server generates log entries with varying levels of severity—from informational to warning to severe errors. From the Application Server Control console, you can easily view messages in the log files for any component by navigating to the home page of the component.

In addition to viewing the log files via the Application Server Control console, you can download the log files to your local hard disk and use any file viewer or editor to browse their contents.

In Oracle Application Server 10*g* Release 1, the log files were stored in the local file system in XML format. In Oracle Application Server 10*g* Release 2, you can store the log files in XML format in a text file or in the farm's repository database. This repository is the *diagnostic message database repository*. The Log Loader component collects the log messages from each instance and component within the farm and loads them into the diagnostic message database repository. The Log Loader labels each entry into the database repository with an instance identifier to distinguish the source of the log message.

Even if the Log Loader process or the database repository fails, you can still view the log messages saved in the local log file; the local file will have diagnostic messages to help you debug why the Log Loader or the repository connection is unavailable!

When you click the Logs link on the instance home page, you will see the log search screen in Figure 3.11. For this search, you want to see messages for the HTTP Server and Database components.

FIGURE 3.11 Log files search page

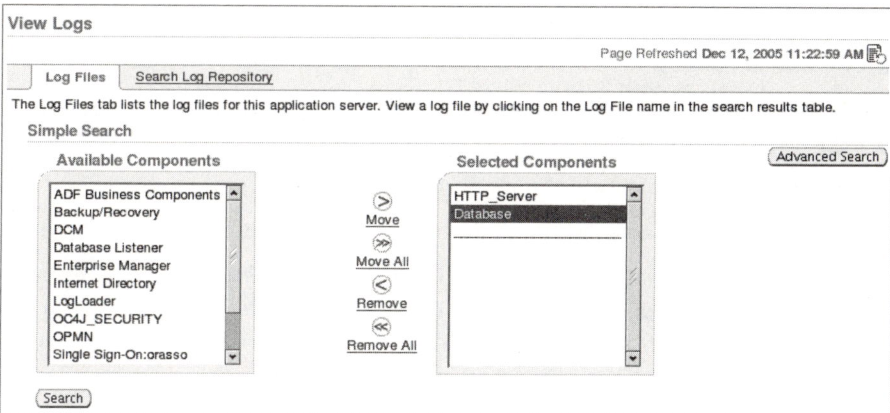

When you initiate the log file search by clicking the Search button, you will see the log messages for the selected components. You can see the results from the search in Figure 3.11 in Figure 3.12.

Clicking a Log File link in column four of the results shows the entire contents of the log file itself. Clicking the Advanced Search button in Figure 3.11 allows you to refine your search by the type of log file entry instead of just the component type.

FIGURE 3.12 Log files search results

Search

Results: 120 Log Entries Retrieved

Component Type	Component Name	Log Type	Log File	Modified	Size (bytes)
HTTP_Server		Server	redirected output/errors	December 12, 2005 10:10:40 AM CST	2677
HTTP Server (Main)	asinfra:7777	Error	error_log	November 8, 2005 12:47:24 AM CST	0
HTTP Server (Main)	asinfra:7777	Error	error_log.1131408000	November 8, 2005 12:47:26 AM CST	297
HTTP Server (Main)	asinfra:7777	Error	error_log.1131451200	November 8, 2005 3:46:31 PM CST	1328
HTTP Server (Main)	asinfra:7777	Error	error_log.1131494400	November 8, 2005 6:14:05 PM CST	667

Using Command-Line Tools

Nearly every function you perform with the Application Server Control interface you can perform with an equivalent command-line tool and vice versa. The exceptions are rare, but they emphasize the need to be able to use the command-line tools under certain circumstances. For example, you cannot use the Application Server Control interface unless you start it first with the `emctl` command!

The three most common command-line tools in the Oracle Application Server environment are as follows:

`emctl` Start, stop, or check the status of the Oracle Application Server console, and configure console and agent settings.

`dcmctl` Create or join clusters and maintain instance configuration.

`opmnctl` Start, stop, or check the status of an instance, a cluster, or components.

In the following sections, I will present a brief overview of each tool with examples of how to use them. Table 3.1 gives you an overview and comparison of the management tasks you are likely to perform on a regular basis and which tools you can use to perform those tasks.

TABLE 3.1 Management Tasks and Their Corresponding Tools

Management Task	Database Control	Application Server Control	`emctl`	`dcmctl`	`opmnctl`
Start or stop a database instance	X				
Start or stop Database Control or Application Server Control			X		
Secure communications with SSL			X		

TABLE 3.1 Management Tasks and Their Corresponding Tools *(continued)*

Management Task	Database Control	Application Server Control	`emctl`	`dcmctl`	`opmnctl`
Start, stop, or restart instances and components		X			X
Start, stop, or restart clusters		X			X
Create OC4J instances		X		X	
Create or join clusters		X		X	
Deploy, undeploy, or redeploy applications		X		X	
Enable or disable components		X			
Obtain status of instances or components		X			X
Archive and restore versions of configurations				X	
Configure installed (and unconfigured) components		X			

The *emctl* Utility

One of the most common uses for the `emctl` utility is to start and stop the Application Server Control interface. In addition, you can use `emctl` to enable secure console communications between a client and the console. Finally, you can change the port values for the Oracle Application Server Management Agent (OMA), the Application Server Control console, and the OC4J port used by the console's OC4J instance. I will show you examples of these commands in action in the following sections.

Starting and Stopping Application Server Control

In Chapter 2, I provided a custom script you can use to start and stop all components of Oracle Application Server when the host boots. The Infrastructure startup script to perform these steps looks like this:

```
# start database listener
lsnrctl start
# start metadata repository database
dbstart
```

```
# start database console
emctl start dbconsole
# start infrastructure instance processes
opmnctl startall
# start AS console
emctl start iasconsole
```

Notice that `emctl` starts both the Application Server Control console and the Database Control console. The script you use to shut down all components, including Application Server Control, is similar to the startup script except you shut down the components in reverse order and you substitute `stop` for `start` in all commands:

```
# stop AS console
emctl stop iasconsole
# stop infrastructure instance processes
opmnctl stopall
# stop database console
emctl stop dbconsole
# stop metadata repository database
dbshut
# stop database listener
lsnrctl stop
```

You can also use the `emctl` command to check the status of AS Control, as in this example:

```
[oracle@asinfra oracle]$ emctl status iasconsole
Oracle Enterprise Manager 10g Application Server Control
      Release 10.1.2.0.2
Copyright (c) 1996, 2005 Oracle Corporation.  All rights reserved.
http://asinfra:1156/emd/console/aboutApplication
Oracle Enterprise Manager 10g Application Server Control is running.
------------------------------------------------------------------
Logs are generated in directory /u01/app/oracle/as10gHome/sysman/log
[oracle@asinfra oracle]$
```

The management agent for Oracle Application Server starts or stops automatically when you start or stop Application Server Control using `emctl`.

Enabling SSL for Application Server Control

By default, communications between your web browser and the Application Server Control console use an unsecure HTTP protocol; in addition, communications between the local management agent and the console are not secure. While this may not be a problem within an internal corporate network, you do not want these unsecured communications channels if you are using a public network. To secure these communications, you can use the `emctl` command. First, you stop the console process as follows:

```
[oracle@asinfra oracle]$ emctl stop iasconsole
Oracle Enterprise Manager 10g Application Server Control Release 10.1.2.0.2
Copyright (c) 1996, 2005 Oracle Corporation.  All rights reserved.
http://asinfra:1156/emd/console/aboutApplication

Stopping Oracle Enterprise Manager 10g Application Server
➥   Control ...   ...  Stopped.
```

Next, use the `secure` option of `emctl` to set up the secure certificate and agent:

```
[oracle@asinfra oracle]$ emctl secure iasconsole
Oracle Enterprise Manager 10g Application Server Control Release 10.1.2.0.2
Copyright (c) 1996, 2005 Oracle Corporation.  All rights reserved.
http://asinfra:1156/emd/console/aboutApplication
Generating Standalone Console Root Key (this takes a minute)...   Done.
Fetching Standalone Console Root Certificate...   Done.
Generating Standalone Console Agent Key...   Done.
Storing Standalone Console Agent Key...   Done.
Generating Oracle Wallet for the Standalone Console Agent...   Done.
Configuring Agent for HTTPS...   Done.
EMD_URL set in /u01/app/oracle/as10gHome/sysman/config/emd.properties
Generating Standalone Console Java Keystore...   Done.
Configuring the website ...   Done.
Updating targets.xml ...    Done.
```

Finally, restart the console:

```
[oracle@asinfra oracle]$ emctl start iasconsole
Oracle Enterprise Manager 10g Application Server Control Release 10.1.2.0.2
Copyright (c) 1996, 2005 Oracle Corporation.  All rights reserved.
https://asinfra:1156/emd/console/aboutApplication
Starting Oracle Enterprise Manager 10g Application Server
➥   Control ....... started successfully.
[oracle@asinfra oracle]$
```

The Application Server Control console is now only available with the HTTPS protocol, as you can see in Figure 3.13.

FIGURE 3.13 Accessing Application Server Control console using HTTPS

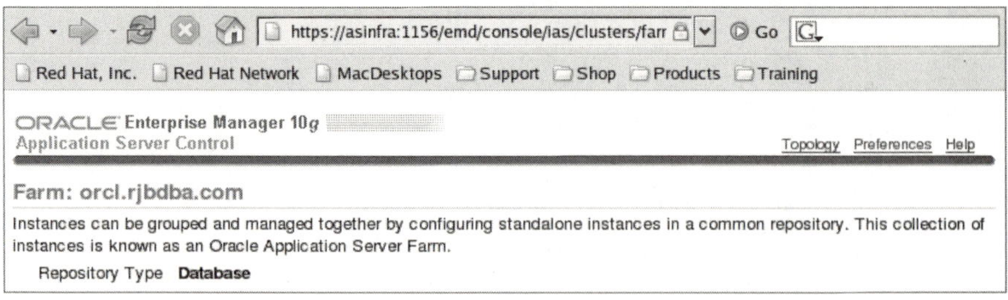

The first time you access the secure page, you must accept the secure certificate from OracleAS by clicking the Accept button. The information on the certificate ensures that all future communications between your browser and OracleAS are encrypted and secure.

Changing Port Values

You may have noticed that you cannot change some of the port numbers from the Ports tab of the instance home page:

- Management Agent port
- Application Server Control Console port
- Application Server Control RMI port
- All OPMN ports
- HTTP Server diagnostic port

You can see in Figure 3.14 that the port numbers are not editable using the web interface.

FIGURE 3.14 Application Server Control console unchangeable ports

oca	AJP	12501	12501-12600	
OPMN	ONS Remote	6200	6200-6299	
OPMN	ONS Request	6003	6003-6099	
OPMN	ONS Local	6101	6100-6199	
Oracle Enterprise Manager 10g	Application Server Control	1156	1156;1810-1829	
Oracle Enterprise Manager 10g	Oracle Management Agent	1157	1157;1830-1849	
Oracle Enterprise Manager 10g	Application Server Control RMI	1850	1850-1869	
Oracle HTTP Server	Diagnostic	7200	7200-7299	
Oracle HTTP Server	Listen	7777	80;7777-7877	

Because AS Control uses these port numbers directly, changing them via the web interface would cause the web session to fail at some point during the change process; as a result, you must change these port numbers using the `emctl` command while the AS Control console is closed.

1. Stop the console using `emctl stop iasconsole`.
2. Change each port with `emctl config`:
   a. `emctl config agent port` <port_number>
   b. `emctl config iasconsole port` <port_number>
   c. `emctl config iasconsole rmiport` <port_number>
3. Start the console using `emctl start iasconsole`.

Real World Scenario

Changing Application Server Control Console Ports

As part of planning for a server consolidation project, we realized that two different infrequently used middleware instances of Oracle Application Server were to reside on the same host. In preparation for the move, we decided to change the three console-related ports on the target host using `emctl` and make sure everything was working before installing the second instance on the target host.

First, we confirmed the three port numbers already in use using the Ports tab on the instance home page. The following list includes the old and new port numbers:

Port Type	Old Port	New Port
Mgmt Agent	1156	1810
AS Console	1157	1830

Next, we stopped the console, changed the port numbers, and restarted the console:

```
[oracle@asmw oracle]$ emctl stop iasconsole
Oracle Enterprise Manager 10g Application Server Control Release 10.1.2.0.2
Copyright (c) 1996, 2005 Oracle Corporation.  All rights reserved.
http://asmw:1156/emd/console/aboutApplication

Stopping Oracle Enterprise Manager 10g Application Server
➥   Control ...   ... Stopped.
[oracle@asmw oracle]$ emctl config agent port 1810
Oracle Enterprise Manager 10g Application Server Control Release 10.1.2.0.2
Copyright (c) 1996, 2005 Oracle Corporation.  All rights reserved.
Oracle Enterprise Manager 10g Agent configuration update succeeded.
[oracle@asmw oracle]$ emctl config iasconsole port 1830
Oracle Enterprise Manager 10g Application Server Control Release 10.1.2.0.2
Copyright (c) 1996, 2005 Oracle Corporation.  All rights reserved.
http://asmw:1156/emd/console/aboutApplication
```

```
Oracle Enterprise Manager 10g Application Server
➥ Control configuration update succeeded.
[oracle@asmw oracle]$ emctl config iasconsole rmiport 1851
Oracle Enterprise Manager 10g Application Server Control Release 10.1.2.0.2
Copyright (c) 1996, 2005 Oracle Corporation.  All rights reserved.
http://asmw:1830/emd/console/aboutApplication
Oracle Enterprise Manager 10g Application Server
➥ Control configuration update succeeded.
[oracle@asmw oracle]$ emctl start iasconsole
Oracle Enterprise Manager 10g Application Server Control Release 10.1.2.0.2
Copyright (c) 1996, 2005 Oracle Corporation.  All rights reserved.
http://asmw:1830/emd/console/aboutApplication
Starting Oracle Enterprise Manager 10g Application Server
➥ Control ...... started successfully.
[oracle@asmw oracle]$
```

Clicking on the instance `mw01.asmw` on the Farm page worked with no additional editing or configuration—the `emctl` command automatically updated the instance metadata in the farm repository as well as the link to the instance with the new port number.

Because we was able to test out some of the migration steps ahead of time, we had a higher confidence level when we performed the actual consolidation.

OPMN and the *opmnctl* Utility

The `opmnctl` utility is the command-line configuration utility for the *Oracle Process Manager and Notification Server* (OPMN). OPMN is the centralized process management mechanism of Oracle Application Server and manages every Oracle Application Server component except for the Metadata Repository and Application Server Control. It is installed and configured with every Oracle Application Server installation type.

OPMN consists of the following components that process and share information both within an OPMN server and between OPMN servers on different instances:

Oracle Process Manager (PM) The PM starts and stops processes; it restarts processes when detecting failure of a process.

Oracle Notification Server (ONS) As the name implies, ONS manages notifications and other information between Oracle Application Server processes.

Process Manager Modules Process Manager Modules are specific to the controlled component and handle outgoing communication for the managed component.

You can use either AS Control or the `opmnctl` utility to start or stop application server components. Using `opmnctl`, you can check the status of the managed processes as well as start the OPMN process itself, start or stop one component, or start or stop all components in an instance.

Table 3.2 shows you the most common options for the `opmnctl` command.

TABLE 3.2 opmnctl Common Options

Option	Purpose
start	Start OPMN
startall	Start OPMN and all managed processes
stopall	Stop OPMN and all managed processes
startproc	Start a single managed process
stopproc	Stop a single managed process
restartproc	Restart a single managed process
status	Show the status of all managed processes

To start, stop, or restart a process, you first need to know the name of the process; you can get the list by using the `opmnctl status` command. Here are the results of that command on the instance `mw01.asmw`:

```
[oracle@asmw oracle]$ opmnctl status

Processes in Instance: mw01.asmw
-------------------+--------------------+---------+---------
ias-component      | process-type       |     pid | status
-------------------+--------------------+---------+---------
DSA                | DSA                |     N/A | Down
LogLoader          | logloaderd         |     N/A | Down
dcm-daemon         | dcm-daemon         |   19718 | Alive
OC4J               | home               |   18762 | Alive
OC4J               | OC4J_Portal        |   18763 | Alive
WebCache           | WebCache           |   18735 | Alive
WebCache           | WebCacheAdmin      |   18718 | Alive
```

```
HTTP_Server         | HTTP_Server        |   18725 | Alive
wireless            | performance_server |   18824 | Alive
wireless            | messaging_server   |   18825 | Alive
wireless            | OC4J_Wireless      |   18826 | Alive

[oracle@asmw oracle]$
```

To stop the Web Cache component, use the `opmnctl stopproc` command with the applicable `process-type` as follows:

```
[oracle@asmw oracle]$ opmnctl stopproc process-type=WebCache
opmnctl: stopping opmn managed processes...
[oracle@asmw oracle]$
```

Checking the status of the Web Cache component, you see that it stopped:

```
[oracle@asmw oracle]$ opmnctl status

Processes in Instance: mw01.asmw
-------------------+--------------------+---------+---------
ias-component      | process-type       |     pid | status
-------------------+--------------------+---------+---------
DSA                | DSA                |     N/A | Down
LogLoader          | logloaderd         |     N/A | Down
dcm-daemon         | dcm-daemon         |   19718 | Alive
OC4J               | home               |   18762 | Alive
OC4J               | OC4J_Portal        |   18763 | Alive
WebCache           | WebCache           |     N/A | Down
WebCache           | WebCacheAdmin      |   18718 | Alive
HTTP_Server        | HTTP_Server        |   18725 | Alive
wireless           | performance_server |   18824 | Alive
wireless           | messaging_server   |   18825 | Alive
wireless           | OC4J_Wireless      |   18826 | Alive

[oracle@asmw oracle]$
```

To start the process again, use the `opmnctl startproc` command:

```
[oracle@asmw oracle]$ opmnctl startproc process-type=WebCache
opmnctl: starting opmn managed processes...
[oracle@asmw oracle]$
```

Finally, you check the status one more time:

```
[oracle@asmw oracle]$ opmnctl status

Processes in Instance: mw01.asmw
-------------------+--------------------+---------+---------
ias-component      | process-type       |     pid | status
-------------------+--------------------+---------+---------
DSA                | DSA                |     N/A | Down
LogLoader          | logloaderd         |     N/A | Down
dcm-daemon         | dcm-daemon         |   19718 | Alive
OC4J               | home               |   18762 | Alive
OC4J               | OC4J_Portal        |   18763 | Alive
WebCache           | WebCache           |   30902 | Alive
WebCache           | WebCacheAdmin      |   18718 | Alive
HTTP_Server        | HTTP_Server        |   18725 | Alive
wireless           | performance_server |   18824 | Alive
wireless           | messaging_server   |   18825 | Alive
wireless           | OC4J_Wireless      |   18826 | Alive

[oracle@asmw oracle]$
```

You can start and stop groups of components by using `ias-component` instead of `process-type` in the `opmnctl` command; for example, you can `use ias-component=wireless` instead of three separate commands using the three different wireless process types. Notice that the OracleAS Web Cache process is up and running with a new process ID (PID); restarting the component starts a new Unix process.

DCM and the *dcmctl* Utility

Earlier in this chapter, we introduced Distributed Configuration Management, or DCM, as a management framework for Oracle Application Server that helps you manage multiple application server instances. DCM can not only manage farms and clusters as a unit, it can also manage the configuration of individual components.

As with most, if not all, of the management tools available for Oracle Application Server, there is both an Application Server Control interface and a command-line interface for DCM; the command-line interface for DCM is `dcmctl`. The process of archiving and restoring configurations is only available with the command-line interface.

The DCM configuration information resides in a repository, which can be a database repository or a file-based repository. In either case, the `dcmctl` command accesses and maintains the metadata in the repository regardless of its type.

If you use a database repository, it resides in the DCM schema in the farm's Infrastructure database. For a file-based repository, it resides in the directory `$ORACLE_HOME/dcm/repository` on the host where the middleware instance is installed.

Table 3.3 shows you the most common options for the `dcmctl` command.

TABLE 3.3 `dcmctl` Common Options

Option	Purpose
`listComponents`	List managed components
`start`	Start a component
`stop`	Stop a component
`resyncInstance`	Refresh configuration from the repository
`updateConfig`	Update repository information from local configuration
`createComponent`	Create a new OC4J instance
`deployApplication`	Deploy a J2EE application
`undeployApplication`	Undeploy a J2EE application

If you plan to use the `dcmctl` command on a regular basis, add the directory `$ORACLE_HOME/dcm/bin` to your `PATH` environment variable.

In the following example, you want to see the managed components on the instance `mw01.asmw`:

```
[oracle@asmw oracle]$ dcmctl listcomponents
1
Component Name: home
Component Type: OC4J
Instance:       mw01.asmw
2
Component Name: HTTP_Server
```

```
Component Type: HTTP_Server
Instance:       mw01.asmw
3
Component Name: OC4J_Portal
Component Type: OC4J
Instance:       mw01.asmw
4
Component Name: OC4J_Wireless
Component Type: OC4J
Instance:       mw01.asmw
5
Component Name: OC4J_Wireless
Component Type: Wireless
6
Component Name: messaging_server
Component Type: Wireless
7
Component Name: performance_server
Component Type: Wireless
8
Component Name: WebCacheAdmin
Component Type: WebCache
9
Component Name: WebCache
Component Type: WebCache
[oracle@asmw oracle]$
```

If you use `dcmctl` commands to make changes to your cluster or farm configuration, you must restart the Application Server Control console. In addition, the `dcmctl` command only operates on the instance in the same installation where the `dcmctl` command itself is located. Finally, you can use `dcmctl` in batch mode to run several commands at the same time. The following command runs the commands in the file `redeploy.dsh` in batch mode:

```
[oracle@asmw] $ dcmctl shell -f redeploy.dsh
```

Here is a sample `dcmctl` batch file that creates and starts a component:

```
createcomponent -ct oc4j -co newcomponent1
start -co newcomponent1
exit
```

Notice that you do not need to specify `dcmctl` on any lines within the batch file.

Summary

Every powerful application server needs the accompanying powerful toolset to manage it. In the first part of this chapter, we reviewed the web-based toolsets that you can use to manage nearly every aspect of Oracle Application Server.

First, we provided a detailed comparison of three management tools: OEM 10*g* Database Control, OEM 10*g* Application Server Control, and OEM 10*g* Grid Control. You use Database Control to manage all aspects of a single Oracle 10*g* database instance or an Oracle 10*g* database cluster. Application Server Control manages an application server farm, its instances, and all components of each instance. Grid Control replaces all functionality found in Database Control, facilitating the management of multiple databases and application servers across the enterprise in a single console. Links within the Grid Control console connect to Application Server Control instances for configuring and maintaining each instance.

Before we delved more deeply into each Application Server tool, we presented an overview of the Application Server Control architecture. Each installation of Oracle Application Server includes a web-based interface. Underneath the web interface is Distributed Configuration Management to manage a farm and its instances, Oracle Process Manager and Notification Server to manage the processes associated with each component, Dynamic Monitoring Service to continuously collect status and performance information, and Oracle Management Agent to communicate status between a component and either Application Server Control or Grid Control.

Next, we presented a walk-through of the highest-level pages available in the Application Server Control console. The Farm page shows all instances that share a common repository; drilling down into an instance exposes the instance's components as well as host CPU and memory statistics. From the instance home page, you can start, stop, or restart one or all instance components as well as review performance metrics by drilling down one more level.

Application Server Control also includes Topology Viewer, a graphical representation of all instances and components in the farm. Topology Viewer includes zoom and pan capabilities to provide a subset of components in the navigation pane. From each graphical component in the navigation pane, you can start, stop, or restart any component or expand and collapse any instance and its subcomponents.

In the last part of the chapter, we covered some of the most important command-line tools available: `emctl`, `opmnctl`, and `dcmctl`. The `emctl` tool starts and stops Application Server Control and Database Control as well as configuring ports that you cannot configure via the web interface. `opmnctl` starts and stops OPMN as well as starting, stopping, or restarting individual instance components. `dcmctl` creates new components as well as deploying or undeploying J2EE applications; `dcmctl` also manages and archives instance configuration information, a feature only available in the command-line interface.

Exam Essentials

Understand the differences between OEM 10*g* control tools. Be able to explain the purpose and interrelationships between Database Control, Application Server Control, and Grid Control. Identify which components Grid Control controls and which components Application Server Control controls when you deploy Grid Control.

Describe the components of the Application Server Control architecture. Understand how to use the console to navigate the instance hierarchy. Define the purpose and interaction of Distributed Configuration Management (DCM) with Oracle Process Manager and Notification Server (OPMN), Dynamic Monitoring Service (DMS), Oracle Management Agent (OMA), and the Oracle Management Watchdog process. Explain the difference between a local agent process and a Grid Control agent.

Explain how Log Loader works. Describe the types of logging produced from instance components and where the log files reside. Understand how Log Loader moves the local log files to the repository.

List the Application Server Control page types. Understand the difference between the Farm page, the instance home page, the host computer home page, and the component home page and how to navigate among them. Be able to identify the overall host resource usage and the percentage of the host resources used by the application server instance.

Understand how to start, stop, and restart components. Be able to use both the instance home page and the component home page to start, stop, or restart a component. Be able to start, stop, or restart all components at once. Identify which components you cannot stop or start using Application Server Control.

Explain the purpose of Topology Viewer. Understand the features of Topology Viewer and how to use the different panes within Topology Viewer. Be able to navigate within the farm as well as collapse and expand components within an instance. Enumerate the node types and their purpose. Explain how to switch between a Java-based and an HTML-based Topology Viewer.

Enumerate and explain each Application Server command-line tool. Explain the functionality that is only available via the command-line tools. Explain the differences among `emctl`, `opmnctl`, and `dcmctl` and how to perform the equivalent operations in Application Server Control. Show how to use `emctl` to secure communications between the administrative web client and the Application Server Control process.

Review Questions

1. OEM 10*g* Grid Control manages which of the following products and versions? (Choose all that apply.)
   - **A.** Oracle Application Server 9i Release 2
   - **B.** Oracle Database 9i Release 2
   - **C.** Oracle Database 10g Release 1
   - **D.** Oracle Database 10g Release 2
   - **E.** Oracle Application Server 10g Release 1
   - **F.** Oracle Application Server 10g Release 2

2. Which command-line tool starts and stops components within an application server instance?
   - **A.** `oidctl`
   - **B.** `dcmctl`
   - **C.** `emctl`
   - **D.** `opmnctl`
   - **E.** `dmstool`

3. You can start, stop, or restart any component of an instance using all but which of the following methods? (Choose all that apply.)
   - **A.** Using the `opmnctl` command line tool
   - **B.** Clicking an icon in Topology Viewer
   - **C.** Using the component's home page
   - **D.** Using the Farm page
   - **E.** Using the instance home page
   - **F.** Using the Application Server page of Grid Control
   - **G.** Using the `dcmctl` command-line tool
   - **H.** Using the `emctl` command-line tool

4. In the following diagram is a portion of the Ports configuration page. Why are three of the OEM components' port numbers not editable?

Oracle Enterprise Manager 10g	Application Server Control	1156	1156;1810-1829	
Oracle Enterprise Manager 10g	Oracle Management Agent	1157	1157;1830-1849	
Oracle Enterprise Manager 10g	Application Server Control RMI	1850	1850-1869	
Oracle HTTP Server	Diagnostic	7200	7200-7299	
Oracle HTTP Server	OCA Mutual Authentication (SSL)	6601	4400-4419	

A. The components have not yet finished starting up.

B. Editing these port numbers would crash the web interface.

C. The administrator who logged in to this page does not have the privileges to edit these port numbers.

D. All of the alternate port numbers for these components are in use and therefore you cannot change the port numbers.

5. You want to change the three ports for Application Server Control because of a port conflict with a new application whose port numbers are hard-coded. Because you cannot use the Application Server Control itself to change these port numbers, you must use a command-line utility to change them. Which of the following command-line sequences achieves the desired results? (Choose the best answer.)

A.
```
opmnctl stop iasconsole
opmnctl config agent port 1810
opmnctl config iasconsole port 1830
opmnctl config iasconsole rmiport 1851
opmnctl start iasconsole
```

B.
```
emctl stop iasconsole
emctl config agent port 1810
emctl config iasconsole port 1810
emctl config iasconsole rmiport 1810
emctl start iasconsole
```

C.
```
emctl stop iasconsole
emctl config agent port 1810
emctl config iasconsole port 1830
emctl config iasconsole rmiport 1851
emctl start iasconsole
```

D.
```
emctl stop dbconsole
emctl config agent port 1810
emctl config dbconsole port 1830
emctl config dbconsole rmiport 1851
emctl start dbconsole
```

6. The Topology Viewer is available in which of the following versions? (Choose all that apply.)
   A. XML
   B. HTML
   C. Java applet
   D. HTTP
   E. Java Server Page

7. Which of the following areas does not exist on the Topology Viewer page?
   A. The navigator pane
   B. The topology pane
   C. The configuration and search area pane
   D. The host pane

8. Your Application Server Farm comprises two instances: an Infrastructure instance and a middleware instance. You are viewing these instances in the HTML version of Topology Viewer with both nodes expanded. You click on the lower-right corner of each instance to collapse the node. How many nodes do you see in the topology pane?
   A. 2
   B. 3
   C. 4
   D. 1
   E. You cannot collapse the nodes in the HTML version, only the Java version.

9. Which of the following options are available on a Topology Viewer node when you click on a process node? (Choose all that apply.)
   A. Go to Home Page
   B. Start
   C. Expand Node
   D. Restart
   E. Collapse Node
   F. Stop
   G. Expand All
   H. Delete Node

10. When you use the HTML version of the Topology Viewer, which of the following options are available on a node when you click on the arrow next to any parent node? (Choose all that apply.)

A. Expand All

B. Start

C. Expand Node

D. Restart

E. Collapse Node

F. Stop

G. Go to Home Page

H. Delete Node

11. In Oracle Application Server 10*g* Release 2, log files can be stored in which of the following formats? (Choose all that apply.)

A. In the Infrastructure database as a table

B. As an MS-Word or RTF document when downloaded to the client

C. In a comma-delimited format for import into MS-Excel

D. In an XML format in a text file

E. In an HTML format in a text file

12. Which of the following statements is not true about the Log Loader process?

A. If the Log Loader process fails, you have to restart it before you can view log files.

B. If the Log Loader process fails, you can view local copies of the log files.

C. Log Loader collects messages from all components within an instance.

D. Log Loader collects messages from all instances within a farm.

13. Which of the following command-line tools can create a cluster?

A. `opmnctl`

B. `dcmctl`

C. `emctl`

D. `dmstool`

E. `oidctl`

14. The `opmnctl` command can check the status of which elements of Oracle Application Server? (Choose all that apply.)

A. Instance

B. Cluster

C. Infrastructure database

D. Components

E. Host CPU usage

F. Farm

15. Identify the only tool that can start or stop both Database Control and Application Server Control.

    A. `asctl`

    B. `dbctl`

    C. `opmnctl`

    D. `emctl`

    E. `dcmctl`

    F. `cnctl`

16. Which of the following functions are not available through Application Server Control? (Choose all that apply.)

    A. Start Database Control

    B. Join a cluster

    C. Disable an instance component

    D. Archive and restore instance configurations

    E. Stop Application Server Control

    F. Restart a cluster

17. You check the status of your instance and see the following:

```
Processes in Instance: mw01.asmw
-------------------+--------------------+---------+---------
ias-component      | process-type       |     pid | status
-------------------+--------------------+---------+---------
DSA                | DSA                |     N/A | Down
LogLoader          | logloaderd         |     N/A | Down
dcm-daemon         | dcm-daemon         |   19718 | Alive
OC4J               | home               |   18762 | Alive
OC4J               | OC4J_Portal        |   18763 | Alive
WebCache           | WebCache           |    4096 | Alive
WebCache           | WebCacheAdmin      |    4089 | Alive
HTTP_Server        | HTTP_Server        |   18725 | Alive
wireless           | performance_server |   18824 | Alive
wireless           | messaging_server   |   18825 | Alive
wireless           | OC4J_Wireless      |   18826 | Alive
```

You decide to stop all Web Cache components. Which commands did you use to check the status of the instance and stop the Web Cache components? (Choose the best answer.)

A. `emctl status`
`opmnctl stopproc ias-component=WebCache`

B. `opmnctl status`
`opmnctl stopproc pid=4096`
`opmnctl stopproc pid=4089`

C. `opmnctl status`
`opmnctl stopproc ias-component=WebCache`

D. `emctl status`
`opmnctl stopproc process-type=WebCache`
`opmnctl stopproc process-type=WebCacheAdmin`

E. `opmnctl status`
`opmnctl stopproc ias-component=WebCache`
`opmnctl stopproc ias-component=WebCacheAdmin`

18. Which of the following commands will synchronize an instance configuration from the repository?

A. `dcmctl syncInstance`

B. `opmnctl resync`

C. `opmnctl resyncInstance`

D. `dcmctl resyncInstance`

E. `dcmctl sync -type instance`

F. `opmnctl sync -type instance`

19. Which of the following are not components of Oracle Process Manager and Notification Server (OPMN)? (Choose all that apply.)

A. Process Manager Modules

B. Oracle Process Manager

C. Oracle Notification Server

D. Process Configuration Manager

E. Log Loader

20. Oracle Process Manager and Notification Server controls every Application Server component except for which of the following? (Choose four.)

A. Oracle Enterprise Manager 10*g* Application Server Control

B. Metadata Repository

C. OracleAS Web Cache

D. Oracle HTTP Server

E. Oracle Enterprise Manager 10*g* Database Control

F. Oracle Enterprise Manager 10*g* Grid Control

Answers to Review Questions

1. A, B, C, D, E, F. OEM 10*g* Grid Control manages all supported versions of Oracle Database, Oracle Application Server 9*i* Release 2, and Oracle Application Server 10*g* Release 1 and 2.

2. D. The `opmnctl` tool starts, stops, and restarts components within an application server instance in addition to automatically starting application server components that terminate unexpectedly.

3. D, F, G, H. You can use the `opmnctl` utility, the Topology Viewer, the component's home page, and the instance home page to stop, start, or restart a component.

4. B. Changing these port numbers on this page would terminate the Application Server Control. You must use `emctl` to change these port numbers and restart Application Server Control.

5. C. To change the ports, you must first stop the console if it is already running. Use the emctl command to configure new port numbers; then restart the console. Option A is not correct because you can only configure these ports with the emctl command, not the opmnctl command. Option B is not correct because each component must have its own port number. Option D is not correct because you are configuring the Application Server Control console, not the Database Control console.

6. B, C. Topology Viewer is available in an HTML version and a Java applet version. If you use the Java version, you can configure the component colors on the page.

7. D. There is not a host pane on the Topology Viewer page; however, the component nodes automatically show host memory and CPU statistics.

8. B. When you collapse all instance nodes, you see the farm node and the instances belonging to the farm.

9. A, B, D, F. For a process node, you can go to the process home page, start the process, stop the process, or restart the process.

10. A, B, C, D, E, F. For a parent node, you can expand all nodes below the parent node if the node is collapsed, start the node's process, expand only the immediate child nodes if the node is collapsed, restart the node's process, collapse the node, or stop the node's process.

11. A, D. Log files are stored either in XML format in a local file system or in the Infrastructure database. In previous versions of Oracle Application Server, the only option was an XML file.

12. A. If the Log Loader process fails, you can review local copies of the log files; the local log files will have information on the failed process. In addition, local log files can help you debug other problems with the diagnostic message database repository.

13. B. The `dcmctl` tool can create a cluster, join existing instances into a cluster, and maintain instance configuration.

14. A, B, D. The `opmnctl` command can check the status of an instance, a cluster, and the instance's components.

15. D. The `emctl` command-line tool is the only tool that can start or stop both Database Control and Application Server Control. The `opmnctl` tool starts and stops instances and components as well as checking the status of an instance or its components. The `dcmctl` tool creates clusters or joins clusters as well as maintains configuration information. There are no such tools as `asctl`, `dbctl`, and `cnctl`.

16. A, D, E. Only the `emctl` tool can start or stop both Database Control and Application Server Control; `dcmctl` archives and restores instance configuration. You can join a cluster from the Farm page and disable a component from the instance home page. You can restart a cluster from Application Server Control or by using the `opmnctl` command.

17. C. The easiest way to stop all Web Cache components is to use the `ias-component` option. You cannot use the `emctl` command to check component status. You can use the `process-type` option to stop each individual process, but this means you will type an extra command. There is no component called `WebCacheAdmin`; it is a process type.

18. D. The `dcmctl resyncInstance` command synchronizes the instance configuration from the repository. The other commands are syntactically incorrect; in addition, the `opmnctl` command is not used for configuration management.

19. D, E. There is no component called Process Configuration Manager. Log Loader is not part of OPMN.

20. A, B, E, F. OPMN controls every Oracle Application Server component except for the Metadata Repository, Application Server Control, Database Control, and Grid Control.

Chapter 4

Performing HTTP Server Configuration and Management Tasks

ORACLE APPLICATION SERVER 10*g* ADMINISTRATION I EXAM OBJECTIVES COVERED IN THIS CHAPTER:

✓ **Managing and Configuring Oracle HTTP Server**

- Explain the Oracle HTTP Server processing model
- Describe the Oracle HTTP Server modules
- Specify the server and file locations for Oracle HTTP Server (OHS)
- Control the number of processes and connections, manage network connection for OHS
- Configure and use OHS log files

✓ **Configuring Directives and Virtual Hosts**

- Describe the configuration directories and their scope
- Describe the process of merging containers and contents
- Configure directories and enable directory indexes
- Describe the process of setting up virtual hosts
- Use configuration directives such as Option, Alias, and Script Alias

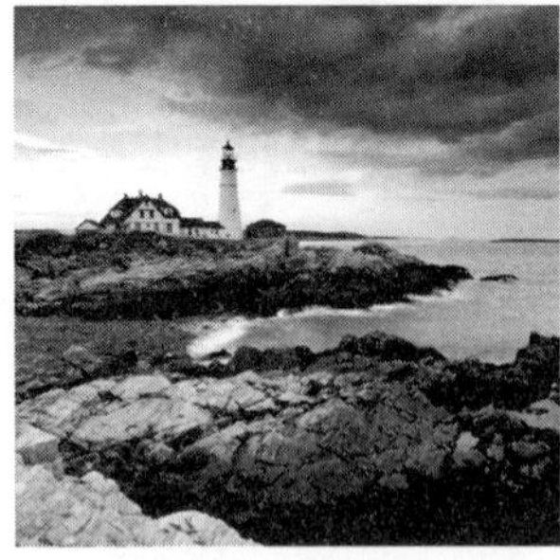

Oracle HTTP Server, also known as OHS, is a key component of Oracle Application Server 10*g* (OracleAS). Built upon the open-source Apache version 1.3, OHS extends the functionality of Apache to include support for Oracle Procedural Language/Structured Query Language (PL/SQL) and integration with OracleAS Single Sign-On (SSO).

In the first part of this chapter, we'll present an in-depth discussion of OHS. We will list the most commonly used pluggable modules for OHS, including Oracle and non-Oracle sourced modules. We'll also show you how to start and stop OHS using both the command-line interface and the GUI, Oracle Enterprise Manager 10*g* Application Server Control (AS Control). In addition, we'll show you how to check the health of the server as well as the contents of the log files. Finally, we'll show you how to manage client requests in a timely manner to ensure high availability and scalability.

In the second part of this chapter, we'll approach the topic of server directives from several different angles. First, we'll give you an overview of where directive files are stored in the OHS directory tree. Alternatively, we'll classify directive types into configuration directives, container directives, and block directives. Along with each classification, we'll summarize the most important directives with a brief description of their purpose. Finally, we'll present several scenarios using the directives in combination to see how they are used in a production environment.

In the last part of the chapter, we'll show you how OHS uses virtual hosts to support multiple websites on one server using only one instance of OHS. You can create both IP-based and name-based virtual hosts; we'll show you how to create these hosts using the AS Control GUI.

Managing Oracle HTTP Server

Oracle HTTP Server, or OHS, is based on the open-source Apache Web Server version 1.3. OHS serves both static and dynamic content; you can generate the dynamic content using Java, C, C++, PHP, Perl, or Oracle PL/SQL. OHS also integrates OracleAS Single Sign-On (SSO) and is cluster ready to ensure high availability. OHS also includes plug-ins to permit integration of OracleAS with non-Oracle HTTP servers.

Oracle supports a stand-alone version of OHS based on Apache Web Server version 2.0.

In the following sections, we'll cover the general HTTP architecture model and how it creates processes on both Linux and Windows platforms. Next is an introduction to OHS modules, including Oracle-specific modules written expressly to support OHS functions such as PL/SQL programming.

Once you are familiar with the components of OHS, you need to know how to manage client connections and the operating system processes that support the connections. We'll give an overview of the global configuration parameters you will use to control processes and connections. Later in this chapter, you'll see how these parameters, or directives, fit in with the other directives you specify in OHS's configuration files.

Next, we'll give you a quick tour with some hands-on examples:

- Using the OHS home page within OEM 10*g* Application Server Control (AS Control)
- Starting and stopping OHS
- Editing configuration files
- Retrieving server status
- Reviewing and understanding log files
- Managing client connection requests

Finally, we'll give a brief overview of some advanced server properties as well as some of the differences between Apache HTTP Server 1.3 and 2.0.

Understanding the HTTP Server Architecture

Oracle HTTP Server consists of several components and is an important and required part of any OracleAS installation. Figure 4.1 shows two servers (hosts) running OracleAS components, with components on the second server accessing a third server containing the database.

One of the servers is dedicated to running OracleAS Web Cache. The other server hosts the OHS *modules* (also known as *mods*) along with other OracleAS components. A *module* implements and extends the basic functionality of OHS by, for example, providing security, running Java applications, and supporting Web-based Distributed Authoring and Versioning (WebDAV).

In the next section, we'll give you an overview of the most common OHS modules and their purpose.

OHS's processing model is slightly different depending on the operating system platform. On the Unix or Linux platform, when OHS is started, a single control process launches several child processes that listen for client requests; to enhance security, each child process should run with fewer privileges than the parent process. You use the Apache directives `User` and `Group` to set the privileges for child processes. The process ID of the parent process is stored in `$ORACLE_HOME/Apache/Apache/logs/httpd.pid` by default.

On Windows platforms, OHS launches a single control process and a single child process; the child process creates multiple threads to listen for client requests. As with the Unix/Linux platform, the child process runs with only enough privileges to access and serve the web server's content.

FIGURE 4.1 A typical OracleAS environment

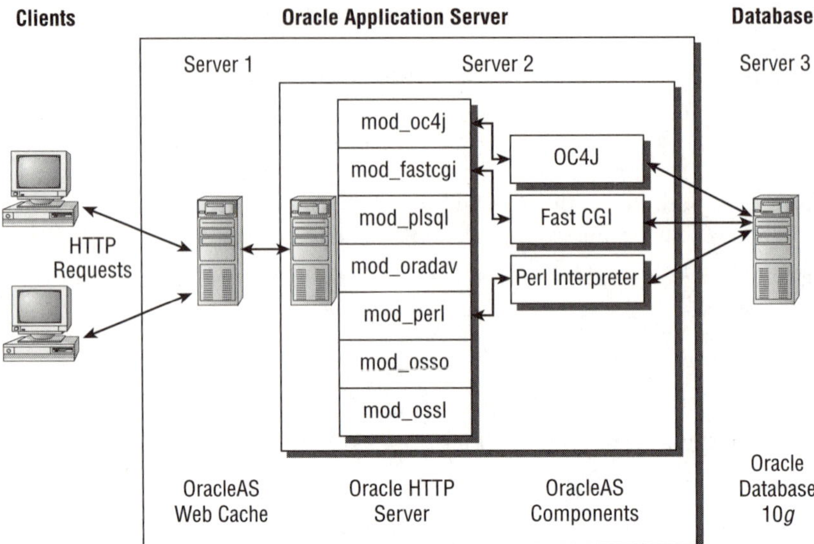

The threaded processing model is not unique to Oracle's implementation of OHS on the Windows platform; conventional programming practices on Windows dictate one or a few distinct processes and many threads within each process instead of individual processes for each asynchronous task within an application.

Overview of Oracle HTTP Server Modules

The Apache HTTP server's biggest strength is its extensibility; the core Apache executable code contains only a small number of features, such as directory filtering, error logging, and connection management. Modules provide everything else. The modules provided by OHS fall into one of three categories:

- Standard compiled modules provided with the open-source distribution of Apache, such as `mod_security`, which shields all applications behind OHS from intrusion attempts
- Open-source modules enhanced by Oracle to provide higher integration with OHS, such as `mod_oradav`, enhanced beyond `mod_dav` from the generic Apache distribution
- Modules specific to OHS, such as `mod_plsql`

A complete list of modules included with the standard Apache HTTP server distribution can be found at `httpd.apache.org/docs/1.3/mod/index.html`.

In Chapter 1, we introduced the most common OHS modules. Table 4.1 lists the modules included in the OHS distribution, either specific to OracleAS or enhanced from the base version for OracleAS.

TABLE 4.1 Oracle-Provided and Enhanced Modules

Module Name	Oracle Specific	Description
`mod_dms`	Y	Monitors the performance of website components within Oracle DMS (Dynamic Monitoring Service)
`mod_oc4j`	Y	Routes requests from OHS to Oracle Containers for J2EE (OC4J)
`mod_php`	N	Supports PHP scripting with extensions for optimized Oracle Database 10*g* access
`mod_plsql`	Y	Enables Oracle PL/SQL procedures connecting OHS to the PL/SQL Gateway
`mod_ossl`	Y	Provides strong cryptography for OHS (Oracle SSL)
`mod_osso`	Y	Interface to Oracle SSO; if the requested resource is protected, retrieves OHS user cookie to prevent reauthorization
`mod_oradav`	Y	Based on `mod_dav`, provides distributed authoring and versioning to OHS; web content can be managed by multiple authors for checkout, edit, and check-in
`mod_security`	N	Shields applications from intrusion attempts

Later in this chapter, you will step through a practical example of how to enable and configure `mod_security`.

Configuring and Managing Oracle HTTP Server

There are several aspects of OHS that you must master to be an effective system administrator. First, you must understand the OHS directory structure as well as the contents and the purpose of the files within it.

Next, you must be able to manage the OHS process itself—starting, stopping, and restarting OHS using either AS Control or the `opmnctl` command-line utility. In addition, you must be able to configure the number of processes and connections for each instance of OHS to handle both routine and unexpected website traffic.

You configure your web server primarily via directives in the configuration file; we'll provide a brief introduction to directives in this section and provide an in-depth look at the most important directives later in this chapter.

Monitoring the status of OHS is another tool you use to ensure your success. You must know how to proactively check the status of your web server using the AS Control GUI interface, command-line tools, and server log files.

Defining Directives

OHS directives are the key components you must understand to successfully and efficiently configure OHS. A *directive* is an OHS configuration instruction or a block of instructions with a header and a footer that you place in `httpd.conf` and other files with a `.conf` extension, or the filename `.htdocs`, to determine the behavior of the server. You will find out more about `httpd.conf` in the section "Oracle HTTP Server Configuration Files" later in this chapter. In addition, we will provide an in-depth look at server directives in the second half of this chapter, "Understanding Server Directives."

In the following sections, however, we will introduce a few specific server directives that you need to know to understand the overall architecture of OHS.

Oracle HTTP Server Directory Structure

OHS is installed in `$ORACLE_HOME/Apache`. The directories at the first level contain subdirectories with configuration information for all modules plus another `Apache` directory. The second `Apache` directory contains subdirectories and their contents as follows:

`htdocs` HTML scripts and any other web content for public consumption

`conf` OHS configuration files

`logs` Log files for both successful and unsuccessful website access

`bin` OHS executables

`cgi-bin` CGI scripts in Perl, C++, Java, and so forth that can be executed by OHS for web clients

`libexec` Shared library files for modules

`fastcgi` `fastcgi` runtime libraries for building `fastcgi` applications

`fcgi-bin` `fastcgi` scripts

`icons` Icons used by OHS for displaying status, information, or error messages

`include` Header files for building custom OHS modules

`man` Online manual pages for OHS

`mod_perl` Sample code for `mod_perl`, libraries, and `man` pages

`php` Sample code for `mod_php`, libraries, and `man` pages

Do not place any files other than web content in the `htdocs` directory since this entire directory tree is available to the public.

Figure 4.2 shows the directory structure containing the OHS files and content. `$ORACLE_HOME` is defined as `/u01/app/oracle/as10gHome`.

Several server directives specify locations within the OHS directory structure. Table 4.2 lists the key file and directory directives. You can use some of these directives for the primary server configuration only; two of these directives are available at both the primary server and virtual hosts, if any. You specify these directives in `$ORACLE_HOME/Apache/Apache/conf/httpd.conf`.

For example, the primary server and any virtual servers have their own directory for serving web files and therefore have different values for `DocumentRoot`; the `PidFile` directive makes sense only at the primary server level since there is only one process ID that initiates child processes for the primary server and all virtual servers.

FIGURE 4.2 OHS directory structure in a Linux environment

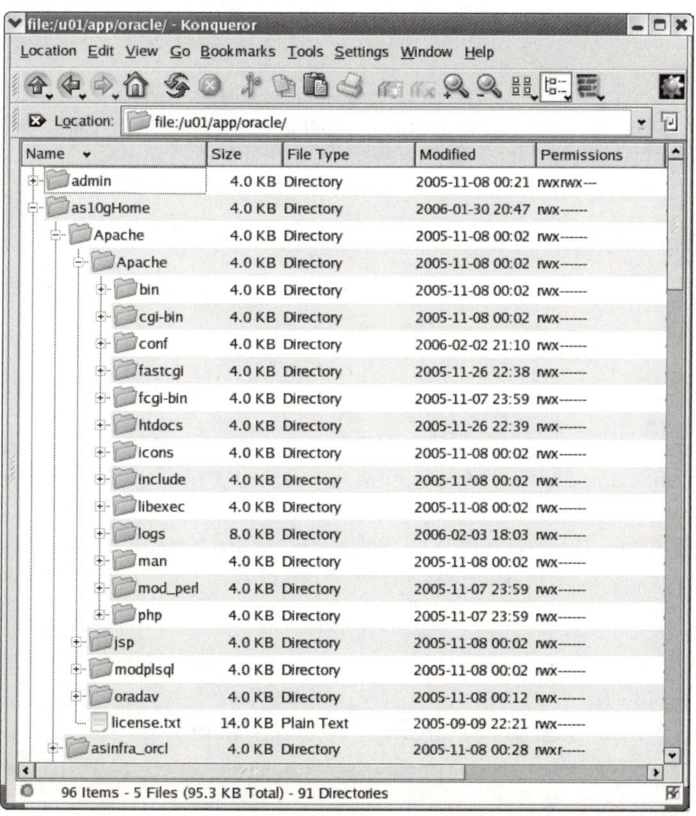

TABLE 4.2 OHS File- and Directory-Related Directives

Directive Name	Available for Virtual Host?	Description
ServerRoot	N	The main (parent) directory where OHS stores its log files, configuration files, and served documents. For other directives, defined with a relative path, ServerRoot is used as the default root.
PidFile	N	The location of the file containing the process identification number of the primary control process. If this directive does not start with /, it is relative to the ServerRoot directory.
CoreDumpDirectory	N	The directory where OHS stores core dumps in case of a server crash; if this is not specified, it defaults to ServerRoot.
DocumentRoot	Y	The directory where OHS serves web content files. The default value is htdocs, relative to ServerRoot.
ErrorLog	Y	The directory where OHS records access or errors. The default is logs/error_log, relative to ServerRoot. You can also specify an explicit pathname starting with /.

Here is the line from `httpd.conf` specifying the value for the `ServerRoot` directive in the Global Environment section:

```
ServerRoot "/u01/app/oracle/as10gHome/Apache/Apache"
```

Oracle HTTP Server Configuration Files

You use two operating system text files to configure all aspects of OHS: `httpd.conf` and `.htaccess`. There is only one copy of `httpd.conf` to control global aspects of the primary web server and all virtual servers; every directory containing content can optionally have a `.htaccess` file. In addition, `httpd.conf` typically references other configuration files using the `Include` directive for ease of maintenance. These referenced files include `oracle_apache.conf` and `mime.types`.

httpd.conf

The primary configuration file for OHS and any Apache HTTP server is `httpd.conf`. For OHS, this file is located by default in the directory `$ORACLE_HOME/Apache/Apache/conf`.

This file is logically divided into three areas: the global environment, the main server configuration, and virtual hosts.

GLOBAL ENVIRONMENT

The section labeled Global Environment contains directives that affect the overall operation of the Apache HTTP server, such as the number of concurrent connections or the location of other configuration files.

Here is the beginning of the Global Environment section:

```
### Section 1: Global Environment
#
# The directives in this section affect the overall
# operation of Apache,
# such as the number of concurrent requests it can handle
# or where it
# can find its configuration files.
#


#
# ServerRoot: The top of the directory tree under which the server's
# configuration, error, and log files are kept.
#
# NOTE!  If you intend to place this on an NFS (or otherwise network)
# mounted filesystem then please read the LockFile documentation
# (available at <URL:http://www.apache.org/docs/mod/core.html#lockfile>);
# you will save yourself a lot of trouble.
#
# Do NOT add a slash at the end of the directory path.
#
ServerRoot "/u01/app/oracle/as10gHome/Apache/Apache"
#
#
# Timeout: The number of seconds before receives and sends time out.
#
Timeout 300
#
# KeepAlive: Whether or not to allow persistent connections (more than
# one request per connection). Set to "Off" to deactivate.
#
KeepAlive On
#
# MaxKeepAliveRequests: The maximum number of requests to allow
# during a persistent connection. Set to 0 to allow an unlimited amount.
# We recommend you leave this number high, for maximum performance.
```

```
#
MaxKeepAliveRequests 100
#
# KeepAliveTimeout: Number of seconds to wait for the next request from the
# same client on the same connection.
#
KeepAliveTimeout 15
#
```

Note that the `ServerRoot` directive specifies the root directory for all OHS files except for the served documents; you define the root directory for served documents in the main server configuration section.

MAIN SERVER CONFIGURATION

The directives in this section apply to the primary web server hosted by this instance of OHS. These directives provide the default values for any virtual hosts that don't override the values in the primary web server. Here are a few directives from the main server configuration file:

```
### Section 2: 'Main' server configuration
#
# The directives in this section set up the values used by the 'main'
# server, which responds to any requests that aren't handled by a
# <VirtualHost> definition.  These values also provide defaults for
# any <VirtualHost> containers you may define later in the file.
#
# All of these directives may appear inside <VirtualHost> containers,
# in which case these default settings will be overridden for the
# virtual host being defined.
#
# If your ServerType directive (set earlier in the 'Global Environment'
# section) is set to "inetd", the next few directives don't have any
# effect since their settings are defined by the inetd configuration.
# Skip ahead to the ServerAdmin directive.
#


#
# Port: The port to which the standalone server listens. For
# ports < 1024, you will need httpd to be run as root initially.
#
# This port is used when starting without SSL
Port 7777
Listen 7777
```

```
#

#
ServerName asinfra
#
# DocumentRoot: The directory out of which you will serve your
# documents. By default, all requests are taken from this directory, but
# symbolic links and aliases may be used to point to other locations.
#
DocumentRoot "/u01/app/oracle/as10gHome/Apache/Apache/htdocs"
#
```

The `DocumentRoot` directive, the directory out of which you serve the web server's documents, can reference any directory on any file system accessible on the server as long as the user account you use to run OHS (usually `oracle`) has read access to the directory containing the content.

VIRTUAL HOSTS

This section defines one or more websites, or *virtual hosts*, that respond to IP addresses or hostnames other than the main server's IP address or hostname. In other words, your server can host multiple websites on the same physical server.

The default `httpd.conf` file that is included with OHS contains a template for creating a virtual host, as you can see in this excerpt from `httpd.conf`:

```
### Section 3: Virtual Hosts
#
# VirtualHost: If you want to maintain
#    multiple domains/hostnames on your
# machine you can setup VirtualHost containers for them. Most configurations
# use only name-based virtual hosts so
#   the server doesn't need to worry about
# IP addresses. This is indicated by the asterisks in the
#   directives below.
#
# Please see the documentation at <URL:http://www.apache.org/docs/vhosts/>
# for further details before you try to setup virtual hosts.
#
# You may use the command line option '-S' to verify your virtual host
# configuration.

#
# Use name-based virtual hosting.
#
```

```
#NameVirtualHost *
#NameVirtualHost 12.34.56.78:80
#NameVirtualHost 12.34.56.78

#
# VirtualHost example:
# Almost any Apache directive may go into a VirtualHost container.
# The first VirtualHost section is used for requests without a known
# server name.
#
#<VirtualHost *>
#     ServerAdmin webmaster@dummy-host.example.com
#     DocumentRoot /www/docs/dummy-host.example.com
#     ServerName dummy-host.example.com
#     ErrorLog logs/dummy-host.example.com-error_log
#     CustomLog logs/dummy-host.example.com-access_log common
#</VirtualHost>
#<VirtualHost _default_:*>
#</VirtualHost>
```

Creating multiple virtual hosts on a single server is a great way to load balance multiple websites with different peak load times. This makes more efficient use of your existing server, delaying the purchase of new hardware and simplifying your maintenance tasks at the same time.

.htaccess

A `.htaccess` file can exist in any directory under the directory specified by the `DocumentRoot` (the web server content home directory) directive in `httpd.conf`. The directives in the `.htaccess` file in a given directory override the directives in `httpd.conf` or in the `.htaccess` file in the parent directory; the directives in `.htaccess` are the same directives allowed in `httpd.conf`.

You can disable all `.htaccess` files by using the `AllowOverride` directive in `httpd.conf`. In addition, the `AccessFileName` directive specifies a different name for the `.htaccess` file.

A typical scenario for using `.htaccess` is to allow content providers more control over the content in their directories when they don't have access to the main configuration file `httpd.conf`. This also reduces the workload for the OHS administrator. However, in general, you should avoid using `.htaccess` because OHS must read the contents of `.htaccess` in addition to all parent directories containing `.htaccess` every time the directory is accessed by a client request.

Other Configuration Files

For ease of maintenance and understanding, `httpd.conf` uses the `Include` directive to reference configuration files specific to the Oracle-provided modules as well as to the commonly available modules. Figure 4.3 shows the hierarchy for included configuration files.

FIGURE 4.3 httpd.conf-included configuration file hierarchy

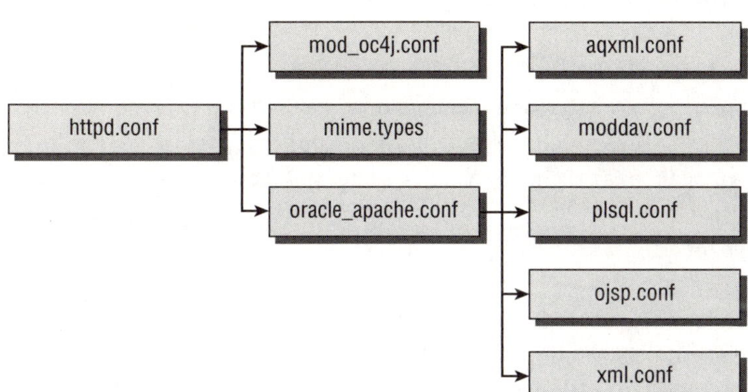

At the first level, `httpd.conf` uses an `Include` directive for these configuration files:

`mod_oc4j.conf` Configures and loads module `mod_oc4j`. This module routes requests from OHS to Oracle Containers for J2EE (OC4J) applications.

`mime.types` Contains the Internet media types that OHS sends to the client for each file extension. For example, the following entry in `mime.types` directs the web browser to use the `msword` application to process documents with an extension of `.doc`: application/msword doc

`oracle_apache.conf` Includes configuration files for all supported Oracle-supplied modules, described in the next paragraph.

At the second level, the configuration file `oracle_apache.conf` contains `Include` directives for these configuration files:

`aqxml.conf` Enables and configures Oracle Advanced Queuing.

`moddav.conf` Configures and loads the module `mod_oradav`, Oracle's extension to web-based distributed authoring and versioning of web documents, `mod_dav`.

`plsql.conf` Configures and loads the PL/SQL module. This file is located in `$ORACLE_HOME/Apache/modplsql/conf`.

`ojsp.conf` Configures Java Server Pages. This file is located in `$ORACLE_HOME/Apache/jsp/conf`.

`xml.conf` Associates any file with the `.xsql` extension with the XSQL servlet. This servlet makes it easy to build dynamic XML pages using standard SQL queries. This file is located in `$ORACLE_HOME/xdk/admin`.

Here are the contents of `oracle_apache.conf`:

```
include "/u01/app/oracle/as10gHome/ultrasearch/
➥ webapp/config/ultrasearch.conf"
```

```
# Advanced Queuing - AQ XML
include "/u01/app/oracle/as10gHome/rdbms/demo/aqxml.conf"
#
#Directives needed for OraDAV module
include "/u01/app/oracle/as10gHome/Apache/oradav/conf/moddav.conf"
include "/u01/app/oracle/as10gHome/Apache/jsp/conf/ojsp.conf"
include "/u01/app/oracle/as10gHome/Apache/modplsql/conf/plsql.conf"
# Oracle uix
include "/u01/app/oracle/as10gHome/uix/uix.conf"
#OiD DAS module
include "/u01/app/oracle/as10gHome/ldap/das/oiddas.conf"
#Directives needed for SSO module
include "/u01/app/oracle/as10gHome/sso/conf/sso_apache.conf"
#Directives needed for OCM module
include "/u01/app/oracle/as10gHome/Apache/Apache/conf/ocm_apache.conf"
```

Splitting up the configuration files into this hierarchy makes the configuration easier to understand and to maintain. Turning off PL/SQL support within the OraDAV module is as easy as commenting out one line in `oracle_apache.conf` and restarting OHS.

Using the Oracle HTTP Server Home Page

Using the OHS home page, you can manage most, if not all, aspects of the server. From the instance home page, click the `HTTP_Server` link in the System Components section and you will see the OHS home page, shown in Figure 4.4.

The OHS home page has three tabs: the Home tab, the Virtual Hosts tab, and the Administration tab.

Home

The OHS home page shows you the general status of the server, such as whether it is up or down and when it was last restarted. In addition, you see a current snapshot of the CPU and memory usage as well as average throughput statistics. You can use the home page to start, stop, or restart OHS.

Virtual Hosts

Using the Virtual Hosts page, you can add, delete, and manage any virtual hosts configured with this instance of OHS.

Administration

The Administration page is where you perform OHS server property configuration, such as changing the document root, port numbers, and number of concurrent connection processes as well as editing configuration files. You can see the Administration tab of the OHS home page in Figure 4.5.

FIGURE 4.4 Oracle HTTP Server home page

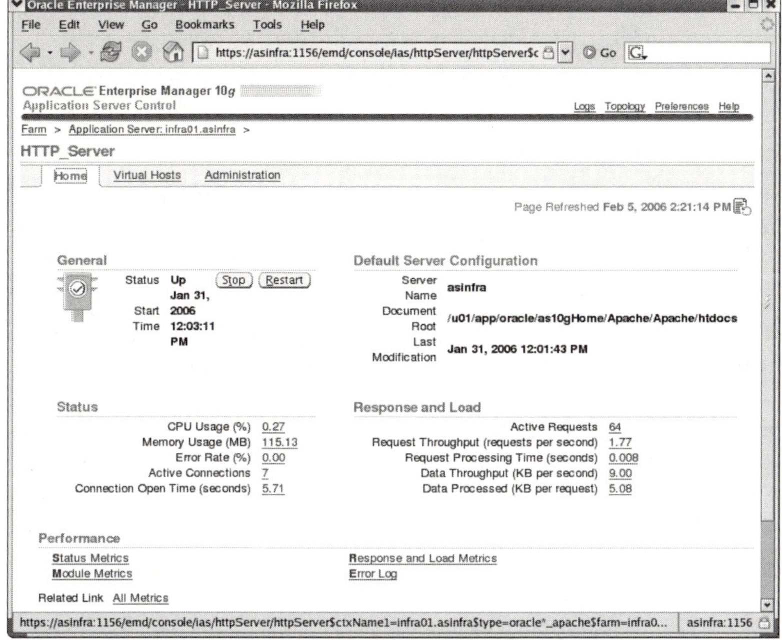

FIGURE 4.5 Oracle HTTP Server Administration page

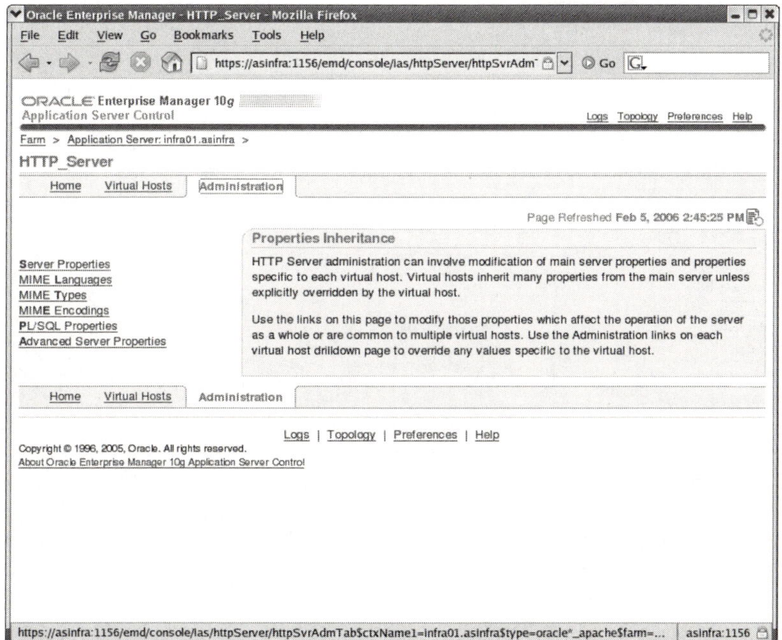

For example, to configure general server properties, click the `Server Properties` link (see Figure 4.5) and you see the Server Properties page in Figure 4.6.

When you install OHS, you do not have an opportunity to specify an email address for receiving status and error conditions. To specify an email address, follow these steps:

1. On the Server Properties page (Figure 4.6), enter the administrator's email address in the Administrator E-Mail text box.
2. Scroll to the bottom of the page and click Apply.
3. Click Yes when you see the Confirmation page. This will restart OHS. After a few moments, OHS will be up and running with the new value for Administrator E-Mail.

Starting and Stopping Oracle HTTP Server

On the OHS home page, you can start, stop, and restart the server by clicking the Start, Stop, or Restart buttons, as you might expect. Figure 4.4 shows the server currently available, so you could either stop or restart it.

If you do not have access to a web browser or you need to change the status of OHS in a batch job, you can use the `opmnctl` command to start, stop, or restart OHS in addition to checking its status. In Chapter 3, we showed you how to use `opmnctl` to start, stop, or restart any OracleAS component; OHS is no exception.

FIGURE 4.6 Oracle HTTP Server Server Properties page

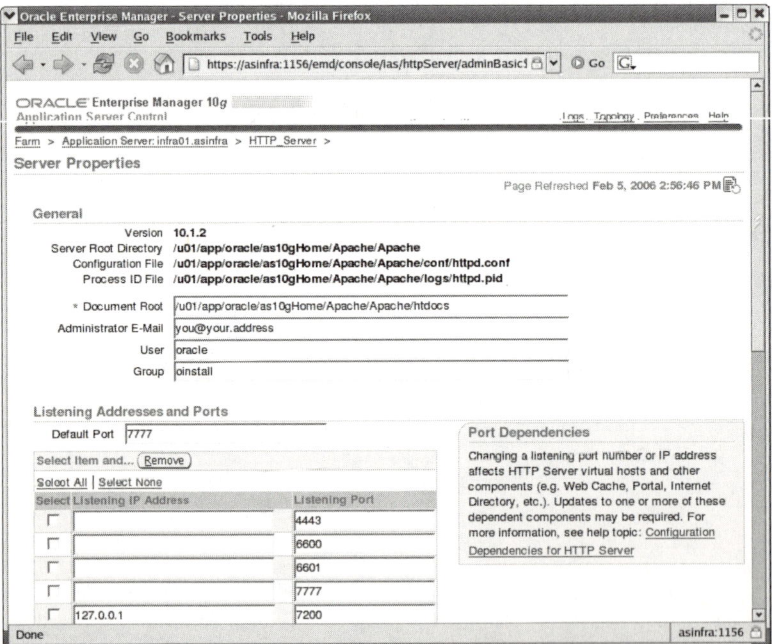

To run the opmnctl command, you must be in the directory $ORACLE_HOME/opmn/bin or have $ORACLE_HOME/opmn/bin in your PATH environment variable. To restart OHS, you use this command:

```
opmnctl restartproc process-type=HTTP_Server
```

To check the status of only OHS, you use the status option:

```
[oracle@asinfra oracle]$ opmnctl status process-type=HTTP_Server

Processes in Instance: infra01.asinfra
-------------------+--------------------+---------+---------
ias-component      | process-type       |     pid | status
-------------------+--------------------+---------+---------
HTTP_Server        | HTTP_Server        |   15788 | Alive

[oracle@asinfra oracle]$
```

If you want to check the status of all components within this instance, leave off the process-type argument to the opmnctl command.

The argument to process-type is case sensitive. The command opmnctl status process-type=hTTP_sERVER returns no results!

Managing Processes, Connections, and Client Requests

The maximum number of processes available to OHS on your server is not unlimited, but you want to ensure that connected users receive a prompt reply to requests for Web content. In addition, the server may have other applications that may compete with OHS for resources. As a result, you need to manage processes and connections for OHS.

In a Unix/Linux environment, you use the following directives in the global environment section of httpd.conf:

StartServers The number of child server processes created when OHS starts; the default value is 5.

MaxClients The number of simultaneous client requests; the default value is 150.

MaxRequestsPerChild The number of requests that a child process will process before it terminates and restarts. The default value is 0; the process never exits until the server is shut down.

MaxSpareServers The maximum number of child processes that are running but not in use. The default value is 10.

MinSpareServers The minimum number of child processes that should be kept running, even with no active client requests. The default value is 5.

KeepAlive Valid values are On and Off. If this is set to On, the connection between the client and the server is maintained for the length of time specified in KeepAliveTimeout to reduce latency for multiple requests within the same session. When KeepAlive is Off, the client must reestablish the connection with the server for each request.

KeepAliveTimeout The maximum amount of time the server will wait for subsequent requests on a persistent connection with a client when KeepAlive is On. The default value is 15 seconds.

MaxKeepAliveRequests The maximum number of requests allowed within a client connection when KeepAlive is On. The default value is 100.

For Windows operating systems, you use these directives:

ThreadsPerChild The number of threads within each child process. Since OHS creates only one child process under Windows, this directive limits the overall number of simultaneous requests. The default value is 50.

KeepAlive, KeepAliveTimeout, and MaxKeepAliveRequests These are the only other directives allowed in Windows operating systems for controlling client connections; they operate the same as they do in Unix/Linux.

Using AS Control, you can change the values for these directives when you navigate to the HTTP Server home page from the instance home page, click the Administration tab, and then click the Server Properties link. At the bottom of the page, you can see the settings related to processes and connections (see Figure 4.7).

FIGURE 4.7 Oracle HTTP Server Server Properties page

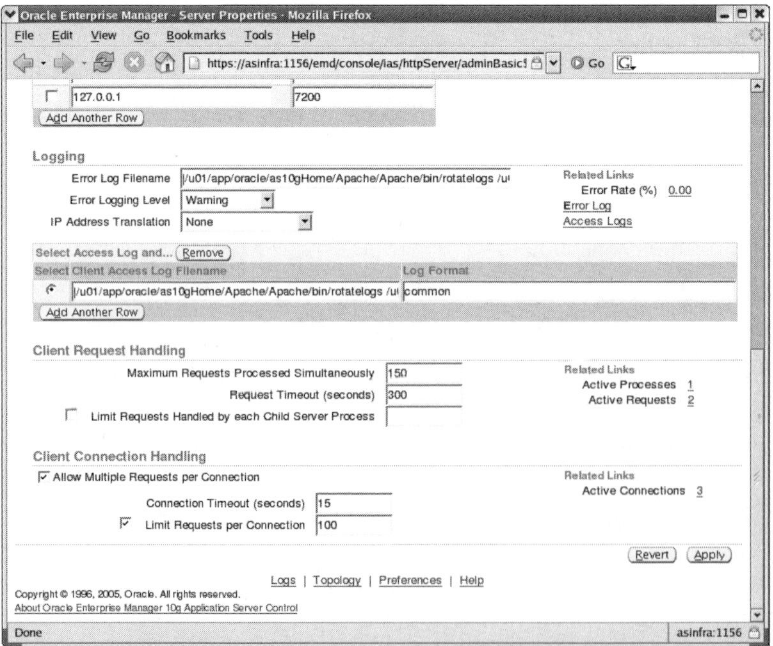

Retrieving Server Status

To retrieve server status statistics in a readable form, use the `Status` module. Within the `Location` block directive, you enable the `Status` module and restrict access to the server status to a single IP address, 192.168.2.82 in this example:

```
<Location /server-status>
   setHandler server-status
   order deny,allow
   deny from all
   allow from 192.168.2.82
</Location>
```

Once you place the `Location` directive in `httpd.conf` and restart OHS, you can access the status page using this URL:

```
http://asinfra:7777/server-status
```

Port number 7777 is the default OHS listening port for an infrastructure installation. Figure 4.8 shows what you see in your web browser for server status.

FIGURE 4.8 Oracle HTTP Server server status page

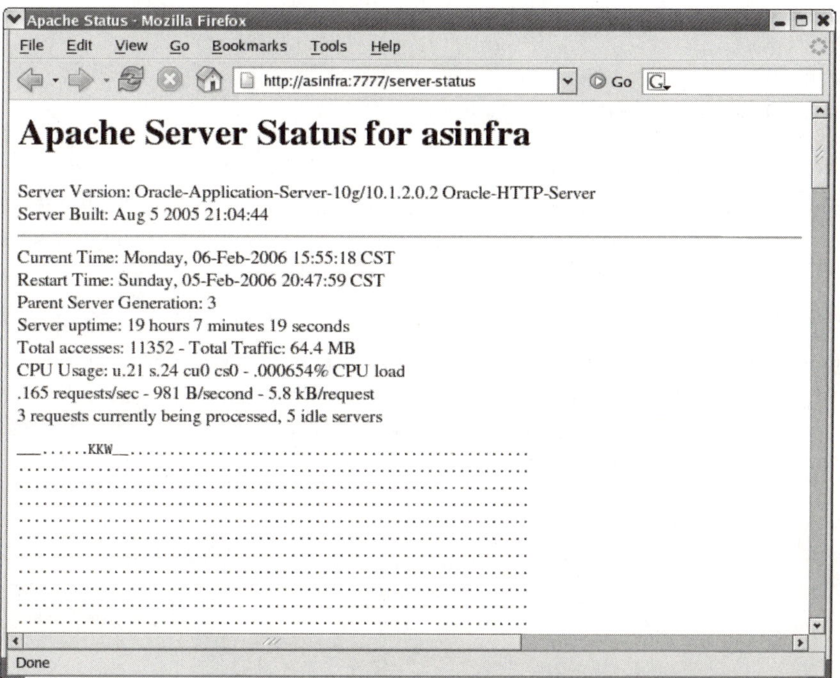

If you want to refresh the page on a periodic basis and your web browser supports it, you can add the refresh option to the URL:

```
http://asinfra:7777/server-status?refresh=60
```

In addition, the OracleAS Administration Service collects usage and performance statistics from all OracleAS components, including OHS. Here are the metrics collected for OHS:

Active Requests Total current active requests

Request Throughput Requests processed per second

Request Processing Time Average number of seconds required to process requests

Configuring Server Access

These basic directives in `httpd.conf` control the addresses, ports, and names at which the web server listens for requests:

`Listen` Allows the server to listen for requests on more than one IP address, one port, or both. You can have more than one `Listen` directive in `httpd.conf` to specify multiple IP address and port combinations. By default, OHS responds to requests on all interfaces but only on the port given in the `Port` directive. If you specify any ports in a `Listen` directive, then the `Port` directive is ignored. In this example, to listen for requests only on port 8080 of the interface with IP address 192.168.2.50 and port 80 of the interface with IP address 192.168.2.51, use these `Listen` directives:

```
Listen 192.168.2.50:8080
Listen 192.168.2.51:80
```

All other interfaces as well as any ports specified in the `Port` directive are ignored.

`Port` You can specify only one `Port` directive per configuration. By default, OHS listens for requests on all interfaces with the port you specify with the `Port` directive. If you specify a port as part of a `Listen` directive, the `Port` directive is ignored.

`ServerName` Sets the hostname of the server; OHS uses it to create redirection URLs.

`UseCanonicalName` You construct the canonical name of a server using the `ServerName` and `Port` directives. OHS uses the canonical name when redirecting a URL to the same server. When it is set to `On`, the default, OHS ignores any hostname or port in the request header. If this directive is set to `Off`, the request may specify a different hostname or port.

You can find more information about using server directives later in this chapter and at `httpd.apache.org/docs/1.3/mod/directives.html`.

Configuring Server Privileges

There are several general directives that control your website's security. You want to be able to deliver content to clients, but at the same time, you want to minimize the exposure of your system to those same clients in the case of an unintentional or intentional breach of security. The OHS control process runs as `root` but spawns off child processes using a user with fewer privileges, such as the `oracle` user. Here are the most important privilege and server-related directives:

`User` OHS serves content using this user account. This account should not be able to access any files on the server not intended for public consumption; in addition, this account should not be able to execute any code not meant for `httpd` requests. By default, OHS uses `oracle` for this directive.

`Group` OHS serves content and runs with the group privileges of this account. Content not available with the `User` directive account privileges will be available if the content has group permissions defined by the `Group` directive.

`ServerAdmin` Sets the email address included with error messages that clients see.

`ServerTokens` Controls the level of information returned to clients in informational or error messages. Here are the possible values for `ServerTokens`:

- **`full`** The server provides the server name (Apache), version, operating system, and installed modules. This is the default.
- **`min` (minimal)** The server provides the server name (Apache) and version.
- **`prod` (product)** The server provides only the server name (Apache).
- **`OS` (operating system)** The server provides the server name, version, and operating system.

In Figure 4.6, you can see how you can change the `User`, `Group`, and `ServerAdmin` directives on the Server Properties page using the User, Group, and Administrator E-Mail fields respectively.

Understanding Server Logs

Log files are key elements you use to assess the health and performance of your server. In the following sections, we'll review all aspects of OHS logs that you need to understand to be an effective administrator.

First, we'll review the basic directives you need to know to configure the individual log filenames.

Log File Locations

OHS creates all of its log files, by default, in the directory defined by a combination of the `ServerRoot` directive and the relative path defined by the individual log file location directive. As a result, by default, log files reside in `$ORACLE_HOME/Apache/Apache/logs` unless overridden by a particular log file's directive with a different relative or absolute path.

Table 4.3 shows the server log location directives and the log filenames they control.

TABLE 4.3 OHS Log File Directives and Filenames

Directive Name	Default	Directive Description
`PidFile`	`logs/httpd.pid`	The directory and filename where OHS keeps the process ID of the parent `httpd` process; this parent process starts all child processes.
`TransferLog`	`logs/access_log`	The directory and filename where OHS logs all requests.
`CustomLog`	`logs/access_log`	Same as `TransferLog` with a custom format for the entries in the log file.
`SSLLog`	`logs/ssl_engine_log` `logs/ssl_request_log`	The directory and filename where OHS saves messages from the SSL Engine process and all SSL requests respectively. In addition, the OHS records these error messages in `ErrorLog`.
`ErrorLog`	`logs/error_log`	The directory where OHS records server access or errors. `ErrorLog` can have different values for the primary server and each virtual server.

Logging Level

Controlling the amount of logging for your servers is another important aspect of system administration: You want to have enough logging to either proactively or reactively tune or configure your server efficiently but not so much logging that you might miss an important message in a virtual sea of log messages or you run out of disk space! In addition, you will adjust the logging level depending on the circumstances, as in the following examples:

- Turn on full logging after you install a new server or make configuration changes.
- Show debugging messages when you have system problems that require a more detailed log.
- Increase logging levels when you suspect a security breach.
- Decrease logging levels during high-usage periods.

You can assign a different log file for the main server and each virtual server. Table 4.4 shows the assigned level number, the name of the level itself, and an example of the types of conditions that generate log entries at that level.

The logging levels are cumulative; the value you assign to `LogLevel` includes logging at all lower levels. For example, if you set `LogLevel` to `Error`, the log file will also contain all messages from the `Crit` and `Emerg` levels.

TABLE 4.4 OHS LogLevel Directive Values

Level Number	Level Name	Level Description
1	Emerg	Emergency—system down or unusable
2	Crit	Critical—limited system functionality
3	Error	Error—missing or corrupted configuration files, unexpected conditions, abnormally terminated sessions
4	Warn	Warning—unexpected but nonfatal condition, recoverable
5	Notice	Normal but significant condition—unexpected client connection errors
6	Info	Informational—performance issues and tuning recommendations
7	Debug	Debug messages—every OHS process detail

Here is an excerpt from `httpd.conf` that shows the default logging level and location when you install the server:

```
#
# ErrorLog: The location of the error log file.
# If you do not specify an ErrorLog directive within a <VirtualHost>
# container, error messages relating to that virtual host will be
# logged here.  If you *do* define an error logfile for a <VirtualHost>
# container, that host's errors will be logged there and not here.
#
ErrorLog "|/u01/app/oracle/as10gHome/Apache/Apache/bin/rotatelogs
➥ /u01/app/oracle/as10gHome/Apache/Apache/logs/error_log 43200"
#
# LogLevel: Control the number of messages logged to the error_log.
# Possible values include: debug, info, notice, warn, error, crit,
# alert, emerg.
#
LogLevel warn
#
```

You can filter only certain logging events from the `error_log` file using the `grep` or `egrep` commands (`egrep` allows for conditional expressions in the search string). In the first example, you want to see only the `Error` entries:

```
[oracle@asinfra logs]$ grep '\[error\]' error_log
[Sun Nov 13 13:54:47 2005] [error] [client 192.168.2.82]
➥ [ecid: 1131911680:192.168.2.82:18930:0:6069,0] mod_plsql:
➥ /pls/orasso/htp.p HTTP-503 ORA-12154 ORA-12154:
➥ TNS:could not resolve the connect identifier specified\n
[Sun Nov 13 13:59:40 2005] [error] [client 192.168.2.82]
➥ [ecid: 1131911980:192.168.2.82:19718:0:6269,0] mod_plsql:
➥ /pls/orasso/htp.p HTTP-503 ORA-3113
➥ Call to WPG_SESSION API Failed.
[Sun Nov 13 14:03:34 2005] [error] [client 192.168.2.82]
➥ [ecid: 1131912213:192.168.2.82:19983:0:5895,0] mod_plsql:
➥ /pls/orasso/htp.p HTTP-503 ORA-12154 ORA-12154:
➥ TNS:could not resolve the connect identifier
➥ specified\n
[Sun Nov 13 14:04:41 2005] [error] [client 192.168.2.82]
➥ [ecid: 1131912280:192.168.2.82:18933:0:6237,0] mod_plsql:
➥ /pls/orasso/htp.p HTTP-503 ORA-12154 ORA-12154:
➥ TNS:could not resolve the connect identifier
➥ specified\n
[Sun Nov 13 14:09:40 2005] [error] [client 192.168.2.82]
➥ [ecid: 1131912580:192.168.2.82:19983:0:5899,0] mod_plsql:
➥ /pls/orasso/htp.p HTTP-503 ORA-12154 ORA-12154:
➥ TNS:could not resolve the connect identifier
➥ specified\n
[oracle@asinfra logs]$
```

In the next example, you want to see only the `Notice` or `Warn` messages:

```
[oracle@asinfra logs]$ egrep '\[notice\] | \[warn\]' error_log
[Sun Nov 13 14:27:29 2005] [notice] FastCGI: process manager
➥ initialized (pid 4265)
[Sun Nov 13 14:27:30 2005] [notice]
➥ Oracle-Application-Server-10g/10.1.2.0.2
➥ Oracle-HTTP-Server configured --
➥ resuming normal operations
[Sun Nov 13 14:27:30 2005] [notice] Accept mutex: fcntl
➥ (Default: sysvsem)
[Sun Nov 13 14:31:09 2005] [notice] FastCGI:
➥ process manager initialized (pid 5628)
```

```
[Sun Nov 13 14:31:10 2005] [notice]
➥ Oracle-Application-Server-10g/10.1.2.0.2
➥ Oracle-HTTP-Server configured --
➥ resuming normal operations
[Sun Nov 13 14:31:10 2005] [notice] Accept mutex: fcntl
➥ (Default: sysvsem)
[Sun Nov 13 14:31:10 2005] [warn]
➥ long lost child came home! (pid 4269)
[oracle@asinfra logs]$
```

Log Formats

We hinted at log formatting earlier in this chapter when we talked about the `CustomLog` directive. The directive `LogFormat` specifies how you construct each log entry using keywords beginning with %. You use `CustomLog` and `LogFormat` to specify different log formats for the server and each virtual server.

Table 4.5 shows the possible substitution variables recognized in a `LogFormat` directive.

TABLE 4.5 OHS `LogFormat` Directive Substitution Variables

Substitution Variable	Name	Description
%h	Remote host	Client domain name or IP address
%l	Remote name	Client identity information
%u	Remote user	User ID if the site is password protected
%t	Date and time	Date and time in DD/MM/YYYY:HH:MI:SS format
%r	First line of request	Request line from the client in double quotation marks supplied by `LogFormat`
%s	Status	Three-digit status code returned to the client
%b	Bytes sent to client	Number of bytes sent to the client, excluding HTTP headers

The default log entry format is *Common Log Format (CLF)*, and it looks like this in `httpd.conf`:

```
LogFormat "%h %l %u %t \"%r\" %>s %b" common
```

The common at the end of the LogFormat directive is a *nickname*; you use this nickname in subsequent LogFormat or TransferLog directives as shorthand instead of repeating the format string.

When you install OHS, several LogFormat directives create nicknames as follows:

```
LogFormat "%h %l %u %t \"%r\" %>s %b
➥ \"%{Referer}i\" \"%{User-Agent}i\"" combined
LogFormat "%h %l %u %t \"%r\" %>s %b" common
LogFormat "%{Referer}i -> %U" referer
LogFormat "%{User-agent}i" agent
```

The access_log log file uses the common log format, as you can see in these examples from the access log:

```
192.168.2.82 - - [25/Jan/2006:23:23:49 -0600]
➥ "GET / HTTP/1.1" 200 19718
192.168.2.82 - - [25/Jan/2006:23:23:49 -0600]
➥ "GET /ohs_images/portals.css HTTP/1.1" 200 14795
192.168.2.82 - - [25/Jan/2006:23:23:49 -0600]
➥ "GET /ohs_images/space.gif HTTP/1.1" 200 43
192.168.2.82 - - [25/Jan/2006:23:23:50 -0600]
➥ "GET /ohs_images/9iAShome_banner_2.gif HTTP/1.1" 200 11045
```

Changing Error Log Properties

You can configure most aspects of OHS and OracleAS using one of the AS Control web pages. Configuring error log properties is no exception: From the OHS home page, click the Administration tab and click Server Properties. Scroll down to the middle of the page and you will see the Logging section (see Figure 4.9).

On this page, you can easily change the location of the error log and access log; on this server, the log format uses the common nickname to specify the log format to use. In addition, you can set the logging level as well as how to handle translation of IP addresses when a client sends an IP address instead of a domain name with the request.

Adding an Access Log File

An *access log* records basic information about every transaction processed by OHS. You can configure an access log to generate statistical reports on usage reports by domain, user, time of day, and so forth. By default, an OHS installation creates a single access log using the common format. Table 4.5 shows the elements contained in the log file.

In some situations, you may want an additional log file to contain a subset of the elements listed previously or you may want to send this log file to a common repository that needs the log file in a specific format. In Figure 4.9, you see the default access log defined in the Logging section; let's say you want to continue using this log and create another copy of the access log in a different format. Click the Add Another Row button and specify the location for the second access log file and the log format. To start creating the log file, click the Apply button near the bottom right of this page. Finally, click Yes to restart OHS and use the new log file.

FIGURE 4.9 Oracle HTTP Server logging configuration section of the Server Properties page

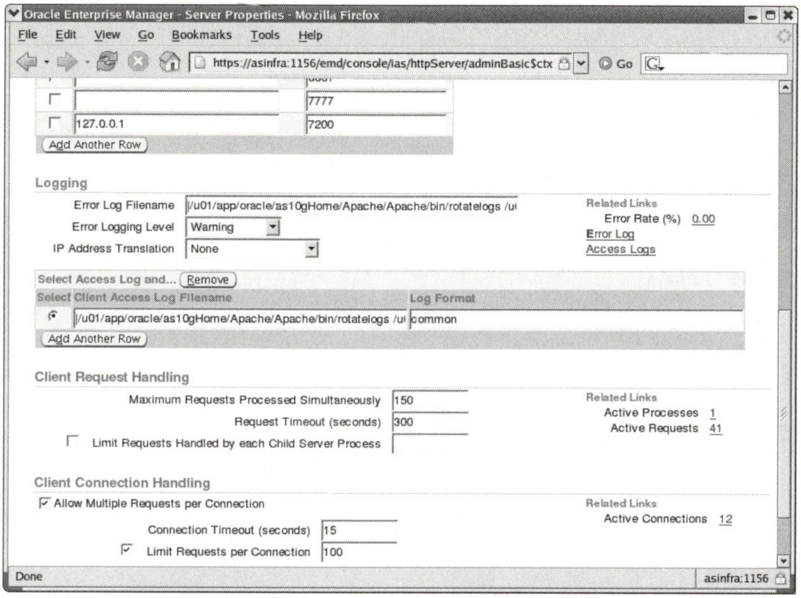

Rotating Log Files

Because the size of the log files can easily exceed hundreds of megabytes over a period of days even on a moderately active server, Oracle recommends that you rotate, archive, and optionally delete the log files on a periodic basis. However, the log files remain locked by OHS until you restart it; unless you have the luxury to restart your HTTP server on a regular basis, you must use another method to divide your log files into more manageable chunks.

As with most Linux- and Unix-based applications, you can send the output of the application to a file, to a pipe, or to standard output. A *pipe* is a Unix/Linux OS construct that redirects output to another process instead of the default standard output location, which is usually your terminal screen. Using a pipe and the Unix/Linux `rotatelogs` command, you can easily manage your log files without restarting OHS. Here is the syntax of the `rotatelogs` command:

```
rotatelogs logfile [rotationtime [offset]] | [filesizeM]
```

The parameters for `rotatelogs` are as follows:

`logfile` The path and base filename for the log file. The `rotatelogs` command appends the time in seconds to the end of the filename to ensure uniqueness.

`rotationtime` The time between log file rotations, in seconds.

`offset` The number of minutes offset from UTC.

`filesizeM` As an alternative to specifying the period between rotations, you can specify the file size at which `rotatelogs` will rotate the logs.

In Figure 4.9, the default log file destination uses a Unix/Linux pipe with the `rotatelogs` command to configure the default log file destination. Alternatively, you can use the `CustomLog` directive to change or create a log file destination, as in this example:

```
CustomLog "|/u01/app/oracle/as10gHome/Apache/Apache/bin/rotatelogs
➥ /u01/app/oracle/as10gHome/Apache/Apache/logs/access_log 43200"
➥ common
```

OHS sends the output via a Unix/Linux pipe to the `rotatelogs` command; the `rotatelogs` command renames and rotates the file `access_log` every 43,200 seconds, or 5 days, regardless of its size. Here is a sample directory listing of the log files created with the `rotatelogs` command:

```
[oracle@asinfra logs]$ ls -lt
-rw-r--r--    1 oracle   oinstall     6498 Feb 25 18:16
➥ access_log.1140912000
-rw-r--r--    1 oracle   oinstall     9998 Feb 25 18:16
➥ access_log2.1140912000
-rw-r--r--    1 oracle   oinstall   284442 Feb 25 17:58
➥ access_log.1140868800
-rw-r--r--    1 oracle   oinstall   437442 Feb 25 17:58
➥ access_log2.1140868800
-rw-r--r--    1 oracle   oinstall   284442 Feb 25 05:57
➥ access_log.1140825600
-rw-r--r--    1 oracle   oinstall   437442 Feb 25 05:57
➥ access_log2.1140825600
-rw-r--r--    1 oracle   oinstall   282756 Feb 24 17:56
➥ access_log.1140782400
-rw-r--r--    1 oracle   oinstall   434856 Feb 24 17:56
➥ access_log2.1140782400
-rw-r--r--    1 oracle   oinstall   284802 Feb 24 05:58
➥ access_log.1140739200
```

On this server, the administrator created a second log file with the name `access_log2` and the nickname `combined` using the following server directive:

```
CustomLog "|/u01/app/oracle/as10gHome/Apache/Apache/bin/rotatelogs
➥ /u01/app/oracle/as10gHome/Apache/Apache/logs/access_log2 43200"
➥ combined
```

Leveraging Advanced Server Properties

Occasionally, you may need to make minor edits directly to one of OHS's many configuration files. AS Control makes this process relatively painless. To access the OHS configuration files, navigate to the OHS home page and click the Administration tab; then click the `Advanced Server Properties` link. You will see the web page shown in Figure 4.10.

FIGURE 4.10 Editing OHS configuration files using AS Control

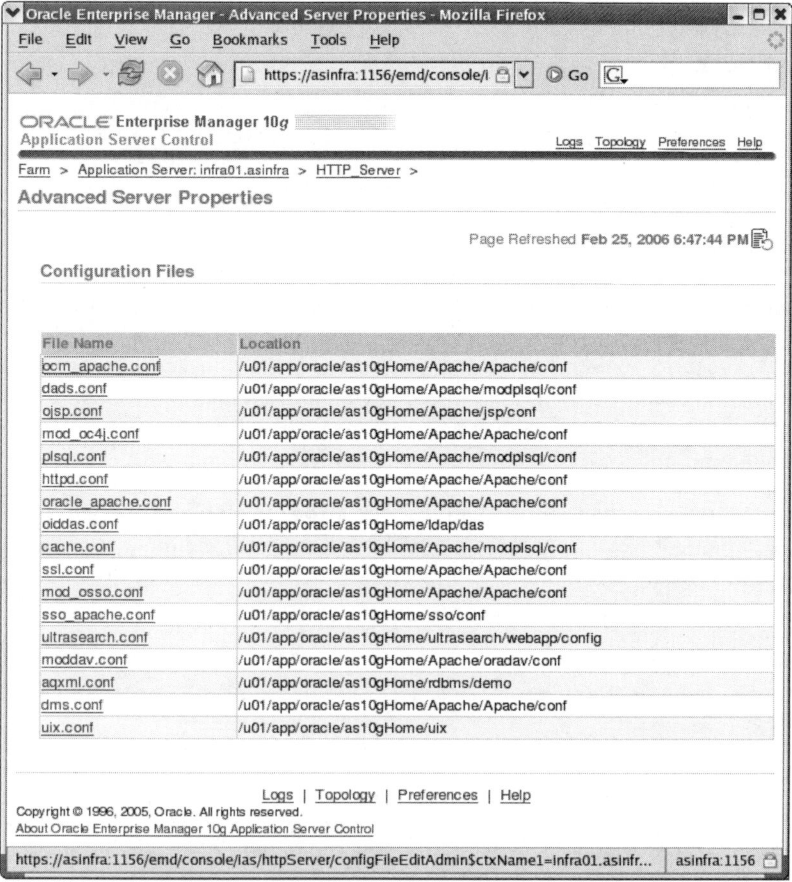

Click the link corresponding to the configuration file you need to edit and you see a text editor web page. After you save the changes, AS Control will restart the component that uses the configuration file, if necessary.

Understanding Apache HTTP Server 2.0

OHS is included as part of the OracleAS installation, but you can also install OHS as a stand-alone component. Two stand-alone versions are available: one based on Apache 1.3 and the other based on Apache 2.0. The stand-alone version based on Apache 1.3 is the same version available with every OracleAS installation. You may want to use either stand-alone version for the following reasons:

- You don't want to use Java on your web server for security reasons.
- You don't need clustering in your environment.
- You don't need AS Control.

OHS based on Apache 2.0 is a complete rewrite of Apache 1.3 and includes many features you may need in your environment:

- Support for Internet Protocol version 6 (IPv6)
- Enhanced modules
- Improved performance in a Windows environment

Future versions of OracleAS will include OHS based on Apache 2.0.

Real World Scenario

Maximizing Website Security While Minimizing Application Changes

As part of a new security initiative at your organization, you are tasked with enhancing the security of your web-based applications, which have lately been compromised by cross-site scripting and SQL insertion attacks. Since there are over a hundred web applications, you are hesitant to spend months making changes to each individual application.

One of your co-workers on the security team suggests you look into the open-source module `mod_security`, which integrates easily with OHS. If you use `mod_security` to prevent attacks at the entry point to your HTTP server, you will not have to change individual applications. `mod_security` includes the following security measures and features:

- Normalizes paths and parameters before sending to HTTP server, removing multiple slash characters, removing directory self-references, and decoding URL-encoded characters
- Performs administrator-supplied filtering and complex rules using regular expressions
- Intercepts contents transmitted in both `GET` and `POST` method commands
- Logs details for every request for later analysis, if desired
- Filters out characters that do not fall within a certain range, such as null bytes or non-printing characters
- Tailors configurations for specific applications

For a default installation of OHS, `mod_security` is included but not configured to load during OHS startup. (You can get the latest version and instructions for compiling it from `www.modsecurity.org/download`.) To load `mod_security` at startup, edit the file `$ORACLE_HOME/Apache/Apache/conf/httpd.conf` and add the following line after the last `LoadModule` directive:

```
LoadModule security_module libexec/mod_security.so
```

Before you restart the HTTP server, you need to add the filtering rules for `mod_security`. Using the `IfModule` block directive (we cover directives in more detail later in this chapter), add the following at the end of `httpd.conf`:

```
<IfModule mod_security.c>
   # Turn the filtering engine On or Off
   SecFilterEngine On

   # Change Server: string
   SecServerSignature " "

   # Make sure that URL encoding is valid
   SecFilterCheckURLEncoding On

   # This setting should be set to On only if the Web
   #    site is using the Unicode
   #    encoding. Otherwise it may interfere with the
   #    normal Web site operation.
   SecFilterCheckUnicodeEncoding Off

   # Only allow bytes from this range
   SecFilterForceByteRange 1 255

   # The audit engine works independently and
   #    can be turned On of Off on the per-server or
   #    on the per-directory basis. "On" will log
   #    everything,
   # "DynamicOrRelevant" will log dynamic requests or
   #    violations,
   # and "RelevantOnly" will only log policy
   #    violations.
   SecAuditEngine RelevantOnly

   # Specify the name of the audit log file
   SecAuditLog /var/log/httpd/audit_log

   # Should mod_security inspect POST payloads
   SecFilterScanPOST On

   # Action to take by default
   SecFilterDefaultAction "deny,log,status:512"

   # Require HTTP_USER_AGENT and HTTP_HOST in all
```

```
    #    requests
    #SecFilterSelective "HTTP_USER_AGENT|HTTP_HOST" "^$"

    # Prevent path traversal (..) attacks
    #SecFilter "../"

    # Weaker XSS protection but allows common HTML
    #    0tags
    #SecFilter "<[[:space:]]*script"

    # Prevent XSS atacks (HTML/Javascript injection)
    #SecFilter "<(.|n)+>"

    # Very crude filters to prevent SQL injection
    #    attacks
    SecFilter "delete[[:space:]]+from"
    SecFilter "insert[[:space:]]+into"
    SecFilter "select.+from"

    # Protecting from XSS attacks through the PHP
    #    session cookie
    #SecFilterSelective ARG_PHPSESSID "!^[0-9a-z]*$"
    #SecFilterSelective COOKIE_PHPSESSID "!^[0-9a-z]*$"
</IfModule>
```

Alternatively, you can put this code in its own file and use the Apache `Include` directive to keep `httpd.conf` shorter and easier to maintain and read. Several of the filters you are particularly interested in are the `SecFilter` directives to prevent SQL injection: preventing `DELETE`, `INSERT`, or `SELECT` statements as part of the URL string.

After you save the file, restart the HTTP server using either AS Control or the command line. In your web browser, navigate to a known page, such as this one, for example:

```
http://asinfra:7777/quickstart.htm
```

The page appears as it always does. However, when you attempt to put restricted character strings into the URL, even if the application behind that page does not parse it, you are denied access to the page. Try this URL:

```
http://asinfra:7777/quickstart.htm?user=RJB%27;delete%20from%20empl;
```

The browser will return `Internal Server Error` instead of website content.

Understanding Server Directives

In the following sections, we'll dig more deeply into the most commonly used and most important directives and show how directives interact with and control the server configuration depending on which file they reside in or which container directive they appear in.

Directives in the `httpd.conf` and `.htaccess` files apply at the server level and directory level, respectively. At the server level, OHS applies the configuration directives hierarchically; this allows for refinement of OHS behavior at lower levels in the hierarchy.

In addition, we'll show you how directives are logically classified to make them easier to understand and use. OHS classifies directives into three general categories: configuration directives, container directives, and block directives.

Configuration Directive Contexts

OHS applies configuration tiers differently in `httpd.conf` and `.htaccess`. The per-server context applies to `httpd.conf`, and the per-directory context applies to `.htaccess`.

The rules for inheritance within `httpd.conf` are as follows:

- Directives that are outside of any sections in the main server are inherited by other sections unless overridden.
- Directives within virtual host sections apply only to the virtual server and are distinguished by unique combinations of IP address and port pairs.
- Directives within a directory container apply only to that directory and its subdirectories. The directory paths within directory sections are either plain directory paths or regular expressions that evaluate to directory paths.
- File sections contain directives that apply only to files within the enclosing `<Directory>` directive and are either plain filenames or regular expressions that evaluate to filenames.
- URL sections defined by the `<Location>` directive apply to a URL and any locations within that URL and contain either plain relative URLs or regular expressions matching relative URLs.

In Figure 4.11, you see how OHS applies these directives hierarchically in the per-server context. The `<Directory>` directive within the `<VirtualHost>` directive applies only to the virtual host; the `<Files>` directive within the `<Directory>` directive applies only to the `<Directory>` directive and not to any other virtual host or the main server.

For `.htaccess`, when OHS accesses the directory, the rules are applied in the order in which they are defined within `.htaccess`. This context is divided into five subcontexts that are enabled with the `AllowOverride` directive in `httpd.conf`:

`AuthConfig` Controls authorization using module `mod_auth`

`Limit` Controls access restrictions using module `mod_access`

`Options` Controls directory features using module `http_core`

`FileInfo` Controls document attributes using module `mod_mime`

`Indexes` Controls directory indexing using module `mod_index`

FIGURE 4.11 A typical OracleAS environment

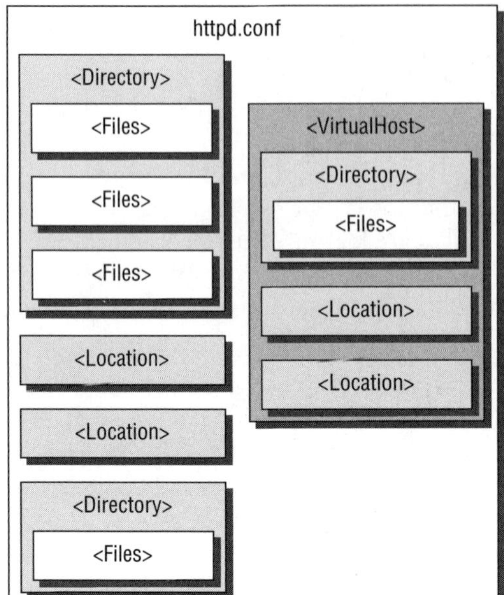

We will provide more detail on these rules, including how you can use `All` and `None` with the `AllowOverride` directive, later in this chapter.

Configuration Directives

In the following sections, we'll provide an in-depth review of the most important *configuration directives* and how to use them. Configuration directives reside within server configuration files and consist of a single line. They define OHS's features available within the context in which they are defined, applying to the entire server or restricted in scope if they are within a container directive.

Options

The `Options` directive is one of the key directives to control features that OHS exposes to the client, such as which file types are recognized within containers and whether OHS follows symbolic links in the file system. Here is a list of all parameters for the `Options` directive and their purpose:

`All` Enables all options except for the `MultiViews` directive and those that are mutually exclusive. This is the default.

`ExecCGI` Permits the execution of CGI scripts; execution is not permitted if the parameter is not set.

FollowSymLinks Permits OHS to follow symbolic links defined on the file system for both files and directories. OHS must have read access to the target file or directory.

SymLinksIfOwnerMatch Overrides `FollowSymLinks` if specified; only follows symbolic links if the permissions of the link match those of the target.

Includes Controls execution of server-side include (SSI) files.

IncludesNOEXEC Permits SSI files like `Includes` but disallows `#exec` and `#include` within CGI scripts.

Indexes If a client request includes a directory on the server that does not have an `index.html` file, provides a formatted list of the requested directory's contents.

Multiviews Supports content-negotiated multiple views. An example of this would be if a page is available in multiple languages and the browser request includes a language preference.

Each of these options can be preceded with a + or - to add or remove it at the level the directive is specified. To clear all inherited and incremental settings as OHS accumulates them further down a directory tree, specify the option without the prefix.

To show you how the `Options` parameters and inheritance works, consider this example with two content directories, one a subdirectory of the other:

```
<Directory /www/content>
   Options Indexes FollowSymLinks
</Directory>

<Directory /www/content/images>
   Options Includes
</Directory>
```

The `Indexes` and `FollowSymLinks` options are in effect for the directory `/www/content`, and only the `Includes` option is in effect for the `/www/content/images` directory because + and - were not used to make incremental changes to the directory above it in the file system. On the other hand, consider this example:

```
<Directory /www/content>
   Options Indexes FollowSymLinks
</Directory>

<Directory /www/content/images>
   Options +Includes -Indexes
</Directory>
```

Because + and - are used to incrementally change the options, the `/www/content/images` directory has the `FollowSymLinks` and `Includes` options.

AllowOverride

`AllowOverride` is the other key directive that controls which OHS features are available, primarily controlling which directives OHS allows in `.htaccess` files to override serverwide directives. The default value for `AllowOverride` is `All`, which means that the contents of every `.htaccess` file is processed.

Here is a list of all `AllowOverride` options:

`All` Enables all overrides. This setting may be a security risk if a client can add or edit a `.htaccess` file in any served directory.

`AuthConfig` Allows user authentication directives such as `AuthName` and `AuthType`.

`FileInfo` Controls file type directives such as `AddType` and `DefaultType`.

`Indexes` Permits directives to disable the override of directory indexing.

`Limit` Allows the use of directives to control host access.

`Options` Enables the use of the `Options` directive for a directory. In general, it is good policy to disable this option to ensure that SSIs and CGIs are not enabled in directories using `.htaccess` when they are disabled in `httpd.conf`.

`None` Tells OHS to ignore all `.htaccess` files.

The process of inheritance for the `AllowOverride` directive follows the same rules as for the `Options` directive, including the use of + and -.

Alias, AliasMatch, and *ScriptAlias*

The module `mod_alias` provides functionality to map directories on the host file system into the document tree in addition to URL redirection. You use the `Alias` and `ScriptAlias` directives to perform the mappings. `AliasMatch` enhances the functionality of `Alias` by enabling regular expressions.

Alias

Aliases allow documents to be stored in locations other than the directory specified by the `DocumentRoot` directive. In this example, the `Alias` directive enables OHS to remap any URL that contains `/register` to `/new_user/reg`:

```
Alias /register /new_user/reg
```

AliasMatch

`AliasMatch` performs the same function as `Alias` except that the first argument can be a Unix/Linux regular expression. This is useful when it is not practical to list all possible aliases explicitly with the `Alias` directive; for example, when you have a directory with thousands of image files. In this example, you have recently converted all of your images from GIF format to JPG format, and moved them from a directory called `photos` to a different directory called `new_photos`:

```
Alias /photos/(.*)\.gif$ /new_photos/$1.jpg
```

ScriptAlias

ScriptAlias functions the same as Alias except that documents in the target directory are treated as applications and executed rather than as documents that are returned to the client. This is useful when you want to enable CGI scripts without using the ExecCGI option and prohibit user-written CGI scripts.

DirectoryIndex

Earlier in this chapter, we introduced the Options Indexes directive to enable a directory listing when the requested directory (a URL with a trailing /) does not contain a file named index.html. The DirectoryIndex directive provides more control over what OHS displays when a client request specifies a directory in the document root. For example, you can use DirectoryIndex to change the default file displayed. In this example, when you enable directory indexing, the default file displayed is index.html. This directive example will look instead for index.htm in any requested directory if index.html does not exist in the requested directory:

```
DirectoryIndex index.html index.htm
```

You can specify multiple options in the DirectoryIndex directive to ensure that if none of these specified default files exists, OHS shows an informational or error message instead of showing the directory contents. Expanding on the previous example, you want to run a CGI script that displays an error message if OHS finds neither index.html nor index.htm:

```
DirectoryIndex index.html index.htm /cgi-bin/NotFound404.cgi
```

IndexIgnore

Even if you want your web clients to see most of the contents of your server directories, there may be files that are not important to the client or you may want to ensure that certain file types do not show up in a directory listing regardless of the directory. To solve this problem, you can use the IndexIgnore directive. The arguments to IndexIgnore are regular expressions. In this example, you want to prevent header files, readme files, backup files, and all files that begin with . and are at least three characters long from appearing in the directory listing:

```
IndexIgnore HEADER* README* *.bak .??*
```

OHS merges multiple IndexIgnore directives that are both in the same directory and inherited from parent directories. In addition, an IndexIgnore directive in the server configuration file httpd.conf cannot be overridden in a .htaccess file.

ErrorDocument

By default, whenever a client requests a file or directory that does not exist on the server or a server error occurs, OHS logs the failed request in the error_log file and returns a short HTML document to the client containing an error code and a description of the error, as you can see in Figure 4.12.

FIGURE 4.12 Default OHS error message page

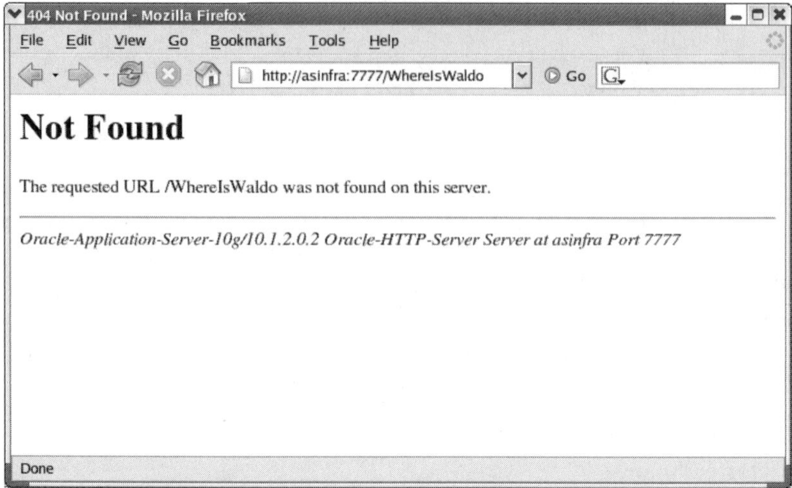

You can modify this behavior with the `ErrorDocument` directive, providing the client with a hard-coded message, another existing document, or a CGI to process the error. In this example, any errors direct the client to a common HTML error page with the 404 error code:

```
ErrorDocument 404 /error_docs/not_found.html
```

To be more succinct, you can provide an error code with a simple hard-coded text message, as in this example:

```
ErrorDocument 404 "We have no idea what the problem is --
➥ your file is missing. Sorry about that.
```

For Apache HTTP Server versions 1.3 and earlier, you must omit the trailing " from an `ErrorDocument` directive that specifies a hard-coded message. Apache HTTP Server 2.0 and later require a trailing ".

Figure 4.13 shows the results when you request a nonexistent document or a server error occurs; this message results from using the `ErrorDocument` directive with a hard-coded message.

You can maximize your flexibility on the error page that the user sees by running a CGI instead of showing a static page when an error occurs, as in this example:

```
ErrorDocument 502 /error_docs/custom_err_page.cgi
```

FIGURE 4.13 OHS error page using a hard-coded message

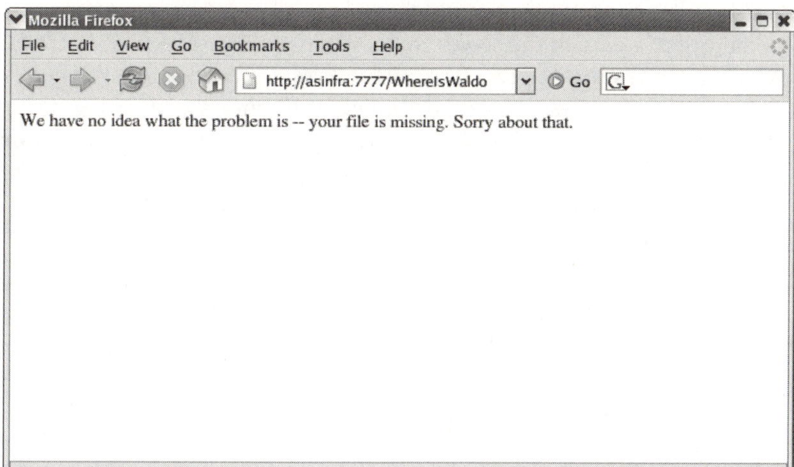

Expires Header

In a web document, the `Expires` header specifies a date beyond which the document is considered out-of-date. Within OHS, the module `mod_expires` controls the `Expires` header. You can use the `ExpiresActive`, `ExpiresDefault`, and `ExpiresByType` directives to provide more granularity and control over document expiration.

ExpiresActive

Using the `ExpiresActive` directive, you can switch on or switch off the `Expires` header within a document:

```
ExpiresActive off
```

ExpiresDefault

The `ExpiresDefault` directive defines a default expiry time for all served files. In this example, all retrieved documents expire 86,400 seconds (1 day) after they are accessed:

```
ExpiresDefault A86400
```

ExpiresByType

The `ExpiresByType` directive provides more control over expiry times, depending on the file type. In this example, GIF files expire 2,419,200 seconds (28 days) after they are created or modified, and JPG files expire 43,200 seconds (12 hours) after they are accessed:

```
ExpiresByType image/gif M2419200
ExpiresByType image/jpg A43200
```

Container Directives

Directives placed in the main configuration file apply to the entire server; if you want to restrict functionality for a part of the server, you use a *container directive*. A container directive is a block of directives enclosed by `<DirectiveName Object>` and `</DirectiveName>` that restrict the scope of a directive based on a number of criteria such as location, filename, and virtual host. Every directive within the container's begin and end tags apply only to the referenced object.

Directory and *DirectoryMatch*

The `Directory` directive matches a physical location within the specified directory and its subdirectories. The `DirectoryMatch` directive works the same as `Directory` except that it allows regular expressions in the directory location argument.

All configuration directives within the `Directory` container apply only to the directory specified in the container header. For example, the following `Directory` directive applies only to the `public_docs` subdirectory within any directory under `/www` relative to the server's `DocumentRoot`:

```
<Directory /www/*/public_docs>
   Options none
   AllowOverride none
</Directory>
```

For any of the directories within the scope of this directive, no options such as allowing CGI file execution or following symbolic links are enabled; in addition, OHS prevents any override of this option by a `.htaccess` file in any of the directories.

Files and *FilesMatch*

The `Files` directive matches specific file types. `FilesMatch` allows for regular expressions in the file specification. These directives operate in a manner very similar to `Directory` and `DirectoryMatch` except that they operate on specific files regardless of the directory they reside in.

You can frequently achieve identical results using `Files` and `FilesMatch`; `Files` uses standard Unix/Linux shell wildcards ? and * and can use regular expressions if you use the prefix ~. For example, you can use this `Files` directive:

```
<Files ~ "\.(gif|jpe?g|tif|png)$ ">
   . . .
</Files>
```

It matches any file with the extensions `.gif`, `.jpg`, `.jpeg`, `.tif`, and `.png`. The `FilesMatch` directive can achieve the same results, as follows:

```
<FilesMatch "\.(gif|jpe?g|tif|png)$ ">
   . . .
</FilesMatch>
```

The Apache documentation recommends using Files with the standard wildcard characters and FilesMatch if you need to specify a regular expression.

Limit and *LimitExcept*

The Limit and LimitExcept directives restrict authentication or restrict access to specific HTTP methods. These directives are rarely used because all of the functionality they provide is available in the module mod_security.

Location and *LocationMatch*

The Location directive matches a *virtual path*; a virtual path is a reference to content within a URL that may not necessarily reside within the server's file system. The LocationMatch directive allows regular expressions in the virtual path.

Here is an example of a LocationMatch container that defines configuration directives for any requests whose URL contains /warehouse/data or /call_center/data:

```
<LocationMatch "/(warehouse|call_center)/data">
   . . .
</LocationMatch>
```

In this example, you use the SetHandler configuration directive within a Location container to enable server status requests only from browsers at oracle.com:

```
<Location /status>
   SetHandler server-status
   Order Deny,Allow
   Deny from all
   Allow from .oracle.com
</Location>
```

Use the Location directive for content outside of the file system; otherwise, use Directory and Files for directory locations and file system files, respectively.

VirtualHost

Earlier in this chapter, we introduced the concept of a virtual host: an additional host or website defined alongside the main server. You define virtual hosts using the container directive <VirtualHost Name|IP [Name | IP]. . .>.

Typically, most options on a virtual host will be the same as on the primary server; as with any container directive, you can override the main server's directives within the VirtualHost directive. The following configuration directives are typically defined within a VirtualHost directive:

- ServerAdmin
- ServerName
- DocumentRoot
- ErrorLog

- CustomLog
- Directory
- Location

OHS supports virtual hosts defined with either IP addresses or names. You can have one or more IP-based virtual hosts and one or more name-based virtual hosts defined within the main server.

Configuring IP-Based Virtual Hosts

As the name implies, you create IP-based virtual hosts by specifying one or more IP:port combinations within the container header. One situation where this is useful is to create a virtual host that responds to the same name on both a public and a private interface, as in this example:

```
<VirtualHost 192.168.66.10 205.143.21.191>
   ServerName www.rjbdba.com
   ServerAdmin oracle@rjbdba.com
   DocumentRoot /www/oradocs/consulting
   ErrorLog /www/logs/error_log
</VirtualHost>
```

Alternatively, you can have several virtual hosts, each defined with a single IP address and unique server name, document root, and error log.

OHS inherits any configuration directives not specified in the `<VirtualHost>` directive from the main server.

Configuring Name-Based Virtual Hosts

In contrast to IP-based virtual hosts, name-based virtual hosts use the `NameVirtualHost` directive to specify the IP address that OHS uses as a target for name-based virtual hosts. In the following scenario, two different websites resolve to the same IP address, 205.143.21.198:

```
NameVirtualHost 205.143.21.198

<VirtualHost 205.143.21.198>
   ServerName www.BobsWidgets.com
   DocumentRoot /www/pricing/retail
</VirtualHost>

<VirtualHost 205.143.21.198>
   ServerName www.BobsWidgets-B2B.com
   DocumentRoot /www/pricing/wholesale
</VirtualHost>
```

Whether a web client uses `www.BobsWidgets.com` or `www.BobsWidgets-B2B.com`, both addresses will resolve to the same IP address and the same OHS server will process the client requests; however, they resolve to different document roots and therefore serve different content.

Using AS Control to Define Virtual Hosts

You can use AS Control to create virtual hosts. From the HTTP Server home page, click the Virtual Hosts tab. As you see in Figure 4.14, you can edit existing virtual hosts and create new ones by clicking the Create button.

FIGURE 4.14 Using AS Control to create a virtual host

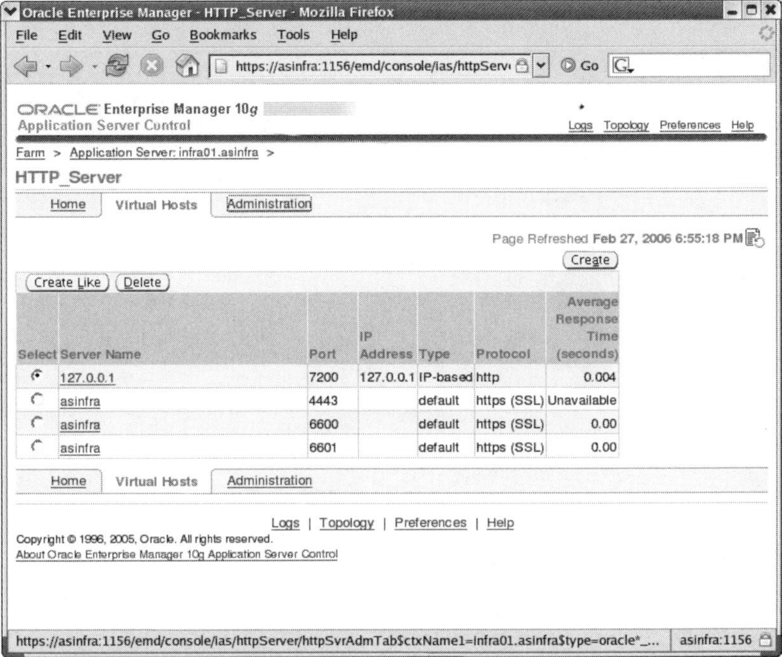

Block Directives

A *block directive* is similar to a container directive in that it is enclosed by `<DirectiveName>` and `</DirectiveName>`, but it does not restrict the scope of the enclosed directives. Instead, OHS parses block directives and adds them to its configuration at startup if the condition specified in the directive is true.

There are two block directives, `<IfModule>` and `<IfDefine>`.

IfModule

The `<IfModule>` directive applies one or more configuration directives within the block if the specified module is enabled on the server. In this example, OHS implements several cache-related configuration directives if the module `mod_mem_cache.c` is compiled into the server:

```
<IfModule mod_mem_cache.c>
   CacheEnable mem /
   MCacheSize 4096
   MCacheMaxObjectCount 100
   MCacheMinObjectSize 1
   MCacheMaxObjectSize 2048
</IfModule>
```

IfDefine

The <IfDefine> directive works similarly to <IfModule>; OHS conditionally executes the enclosed configuration directives depending on a condition. However, the condition is based on parameters you specify on the command line when you start OHS. In this example, you start OHS with the ReverseProxy parameter enabled:

```
[oracle@asinfra]$ httpd -DReverseProxy
```

As a result, if you have the following <IfDefine> block directive defined in httpd.conf, OHS will execute the enclosed LoadModule directives:

```
<IfDefine ReverseProxy>
   LoadModule rewrite_module modules/mod_rewrite.so
   LoadModule proxy_module modules/libproxy.so
</IfDefine>
```

Summary

In this chapter, we presented an overview of Oracle HTTP Server, or OHS, starting with the general architecture of OHS and how the base server, based on the open-source Apache HTTP Server version 1.3, is enhanced by modules. These modules are either generic or enhanced to work more seamlessly with other Oracle products.

You configure OHS using three types of directives: configuration directives, container directives, and block directives. Configuration directives specify OHS's behavior for the main server or a virtual server; container directives contain configuration directives that apply to specific files, directories, or URLs. Block directives contain configuration directives that are enabled depending on parameters enabled when OHS starts.

As with virtually all components of OracleAS, AS Control provides a convenient GUI to manage and monitor all aspects of OHS, such as starting or stopping OHS, creating virtual hosts, centralizing your configuration file maintenance, and viewing or adding log files.

In the second half of this chapter, we delved more deeply into the specifics of each directive type, providing a number of examples and scenarios using the most common directives you will encounter on a daily basis for your main server and any virtual servers. Virtual servers are not only a good way to support multiple websites to take best advantage of your server's resources, they also give you another way to provide failover and redundancy in your environment when you have more than one physical server available.

Exam Essentials

Understand the OHS architecture and its components. Be able to identify the core components of OHS and differentiate them from the generic modules and the Oracle-specific or Oracle-enhanced modules. Enumerate the different parts of the OHS directory structure and where OHS stores configuration files and executables.

Identify the key tools used to manage OHS using either the command line or AS Control. Be able to start, stop, or restart OHS using AS Control and when the server must be restarted when you make configuration changes. Be able to use the `opmnctl` command to perform common server startup, shutdown, and status inquiries.

Use directives to configure and control your main server and any virtual servers. Understand the difference between configuration directives, container directives, and block directives. Know how they interact and how OHS applies the directives within container and block directives depending on the conditions defined in the container or block directive.

Be able to locate, edit, and understand OHS configuration files. Understand the difference between `httpd.conf` and `.htaccess` configuration files. Show how `.htaccess` overrides directives defined at the server level and how you can prevent possible security problems by disabling the use of `.htaccess`. Enumerate the directives that are never allowed in `.htaccess`.

Understand how OHS logging works and how to customize the logging environment. Be able to customize the format of any log file and assign a nickname to the log format. Use access logs to analyze web traffic patterns. Use the Linux `rotatelogs` command to split up your log files based on elapsed time or size, making the log files easier to manage and archive.

Review Questions

1. Identify the primary difference between a Microsoft Windows and a Linux/Unix implementation of OHS. (Choose all that apply.)

   A. On the Windows platform, the child process runs with the same privileges as the control process.

   B. On a Linux/Unix platform, the child process runs with the same privileges as the control process.

   C. On the Windows platform, OHS creates one control process and one child process.

   D. On a Linux/Unix platform, the control process creates at least one child process.

   E. There is no difference other than the difference in file systems between NTFS and EXT3.

   F. On a Linux/Unix platform, OHS creates one control process and several child processes.

2. Given these typical configuration files in an OHS environment, which of the following statements are true about the relationship among these files? (Choose all that apply.)

   `httpd.conf`

   `aqxml.conf`

   `moddav.conf`

   `plsql.conf`

   `ojsp.conf`

   `xml.conf`

   `mime.types`

   `mod_oc4j.conf`

   `oracle_apache.conf`

   A. They are all located in `$ORACLE_HOME/Apache/Apache/conf`.

   B. They are all located in `$ORACLE_HOME/Apache/conf`.

   C. `httpd.conf` uses the `Include` directive for all of the other files.

   D. `httpd.conf` uses the `Include` directive for `mod_oc4j.conf`, `mime.types`, and `oracle_apache.conf`.

   E. `oracle_apache.conf` uses the `Include` directive for `mod_oc4j.conf`, `aqxml.conf`, and `moddav.conf`.

3. Identify the configuration directive you use to change the document root from `htdocs` to `webdocs1`.

   A. `WebRoot "/u01/app/oracle/as10gHome/Apache/Apache/webdocs1"`

   B. `ServerRoot "/u01/app/oracle/as10gHome/Apache/Apache/webdocs1"`

   C. `DocumentRoot "$ORACLE_HOME/Apache/Apache/webdocs1"`

   D. `DocumentRoot "/u01/app/oracle/as10gHome/Apache/Apache/webdocs1"`

   E. `DocumentRootNew "/u01/app/oracle/as10gHome/Apache/Apache/webdocs1"`

4. You have several directories on different file systems that have web content for your web clients. What is the best way to serve this content?

   A. Create a `DocumentRoot` directive for the content directory in each file system.

   B. Create symbolic links to each file system in the `htdocs` directory.

   C. Create a new virtual server to serve the content in each file system with a different definition for `DocumentRoot` in each virtual server.

   D. Create a comma-separated list of all target content directories in the `DocumentRoot` directive.

5. If you use symbolic links in the directory `htdocs`, what configuration directive(s) must you use to ensure that OHS follows the symbolic links successfully?

   A. `Options FollowSymLinks`

   B. `FollowSymLinks All`

   C. `Options FollowSymbolicLinks`

   D. `Options Multiviews`

   E. `Options FollowSymLinksAll`

6. In the content directory `/web_emp/hr` you have a `.htdocs` file with the following directive:

   ```
   Options ExecCGI FollowSymLinks
   ```

   If you want to avoid using the `.htdocs` file in content subdirectories, what directive would you use in `httpd.conf` instead?

   A. You cannot place an equivalent directive in `httpd.conf`; it must reside in `.htdocs`.

   B. `Options /web_emp/hr ExecCGI FollowSymLinks`

   C.
   ```
   <DirectoryMatch /web_emp/hr>
       Options FollowSymLinks
       Options ExecCGI
   </DirectoryMatch>
   ```

   D.
   ```
   <Directory /web_emp/hr>
       Options ExecCGI FollowSymLinks
   </Directory>
   ```

7. Which of the following is not one of the tabs on the HTTP Server home page?

   A. Virtual Hosts

   B. Home

   C. Ports

   D. Administration

8. Using the `opmnctl` command, which of the following commands will restart OHS?
   A. `opmnctl restartproc process-type=http_server`
   B. `opmnctl restart process-type=http_server`
   C. `opmnctl restartproc ias-component=http_server`
   D. `opmnctl restartproc process-type=OHS`
   E. `opmnctl restartproc process-type=HTTP_Server`
   F. `opmnctl restart ias-component=OHS`

9. Identify the configuration file in an OHS installation that contains `Include` directives for Oracle-specific configuration files such as `plsql.conf`.
   A. `apache_oracle.conf`
   B. `apache_mods.conf`
   C. `oracle_only.conf`
   D. `oracle_apache.conf`
   E. `ora_apache.conf`

10. Which of the following directives in the main section of `httpd.conf` will maintain a minimum number of child processes running, even with no active client requests?
    A. `KeepAlive`
    B. `MinChildProcesses`
    C. `MinSpareServers`
    D. `MinRequestsPerChild`

11. Which of the following directives in the main section of `httpd.conf` will enable a persistent connection with a client to reduce latency for multiple requests within the same session?
    A. `KeepAlive`
    B. `MinChildProcesses`
    C. `MinSpareServers`
    D. `MinRequestsPerChild`

12. Which of the following directives is not permitted in a Windows environment?
    A. `KeepAlive`
    B. `MaxKeepAliveRequests`
    C. `MaxClients`
    D. `KeepAliveTimeout`
    E. `ThreadsPerChild`

13. How many `Listen` and `Port` directives can be in `httpd.conf`?
    A. More than one `Listen` directive and only one `Port` directive.
    B. Only one `Listen` directive and more than one `Port` directive.
    C. More than one `Listen` directive and more than one `Port` directive.
    D. Only one `Listen` directive and only one `Port` directive.
    E. You can define `Listen` and `Port` directives only in virtual host containers.

14. Which of the following statements is true about the `AllowOverride` configuration directive? (Choose all that apply.)
    A. The default value for `AllowOverride` is `None`.
    B. `AllowOverride` follows the same rules as the `Options` directive, allowing + and - to fine-tune the enabled overrides at lower directory levels.
    C. `AllowOverride Options` enables use of the `Options` directive in `.htaccess`.
    D. `AllowOverride FileInfo` enables directory listings in the absence of `index.html`.
    E. `AllowOverride Limit` permits restrictions on resolving the target of a symbolic link.

15. You have the following configuration directive in `httpd.conf`:

```
Alias /videos/(.*)\.wmv$ /apple_videos/$1.mov
```

    What is the effect of this directive?
    A. On access, each of the files in the `/videos` directory is converted to a new format in `/apple_videos`.
    B. OHS will redirect a request for `/videos/StarWars.rma` to `/apple_videos/StarWars.mov`.
    C. OHS will redirect a request for `/apple_videos/iPod.mov` to `/videos/iPod.wmv`.
    D. OHS will redirect a request for `/videos/Napoleon.wmv` to `/apple_videos/Napoleon.mov`.

16. What is the difference between the `Files` and the `FilesMatch` directives?
    A. Both `Files` and `FilesMatch` use regular expressions, but `Files` requires a ~ character in front of the search string to indicate that the following string is a regular expression.
    B. Both `Files` and `FilesMatch` use regular expressions, but `FilesMatch` requires a ~ character in front of the search string to indicate that the following string is a regular expression.
    C. You use `FilesMatch` in `.htaccess`, and you use `Files` in `httpd.conf`.
    D. `Files` only uses the standard Linux/Unix wildcard characters ? and *.

17. Virtual hosts can define all of these directives except for which of the following?
    A. `ServerName`
    B. `ServerAdmin`
    C. `CustomLog`
    D. `ErrorLog`
    E. `MaxClients`
    F. `DocumentRoot`

18. Which configuration directive specifies an IP address that can be used by more than one virtual host?

   A. `VirtualHost`

   B. `Port`

   C. `IPVirtualHost`

   D. `NameVirtualHost`

19. You want to conditionally load the module `mod_security` at OHS startup. Which two things must you do to facilitate this? (Choose two answers.)

   A. Use the `IfDefine` block directive.

   B. Use the `IfModule` block directive.

   C. Use `httpd -D` on the Linux command line.

   D. Use AS Control to start OHS.

20. You have the following three `<Directory>` container directives in `httpd.conf`:

```
<Directory /hr/emp>
   Options Multiviews Indexes
</Directory>

<Directory /hr/emp/salaried>
   Options +ExecCGI +FollowSymLinks -Indexes
</Directory>

<Directory /hr/emp/salaried/benefits>
   Options +Includes -Multiviews +SymLinksIfOwnerMatch
</Directory>
```

   In the directory `/hr/emp/salaried/benefits`, which options are in effect?

   A. `Includes SymLinksIfOwnerMatch`

   B. `Indexes Multiviews ExecCGI FollowSymLinks`

   C. `Multiviews ExecCGI FollowSymLinks`

   D. `SymLinksIfOwnerMatch ExecCGI Includes`

   E. `FollowSymLinks SymLinksIfOwnerMatch ExecCGI Includes`

Answers to Review Questions

1. C, F. On both platforms, OHS creates a control process. On Linux/Unix, OHS creates several child processes to listen for requests; the child processes have fewer privileges than the parent process. On Windows, the single child process has fewer privileges and creates multiple threads to listen for requests.

2. A, D. All of these configuration files are located in `$ORACLE_HOME/Apache/Apache/conf`. The primary server configuration file `httpd.conf` uses the `Include` directive to reference `mod_oc4j.conf`, `mime.types`, and `oracle_apache.conf`; in turn, `oracle_apache.conf` uses the `Include` directive to reference `aqxml.conf`, `moddav.conf`, `plsql.conf`, `ojsp.conf`, and `xml.conf`.

3. D. The `DocumentRoot` directive specifies the top-level directory from which OHS serves all web content.

4. B. The easiest way to maintain several content directories on different file systems is to place symbolic links to each file system in the directory specified by the `DocumentRoot` directive, ensuring that the OHS child process has privileges to read the content referenced by the symbolic links.

5. A. `Options FollowSymLinks` will follow symbolic links in `htdocs` as long as OHS has read permission on the target directories and files. Specifying `Options All` will also include the `FollowSymLinks` parameter, among others.

6. D. You can relocate all directives you place in `.htdocs` to the file `httpd.conf` using the `Directory` container directive. Using `.htdocs` is recommended only if the content owner for the directory does not have privileges to modify `httpd.conf`.

7. C. The Ports tab exists on the application server home page but does not appear on the HTTP Server home page.

8. E. You use the `restartproc` option to restart a component, and the `process-type` option must be `HTTP_Server`; the `process-type` parameter value is case sensitive.

9. D. The configuration file `oracle_apache.conf` further subdivides the configuration by module into `aqxml.conf`, `moddav.conf`, `plsql.conf`, `ojsp.conf`, and `xml.conf`.

10. C. The `MinSpareServers` directive maintains a minimum number of child processes, even with no active client requests. The default value is 5.

11. A. `KeepAlive` is `On` or `Off`. If it is `On`, OHS maintains the connection between the client and the server for the length of time specified in the `KeepAliveTimeout` directive.

12. C. The directive `MaxClients` is valid only in a Linux/Unix environment; `ThreadsPerChild` is valid only in a Windows environment.

13. A. OHS allows more than one `Listen` directive in `httpd.conf`. If the `Listen` directive contains a port specification, the `Port` directive is ignored. If only the `Port` directive exists, OHS listens on all interfaces with the specified port number.

14. B, C. The `AllowOverride` directive controls which feature within the server context (`httpd.conf`) can be overridden in the directory context (`.htaccess`).

15. D. OHS will redirect any requests for files with an extension of `.wmv` in the `/videos` directory to files with the `.mov` extension in the `/apple_videos` directory.

16. A. The Apache documentation recommends using `Files` with the standard wildcard characters and `FilesMatch` if you need to use regular expressions.

17. E. `MaxClients` is valid only in the server context and is not allowed in a virtual host.

18. D. `NameVirtualHost` specifies the IP address that OHS uses as a target for name-based virtual hosts.

19. A, C. You use the `IfDefine` block directive to check the value of `-D` specified with `httpd` on the command line.

20. D. You can clear all inherited and incremental settings at a specific directory level by specifying the option without a + or - prefix for any of the options.

Chapter 5

Managing and Configuring OracleAS Web Cache

ORACLE APPLICATION SERVER 10*g* ADMINISTRATION I EXAM OBJECTIVES COVERED IN THIS CHAPTER:

✓ **Managing and Configuring OracleAS Web Cache**

- Start, stop, and restart OracleAS Web Cache
- Change passwords for administrative users and listener ports
- Specify site-to-server mappings
- Create and configure caching rules
- Set up basic invalidation mechanism
- Set up expiration rules
- Configure access and event logs
- Obtain basic performance statistics

Oracle Application Server Web Cache is a key component of Oracle Application Server 10*g* (OracleAS); it can also be a key component for other vendors' application server products. OracleAS Web Cache provides many features not available in most other commercial caching products, such as intelligent caching, page assembly, dynamic web content caching, and compression. In addition, OracleAS Web Cache provides load balancing, failover, surge protection, and clustering capabilities. We'll cover all of these capabilities in this chapter.

In the first part of this chapter, we'll present the architecture of OracleAS Web Cache by showing the flow of requests from the client through the various OracleAS components and back to the client. Along the way, we'll describe the transformation and validation steps for each part of the request. At the same time, we'll describe each component in the OracleAS Web Cache architecture along with its benefits and features.

Every component of OracleAS collects usage and performance statistics, and OracleAS Web Cache is no exception. AS Control tells you everything you need to know to efficiently monitor status, view the most popular cache requests, and tune the cache.

Next, we'll step through the most important configuration options, including port assignments, site definitions, and origin server settings. You can easily configure each of these options using AS Control, except for a few rare cases where you must use command-line tools such as `opmnctl` and custom Oracle-provided shell scripts.

In the middle of the chapter, we'll cover the nuts and bolts of why you use OracleAS Web Cache in the first place: to cache content. Creating and editing caching rules is fast and efficient using AS Control. We'll show you how to compress your cache content and speed delivery of the content even more. In addition, you can cache dynamic content and partial web pages if your site has more than just static content. Conversely, you want to make sure that you expire stale content when the source of the content changes frequently, so we'll show you how to define and edit expiration rules.

In the last part of the chapter, we'll wrap up our discussion with logging: how to configure and analyze both the access log and the event log as well as manage log rollover to keep the size of each log file small and ease the review and archival of the log files.

Understanding OracleAS Web Cache Architecture

OracleAS Web Cache receives both Hypertext Transfer Protocol (HTTP) and Hypertext Transfer Protocol over SSL (HTTPS) requests from clients and delivers the content if it is already cached; if not, it passes those requests on to application servers, receives the content, and passes it back to the client and caches it for future requests from other clients. In Figure 4.1, in Chapter 4, you saw an example of an infrastructure with one server dedicated to web cache duties; because of OracleAS Web Cache's high scalability, you can add any number of additional servers at this tier to improve response time and availability. Here is a list of features we will cover throughout this chapter:

- Static content caching, including HTML files and image files
- Dynamically created read-only content
- HTTP-based invalidation header support in addition to declarative expiration
- Content-aware caching based on HTTP headers and cookies
- Automatic tuning during traffic spikes (surge protection)
- Load balancing, clustering, and failover support
- Compression of large files
- Ability to run on the same or a different server from web servers
- Partial page caching using the Edge Side Includes (ESI) feature

OracleAS Web Cache Request Processing

The URL the client specifies in its HTTP request translates to the IP address (translated using a domain name server) of the server running OracleAS Web Cache. The client does not know the address of the application server that provides the content to the OracleAS Web Cache server. This is beneficial in a secure environment where the application server is behind a firewall; the only requests allowed from outside of the firewall must originate from the OracleAS Web Cache server.

By default, a browser assumes a port number of 80; since the default port for OracleAS Web Cache is 7777, Oracle strongly recommends that you change this port number to 80.

If the requested content is in the cache and is not expired, OracleAS Web Cache sends the content back to the client and does not need to access the application server. If the requested content is not in the cache or is expired, OracleAS Web Cache sends a request to the application server.

The application server, in turn, assembles the requested content and sends it back to OracleAS Web Cache. Finally, the content is sent to the client and retained by OracleAS Web Cache for future requests.

OracleAS Web Cache does not precache any documents or content. All caching occurs when the client requests a document; the document is available in the cache for future requests from the same or other clients. As a result, the first time a client requests a new page or document, the response time may be slightly longer than subsequent requests for the same document.

Ensuring Cache Freshness

Caching web pages and other content provides the client with improved response time, but the speed of page retrieval is irrelevant if the page is out-of-date! Administrators and developers can invalidate content within the OracleAS Web Cache server either by sending an invalidation message or by assigning an expiration time to the document ahead of time.

OracleAS Web Cache also supports HTTP 1.1 validation models by comparing values in the HTTP request header with the values in the cached object's response header; if they do not match, the cached object is stale and a refresh is required. A full discussion of HTTP/1.1 validation is beyond the scope of this book. See `www.w3.org/Protocols/rfc2616/rfc2616.html` for more information.

Dynamic Content Caching

For dynamically generated content, the browser request contains information that OracleAS Web Cache passes to the origin server; in turn, the origin server provides customized (dynamic) content based on the identifying information in the client request. OracleAS Web Cache caches this content just as it caches static content.

The client-specific information can be stored in a client-side cookie and passed with the HTTP request; alternatively, OracleAS Web Cache recognizes embedded URLs when cookies are not used or are disallowed on the client.

Using Edge Side Includes and Partial Page Caching

Edge Side Includes, or ESI, is a markup language similar to Extensible Markup Language (XML) that enables dynamic content assembly of individual content fragments. ESI is an open standard language; you can find out more about ESI at `www.esi.org`.

The flexibility of OracleAS Web Cache permits you to assign caching rules to the template page itself, individual Hypertext Markup Language (HTML) fragments, or both. Performance is enhanced by enabling page assembly in OracleAS Web Cache instead of at the application server level. You can enable a different caching rule for each fragment on a page to further enhance performance.

You can also leverage ESI within Oracle Containers for J2EE (OC4J) by using ESI for Java (JESI). JESI is also an open standard.

Cache Clustering

When you have OracleAS Web Cache running on more than one server as a front end to one or more servers in an application server cluster, you have an OracleAS Web Cache cluster. In addition to providing better response time for your clients, a clustered OracleAS Web Cache environment provides transparent failover detection and cache failover. As a result, your website is also more available if you have more than one OracleAS Web Cache server caching content from your application server.

Administering OracleAS Web Cache

Web Cache administration duties, as a subset of your Oracle AS administrative duties, fall into the following categories:

Starting and stopping OracleAS Web Cache You can use AS Control or command-line tools to perform these tasks, as is the case with most components of OracleAS. In a few rare cases, the functionality of a command-line tool is not available in the web interface.

Adjusting administrative security settings OracleAS Web Cache Security supports separate passwords for administration and invalidation. In addition, you can restrict access for these functions by IP address or subnet.

Monitoring cache statistics and performance The statistics collected by OracleAS Web Cache will help you determine where you are having performance bottlenecks or potential problems in your environment. Even without these statistics, however, OracleAS Web Cache has many features to automatically tune performance, such as surge protection when an unexpected traffic spike occurs.

General configuration tasks You generally perform these tasks once or infrequently shortly after installation. They include configuring ports, specifying origin server settings, and configuring site definitions.

Adjusting cache settings These settings include caching rules to determine which objects are cached.

Expiring content in the cache You can expire content automatically or on demand; in addition, an expired document can recache automatically or the next time a client requests it.

Evaluating event logs The administrator controls how much of the event log is buffered in memory, where OracleAS Web Cache stores the event log, and how often to roll over the event log.

Evaluating access logs All accesses to the website cached by OracleAS Web Cache are recorded in the access log, and these logs are maintained in much the same way as the event logs.

Throughout the rest of this chapter we'll cover these topics in great detail.

Starting and Stopping OracleAS Web Cache

In previous versions of OracleAS, you needed a separate tool, OracleAS Web Cache Manager, to administer OracleAS Web Cache. Starting with Oracle Application Server 10*g* Release 2, you can use AS Control to administer OracleAS Web Cache. Even if you use OracleAS Web Cache in a stand-alone environment, you still have the option to install AS Control to monitor and configure OracleAS Web Cache.

In addition to the AS Control web interface, you have the option of using `opmnctl` on the command line to perform many of your administrative tasks.

Using AS Control

You can start, stop, or restart OracleAS Web Cache in two different places within AS Control: from the instance home page or from the OracleAS Web Cache home page. In Figure 5.1, you see the home page for the instance `mw01.asmw`. To stop, start, or restart OracleAS Web Cache, select the check box next to Web Cache and click the Start, Stop, or Restart button, depending on the current state of OracleAS Web Cache.

If you click the `Web Cache` link in Figure 5.1, you see the OracleAS Web Cache home page in Figure 5.2. In addition to stopping and starting OracleAS Web Cache from this page, you can see how much of the CPU OracleAS Web Cache uses, the status of the cached servers, the cache memory usage, and how many documents are currently in the cache. If the percentage of CPU used by OracleAS Web Cache exceeds 80 percent, you may need to upgrade your server or you may need to move or disable other processes that are using this server.

FIGURE 5.1 An OracleAS installation including OracleAS Web Cache

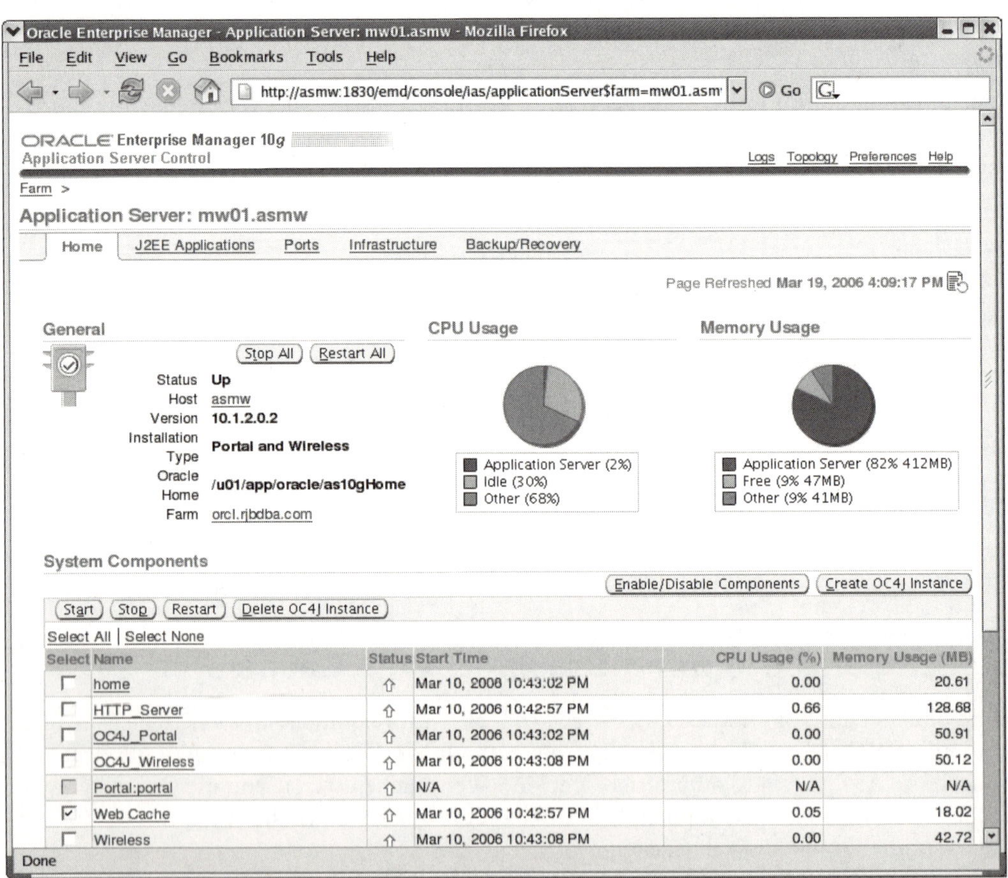

FIGURE 5.2 OracleAS Web Cache home page

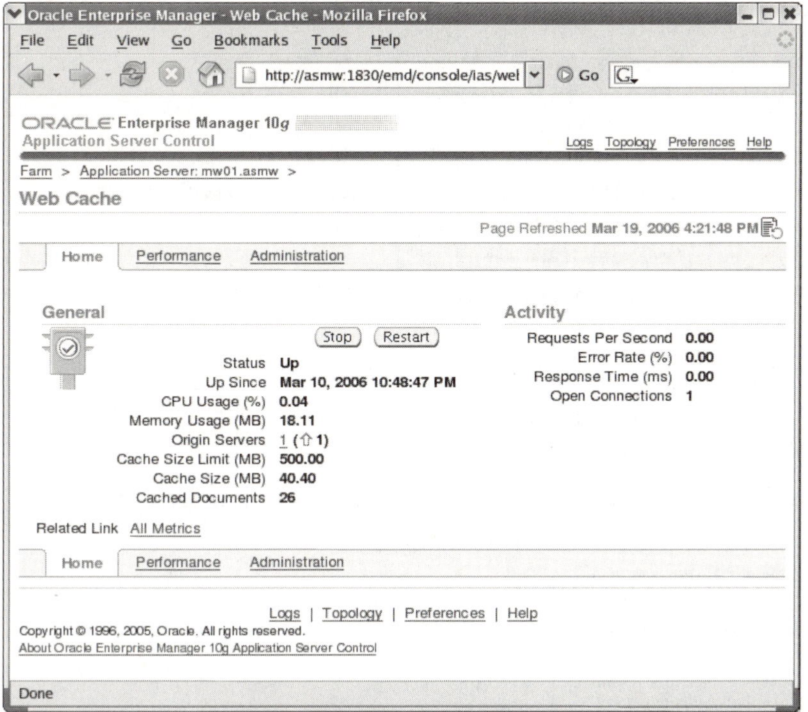

Later in this chapter, you'll discover the functionality behind the other two tabs on this page, Performance and Administration.

Using *opmnctl*

Even though you can use AS Control to perform nearly every routine administrative task in your environment, the `opmnctl` command comes in handy now and then. For example, you may not have access to a web interface when you need to perform a restart of OracleAS Web Cache. In addition, you can use the `opmnctl` command in a `cron` job to perform start, stop, or restart operations during routine system maintenance.

To start, stop, or restart the OracleAS Web Cache process, you first need to know the name of the process; you can get the list by using the `opmnctl status` command. Here are the results of that command on the instance `mw01.asmw` while pointing to the middleware `ORACLE_HOME`:

```
[oracle@asmw oracle]$ opmnctl status

Processes in Instance: mw01.asmw
-------------------+--------------------+---------+---------
ias-component      | process-type       |     pid | status
-------------------+--------------------+---------+---------
```

```
DSA                | DSA                |       N/A | Down
LogLoader          | logloaderd         |       N/A | Down
dcm-daemon         | dcm-daemon         |     19718 | Alive
OC4J               | home               |     18762 | Alive
OC4J               | OC4J_Portal        |     18763 | Alive
WebCache           | WebCache           |     18735 | Alive
WebCache           | WebCacheAdmin      |     18718 | Alive
HTTP_Server        | HTTP_Server        |     18725 | Alive
wireless           | performance_server |     18824 | Alive
wireless           | messaging_server   |     18825 | Alive
wireless           | OC4J_Wireless      |     18826 | Alive

[oracle@asmw oracle]$
```

To stop the OracleAS Web Cache component, use the `opmnctl stopproc` command with the applicable `process-type` as follows:

```
[oracle@asmw oracle]$ opmnctl stopproc process-type=WebCache
opmnctl: stopping opmn managed processes...
[oracle@asmw oracle]$
```

Checking the status of the OracleAS Web Cache component, you see that it stopped:

```
[oracle@asmw oracle]$ opmnctl status

Processes in Instance: mw01.asmw
-------------------+--------------------+---------+---------
ias-component      | process-type       |     pid | status
-------------------+--------------------+---------+---------
DSA                | DSA                |     N/A | Down
LogLoader          | logloaderd         |     N/A | Down
dcm-daemon         | dcm-daemon         |   19718 | Alive
OC4J               | home               |   18762 | Alive
OC4J               | OC4J_Portal        |   18763 | Alive
WebCache           | WebCache           |     N/A | Down
WebCache           | WebCacheAdmin      |   18718 | Alive
HTTP_Server        | HTTP_Server        |   18725 | Alive
wireless           | performance_server |   18824 | Alive
wireless           | messaging_server   |   18825 | Alive
wireless           | OC4J_Wireless      |   18826 | Alive

[oracle@asmw oracle]$
```

To start the process again, use the `opmnctl startproc` command:

```
[oracle@asmw oracle]$ opmnctl startproc process-type=WebCache
opmnctl: starting opmn managed processes...
[oracle@asmw oracle]$
```

Finally, you check the status one more time:

```
[oracle@asmw oracle]$ opmnctl status

Processes in Instance: mw01.asmw
-------------------+--------------------+---------+---------
ias-component      | process-type       |     pid | status
-------------------+--------------------+---------+---------
DSA                | DSA                |     N/A | Down
LogLoader          | logloaderd         |     N/A | Down
dcm-daemon         | dcm-daemon         |   19718 | Alive
OC4J               | home               |   18762 | Alive
OC4J               | OC4J_Portal        |   18763 | Alive
WebCache           | WebCache           |   30902 | Alive
WebCache           | WebCacheAdmin      |   18718 | Alive
HTTP_Server        | HTTP_Server        |   18725 | Alive
wireless           | performance_server |   18824 | Alive
wireless           | messaging_server   |   18825 | Alive
wireless           | OC4J_Wireless      |   18826 | Alive

[oracle@asmw oracle]$
```

You can start and stop all OracleAS Web Cache components by using `ias-component` instead of `process-type` in the `opmnctl` command; to do this, you use `ias-component=WebCache` instead of two separate commands using the two different OracleAS Web Cache process types. Notice that the OracleAS Web Cache process is up and running with a new process ID (PID); restarting the component starts a new Unix process.

If you have a stand-alone OracleAS Web Cache installation, you do not have `opmnctl`; instead, you use the `webcachectl` command:

```
[oracle@asmw oracle]$ webcachectl start
```

Adjusting Administrative Security Settings

You can configure several security options from the OracleAS Web Cache administration page: the `administrator` and `invalidator` passwords, trusted subnets, and the Unix executables owner and group.

Administrator Passwords

After you install OracleAS Web Cache, the default administration password and invalidation password are set to the same value as the OracleAS administration password and are stored in the file `$ORACLE_HOME/webcache/webcache.xml` in encrypted form. Here is an excerpt of the complete `<Security>` tag in this file:

```
<SECURITY>
   <USER TYPE="INVALIDATION"
      PASSWORDHASH="B313A07317FA3F184628AE4D44A1B1072B756B69"/>
   <USER TYPE="MONITORING"
      PASSWORDHASH="B313A07317FA3F184628AE4D44A1B1072B756B69"/>
   <SECURESUBNET ALLOW="ALL"/>
   <DEBUGINFO HEADER="YES" EVENTLOG="NO" HTMLCOMMENT="NO"
       SWITCHSTRING="+wcdebug"/>
   <HTTPREQUEST MAXTOTALHEADERSIZE="819000"
       MAXSINGLEHEADERSIZE="8152"/>
</SECURITY>
```

To change these passwords, start at the page in Figure 5.2 and select the Administration tab; you will see the page shown in Figure 5.3.

FIGURE 5.3 OracleAS Web Cache Administration tab

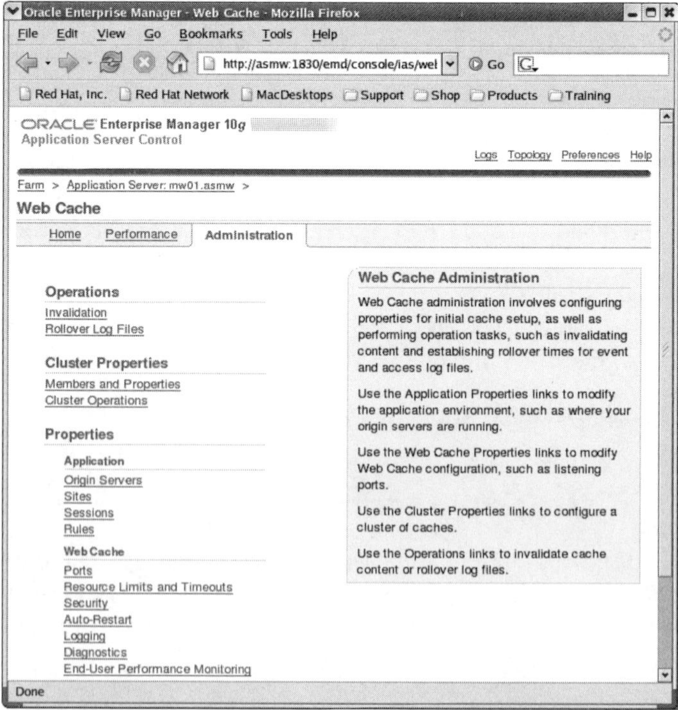

Near the bottom of the Administration page, click the `Security` link and you will see the page shown in Figure 5.4.

On this page, you can change the `administrator` password, the `invalidator` password, or both at the same time. After you specify the old and new passwords, click OK. On the next page, AS Control reminds you to restart OracleAS Web Cache to enable the new passwords.

FIGURE 5.4 OracleAS Web Cache Security page

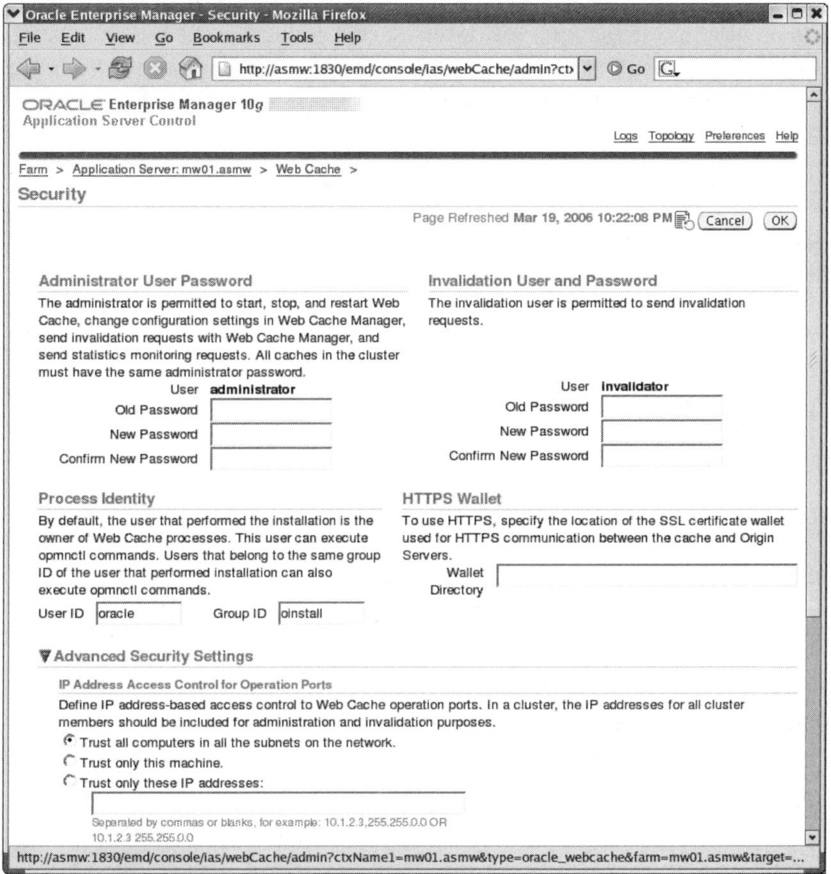

User and Group

When you install OracleAS, the default Unix owner is `oracle` and the default group is `oinstall`; this, of course, applies to OracleAS Web Cache as well. If your environment has specific security requirements or you are installing a stand-alone version of OracleAS Web Cache, you may wish to change the owner and group. To make these changes, start with the page in Figure 5.4. Under the heading Process Identity, enter the desired user ID and group ID. When you click OK, you must restart OracleAS Web Cache for this change to take effect.

To execute `opmnctl` commands, you must be logged in as the new user ID or as a user with the new group ID.

Trusted Subnets

By default, you can perform OracleAS Web Cache administrative tasks from any subnet in the same network as the server running the OracleAS Web Cache processes. To further enhance the security of your network or restrict administration or invalidation to specific IP addresses, start with the page in Figure 5.4 (the Security page).

Scroll down to the bottom of the page and expand the tree labeled Advanced Security Settings. To allow OracleAS Web Cache administrative tasks only from the server running the Web Cache processes, select the Trust Only This Machine radio button; if you want to restrict administration to another address, a list of addresses, or a particular subnet, click the Trust Only These IP Addresses radio button and enter the address list in the text box. For example, if you want to restrict administrative tasks to the user at IP address 192.168.2.81 and IP address 192.168.2.82, use this:

```
192.168.2.81, 192.168.2.82
```

Click OK to implement these changes; AS Control prompts you to restart OracleAS Web Cache so that these changes take effect. If you changed these addresses from a computer not in this list, you will not be able to make any further administrative changes to your Web Cache server. Web Cache stores this list in `webcache.xml`, and the entry for restricted IP addresses now looks like this:

```
<SECURESUBNET ALLOW="LIST_OF_IPS">
   <IP ADDR="192.168.2.81"/>
   <IP ADDR="192.168.2.82"/>
</SECURESUBNET>
```

The previous entry in `webcache.xml` looked like this:

```
<SECURESUBNET ALLOW="ALL"/>
```

Monitoring Web Cache Performance

Optimizing performance is a key goal of any system administrator, and tuning OracleAS Web Cache is no exception. Using OracleAS Web Cache's statistics page, you can see at a glance where the bottlenecks are occurring. Even if you don't catch a performance spike proactively, OracleAS Web Cache surge protection will be able to serve user requests with minimal tradeoff between response time and content consistency.

Understanding Web Cache Statistics

To review instantaneous and cumulative OracleAS Web Cache statistics, click the Performance tab on the OracleAS Web Cache home page, shown in Figure 5.2. You will see the performance statistics shown in Figure 5.5.

FIGURE 5.5 OracleAS Web Cache Performance page

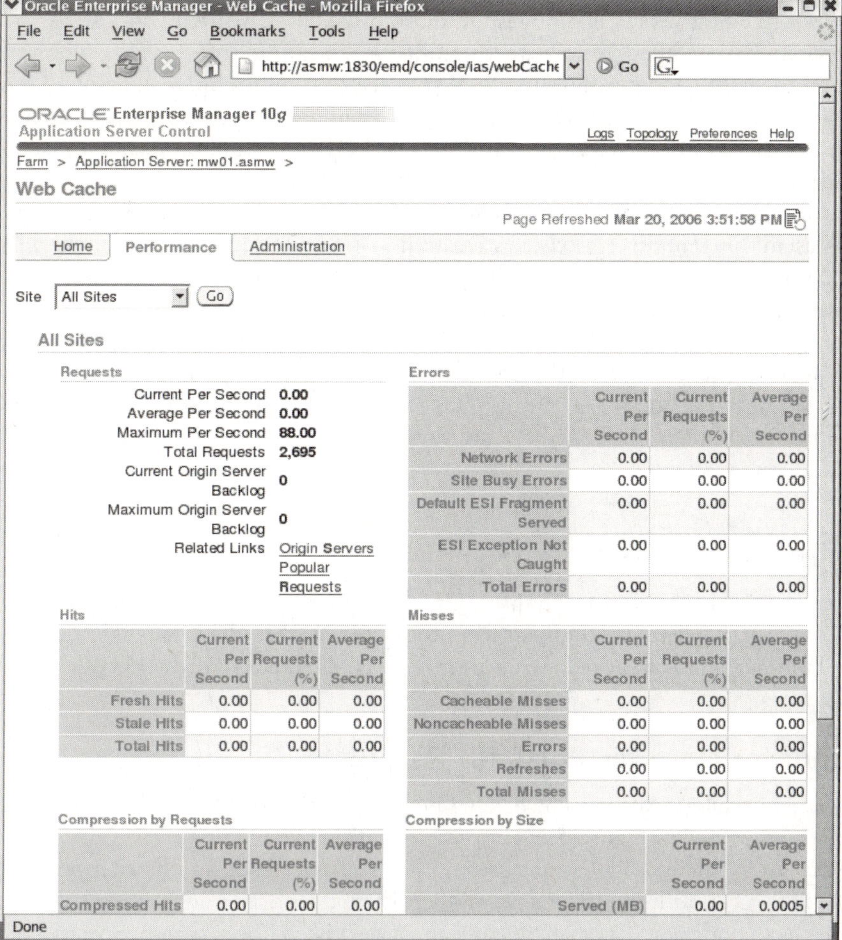

This page includes current, average, and maximum requests per second along with the total number of requests since the last time OracleAS Web Cache started. In addition, you can see statistics for cache hits, cache misses, compression hits, and errors.

Advanced web cache tuning is beyond the scope of this book. For further details, see the Oracle document *Web Cache Administrator's Guide 10*g *Release 2 (10.1.2)* on `technet.oracle.com`.

Leveraging Performance Assurance and Surge Protection

During a spike in website usage, as a system administrator you may face the choice of serving slightly stale content versus no content at all. In most cases, you will choose to serve slightly stale content. This is called *performance assurance*. An example of this would be a stock quote system: A traffic spike may result in quotes that are 20 minutes old instead of 15 minutes old. This is acceptable in most cases as long as the user understands that the quotes are slightly older than expected. In the end, however, you may choose to upgrade your web cache server, application server, or both to satisfy future peak requests.

OracleAS Web Cache makes it easy to balance website performance with content consistency. With minimal input from the system administrator, OracleAS Web Cache will minimize stale content and maximize response time by refreshing the most popular and least valid documents first.

A complementary feature that OracleAS Web Cache leverages during peak demand to prevent an overload of requests on the application server is called *surge protection*. Surge protection enables you to set a limit on the number of concurrent requests that the application server can handle simultaneously. When the number of requests exceeds this limit, subsequent requests are queued.

Configuring Ports

As we mentioned earlier in this chapter, OracleAS Web Cache listens for HTTP requests on port 7777. You can use the administration tools linked from the OracleAS Web Cache home page to configure one or more listener ports as well as to configure other Web Cache administrative ports.

Configuring Listener Ports for Requests

To configure OracleAS Web Cache listener ports, click the `Ports` link shown in Figure 5.3 and you will see the page in Figure 5.6.

As you can see in Figure 5.6 in the Listen Ports section, the default listener port is 7777. You can change this to another port or add another listener port. To add another listener port, click the Add a Row button and a new row appears in the Listen Ports section. Specify the IP address and listener port; if you use an * in the IP address field, Web Cache listens on all IP addresses on the server running Web Cache.

If you set the Protocol drop-down box to HTTP, no further entries are needed; if you specify HTTPS, you must specify the wallet in which the client-side certificates are stored.

Note that you can also delete ports on this page if you no longer need to listen for requests on a particular port.

When you finish adding ports, click the OK button and AS Control prompts you to restart Web Cache to enable the new port numbers.

FIGURE 5.6 OracleAS Web Cache Ports page

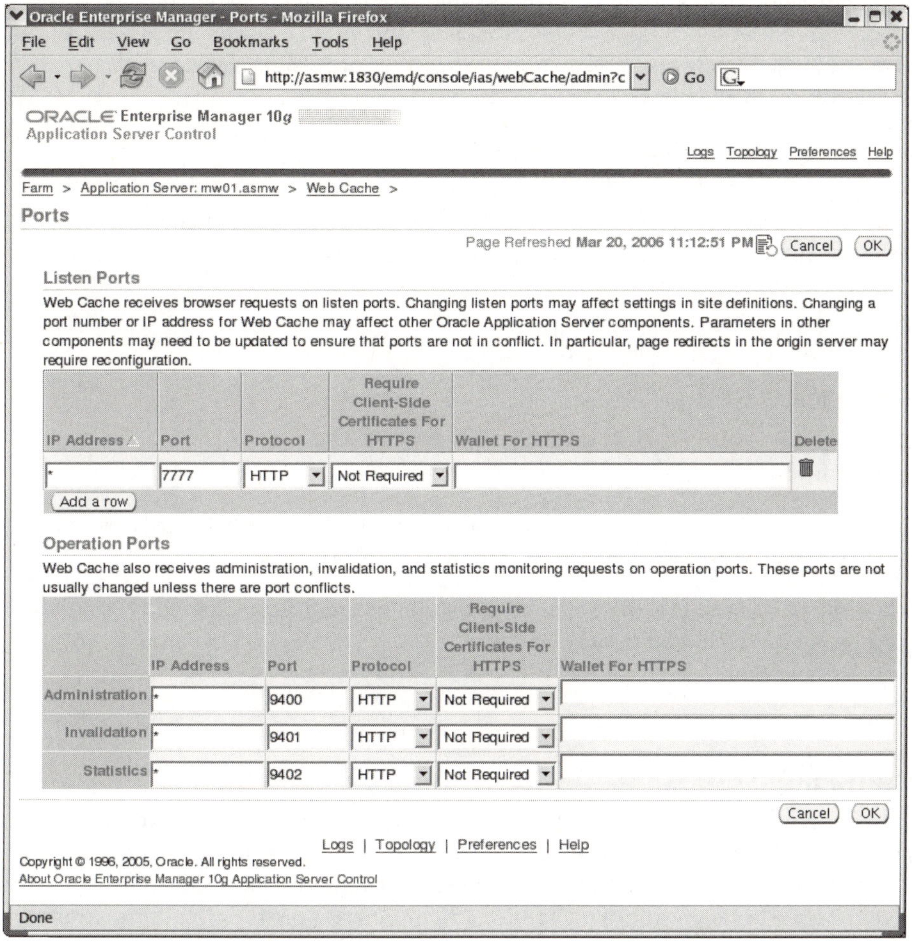

Conforming to Industry Standard Port Assignments

Many of your clients complain that they must append a port number to access some of your sites. Unfortunately, you never configured one of your servers to allow port assignments under 1024. As a result, you could not assign port 80, the default HTTP port number, as one of your listener ports.

If you want to use port 80 for one of the listeners, you must run a special script file as the root user since port numbers less than 1024 are reserved for use by privileged processes under Unix. To give Web Cache access to these ports, first stop all Web Cache processes using AS Control or the opmnctl command. Next, run the shell script $ORACLE_HOME/webcache/bin/webcache_setuser.sh as follows:

```
[root@asmw root]# cd $ORACLE_HOME/webcache/bin
[root@asmw bin]# ls -l webcached
-rwx------    1 oracle   oinstall  3565525 Nov  8 09:12 webcached
[root@asmw bin]# ./webcache_setuser.sh setroot oracle

setroot task completed successfully.

[root@asmw bin]# ls -l webcached
-rwsr-x---    1 root     oinstall  3565525 Nov  8 09:12 webcached
[root@asmw bin]#
```

Note that the setuid bit s is now set on the webcached executable; in other words, even though the oracle user still owns webcached, it will run with root privileges.

After this process is complete, log out and log back in as the oracle user and restart Web Cache. You can now assign port numbers under 1024 to any Web Cache process, including your client listener port.

Changing Operation Ports

You can change the Web Cache port numbers for administration, invalidation, and statistics under the Operation Ports section on the same page you used to configure listener ports (Figure 5.6). The rules for updating these port numbers are the same as for configuring listening ports except that you cannot add or delete a port; each administrative function requires one and only one port.

If you want to use a port number less than 1024 for one of these administrative operation ports, you must use the same procedure we presented in the previous section for defining a listener on port 80.

Specifying Origin Server Settings

As part of your administrative duties, you configure OracleAS Web Cache with one or more applications or websites whose content Web Cache will cache.

To configure OracleAS Web Cache origin servers, click the Origin Servers link on the Administration page (Figure 5.3) and you will see the page shown in Figure 5.7.

FIGURE 5.7 OracleAS Web Cache Origin Servers page

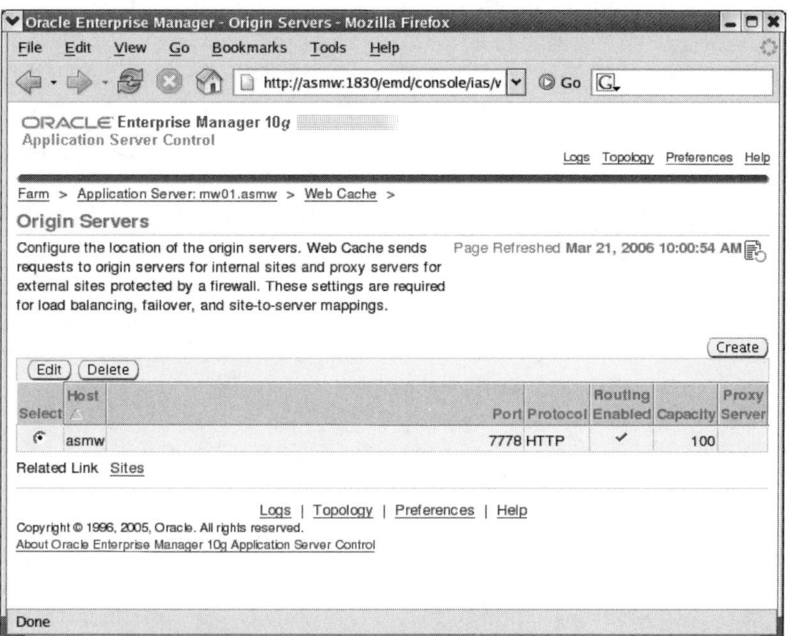

In this example, the Web Cache server caches content from the HTTP server in the instance `asmw` on port 7778. Note that a client will not access `asmw` at port 7778 directly; it will use the address of the Web Cache server and the associated port number. In fact, typically you will disable access to the origin server to every IP address except for the Web Cache server. The instance `asmw` is configured to handle 100 concurrent connections; this is calculated ahead of time using common load testing techniques.

To add a new origin server to this Web Cache server, click the Create button shown in Figure 5.7 and you will see the Create Origin Server page shown in Figure 5.8.

On the Create Origin Server page, enter the following values:

Host The hostname of the application or proxy server.

Port The port number at which the application or proxy server receives requests from Web Cache.

Capacity The maximum number of concurrent connections that the application or proxy server can accept.

Routing Enabled Controls whether the cache sends requests to the origin server.

Protocol Select either HTTP or HTTPS.

FIGURE 5.8 OracleAS Web Cache Create Origin Server page

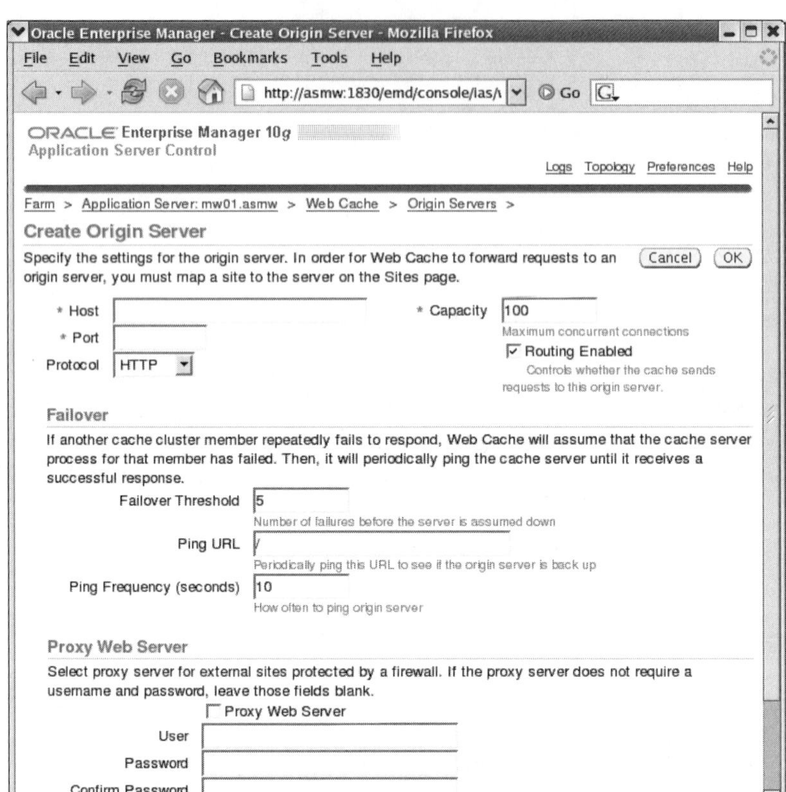

Failover Threshold The number of allowed continuous failures before Web Cache considers the origin server unavailable; the default value is 5.

Ping URL The URL that Web Cache will use to check the health of an origin server whose threshold has been exceeded. Alternatively, you can use a URL that checks the application logic on the origin server and returns HTTP 200 or 500 status codes.

Ping Frequency The number of seconds between ping requests when the failover threshold has been exceeded.

Click OK to add the origin server to the list of servers that this Web Cache instance will cache. Web Cache forwards requests to this origin server only if you map the origin server correctly on the Site to Server Mapping page, which we will discuss in the next section. If you do not map it correctly, Web Cache ignores this origin server.

Configuring Site Definitions

OracleAS Web Cache caches and optionally assembles dynamic content from one or more origin servers. When Web Cache receives a request, it uses one of the following elements to determine where to go for the content if it is not already in the cache:

- The `Host` request-header from the request URL
- The Host portion of the requested URL
- The `src` attribute of the ESI tag

To define the site-to-origin server mappings, click the `Sites` link on the Administration (Figure 5.3) and you will see the page in Figure 5.9.

To add a new site mapping, click the Create button in the Named Sites Definitions section; you see the page in Figure 5.10.

FIGURE 5.9 OracleAS Web Cache Sites page

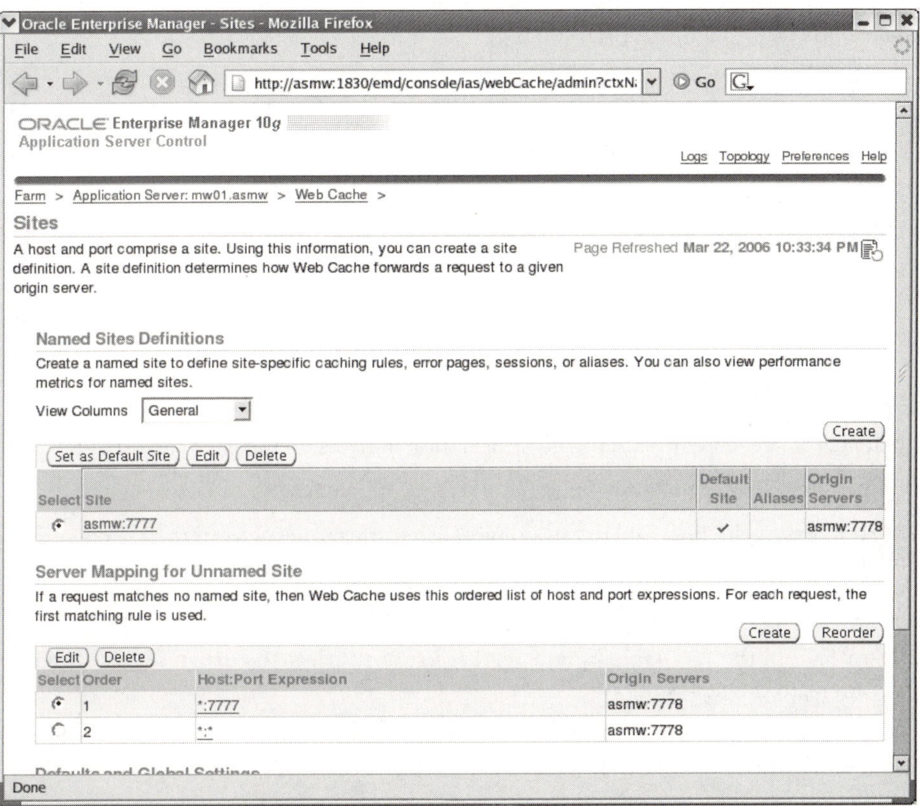

FIGURE 5.10 OracleAS Web Cache Create Named Site page

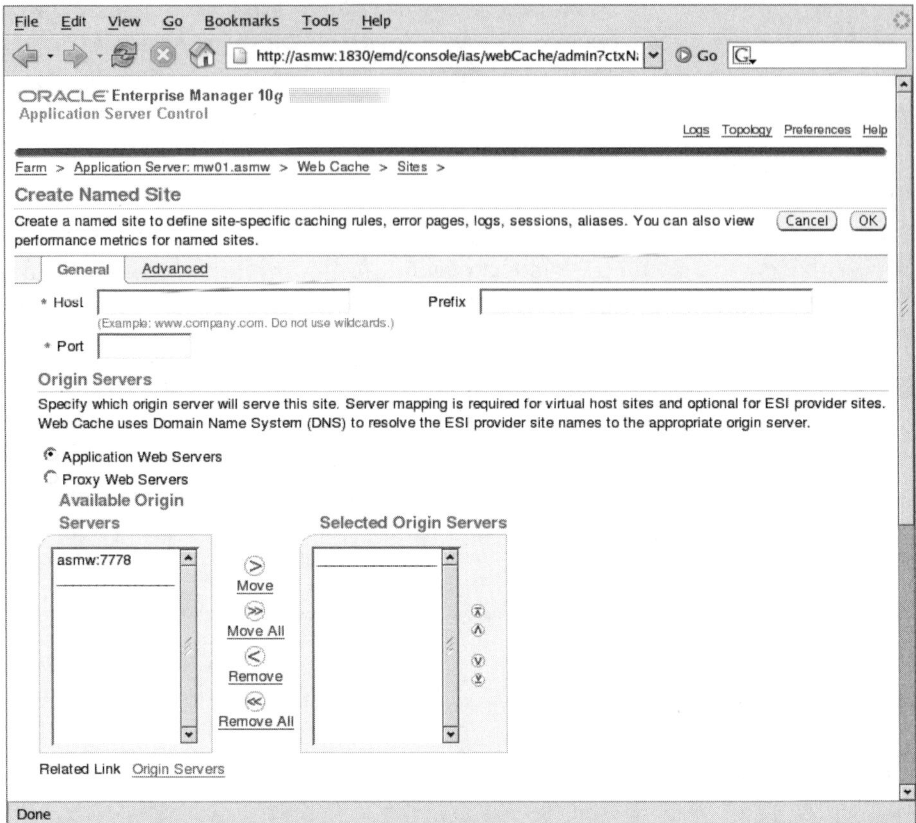

To add a new site, enter the following information in fields on the page shown in Figure 5.10:

Host The hostname of the new site; clients will use this name to retrieve content.

Port The name of the port where the site will listen for requests from the clients.

Prefix A path prefix to distinguish multiple sites with the same hostname cached by the same Web Cache server.

Origin Servers In the Available Origin Servers list box, select the origin server(s) that will supply content to the new site.

Aliases Add any aliases for this site. For example, you may want to respond to a site with or without a `www.` prefix.

In the Available Origin Servers list box, move one or more available origin servers to the Selected Origin Servers list box. Click OK to save this site; AS Control will prompt you to restart Web Cache.

Configuring Caching

Caching rules specify which content you should cache; whether you cache some or all content from an origin server depends on the size of each document and how often a client accesses the document. If you have enough memory on your Web Cache server to cache all content, then you would not need any caching rules! In nearly every situation, however, your memory capacity is limited and you must optimize client response time by deciding which content to cache.

Once you decide which objects to cache, you can further enhance response time and minimize bandwidth usage by delivering compressed content to the client. Web Cache will deliver content compressed using the `zlib` compression method if the client browser supports this method.

You also have the ability to cache multiple versions of a document; you can cache and serve different versions of the same document depending on the existence and value of a cookie stored on the client. In contrast to caching multiple versions of the same document, you can also cache partial pages; this is useful if all clients retrieve one part of a page but other parts are customized for each client.

Using Caching Rules

OracleAS Web Cache contains a number of default caching rules that are a good starting point for your environment. In the following sections, we'll give you a brief overview of how Web Cache prioritizes cache rules, the predefined cache rules, how to edit the predefined cache rules, and how to create new rules.

Caching Rules Overview

Web Cache caches using the following rules, with the first rule having the highest priority:

1. Static documents
2. Multiple-version URLs
3. Personalized pages
4. Pages that support session tracking
5. HTTP error messages
6. URLs that match regular expressions
7. URL trees that contain a document or a subtree

All caching rules are URL expressions; you specify the caching rules in these formats:

- Unix regular expressions
- File extensions
- Path prefixes

If the expression evaluates to more than one document, or even one or more complete directories, it is called a *subtree* of URLs.

Understanding Predefined Caching Rules

To view the predefined caching rules, click the `Rules` link on the Administration page (Figure 5.3) and you will see the page shown in Figure 5.11.

FIGURE 5.11 OracleAS Web Cache Rules page

File Edit View Go Bookmarks Tools Help

http://asmw:1830/emd/console/ias/webCache/admin?ctxl Go

ORACLE Enterprise Manager 10*g*
Application Server Control

Logs Topology Preferences Help

Farm > Application Server: mw01.asmw > Web Cache >

Rules

Rules instruct the cache how to react to each request. A rule has two parts: Selector and Instructions. A request is compared with the Selectors. If there is a match, then the cache follows the Instructions. Rules are ordered; only the first matching rule is honored.

Page Refreshed Mar 23, 2006 5:35:47 PM

View Site asmw:7777 View Columns Overview (Create) (Reorder)

(Create Like) (Edit) (Delete)

Select	Order	Name	Selector Summary	Enabled	Instructions: Cache	Instructions: Summary
(•)	1	cache_wireless_rm	Reg: /ptg/rm	✓	✓	Expires: As Specified in HTTP Header, Refresh: Immediately Sessions: PAsid, PAconnxn, PAuserid
( )	Global 1	cache image	Reg: \.(gif|jpe?g|png|bmp)$	✓	✓	Expires: Max Time in Cache, 60 Minutes, Refresh: Within 6 Minutes
( )	Global 2	cache compress css	Ext: .css	✓	✓	Compress, except Netscape 4.x Expires: Max Time in Cache, 5 Minutes, Refresh: Immediately
( )	Global 3	cache uix-jdev js	Reg: /jsLibs/.*\.js$	✓	✓	Expires: Max Time in Cache, 5 Minutes, Refresh: Immediately
( )	Global 4	cache compress js	Ext: .js	✓	✓	Compress, except Netscape 4.x Expires: Max Time in Cache, 5 Minutes, Refresh: Immediately
( )	Global 5	cache compress html	Reg: \.html?$	✓	✓	Compress Expires: Max Time in Cache, 5 Minutes, Refresh: Immediately
( )	Global 6	cache swf	Ext: .swf	✓	✓	Expires: Max Time in Cache, 60 Minutes, Refresh: Within 6 Minutes

Related Link Expiration Policies

Done

Using this page, you can create a new rule or reorder existing rules. Caching rules are applied in the order on this page; consider the first and second rules on this page:

```
/ptg/rm
\.(gif|jpe?g|png|bmp)$
```

If a client requests a document with the name `/ptg/rm/home.gif`, the caching rule for `/ptg/rm` is applied and Web Cache ignores the second rule. However, for any other image files that are not in the directory `/ptg/rm`, Web Cache uses the second rule.

Creating and Editing Caching Rules

To add a new caching rule, click the Create button shown in Figure 5.11. In the screen shown in Figure 5.12, you must provide the following information:

General Name and description of the rule

Site Rules applied to content on this site

Selector Unix regular expression, file extensions, or paths

Instructions Turn caching on or off; if caching is on, when to expire cached documents falling under this rule

Compression Turn compression on or off; if on, restrict compression to some browsers

FIGURE 5.12 OracleAS Web Cache Create Rule page

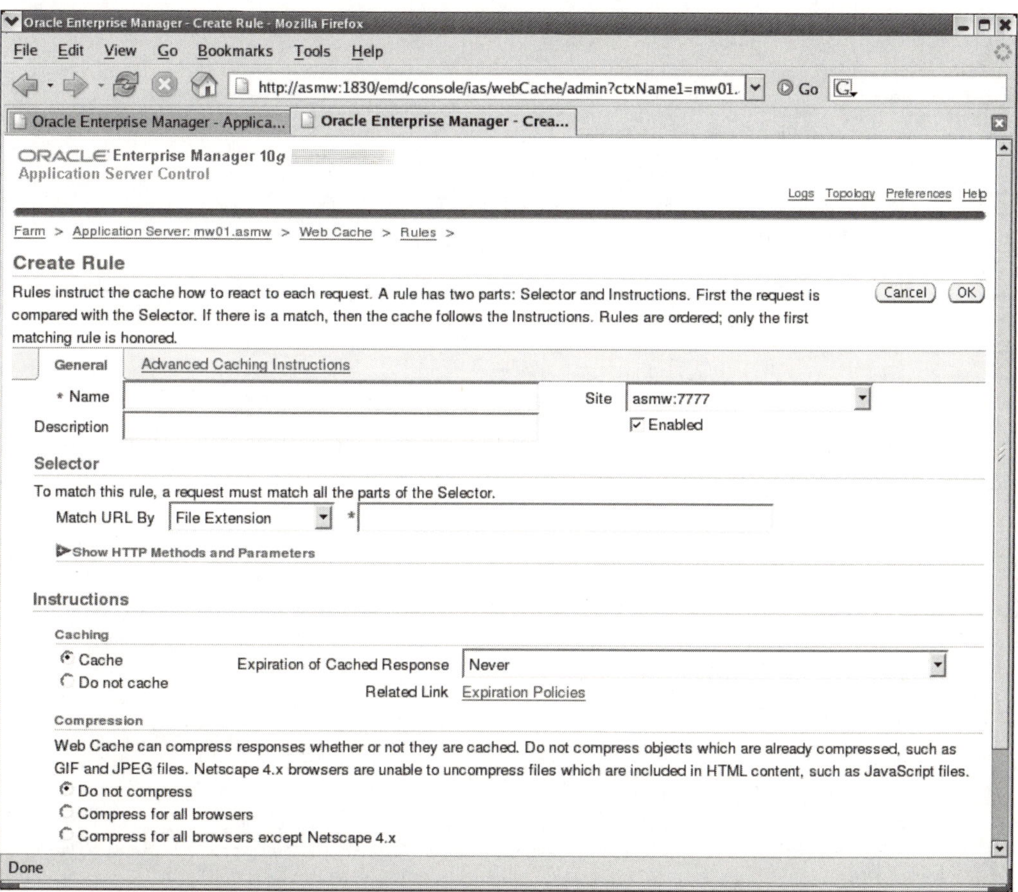

The Enabled check box is handy when you want to turn this cache rule off without deleting the rule; you can reuse this rule later by simply reenabling it and restarting Web Cache.

To edit an existing rule, start on the Rules page (Figure 5.11), select the rule to edit, and click the Edit button. In the page shown in Figure 5.13, you edit the cache image rule.

Because these image types are already compressed, this rule does not compress these documents before sending them to the client. If you click the `Advanced Caching Instructions` link, you see the page shown in Figure 5.14.

This page gives you many ways to further customize and optimize content delivery to the client:

Cache Multiple Versions of an Object Cookies stored on the client can trigger customized content to the client.

For Other HTTP Headers Change the response based on the existence and value of additional HTTP headers in the request: for example, the client may request a response in a particular language.

FIGURE 5.13 OracleAS Web Cache Edit Rule page

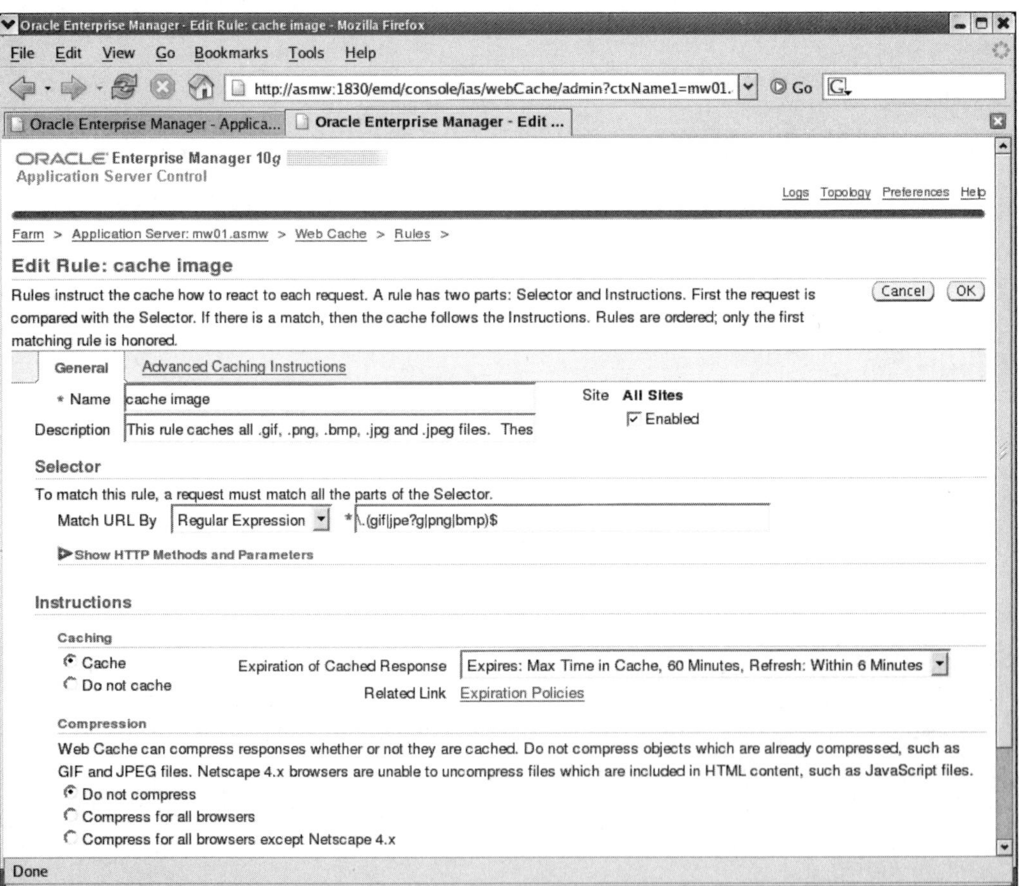

FIGURE 5.14 OracleAS Web Cache Advanced Caching Instructions page

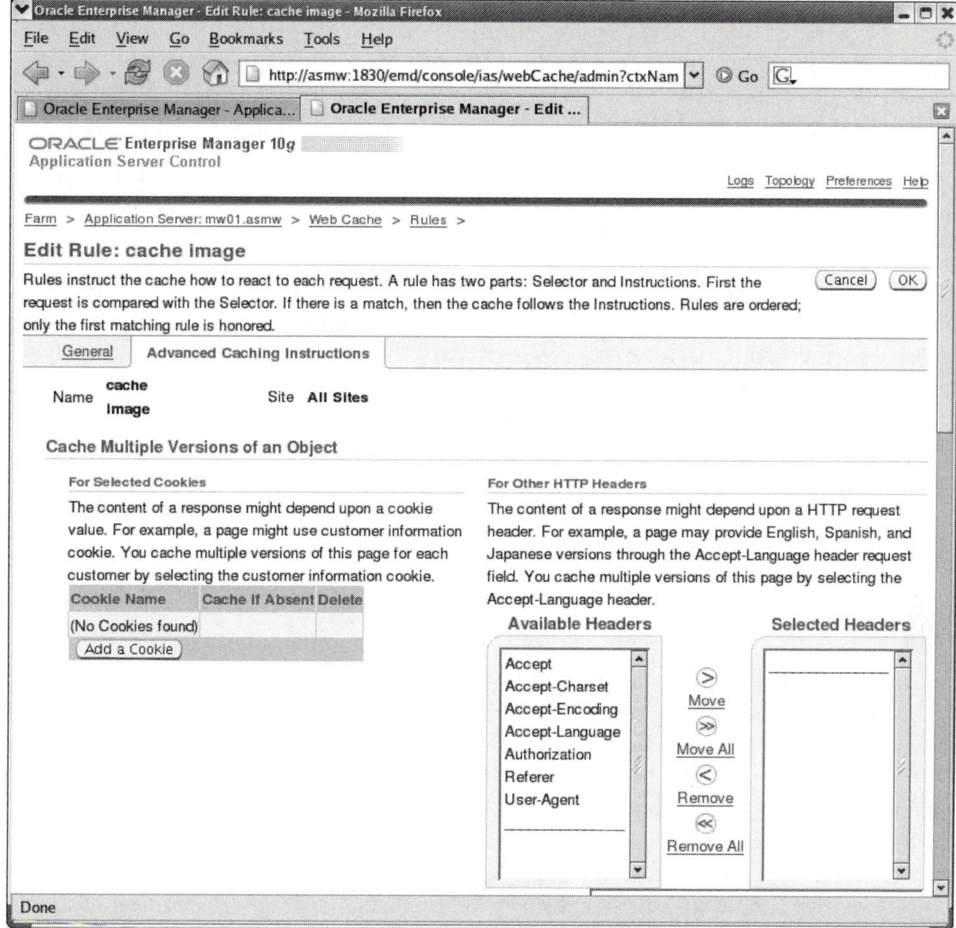

Avoid Unwanted Copies Cache the same content from nonidentical URL strings if the content returned is identical; you specify parameters that Web Cache ignores when comparing URLs.

Process Session Encoded URLs Customize content based on a session ID included in HREF tags in the HTML file.

Session Related Caching Cache objects based on sessions, cookies, embedded URL parameters, or POST parameters.

Cache Error Responses Web Cache does not cache any response code other than an expected 200 OK response; however, to conserve origin server resources, you can use Web Cache to cache error response codes.

ESI Processing You can allow clients to perform ESI processing instead of Web Cache.

Delivering Compressed Content

To speed delivery of content to your clients, you can enable compression of content. Most text-based pages, HTML, XML, and word-processing document files will benefit from compression. OracleAS Web Cache uses the `zlib` compression technique; most, if not all, modern browsers support decompression of content encoded by `zlib`. However, the client must explicitly request compression in the `Accept-Encoding` HTTP header:

```
Accept-Encoding: zlib
```

On average, Web Cache will compress HTML and XML pages to as little as 1/10 their original size. This provides the client with improved response time and reduces network bandwidth; the processing cost on the client to decompress the content is not significant.

Web Cache stores both compressed and uncompressed versions of documents if compression is enabled; in addition, if the origin server marks a document as compressed with the `Content-Encoding` response header, Web Cache will not attempt to compress it further.

One of the many features new to OracleAS 10*g* Release 2 is *content streaming*. The client does not have to wait for Web Cache to receive the entire document from the origin server before sending it; furthermore, Web Cache sends a compressed document to the client in pieces as Web Cache compresses it. The client does not have to wait for Web Cache to compress the entire document before viewing it.

Expiring Content

For most web content you provide to your clients, you can predict how long a cached version of the document should remain cached before it becomes stale; for these documents, you will typically specify an *expiration rule* for a document, a group of documents, or a directory.

Even if the duration of the document validity in the cache varies widely, you can usually determine a minimum duration to balance content accuracy and speed of delivery from the cache. In some cases, however, you may not cache some documents at all due to their extreme volatility from minute to minute. For example, a stock brokerage site will most likely cache its trading terms and conditions document but will not cache any pages that reflect real-time stock price information.

You can set expiration rules in three different ways:

HTTP header Content expiration is based on the `Expiration` header in the document provided by the origin web server. This is the default behavior for a cached document.

Maximum time in cache Expiration is relative to when Web Cache places a document into the cache.

Maximum time since the document was created Expiration is relative to when the document was created. This option requires the origin server to include the `Last-Modified` header in the response.

When a document expires, you can configure Web Cache to either refresh the document immediately or refresh on demand. If you expect that an expired document will be requested again soon, you can improve response time for future client requests by recaching immediately. On the other hand, on a Web Cache server with peak usage periods, you may want to optimize overall performance by recaching a document only when it is requested again. This may cause a slight performance hit for the first client to request the document after invalidation, but it keeps overall cache performance high by not recaching documents that may not be needed immediately.

Defining Expiration Rules

To define or edit an expiration rule, select any existing rule and click the `Expiration Policies` link shown in Figure 5.13. You will see all rules defined for this installation of Web Cache, as in Figure 5.15.

Included on the page are all expiration policies and which defined rules use each policy. For example, image documents fall under the third policy in Figure 5.15: they stay in the cache no longer than 60 minutes, and Web Cache recaches them within 6 minutes. To create a new policy, click the Create button and you see the page shown in Figure 5.16.

FIGURE 5.15 OracleAS Web Cache Expiration Policies page

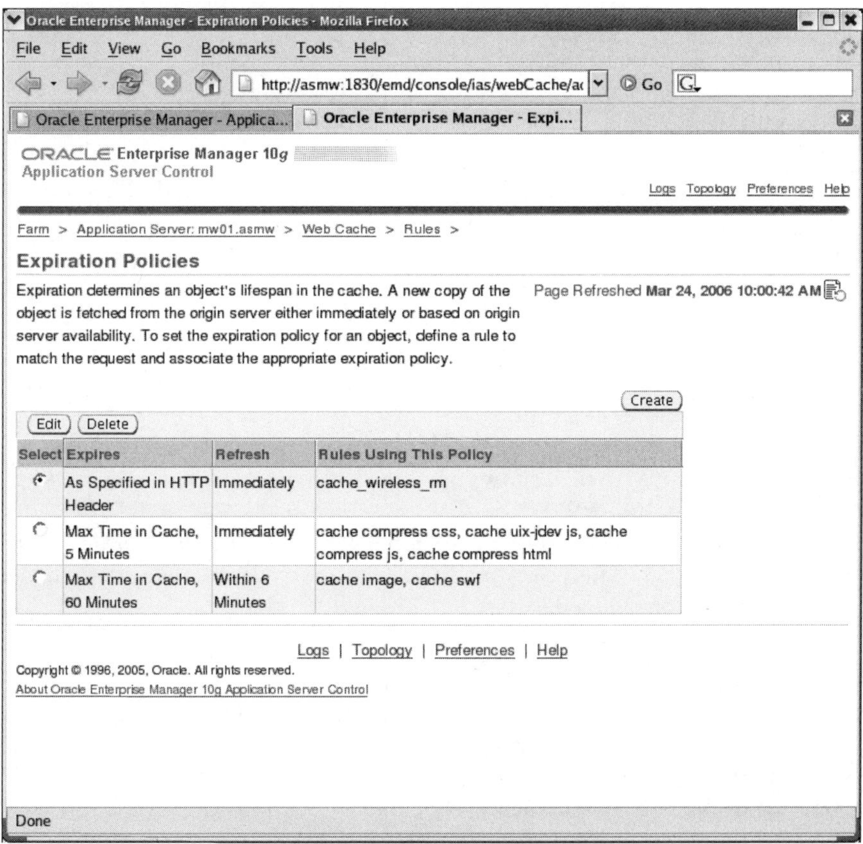

FIGURE 5.16 OracleAS Web Cache Create Expiration Policy page

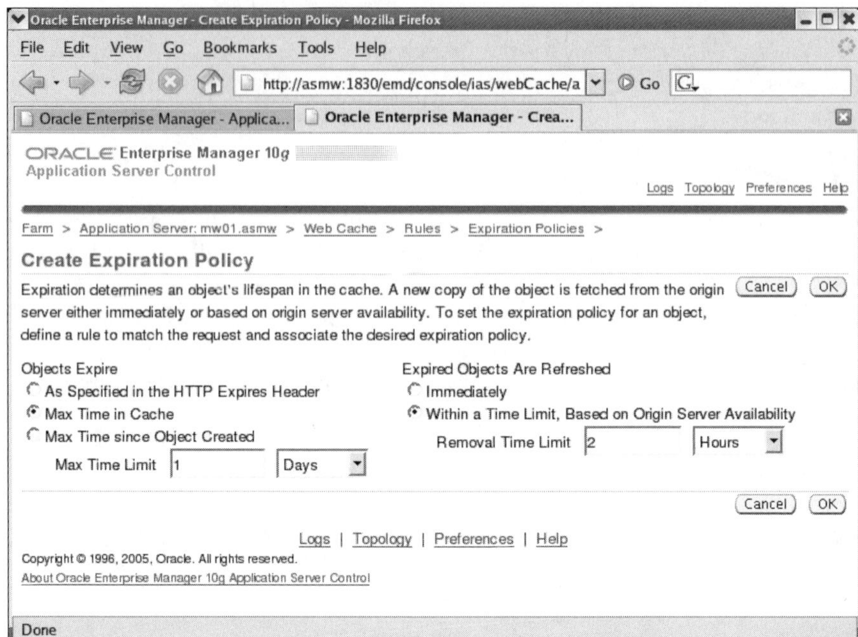

You have a lot of flexibility when expiring documents; you can even define a different expiration policy for each rule, and each rule can apply to an individual document at the origin server if that is practical and each document has different expiration criteria!

On the Create Expiration Policy page, you specify one of the three expiration categories: by HTTP header, time in cache, or time since object creation. If you select the object's creation time, you can set the expiration time relative to creation time to the nearest second.

Next, you define when Web Cache must refresh the object, either immediately or within a specified amount of time after expiration.

After you complete the new policy, click OK. The policy you defined on the Create Expiration Policy page (Figure 5.16) now shows up in the list of policies, as shown in Figure 5.17, and is available after you restart Web Cache.

The new policy expires any documents associated with this policy after 1 day in the cache and refreshes within 2 hours. This policy might be useful for a daily cafeteria lunch menu that becomes stale every day after lunch.

Using Basic Content Invalidation

Content expiration is often not predictable enough to use a fixed expiration time. For example, an online clothing retailer will most likely not know in advance when their mock turtlenecks will sell out; they want to disable the product page or show the mock turtlenecks with a backorder status within moments of their becoming unavailable.

FIGURE 5.17 Updated OracleAS Web Cache Expiration Policies page

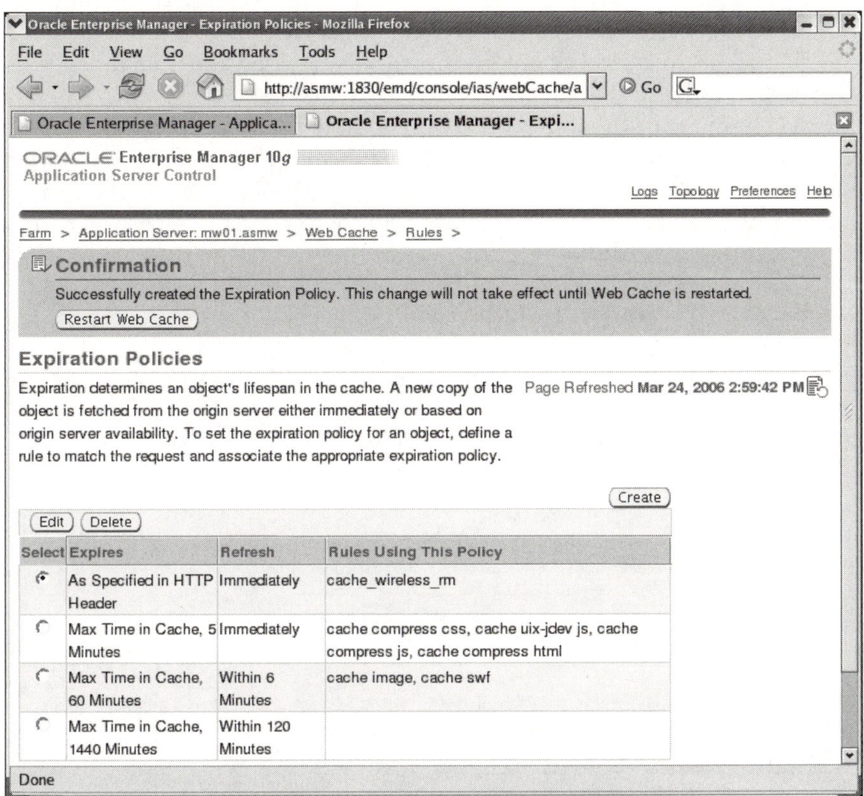

To account for these unpredictable situations, you can use *invalidation messages* to mark these cached pages as stale. Invalidation messages can be sent to Web Cache via several methods that we will present in the following sections. In all cases, however, the form of this message is an HTTP `POST` request with XML data. Here is an example of a `POST` request to invalidate all URLs in the cache that begin with `/core_us_catalog`:

```
POST /x-oracle-cache-invalidate HTTP/1.0
X-Oracle-Cache-Invalidate-URL-Prefix: /core_us_catalog
X-Oracle-Cache-Invalidate-Level: 0
```

An invalidation level of `0` directs Web Cache to never display these pages once they are marked as stale.

Web Cache receives invalidation messages by several methods, including the AS Control Web Cache Administration page, database triggers, automated scripts, applications, `telnet`, or a secondary key specified in an application.

Invalidation Using the Web Cache Administration Page

To invalidate pages manually from the AS Control interface, click the `Invalidation` link in the Operations section on the Administration page (Figure 5.3). You will see the page shown in Figure 5.18. To limit an administrator's duties to web cache invalidation functions, you use the `invalidator` user ID.

Invalidating objects using the web interface takes three steps: selecting the objects to invalidate, specifying when Web Cache should invalidate them, and optionally previewing the objects Web Cache will invalidate before starting the operation.

If you have a stand-alone Web Cache installation, you can use the Web Cache Manager to perform this task.

FIGURE 5.18 Web Cache Invalidation page

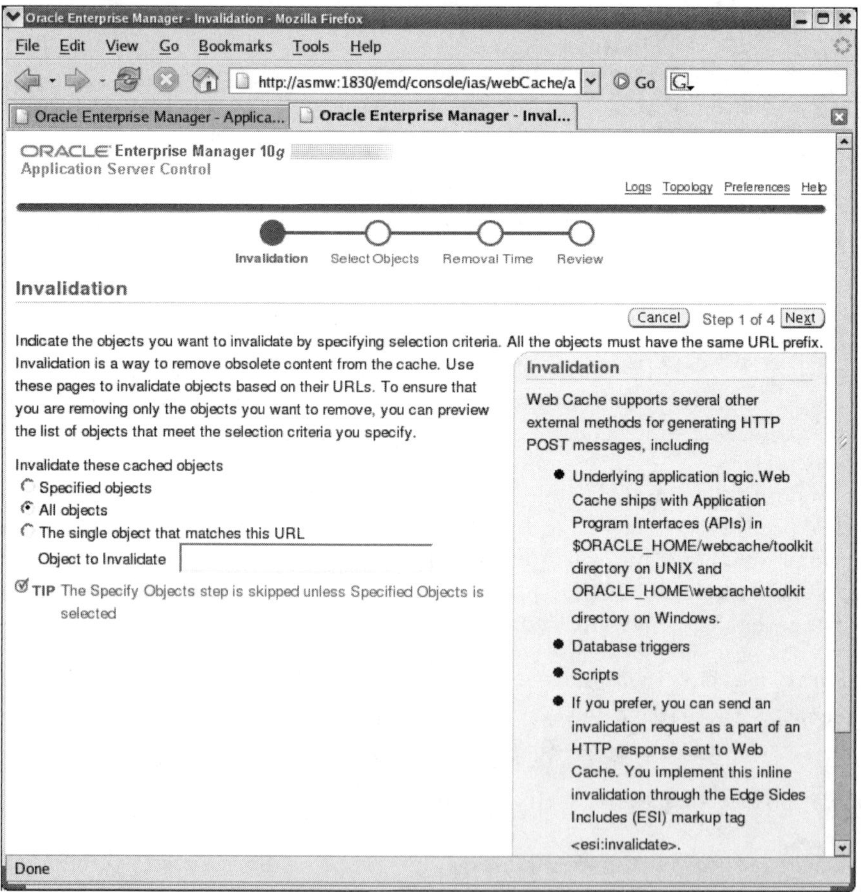

Invalidation Using Database Triggers

Events in the backend database can trigger a change to the cached objects, such as an UPDATE, INSERT, or DELETE in the database. When a database event fires the trigger, the trigger can send an HTTP invalidation message to Web Cache. For example, when a sales promotion is over, you delete a row from the PROMOTIONS table and a database trigger will send an HTTP invalidation message to Web Cache to invalidate any content related to the promotion.

You can use any database that supports triggers and HTTP for Web Cache content invalidation, including Microsoft SQL Server and IBM DB2.

Invalidation Using Automated Scripts

Many sites use Unix shell scripts to update file systems and databases that source a website. To ensure that the cached pages reflect the content of the updated file systems and databases, the shell scripts can send a message to Web Cache instructing it to perform invalidation as its last step after performing its updates.

Invalidation Using Applications

Oracle's Web Cache application programming interface (API) includes functions to automatically create invalidation messages. Embedded Java Server Pages (JSPs) and Java servlets can therefore take advantage of automatically generated invalidation messages when website content is changed.

Invalidation Using the *telnet* Command

Using the `telnet` command is a simple yet effective way to send invalidation messages to Web Cache. Once you know the invalidation port number, the authentication information for Web Cache, and the format for the invalidation messages, you can perform all invalidation operations in text mode. This method is useful when you don't have access to a web browser or any other GUI to connect to Web Cache.

Invalidation Using a Secondary Key

For all of the invalidation methods we've previously discussed, you can use a *secondary key* to specify which content to invalidate. Secondary keys are search keys you can use to specify URLs for invalidation. In addition to using an exact URL or a regular expression that matches a URL, you can use application-specific search keys. Using a secondary key to identify URLs is analogous to using an alternate index on a database table to retrieve rows from the table when you do not know the value of the primary key for the table.

Secondary key invalidation is a new feature of Oracle Application Server 10*g* Release 2.

Logging Events and Accessing Log File Information

All events and error messages are stored in an *event log*. This log will display startup errors such as port conflicts or any other errors that occur while Web Cache is running. By default, Web Cache creates the log file with the name `event_log` in `$ORACLE_HOME/webcache/logs` under the OracleAS middleware home.

In contrast, the *access log* contains entries for the HTTP requests sent to Web Cache. By default, Web Cache creates the access log file with the name `access_log` and stores it in `$ORACLE_HOME/webcache/logs`.

Both log types support the common log format (CLF), the combined format, and a log format specific to Web Cache, the *Web Cache log format (WCLF)*.

For more information on other OracleAS log file formats, see Chapter 4, "Performing HTTP Server Configuration and Management Tasks."

In the following sections, we'll show you how to configure and manage both of these logs, including how to manage the disk space used by the logs. Depending on the level of logging you choose, these log files may use a significant amount of disk space if they are not managed correctly.

Configuring the Access Log and Event Log

To configure the attributes of the access log, start from the Web Cache Administration page in Figure 5.3 and click the Logging link near the bottom of the page. You will see the Logging page shown in Figure 5.19.

On this page, you can change the directory and filename for each log type as well as how often the logs roll over. In addition, you can improve the performance of Web Cache by buffering the log files in memory; when the buffer is full, Web Cache writes the contents to disk. You should turn off this option when you are debugging Web Cache problems and you need to see log file entries immediately.

By default, you can roll over the log files every hour, every day, or every week. Splitting up the log files into more manageable pieces makes it easier to analyze a particular time period and archive log files to tape or another offline medium for historical purposes. When a log rolls over, the existing log is renamed to `event_log_file.yyyymmdd_hhmm` and subsequent log entries are written to an empty log file with the configured log filename. You can create your own custom log rollover frequency by clicking Custom Rollover Schedules at the bottom of the Logging page.

Finally, you have the option to manually roll over the log at any time. Click the `Rollover Log Files` link at the bottom of the Logging page and you will see the page shown in Figure 5.20.

Click the Rollover Event Log button or the Rollover Access Log button to roll over the event log or access log, respectively. The same `Rollover Log Files` link is also available from the Operations section of the Web Cache Administration page.

FIGURE 5.19 Web Cache Logging page

ORACLE Enterprise Manager 10*g*
Application Server Control

Logs Topology Preferences Help

Farm > Application Server: mw01.asmw > Web Cache >

Logging

Page Refreshed **Mar 25, 2006 10:13:31 PM** (Cancel) (OK)

Event Log

The event log contains event and error information. It can help you detect port conflicts, find startup or shutdown issues, and determine what objects or objects have been inserted into the cache. Event logging is always enabled.

Directory /u01/app/oracle/as10gHome/webcache/logs/
Logging Level Notification
Takes effect immediately when OK is clicked.
☑ Buffer in Memory
Takes effect immediately when OK is clicked.
File Name event_log
Time Style Local
Rollover Never
☑ Include Request Details

Access Logs

Access logs contains information about the HTTP requests sent to Web Cache. You can set up access logging for individual sites, overriding the defaults.

☑ Enable Access Logging
Directory /u01/app/oracle/as10gHome/webcache/logs/
☑ Buffer in Memory
Takes effect immediately when OK is clicked.
File Name access_log
Time Style Local
Rollover Never
Format Enhanced Common Log Format (ECLF)
☐ Include ESI Fragment Requests

FIGURE 5.20 Web Cache Rollover Log Files page

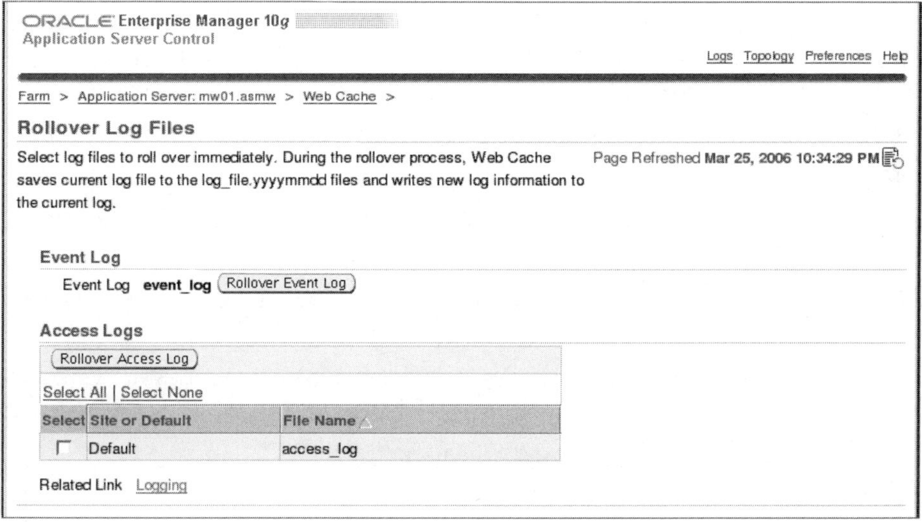

Understanding the Web Cache Log Format

As the name implies, the Web Cache log format (WCLF) is optimized for analyzing end-user performance of Web Cache. It contains most of the fields found in the CLF and the combined format; here is a list of the fields in WCLF and a brief description of each field:

x-req-type Request type

x-date-start Date before Web Cache received the first byte of the request

x-time-start Date when Web Cache received the last byte of the response

c-ip IP address of the browser

s-ip IP address of the Web Cache server

x-auth-id Username of an HTTP authentication request

cs(Host) The hostname of the client that sent the request

cs-method HTTP request method, browser to Web Cache

cs-uri URI, browser to Web Cache

x-protocol Protocol and version from browser request

sc-status Web Cache to browser HTTP status code

bytes Content length of the request

cs-bytes Bytes received from the browser

x-cache Cache status: cache hits, misses, and updates

time-taken Amount of time to the nearest microsecond for the request to complete

r-time-taken Time to the nearest microsecond that Web Cache spent communicating with the origin server when sending a request

x-time-delay Time to the nearest microsecond that Web Cache spent communicating with the origin server when receiving a request

x-os-timeout 0 = origin server did not time out, 1 = origin server did time out

x-ecid ID of the ECID request header

x-cookie(ORACLE_SMP_CHRONOS_ST) Cookie value for the ORACLE_SMP_CHRONOS_ST cookie

x-cookie(ORACLE_SMP_CHRONOS_LT) Cookie value for the ORACLE_SMP_CHRONOS_LT cookie

x-cookie(ORACLE_SMP_CHRONOS_GL) Cookie value for the ORACLE_SMP_CHRONOS_GL cookie

cs(Referer) The previous site visited by the user

cs(User-Agent) The browser used on the client

x-esi-info ESI fragment log message from ESI tags

If you need to log information in both CLF and WCLF for two different types of analyses, you can specify your own custom access log format by clicking the `Custom Access Log Formats` link near the bottom of the Logging page.

Summary

In this chapter, we presented an overview of the OracleAS Web Cache, starting out with a general overview of Web Cache and how it processes client requests for content by checking its cache and contacting the origin server if the copy of the requested content is stale or not in the cache. The overview also included a summary of how Web Cache handles dynamic content caching and Edge Side Includes (ESI) technology to cache partial pages.

You configure Web Cache using AS Control, the `opmnctl` command, or a combination of the two, depending on the situation. Security and administrative capabilities are granular in Web Cache by assigning different administrative accounts for different administrative functions in addition to restricting administrative functions to a particular set of IP addresses.

Other administrative functions include monitoring Web Cache performance and understanding Web Cache statistics available via the AS Control Web Cache home page. In addition, you can easily use the AS Control interface to configure listening and operation ports.

Once we laid the groundwork, we provided an in-depth discussion of how you configure caching, the reason you use Oracle Web Cache! We reviewed the default cache rules, how to change them, and how to create new rules. To further enhance your understanding of Web Cache's technology, we showed you how to reduce content delivery time by compressing documents that will benefit from compression technology, such as XML or word processing documents.

In the last part of this chapter, we reviewed the many ways you can automatically or manually invalidate content using a number of methods, including database triggers, scripts, or manually using the Web Cache administration pages. Finally, we reviewed how events and errors are recorded in log files in a manner similar to other components of OracleAS.

Exam Essentials

Understand the Oracle Web Cache architecture and its components. Be able to identify the core components of Web Cache and how Web Cache ensures freshness of objects in the cache. Describe the different types of content cached by Web Cache and the Oracle components and technologies you can use to cache content.

Describe the different ways to configure Web Cache's security. Understand how to change administrative passwords and divide administrator responsibilities. Be able to restrict administrative capabilities based on user, group, and IP address.

Know where to find Web Cache performance statistics. Be able to navigate to the Web Cache statistics pages and identify potential performance bottlenecks. Understand and compare the Web Cache high availability features surge protection and performance assurance.

Be able to configure ports, origin servers, and site definitions. Configure both the operational ports and the request listening ports. Understand the dependencies between configuring site definitions and origin servers.

Understand how to construct Web Cache caching rules. Understand the type of content cached by the predefined caching rules and how to add new rules. Be able to explain how content compression works and where it provides the most benefit.

Describe how to expire content using several different methods. List the different methods you can use to expire content and how to automate them. Be able to define expiration rules using the Web Cache administration pages.

Understand how Web Cache logging works and how to customize the logging environment. Be able to customize the format of the event log and the access log files and change the log format. Explain the differences among the different log file formats and when to use them. Describe how log rollover works, how to automate log management, and how to manually roll over either of the logs.

Review Questions

1. When does Web Cache cache a document? (Choose all that apply.)
   - **A.** When Web Cache starts up and the documents are marked as cacheable
   - **B.** When Web Cache is idle and documents are precached
   - **C.** When a client first requests a document
   - **D.** Immediately when an expiration policy applies to a document and there is no explicit refresh time specified
   - **E.** When a database trigger sends an invalidation message
   - **F.** When the administrator manually invalidates a document

2. Web Cache can deliver dynamic content to a client depending on a value stored in a client-side cookie. If the client restricts the use of cookies, what other method can be used to customize a client's content? (Choose the best answer.)
   - **A.** The client can receive different content based on its source IP address.
   - **B.** Cookies are the only way to deliver custom content to clients unless they use HTTPS.
   - **C.** Web Cache can use values stored in the ESI request.
   - **D.** It can use parameters embedded in the URL request.

3. Which of the following is not true about ESI?
   - **A.** ESI enables dynamic content assembly of page fragments.
   - **B.** JESI is a version of ESI that you use with OC4J and is an open standard.
   - **C.** ESI stands for Edge Side Includes.
   - **D.** ESI was developed by Oracle for use with Web Cache and is now an open standard.
   - **E.** You code ESI in a language similar to XML.

4. Which of the following commands will restart Web Cache? (Choose the best answer.)
   - **A.** `opmnctl startproc ias-component=WebCache`
   - **B.** `opmnctl restartproc ias-component=WebCache`
   - **C.** `opmnctl startproc process-type=WebCache`
   - **D.** `opmnctl restartproc process-type=WebCache`

5. Which of the following two administrator accounts do you use for maintaining the Web Cache environment?
   - **A.** `administrator` and `invalidator`
   - **B.** `administration` and `invalidation`
   - **C.** `ias_admin` and `invalidator`
   - **D.** `administrator` and `ias_admin`

6. Identify one of the reasons why you would change the default owner and group for the Web Cache processes.
   A. Oracle AS 10*g* Release 2 requires Web Cache to have a different owner than the rest of the AS components because the administrator tools are not integrated into AS Control.
   B. When you install Web Cache as a stand-alone product, the default owner is `root` and the default group is `root` and you don't want Web Cache to run with too many privileges.
   C. When you install Web Cache as part of an OracleAS infrastructure installation, the default owner is `root` and the default group is `root` and you don't want Web Cache to run with too many privileges.
   D. You want to restrict the privileges for the owner in an environment that runs a stand-alone version of Web Cache and an Oracle database.
7. Which of the following is not one of the tabs on the Web Cache home page?
   A. Performance
   B. Home
   C. Ports
   D. Administration
8. Using the `opmnctl` command, which of the following commands will restart Web Cache?
   A. `opmnctl restartproc process-type=webcache`
   B. `opmnctl restart process-type=webcache`
   C. `opmnctl restartproc ias-component=webcache`
   D. `opmnctl restartproc process-type=WC`
   E. `opmnctl restartproc process-type=WebCache`
   F. `opmnctl restart ias-component=WC`
9. Identify the feature of Web Cache that sets a limit on the number of concurrent requests that an origin application server can handle.
   A. Content streaming
   B. Compressed documents
   C. Performance assurance
   D. Surge protection
   E. Edge side throttling
10. Identify the feature of Web Cache that allows Web Cache to serve slightly stale content instead of no content at all.
   A. Content streaming
   B. Compressed documents
   C. Performance assurance
   D. Surge protection
   E. Edge side throttling

11. Web Cache can use all but which of the following sources to determine where to get content?

    A. A client-side cookie

    B. The `Host` request header

    C. The `src` attribute of the ESI tag

    D. The `Host` portion of the requested URL

12. When you define a Web Cache site in AS Control, which of the following is not a valid parameter for a site?

    A. Prefix

    B. Origin server

    C. Host

    D. Protocol

    E. Port

13. Place the following caching rules in ascending order of priority:

    1. URLs that match regular expressions
    2. Personalized pages
    3. Pages that support session tracking
    4. Static documents
    5. Multiple-version URLs
    6. URL trees that contain a document or a subtree
    7. HTTP error messages

    A. 4, 5, 2, 3, 7, 1, 6

    B. 5, 4, 2, 3, 7, 1, 6

    C. 2, 4, 5, 6, 1, 7, 3

    D. 4, 2, 7, 1, 3, 5, 6

14. Which of the following is not a valid caching rule?

    A. `.doc`

    B. `\.(gif|tif?f)$`

    C. `\.html?$`

    D. `/www/us/overstocks`

    E. `.zip`

    F. All of these are valid caching rules.

15. By default, the only response code from the origin server that Web Cache caches is which of the following?
    A. 404
    B. 400
    C. 401
    D. 200
    E. 501

16. You can automatically expire a document using all but one of the following methods.
    A. By using the Invalidation page in Web Cache Administration
    B. Using the `Expiration` HTTP header
    C. Using a duration relative to when the document was placed in the cache
    D. Using the document creation date

17. Invalidation messages can be sent using all but which of the following methods? (Choose the best answer.)
    A. The Web Cache Invalidation page
    B. Database triggers
    C. Applications written using the Web Cache API
    D. Automated Unix shell scripts
    E. The Unix `telnet` command
    F. A secondary key
    G. All of the above methods can send invalidation messages.

18. Your event log file rolls over on March 26, 2006, at 8:45 p.m. The defined filename of the active event log is `event_error_log`. What is the name of the file after it is renamed?
    A. `event_log_file.20060326_0845PM`
    B. `event_error_log.200603262045`
    C. `event_error_log.20060326_2045`
    D. `event_log_file.20060326_2045`

19. Your website contains product attributes and inventory levels for the items you sell. When an inventory control Java application updates or deletes a product from the database, you want to invalidate the product page for that item. Which of the following methods is the best method to invalidate this content?
    A. Use a database trigger.
    B. Use a Java application written with the Web Cache API.
    C. Use `telnet` from a shell script.
    D. Use the product description as a secondary key to manually invalidate the content.

20. When you define a Web Cache site in AS Control, which of the following is not a valid parameter for a site?

   A. Prefix

   B. Origin server

   C. Host

   D. Aliases

   E. Port

Answers to Review Questions

1. C, E, F. Web Cache does not precache documents; it caches documents only when they are requested by a client. There are many ways to invalidate a document; the refresh depends on the time delay specified in the policy that applies to the document.

2. D. If cookies are disallowed on the client, you can save identifying information for the client in the URL itself.

3. D. ESI was developed as an open-source product, but it was not developed by Oracle.

4. D. Using `restartproc` will kill the existing Web Cache process and create a new Unix process for Web Cache. You use `startproc` only if the process is already stopped. If you use the `ias-component` parameter, you stop all Web Cache–related processes, not just Web Cache itself.

5. A. The `administrator` account is permitted to start, stop, and restart Web Cache, change configuration settings, and send invalidation requests. The `invalidator` account is only permitted to send invalidation requests.

6. D. On a server with many different Oracle products installed, you may want to change the owner of a stand-alone Web Cache installation to ensure that the administrator cannot intentionally or unintentionally make changes to any other installed Oracle products on the server.

7. C. The Ports tab exists on the application server home page but does not appear on the Web Cache home page.

8. E. You use the `restartproc` option to restart a component, and the `process-type` option must be `WebCache`; the `process-type` parameter value is case sensitive.

9. D. Surge protection enables you to set a limit on the number of concurrent requests that the application server can handle simultaneously. When the number of requests exceeds this limit, subsequent requests are queued.

10. C. During a spike in website usage, as a system administrator you may face the choice of whether to serve slightly stale content versus no content at all. In most cases, you will choose to serve slightly stale content.

11. A. Web Cache uses all of the sources listed except for a client-side cookie to determine which origin server to use for content retrieval if it is not already in the cache.

12. D. To add a new site for Web Cache in AS Control, you must specify the host, port, prefix, origin servers, and, optionally, any aliases.

13. A. Static documents are cached with the highest priority and URL trees that contain a document or a subtree are the lowest. If a document applies to more than one rule, Web Cache caches the document using the rule with the highest priority.

14. F. All caching rules are URL expressions; you specify the caching rules as either a Unix regular expression, a file extension, or a path prefix.

15. D. Web Cache does not cache any response code other than an expected 200 OK response.

16. A. You can expire content using the Invalidation page, but it is not automatic; it is a manual process.

17. G. You use these methods for invalidation when content expiration is not predictable enough to use a fixed expiration time.

18. D. Regardless of the name of the active log file, the rolled-over log file always begins with `event_log_file` and has a time-stamp suffix in the format `yyyymmdd_hhmm`.

19. A. You can send an invalidation message from any database that supports triggers and HTTP.

20. D. To add a new site for Web Cache in AS Control, you must specify the host, port, prefix, origin servers, and, optionally, any aliases.

Managing and Configuring OracleAS Portal

ORACLE APPLICATION SERVER 10*g* ADMINISTRATION I EXAM OBJECTIVES COVERED IN THIS CHAPTER:

✓ **Managing the OracleAS Portal**

- Describe OracleAS Portal Administrative Services
- Describe tools to monitor the OracleAS Portal instance
- Manage OracleAS Portal users, groups, and schemas
- Administer the portlet repository
- Perform export and import of portal content

✓ **Configuring OracleAS Portal**

- Describe OracleAS Portal configuration tasks
- Configure the Self-Registration feature to enable users to create their own portal accounts
- Configure OracleAS Portal for WebDAV
- List the configuration modes of the Oracle Portal Configuration Assistant (OPCA)
- Configure language support
- Configure the OracleAS Portal instance dependencies by using the Portal Dependency Setting file

One of the most popular components in the Oracle Application Server 10*g* (OracleAS) suite is the portal feature. It provides end users and developers alike with the ability to call other websites or other web content into one central page. End users can customize the look and feel of their home page to include the pieces that they use most often and order that content in a way that is most intuitive to them. In this chapter, we will look at managing this powerful tool so that your users can have the most flexible interface possible.

Just as with everything else it builds, Oracle has built a central administrative interface for portal administration that allows you to monitor and configure portals and portlets from one browser-based application. You can use this interface to administer Single Sign-On, directory integration, and various other security features as they relate to portals. The Portal User Interface Administration screen in the Application Server Control console can help you perform all of the necessary configuration and administration tasks that you will face in your day-to-day administration duties. Notice that the Portal Administrative Services are a part of the overall central interface, the Application Server Control console. This means that you have one central location from which you can administer not only the portal, but also all of your application server administration tasks.

In this chapter, we will discuss how you can use this interface to help you manage portal users and groups, set up security associated with those users and groups, configure multiple language support (which is becoming more important as companies are pushing content out multinationally and globally), and configure mobile support. We will even look at how you can migrate content between different portal instances so you can manage code migration throughout your systems more efficiently and effectively, and we'll look at monitoring performance of the portal instances once your users are beginning to access them.

Managing OracleAS Portal

In order to perform most administrative tasks in the OracleAS Portal instance, you first have to log in to the portal as a portal administrator. This is probably painfully obvious, but it is a necessary step.

Once you are logged in, you use the administrative portlets that you find there to perform your basic administration tasks. Remember that even though this is a simple interface, it doesn't mean that a lot of thought and planning shouldn't go into what you end up doing here. Create a playground for yourself where you can try things out and see what does and doesn't work, but for real systems, plan before you build. Some of the tasks you will perform will need to be accomplished either through the Application Server Control interface or by running the provided configuration scripts. These scripts would have been copied into your infrastructure Oracle Home directory during the installation of Portal, so they should be easy to find.

OracleAS Portal Administrative Services provide you and your other administrators with Application Server Control–based interfaces through which you can set up and maintain your portal environment. When you couple these interfaces with the basic configuration scripts, you have a full menu from which to choose.

Managing the Portal Instance Using Application Server Control

The first, and often the most turned to, administrative interface is the Oracle Enterprise Manager 10*g* Application Server Control (better known as Application Server Control) interface. Application Server Control is automatically installed every time you install OracleAS. If you install OracleAS 10 times on the same server, by default it installs an Application Server Control interface for each instance. You and your fellow administrators can use Application Server Control to monitor and administer the OracleAS Portal instance. It provides you with the necessary tools to manage, monitor, and administer the portal instance.

In the System Components section of the OracleAS instance home page, shown in Figure 6.1, you can find entries related to the OracleAS Portal instance: `OC4J_Portal` and `Portal:portal`.

`OC4J_Portal` is an Oracle Containers for J2EE (OC4J) instance that contains all of the web applications related to the OracleAS Portal instance. Because OC4J is J2EE 1.4 compatible, and because it runs on standard J2EE distributions, it maintains its ease of use, its portability, and its flexibility as a programming interface of choice while remaining a scalable and high-performance solution for any production environment. `OC4J_Portal` includes the Parallel Page Engine (PPE), a multithreaded servlet deployed on top of the OC4J instance. The Parallel Page Engine really comes into its own when deployed in a server farm where the disparate engines can work together to retrieve content from the various portlet providers, manage caching, and assemble and deliver pages quickly to the end users without the users even having to be aware that the farm exists.

The OC4J instance gets configured automatically during portal installation and is started up as installation completes. There is little regarding configuration that you need to be concerned with, and you can start and stop `OC4J_Portal` the same way that you start and stop the other OC4J instances.

`Portal:portal` is your link to the home page of the OracleAS Portal instance in the Application Server Control. This should be the first place you go to check the condition of the OracleAS Portal instance. It is also a place that you should make a habit of checking periodically to ensure the health of your portal. Proactive maintenance is more important than reactive maintenance. From this portal home page you can manage and monitor the components that make up the OracleAS Portal instance, including the Oracle HTTP server, `mod_plsql`, Web Cache, and providers.

FIGURE 6.1 The System Components section of the OracleAS instance home page

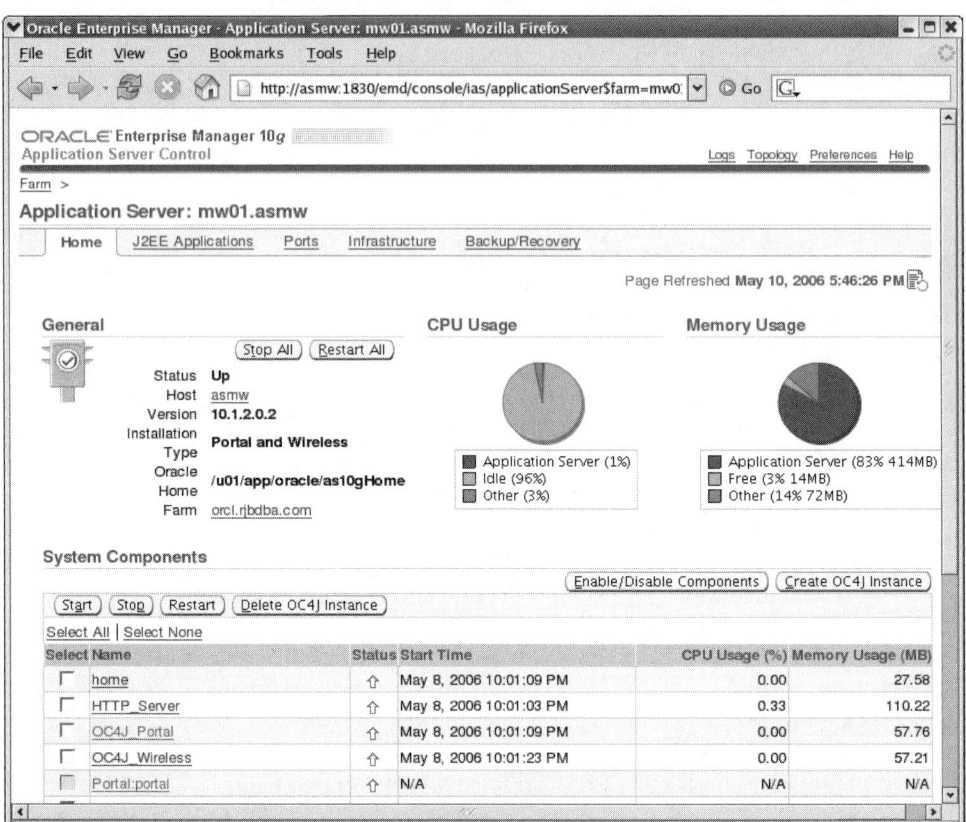

The OracleAS Portal Instance Home Page

As you can see in Figure 6.1, from the home page of the OracleAS Portal instance you can view the overall status of your portal instance, view data on how the instance is using the Application Server Metadata Repository, and check the overall status of all of the other OracleAS components on which the portal instance depends. You also can view the severity status for errors associated with the components that are used by your portal instance; the ability to do this quickly and in a central location is often one of the most important features of the interface.

From the Parallel Page Engine Service home page, shown in Figure 6.2, you can view and monitor the status of the Parallel Page Engine (PPE) or any of the components registered with the portal instance providers. From here you can go to the portlet providers' home pages, where you can monitor and view the status of the portlet providers.

FIGURE 6.2 The Parallel Page Engine Service home page

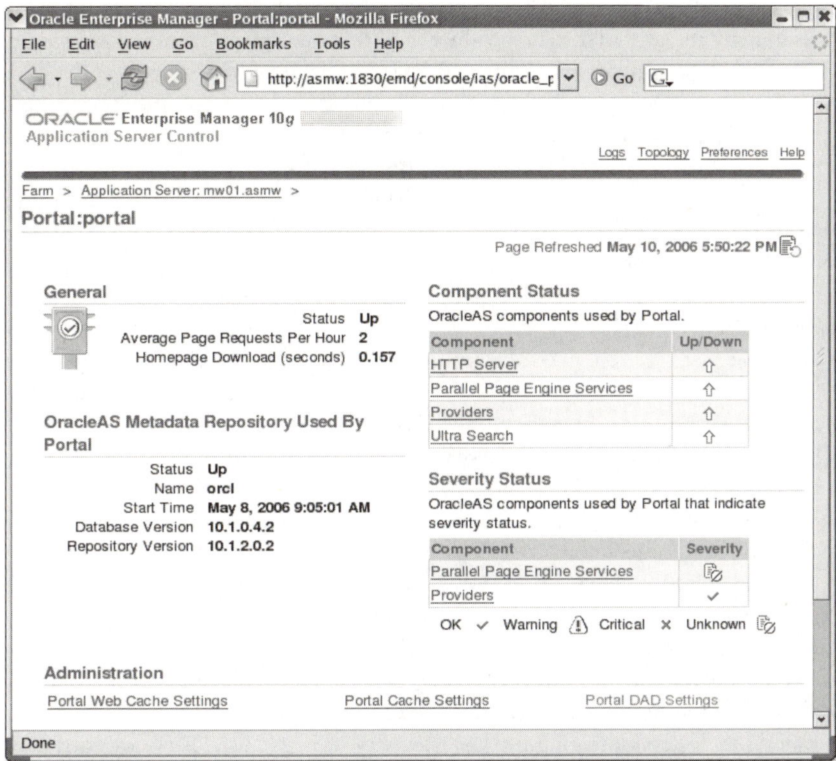

The PPE, an often-used component of the OracleAS Portal middle tier, is a shared server process servlet engine that runs in the OracleAS Containers for J2EE and services page requests. The PPE reads page metadata, calls the appropriate providers for the requested portlet content, accepts provider responses, and assembles the requested page in the specified page layout.

Whenever a user requests a page from OracleAS Portal, the request is made, naturally, from the browser and is forwarded to the Oracle HTTP Server listener and processed as normal. The returned page is likely composed of many types of portlets (an area of a portal page that contains data from a given data source). In this process, the PPE obtains the page metadata from the OracleAS Metadata Repository (the infrastructure database) and is responsible for assembling the portlets as they are returned to the user.

The Administration section of the PPE Service home page contains the Portal Web Cache Settings link, through which you can reconfigure the portal instance when you make changes to the Web Cache configuration.

The `Portal End User Default Homepage` link is located in the Related Links section and takes you to the Welcome page of the OracleAS Portal instance.

The `All Metrics` link on this page provides you with a single list of the metrics available for the portal instance.

Monitoring the OracleAS Portal Instance

Several tools are available for you to use to monitor the portal instance. Oracle is very good at providing tools that are integrated into its products and that are tuned for monitoring and administering its products. Application Server Control, OracleAS Portal activity reports and logging services, and OracleAS Portal performance reports typically are the primary tools that are employed.

You probably don't have a lot of spare time to just sit and watch what a system is doing, but by taking the time to sit and monitor the portal instance, you can start to better analyze and understand the types of activities and the volume of data and transactions that are taking place on your portal. Once you fundamentally understand this information, you can start to make better, more-informed choices concerning the portal instance that you are dealing with and take well-timed administrative actions that will be necessary to improve performance, throughput, usability, navigation, available features, and more.

Application Server Control provides immediately accessible tools that you can use to monitor your portal instance, start and stop services, view logs and ports, and access configuration settings, security settings, and performance metrics related to your portal instance.

The OracleAS Portal activity reports assist you in analyzing the data stored in the Activity Log tables and Activity Log views. These views are created automatically and exist in the portal instance; access to the views is granted to public. The logs themselves, however, are secured according to the portal object's security. You can even create your own reports from these views. They are, after all, simply views, and they can be used as you would any other view.

OracleAS Portal logging services are your tool for logging objects and actions on objects in Portal and later generating the data that can be used in your activity reports. OracleAS Portal logging services collect information about the events that you choose to register in your instance and store that information in the Activity Log tables. You can pick and choose which events are logged in the Activity Log tables by managing the Log Registry records in the Services portlet.

OracleAS Portal performance reports can be generated based on statistics collected by the `mod_plsql` performance logging service by running the Performance Reporting SQL scripts that are located in the `$ORACLE_HOME/portal/admin/plsql/perf` directory.

Make sure that you read the `README.html` file found in the `$ORACLE_HOME/portal/admin/plsql/perf` directory to find the instructions on how to load the logging data into the database and how to generate the performance reports.

Managing the Portal Instance Using Administrative Portlets

To perform the various administrative functions, you have to log in to the OracleAS Portal instance as an administrator. By default, the Portal Builder page is displayed after you have logged in to the portal.

OracleAS Portal administrative portlets are grouped based on their functions into three subtabs on the Administer tabbed page and are integrated with the other OracleAS components.

The Portal tab allows you to create portal users and groups, configure global settings for the entire portal instance, export and import OracleAS Portal objects, and administer other services. These other services that you can administer include the SSO server, Delegated Administration Services, Oracle Ultra Search, OracleAS Web Cache, and proxy settings.

The Portlets tab lets you manage the Portal Repository, which stores information about the various types of registered providers (we will cover these further shortly) and portlets in the portal. You also can use the functions on this tab to register new remote providers and provider groups.

The Database tab provides you with an interface through which you can create and edit individual database schemas and database roles and monitor database information (initialization parameters, memory consumption, and storage details). Although much of what you will administer will be connected directly with the middle tier components, remember that you have an infrastructure database that is part of the installation and you will need to have at least a working knowledge of database administration concepts in order to do an effective job working with OracleAS. You can take steps in the database to allow the portals and other application server components to perform more efficiently and effectively.

Managing Passwords for Portal Schemas

Although there are components that reside primarily on the middle tier, the OracleAS Portal product resides almost exclusively in the Oracle database. This means that you have to become familiar with database administration tasks like creating and maintaining schemas and passwords.

A schema is also known as a database user account. These accounts are used to store database schema objects (tables, views, stored procedures) and to provide database access for the human assigned (either directly or indirectly) to those objects.

During your installation, several predefined schemas are automatically created in the database for you:

`PORTAL` The `PORTAL` schema is the product schema for the OracleAS Portal. It contains all of the database objects associated with the Portal Repository as well as all of the associated PL/SQL code necessary to facilitate connectivity of the portals. This is, by design, a highly privileged database schema, and its job is to act as a proxy for the interaction between the middle tier and the database. Because of the advanced privileges that are granted to this account, it is important to ensure that only those who have a legitimate need to access the account can do so. This account allows the middle tier to have secure access to all of the other schemas in the database.

`PORTAL_PUBLIC` The `PORTAL_PUBLIC` schema is the schema that portal users map to by default. Because portal users don't have individual database schemas or database accounts, each portal user must be mapped to a database schema. The schema that these users map to should be something other than the product schema because of all of the security considerations and advanced privileges that are associated with the PORTAL_PUBLIC account.

`PORTAL_DEMO` The `PORTAL_DEMO` schema contains the OracleAS Portal demonstration code. This schema is often left in place for developers and programmers to learn what they can do with portals and how they can go about doing it.

`PORTAL_APP` The `PORTAL_APP` schema contains the OracleAS Portal applications.

The passwords for these schemas are specified at installation and are randomized and stored in the Oracle Internet Directory. You can retrieve these passwords using Oracle Directory Manager.

```
Entry management > cn=OracleContext > cn=Products >cn=IAS >
   cd=IAS Infrastructure Database > orclReferenceName=
   database > cnOrclResourceName=PORTLA_PUBLIC
```

These passwords must be changed using Application Server Control. To do so, follow these steps:

1. Click on the Infrastructure tab on the home page of the middle tier OracleAS instance.
2. In the Metadata Repository section, click the `Change Schema Password` link.
3. On the Change Schema Password page, select the schema whose password you want to change and enter a new password in the Password field. Retype the password in the Confirm Password field and click OK.

If the change was successful, you should receive the following confirmation message:

```
The operation Change Schema Password was successful.
```

You can map a new or existing application to schemas currently in the Oracle database where OracleAS Portal is installed. It is important to note that when you create the schema, you need to select the Application Schema check box so the schema and the database have the support necessary to allow applications to be built in the schema.

Whenever you create an Oracle Portal user, you also map that user to a database schema. By default, the schema that all users get mapped to is `*portal*_public`. (`*portal*`, in this case, is the schema where Oracle Portal is installed.) You can, however, map some or all of your users to another schema if you selected the Use This Schema for Portal Users check box when you created the schema. This check box tells the Oracle database to create all of the structures necessary to support the use.

OracleAS Portal provides you with two methods for creating portal schemas in your database.

Probably the simplest way is to use the schema portlet that is provided for you on the Oracle Portal home page. This portal walks you through all of the information that will be needed to create the schema in the database so it will be available to you to use as a portal schema.

Alternatively, you can use the Database Objects Navigator to create the schema and specify that it will be used as a portal schema.

Either way, you will be able to set up the new schemas to support your portal applications. This will enable you to use even an existing schema as a portal schema simply by providing the additional information necessary to make it all work. You can very quickly start building applications and new portal users associated with the new schemas.

Remember, you have to have the `CREATE ALL SCHEMAS` global privilege to create a schema. By default, all members of the DBA group have this privilege.

Managing Portal Users and Groups

Three different kinds of users come into play with Portal: SSO users, portal users, and database users.

A Single Sign-On user account can access applications by using a single user ID and password. SSO Server administrators create these users on the Administer tab of the Oracle Portal home page. (These SSO Server administrators also have to be OracleAS Portal administrators.)

A portal user account is usually simply referred to as a user account. It establishes user details, preferences, and privileges specifically within OracleAS Portal. These accounts don't have any direct privileges in the database. Ironically, because OracleAS Portal pages are displayed only by executing database-stored procedures, the OracleAS Portal user account has to be able to execute (via database-granted Execute privileges) on those procedures. To accomplish this, the OracleAS Portal user account has to be associated with a database schema that has the correct privileges granted to it.

An Oracle database user account (also known as a schema) is what stores the database objects, applications, and components and also what determines a user's database-level privileges. Database administrators create Oracle database schemas using either SQL commands or the Schemas portlet on the Database tab of the Oracle Portal home page

Portal users are set up as SSO user accounts. This allows users to access multiple applications using OracleAS Portal by providing their credentials just once. Although this might not seem like an important point for many administrators, it is a big deal for most users.

To manage the users' information and their associated group information (the information that pertains specifically to the portal environment), OracleAS Portal creates user profiles and group profiles for each and stores that information in the Oracle Internet Directory within the Portal Repository. These profiles are created automatically whenever the portal administrator first tries to edit the user profile or the group profile of a user or group. These profiles also are created the first time a user attempts to log in to OracleAS Portal using their credentials. Often, administrators will allow the profiles to be created automatically, saving time and effort.

The following portal users are created automatically during installation. The administrator needs to do nothing to create these other than install the software:

ORCLADMIN This is created for the OracleAS administrator. This user profile has the highest level of privileges in the portal. Some of the portal tools (for example, the critical SSO Server Administration portlet that will help set up the SSO settings for the portal users) are available only for this user.

PORTAL This user is the privileged OracleAS Portal superuser, kind of like system in the database or sysadmin in an E-Business Suite implementation. This user has been granted all of the privileges available in the portal.

PORTAL_ADMIN This privileged OracleAS Portal user has the most administrative privileges of all normal portal users short of the administrator and is created as the PORTAL user when the portal is installed into a schema called PORTAL. These privileges, however, exclude anything that would enable the user to grant themselves higher privileges or access the database administration features (schema creation and management). Typically, this type of user is intended to be for administrators who manage and provision portal users.

PUBLIC This user identifies unauthenticated access to the portal. All of the sessions, before authentication, use this account to access the database.

The orcladmin OID superuser and the orcladmin portal user are two *different* users that are stored in the same directory.

It is important to remember that whenever you grant a user the ability to manage privileges on any portal's home page, they are granted full privileges over that particular portal. The user cannot edit, delete, or even view any other Oracle Instant Portal unless they have been granted explicit permission to do so. They can, however, do any and all of the following:

- Create new users.
- Delete any user in the Manage User Rights dialog box, even those they did not create. (This is probably the single most important reason to restrict the number of users who have Manage privileges on a home page.)
- Create new Oracle Instant Portals.

If you want a user that was created through OracleAS Portal to have access to an Oracle Instant Portal, you must first add the user to the OIP_AVAILABLE_USERS group; then use the Manage User Rights dialog box to grant the appropriate privileges to the user.

The initial password for the ORCLADMIN user, the portal user, and the portal_admin portal users is the same as the password supplied for the ias_admin user during the installation of the OracleAS Infrastructure.

The default portal groups include the following basic groups:

OIP_USER_ADMINS A group of users who can install new Instant Portals. ORCLADMIN and PORTAL are both members of this group.

OIP_AVAILABLE_USERS A group of users who can access the Instant Portals and who appear in the Manage User Rights dialog box. Neither ORCLADMIN nor PORTAL is a member of this group, and therefore they don't appear. This is very important for securing the portals because you don't want anyone to accidentally (or accidentally on purpose) delete the administration IDs.

AUTHENTICATED_USERS A group that provides a convenient mechanism for assigning the default privileges that you want every logged-in user to have in the portal. AUTHENTICATED_USERS can log in to the portal, create all pages, and create all styles. By default, this group includes the <portal_schema> group and the <portal_schema>_ADMIN group.

DBA Members of this group have the maximum privilege level in the system; this is the only group that is allowed to manage the database through the Portal interface. All global privileges are granted to this group, including all of the "manage all" privileges. Initially, the group has exactly one user, the user with the name of the <product_schema> (portal, for example).

PORTAL_ADMINISTRATORS A group that includes users with most of the global privileges (except the database-related privileges). Group members can complete any task that is contained wholly within the middle tier except editing groups that they are not named explicitly as owning (and PORTAL_PUBLISHERS and PORTAL_ADMINISTRATORS). Members do not have any of the necessary privileges to administer OracleAS Single Sign-On. This group initially includes the PORTAL_ADMIN user and the DBA group.

PORTAL_DEVELOPERS Members of this group have privileges to build and manage local database providers and their portlets as well as shared components. They can create all Portal database providers and manage all shared components. The DBA group and the **portal_schema** group are members of the PORTAL_DEVELOPERS group.

PORTLET_PUBLISHERS This group includes users who have privileges to add portlets to Portal pages and make the portlets available to other portal users. They can publish pages, publish navigation pages, and publish Portal DB provider portlets to the OracleAS Portal. The PORTLET_PUBLISHERS group contains the PORTAL_ADMINISTRATOR group as well as the *portal_schema* group.

The default groups also include the following groups that support OracleAS Reports Services:

RW_BASIC_USER Users assigned to this group can execute already deployed reports and view less-detailed error messages than members of the other groups if their authentication fails the security checks.

RW_POWER_USER In addition to the privileges assigned to the RW_BASIC_USER, users in this group receive more-detailed error messages from the OracleAS Reports Services if they fail security checks.

RW_DEVELOPER Continuing to build on the privileges of the less-authorized users, the RW_DEVELOPER adds to the privileges available to the RW_POWER_USER; this user can run special web commands necessary to generate the Oracle Reports environment. If this user's security check fails, they will be able to view detailed error messages.

RW_ADMINISTRATOR One step more privileged than the RW_DEVELOPER, the RW_ADMINISTRATOR group has access to all of the administrator's functionality in Oracle Reports Queue Manager, can administer reports built with Oracle Reports, and can administer printer and server definitions. This means that members of this group not only can manage the server queue and perform rescheduling, but also can delete and record jobs in the server. RW_ADMINISTRATORs can create, update, and delete the registered report definition files and servers. These administrators also can navigate to the Access tab on the Components Management page, where they can specify who can or cannot access a particular report and assign security privileges. These users will receive full error messages when they are generated.

Every user who needs access to reports built with Oracle Reports and deployed to the OracleAS middle tier should belong to one of these groups. Further, the portal administrator needs to grant appropriate portal privileges to the reports-related groups.

Managing User and Group Profiles

To manage user profiles and group profiles, administrators use the Portal User Profile portlet (for user profiles) and the Portal Group Profile portlet (for group profiles).

Portal users and groups are stored in the OID. The management interface is provided by Delegated Administration Services (DAS) and is used to enter information about your portal users and groups into the OID. The OracleAS administrators and portal administrators can access DAS using a direct URL or via the User and Groups portlets from the Administer tab on the OracleAS Portal Builder page.

Creating Portal Users

When you create a new user, you are (in effect) creating nothing more than a new Single Sign-On user account in the OID that will be used by the user you are provisioning. You provision this new user via the User portlet. (In Chapter 9, we will discuss how the OID is the Lightweight Directory Access Protocol [LDAP] server that is installed with your OracleAS installation.) When you create the new user, you will need to enter some basic information for them, including username, password, and email address. Although many administrators choose to maintain minimal necessary information on the users that they create, you can optionally enter other information as well. You can enter job-related details (such as job title and description), telephone number, and location address. Some administrators are even willing to maintain photographs in GIF or JPG format as a way to provide better identification of users to others in the organization.

You can now assign the newly created user to one of the existing portal groups. You can assign fine-grained portal privileges to each user to augment those that are provided based on the group to which they were assigned. There is also a section in this area where you can enter individualized resource access information for the user associated with Forms and Reports applications as well as default connection string information necessary to allow a user to attach to the data source that should be used when running reports. This is particularly important when you have multiple data sources along with reports for which a particular data source needs to be accessed.

Editing Portal User Profiles

The Portal User Profile portlet enables you to define a user's information in that OracleAS Portal instance. It is very interesting that OracleAS is such a big user of its own portlets. It says something about the faith that Oracle puts in its applications.

On the Preferences tabbed page, you can configure the following user profiles:

Allow User to Log On This is a handy little profile setting for users to have. It is rather difficult for them to get much computing done in the portlet if they can't log on. However, it is also handy for administrators to have the ability to deny the user from logging on if for some reason that user ID needs to be disabled temporarily (for reasons such as administrative activities, maintenance, or temporary account locking). A simple check box is all that it takes to enable or disable the user from logging on.

Database Schema Remember, portal users don't have any direct database privileges. This can create problems when you remember that portal pages are displayed by virtue of executing stored database procedures. This means that portal users who don't have database privileges, or even direct database connectivity, must have execute privileges on those procedures. This can create problems of the "you just can't get there from here" kind. To overcome these issues, each portal user must be associated with a database schema that has the appropriate privileges necessary to display the necessary portal pages. Recall that, by default, new portal users are associated with the `PORTAL_PUBLIC` schema.

Default Group The default group determines the preferences for the user if no personal preferences are specified.

Default Style You can preselect the style that should be used as all users' default style. The default style is used when pages are set to the user's default style and a given user doesn't have a default style selected. The selection can be made either directly by the user or indirectly by the administrator for them. If these choices aren't made, and if a group's default style isn't set, the system default style is used. If the users decide that they don't like what you selected for them (or that you maybe haven't selected for them), they can change this setting on the Account Information page on their own. This can free you, the administrator, to do other administration tasks and can provide a level of autonomy for the end users and a way to express their individuality.

Default Home Page The default home page setting provides the first page that will be displayed to the user after they log in to the OracleAS Portal (so it will not affect the home page that the browser identifies as the user's preference). These two pages can be the same, but they don't have to be. If the user specifies a personal home page as their portal home page, that page is displayed when the user logs in. However, if the user fails to specify one, the default home page assigned to the user is displayed. If the user is assigned to a group and doesn't specify a home page, the default home page of the group is displayed. If no default home page is assigned to the user (either by the administrator or by the user) and the group to which the user belongs does not have a default home page assigned to it, then the system's default home page will be displayed. Notice the pattern? Make note of it: The pattern—if not user, then group, if not group, then system—is the hierarchy that you should remember.

Default Mobile Home Page Similar to the Default Home Page (but with different ramifications), you can set the Default Mobile Home Page attribute if mobile support is enabled in the portal. With the mobile page design global setting enabled, you can specify a certain home page to be displayed when the portal is accessed using a mobile device. If you select Default Mobile Home Page here, it will override the setting of the user's default group. You can't enter your own values into this parameter; you just have to pick from a list of values that are appropriate. This parameter is available only if mobile support is enabled.

Clear the Cache in Web Cache for User If you select this check box, it will invalidate the pages associated with the user in the Web Cache and will force generation of new pages for the user. This feature can be important when users change job descriptions, resulting in default group changes. You will want them to be able to view the information associated with the new group, not the old—perhaps to help keep their concentration focused on the new job or to tighten security. It won't remove the memories of the data already seen, but it will keep secure the data that has been added since the changeover. This attribute can be set back at a future point in order to leverage the Web Cache features.

Mapping Portal Users to a Custom OracleAS Portal Access Schema

There may be times that you will want to map a portal user to a database schema that is different than the default portal schema but still provides similar privileges as the default portal access schema (`PORTAL_PUBLIC`). This can happen when a company has legacy database applications that should be accessed by only a limited number of portal users. Allowing `PORTAL_PUBLIC` to access the other systems would open them up to too many people. In a case like this, when you need to add an additional layer of security, you might want to create a new custom portal access schema that can either only access the legacy application or potentially access both. Naming conventions should, of course, be followed if they exist in your organization, but descriptive names for portal schemas are better than terse cryptic ones. In this case, something like `mylegacy_portal` might be appropriate.

This custom OracleAS Portal access schema should be granted all of the necessary database privileges from an application product schema to be able to run the application code and access the appropriate application data in addition to being granted whatever other privileges are necessary to meet the business requirements.

To map the portal user to a custom OracleAS Portal access schema, perform the following steps:

1. Create the custom schema in the database and grant it the appropriate privileges.
2. Add the custom OracleAS Portal access schema to the list of database schemas to which the users can map. This means that in the Schemas portlet, select a database schema, click Edit, and select the Use This Schema for Portal Users check box. Then apply the changes.
3. Now, edit the user profile necessary to provide the applicable access and select the custom portal access schema in the Database Schema field.

Creating Portal Groups

There will be times when the preseeded groups (the groups that come by default with the portal installation) will no longer suffice in your implementation. When this occurs, you will need to create a new custom portal group. When you create a new portal group, you specify basic information such as name, display name, and a description of the group, and you specify the visibility of the group as either public or private. If you specify private, the group will be visible only to its owners; specifying public will allow it to be seen by everyone. The default visibility is public. If you specify the new group to be privileged, you can then assign privileges to the group.

The group's creator is the automatic group owner. You can specify additional owners for the group now or at a later time. New users can be assigned as group members and privileges can be assigned to the group.

Editing Portal Group Profiles

The Portal Group Profile portlet provides an interface through which you can make alterations and define and alter group information that pertains specifically to the portal instance in question. As with the Portal User Profile portlet, you can set the default home page for users who have the group set as their default group. Users who set their own home page will override this setting.

You can specify a default style for the portal pages or other global privileges for the group in the same manner.

Remember, if your users don't customize their own settings, the default user settings or the group settings will take over; failing this, the settings will go to the group defaults.

Assigning Privileges to OracleAS Portal Users and Groups

Oracle allows you, as the administrator, as well as security administrators in your organization to decide at what level of granularity you want to control access. You can assign privileges at the user level or the group level. There are two distinct groups of privileges that can be assigned to portal users.

Oracle Application Server Privileges are those that enable users to perform user and group management, assign access rights to other users and groups, and configure user entries and subscriber information by using the Delegated Administration Service. These privileges are stored in OID along with the user or group information.

OracleAS Portal object privileges give a user or a group a certain level of access on a particular instance of a portal object rather than on all objects of that type. This can allow you the freedom to customize the security to the extent that it is necessary in your organization.

User and Group Lists of Values

User, Group, Portal User Profile, and Portal Group Profile portlets include lists of values (LOVs) for users and groups. These must be populated with information that is stored within the directory. Just as with any LOV, the data have to come from somewhere, either typed directly into the list or generated from existing data.

User and Group LOVs work efficiently in OracleAS Portal 10*g* through the implementation of a new callback method. Oracle Delegated Administration Services posts the selected values to the callback method in the portal's domain to avoid cross-domain JavaScript issues that were a plague in the past. This callback method requires support from both OracleAS Portal and Oracle Delegated Administration Services. This support is available in Oracle Application Server 10*g* Release 2 of these components.

If you have upgraded from an earlier version of OracleAS Portal 10*g* R2 or if OracleAS Portal is used against an older version of Oracle Delegated Administration Services that does not support the callback method, you must perform the following configuration steps:

1. Execute `secjsdom.sql` to reset the common domain to the one that was defined originally.
2. If OracleAS Portal was configured to use the locally deployed Oracle Delegated Administration Services servlet, reconfigure it to point to the Infrastructure tier by running the `secdaslc.sql` script.

The Portlet Repository

The Portlet Repository stores registration information about providers and their portlets that are available in the OracleAS Portal instance. The Portlet Repository is created during installation, and the initial Portlet Repository stores information about the built-in providers and their portlets that are installed and configured for administration, development, and general use by different groups of portal users.

When you register a new provider, information about that provider and its portlets is automatically added to the Portlet Repository.

The Portlet Repository is implemented as a part of the Portal Repository in the portal product schema. To display the Portlet Repository to portlet users, OracleAS Portal is shipped with a special page group (the Portlet Repository page group). This page group's content populates the Add Portlets page that is displayed when the portal user wants to add a portlet to a portal page. What the portal user can see on the Add Portlets page depends on the user's portal privileges as the portal administrator defines them.

Accessing the Portlet Repository

The Portlet Repository can be accessed from the Providers tabbed page of the Portal Navigator. All providers that are available in the portal instance are grouped into three provider groups:

Locally Built Providers Providers that were created by using the tools available in the OracleAS Portal. When a portlet developer creates a form portlet or a report portlet using Portlet Builder, a new database provider is created in the Locally Built Providers group. The registration of these locally built providers is handled by the portal instance internally.

Registered Providers Providers that have been registered with the OracleAS Portal instance through the registration process by the portal administrator.

Provider Groups The logical collection of web providers that is defined by a remote Provider Group Service. Once a provider is registered, a Provider Group simplifies the process of registering the providers in the group.

Managing the Portlet Repository

You can perform many management tasks associated with the Portlet Repository, including registering providers, updating provider registration information, refreshing the Portlet Repository and any individual providers, and organizing the Portlet Repository page group.

Registering providers is the most frequent management task that most portal/portlet administrators have to perform. Registration of providers adds information about providers and their portlets to the Portlet Repository. Portlet developers typically submit the setup instructions that include registration details about the provider when they are migrating their applications through different environments.

When you update registration details about existing providers in the system in the Portlet Repository, you can update the display name or time-out message, or you can change access to the provider for portal users.

When there are changes in provider implementation (such as new portlets added to the provider) you, as the administrator, will need to refresh the provider registration information in the Portlet Repository. You can accomplish this in either of two ways. First, you can refresh an individual provider, which is cheaper and less time consuming (from a people perspective and a CPU perspective). When you refresh an individual provider, the portal contacts the provider in question and updates the list of the provider's portlets in the repository. The second option, refreshing the entire Portlet Repository, updates all of the information about all of the providers that are registered in the repository. This can be very time and resource intensive, particularly if the Portlet Repository is sizeable. This full refresh should be performed when the load on the OracleAS Portal instance is minimal. During the task, the portal contacts all of the registered providers and updates their registration information in the Portlet Repository.

Let's face it, administrators as well as end users like to be able to customize their interfaces. They like to be able to group their pages and organize them to best meet their own likes and needs. This can add greatly to everyone's ability to effectively do their job. You or your users can customize the display of the Portlet Repository by organizing the Portlet Repository page group content. This can ease the way for everyone to locate their most used and required portlets. This is particularly important when you have many portlets that relate to a similar theme.

Most organizations will have multiple portlets on any one given subject area. This is really as it should be—modularizing applications so you can have a finer level of security over time. To accomplish this, you can create one big page (such as accounting, accounts payable, accounts receivable, human resources, marketing, or sales). In a perfect world, that page should be named something logical relating to all of the information on it. Then, within the Portlet Repository page group, you can move portlet items from their original pages to this central page as appropriate to the theme. You can even create links to other similarly organized pages to further add to the granularity of security to each additional layer.

To further drive security as far into the application as possible, you can secure access to the content of the Portlet Repository by granting access to the pages themselves and further to the portlet items of the Portlet Repository page group. Typically, users will try to get to things if those things are there. If people in marketing, for example, see in the list of values the entry for accounts receivable, they may decide that they ought to be able to see the effect of what they are doing on the overall organization. This is normal human nature to an extent. However, it is also typically not something the business sees as appropriate. Allowing different portal users to see different lists of values will limit these tendencies by not allowing them to even see the portals and portlets that they haven't been granted privileges to see. You set these privileges on the Add Portlets page and the differences are based on their privileges in the Portlet Repository page group. All of the options can be grouped behind the scenes to make security and application administration simpler.

Refreshing the Portlet Repository

There will come a time when you have to refresh your Portlet Repository. The Portlet Repository portlet enables you to display the Portlet Repository, refresh the Portlet Repository, or view the Portlet Repository Refresh Log.

When you refresh the Portlet Repository, registration information about your providers and their portlets will be updated in the repository. This involves creating portlet items for each new portlet along with the portlet translations.

Exceptions will be raised during the refresh process if any error conditions occur. These exceptions are captured in the Refresh Log.

A side effect of this process is that all pages that contain any of the updated portlets will have their page caches invalidated.

Displaying the Portlet Repository Page Group

So, the Portlet Repository page group is a wonderfully handy tool. It displays information about the portlets that are available in the portal instance. It is not much different from any of the other page groups in OracleAS Portal; it is organized in a hierarchy of portal pages and displays information about available portlets as portlet items. But the question remains: How do you get there from here?

It's simple: You can view the Portal Repository page group from the Portal Navigator or from the Portlet Repository administrative portlet.

Organizing the Portlet Repository Page Group

Think you're stuck with the out-of-the-box, vanilla Portlet Repository page group? Do you know that the page group is utilitarian but wish you could personalize and customize the interface to make better use of your overall administration time? Fear not; this too is customizable.

You can create standard pages, move portlet items between pages, and rearrange portlet items within a page. You can edit the Portlet Repository style or the Portlet Repository template.

Whenever you register a new provider, a new portal page is created under the Portal Staging Area page in the Portlet Repository page group. The new page's name is the same as the provider's display name, and the new page contains the portlet items for each of the provider's portlets.

You can reorganize the content of the Portlet Repository page group to help your portal users more easily browse the Portlet Repository. You could even apply a corporate style to the Portlet Repository pages. You can create additional pages within it, rearrange portlet items on the pages, move portlet items between pages, change the appearance of the Portlet Repository by editing the style, or change the layout of all the pages by editing the layout of the Portlet Repository page template.

Securing the Portlet Repository Page Group

Security, today more than ever, is uppermost in the minds of many administrators and many more managers in the organization. In the Portlet Repository page group, users are allowed to see all of the providers and portlets that they have privileges to view. If you don't limit the privileges, you don't limit the providers and portlets users can view. Not only do you have the ability to control access to providers by editing their registration information, but you also can secure the information about the available portlets by controlling user access to the Portlet Repository page group.

It is important that you have the ability to control which users can access which pages in the Portlet Repository page group by granting privileges in the Access Settings section of the Access tabbed page.

You can also control the security settings at the portal level, thereby controlling who can even see the portlet on a page. This is accomplished by editing the portlet item access privileges in the Portlet Repository on the Edit Portlet page.

Registering a Provider

Before you can use the portlets, you need to register a provider with the portal. Provider registration puts a fancy-sounding slant on the process that you use to inform OracleAS Portal about how users can access the provider. These providers are registered through the OracleAS Portal Web user interface. Once it is registered, the provider and all of its portlets become available in the Portlet Repository and are listed in the OracleAS Portal Navigator. Portlets can then be deployed to OracleAS Portal through web providers, Web Service for Remote Portlets (WSRP) producers, or database providers.

Whenever you register a new provider, you define the provider connection information that allows the provider to be contacted by the portal. The provider returns registration information to the portal. This information includes the list of the provider portlets and their attributes.

During the process of registration, the provider can perform provider-level initializations (load error messages and strings to be used in the portlets). The portal saves the provider registration information in the Portlet Repository, creates a new page in the Portlet Repository page group, and adds the portlet items for each of the provider portlets to that page. Finally, the portal grants the Manage privilege on the provider to the user who registers the provider and sets the provider's status to ONLINE.

Updating the Provider Registration Information

You can use the Remote Providers portlet to do much of the maintenance associated with provider registration. Through this interface, you can update previously registered providers. You can either enter the provider name in the Name field or select the provider from the pop-up list that is displayed when you click the List icon next to the Name field.

By clicking the Edit button, you open the Edit Provider Registration page. This page contains three tabs on it:

Main The Main tab enables you to change the display name of the provider or enter information about how long to wait for a response from the provider.

Connection The Connection tab lets you edit the connection information of the provider.

Access The Access tab allows you to control the security of the provider by selectively granting access to the provider to portal users and groups. You can take a provider offline when it is temporarily unavailable. The portal does not contact the provider until the provider comes back online. In the Cache Invalidation section of the Access tab, you can clear the Web Cache entries for the provider to make sure that the changes you make are effective immediately rather than when the cache flushes naturally.

If you need to update a WSRP type of provider, the Edit Provider Registration page provides you with the following two additional tabs:

Properties The Properties tab enables you to enter values for registration properties for producers that have them.

User Categories The User Categories tab enables you to map WSRP producer user categories to portal groups unless it is one of the standard categories that is already mapped to portal groups by default.

In production environments, provider deployment and the registration process should be kept strictly under the control of the portal administrator.

Database Providers

In this discussion, database providers are PL/SQL packages that communicate with OracleAS Portal. PL/SQL portlets are program units that are used to implement the business logic and produce HTML output. Both database providers and PL/SQL portlets use application programming interfaces (APIs) from the Portal Developer Kit (PDK) and Web PL/SQL Toolkit.

In the OracleAS Portal architecture, the portal never actually communicates with a portlet directly. Portals talk to the providers. The database provider is a PL/SQL package that implements communication methods that are required by OracleAS Portal. These methods are used to retrieve information about, or to display, the provider's portlet.

PL/SQL portlets, in turn, communicate with OracleAS Portal through the database provider, which is implemented in PL/SQL and is deployed in the Oracle database where the portal is installed. You have to register the database provider explicitly.

Data driver portlets, which are built with Portlet Builder, communicate with OracleAS Portal through database providers. You do *not* need to register the Portal Builder providers with OracleAS Portal explicitly. They are registered automatically by OracleAS Portal.

Portal developers, much like many web programmers, use APIs. However, portal developers use the APIs that are specified in the PDK and the Web PL/SQL Toolkit to code the database providers and the PL/SQL portlets.

Installing the Database Provider and Its PL/SQL Portlets

When you install the database provider and its associated portlets, you first need to create a provider schema in which to store the PL/SQL packages. It is highly recommended that this schema not be the same one where the OracleAS Portal is installed. The following script creates the `oradbabc` user and grants the necessary privileges to the user associated with the provider:

```
Create user <oradbabc> identified by <mypassword>;
Grant connect, resource to <oradbabc>;
```

Now that you have a user, you need to create the necessary synonyms to the objects in the OracleAS Portal PL/SQL APIs stored in the portal schema. To do this, log in to the portal schema and grant the privileges to call the PL/SQL APIs to the provider schema. This is accomplished by running the `provsyns.sql` script that you can find in the `%ORACLE_HOME%\portal\admin\plsql\wwc` directory for the OracleAS portal instance, as follows:

```
Connect portal/portal_pass
@provsyns.sql oradbabc
```

You only have to grant execute privileges on the OracleAS Portal PL/SQL APIs once per provider schema.

Next you need to install the PL/SQL packages of the database provider and its PL/SQL portlets in the new provider schema. To do this, log in to the database as the new provider and run the scripts necessary to create the database provider and its PL/SQL portlets. The `new_database_provider.sql` script should contain the PL/SQL code that creates packages for the database provider and its PL/SQL portlets:

```
connect oradbabc/mypassword
@new_database_provider.sql
```

The `new_database_provider.sql` script needs to be supplied by whoever is supplying you with the new database provider.

Registering the Database Provider with OracleAS Portal

More GUI tools! To register the database provider with OracleAS Portal, do the following:

1. Log in to the OracleAS Portal as the portal administrator and click on the Administer tab on the Portal Builder page.
2. Click on the Portlets subtab.
3. Click the `Register a Provider` link in the Remote Providers portlet.
4. You are now presented with the Register Provider Wizard. In the Register Provider Wizard, enter the values for the following database provider properties:
   a. Name is a unique name. This name can be up to 200 characters for the database provider.
   b. Display Name is the name that appears on the Add Portlets page with the provider's portlets listed under it.

c. Timeout is the number of seconds that OracleAS Portal should attempt to connect to this provider before displaying the time-out message.

d. Timeout Message is the text of the message that you want to display whenever the OracleAS Portal cannot establish contact with the database provider within the number of seconds specified in the Timeout field.

e. Implementation Style is the type of implementation style chosen for this provider. In this case, choose Database.

5. Click Next to get to the next step of the wizard. On this page, the display that you see depends on the provider implementation style that you selected in the previous step (in this case, database).

6. The display will request that you enter the values for the following:

   a. Owning Schema is the name of the provider schema that you configured.

   b. Package Name is the name of the PL/SQL package that is responsible for implementing the provider.

   c. Login Frequency is the variable that determines the frequency of the calls that OracleAS Portal makes to the provider in order to perform its special processing before any part of the portlet is executed. This is typically not an arbitrary number but is specified in the provider documentation. Typically, the value gets set to Never.

7. At this point, click Finish to complete the provider registration.

Using a WSRP Provider

WSRP is a communication protocol that is often used between portal servers and their portal containers. Another protocol that can be used is Java Specification Request (JSR) 168. JSR 168 is a Java API that can be used to enable portlets to work with portals (`javax.portlet.package`).

The combination of these different protocols with the standard protocols allows developers to provide a wider variety of portlets to the end users of the organization. The overall combination allows you to integrate applications from any internal or external source as portlets.

The WSRP standard can be used for communication between portlets and the OracleAS Portal Server. It is a web services standard that provides you with the ability to integrate GUI user-facing web services with portals or other web applications. It enables the interaction and interoperability between containers that conform to the standard and any WSRP portal. These standards-compliant containers can be based on any particular language (Perl, Java, or .NET, for example). These portlets, which are WSRP enabled, can then be rendered on any portal that supports the standard.

WSRP producers contain all of the information that is, necessarily, specific to them. This includes the Web Services Description Language (WSDL) URL and any session handling information that is supplied by the producers.

JSR 168 provides the descriptions associated with the Java Portlet API that are necessary for building portlets.

Registering a WSRP Provider

Registration of a WSRP is little different from registration of a database provider:

1. Log in to OracleAS Portal as the portal administrator.
2. Click on the Portlets subtab
3. Click the `Register a Provider` link in the Remote Providers portlet.
4. In the first step of the wizard, enter provider-specific properties such as name, display name, time-out value, and time-out message, and then select WSRP as the implementation style. With the exception of selecting WSRP as the implementation style, this should sound familiar so far.
5. Click Next to proceed to the next step of the wizard.
6. In the WSDL URL field, enter the URL of the Web Services Description Language (WSDL) document that contains the relevant description of the WSRP provider.
7. Click Next.
8. At this point, the portal fetches the WSDL document that you referenced in the URL and retrieves from it the provider information.

If you need to add any required property values, or if you need to set specific security for the relevant provider, you can look to the *Oracle Application Server 10*g *Release 2 (10.1.2) Portlet Developer Guide.*

Web Providers

Web providers are J2EE applications that are distributed by portlet developers as Enterprise Archive (EAR) files. An EAR file is little more than a Java Archive (JAR) file that contains a J2EE application. To clarify, realize that a J2EE application is simply a group of web modules that work together to perform as a single entity. A web module consists of one or more resources (HTML files, Java class files, XML files, etc.). Web modules are packaged in Web Archive (WAR) files. Looking at it from a top-down view, EAR files contain JAR files and WAR files. Packaging resources in WAR files, JAR files, and eventually EAR files makes it easier to reuse and reassemble components as new J2EE applications and distribute them to new environments. (There's no need to reinvent the wheel when there are so many perfectly good wheels already lying around the organization.)

Web providers may live on the same application server as OracleAS Portal or on a remote application server. For that matter, they can even be grouped together anywhere on the network that is accessible from the application server. This can be another key feature you can use to enhance your organization's ability to tighten security. By placing the web providers on a highly secured and separate server, you can obfuscate their location and add another layer of hoops that anyone might have to jump through in order to compromise the system.

OracleAS Portal Developer Kit provides you with a Java framework that simplifies the task of building web providers. Because they can be deployed to a J2EE container, there is no additional load location on the OracleAS Portal Repository database. They can be deployed on the OracleAS middle tier just like any other J2EE application.

Web providers can not only use J2EE for deployment of their applications, they can also use most open standards (XML, SOAP, HT). These standards can be allowed to communicate effectively and efficiently with the OracleAS Portal interface. If you want your portlet applications to be able to talk to other web providers, you create a provider that manages the portlets and that can also communicate with the OracleAS Portal using Simple Object Access Protocol (SOAP).

Testing Web Providers

Once you have set up a web provider, you need to test the setup to make sure that you are seeing anticipated behavior. This should always be a part of your employment process. To test the web provider, enter the URL of the provider adapter servlet in the following format:

```
http://<host.name:port>/<context_root>/<providers>
```

If your deployment succeeded, you should see a test page returned to your browser. It is possible that access to the provider test page can be denied. You can specify the default value of the `showTestPage` Java Naming and Directory Interface (JNDI) variable in the `web.xml` file that is located in the middleware code tree in `Oracle_Home` in the `sysman/webapps/default/WEB-INF` directory. The following code snippet shows an example of this:

```
<env-entry>
   <env-entry-name>
   oracle/portal/sample/showTestPage
   </env-entry-name>
<env-entry-type>java.lang.String<env-entry-type>
<env_entry-value>true</env-entry-value>
</env-entry>
```

If the test page is disabled, you will get a "403 Forbidden" error message as opposed to a "404 File Not Found" response to the test page request.

Registering Web Providers

Web providers contain information that is specific to a particular type of provider, such as the URL of the provider, the user's identity that is communicated to the provider, and proxy information. Since web providers can reside on any host in the network that is accessible from the OracleAS Portal, the administrator must specify, along with the URL, whether the portlet provider takes advantage of any of the session-handling PDK Java-specific services.

Here's how to register the provider:

1. In the Remote Providers portlet, click the `Register a Provider` link to launch the Register Provider Wizard.

2. Enter the provider properties of name, display name, time-out, and time-out message and select the implementation style of Web.
3. Click Next to proceed to the final step of the wizard.
4. In the final step of the wizard, for the web style provider, define the provider's general properties. (The URL property is the only property that actually depends on the environment in which it is deployed.) This is the URL that you have to enter when testing the web provider. When you enter the URL, you need to omit the web service name from the end of the URL. No values should be entered in this step other than the URL and the values provided by the portlet developer in the web provider installation instructions.

Adding a Portlet to the Portal Page

Once you have installed and registered the portlet, the PL/SQL portlet can be added to a portal page. To accomplish this, you need to edit your portal page:

1. Select the portlet region in which you want the portlet to appear and click the Add Portlet icon.
2. In the Add Portlets window, select the portlet that you want to display on your page.
3. Click the portlet title link and add it to the region.
4. Click OK.

The portlet will now be displayed on your page.

The Portlet Staging Area page of the Portlet Repository is where the portlets appear when a provider is first registered with the portal.

Exporting and Importing Objects in OracleAS Portal

Much like an Oracle database, OracleAS Portal provides a set of utilities to import and export data. In the case of Portal, they are to help you as the administrator migrate portal content between different OracleAS Portal instances. A prime example of when this would be beneficial is when you need to update or copy portal objects among development, testing, system integration testing, user acceptance testing, and production environments as you promote the code through your organization.

You can use import/export to support your attempts to stage your content on one or more preproduction instances before they are deployed in the production environments. If you have created a cloned production instance in preparation for migrating code into the production instance, you can migrate your code and its supporting objects using export from one environment and import into the other as a way to simply drop all of the new code into the environment at one time. By exporting from several disparate instances into one central instance, you can consolidate your applications and your maintenance in one central location.

All this being said, by this time you should know that exporting and importing, by their very nature, are a way to deploy absolutely identical content on multiple locations, or one central location, at one time. The only caveat in all of this is that the databases that you are importing to and exporting from need to be the same version.

Exporting objects from the source instance starts with the creation of a transport set. Once you have created the transport set, you populate it with the objects that you need to export from one environment in preparation for importing it into another environment.

What is a transport set? It is nothing more than a collection of OracleAS Portal objects grouped for export from a source instance or import into a target instance. It can contain one object or multiple objects of a particular type, such as multiple page groups or pages.

Once you have gathered all of the objects that need to be in your transport set, you generate the export/import script in EXPORT mode. When run in EXPORT mode (`-mode = export`), this script will create a dump file (`.dmp`) that will contain the transport set. For anyone with a database administration background, this naming convention and the associated utilities should look somewhat familiar. Imports use dump files and exports produce them. The export/import of objects relies on the same export/import utilities that have long been a mainstay of the Oracle database.

At this point, you need to manually transfer this dump file to a location that is accessible by the instance into which you want to import the objects. This can be done by using network-attached storage, remote-mounting the file system to the new location, or physically transferring the file via removable media.

Once the file is in a location that is readable by the target instance, import the dump file using the export/import script in IMPORT mode (`-mode = import`).

Finally, now that you have imported the new objects into the target database, you need to merge these new objects into the target instance using the Export/Import Transport Set portlet.

Creating a Transport Set

How, then, do you create a transport set? You simply log in to the Portal Navigator as an administrator and select a portal object that you want to have in your transport set. Click the Export action and provide a name for your transport set. Although you may be tempted to name your transport sets something based on your current tastes, it is much better to have a naming convention in place and to use that convention to maintain your transport set names. One naming convention that we like is `<TS_myinitials_date_schema>`, so you'll end up with something like `TS_ajw_02jan06_portal1`.

Now that you have a name, you can save the transport set so you can add more objects to it either now or later, or you can use it now and export it out for use.

You can select objects starting at the topmost level in the object tree, the page groups, or you can export individual objects (categories, styles, perspectives); however, if you choose not to export the entire page group, the page group has to already exist in the target instance. For this reason, the first time you export, you must always export and then import the entire page group. It is also advantageous to export and import entire page groups whenever you are doing this maintenance so you are sure that you have all of the associated code and nothing gets missed.

Whenever you export a page group, not only do you export all of the objects within that page group, but also all of the shared objects that are referenced by that page group. OracleAS

Portal will attempt to register these objects (pages, categories, perspectives, styles, custom types, providers, ACLs) that are associated with the page groups during the migration of the metadata. If the provider cannot be contacted during registration, it will not be migrated and there will be associated messages written to the log file.

Editing a Saved Transport Set

There will be times when you need to take a saved transport set and edit it. This is simple, if you navigate to the Export/Import Transport Set portlet. From there, select the transport set that you need to manipulate from the list of available saved transport sets.

You can use the interface to modify the security associated with selected portal objects in the set, remove any object that you don't need to export/import, or add new objects to the transport set.

Exporting a Transport Set

Once you have at least one saved transport set, you can start an export. Select the transport set from the list of saved sets and export it by clicking the Export Now button in the Edit Transport Set Wizard. Once it is exported, it is considered to be complete and can therefore no longer be edited. At this point, Portal considers the transport set to be exported; however, all that has really happened is that a script has been generated by the wizard that you can copy into your Unix box or your Windows machine's command window and use to perform the actual export.

You run this script in EXPORT mode to generate the dump file that contains the references to the transport set that is ready for migration. When you run the script, it is necessary to provide the following parameters:

-mode The export/import script mode; for export this parameter must be set to `export` (for import it must be set to `import`).

-d The name of the dump file.

-c The connection string needed to connect to the database that contains the source OracleAS Portal instance. If this is not correctly qualified, the export will fail.

-s The portal schema from which you are exporting. This will typically be the `portal` schema unless you have defined other custom portal schemas in your environment.

-p The password for the schema identified by the `-s` parameter. This password can be extracted from OID if necessary.

Importing a Transport Set

Running the script created in the source instance in IMPORT mode (`-mode = import`) will load the dump file, not the target portal instance.

To import a transport set, you take the exported dump file to the target instance and run the import utility with the same parameters you used in EXPORT mode. This will make the file ready, in the target instance, to be incorporated into the target environment.

The import script contains an optional parameter, `-company`, that can be specified if you are importing what was provided from a hosted environment. The default for this parameter assumes that you are exporting and importing internally and is therefore `none`.

There are a few other differences between importing and exporting:

-s The schema in the target instance from which you exported the transport set

-pu The portal user that will log in to the target OracleAS Portal instance. This is often the same as the `-s` parameter, but it still must be specified.

-p The source instance's password for the portal schema.

-pp The password for the target instance's portal user identified in `-pu`.

Once the file has been imported, you then can log in to the target OracleAS Portal instance as one of the portal administrators and navigate to the Administer tab of the Builder page. On this tab, you can select from the list of already imported transport sets in the Export/Import Transport Set portlet and click Import.

Before it allows you to start the import, the wizard gives you the opportunity to set which of the three import modes that you want to use:

Overwrite Mode This will cause existing objects with the same name as objects in the transport set to be overwritten. This is a good mode to use when you are migrating code from one instance to another and you know that you want to have all changes incorporated into the target instance. It does mean, however, that you have to be sure that you always use unique naming when you name objects.

Ignore Warnings During Import Use this mode when you want to ignore warnings that would ordinarily be raised during the import process. This mode will isolate those objects that cause errors to be raised and import successful objects.

Check-Only This can be used (and really should be used first) whenever you import a new transport set. It allows you to see what would have been done if you had just imported the set but without any of the actual ramifications occurring. During a check-only run, no changes will actually occur on the target instance; instead, you will be able to review those objects that would have been overwritten or reused. This can allow you to make intelligent and informed decisions as to whether to actually take the final step of starting the import.

You can check your import's progress by keeping an eye on the log files that are being generated and analyzing any errors that may present themselves in the files.

It is important to note here that you don't actually have to import all of the transport sets that you export. One handy use of exported transport sets is as a backup for existing instance portals. These can be brought out if someone decides that they are going to make alterations to an existing set of pages and then decides that they didn't really mean to make the changes after all.

Alternatively, when it comes time to mothball a page group, exporting it in a transport set is a good way to assure that you can get it back when someone decides that they really weren't ready to have the page group deleted after all. Just as exporting a database schema before you drop its contents is a good way to cover yourself when someone asks you to do this kind of maintenance, it is just as good a practice to export a transport set of the pages to be deleted before actually deleting them. It can save you a lot of time and aggravation later.

Investigating Transport Sets

There will likely come a time when you need to be able to view information about an existing transport set without actually having to do anything with it. You may need to simply view the status of a bunch of transport sets that are in a given portal instance. You may need to take a look at the logs of import or export actions to make some decisions on administration of your instance, or you may need to figure out which transport sets can be deleted from your portal instance or which ones might be available to you that you could simply reuse.

These are all actions that are available through the Export/Import Transport Sets portal interface.

Configuring OracleAS Portal

In this section we will look at configuration tasks as they apply to the OracleAS Portal. We will set up self-registration and search features, look at what it will take to configure languages as well as mobile and OraDAV support for portal access, and look at the tasks surrounding relinking the portal instance with the other OracleAS components.

We will use the administrative services that we have already discussed in this chapter to perform most of the tasks needed to perform the configuration. You use the administrative user interface in the OracleAS Portal along with the Oracle Application Server Control. Again, you can also use the configuration scripts in the infrastructure Oracle Home directory on the Middle tier.

Configuring the Self-Registration Feature in OracleAS Portal

It is often a requirement of organizations that users should be able to create their own portal user accounts. In order to facilitate this, you configure the self-registration feature; after you complete the process, a self-registration link appears in the Login portlet.

It is also often necessary to have an approval process in place to oversee the self-registration so users can't log in to their account until it has been approved. Once the account has been either approved or rejected, the user who made the self-registration request will be notified by email.

If your organization doesn't require approval for the self-registration of users, your users will be able to log in to their new portal immediately after registration.

User Actions

When the user makes the self-registration request, they open a portal page containing the Login portlet and click the `Create New Account` link. The self-registration form (shown in Figure 6.3) will then be displayed, where the user will enter their preferred username, password, email address, and any optional personal information that they choose to enter (first name, last name, contact phone number). If the organization does not require that new portal accounts be approved, the portal account will be created immediately after the request has been submitted. If the organization does require approval, the request is sent to the portal administrator for approval. If it is approved, the account is created and the user can log in to the portal; if the request is rejected, the user will be denied access to the portal. Regardless of what the status of the request ends up being, the user will be notified by email of the outcome. If the account is created, the user will log in to the portal using their username and password.

Administrative Actions

If you are the portal administrator, you can set up self-registration so that your users can request portal accounts. In the Services portlet on the Portal subtab of the Administer tab on the Portal Builder page, click Global Settings. In the Self-Registration Options section, as in Figure 6.3, select Enable Self-Registration. If you select No Approval Required, users will be able to log on to the portal immediately after they register. If you select Approval Required, self-registered users need to be approved before they can log on to the portal. Click Configure if you need to set up the approval process. In the Recipients field, enter the names of all of the users and/or groups that you want to approve the self-registered users. The names of users and groups need to be separated by a semicolon (;).

FIGURE 6.3 The self-registration form

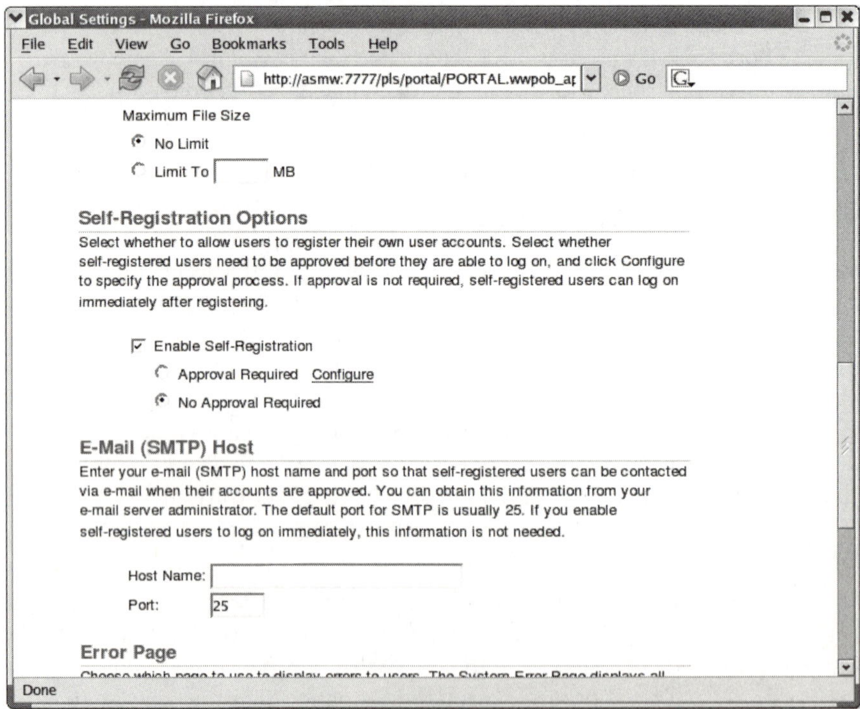

Table 6.1 lets you compare and contrast the different ways to register users. Determining your purpose ahead of time will allow you to make intelligent decisions regarding how you want your users to be registered with the application.

TABLE 6.1 Methods of Registering Users

Authentication Type	When to use
Self Registration No Approval Needed	Use this when you want to allow any user to register themselves and immediately use the application. This would work well for an online application with minimal security implications.
Self Registration Approval Required	Use this when you want people to be able to register themselves but you need to maintain a tighter rein on security.
Administrator Registered Accounts	Use this when it is important that you not only control who can get to an application, but also when you need a more granular control over security privileges and when you want to make sure that the application cannot be accessed by the general public.

In the Routing Method radio group, choose "One at a time, all must approve" if you need each user and/or group to be notified in turn. Each of the approvers must approve the self-registered users before they can log on. If instead you choose "All at the same time, all must approve," all of the users and groups will be notified at the same time and every user or group must approve the user before they can log on. Finally, if you choose "All at the same time, only one must approve," the users and groups will be notified at the same time; however, only one of the approvers needs to approve the self-registered user before the user can log on. Click Add Step if you need to add more steps to the approval process. Click OK when you are ready to return to the Global Settings screen. In the E-Mail (SMTP) Host section, enter the hostname and port of the email server so that the self-registered users can be informed by email when their accounts are either accepted or rejected. Click OK to finish.

You do not need to change any other settings on this tab or on any of the other tabs on this screen.

The final approver in the approval chain must have an email address that is defined in Oracle Internet Directory as well as sufficient privileges necessary to enable self-registration of users. If you need to provide the user with this privilege, grant Allow User Editing to the approver.

If there is no Login portlet on the portal home page, you need to add the Login portlet to the page. By default, the Login portlet can be found on the SSO/OID page under the Administration page of the Portlet Repository.

1. Next to the Login portlet, click the Actions icon and click Edit Defaults.
2. Select Enable Self-Registration.
3. In the Self-Registration Link Text field, enter the text that you want users to click to register the portal. If you leave the Self-Registration URL field blank, users will use OracleAS Portal's own self-registration screen. If you have created your own self-registration screen, you can enter the URL of this screen.
4. Click OK.

Configuring OraDAV Support for OracleAS Portal Access

Web-based Distributed Authoring and Versioning (WebDAV), much as the name implies, is a Hypertext Transport Protocol (HTTP) extension that supports distributed authoring and versioning, reading, writing, creating, editing, and moving documents on a server or between servers. It is a standard that will allow the Web to become a truly global interface through which users can interact with content that can be checked out, edited, and checked back in to a URL address. This will allow auditing and change control of documents that may reside anywhere that is network accessible and for which a given user or group of users have been granted appropriate permission. The `mod_dav` module is Apache's native module that supports this read and write access to the files.

Oracle's HTTP Server helps to extend this implementation of native `mod_dav` through the `mod_oradav` module. This module supports connections to the Oracle database as a facility to assist the read and write operations on the content and assists with locking queried documents in the accessed schemas. In order for this extension to the Apache facilities to function, the OraDAV driver must be installed because the `mod_oradav` module calls the driver as a means to map the WebDAV activity to database activity.

When you install OracleAS, all of the OraDAV parameters that are required to enable the database content to be accessed through either the web browser or a WebDAV client are installed as well. If these automatically installed parameters are not sufficient to meet your organizational needs, you can modify the values and also specify values for any optional parameters needed by your organization.

Very similar to the database access descriptor (DAD) configuration file that is used to assist with the configuration of Portal, WebDAV has its own configuration file located in the infrastructure `$ORACLE_HOME/Apache/oradav/conf/` directory. The `oradav.conf` file contains the configuration parameters starting with `DAV` and `DAV`*`Param`*. These parameters are specified with `<Location></Location>` directives pointing to the portal schema. (By default, the URL for the OracleAS Portal DAV is `http://<host:portal>/<dav_portal>/portal.`) This URL enables other WebDAV clients to access portal data. The `dav_portal` portion of the URL is the default name of a virtual directory that is used to differentiate between the portal accesses through a WebDAV client. Compare this to portal access that uses the `pls` virtual directory portal DAD of the portal installation.

The mod_oradav file is configured either through the Application Server Control (recommended) or by manually editing the file using any standard text editor. Just as when you make changes to the dads.conf file, whenever you make change to the oradav.conf file you need to restart the HTTP server and the OC4J_Portal for the changes to take effect.

The parameters that you will be most concerned with in the oradav.conf file will specify the DB connection, the OraDAV driver, and the password and package name:

```
<Location /dav_portal/portal>
DAV Oracle
DAVParam ORASERVICE cn-iasdb, cn=oraclecontext
DAVParam ORAUSER portal
DAVParam ORACRYPTPASSWORD Th1s15mypAssw0rd==
DAVParam ORAPACKAGENAME portal_schema.wwdav_api_driver
</Location>
```

Before you make manual changes to the configuration file, first make a copy of the file. This way, if anything goes wrong, you can get back your old configuration.

You include the oradav.conf configuration file in the httpd.conf file by using the include statement.

Users will connect to a WebDAV portal using the same user ID and password that they use in the portal itself.

It is important to remember that, if the portal is housed in a hosted environment, users will also need to add their company information to their username: <username>@<company>.

Configuring Language Support

Because fewer and fewer organizations today are completely localized, and because more and more organizations that are local are becoming more multilingual, Oracle has provided support for 29 languages in OracleAS and its Portal interface.

The most expeditious way of configuring languages is to install all that are likely to be relevant during the initial installation. However, to configure any languages that were not installed by the Universal Installer, you can use the ptllang tool:

```
ptllang -lang <language_code> [-s <portal_schema>]
   [-sp <portal_schema_password>] [-c <connect_string>]
   [-log <logfile_directory_name>] [-lang <language>]
```

The ptllang script needs to be run once for every language that you need to configure. The script is located in the infrastructure or portal $ORACLE_HOME/assistants/opca directory and is run as a shell scrip on Unix. For example, to install Spanish you would use the following:

```
ptllang.sh -s <portalschema> -sp <mypass>
-c <myhost.domain.com:1521:databaseserver> -lang sp
```

Then you can pass the following parameters to the utility:

-s The portal schema name

-sp The portal schema password

-c The connection string to the Metadata Repository database

-log The log file directory

-lang The abbreviation for the language you want to install

For a portal repository whose version is 10.1.4, you must run ptllang.sh from the Metadata Repository Upgrade Assistant CD-ROM.

Once you have configured Portal for the language support that you need, you can use the Set Language portlet to allow selected languages to be used for given portal sessions as well as selected territories for the selected languages. (This allows you to determine localization settings such as date format, currency, and decimal formats, if these are enabled by the page designer.)

After the language has been set, it can be chosen as a preferred language for portal sessions by using the Set Language portlet in the OracleAS Portal (which displays a list of installed languages as links). Simply clicking the appropriate link will set the language for the portal session. The Set Language portlet updates the login_nls cookie value, tying the language to the session on the specific browser containing the cookie. Further, by selecting a preferred language for your portal session, the user can choose the implied territory that will be used for their portal session. Territories are typically enabled by the page designer by setting the default properties of the Set Language portlet. This means that they don't require additional configuration by the portal administrator. Territories, like languages, show up as a list of links in a separate section of the portlet.

If you don't select the Enable Territory Selection check box while editing the values on the Set Portlet Setting screen, then the territory defaults to the most common settings for the chosen language. The list of territories offered to users depends on the language that they choose.

If the database is to support multiple languages, it should be created with Unicode (UTF8) character sets.

Configuring OracleAS Portal Dependencies

OracleAS Portal depends on several other components (primarily Web Cache and Oracle Internet Directory). Understanding these dependencies becomes important because fine-tuning likely will need to be done to configure these components after the application server is installed.

To allow you to configure these changes, OracleAS Portal introduces the Portal Dependency Settings file. Portal stores its dependencies on the myriad of OracleAS components in this Portal Dependency Settings file, `iasconfig.xml`, which is located in the infrastructure `$ORACLE_HOME/portal/conf` directory. This file stores all of the configuration data from all of the dependent components in this central location. The contents of the file are updated whenever any configuration changes are made on any of the dependent components.

You can view this file in any text editor and discover the settings that are being used by the OracleAS Portal instance. Further, you can use this file as a means to update the settings in the Metadata Repository.

The Portal Dependency Settings tool (`ptlconfig`), which you can use to update the configuration settings in the `iasconfig.xml` file, is located in the same directory as the configuration file.

The Portal Dependency Settings file, obviously an Extensible Markup Language (XML) file, is made up of a number of elements that describe the different settings of specific OracleAS components and the dependencies that the portal instance has on them. The definition of this file is modeled in the `iasconfig.xsd` schema. This is also located in the infrastructure `$ORACLE_HOME/portal/conf` directory.

A complete list of elements and the descriptions of the elements can be found in the Portal Dependency Settings file that resides in the *Portal Configuration Guide*'s Appendix A (Using the Portal Dependency Settings Tool and File).

The following is an example of the `iasconfig.xml` file:

```
- <IASConfig XSDVersion="1.0">
- <IASInstance Name="iasportal.localhost"
   Host="localhost">
  <OIDComponent
   AdminPassword="@BSKMZqEY0OS1TqufT4qndx4il4WNilCvpQ=="
   AdminDN="cn=orcladmin" SSLEnabled="false" LDAPPort="389" />
  <WebCacheComponent ListenPort="80"
   InvalidationPort="9401"
   InvalidationUsername="invalidator"
   InvalidationPassword="@Bcs40KHZfjHOidUDSDioz1nxjLLLzC901A=="
   SSLEnabled="false" AdminPort="9400" />
  <EMComponent ConsoleHTTPPort="18101" SSLEnabled="false" />
  </IASInstance>
- <PortalInstance DADLocation="/pls/portal"
   SchemaUsername="portal"
   SchemaPassword="@Bcs40KHZfjHOFJuxiZw6LK001HZAa0A3qg=="
   ConnectString="cn=orcl,cn=oraclecontext">
  <WebCacheDependency ContainerType="IASInstance"
   Name="iasportal.localhost" />
  <OIDDependency ContainerType="IASInstance"
   Name="iasportal.localhost" />
```

```
<EMDependency ContainerType="IASInstance"
 Name="iasportal.localhost" />
</PortalInstance>
</IASConfig>
```

You can use the `ptlconfig` script as a tool to help you update your Metadata Repository for a specific portal instance. This will help you to update the specific instance that you have defined in your Portal Dependency Settings file. It can also help you to encrypt all of your plain-text passwords that are stored in the `iasconfig.xml` file itself. This can be especially important on a server that either is easily accessible or for which you don't have control over the security.

You can use the same utility to update the Web Cache, OID, and Enterprise Manager as well as OracleAS Portal data that are defined in the settings file or to create and delete provisioning profiles in the OID of the portal instance.

You can choose to run `ptlconfig` in one of three modes. Choose configuration mode to update a specific portal instance from the file:

```
ptlconfig -dad portal -sso -host my.host.com
   -port 7787 -ssl
```

Choose encryption mode to encrypt the text passwords:

```
ptlconfig -encrypt
```

Or choose load mode to create and update the entries in the `iasconfig.xml` file with the active settings of the specifically named schema:

```
ptlconfig -load -schema portal30 -pw mypass
   -conn my.host.com:1521:infra2 -lp 4889
```

Regardless of the option you choose, the `pltconfig.log` file will be created in the infrastructure `$ORACLE_HOME/portal/logs` directory and will contain a record of all of the operations performed on the Metadata Repository. It is often wise to version-control this file and store it in a secondary location as an audit trail of what occurred to the file and when.

The flags that are relevant to the `ptlconfig` utility are as follows:

-all Updates all portal instances from the file

-dad Provides the name of the portal DAD (database access file)

-encrypt Encrypts any plain-text passwords that exist in the file

-wc Updates the Web Cache data as defined in the file

-oid Updates the Internet Directory data as defined in the file

-site Updates the listening host and port as defined in the file

-em Updates the Enterprise Manager as defined in the file

You can also configure Web Cache independently of the `ptlconfig` utility. You can define the Web Cache settings that you want OracleAS Portal to use from within the Application Server Control center. Whenever you update the Web Cache properties, the Portal Dependency Settings file is automatically updated.

If you navigate to the Application Server Control Portal home page, click the `Portal Web Cache Settings` link under the Administration tab, and modify the Web Cache information on the Portal Web Cache Settings page, the Portal's perspective on these properties changes and `iasconfig.xml` changes but the Web Cache settings in the `webcache.xml` file do not change. If you want to make the same, associated changes in this file, you need to navigate back to the Web Cache Administration page and make the appropriate changes there.

Summary

OracleAS Portal is one of the most widely used and versatile aspects of an OracleAS infrastructure install. It provides developers with added functionality and versatility in the products that they deploy. It provides administrators with the flexibility to allow users to customize their own application interface and to some extent the way that their applications behave on their computer.

Not only does Oracle provide you with a powerful interface, but also with powerful and flexible tools with which to monitor and configure the portal instance.

By understanding how this component works and how it can be leveraged by your organization to meet continuously changing business needs, you can provide to your end users the functionality that they need to meet the demands of their busy schedules.

In this chapter, we looked at the components of the portal instance, along with its users, groups, and repository.

We looked at creating new users and groups and how to maintain the ones that you have. We discussed allowing new users to self-register and providing the organization with the flexibility to allow users to either create their accounts on-the-fly or have their accounts approved along the way.

In order to prepare you for your exam experience, we showed you how to manage the OracleAS Portal and all of its components using the Oracle-provided interfaces and configuration files.

By now you should have a basic understanding of the OracleAS Portal Administrative Services and how to use them to manage the portal instance.

Also, you have learned how to identify the tools that you use to monitor the portal instance and have a basic understanding of how to use each. You should also be able to identify the tools that are necessary to create and manage portal users, groups, and schemas and the portal repository itself.

To add to your DBA repertoire, it's important to be able to understand and describe how and why to export portal content and then import that content into a different location.

Finally, in order to provide added flexibility for your developers, we have discussed adding and configuring providers in your environment and setting additional languages to provide your content to additional locations and different sets of users.

Exam Essentials

Describe the services that can be used in connection with OID. Be able to describe the support services that you can use as an administrator to manage the OracleAS Portal services. Understand the differences among these services and how to configure and manage each.

Describe managing OracleAS Portal. Be able to describe in detail the components of OracleAS Portal and how to manage the portal instance and its interfaces using the provided utilities.

Understand OracleAS Portal Administrative Services. Describe Portal Administrative Services, the components that are involved, and how to use this tool to manage the portal instance.

Identify and understand the tools used to monitor the OracleAS Portal instance. Describe the different tools and how to use them to monitor the portal instance. This will be important in your ability to tune and provide a highly available interface for users.

Be able to manage OracleAS Portal users, groups, and schemas. Describe the tools used to create and manage users and groups as they apply to the Oracle Application Server Portal.

Understand how to administer the portlet repository. Know how to configure and administer the portlet repository. Describe the available tools and how to use them.

Describe how to perform export and import of portal content. Describe the steps necessary to perform an export and an import of portal content and why you might want to do that.

Be able to configure OracleAS Portal. Describe the steps and the tools necessary to administer Oracle Application Server Portal.

Describe OracleAS Portal configuration tasks. Describe configuration tasks associated with OracleAS Portal, as well as the tools and utilities that can be used for the tasks.

Understand the self-registration feature so that users can create their own portal accounts. Describe how to configure the portal to allow for user self-registration and how users go through the steps necessary to self-register.

Explain how to configure OracleAS Portal for WebDAV. Describe WebDAV and OraDAV. Understand how you can configure your portal instance to make the best use of this technology and why you might want to do so.

Understand how to provide language support. Describe the steps necessary to configure multiple language support on the portal instance, both at the time of install and at a later time.

Describe how to configure OracleAS Portal instance dependencies by using the Portal Dependency Setting file. Describe the steps necessary to configure portal instance dependencies using the `ptlconfig` utility in connection with the Portal Dependency Settings file.

Review Questions

1. Which of the following is/are not one of the portal default groups? (Choose all that apply.)
   - A. authenticated_users
   - B. dba
   - C. sysadmin
   - D. portal_developers
   - E. rw_power_users
   - F. portal_administrators
2. What is the name of the utility used to configure the portal instance dependencies?
   - A. prtlconfig
   - B. oidconfig
   - C. oasconfig
   - D. iasconfig
   - E. ias_admin
3. Which entries can you find in the System Components section of the OracleAS instance home page relating directly to portals? (Choose all that apply.)
   - A. OC4J:Portal
   - B. Portal Instance
   - C. Portal:Portal
   - D. Web Portal
4. In what configuration file does OracleAS store its portal dependencies? (Choose all that apply.)
   - A. iasconfig.xml
   - B. Portal Dependency Settings file
   - C. webcache.xml
   - D. Portal configuration file
   - E. OC4J.xml
5. When Oracle Delegated Administration Services is used, what script resets the common domain to the one that was defined originally?
   - A. ptlconfig
   - B. secjsdom.sql
   - C. utlrp.sql
   - D. WSRP
   - E. All of the above

6. The __________________ and the __________________ are used to manage users and groups.
   - A. Portal User Profile portlet, Portal Group Profile portlet
   - B. Portal Group Profile administration page, Portal User Profile portlet
   - C. Portal Group Profile portlet, Portal User Profile Administration page
   - D. Portal User Profile administration page, Portal Group Profile administration page
   - E. All of the above
   - F. None of the above

7. What is the default portal group that provides a convenient mechanism for assigning the default privileges that you want every logged in user to have in the portal?
   - A. `AUTHENTICATED_USERS`
   - B. `DBA`
   - C. `PORTAL_ADMINISTRATORS`
   - D. `PORTAL_DEVELOPERS`
   - E. `PORTLET_PUBLISHERS`

8. Members of this group have the maximum privilege level in the system.
   - A. `DBA`
   - B. `AUTHENTICATED_USERS`
   - C. `SYSTEM`
   - D. `SYSADMIN`
   - E. `PORTLET_PUBLISHERS`

9. This group includes users who have received more detailed error messages from the OracleAS Reports Services in addition to the privileges assigned to the `RW_BASIC_USER`.
   - A. `DBA`
   - B. `AUTHENTICATED_USERS`
   - C. `RW_POWER_USER`
   - D. `SYSADMIN`
   - E. `PORTLET_PUBLISHERS`

10. Which Reports Service group has access to all of the administrator's functionality in Oracle Reports Queue Manager, can administer reports built with Oracle Reports, and can administer printer and server definitions?
    - A. `DBA`
    - B. `RW_POWER_USER`
    - C. `RW_ADMINISTRATOR`
    - D. `SYSADMIN`

11. What do you have to do before you can use the portlets?
   A. Register a provider with the portal.
   B. Log in as the portal administrator.
   C. Launch the portal administrator page.
   D. Launch the application server administration page.
   E. Launch Enterprise Manager.

12. Which of the following is not a portal provider?
   A. Database provider
   B. Application server provider
   C. WSRP provider
   D. Web provider

13. What two modules help support distributed authoring and versioning?
   A. `mod_pls`
   B. `mod_sso`
   C. `mod_av`
   D. `mod_dav`
   E. `mod_oradav`

14. What parameters will you be most concerned with in the `oradav.conf` file? (Choose all that apply.)
   A. `DAV`
   B. `DAVParam`
   C. `dads.conf`
   D. `Include`

15. What two utilities can be used to configure language support in the portal instance?
   A. `ptllang`
   B. `ptlconfig`
   C. `xmlconfig`
   D. Universal Installer
   E. Database Upgrade Assistant
   F. All are available tools

16. When is the best time to install language support to minimize the amount of time and work necessary?
   A. Whenever you need them
   B. At the beginning of a migration period
   C. When you install the application server software
   D. Whenever developers ask for them
   E. Whenever users ask for them

17. What do you have to create before you can export portal objects out of a source instance?

    A. The Export database utility

    B. Your target instance

    C. Transport sets

    D. Dump files

18. Which database utility exports and imports portal objects?

    A. Transport sets

    B. Export/import

    C. Transportable tablespaces

    D. Transport set creation

19. If your organization has a requirement that users should be able to create their own portal user accounts, what should you do?

    A. Give all of your users administrative accounts.

    B. Configure everyone that connects to be system administrators.

    C. Configure self-registration.

    D. Teach everyone how to log in to the administrative portal and create their own accounts.

20. Where can you find the elements that describe the different settings of specific OracleAS components and the dependencies that the portal instance has on them?

    A. `iasconfig.xml`

    B. `config.xml`

    C. `ias.config`

    D. `iasconfig.conf`

Answers to Review Questions

1. C. sysadmin is not one of the default portal groups; all of the others are.
2. A. prtlconfig, in connection with the iasconfig.xml file, is used to configure instance dependencies.
3. A, C. OC4J:Portal and Portal:Portal are the two portal entities that appear on the OracleAS instance home page.
4. A, B. OracleAS stores its portal dependency in one file. This file is referred to as either of two names, the iasconfig.xml and Portal Dependency Settings file.
5. B. secjsdom.sql resets the common domain to the one that was defined originally.
6. A. The Portal User Profile portlet and the Portal Group Profile portlet are used to manage users and groups.
7. A. AUTHENTICATED_USERS is the portal group that you use to help you with the administrative task of assigning the default privileges that you want every logged-in user to have in the portal.
8. A. Members of the DBA group have the maximum privilege level.
9. C. In addition to having the privileges assigned to the RW_BASIC_USER, users in the RW_POWER_USER group includes have received more detailed error messages from the OracleAS Reports Services.
10. C. The RW_ADMINISTRATOR group has all of these features.
11. A. Before you can use the portlets, you have to register a provider with the portal.
12. B. There is no application server provider that is a portal provider.
13. D, E. mod_dav and mod_oradav help support distributed authoring and versioning. mod_dav is standard Apache and mod_oradav is the Oracle extension to that module.
14. A, B. When setting up OraDAV, you will be most concerned with the DAV and DAVParam parameters.
15. A, D. If the languages are not configured by the Universal Installer, they need to be configured by the ptllang utility before they can be used.
16. C. The best and simplest time to install any languages is when you are installing the application server software because the installer takes care of all of the configuration details automatically.
17. C. You have to create and save a transport set before you can export the content.
18. B. When you export and import portal objects, you are using the export/import database utilities that have been a part of the Oracle database for many releases.
19. C. If your organization requires that users can register themselves, you need to configure the instance for self-registration.
20. A. The file that has the settings for OracleAS components and their dependencies is iasconfig.xml.

Deploying Application Server Applications

ORACLE APPLICATION SERVER 10*g* ADMINISTRATION I EXAM OBJECTIVES COVERED IN THIS CHAPTER:

✓ **Managing and Configuring OC4J**

- Create OC4J instances
- Start and stop OC4J instances
- Enable or disable application startup
- Configure OC4J instance properties
- Configure web site and JSP properties
- Edit OC4J configuration files

✓ **Deploying J2EE Applications**

- Deploy Web applications to the Oracle Application Server
- Configure data sources to be used in OC4J
- Provide necessary mappings for an Oracle database
- Deploy J2EE applications
- Deploy and register web providers

This chapter will cover the deployment of applications. Primarily, applications in Oracle Application Server 10*g* (OracleAS) consist of either PL/SQL programs or Java 2 Platform, Enterprise Edition (J2EE) programs. J2EE programs are deployed on Oracle Containers for J2EE (OC4J) instances. Therefore, before we can cover the deployment of these applications, we will discuss the ins and outs of OC4J instances.

Many organizations have standardized on either PL/SQL applications or J2EE applications. This typically means that the OracleAS administrator will have a preference for the area they deal with most often. This does not mean, however, that you should not understand what is going on with the other applications. This will allow you not only to pass your exams, but also to have a deeper understanding of how different applications work and how different organizations deal with the challenges that come up every day. It will also help prepare you, should you ever find yourself in a different organization or should you find your organization changing its direction, to deal with these changes in a proactive and highly responsive manner.

Configuring and Managing OC4J Applications

Oracle Containers for *J2EE (OC4J)* is Oracle's core J2EE runtime component of Oracle Application Server. This component is J2EE 1.4 compliant and runs on the standard J2EE platform. OC4J is easy to use and improves a developer's productivity, given its rich library of functions, component-based approach, and compatibility with the thousands of other OC4J applications available. It is designed to be highly scalable and available for the most demanding distributed application environments.

As with most of the OracleAS components, you can manage OC4J either from the AS Control GUI interface or from the command line. AS Control's GUI interface is the preferred method for monitoring and troubleshooting OC4J instances in real time and interactively. Alternatively, you can use the command-line tools `dcmctl` and `opmnctl` to perform similar operations when a web browser is not available or you need to perform these operations in a nightly batch job.

In the following sections, we'll first give you an overview of how the industry-standard J2EE platform works. Next, we'll show you how to create an OC4J instance, and as you might expect, we will also cover the basics of managing OC4J instances using the command line and AS Control.

Understanding the J2EE Architecture

To effectively manage your OC4J environment, you need to have at least a basic understanding of the J2EE architecture and its components. In the following sections, we'll give you a brief overview of each tier and how the tier's components (not surprisingly) correspond to the components in OracleAS. In addition to describing each tier, we'll give you an overview of Enterprise JavaBeans (EJB). Finally, we'll describe the differences among and uses of JAR, WAR, and EAR files.

In a nutshell, J2EE is a multitiered, distributed application model that supports the development, deployment, and execution of application components. The model supports as few as two tiers and as many as four or even five tiers, depending on the size, complexity, and business needs of your organization. The number of tiers can even change on a regular basis to reflect unexpected changes in the business environment or seasonal customer demand; the J2EE component model makes it easy to move components or collapse tiers with minimal changes to existing applications.

Client Tier Components

As you might expect, a web browser is the primary client tier component in a J2EE environment. The web browser downloads dynamic or static content from the web tier; the dynamic content comes from servlets and Java Server Pages (JSPs) that reside in the web tier.

The other type of client tier component is an application that runs on a client machine but does not use a web browser. These application components can run either in a GUI-based application or on a command line; in either case, they connect to a business-tier servlet component on the web tier using a Hypertext Transfer Protocol (HTTP) connection.

Middle Tier Components

The middle tier is also known as the web tier. Middle-tier components are either servlets or JSPs that can statically or dynamically generate Hypertext Markup Language (HTML), Extensible Markup Language (XML), or Wireless Markup Language (WML) documents. JSPs ease dynamic content generation by using Java as the scripting language within an HTML page.

These web components can access the business-tier components in Enterprise JavaBeans (EJB), which in turn access the database using Java Database Connectivity (JDBC) function calls.

EIS Tier Components

The Enterprise Information Service (EIS) tier consists primarily of a database, such as Oracle Database 10*g* or even non-Oracle databases such as DB2 or Microsoft SQL Server. You use a database in a J2EE environment to persist session information, customer profile data, sales history, and so forth.

Enterprise JavaBeans (EJB)

Enterprise JavaBeans is an architecture that supports transactional applications that access, for example, an Oracle database. EJB developers spend most of their time supporting the execution of the business logic instead of on database-related issues such as transaction support, security, remote object access, and so forth.

JAR, WAR, and EAR Files

To make application deployment easier, you deploy applications in one of three types of files, depending on the type of file and where they are deployed: JAR, WAR, and EAR files. In many ways, all three of these files are like a ZIP file or a TGZ file on Windows or Linux: They provide an easy way to manage a large number of files using a single operating system file, maintaining the original file directory structure and optionally providing file compression to save space and network bandwidth when the file is copied to another server.

JAR Files

Java Archive (JAR) files make it easy not only to archive and distribute files, but also to deploy and encapsulate libraries, server components, plug-ins, and image files. The JAR file itself maintains the original directory structure of the files in the archive as well as instructions on how to access the files in the JAR. JAR files have the extension `.jar`.

WAR Files

Web Archive (WAR) files are similar to JAR files except that they store web components for a J2EE application. As you might expect, the extension for a WAR file is `.war`. In a typical WAR file you will see HTML documents, servlets, JSPs, and applet class files. The top-level directory in a WAR file is the `document-root` directory of the application. The subdirectory of `document-root` is called `WEB-INF` and contains tag library descriptor files, server-side classes, the application deployment descriptor in XML format, and a `lib` directory containing JAR files.

EAR Files

An *Enterprise Archive (EAR)* file is a JAR file that contains the web modules of a J2EE application; each web module contains HTML files, class files, and XML files. It can contain both regular JAR files and WAR files, plus an application descriptor called `application.xml` that describes the contents of the EAR file. As you might expect, EAR files have the extension `.ear`.

Creating and Managing an OC4J Instance

Whenever you install OracleAS, you have one default OC4J instance. This instance is named `home`. If it turns out that you don't have sufficient instances of OC4J for your environment, you can easily create new instances, provided that you give each its own unique name (unique not necessarily to your overall environment, but within the application server instance). In the following sections, we'll show you how to create and manage OC4J instances both from the command line and using AS Control.

Creating an OC4J Instance Interactively

In the Application Server Control center, simply go to the OracleAS instance in which you want to create your new OC4J instance and click the Create OC4J Instance button. In the field next to the OC4J Instance Name tag (shown in Figure 7.1), enter the name of your new OC4J instance and click the Create button. Confirm the creation on the confirmation page and you will see the page in Figure 7.2 until creation is complete.

At the same time the instance is created, a directory is created in the infrastructure's ORACLE_HOME in the j2ee subdirectory with the same name as the instance you created. This instance will now show up on the application server instance page in the System Components section, as you can see in Figure 7.3.

FIGURE 7.1 Create OC4J Instance page

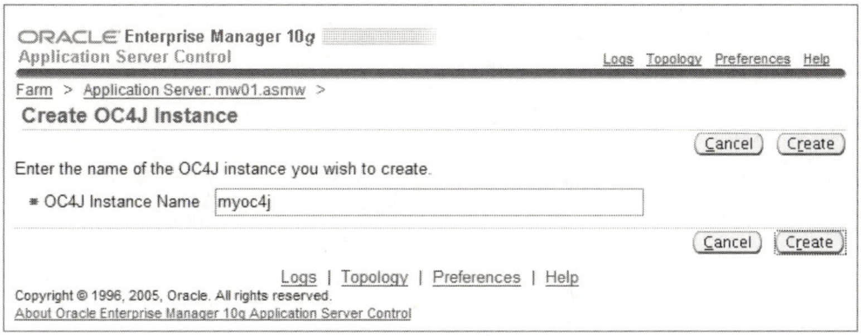

FIGURE 7.2 Create OC4J Instance progress page

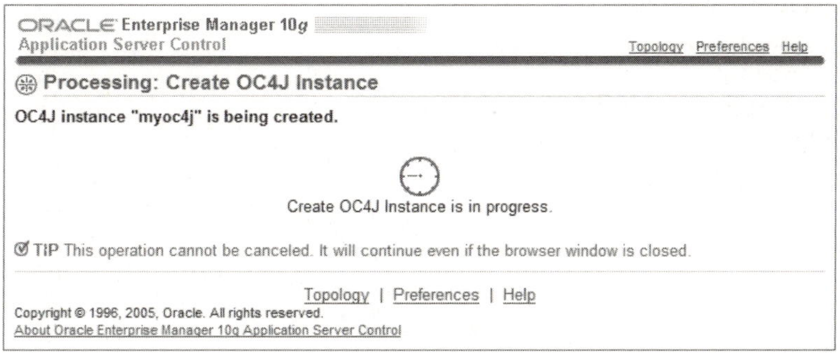

FIGURE 7.3 The System Components section of the AS Control home page

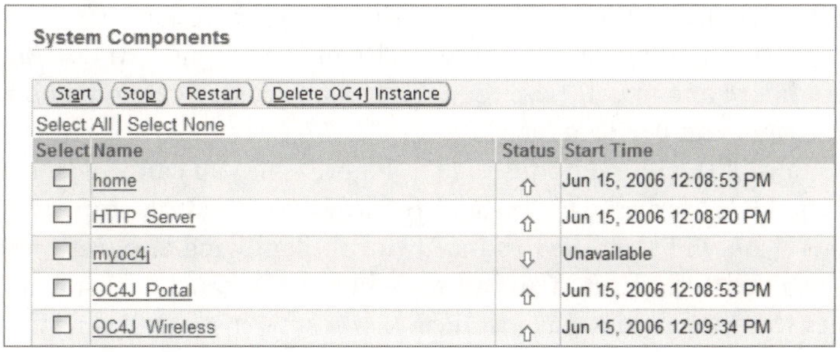

Select	Name	Status	Start Time
☐	home	⇧	Jun 15, 2006 12:08:53 PM
☐	HTTP_Server	⇧	Jun 15, 2006 12:08:20 PM
☐	myoc4j	⇩	Unavailable
☐	OC4J_Portal	⇧	Jun 15, 2006 12:08:53 PM
☐	OC4J_Wireless	⇧	Jun 15, 2006 12:09:34 PM

Although the new OC4J instance has been created, it is not started automatically. You need to start it before you can use any applications that have been deployed on it and before you can deploy any applications to it. To start it, click the check box next to the new instance and click the Start button, as has been done in Figure 7.4. After you start the instance, you can see the new status of the instance, as in Figure 7.5.

FIGURE 7.4 Starting a new OC4J instance

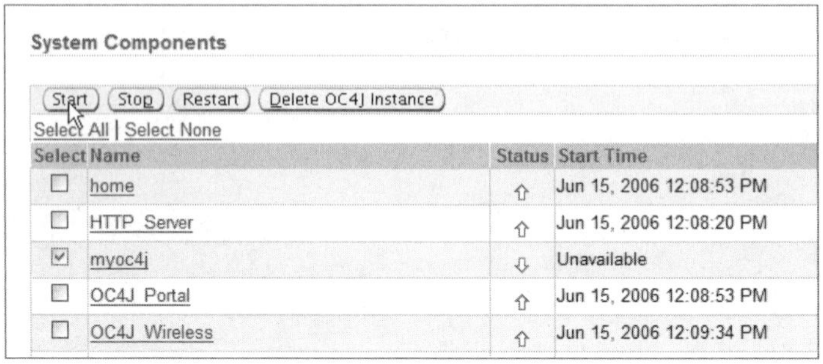

System Components

(Start) (Stop) (Restart) (Delete OC4J Instance)

Select All | Select None

Select	Name	Status	Start Time
☐	home	⇧	Jun 15, 2006 12:08:53 PM
☐	HTTP_Server	⇧	Jun 15, 2006 12:08:20 PM
☑	myoc4j	⇩	Unavailable
☐	OC4J_Portal	⇧	Jun 15, 2006 12:08:53 PM
☐	OC4J_Wireless	⇧	Jun 15, 2006 12:09:34 PM

FIGURE 7.5 New status of the OC4J instance

System Components

(Start) (Stop) (Restart) (Delete OC4J Instance)

Select All | Select None

Select	Name	Status	Start Time
☐	home	⇧	Jun 15, 2006 12:08:53 PM
☐	HTTP_Server	⇧	Jun 15, 2006 12:08:19 PM
☐	myoc4j	⇧	Jun 15, 2006 11:38:45 PM
☐	OC4J_Portal	⇧	Jun 15, 2006 12:08:53 PM
☐	OC4J_Wireless	⇧	Jun 15, 2006 12:09:34 PM

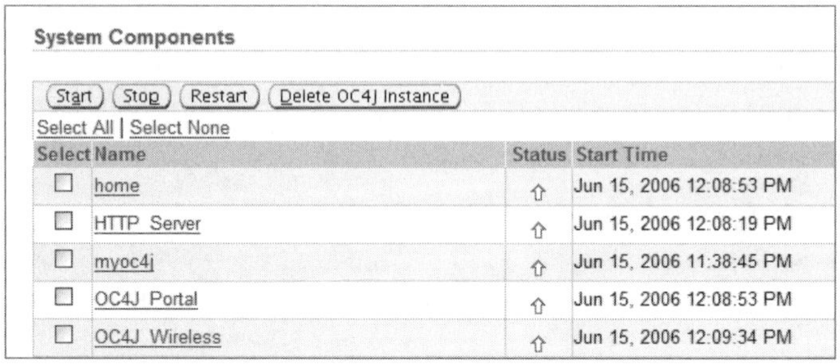

Managing an OC4J Instance Interactively

When it comes time to manage your new OC4J instance, you can accomplish this with the OC4J home page of the Application Server Control, shown in Figure 7.6.

Through this page, you can administer all of the J2EE environment settings. Among the things that you can configure and manage are the OC4J instance, services and their resources, security, availability, usage, and performance.

On the General section of the OC4J home page in Figure 7.6, you can view a snapshot of the current status of the OC4J server. This page also allows you to start, stop, or restart the OC4J server. From here you will start the instance prior to deploying applications to it and restart it to allow changes to take effect. You can see when the instance was started and how many virtual machines were assigned to the instance. If you start instances using this method, you will be presented with a confirmation page verifying that the restart is in progress, as shown in Figure 7.7, and the status of the OC4J instance changes to "up" in the General area.

FIGURE 7.6 The System Components section of the AS Control home page

ORACLE Enterprise Manager 10g
Application Server Control
Logs Topology Preferences Help
Farm > Application Server: mw01.asmw >
OC4J: myoc4j
Home Applications Administration
Page Refreshed Jun 15, 2006 11:41:43 PM
General
Status Up
Stop Restart
Start Time Jun 15, 2006 11:38:47 PM
Virtual Machines 1
JDBC Usage
Open JDBC Connections 0
Total JDBC Connections 0
Active Transactions 0
Transaction Commits 0
Transaction Rollbacks 0
Status
CPU Usage (%) 0.16
Memory Usage (MB) 21.20
Heap Usage (MB) 5.06
Response - Servlets and JSPs
Active Sessions 0
Active Requests 1
Request Processing Time (seconds) Not Yet Available
Requests per Second Not Yet Available
Response - EJBs
Active EJB Methods 0
Method Execution Time (seconds) 0.00
Method Execution Rate (per second) 0.00
Related Link All Metrics
Home Applications Administration
Logs | Topology | Preferences | Help
Copyright © 1996, 2005, Oracle. All rights reserved.
About Oracle Enterprise Manager 10g Application Server Control

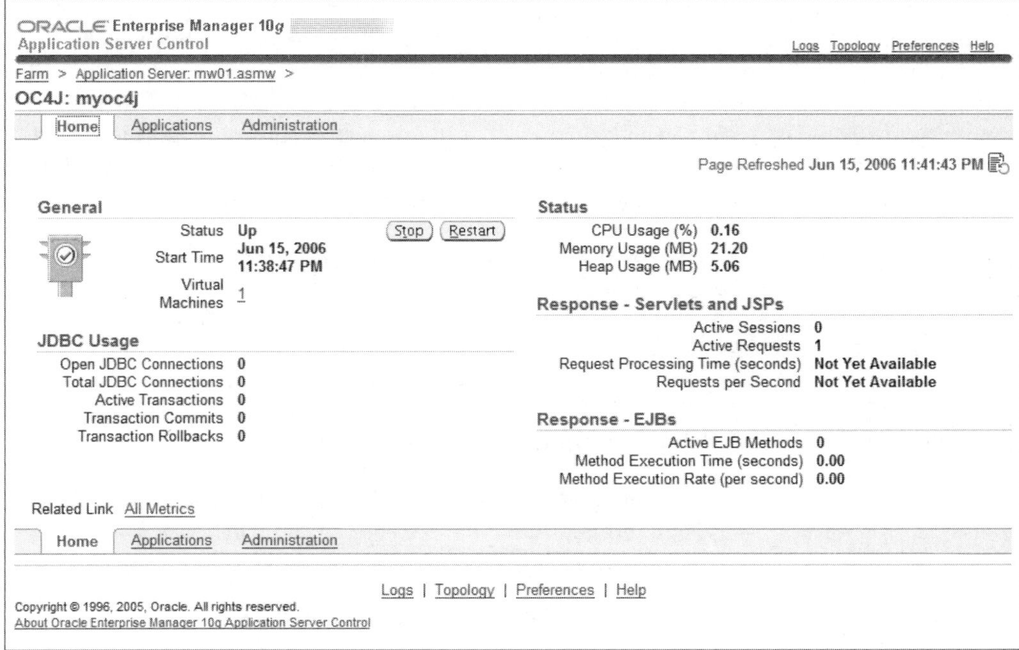

FIGURE 7.7 OC4J instance status change

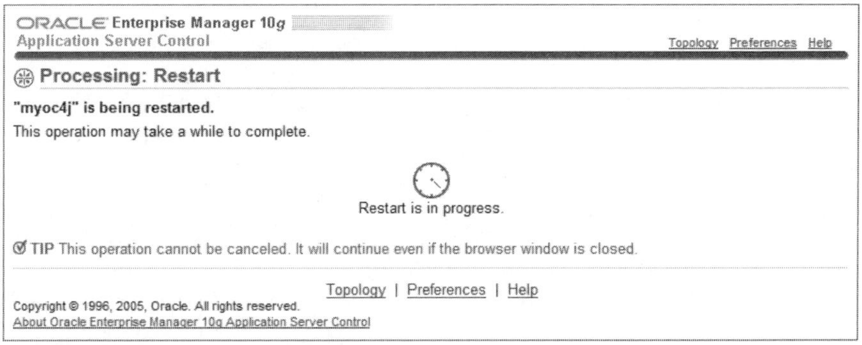

ORACLE Enterprise Manager 10g
Application Server Control
Topology Preferences Help
Processing: Restart
"myoc4j" is being restarted.
This operation may take a while to complete.
Restart is in progress.
TIP This operation cannot be canceled. It will continue even if the browser window is closed.
Topology | Preferences | Help
Copyright © 1996, 2005, Oracle. All rights reserved.
About Oracle Enterprise Manager 10g Application Server Control

The Status section of the OC4J home page gives you a quick look at the performance of the server (including CPU usage, memory usage, and heap usage).

The JDBC Usage section gives you a glimpse into the number of open JDBC connections, the number of active current transactions, and the number of commits and rollbacks. The number of commits and rollbacks is cumulative.

The Response - Servlets and JSPs section shows you information about currently active sessions, currently active requests, and the average processing time for historic requests in seconds. Statistics include the number of requests processed per second. Although this is not an exhaustive set of information on performance that can be used for tuning, it might well be used for determining whether tuning is in order.

The Response - EJBs section provides transactional details about the OC4J Enterprise JavaBeans. Information in this section includes active EJB methods, method execution time in seconds, and method execution rate per second. Again, this information isn't exhaustive, but it can be indicative of problem areas that you can research more thoroughly should the need arise.

Creating an OC4J Instance from the Command Line

To create the same instance using the command-line utility, you use the `dcmctl` command with the `createComponent` option.

Using `dcmctl` When the Browser Is Not Available

On very short notice, you need to create a new OC4J instance but do not have access to a web browser; all you have is access to a terminal session. To create an OC4J instance called `myoc4j2`, the command would be as follows:

```
[oracle@asmw oracle]$ dcmctl createComponent -ct oc4j -co myoc4j2

1
Component Name: myoc4j2
Component Type: OC4J
Instance:       mw01.asmw
[oracle@asmw oracle]$
```

This will create the `myoc4j2` instance along with the directory to store the files for the component itself. The `-ct` option specifies the type of component, in this case `oc4j`; the `-co` option specifies the component name.

Once the instance is created, you can use the `dcmctl` command to list the available components on this application server instance:

```
[oracle@asmw oracle]$ dcmctl listcomponents
1
Component Name: HTTP_Server
Component Type: HTTP_Server
Instance:       mw01.asmw


. . .
```

```
5
Component Name: myoc4j
Component Type: OC4J
Instance:       mw01.asmw

6
Component Name: myoc4j2
Component Type: OC4J
Instance:       mw01.asmw

. . .

11
Component Name: WebCache
Component Type: WebCache

[oracle@asmw oracle]$
```

You can look at the subdirectories of the j2ee directory by simply using common operating system commands to make sure that the directories exist:

```
[oracle@asmw oracle]$ cd $ORACLE_HOME/j2ee
[oracle@asmw j2ee]$ ls
deploy.ini   j2eetargets.xml   myoc4j2
OC4J_Portal     properties
home          myoc4j             oc4j
opmn.xml   OC4J_Wireless
[oracle@asmw j2ee]$
```

Managing an OC4J Instance from the Command Line

If you need to start or stop the OC4J instance without the benefit of the GUI tools, you can easily do this with the command-line tool opmnctl using the following format:

```
opmnctl startproc process-type=myoc4j
```

To stop the myoc4j instance, you can use a similar command:

```
opmnctl stopproc process-type=myoc4j
```

If you need to start or stop all of the OC4J instances associated with your given OracleAS instance, the following commands can be used:

```
opmnctl startproc ias-component=OC4J
opmnctl stopproc ias-component=OC4J
```

Enabling and Disabling an OC4J Instance

There are times when you need to enable or disable an OC4J instance; for example, there may be components that you simply don't want to have running to save on system overhead. Sometimes you don't need an instance anymore because an application has completed its life cycle or because it has been decommissioned.

To disable a component, you can use the OracleAS instance page and click the Enable/Disable Components button, as you can see in Figure 7.8.

FIGURE 7.8 The Enable/Disable Components button

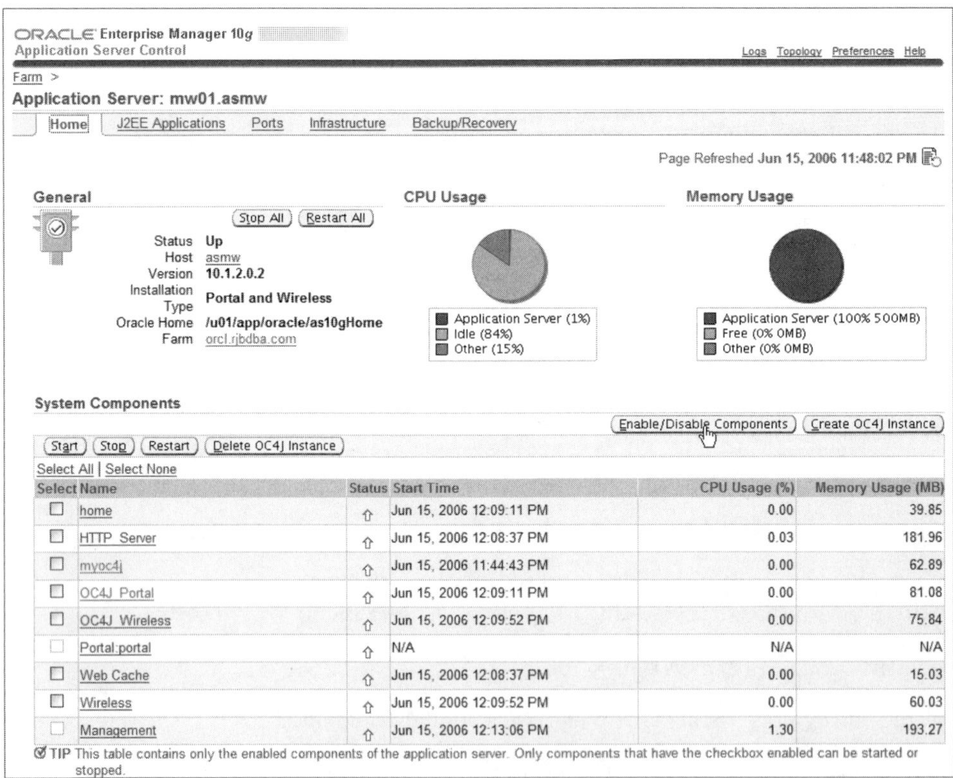

In Figure 7.9, you can see the Enable/Disable Components page. You can select the component that you want to disable from the list of enabled components. Click the `Move` arrow (>) to move the selected component to the Disabled Components list. If you click the dual arrow (>>) `Move All` link, you can move all of the components from the Enabled Components list to the Disabled Components list.

Did you change your mind? You can select a disabled component from the Disabled Components list (see Figure 7.10) and click the `Remove` arrow (<) or the `Remove All` arrow (<<) to put one, more than one, or all of the disabled components back to the Enabled Components side.

Taking advantage of the efficiencies built into many Oracle tools, if you disable any component that has subcomponents, such as applications deployed, the subcomponents will be stopped gracefully and disabled with the parent component.

FIGURE 7.9 The Enable/Disable Components page

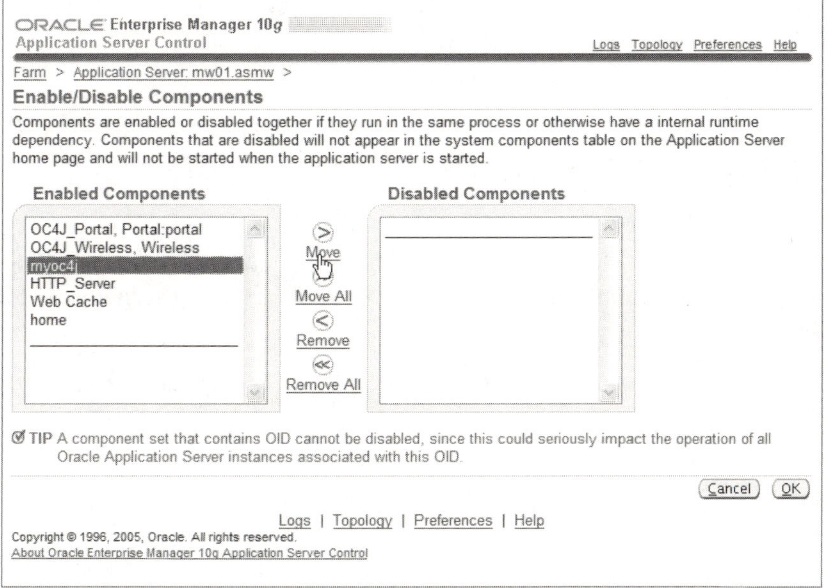

The Basics of OC4J

Now that we have showed you how to create and enable (or disable) OC4J instances and how to start and stop the OC4J instances, we will show you how to configure the instances. There are several configuration files that work together to make the instances work efficiently.

OC4J instances can each contain multiple J2EE applications, and the web applications communicate between OHS and OC4J using `mod_oc4j`. One set of configuration files is used to make `mod_oc4j` work effectively. These files reside in the `$ORACLE_HOME/Apache/Apache/conf` directory. OC4J server configuration files contain information that is OC4J specific and contain parameters that are meant to configure OC4J servers. These files point to J2EE configuration files.

FIGURE 7.10 Reenabling a component

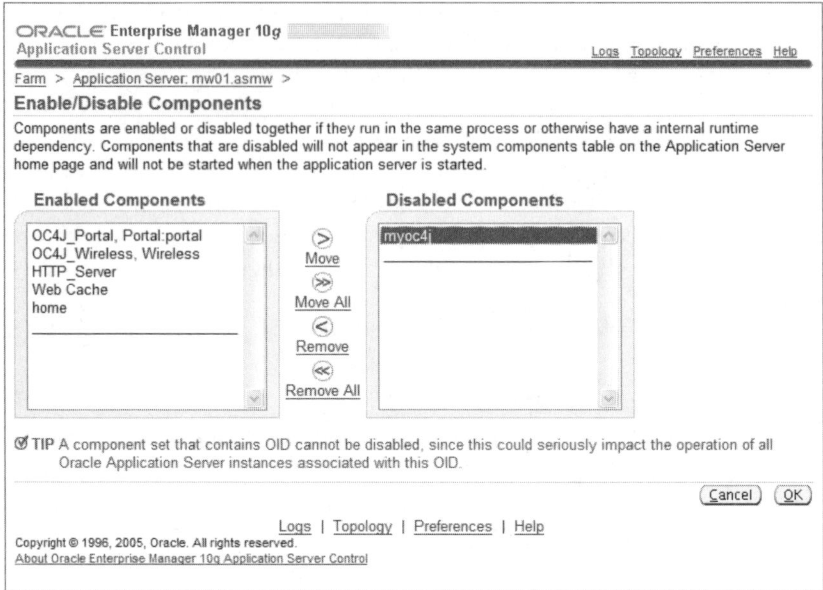

The primary files in an instance configuration are in the following sections. In most cases, we will provide a short sample of the contents of each file. Here is the hierarchy for the files that follow:

- `server.xml`
  - `rmi.xml`
  - `jms.xml`
  - `application.xml`
    - `principals.xml`
    - `data-sources.xml`
  - `global-web-application.xml`
  - `default-web-site.xml`

We will provide details on the files you will typically maintain in the following sections. Two other files, `jazn.xml` and `jazn-data.xml`, describe the security configuration when you use Java Authentication and Authorization Service (JAAS).

server.xml

The `server.xml` file has an entry for every application that is deployed. All directory references in this file are relative to the `$ORACLE_HOME/j2ee/home/config` directory (where the `server.xml` file is located). The `application-directory` attribute in the `server.xml` file specifies the directory in which you will store your applications' Enterprise Archive (EAR) files. If you do not specify anything outside of the default directory, the EAR files will be stored in the `$ORACLE_HOME/j2ee/home/applications` directory.

The `deployment-directory` attribute specifies where your OC4J instance-specific files will be permanently stored. This attribute is not a global attribute but is application specific. This means that there needs to be a `deployment-directory` attribute for each and every application that you deploy.

The `application-auto-directory` attribute specifies where files go that are automatically deployed whenever there is no need for action from any administrator. This is primarily for developers and should not be enabled on a production server. Leaving this parameter enabled can be a security concern because no administrative intervention is necessary to perform the deployment.

The `application` parameter specifies where the application archive (the EAR file) will be located.

Here is an example of the file `server.xml`:

```
<?xml version="1.0"?>
<!DOCTYPE application-server PUBLIC "-//Oracle//DTD OC4J
   Application-server 9.04//EN"
   "http://xmlns.oracle.com/ias/dtds/application-server-9_04.dtd">
<application-server localhostIsAdmin="true"
 application-directory="../applications"
 deployment-directory="../application-deployments"
 connector-directory="../connectors"
>
   <rmi-config path="./rmi.xml" />
   <sep-config path="./internal-settings.xml" />
   <jms-config path="./jms.xml" />
   <javacache-config path="../../../javacache/admin/javacache.xml" />
   <j2ee-logging-config path="./j2ee-logging.xml" />
   <log>
      <file path="../log/server.log" />
   </log>
   <transaction-config timeout="30000" />
   <java-compiler name="javac" in-process="false"
   extdirs="C:\OraHome_2\jdk\jre\lib\ext" />
   <global-application name="default" path="application.xml" />
   <application name="portletapp" path="../applications/portletapp.ear"
   auto-start="true" />
   <application name="BC4J"
   path="../applications/BC4J.ear"
   auto-start="true" />
```

```
    <application name="ADFBCManager" path="../applications/ADFBCManager.ear"
    auto-start="true" />
    <application name="IsWebCacheWorking"
    path="../applications/IsWebCacheWorking.ear"
    auto-start="true" />
    <global-web-app-config
    path="global-web-application.xml" />
    <web-site default="true"
    path="./default-web-site.xml" />
    <cluster  id="248105886" />
</application-server>
```

application.xml

Modules for each application defined in `server.xml` are defined in the `application.xml` file. The contents of this file follow:

```
<?xml version="1.0" standalone='yes'?>
<!DOCTYPE orion-application
   PUBLIC "-//Evermind//DTD J2EE Application runtime 1.2//EN"
   "http://xmlns.oracle.com/ias/dtds/orion-application-9_04.dtd">
   <!--
   The global application config that is the parent of all
   the other applications in this server.
   -->
<orion-application autocreate-tables="true"
   default-data-source="jdbc/OracleDS">
    <web-module id="defaultWebApp" path="../../home/default-web-app"/>
    <web-module id="dms" path="../../home/applications/dms.war"/>
    <commit-coordinator>
        <commit-class class=
   "com.evermind.server.OracleTwoPhaseCommitDriver"/>
        <property name="datasource" value="jdbc/OracleDS"/>
 <!--
   Username and password are the optional
   properties replace with your
   commit_co-ordinator_super_user
          <property name="username"
           value="system" />
           <property name="password"
           value="->pwForSystem" />
  -->
```

```
 </commit-coordinator>
 <persistence path="../persistence"/>
 <!--
Path to the libraries that are installed
on this server.
These will be accesible for the servlets,
EJBs etc
-->
 <library path="../applib"/>
 <library path="../../../BC4J/lib"/>
 <library path="../../../jlib/ojmisc.jar"/>
 <library path="../../../ord/jlib/ordim.jar"/>
 <library path="../../../ord/jlib/ordhttp.jar"/>
 <library path="../../../jlib/jdev-cm.jar"/>
 <library path="../../../lib/dsv2.jar"/>
 <library path="../../../lib/xsu12.jar"/>
 <!-- Path to the taglib directory that
      is shared
      among different applications.
 -->
 <library path="../../../j2ee/home/jsp/lib/taglib"/>
 <library path="../../../uix/taglib"/>
 <library path="../../../lib/oraclexsql.jar"/>
 <library path="../../../lib/xsqlserializers.jar"/>
 <!--
     Comment the following element to use
     principals.xml
  -->
 <principals path="./principals.xml"/>
 <log>
     <file path="../log/global-application.log"/>
     <!--
       Uncomment this if you want to use
       ODL logging capabilities
       <odl path="../log/global-application/"
        max-file-size="1000"
        max-directory-size="10000"/>
      -->
 </log>
 <jazn provider="XML"
       location="./jazn-data.xml"/>
```

```
    <data-sources
         path="data-sources.xml"/>
    <connectors
         path="./oc4j-connectors.xml"/>
    <namespace-access>
        <read-access>
            <namespace-resource root="">
               <security-role-mapping>
                 <group name="administrators"/>
               </security-role-mapping>
            </namespace-resource>
        </read-access>
        <write-access>
            <namespace-resource root="">
                <security-role-mapping>
                  <group name="administrators"/>
                </security-role-mapping>
            </namespace-resource>
        </write-access>
    </namespace-access>
</orion-application>
```

The `application.xml` file references `principals.xml` and `data-source.xml` as include files.

default-web-site.xml

The `default-web-site.xml` file is the container file for all of the configuration settings for the default website. By using the `<web-site parameter list>` directive, you control the configuration settings for the website. The key parameters for the directive are as follows:

port The port for the instance where the content will be found (default is 3000).

protocol The protocol used for communication between the OC4J instance and its corresponding mod_oc4j.

display_name The administration display name.

default-web-app The application to be displayed if no application name is passed in as a parameter. This particular application is bound to the root of the tree in which the application is located.

web-app This parameter binds a web module from J2EE to a virtual directory path in the file system.

access-log The location for the access log.

Here is an example of a typical default-web-site.xml file:

```
<?xml version="1.0" standalone='yes'?>
<!DOCTYPE web-site PUBLIC "OracleAS XML Web-site"
   "http://xmlns.oracle.com/ias/dtds/web-site-9_04.dtd">
<!-- change the host name below to your own host name. Localhost will -->
<!-- not work with clustering -->
<!-- also add cluster-island attribute as below
<web-site host="localhost" port="0"  protocol="ajp13"
          display-name="OracleAS Java Web Site" cluster-island="1" >
-->
<web-site port="0"  protocol="ajp13"
          display-name="OracleAS Java Web Site">
        <!-- Uncomment the following line when using clustering -->
   <!-- <frontend host="your_host_name" port="80" /> -->
   <!-- The default web-app for this site, bound to the root -->
   <default-web-app application="default"
   name="defaultWebApp" root="/j2ee" />
   <web-app application="default" name="dms"
   root="/dmsoc4j" access-log="false" />
   <!-- Access Log, where requests are logged to -->
   <access-log path="../log/default-web-access.log" />
   <!-- Uncomment this if you want to use ODL logging capabilities
   <odl-access-log path="../log/default-web-access"
   max-file-size="1000" max-directory-size="10000"/>
   -->
</web-site>
```

jazn.xml and *jazn-data.xml*

Two other files, jazn.xml and jazn-data.xml, deal with security surrounding Java Authentication and Authorization Service (JAAS). Configuration of these files, unless you use JAAS, is not necessary and will be ignored. In these files, you will find information about passwords, providers, and credential keys. Much of the code in either of these files is commented out and the functionality is therefore very adaptable. You can create a very versatile system simply by choosing which parameters you need to uncomment based on the needs of your business.

Configuring OC4J Using Application Server Control

You can use Application Server Control (AS Control) to, among other things, configure the OC4J instances. From the OC4J home page in AS Control, all you need to do is select the

Administration tab. This will take you to the OC4J Administration page shown in Figure 7.11; from there you can configure the instances and drill down to other administrative pages. Using the Administration pages is the preferred way of altering the contents of the previously described XML files, as you might expect. However, you can always edit XML files in a text editor after first creating a backup and taking care to follow the established tags in the file.

From the OC4J Administration page, you can access the Server Properties page shown in Figure 7.12 by clicking the `Server Properties` link. On this page you can alter the properties associated with the currently selected OC4J container.

The Server Properties page is where you can view the name, server root, configuration file, default application name, and default application path; however, since they are set up at configuration time for the OC4J instance, they can't be altered on this page. You can, however, alter the default web module properties, which give you the location of the file that you are using to define the global properties associated with all of your web modules. (Recall that, by default, this is the `global-web-applications.xml` file.) You also can change the application directory. (Again, recall from our configuration file discussion earlier in the chapter that this is the directory where your EAR files are located for all of the deployed applications.) You also can alter your deployment directory.

FIGURE 7.11 OC4J container Administration tab

FIGURE 7.12 Server Properties page

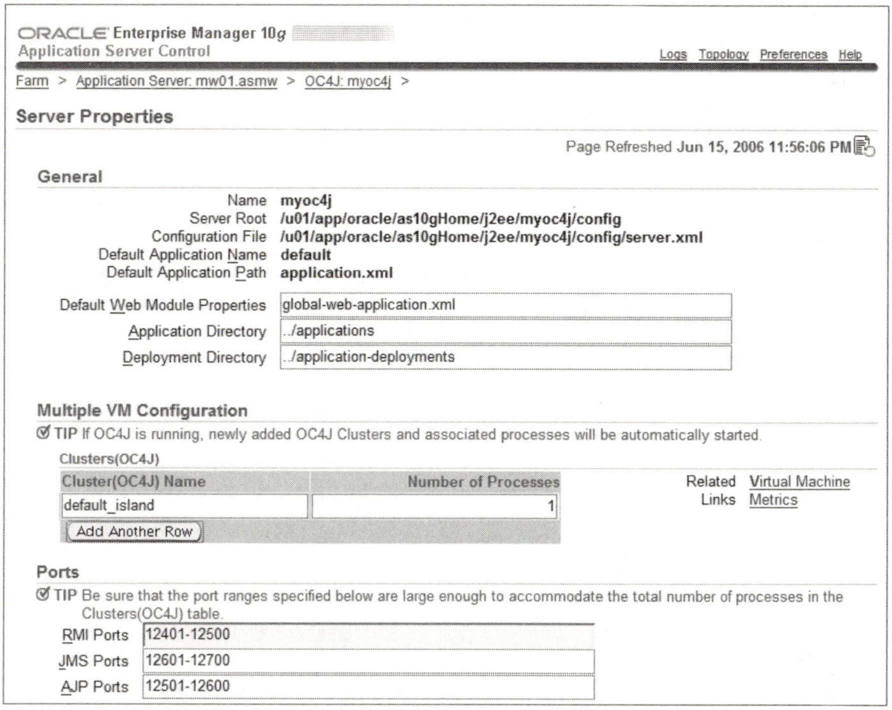

Application Deployment and Maintenance

Often developers and administrators are concerned about the difficulties of application deployment on an OracleAS server, particularly if this is a new implementation; however, deployment is quite simple. You can either deploy automatically using AS Control or the command-line utility `dcmctl` (never thought using the command line would be considered automatic, did you?) or manually by modifying the configuration files and then unpacking the EAR file in the deployment directory.

Using AS Control for Deployment

If you use AS Control, there is a wizard to help you through the deployment process. The Deploy Application Wizard (accessed from the OC4J home page) deploys either EAR files or WAR files. When you click the Applications tab shown in Figure 7.11, you'll see the applications deployed in the selected OC4J instance, as shown in Figure 7.13.

To deploy a new application, you click either the Deploy EAR File or Deploy WAR File button, and you will see the Deploy Application page shown in Figure 7.14.

FIGURE 7.13 OC4J container deployed applications

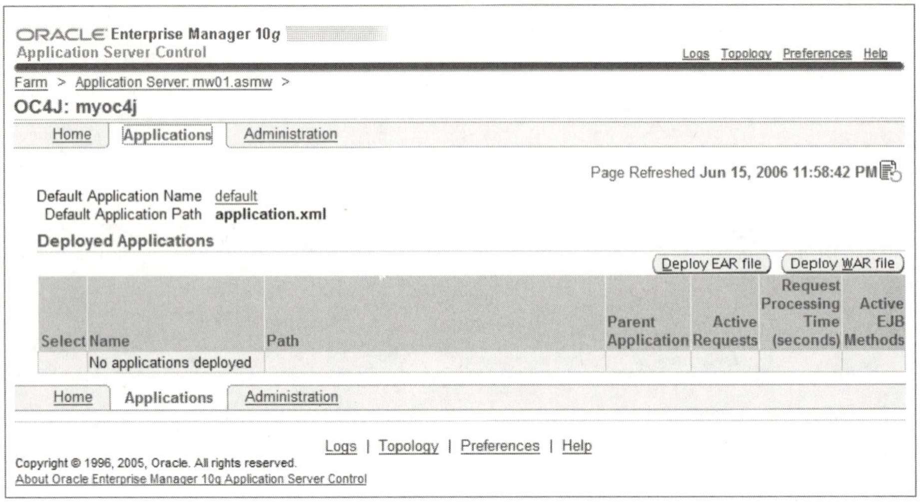

FIGURE 7.14 The Deploy Application page for J2EE

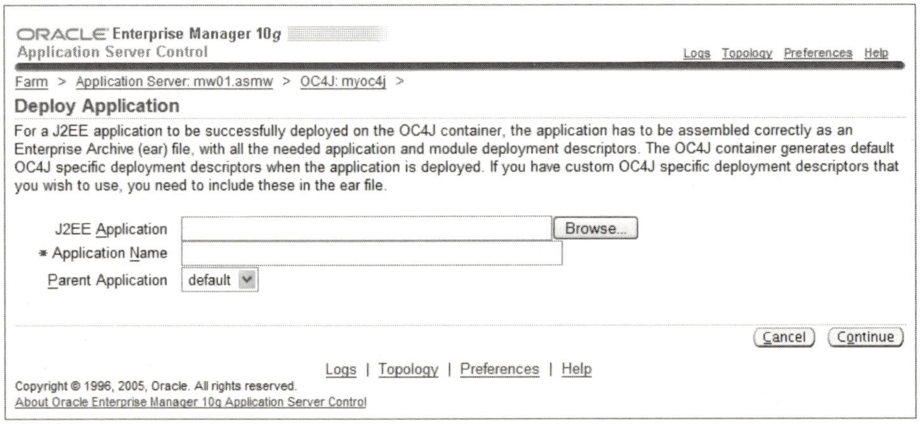

On this page, you browse for the EAR or WAR file and specify the unique name for the application and the parent application name. When you click the Continue button, AS Control deploys the application into the OC4J container. Figure 7.15 shows the applications deployed within the `OC4J_Wireless` container.

Clicking the `Wireless` link shown in Figure 7.15 will take you to the web modules associated with the wireless application, as shown in Figure 7.16.

FIGURE 7.15 OC4J_Wireless deployed applications

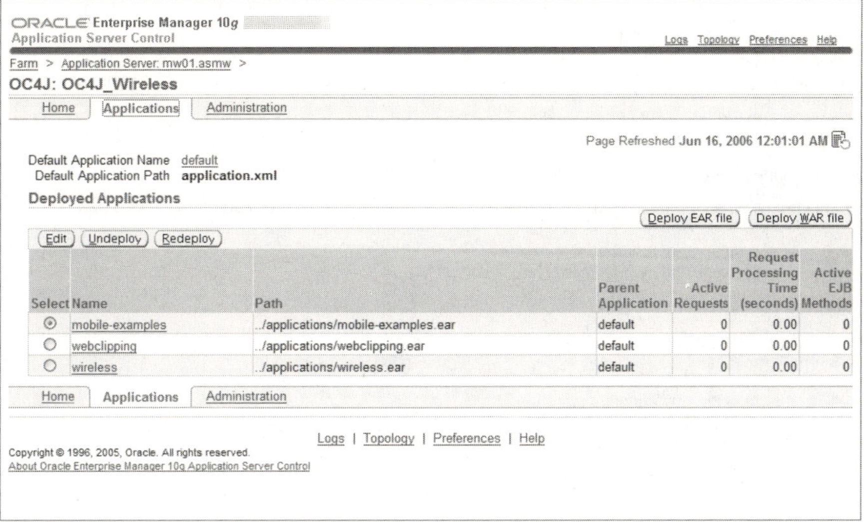

FIGURE 7.16 Wireless web modules

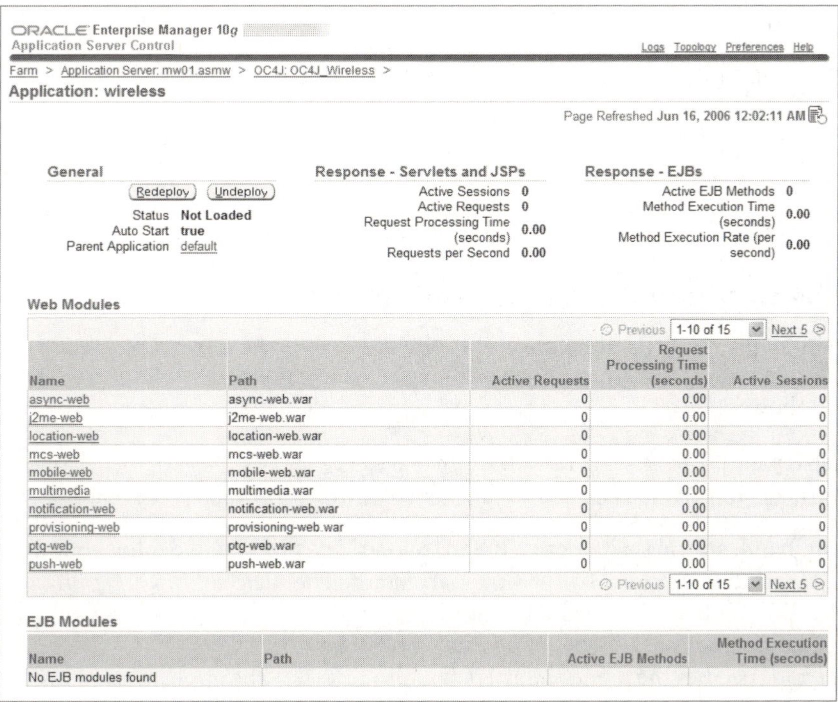

Drilling down one more level, you can click the `multimedia` web module link and see the details of the multimedia web module shown in Figure 7.17.

Most, if not all, of these pages give you valuable performance metrics that you can use for capacity planning and performance tuning.

FIGURE 7.17 Multimedia web module status and servlets

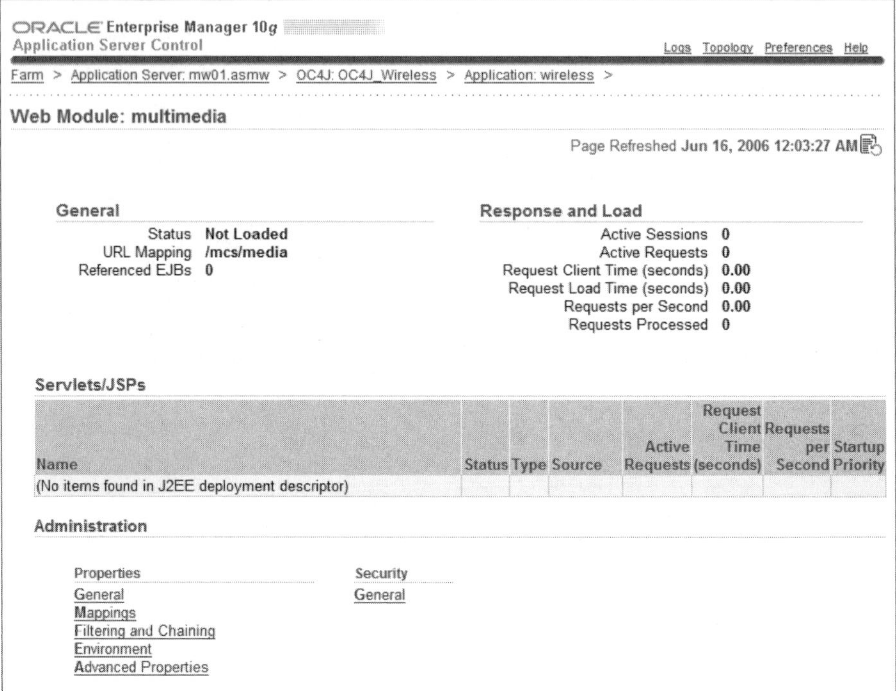

Using the Command Line for Deployment

You can also deploy your J2EE application "the old-fashioned way." The `dcmctl` utility allows you to manually deploy, remove, or redeploy your application files. An example of the command follows:

```
dcmctl deployApplication -file < war or ear file path>
➥ -a <application name> -co <OC4J instance name> -rc <application name>
```

This command, starting with `dcmctl deployApplication`, will deploy your application to the OC4J instance specified by the `-co` parameter. The file that you are going to use for your application (either WAR or EAR) should be local to the system where you are running the `dcmctl` command.

The `-rc` tag specifies the name end users will use to access the application. This tag is used only if it is a WAR file.

The `dcmctl redeployApplication` command will redeploy an already deployed application; finally, the `dcmctl undeployApplication` deletes an already deployed application.

Databases and J2EE

J2EE applications may or may not need to make use of a database for their operation or their data. Many, naturally, do use databases because the need for reliable and persistent data is critical to most applications (and not just J2EE applications).

By definition, J2EE applications are designed to be very portable (recall that Java is operating system independent from its origins). This means that the servlets (JSPs, ASPs, and PSPs) as well as the EJB have to be able to communicate with their target database.

As a security precaution, and to assure true portability, the connection details that you use to allow communication with the database should not be stored in the application code. Although not storing the connection string in the code seems to be counterintuitive to many application developers, most know that they should use a logical representation of the database embedded within their code and then allow the deployer to map this to the physical data source. The source (the connection string) is stored in the Java Naming and Directory Interface (JNDI) tree. The J2EE application retrieves this connection information using the `java.sql.DataSource` object with the published name. This information is then pulled into the variable in the code and used to connect to the database. The location of the tree is in the file `data-sources.xml` that we presented earlier in this chapter.

Enterprise JavaBeans

Enterprise JavaBeans (EJB) is modular, fully portable application code created in an object-oriented architecture (allowing for reuse of code and to help us all keep from having to reinvent the wheel). EJBs enable rapid development of distributed and secure Java applications; they are server-side components that are deployed on a J2EE architecture. EJBs are typically constructed so that the developers are closely modeling the business model rather than just trying to answer a discrete need.

EJBs are typically packaged as Java Archive (JAR) files, and the deployment-specific and run-time behavior information is typically stored in the `ejb-jar.xml` file. As you may already have noticed, Oracle makes extensive use of industry-standard application components, including JAR, EAR, and WAR files, as well as XML files as a means of configuring the application server itself and the components that come into play when different organizations use different components.

EJBs can be deployed on any J2EE-compliant server, which all of our OC4J instances are. Although the EJB module does not need to be modified in any way to be launched on the OC4J instance, it does need to be mapped to its new server environment, which you can accomplish by configuring the new EJB in the `orion-ejb-jar.xml` file. The EJBs (and their JAR files) should then be packaged into an EAR file and deployed to your OracleAS.

Deploying PL/SQL Applications

When it comes time to configure your PL/SQL applications, it is important that you understand all of the pieces and processes necessary to get them working effectively and efficiently.

Configuring *mod_plsql*

mod_plsql is a key component in the Oracle 11*i* E-Business Suite. Based on a modified OracleAS, 11*i* uses mod_plsql to a great extent as a means to connect the browser to an Oracle database and execute stored program units. This process is the same in the full version of the application server.

mod_plsql requests become associated with a database by means of a database access descriptor (DAD), a file that contains a relevant set of configuration parameters used to allow the request to access the database. The parameters that can be found in the DAD file include the database alias (the official Net8 service name), a connection string needed to connect to the database (particularly if the database is remote), and the procedure necessary for uploading and downloading documents.

Although the PL/SQL program units that get called can do any of the database processing in the database, just as any PL/SQL program unit can, typically they return HTML data to the client to help populate web pages.

In an attempt to simplify mod_plsql, Oracle provided the environment with the PL/SQL Web Toolkit. This toolkit is the preliminary set of packages that developers can pull into their own designed packages, functions, and procedures to get information about the initial request and to reconstruct the result and the HTML tags that will be necessary to display the resulting pages appropriately. This toolkit is typically installed in the SYS schema and is available for use by developers who are granted access by administrators.

Although you probably aren't a web developer at the same time you are an administrator, you may be called upon to mentor those who are. You can point these developers to resources in the PL/SQL Web Toolkit Reference for further information.

There are two ways to generate an HTML page using PL/SQL. First, you can create a static HTML page and embed PL/SQL code within it. This page can be compiled into a PL/SQL server page. Although you can easily call procedures from the toolkit, you cannot generate the entire HTML output. If you have considerable existing HTML code and your organization has decided that there needs to be dynamic content or that the HTML pages must work as a front-end interface to database applications, this is the alternative that you would be most apt to follow. Alternatively, you can create a complete stored procedure that can produce the HTML tags to format the output by calling the HTP, HTF, or OWA_% package in the toolkit. This alternative would most likely be chosen by an organization that has an existing source of PL/SQL code that can produce formatted output. In this case, it is easy enough to produce the HTML tags by setting your PRINT statements to call the HTP package of the PL/SQL Web Toolkit.

Several files are involved in the configuration of the mod_plsql module. Because mod_plsql is accessed either directly or indirectly by Apache, the configuration files are called indirectly from the httpd.conf file, which is the primary configuration file for Apache.

httpd.conf

httpd.conf has several include files (or files accessed as a container directive); oracle_apache.conf (discussed in the following section) is one of these. The following is a snippet from a working httpd.conf file that shows several include files:

```
# Include the mod_oc4j configuration file
include "C:\OraHome_2\Apache\Apache\conf\mod_oc4j.conf"
# Include the mod_dms configuration file
include "C:\OraHome_2\Apache\Apache\conf\dms.conf"
# Loading rewrite_module here so it loads before mod_oc4j
LoadModule rewrite_module modules/ApacheModuleRewrite.dll
# Include the SSL definitions and Virtual Host container
include "C:\OraHome_2\Apache\Apache\conf\ssl.conf"
# Include the mod_osso configuration file
include "C:\OraHome_2\Apache\Apache\conf\mod_osso.conf"
# Include the Oracle configuration file for custom settings
include "C:\OraHome_2\Apache\Apache\conf\oracle_apache.conf"
```

httpd.conf is a large file—too large to include in its entirety here. It can be found in the $ORACLE_HOME/Apache/Apache/conf directory. As an OracleAS administrator, you should get to know this file intimately.

As you can see, the configuration files are named logically based on what they are used to configure. mod_osso.conf configures mod_osso, for example.

oracle_apache.conf

One of the main included configuration files in this directive is oracle_apache.conf. Primarily, this file is full of directives of other configuration files. Because it has such a tight purpose, it is a small file. The following are the contents of a working oracle_apache.conf file on the Windows platform:

```
include "D:\OraHome\ultrasearch\webapp\config\ultrasearch.conf"
# Advanced Queuing - AQ XML
include "D:\OraHome\rdbms\demo\aqxml.conf"
#
#Directives needed for OraDAV module
include "D:\OraHome\Apache\oradav\conf\moddav.conf"
include "D:\OraHome\Apache\modplsql\conf\plsql.conf"
include "D:\OraHome\Apache\jsp\conf\ojsp.conf"
# Oracle uix
include "D:\OraHome\uix\uix.conf"
#OiD DAS module
include "D:\OraHome\ldap\das\oiddas.conf"
```

```
#Directives needed for SSO module
include "D:\OraHome\sso\conf\sso_apache.conf"
#Directives needed for OCM module
include "D:\OraHome\Apache\Apache\conf\ocm_apache.conf"
```

plsql.conf

Notice the `plsql.conf` file in the `oracle_apache.conf` file. This, one of the primary configuration files for `mod_plsql`. `plsql.conf`, located in your `$ORACLE_HOME/Apache/modplsql/conf` directory, is also not a large file. It contains the configuration directives that are necessary to load `mod_plsql` into the Apache HTTP server:

```
#==============================================
#  mod_plsql configuration file
# ========================================
# 1. Please refer to plsql.README for a description
#    of this file
# 2. Parameters in this file have to be configured
#              manually
# ========================================
# Configure Oracle HTTP Server to load mod_plsql
LoadModule plsql_module D:\OraHome\bin\modplsql.dll
# Load in mod_plsql directives only if
#mod_plsql is loaded
<IfModule mod_plsql.c>
# ========================================
# Global Settings Section :
# Directives that apply to all DADs
# ==========================================
    PlsqlLogEnable Off
    PlsqlLogDirectory D:\OraHome\Apache\modplsql\logs
# PlsqlIdleSessionCleanupInterval 15 (default)
# PlsqlDMSEnable On (default)
# ============================================
# Database Access Descriptors Settings Section
# ============================================
  include "D:\OraHome\Apache\modplsql\conf\dads.conf"
# ============================================
# Cache Settings Section
# ============================================
  include "D:\OraHome\Apache\modplsql\conf\cache.conf"
</IfModule>
```

The LoadModule plsql_module directive:

```
LoadModule plsql_module D:\OraHome\bin\modplsql.dll
```

indicates that Apache should load the modplsql library when it loads so your implementation can make use of the mod_plsql module. It is important to remember that any changes that you make to this file require that Apache be restarted because the module is not pulled in dynamically when the configuration file is changed.

Notice that the global settings for mod_plsql contain the include directives for the dads.conf file. This file provides configuration directives for database connectivity.

Notice that the plsql.conf file is organized in much the same manner as the httpd.conf file. It has different sections, each pertaining to different aspects of the configuration and settings for the sections. It starts out with general sections that contain the directives that apply to mod_plsql overall, at the highest level.

Configuring DADs Using *dads.conf*

One of the other primary files, and one of the most significant included files in the plsql.conf file, is the dads.conf file. Like all of the other .conf files, dads.conf contains those settings that pertain directly to database access descriptor (DAD) files.

DAD files are the specific sets of values that provide information to mod_plsql so it can connect successfully to the target database (regardless of where that database might be) and successfully fulfill the request from the end user.

A working dads.conf file follows:

```
# ============================================
#  mod_plsql DAD Configuration File
# =============================================
# 1. Please refer to dads.README
# for a description of this file
#=============================================
# Note: This file should typically be included
# in your plsql.conf file with
# the "include" directive.
# Hint: You can look at some sample
# DADs in the dads.README file
# =============================================
<Location /pls/orasso>
SetHandler pls_handler
Order deny,allow
Allow from All
AllowOverride None
PlsqlDatabaseUsername orasso
```

```
PlsqlDatabasePassword @Baffp9iwB1RI7v4q3/3aqf/Si/rpVoOSiw==
PlsqlDatabaseConnectString cn=orclas,cn=oraclecontext NetServiceNameFormat
PlsqlNLSLanguage AMERICAN_AMERICA.AL32UTF8
PlsqlAuthenticationMode SingleSignOn
PlsqlSessionCookieName orasso
PlsqlDocumentTablename orasso.wwdoc_document
PlsqlDocumentPath docs
PlsqlDocumentProcedure orasso.wwdoc_process.process_download
PlsqlDefaultPage orasso.home
PlsqlPathAlias url
PlsqlPathAliasProcedure orasso.wwpth_api_alias.process_download
</Location>
```

Notice in the comments that it suggests that you read the `readme` file. I know that these files are low on your reading list, but most Oracle `readme` files contain very valuable information that can make your life much easier.

DAD files not only contain information necessary for your middle tier to connect to the database, they also contain parameters that help Apache and `mod_plsql` work efficiently together to fulfill `mod_plsql` requests in the database.

All web-based applications that use the PL/SQL Web Toolkit have to have a DAD available in order to even invoke their applications. This is true in any OracleAS-based application and in any current E-Business Suite application.

The following parameters are specified in the DAD files:

PlsqlDatabaseUsername The username that has permission to log in to the database. Unless your parameter `PlsqlAuthenticationMode` (discussed later in this list) is set to something other than `Basic`, this parameter is mandatory and (if you are using SSO) has to be the name of the schema owner.

PlsqlDatabasePassword The password associated with the username in the previous parameter. This is also mandatory if you are setting `PlsqlAuthenticationMode` to `Basic` and is the schema owner if you are using SSO.

It is important to remember that the DAD file needs to be kept protected because it is typically an easily readable entry in an easily readable file.

PlsqlDatabaseConnectString The connection string necessary for `mod_plsql` to connect to the database. Obviously, if this is a database access descriptor file, it needs to provide the information necessary to connect to the database. If the parameter is not specified, `mod_plsql` assumes (rightly or wrongly) that the connection is in the format <host:port:sid> or that it is resolvable by Net8. This parameter can take several distinct values:

ServiceNameFormat <host:port:servicename>

SidFormat <host:port:sid>

TNSFormat A TNS alias that is resolvable by Net8 and that can be accessed successfully by `tnsping` or `sqlplus`

NetServiceNameFormat A valid net service name that can successfully resolve to a database connect descriptor

PlsqlAuthenticationMode The authentication mode that needs to be used by the application that is attempting to access the database through the DAD. The value for this can be any of the following:

Basic This is the default value and should be used when you want to be able to use dynamic authentication. If this is set, the DAD username and password have to be omitted from the string.

SingleSignOn Used for OracleAS Portal.

GlobalOwa Provided for backward compatibility.

CustomOWA Used by a very small number of applications (see *HTTP Server Administration Guide 10*g for more information).

PerPackageOwa Used by a very small number of applications (see *HTTP Server Administration Guide 10*g for more information).

Invoking a PL/SQL Application

Once you have created your PL/SQL application and you have configured your DAD file to allow you to connect to the database with the application, it is time to test your application and launch it the way that your end users will launch it. Quite simply, you launch a PL/SQL application by typing the URL into the browser. The following URL is a generic representation of the way the application is called:

```
<protocol>://<host>:<port>/<path>/
<package.procedure>?<param1>=<value1>&<param2>=<value2>&<param3>=<value3>
```

In this URL, the generic representations are replaced as follows:

protocol This can be either `http` for standard connections or `https` for SSL secured connections.

host The fully qualified domain name of the machine where the web server runs.

port The port on which the application server is listening. If this is omitted, the port is assumed.

path The virtual path to handle PL/SQL requests. This is the parameter in the `<Location>` container for the DAD file that the PL/SQL request uses to connect.

package The PL/SQL package containing the stored procedures that the application comprises.

procedure The name of the stored procedure that the application will run. It must be a procedure so it can return a screen instead of a single value. Any parameters can only be `IN` arguments.

It is, of course, possible to successfully retrieve a page without specifying a schema, a package, or a stored procedure name when the URL is specified. To accomplish this, the location container associated with the virtual path (/plsqlapp) has to contain the PlsqlDefaultPage directive. The directive specifies the default procedure that should be used if the URL call does not contain a schema/package/procedure. This example sets the default page to hrschema.homepage:

```
<Location /pls/plsqlapp>
SetHandler pls_handler
...
PlsqlDefaultPage hrschema.homepage
</Location>
```

PL/SQL Server Pages

PL/SQL Server Pages (PSPs) are an extension of the PL/SQL Web Toolkit. They allow PL/SQL to be used as a scripting language within HTML files just like Active Server Pages (ASPs), JavaServer Pages (JSPs), and PHPs. The PSPs containing the PL/SQL scripting are loaded into and published from the Oracle 10*g* database. (They are, after all, PL/SQL constructs.)

You (as the application server administrator) probably won't be involved with creating the PSPs or even with loading them into the database, but you will eventually need to help an application developer with them, since the application developers assume you know about everything under the Oracle Application Server subject area!

In order to load these PSPs, you first need to create the PL/SQL file with a .psp extension. This file can have text, tags, and even PSP directives interspersed with PL/SQL declarations and scripts and script snippets. At times PSPs are nothing more than HTML files. It is the compilation of these files as a PSP that produces the resulting stored procedure. This stored procedure then outputs the same HTML file that would be output if the same procedure were run using the PL/SQL Web Toolkit.

The PSP can be as simple as all straight static HTML or as complex as a procedure that generates all of the content of a given web page complete with markup tags for the title, body, and all levels of headings and breaks.

Once you have compiled the file into a PSP with a .psp extension, you need to get it loaded into the database. (After all, what good is a PL/SQL package if it is not resident in the database?) The command that accomplishes this is as follows:

```
loadpsp -replace -user scott/tiger@mydb target_psp.psp
```

- scott is the database user.
- tiger is the database user's password.
- mydb is the database name as it appears in the tnsnames.ora file.
- target_psp.psp is the name of the stored procedure that is being uploaded.

You can now freely and easily access the procedure by entering the URL for that procedure:

```
http://my.co:80/pls/mydad/target_psp
```

- `my.co` is the DNS name of the server.
- `80` is the port on which Apache is listening.
- `mydad` is the name of the DAD file to be used.
- `target_psp` is the name of the stored procedure.

It is important to remember that you cannot accomplish everything with PL/SQL, however. It's true that when you have a hammer everything looks like a nail (or like a Phillips head screw depending on your development style), but it is also important to remember that you need to always match the tool to the problem.

For that reason, Oracle also includes, by default, the ability to use the Common Gateway Interface (CGI) to provide dynamic content to a web page. We covered CGI applications previously in Chapter 4.

Summary

There are many different kinds of web applications that you can configure to run on your application server. Not only can you configure typical PL/SQL applications to be called through the application server, you also can set up OC4J instances so you can call Java applications.

In this chapter, you learned what PSPs are and how to configure and deploy them. This information is good to know not only for your OracleAS installation, but also as general background knowledge on how applications are deployed in an application server environment. Although many shops will choose to go with Java applications despite the performance gains that might be made with PSP applications, the understanding of how you deploy PSP applications will come in handy.

We then looked at creating and maintaining an Oracle Containers for J2EE (OC4J) instance. You learned how to use `dcmctl` and the GUI interface as a means for configuring and creating OC4J instances. We looked at the files that go into making up your OC4J environment and how those files interact to modularize your configuration.

Once we described how to create an OC4J instance, we showed how to deploy J2EE applications that will ride on that instance. These applications are highly portable and can be run nearly anywhere. This will benefit not only your organization, but also your end users because portability means that you can move the application from one server to another without having to totally recode content to match the syntax of a different operating system.

Exam Essentials

Know how to configure OC4J. Be able to configure OC4J using either the GUI or the command-line tool. When using command line, understand what the different flags represent.

Understand how to create an OC4J Instance. Understand how the different XML files work together to provide the underpinnings of the instance and what the key files do for your instance.

Be adept at enabling OC4J Instances. Be able to describe how to enable and disable OC4J instances in your environment. Also, be able to explain when you might want to do this.

Understand OC4J Configuration Basics. Describe the basic configuration steps involved in an OC4J instance and what the different background configuration files are that support this.

Be able to configure OC4J Using Application Server Control. Be able to configure OC4J using either the command-line tools or the Application Server Control GUI.

Understand how to deploy J2EE Applications. Describe the different components in a J2EE application and determine where each will reside on the server and what flags in the configuration files control this destination.

Know how to deploy Web Application Modules Using `dcmctl`. Describe the process of deploying application modules using the command-line tools. Understand the meaning of the different flags.

Thoroughly understand the J2EE Architecture. Describe the J2EE architecture and what the different components do.

Understand the interface between databases and J2EE. Understand how a database provides the infrastructure on which a J2EE application runs and how connectivity to that database is accomplished.

Understand the purpose and uses of Enterprise JavaBeans. Describe Enterprise JavaBeans and understand when they are appropriate. Be able to describe when they might be appropriate to use.

Describe the relationship between EJB and OC4J. Describe how Enterprise JavaBeans and OC4J work together in a successfully deployed application.

Know how to deploy J2EE Applications Using Application Server Control and `dcmctl`. Understand how to deploy J2EE applications either with the command-line tools or the GUI interface. Understand how the background configuration files play into this deployment.

Review Questions

1. What is a PSP?

   A. Passive Server Pages

   B. Perl Server Pages

   C. PL/SQL Server Pages

   D. Portable SQL Procedures

2. What component does Oracle add to enhance Apache to assist in performing processing on PL/SQL code?

   A. `mod_oracle`

   B. `mod_database`

   C. `mod_pl/sql`

   D. `mod_plsql`

   E. `mod_as`

3. What Apache-provided module extends the functionality of standard Apache to assist the Perl interpreter with parsing Perl code?

   A. `mod_sso`

   B. `mod_perl`

   C. None; it is standard functionality.

   D. `mod_plsql`

4. What module, provided by third parties and packaged by Oracle with its application, supports the use of FastCGI?

   A. `mod_cgi`

   B. `mod_fcgi`

   C. `mod_fastcgi`

   D. `mod_gateway`

   E. `mod_perl`

5. What benefit can you derive from using FastCGI? (Choose all that apply.)

   A. Eliminate resource overhead

   B. Improve security

   C. Language independence

   D. Scalability

6. What does mod_plsql use to help it connect to the appropriate database?
   A. MOM file
   B. DAD file
   C. Configuration descriptor file
   D. mod_fastcgi
   E. All of the above
   F. None of the above
7. What is the name of the Oracle-provided set of tools, functions, procedures, and packages that assists with the creation of PSPs?
   A. mod_plsql
   B. PL/SQL Web Toolkit
   C. Java Developer's Tool Kit
   D. Oracle Development Kit
8. What is the primary file that is accessed by Apache and that contains the include directive for many other files?
   A. mod_plsql
   B. apache.config
   C. HTTP.conf
   D. httpd.conf
9. How do you configure the parameters in the plsql.conf file?
   A. Via the Application Server home page.
   B. Use the PL/SQL Web Toolkit.
   C. Manually.
   D. You can't configure the parameters in the plsql.conf file.
10. What file do you fix to configure your DAD files?
    A. dad.conf
    B. dads.cfg
    C. dads.config
    D. dads.conf
11. Why should you put your DAD files in a protected location?
    A. They are easily corrupted.
    B. They are plaintext and easily readable.
    C. They can be lost or deleted easily.
    D. It is sometimes hard to remember where you put them.

12. What modules could possibly handle requests for CGI scripts? (Choose all that apply.)
    A. `mod_oc4j`
    B. `mod_cgi`
    C. `mod_perl`
    D. `mod_fastcgi`
13. What process does FastCGI use to speed up performance?
    A. It uses server pooling.
    B. It spawns multiple threads.
    C. It spawns a new process for every script.
    D. It runs on another server.
    E. It performs more fetches than regular CGI.
14. What component of the application server is J2EE 1.4 compliant?
    A. WAR
    B. JRE
    C. OC4J
    D. CGI
15. What is the name of the default OC4J instance that gets installed with OracleAS?
    A. `test`
    B. `dev`
    C. `orahome`
    D. `home`
16. What section of the OC4J home page shows you the current status of the OC4J server and allows you to start, stop, and restart the OC4J instance?
    A. Status
    B. Stat
    C. Administration
    D. General
17. What is the command that you use to start the OC4J instance at the command line?
    A. `dcmctl`
    B. `opmnctl`
    C. `oractl`
    D. `oc4jctl`

18. What module helps communicate between OHS and OC4J?

A. `mod_plsql`

B. `mod_ohs`

C. `mod_oc4j`

D. `mod_j2ee`

19. What is stored in the specified `deployment-directory`?

A. Instance-specific files

B. Deployed WAR files

C. Deployed J2EE files

D. Deployed EAR files

20. `Application-auto-directory` specifies the directory that stores what?

A. All files for an application

B. All WAR files on the server

C. Automatically deployed files for an OC4J instance

D. All files for an OC4J instance

Answers to Review Questions

1. C. PSPs are PL/SQL Server Pages. PSPs are PL/SQL code modules that provide static and dynamic content for your application.

2. D. The `mod_plsql` module is how Oracle extends the functionality of the Apache web server to assist with the access and processing of database information in the web pages.

3. B. `mod_perl` forwards Perl requests to the Perl interpreter, which is embedded in the Oracle HTTP server.

4. C. `mod_fastcgi` supports the FastCGI protocol.

5. A, B, C, D. All of these are benefits derived from using FastCGI.

6. B. `mod_plsql` uses the database access descriptor file (DAD file) to help it connect to the appropriate database.

7. B. Oracle provides the PL/SQL Development Web Toolkit, which is the preliminary package that developers can pull into their own designed packages, functions, and procedures to get information about the initial request, to reconstruct the result, and to access the HTML tags that will be necessary to display the resulting pages appropriately.

8. D. The `httpd.conf` file calls (either directly or indirectly) many other configuration files.

9. C. Parameters in this file have to be configured manually.

10. D. The `dads.conf` file is used to set the parameters for your DAD file.

11. B. DAD files need to be in a protected location because they contain sensitive information that could be easily readable by someone with less than honorable intentions.

12. B, D. CGI script requests could be handled by either `mod_cgi` or `mod_fastcgi`.

13. A. FastCGI speeds up applications by pooling processes in a pool of running servers.

14. C. Oracle Containers for J2EE is the Oracle runtime component that is J2EE 1.4 compliant.

15. D. The instance named `home` is installed by default when you install OracleAS.

16. D. On the General section of the OC4J home page you can view a snapshot of the current status of the OC4J server and start, stop, or restart the OC4J server.

17. B. `opmnctl startproc` starts the OC4J instance.

18. C. Web applications communicate between OHS and OC4J using `mod_oc4j`.

19. A. OC4J instance-specific files are stored in this directory for each deployed application.

20. C. The `application-auto-directory` attribute specifies where files go that are automatically deployed whenever there is no need for action from any administrator.

Managing Secure Access to the Application Server

ORACLE APPLICATION SERVER 10*g* ADMINISTRATION I EXAM OBJECTIVES COVERED IN THIS CHAPTER:

✓ **Managing and Configuring OracleAS Certificate Authority**

- Explain Public Key Infrastructure
- Describe Oracle Public Key Infrastructure Management tools
- Describe OracleAS Certificate Authority
- Explain OracleAS Certificate Authority Architecture
- Access OCA Administration Pages
- Access OCA User Pages

✓ **Securing OracleAS Components Using SSL**

- Explain Oracle wallet manager functionality
- Manage wallets
- Upload and download wallets
- Manage user certificates
- Manage trusted certificates
- Enable Oracle HTTP Server, SSO, Web Cache, and Portal to use SSL

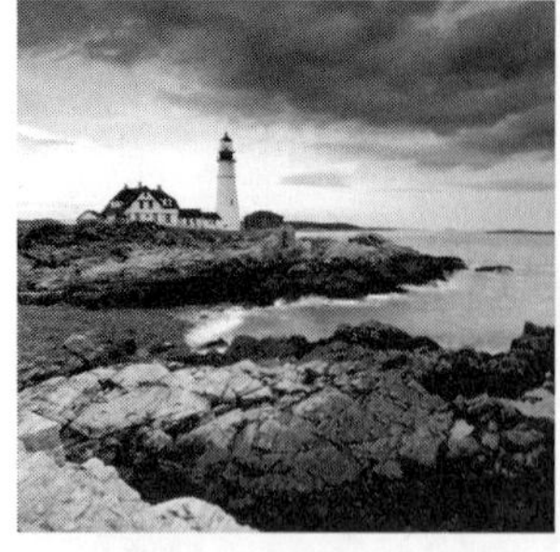

Oracle's integrated security services work together to assure that your Internet and intranet applications are as secure as possible. Because of the tightly integrated components, Oracle Application Server 10*g* (OracleAS) can be the single solution necessary for an organization to venture into not only the present, but also the future.

Although security in such a widely networked environment can be even more complex than the necessary programming efforts, breaking down the overall security of OracleAS into its components will help you better understand not only their inner workings, but also the workings of the security features as a whole.

In the first half of this chapter, we will discuss security as it applies in a networked environment, be it Internet or intranet (collectively known as I*net). We will discuss the components of an I*net environment, including the components that are specific to the OracleAS security infrastructure. In the second half, we will cover the use of several of these components to configure OracleAS security features.

Security in an Internet Environment

Privacy of communication, whether spoken or data related, is essential to business. This is no less true in an Internet environment than in any other. The importance of taking whatever steps are necessary to assure this privacy cannot be overstated. With the advent of mass usage of the Internet in business, security risks associated with data communication become more of an issue nearly every day. What are these threats?

Security risks in an Internet business can be divided into the following categories:

Data tampering and fraud Distributed environments like the Internet bring with them the potential for anyone, particularly a malicious third party, to tamper with your data as it moves between locations. This can be done in a multitude of ways. Some good examples are altering the name on a transaction to reroute funds and changing the amount on a banking transaction from maybe $100 to $1000 or $10,000.

Eavesdropping and data theft This often deals with the storage and transmittal of data. Users need to be assured that their data are being stored and transmitted securely. This includes, but is not limited to, making sure that sensitive information (like Social Security numbers and credit card information) cannot be stolen. Network watching programs can easily be installed without anyone's knowledge and eavesdrop on network traffic. This kind of packet observation program can be customized to find and steal usernames, passwords, credit card information, or any other relevant personal information that a person might be looking for.

Falsifying user identities Nearly everyone today is concerned with identity theft. It is, in fact, becoming one of the greatest threats to users of the Internet. Criminals steal personal data (such as bank account numbers, driver's license numbers, and Social Security numbers) and set up illegal accounts in someone else's name. Consider how many times you have had to enter any of this information into an interface, Internet or intranet, to complete a transaction.

Password-related threats How many passwords do your users have to remember? Even in a small organization, users have to remember multiple passwords. And that is just for work. How many more do you have to remember to allow you to pay your bills online or log into your library account or your Amazon.com account? All of these passwords are necessary to help with the *authentication* of user access. As a result of the need for a growing number of passwords, people often do things to help themselves while inadvertently compromising password security. They may select easily guessed passwords. Names of spouses, children, pets, or fictional characters are often used; these, along with words easily found in a dictionary, are vulnerable to dictionary attacks. Users also may standardize all of their passwords so that they are the same on every machine and every website, resulting in potentially vast exposure in the event that even one password is compromised. They may use passwords with very slight variations that can easily be derived from other known passwords (like april, @pril, and apr1l). Think complex passwords are a solution? Users with complex passwords often write them down and leave them in locations where any attacker could easily find them (such as in a file on the computer or taped to the writing drawer or under their keyboard on their desk). They could forget them too, causing costly administration and support efforts.

Unauthorized use of data It is the role of any application server to mediate access between the end users and the backend databases. Once the application server has done its job, the database's access controls take over and the user's database privileges allow access to the tables, columns, and rows for data that are supposed to be accessible to that user. The ability or inability of the application server to fulfill its job can mean that the database either is protected from harm or is open and vulnerable to access from outside agents.

Although no one piece of the networking puzzle will stop all unauthorized use of data, neither can any piece be ignored. Anyone with a strong enough desire to use your data in inappropriate ways will be able to find paths into the system through any weakness. No piece is inherently less secure than any other. As long as you understand that as an administrator, you will be far better equipped to make your piece of the puzzle as secure as possible.

Lack of accountability Technology can go only so far on its own. If the system administrator is unable to track users' activities, then the users cannot necessarily be held responsible for their actions. One of the most dangerous things in a system is the combination of a user with just enough knowledge and ability to be dangerous and nobody watching them while they play. Therefore, there needs to be some reliable way to monitor who is doing what with the data. A logging service can be called on to audit security-related events if necessary. Database auditing also can be used.

Hacking Hackers are a unique breed. They may try to corrupt your website or your database, or they may try to steal web connections and redirect those connections to a different site (fooling the end user into believing the resulting site is something other than what it is). To prevent corruption, you can control access tightly to administrative functions that govern the content of your company's site. You can use *authorization* and *encryption* as a means to protect against stolen web connections, and you can investigate suspicious traffic or lack of traffic to your company's site to determine if hacking is going on.

Denial of service attacks What good is a website or an application if it is not accessible to its targeted authorized end users? Although system security does not alone ensure the ultimate availability of any given system, without security, that availability is guaranteed to disappear at some point. Users and many administrators feel that availability is the same as continuity of service. They believe that being able to access a site whenever they want to implies availability. If the website, application, and database are all available all of the time, that should be enough, right? Maybe. Security vulnerabilities can compromise any system's availability. Security in the configuration and allocation of resources, security in the accessibility of those resources, and security in the unavailability of the system to those without legitimate reasons to access it all play a part in an application's availability. All systems should be set up in such a way that any vulnerabilities of the system are protected so that malicious intruders cannot exploit them.

Security Services in an Internet Environment

Many fundamental security services are required in any multiuser networked environment. These services include, but are not limited to, the following:

Authentication This occurs after users or systems request access to services or data; it is the process that enables the target system to verify the identity of the user or the system that is requesting access.

Authorization This is required for effective and efficient access control. This process determines the privileges that users and other systems have for accessing resources.

Delegation This is the ability to allow a user or application to perform a task that would ordinarily require higher authorization than they currently have.

Access control This is the limitation of any given user's access privileges so that they can see only what they need to be able to see in order to perform the tasks that they are allowed to perform. On the basis of the authentication of identity and the authorization of privileges granted by the previous three services, a system grants access to resources (hardware, software, and data) in ways that are consistent with security policies that are defined for those resources.

Data protection This control uses encryption mechanisms to prevent unauthorized users from accessing sensitive or secure data (such as passwords or sensitive health or financial data). Encryption is not the only method of controlling access to data, however; you or another administrator can assign roles to a given user or a group of users at either the operating system level or the database level, depending on the security your organization is attempting to control. In the database, views can be used to enforce security by limiting the user to seeing only the data that meet the "where" criteria in the view's definition. Fine-grained access control can be used at the database level as well, as can virtual private databases. But these only control access to the data at the source;

they really don't protect that data or prevent access to that data as they pass over the network from the source to the destination.

OracleAS addresses these challenges in an e-business in several ways. Among the best ways to reduce the security risks on the Internet (and indeed, on an intranet as well) is to provide multiple layers of security mechanisms to make sure that security can remain strong even in the event of the failure of a single mechanism. The ability to rest assured that security remains intact and critical information will remain uncompromised even if there is a failure in one of the layers is often referred to as deep data protection. OracleAS provides for this type of protection through data encryption, broad and extensive auditing offerings, and access control.

Regardless of the number of anticipated users, security mechanisms must be scalable and scaled to Internet size, able to support many thousands or even millions of users. This scalability needs to be practical to administer while remaining robust. OracleAS provides several security features that are customizable to meet this need for any size application. Proxy authentication, support for established Internet standards (such as Secure Sockets Layer, or SSL) and relevant public key infrastructure (PKI) standards, Java security, and enterprise-wide user security features (such as directory-based privilege management) round out Oracle's robust offerings to meet the Internet-scale security requirements.

OracleAS's secure hosting and data exchange features enable economical and secure partitioning of data access by either customers or other users while allowing for secure data sharing among different communities of interest. This is accomplished through PKI and enterprise user security.

OracleAS Security Architecture

OracleAS implements its security features in every one of its components, from the Web Cache clear through to the backend database. Each OracleAS component integrates its security features into the entire application server.

In the following sections, we will discuss these components and how they integrate their security features to make OracleAS an even more secure product.

Secure Sockets Layer

Secure Sockets Layer (SSL) is an industry-standard protocol for securing network connections. SSL authenticates a user's identity through the exchange of certificates. It protects data not when it resides in the database but rather while it is being transmitted. This is accomplished using encryption, authentication, and data integrity algorithms. OracleAS supports SSL versions 2 and 3 and Transport Layer Security (TLS) version 1. The technologies for this are rooted in public key encryption, the only feasible way to implement security over an insecure network.

Data integrity is a mechanism for verifying that all of the data transmitted is correctly received. The client hashes the message into a digest, using a hash function, and sends this message digest to the server. The server hashes the same message into a digest and compares the two resulting digests. It is not possible to produce the same digest from two different messages, even if the only difference in the messages is a difference in white space. Therefore, if for any reason the two digests don't match identically, this is an indication that someone tampered with the message. One of the hash functions supported by SSL is SHA1. SHA1 is a Secure Hash Algorithm, and is the mostly commonly used member of a family of cryptographic hash functions, used in SSH, SSL and many other communication protocols.

It is far beyond the scope of this chapter, or even this book, to adequately discuss all the areas an administrator should understand concerning cryptography, how it works, and its ramifications. Additional sources of information can be found at the RSA website (`www.rsasecurity.com/rsalabs/pkcs/`), Wikipedia (`http://en.wikipedia.org/wiki/Public-key_cryptography`), Webopedia (`www.webopedia.com/TERM/P/public_key_cryptography.html`), and Sun's site (`http://docs.sun.com/source/816-6154-10/contents.htm`). These resources can provide a general explanation of what cryptography and public key encryption are so you can have a fuller background on the concept. If you really want an adventure in learning, there is a 10-part cryptography concepts lesson at faq.org (`www.faqs.org/faqs/cryptography-faq`) that is very interesting to read, if a little deep.

SSL is the standard protocol for network Transport layer security. It provides for secure communication between the client and the server by allowing authentication, the use of digital signatures to prove integrity, and encryption to provide privacy.

The certificate authority (CA) is a third-party authority whose job it is to issue, renew, and revoke authentication or digital certificates. One of the most well-known CAs is VeriSign. Digital certificates are the electronic means of establishing credentials when processing transactions over the Internet. Certificates are issued by authorized CAs and contain the name, the serial number, the encryption date, a copy of the certificate holder's public key (the key that is used for encrypting and decrypting messages and digital signatures), and the digital signature of the certificate issuing authority. These certificates for SSO users can be stored in the Oracle Internet Directory (OID).

OracleAS provides OracleAS Certificate Authority (OCA) to allow you to create and manage certificates for use in Oracle software. OCA provides administrators with a simple, easy-to-use web-based interface through which a user can submit online requests, provide authentication information, and acquire a certificate. As a part of the OCA architecture, a server administrator can also use Oracle Wallet Manager (OWM) to create, acquire, use, and store certificates. Wallet owners use Oracle Wallet to manage the credentials of clients.

Using simple authentication alone, however, can pose serious security risks for applications and their supporting data. If a hacker can access an account, they can do immeasurable damage. As a means to avoid, or allay, such attacks, SSL can be used instead of simple usernames and passwords to authenticate.

Cryptography

Cryptography is a field of study involving the use of mathematical and linguistic techniques for the purpose of securing data communication. Historically it has concerned itself primarily with encryption, and this is the frame of reference we will use.

Encryption is the method used to scramble or unscramble data. Different encryption algorithms can be used to encrypt messages, including Advanced Encryption Standard (AES), RC4 (a variable key-size stream cipher designed by Rivest for RSA Security), and Triple Data Encryption Standard (3DES). TLS is a protocol that provides facilities for private communications over the Internet and enables client/server applications to communicate in ways that prevent eavesdropping, tampering, and message forgery.

SSL provides message integrity, authentication, and encryption based on the concept of public key cryptography. Public key cryptography (or asymmetric key cryptography) allows users to communicate securely without having prior access to a shared secret key. This is done using a pair of cryptographic keys designed as public key and private key. These keys are related mathematically.

In public key cryptography, the private key (the key that encrypts or locks the message) is kept consistently secret while the public key (the key that is used to decrypt or unlock the message) is widely distributed and is itself stored encrypted. Given a public key, it should be impossible to deduce the private key.

In OracleAS, the public key often is stored with other security credentials in Oracle Wallet. The private key is randomly generated when the server and the client first establish an SSL connection. It is generated specifically for a given session and is not stored.

Public key algorithms do not authenticate the identities of the communicating parties. To verify that the owner of the public key is who they say they are, digital signatures are typically used.

Digital signatures are electronic signatures that can be used to authenticate the identity of the sender of the message or the signer of a document. Although the end product is still authentication, digital signatures should not be confused with digital certificates. Digital signatures can be used to ensure that the content of the original message or document arrived at its destination unchanged and can be used to hold the originator legally responsible for the document, just as a physical signature can hold the signer legally responsible for something they signed physically. It can be used, literally, in the stead of a physical signature and can be as legally binding.

Credentials and Their Storage

Authentication is used to provide the identity of one party to another party. Whenever a client requests an SSL session, the server sends certificates to the client. The client verifies that the server is authentic by validating the server certificate. The server can also require the client to have a certificate in order to authenticate the identity of the client.

Digital certificates are the electronic counterpart of the proof of identification that is often requested at airline ticket booths and other official points. Driver's licenses, passports, and official membership cards are your way of identifying yourself when you are standing face-to-face with someone. Digital certificates are your way of identifying yourself electronically when you are dealing computer-to-computer. They electronically prove your identity and your right to access information or services. They are also known as digital IDs and are used to bind the unique pair of electronic keys that are used to encrypt and decrypt messages and to sign digital documents. Digital certificates are also a means by which transactions over the Internet are made legally binding.

Digital IDs make it possible to absolutely verify someone's claim that they have the right to use a given key, making it easier to prevent people from using fake keys to impersonate other users. They enable secure authentication of users, ensure the integrity of transmitted data, and prevent unauthorized access to information at either the transmission level or the storage layer. When used in conjunction with encryption, digital IDs provide a far more complete security solution by assuring the identity of all of the parties taking part in any given transaction. They do this by incorporating into the digital ID the owner's public key and name, the expiration date of the public key, the name of the issuer and the certificate authority associated with it, the serial number of the digital ID, and the digital signature of the issuer.

Web Cache

OracleAS Web Cache can be configured to support Hypertext Transfer Protocol over Secure Socket Layer, or HTTP over SSL (HTTPS). HTTPS is a web protocol that encrypts and decrypts user pages requesting information as well as the pages that are returned by the web server to the requesting browser. This web cache (a service running on an independent server or as a separate service on the middle tier) is positioned between the client and the primary HTTP service that accesses the content and is intended to retrieve cached frequently accessed pages or partial pages. Figure 8.1 shows an example of how a Web Cache architecture can be added to an existing set of application servers to allow for more rapid response time for providing predefined types of content to the user and to limit the added calls to the database and the additional network traffic to the servers.

OracleAS Web Cache's security features can be implemented by restricting administration, by using SSL, and by enabling SSL acceleration.

Administration restriction can be implemented by password authentication, port control, and restriction of IP addresses and subnets.

SSL is a standard for Transport layer security. Recall that SSL provides a vehicle for authentication, encryption, and data integrity. By allowing OracleAS's Web Cache to support SSL, Oracle provides the facility to cache pages for the HTTPS protocol requests.

SSL can put a strain on the server's CPU and can slow down the overall performance of the application. The computers involved in the transaction have to agree on protocols and perform the initial handshake and key exchange that contribute nothing to the data throughput of the interaction. And, every packet of information has to include the necessary information that SSL adds to ensure security in addition to being encrypted with the other pieces of information that must be added to the data to ensure that the data is routed to the appropriate destination. With every additional operation, additional strain is placed on the server. Although the additional CPU load for each operation may appear negligible, on a busy server, they can add up.

FIGURE 8.1 Web Cache architecture

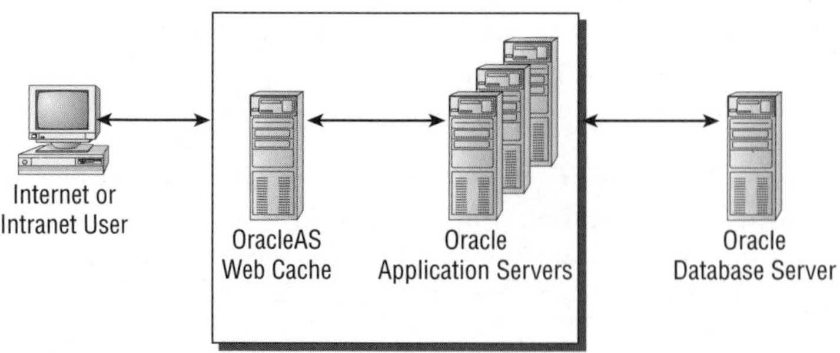

To help performance, OracleAS supports nCipher's BHAPI-compliant hardware on servers running OracleAS Web Cache and the Oracle HTTP server. The Bluemagic Host Application Programming Interface (BHAPI) is a programming interface that helps make it easier for hardware coprocessors to handle some of the additional load. This nCipher hardware offloads the key exchange processing from the CPU, thereby alleviating much of the strain and improving throughput and response time.

HTTP/HTTPS

Oracle's HTTP server supplies services for either HTTP or HTTPS and (through plug-ins) routes requests for authentication and authorization.

Oracle Containers for J2EE (also known as OC4J) provides facilities for Java Runtime Environments for OracleAS components. The Java Authentication and Authorization Service (JAAS) provider ensures both secure access to and execution of Java applications as well as the integration of Java-based applications with OracleAS's Single Sign-On facilities.

Oracle's HTTP server controls access to resources through basic authentication, by authentication through OracleAS Single Sign-On using `mod_osso` (based on the request), through the use of filters, or through the use of the SSL protocol.

Oracle's HTTP server allows users to access OracleAS using standard web protocols. The HTTP listener supports both HTTP and HTTPS. Further, Oracle's HTTP server security infrastructure provides the following *modules* to assist with security configuration:

`mod_auth` Authentication based on username and password.

`mod_access` Server access control based on request.

`mod_security` Noninvasive method to define filters used to detect anomalies such as SQL injections and to prescribe appropriate actions when such anomalies are detected.

Oracle adds the following modules to the standard HTTP modules:

`mod_ossl` Authentication and encryption with X.509 client certificates over SSL. X.509 is a widely employed standard used for defining digital certificates.

`mod_osso` Enables Single Sign-On authentication for web applications.

Java Authentication and Authorization Service

OracleAS's flexibility has been enhanced by the introduction of a comprehensive and fully integrated security framework that will support all of the OracleAS components as well as third-party and custom applications that organizations choose to deploy through OracleAS. This framework is based on OracleAS's Single Sign-On authentication as well as Oracle Internet Directory (OID) for authorization of users and for user provisioning. Adding JAAS for security services in J2EE allows for an even more highly customizable and flexible architecture.

OracleAS's JAAS provides key security services to Java programmers by allowing them to use authentication to identify users, authorization as a way to limit what those users can do, and delegation to enable code to run securely.

Let's face it: Java development is becoming central to the Web. Because of this, Java security is a vital feature of any application server. OracleAS meets this need through OracleAS

JAAS Provider. JAAS Provider supplies core security services critical for developing Java-based applications for OracleAS. It enables security for OC4J to enforce security constraints for Web servlets, JavaServer Pages (JSPs), and Enterprise JavaBeans (EJB) components.

JAAS supports two different provider types: XML-based providers and LDAP-based providers (Extensible Markup Language and Lightweight Directory Access Protocol, respectively). These provider types implement a repository for secure central storage, retrieval, and administration of provider data. The provider data consists of users and roles (realms) and JAAS policies (permissions).

So, what is the difference between the two provider types? XML-based providers are used for lightweight storage of the security information in XML files. LDAP-based providers use OID as their storage repository for security information. XML-based providers should be used for those deployments that do not use Oracle Identity Management. For those that do employ Oracle Identity Management, JAAS can leverage this feature and can provide Single Sign-On authentication and authorization and users can be provisioned using Oracle Delegated Administration Services (DAS). This has the benefit of utilizing a common framework for both authentication and authorization, and it eases the integration with other Oracle products and allows support for user information management in a secure and highly available directory service.

Oracle Identity Management

With the growth of larger and larger organizations, globalization, and virtually 24/7 operations on global networks, there is an even more critical need for security solutions that allow for ease of use for the end user while maintaining the highest possible security for applications. OracleAS meets this need through the use of Oracle Identity Management.

Oracle's Identity Management provides an integrated infrastructure of directory, security, and user management functionality on which OracleAS products rely. It includes Oracle Internet Directory (OID), Delegated Administration Services (DAS), and Single Sign-On (SSO).

OID allows the centralized user management required in most global organizations. Users are defined centrally in OID, and all Oracle Identity Management components as well as the applications involved in the organization share the definition of user identity and their credentials, profiles, and preferences. This eases the maintenance load for administrators while also simplifying the issues that users often have with multiple authentications.

Whereas OID allows you to centrally administer users, Oracle's Delegated Administration Services allows you to delegate administrative functions to different administrators. By using a self-service interface, end users can update their preferences and profiles and reset their passwords. Directory administrators can use the same self-service interface to create and manage both users and groups.

If you choose to implement OracleAS Single Sign-On, your users can log into the Application Server Environment as well as any other web application by using a single username and password. The Single Sign-On consists of specific logic in the OracleAS database, the Oracle HTTP server, and the OC4J server that together enable users to log securely into the different applications. Two distinct types of applications can be authenticated through OracleAS Single Sign-On—OracleAS applications, naturally, which are called partner applications, and external applications. Oracle's `mod_osso` is an Oracle HTTP Server module that provides the facilities for the integration of the single sign-on server to authenticate users to either kind of application.

Portal

OracleAS Portal provides an interface infrastructure that allows you to create and manage web pages. Portal enables multiple web pages to be displayed on a single portal page with links to content through Java applications. Portal uses OracleAS's Single Sign-On to provide secure access to its content and applications.

OracleAS Portal provides a comprehensive security model that enables administrators to control exactly what users can see and change on the organization's website. It brings together many of the components of OracleAS's security features, including the following:

- OracleAS's Single Sign-On authenticates users.
- `mod_osso` redirects those authentication requests to OracleAS's Single Sign-On and keeps track of the user activity in any given application.
- Web Cache serves pages generated by Portal.
- OID is the storage repository for user credentials and group memberships.
- Oracle's Delegated Administration Services adds or updates existing information stored inside the directory.

Before your users log into OracleAS Portal, they can view only the public content. This can include public portlets or static content. When a user first attempts to log into the Portal, if they have not yet been authenticated with OracleAS Single Sign-On, they are asked for a username and password. This authentication information is redirected to Single Sign-On for authentication. Once the user is logged in, their credentials are verified against those in OID.

Once the user is successfully authenticated, Single Sign-On creates a Single Sign-On session cookie. After this cookie and the session are created, it is critical for the Portal application to determine the pages and objects for which the user has the necessary privileges to access. The access control lists (ACLs) for all portal objects are stored in the Portal Schema in the Metadata Repository. When a user first logs into the portal, user and group information is read from the directory and cached in the same repository as the ACL.

Oracle Delegated Administration Services generates an administration interface to allow the user direct access to OID, thereby simplifying the provisioning of users and groups in OID for use in Portal.

Finally, Portal leverages the components in connection with the Oracle 10*g* database to provide strong protection for your portal applications.

Managing and Configuring OracleAS Certificate Authority

Simply having certificate authorities and the certificates that result from them at your disposal is a strong tool, but as with most power, the real strength is in your ability to manage it. The following sections will show you how to configure your OracleAS Certificate Authority

(OCA) component and use it to manage certificates. Through this tool, you will request and manage certificates to assist in the security of your system.

We will discuss further the tools and techniques that you can employ to manage and configure your OCA.

Oracle PKI Management Tools

Before an organization can begin to implement a public key infrastructure (PKI), it must first acquire a certificate to use for authentication. This involves multiple steps. First, the organization must fill in the appropriate details on the request for a certificate and submit it to the proper registration authority. Once the registration authority validates, approves, and returns the form, the organization has to deliver the approved form to a certificate authority, which then processes it and issues a certificate.

OracleAS's implementation of PKI removes these steps, saves an organization time, and avoids delays, thereby lowering costs. It does this by integrating the authentication function, the user repository, and the applications.

OracleAS's PKI components include SSL to transmit communications over the Internet in an encrypted form. Recall that SSL uses public key cryptography to enable not only encryption, but also authentication and data integrity. OID and SSO are also key components of the PKI in OracleAS. OID enables PKI-based Single Sign-On by providing the repository for the credentials used by SSO.

When you install OracleAS, you can configure the installation to include the OracleAS Certificate Authority to manage the complete certificate life cycle. This feature is particularly useful for internal implementations and for testing purposes; it also simplifies the migration from an internal implementation to a public production implementation by requesting a certificate from a trusted third party.

After the certificate is available, it then becomes necessary to have a container in which it can reside. Certificates can reside in any LDAP-compliant directory, or they can reside in a wallet. A wallet is nothing more than a transparent database used to manage authentication data (such as keys and certificates) that is needed by SSL. The Personal Information Exchange Syntax (PKCS#12) is the standard that provides the specifications for these containers. Administrators use a tool such as Oracle Wallet Manager (OWM), a Java-based application that is also used by end users, to manage the security credentials on the server. Wallet owners use OWM to manage the credentials on the client.

OWM creates a wallet that can be opened using the Oracle Enterprise Login Assistant. It ships with trusted certificates from the top-name root authorities (VeriSign, RSA, and GTE CyberTrust) and can also use a site's own in-house certificate authority if one is available. OWM can upload wallets to and download wallets from OID.

Key Features of OCA

OracleAS Certificate Authority uses OID as the storage repository for its certificates. This not only provides for centralized certificate management, it also simplifies the provisioning and revocation tasks. After the user has been provisioned in OID and has been authenticated in the Single Sign-On server, that user can choose to request a digital certificate from the OCA. If the request is made, the certificate is automatically immediately provisioned in the OID, thereby leveraging Single Sign-On to identify the user and populate all of the certificate request's required fields. What's more, the immediacy of this extends to the administrator and the certificate owner's ability to revoke certificates in real time. This means that once the certificate is revoked, all future attempts to use the certificate as a means of authentication will fail. The interface through which this provisioning and revocation of server-side components occurs is OWM. When provisioning, PKCS#10 or PKCS#12 certificates are requested and can be submitted to the OracleAS Certificate Authority or to an external CA to acquire services. Oracle's PKI is designed to operate effectively with the leading PKI vendors to provide an enterprise-wide solution.

OCA Architecture

The OracleAS Certificate Authority can aid your organization a great deal in terms of streamlining processes and cutting costs, but what is its functional structure? What is the underlying architecture on which it rests?

The OCA is linked closely with SSO, utilizing SSO as its authentication tool after the user has been established in OID, and relies on the `mod_osso` component to assist with the SSO authentication of those users. OCA automatically publishes the certificates that it issues to the OID and deletes the entries whenever the certificates are revoked. This limits manual intervention in the process.

OCA uses the OracleAS Infrastructure Metadata Repository as its internal repository for storing not only issued certificates, but also certificate requests and auxiliary information surrounding requested, issued, and revoked certificates.

OCA consists of the registration authority (RA) and the certificate authority (CA). RA consists of the Authorization module and the Policy module.

Authorization module The Authorization module ensures that the user has the privileges that are appropriate to making the request that is being received by OCA. The user that is authenticated by both SSO and SSL automatically has the privilege to either acquire more certificates or revoke existing ones, but only for the same distinguished name (DN). A distinguished name is a unique name for an entry in the directory server. Any user not authenticated by SSO and SSL must be manually approved and has only the privilege to list and request certificates.

Policy module Packages within the Policy module enforce custom restrictions that the OCA administrator creates by editing the OCA configuration file using any text editor.

OID is responsible for publishing issued certificates and deleting revoked certificates.

HTTP Server, via `mod_osso`, is responsible for interaction with Single Sign-On Server.

In OracleAS, Web Cache and HTTP Server communicate with the other initial component as well as with external clients (browsers and other requesting clients). Because there is a need to secure the communication channel, OracleAS can be configured to use SSL, allowing for secure communication via OC4J using Apache Jserv Protocol and for communication with Web Cache through SSL.

It is important to remember that no components of OracleAS installations are configured to use SSL by default. It is up to the administrator, with input from the business, to determine what paths need to be secured. SSL can be configured with enough flexibility to secure only specific paths (for instance, those accessible by the public) while leaving some avenues less secure (such as those used by internal clients).

OCA Configuration Elements

The configuration file `oca.xml` stores the policies used by the Policy module; it is located in the `$ORACLE_HOME/oca/conf` directory. This file is used by the command-line tool (`ocactl`) and by the policy administration modules. It can be edited using any XML editor or, if you are comfortable editing XML files directly, using a text editor.

The following sections describe the elements that can be used to aid in your configuration efforts.

OCA Wallets

OCA needs at least a minimal set of wallets and certificates to operate. The first wallet necessary is the CA Signing Wallet, which is generated automatically by the installer. This wallet holds the signing key and the signing certificate of the OracleAS Certificate Authority. The CA Signing Wallet also can be imported from another certificate authority to set up a new or different CA structure. This structure is hierarchical in nature; if a CA Signing Wallet is imported from somewhere else, it will replace the installed one. The new imported wallet, signing key, and signing certificate will be those signed by the new CA from which you imported it.

The CA SSL Wallet also is automatically created by the installer and is the other wallet that is minimally necessary for OCA. This wallet contains both the SSL certificate and the private key of the server hosting the OCA. This wallet can be either imported from another CA or manipulated via the OWM interface.

Password Store

Most passwords that are used by OracleAS Certificate Authority are generated automatically and are kept in an encrypted Password Store. The encryption is accomplished using the OCA administrator passwords.

All of the passwords kept in this store can be altered via the OCA command-line tool (`ocactl`).

Several passwords that are needed to protect interactions between OracleAS Certificate Authority and other AS entities (like OID, the Oracle database, and SSL) are stored in the Password Store, as are those used to protect sensitive data structures that the CA uses (such as the

CA Signing Wallet and the CA SSL Wallet). The only password that is not automatically generated and stored in the Password Store is the CA administrator password. This password can be changed via `ocactl`.

Care needs to be taken with the OCA administrator password. If it is forgotten, it cannot be recovered using any tool.

The syntax for running OCA is simple. Table 8.1 shows each operation and the command necessary for it.

TABLE 8.1 OCA Syntax

Operation	Command
Start	`$ORACLE_HOME/oca/bin/ocactl start`
Stop	`$ORACLE_HOME/oca/bin/ocactl stop`
Status	`$ORACLE_HOME/oca/bin/ocactl status`

For what may be obvious reasons, it is important that the only way to start and stop the OCA product is through the command-line tool that requires the administrator's password. Figure 8.2 shows what this would look like at a command prompt.

FIGURE 8.2 Starting OCA

```
C:\WINDOWS\system32\cmd.exe - ocactl.bat start
D:\OraHome_3\oca\bin>dir
 Volume in drive D has no label.
 Volume Serial Number is C412-62A6

 Directory of D:\OraHome_3\oca\bin

03/05/2006  09:05 AM    <DIR>          .
03/05/2006  09:05 AM    <DIR>          ..
03/05/2006  09:05 AM               640 cmdeinst.bat
03/05/2006  09:05 AM             3,372 cmdeinst.pl
03/05/2006  09:05 AM               636 cminst.bat
03/05/2006  09:05 AM            11,140 cminst.pl
03/05/2006  09:03 AM               631 ocactl.bat
03/05/2006  09:03 AM             3,452 ocactl.pl
               6 File(s)         19,871 bytes
               2 Dir(s)  185,630,564,352 bytes free

D:\OraHome_3\oca\bin>ocactl.bat start

OracleAS Certificate Authority 10g (10.1.2.1.0)

Copyright (c) 2003, 2005, Oracle Corporation. All rights reserved.

OracleAS Certificate Authority administrator password:
```

Before you can start OCA, Oracle's HTTP server needs to be started and running on the same machine as OCA; OC4J for OCA must be started and running on the same machine as OCA; the Infrastructure Metadata Repository needs to be up and running and accessible; and the OID and, optionally, the SSO server need to be functional and accessible. In a default deployment, all of these components reside in the same Oracle Home. For OracleAS Certificate Authority, it is important that Enterprise Manager not be used for stopping and starting these components, even if you can script it to do so.

Accessing the OCA Interface

After the infrastructure is installed successfully, the OracleAS Certificate Authority server becomes functional. But functional is not very useful unless you can access the administration interface. In order to do this, launch your web browser and enter the URL and port number of your administration server. This information was displayed at the end of your infrastructure installation. The format for this URL look something like this:

```
https://<your.server.name>:<ssl_port>/oca/admin
```

You will likely know your server's name; the port number is available in the `$ORACLE_HOME/install/portlist.ini` file. The entry that you are looking for is the OracleAS Certificate Authority SSL port.

The following is an example of the working contents of a `portlist.ini` file. As you can see, the OracleAS Certificate Authority SSL port is 6600; therefore, the URL in question would be `https://ajw.home.com:6600/oca/admin`.

```
;OracleAS Components reserve the following ports
    at install time.
;As a post-installation step, you can reconfigure
    a component to use a different port.
;Those changes will not be visible in this file.

[System]
Host Name = 192.168.1.100

[Ports]
Oracle HTTP Server port =  7777
Oracle HTTP Server Listen port = 7777
Oracle HTTP Server SSL port = 4443
Oracle HTTP Server Listen (SSL) port = 4443
Oracle HTTP Server Diagnostic port = 7200
Oracle Notification Server Request port = 6003
```

```
Oracle Notification Server Local port = 6101
Oracle Notification Server Remote port = 6200
ASG port = 7890
Log Loader port = 44000
Java Object Cache port = 7000
DCM Discovery port = 7100
Oracle Management Agent Port = 18120
Application Server Control RMI port = 18140
Application Server Control port = 18100
Oracle Internet Directory port = 389
Oracle Internet Directory (SSL) port = 636
Oracle Certificate Authority SSL Server Authentication port = 6600
Oracle Certificate Authority SSL Mutual Authentication port = 6601
Enterprise Manager Console HTTP Port (orclas) = 5501
Enterprise Manager Agent Port (orclas) = 1830
```

When you have successfully launched the OCA administrative interface, you will see the OracleAS Certificate Authority home page, displaying three additional subtabs (see Figure 8.3). If this is your first time accessing this particular administration interface, you must request a certificate to obtain authentication before you can perform administration tasks on the Certificate Management page.

FIGURE 8.3 OCA administration home page

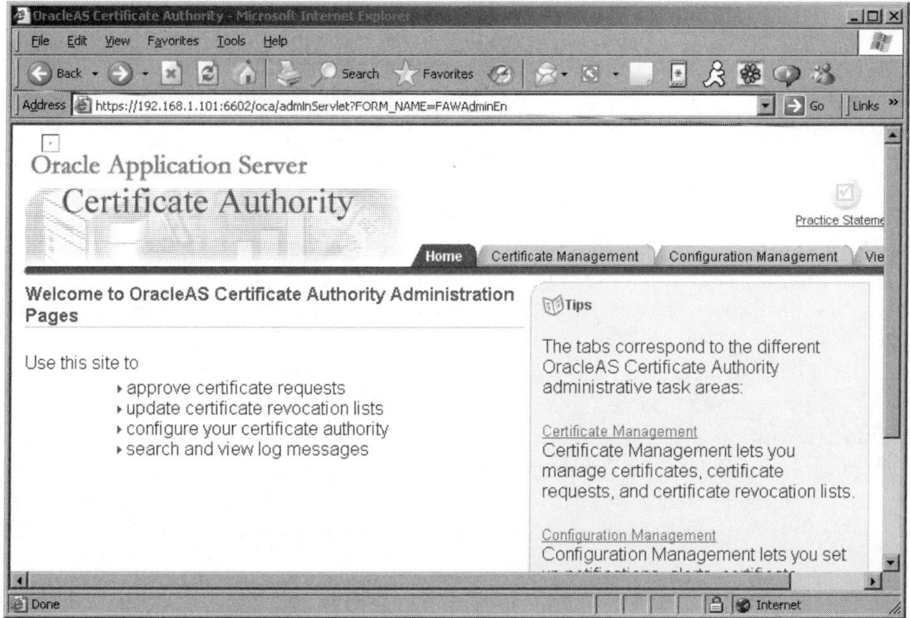

FIGURE 8.4 Certificate request information

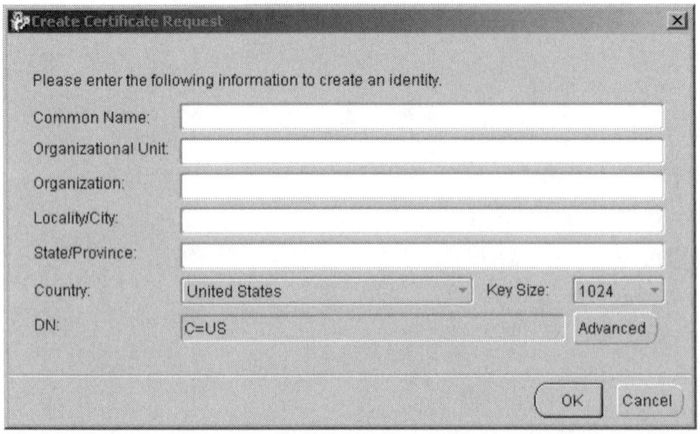

Eight pieces of information are necessary for requesting this certificate (see Figure 8.4):

Common Name The name that you want to have on the certificate.

Organizational Unit The name of the organizational unit or division to which the OCA administrator belongs.

Organization The name of the company or organization to which the administrator belongs.

Locality/City The city where the administrator is located.

State/Province The state or province of the administrator.

Country The country associated with the administrator.

Key Size The encryption strength of the key that will be created in connection with the certificate. Remember that the stronger the key, the more processing must be done in connection with it, so create a key no stronger than necessary to meet your business's needs.

DN This field is typically unchangeable and fills itself in as you fill in the other information.

You must be working at the computer where you intend to use the certificate as the web administrator. OracleAS Certificate Authority must be running. If these are not both true, you will get an error message indicating that you will need to start the OracleAS Certificate Authority first. It is now a matter of simply following the instructions provided to generate the key pair.

Once the certificate is issued, you will need to import it into your browser so that you can access the facilities of the OracleAS Certificate Authority administration interface.

Although the import process into any given browser is different, you will likely be working primarily with Internet Explorer, particularly in preparation for your exam.

Whenever you are presented with an importable certificate, you will see a splash screen similar to Figure 8.5. Answer yes to the question of whether you want to install it.

FIGURE 8.5 Certificate installation screen

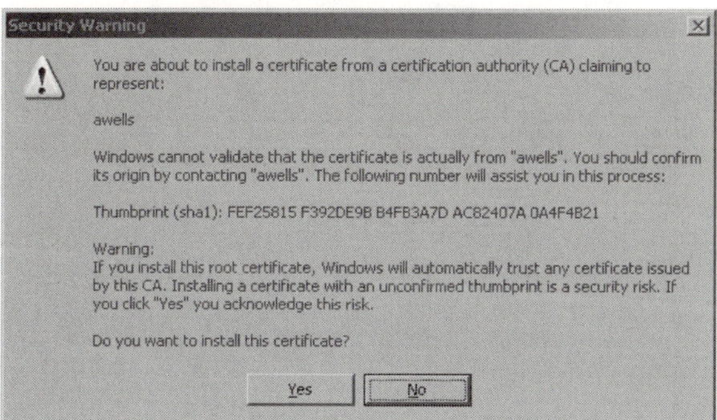

Next you are asked whether you are sure you want to install this certificate because it could be a security risk (see Figure 8.6). The certificate should then be successfully installed.

FIGURE 8.6 Are you sure you want to install it?

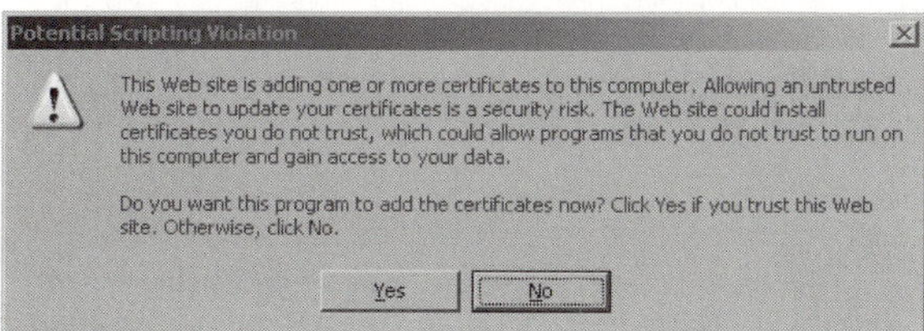

It is as simple as filling out a simple request form. This process replaces all of the steps that would otherwise be needed for PKI certificate acquisition from another CA.

Through the OracleAS Certificate Authority administration interface, you can approve certificate requests, reject certificate requests, search for and list already issued certificates, search for and list certificate requests, revoke existing certificates, and update the Certificate Revocation List (CRL).

The OracleAS Certificate Authority maintains a master list of all certificate requests and their current status (whether pending, rejected, or certified). When the administrator clicks the Certificate Management tab (shown in Figure 8.7), all of the certificate requests that are awaiting action are displayed. The administrator is responsible for approving or rejecting all requests and for managing the CRL. As the administrator, you can perform all actions not only on the certificates that you own, but also on any certificates in the CA. This is particularly important, from a security standpoint, when it becomes necessary to revoke specific certificates when those certificates have been compromised, when they are no longer appropriate, or when the owner of a certificate or certificates has left the company or otherwise put the information in jeopardy.

FIGURE 8.7 Certificate Management tab

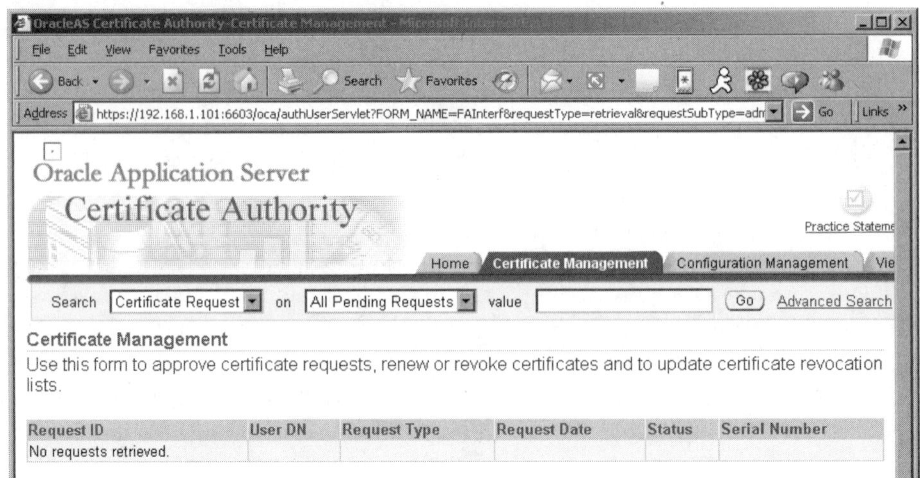

To view, approve, or reject a certificate request, from the Certificate Authority administration home page, click the Certificate Management tab to display the Search for Certificates form. Use the Search drop-down list to find a specific issued or requested certificate. Selecting Select Certificate will display issued certificates. Selecting Certificate Request will display those requested certificates.

Enter the appropriate value into the Search criteria field to search. To retrieve all pending requests, no further specifications are necessary. You can enter the ID/serial number or the request ID for the specific certificate request. For Common Names, you can enter the common name of the certificate requester.

Click Go and the certificate (or certificates) will be retrieved.

To view the details of a certificate, select the certificate you want to review and click View Details. The Certificate page will appear with the certificate's detailed components. Use this page to revoke, renew, or import the selected certificate. If you need to approve a certificate, you can use the contact information to authenticate the requestor of the certificate. Check the validity period and change it if necessary. For subordinate CA certificate issuances, the default path length of 2 is displayed. The certificate path is an ordered nonrepeating list of all certificates starting with a certificate that is used by the relying party's trust root and ending with the target certificate that needs to be validated. The length of 2 indicates that the OracleAS Certificate Authority can have two CAs below it in the certificate chain. If longer paths are required, this path length can be changed.

There are several reasons an administrator will need to revoke a certificate. Revocation should occur when the certificate owner has changed status and no longer has the privileges needed to use the certificate. It also should occur if the private key of the certificate owner has been compromised or if the root CA has ceased operations.

As the OCA administrator, you can renew a user's certificate 10 days before or after it expires, thereby allowing its use to continue without interruption. You can alter the number of days that are allowed before and after expiration, as well.

Expired certificates can be renewed at any time during the number of days specified for the period after the expiration date. After a certificate expires, if it is not renewed during this permitted period, it becomes unusable and *must* be replaced by a certificate acquired by submitting a new certificate request and having it approved.

To renew a certificate, select the certificate, click View Details to display the Certificate page, and click Renew. If the data is still within the established window, the certificate is renewed. If not, an error message appears regarding the expiration of the established window.

Revoking a certificate makes it unusable in your environment. However, this does not mean that the certificate cannot still be misused. If you update the Certificate Revocation List and publish the list of revoked certificates, you can help to assure that the certificate cannot be misused. All applications in your set of trusted environments can use your CRL to prevent anyone from using that certificate in an attempt to authenticate. If an application is using OracleAS CA and OracleAS SSO, the user is prevented from immediate authentication.

To update the CRL, you need to access the OracleAS CA administration home page and click the Certificate Management tab. You will be presented with a sheet that contains, among other things, an Update Certificate Revocation List (CRL) button. Once you click this button, the Update Certificate Revocation List form appears. In the CRL Validity field, enter the number representing the number of days until the next update. Update the signature algorithm by choosing the appropriate algorithm (such as MD5 with RSA or SHA1 with RSA) from the drop-down list. You need to enter the relevant data in the rest of the fields on the page and then click OK. This generates the updated Certificate Revocation List and stores it in the file system. You can review the file or save it by choosing Download CLR and then Import to Browser or Download to your local disk.

The HTTP server uses this list to check the validity of the SSL certificates that it receives, rejecting those SSL connections with any end entity whose certificate is resident on the CRL.

If your environment uses multiple servers, you will need to copy the CRL file to the appropriate location with the appropriate filenames used by those servers as their CRLs. You will need to follow the established steps that have been designated for each server for setting up their CRLs.

You can use the OCA administration interface not only to administer certificates, but also to help you configure the OCA server. From the OCA administration main page, you can see all of the configuration details grouped together and listed on the Configuration Management tab (see Figure 8.8). This tabbed page is further subdivided into three additional tabs that represent different sets of configuration details:

- Notification is used to set and configure the different notification settings for the OCA server.
- General is used to configure the general overall properties for the server, such as logging, tracing, certificate publishing, database settings, and directory settings.
- Policy is used to manage the policies of the OCA server.

FIGURE 8.8 Configuration Management tabbed page

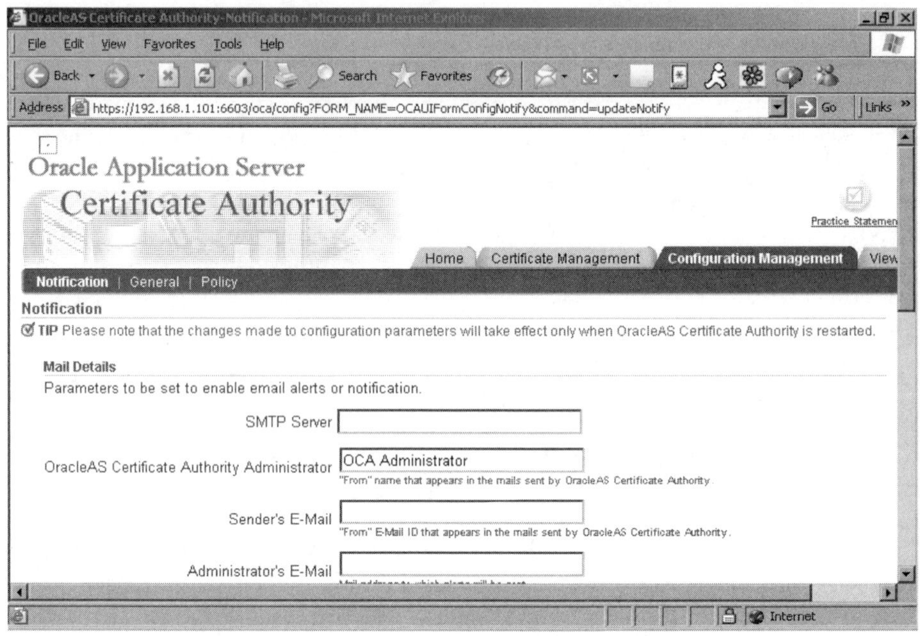

The OCA User Interface

The OracleAS Certificate Authority interface can be used for more than just administration. Users and server entities also use it to acquire certificates and to find any certificates that exist on the system. The URL that they use to access their information is similar to that of the administration pages.

To access the OracleAS CA user home page, shown in Figure 8.9, you first need to launch your web browser and enter the user interface URL. https://<your.server>:<ssl_port>/oca/user is the typical URL format for the page. The resulting page appears with two tabs: User Certificates and Server/SubCA Certificates.

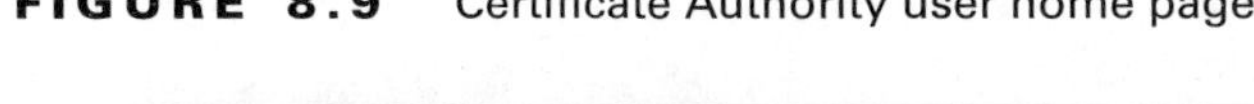

FIGURE 8.9 Certificate Authority user home page

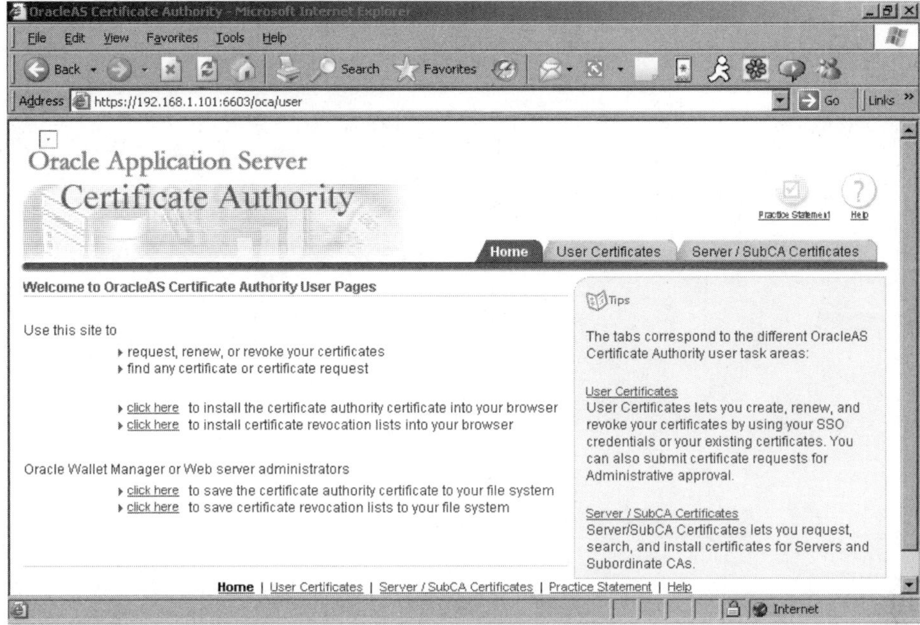

When users in your organization need to access any SSL-enabled website in your enterprise, they will need a user certificate. This certificate authenticates the user to the website. The OracleAS CA User Certificates tab, shown in Figure 8.10, allows you to get such a certificate. After the user gets the certificate, they can import it into their browser and can then access SSL-enabled web sites and applications. When they do, the browser will present the certificate to the page or application as proof of authentication.

When you or the user clicks on the User Certificates tab, the Authentication page will be displayed. From here you determine how you want to be authenticated to the OracleAS CA. You can choose to be authenticated via OracleAS Single Sign-On (based on the user's SSO password), through SSL (based on an already issued SSL certificate of the user), or manually (none of the authentication is automated). If you choose manually, the certificate request form needs to be obtained, filled out, and submitted, and then the user will have to wait for approval from the OCA administrator. This is the only viable option if there is no SSO setup in the system and if there is not already an existing user certificate assigned to that given user.

Single Sign-On

User certificates can be generated automatically if users can identify themselves to the OCA server by using their Single Sign-On username and password. Once a user is authenticated, the OCA server will generate the certificate and allow the user to import it into their browser. This can save administration time because authentication is automatic, and because time is money, it saves on the cost involved in certificate provisioning.

FIGURE 8.10 Certificate Authority User Certificates tab

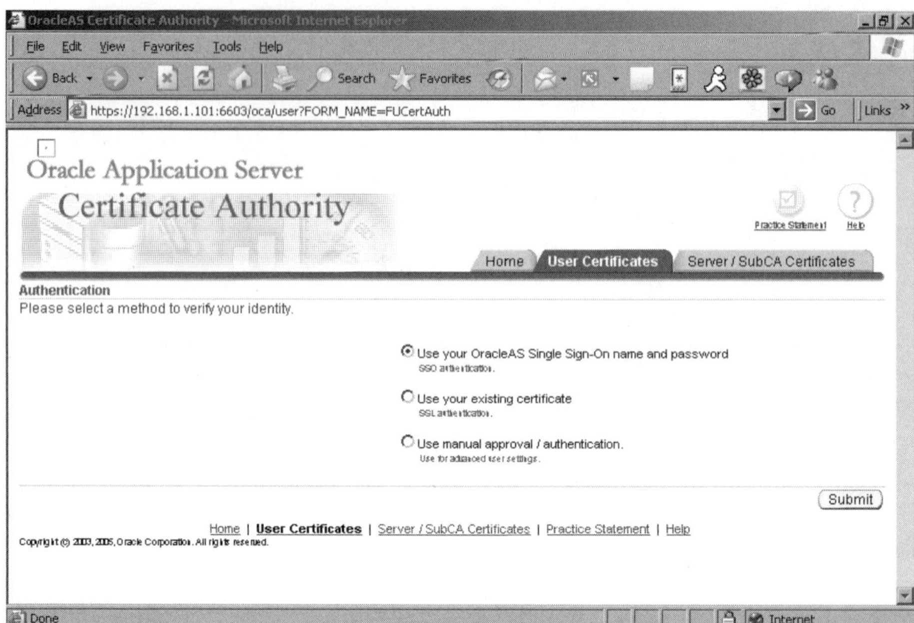

To acquire certificates using SSO, users will need the required SSO information, such as username and password, and then will need to perform the following steps:

1. In the Authentication form, select the Use Your OracleAS Single Sign-On Name and Password option and click Submit. Figure 8.11 shows the SSO authentication form.
2. Enter your SSO username and password. If the information is verified as being correct, the User Certificate - SSO form appears with a list of valid certificates that the user can view the details for. This form will allow the user to renew or revoke these certificates.
3. On the User Certificates - SSO Authentication page, click Get Certificate to display the details necessary on the Certificate Request form. This request form page displays the distinguished name (DN) of the entry in the OID server. This value is not modifiable. Users can enter the appropriate value for Certificate Key Size (in bits) for the key pair to be generated and for Certificate Usage. Certificate Usage is simply the purpose for which the certificate is being requested.
4. Submittal of the Certificate Request form allows the OCA server to generate the certificate and store it in the OID connected to the given user's DN. The Approved Certificate Information page then appears with the certificate information. The requester can now import the certificate into the browser by clicking the `Import to Browser` link.

After the certificate is imported into the browser, it can be used to authenticate the user to any SSL-enabled website within the organization.

FIGURE 8.11 Certificate Authority user SSO authentication screen

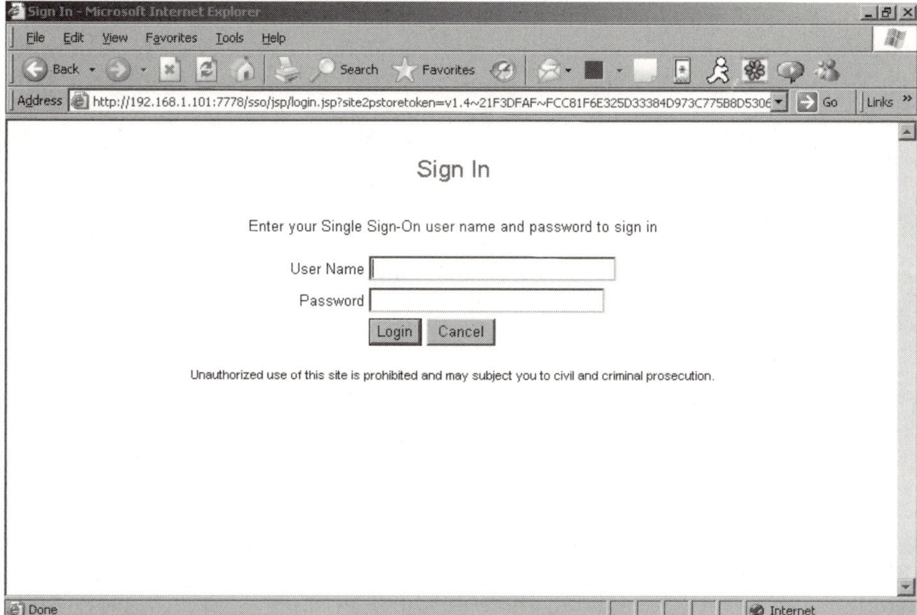

SSL Authentication

When requesting a user certificate, you can also choose to set the authentication type to SSL, which will automate authentication on a preexisting SSL certificate. As in the case of SSO authentication, a certificate is provisioned to the user immediately.

Because not all of the applications in an enterprise are used only by employees of the organization, not all users will be found using SSO or SSL methods. Every employee will be uniquely identified in the OID and they can use this identification to connect to the different applications. If the enterprise is using SSO, certificates can be issued based on the SSO identity. Partners, however, may need to be able to use some of the applications in the enterprise but may not be found in the OID or SSO. If this is the case, it will be difficult for them to gain access to the necessary systems. How do they get around this hurdle and identify with the OCA server? In these cases, manual approval must be used when requesting a certificate. The partner user will have to fill out a Certificate Request form, submit the form, and then wait for approval by the administrator.

Managing User Certificates

After a user's request for a certificate has been processed, regardless of the method chosen for requesting the certificate, the user can manage their certificates. They can review and retrieve certificates from the OCA server, renew a certificate, or revoke a certificate.

Reviewing and Retrieving a Certificate

Once you, as the administrator, notify a user that the requested manual certificate request is approved, the user can search for their certificate request by using the request ID generated at the time of the request. They can check the status of the request, and if the request status displayed is Valid, they can then click View Details to see the content of the approved certificate. They must review the certificate details and then click `Import to Browser` to import the certificate into the browser.

Renewing Certificates

Users also can use OCA user pages to renew certificates. To renew a certificate, the user must first search for their certificate and then click the Renew button. This operation must be performed within the renewal period before or after the certificate's expiration date.

Revoking a Certificate

If a user needs to revoke a certificate, they must first search for the certificate and then click the Revoked button. This action marks the certificate as revoked in the OCA repository and adds it to the CRL the next time the CRL is generated.

Revoking certificates does not remove them automatically from the user's browser database. They need to be manually removed by the user.

Server Certificates

Not only can users obtain certificates, administrators for any server in the network also can obtain certificates for their server. This server certificate enables PKI authentication for that server with other servers or with users. To enable server security, you need a PKCS#10 certificate request. This request is generated using OWM or another third party tool such as OpenSSL reqtool. After generating the server certificate request, you can request a server certificate using the OCA user pages.

Oracle Wallet Manager (OWM)

As mentioned earlier, OWM is a stand-alone Java-based application that allows wallet owners to manage and edit the security credentials on wallets. It also allows security administrators to mange public key security credentials on OracleAS and other Oracle clients and servers and to manage trusted certificates in the system.

OWM is used to create private keys associated with X.509 certificates requiring strong encryption and save them to the file system. It can be used to create certificate requests, install certificates for the entity, and configure trusted certificates for the entity. You can use OWM to create a wallet that can be accessed by OWM, you can upload wallets to an LDAP directory such as OID, or you can download a wallet from a similar directory. You can even import and export directories.

Creating a New Wallet

Using OWM, you can create a new empty wallet that can be used by the OWM tool. You will have to supply a valid password for the new wallet, and that password needs have at least eight alphabetic, numeric, or special characters to make it as difficult as possible to guess.

To start Wallet Manager, navigate to Start, select your Oracle Home under Programs, select Integrated Management Tools, and then select Wallet Manager.

Figure 8.12 shows the information necessary for creating your new wallet. Notice that you have the option of selecting either a standard wallet or a PKCS11 wallet.

Wallets contain user credentials that can be used to authenticate a particular user to multiple databases and application servers. That means that the password needs to be as strong as possible. It is strongly suggested that normal regulations and suggestions on passwords be followed for wallets as with anything else. Further, following organizational security practices in mandating periodic password change is also important.

Once you have created your new wallet, Wallet Manager asks you whether you want to create a certificate, as shown in Figure 8.13.

Choosing to create a new certificate request at this point will provide you with the screen shown in Figure 8.14, where you fill in the specific information related to the certificate that you are requesting and submit the request.

FIGURE 8.12 New wallet creation

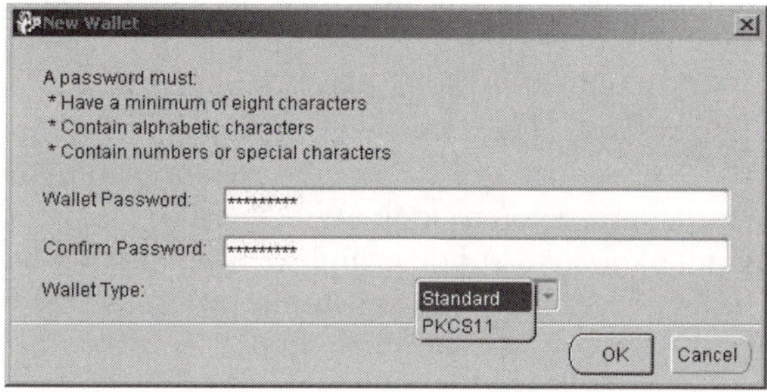

FIGURE 8.13 Prompt to create a certificate screen

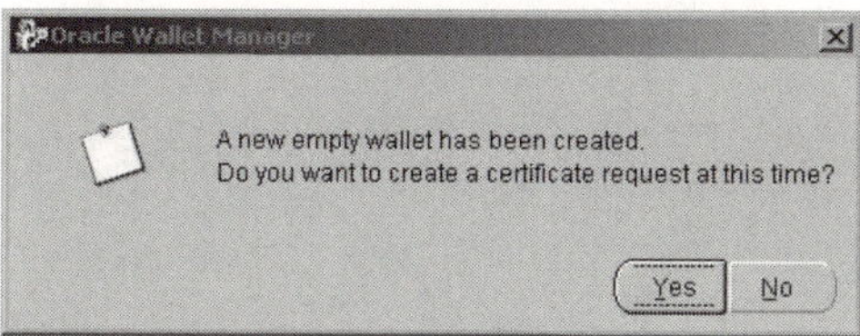

FIGURE 8.14 Create Certificate Request screen

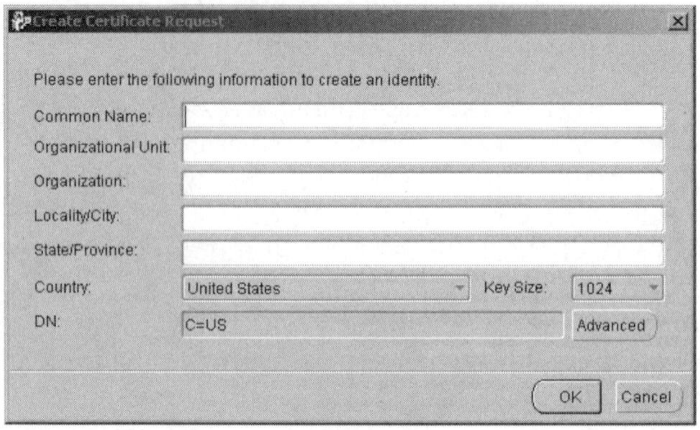

OWM uses two different kinds of certificates, user certificates and trusted certificates. Trusted certificates are any certificates that you can trust, such as a certificate issued by a CA. A wallet comes with some common trusted certificates and you can add more. User certificates are those used by end entities such as end users, clients, and databases. You must install a trusted certificate from the CA before you can install a user certificate issued by that same CA.

As you can see in Figure 8.15, the DN is entered for you automatically as you fill in the other fields, and you have the option of requesting a certificate with a key length from 512 to 4096 bytes, allowing for a wider range of security options.

Finally, you have created your new wallet and are ready to import new certificates, export user or trusted certificates, and remove certificates from your wallet. A look at Figure 8.16 shows that the new wallet already contains several trusted certificates at creation time, as well as the request for a new certificate. We encourage you to look at the interface, play around with it on a test box or in your own sandbox system at home, and see just exactly what you can do and what your options are. The more familiar you are with the interfaces, the better you will do on the exam.

FIGURE 8.15 A fully filled-out certificate request

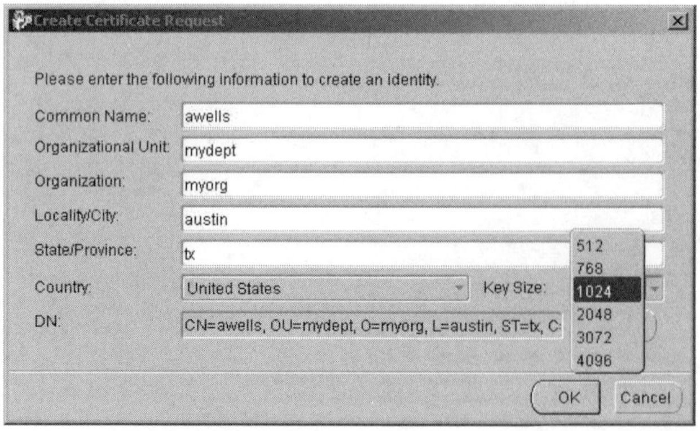

FIGURE 8.16 Wallet Manager with the new wallet open

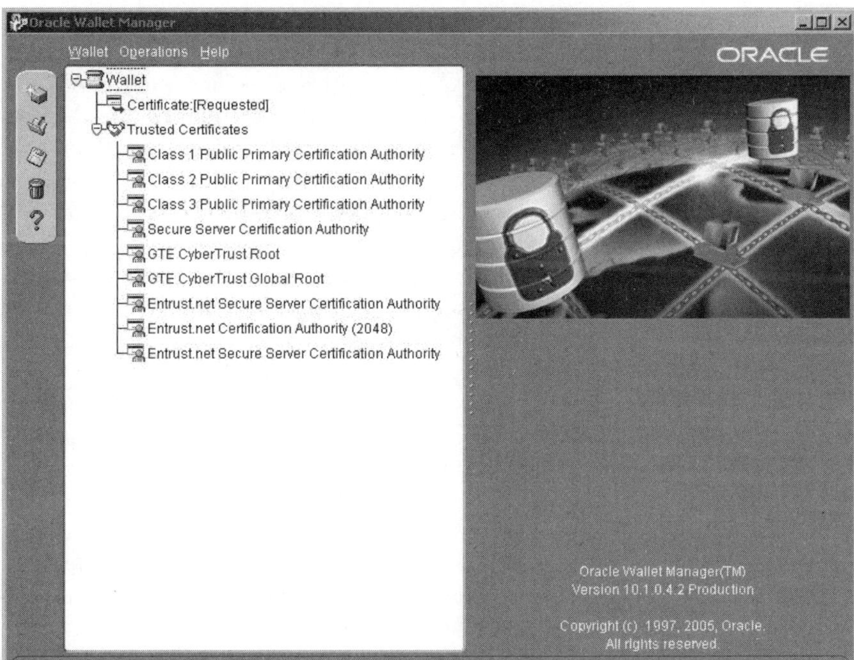

Securing OracleAS Components Using SSL

It is possible to secure nearly every component in the OracleAS stack using SSL. This means that header information that gets sent with every request can be used to determine whether the user has the authority to access the information requested.

The following sections discuss not only how SSL works, but also how to configure it to work with the other security components.

How SSL Works

All this is well and good, we know, but you are dying to find out exactly how SSL really works, aren't you? Think about it this way: Amanda has a web store that sells football jerseys. Adam wants to buy a Steelers jersey.

Adam makes a request to establish a connection with Amanda's web server. Because it is to be a secure connection to the SSL-enabled port on the server, HTTPS is the protocol used rather than HTTP.

Amanda's server asserts its site identity (so Adam is sure that he is buying a jersey from Amanda and not from someone else) by signing its server certificate and sending it to Adam's computer.

Adam's computer uses the server's public key to verify that the owner of the certificate is the same user who signed it (Amanda's computer). His computer verifies the credentials of the CA using the exchanged keys. If the CA is unknown, the user manually verifies that the site certificate was issued by a trusted third party for the requested site (Amanda's jersey store). Once the certificate is verified, the client (Adam's computer) generates a premaster secret (a totally random string of bytes) and encrypts it using Amanda's server's public key. This premaster is then used as the basis for encryption keys and message authentication codes (MACs) and checksums. An encryption algorithm and a hash function are negotiated for encryption and integrity verification between Adam's computer and Amanda's server. A typical example of this premaster secret encryption is encrypting data using Data Encryption Standard (DES), a symmetric encryption scheme, and generating the authentication codes for verification using The Message Digest utility (MD5). MD5 is a hashing algorithm that was designed for 32-bit machines as a way to create digital signatures. It is a one-way hash function. (It converts a message into a fixed string of digits that form the message digest.)

Amanda's server requests a client certificate as a way to authenticate that Adam, not someone else, is requesting the Steelers jersey. If there are multiple certificates, the user chooses which personal certificate to present.

A secure channel is now established between Adam's computer and Amanda's server, with the client's computer generating a session key and using the server's public key as a way to encode the session key to send it securely over the Internet.

This scenario occurs thousands of times a day when people make secure transactions over the Internet. You usually don't think about what is going on behind the scenes when you buy something from Amazon.com or when you pay your credit card bill, but it requires a lot of processing to be assured that your credit card information is as secure as possible. The following sections will discuss in more detail the different elements involved in the communication channel security that goes along with the events we just looked at.

SSL Handshake

At the beginning of their communication session, the client and the server perform a handshake. This handshake executes several important tasks. First, the client and the server decide which cipher suite to use when transmitting messages. Cipher suites (discussed in the next section) are sets of authentication, encryption, and data integrity algorithms that are used to exchange messages between two nodes on a network regardless of the size and complexity of the network.

Second, the server sends its certificate to the client, who verifies that a trusted CA signed it. If client authentication is required at this point, the client sends its certificate to the server, which verifies that a trusted CA also signed the client certificate.

Finally, during the handshake, the client and server exchange key material using public key cryptography and generate a session key from this material. From this point on, all communication between the client and the server is encrypted and decrypted using the session keys and the negotiated cipher.

Cipher Suite

So what is all of this about a cipher suite? The SSL technology supports a variety of encryption protocols. Each choice is called a cipher suite, and each type specifies the type of signature-capable certificate that can be used, the type of symmetric encryption, and the type of signature algorithm (secure hash) that should be used. Signature-capable certificates deal with the authentication and are either RSA or DSS. Symmetric encryption can be RC4, RC2, IDEA, DES, or 3DES. The secure hash or MAC algorithm, dealing with data integrity, can be either MD5 or Secure Hash Algorithm (SHA).

Different cipher suites have different combinations of these components.

OracleAS's Certificate Authority

You can get all of your certificates from CAs such as VeriSign or Thawte; however, as discussed earlier in the chapter, OracleAS also has its own mastercertificate authority, OracleAS Certificate Authority (OCA), and you can use it to set up your own certificate authority. OCA rounds out the Oracle PKI solution by providing you with a certificate authority and a registration authority combined. This combination, accessed through a web interface, is highly integrated with OracleAS.

By utilizing OracleAS Single Sign-On Server, administrators can navigate to the OCA and request a certificate for use in other PKI-based Single Sign-On authenticated applications. The tight integration of OCA with OID and the SSL Server along with other products easily overcomes one of the sticky issues associated with PKI, authentication methods.

Application users who authenticate to Single Sign-On Server can easily obtain a certificate without any existing technical knowledge or understanding of the PKI. New applications can then use these certificates transparently to authenticate the user, thereby providing increased security. If the user had previously been issued an X.509 version 3 certificate, that certificate can be used as the authentication method for the OracleAS Certificate Authority over HTTPS. Additionally, OCA can be used to enforce manual certificate approval. This can be particularly useful if an organization's security policy dictates that requests for certificates have to be manually approved by users.

Managing User Certificates

User certificates must be managed. Management functions include adding a certificate request, submitting the request to a CA, importing the user certificate into a wallet, removing a user certificate from a wallet, exporting a user certificate, and exporting a user certificate request. Figure 8.17 shows the Operations menu in Wallet Manager, where these functions can be performed. We will discuss adding a request, exporting a request, and importing a user certificate into a wallet in more detail in the following sections.

FIGURE 8.17 The Operations menu in Wallet Manager

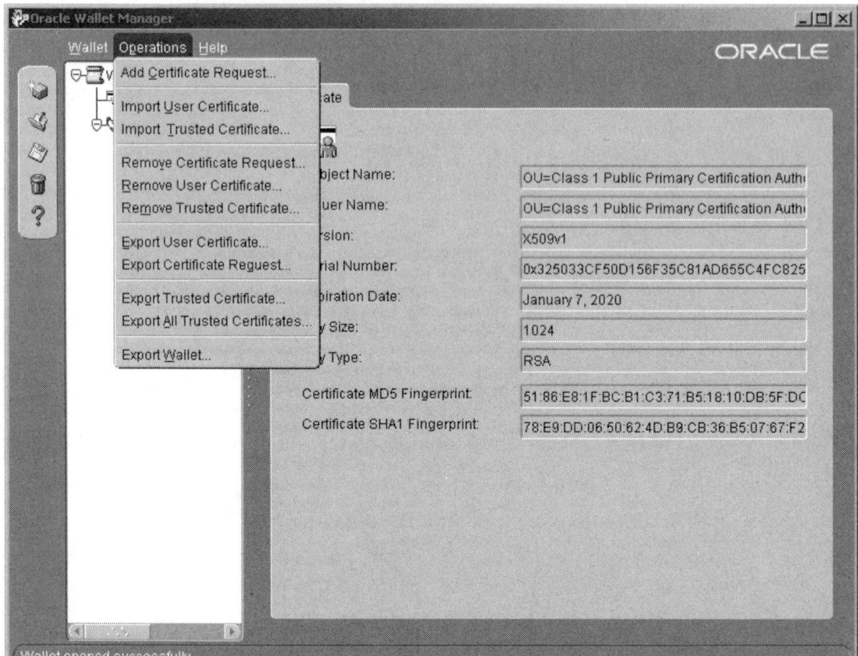

Adding a Certificate Request

In order to obtain a user certificate, you must first create the certificate request. Multiple certificate requests can reside in a wallet. When you use OWM to create multiple certificate requests, it automatically populates the fields on every subsequent request with components from the initial request; you can then go through and edit the values where necessary.

When you use Wallet Manager, the actual request becomes a part of the wallet and can be reused to obtain new certificates when necessary. However, you cannot edit an existing request, only reuse it to request the same certificates.

To create a request, perform the following steps:

1. In Wallet Manager, select Operations ➢ Add Certificate Request.
2. Enter the requested information in the Create Certificate Request dialog box.
3. Click OK.
4. An OWM dialog box appears confirming that the request was successfully created. Either copy the information from this box into an email message and send it to the CA or export the request to a file and email that to the CA.
5. Click OK, and you will be returned to the OWM main window. The status of the certificate has now changed to Requested.

Exporting a User Certificate Request

It is often advantageous for users to create a certificate request and then export it and save it to a file system directory. This is usually done because it separates the act of generating the user certificate request from the act of going to a CA and requesting the certificate. It also enables users to create their own private keys and then export their certificate requests, which can be sent independently to an administrator who may then submit all of the requests to a CA collectively.

If you find that you need to be able to export a certificate request, or if you have users whom you need to instruct on how to export their certificate requests, the following steps are the way to go about that:

1. In Wallet Manager, select Operations ➢ Export Certificate Request.
2. When the Export Certificate Request dialog box appears, select the file system directory to which you want to save your certificate request.
3. Enter a name for the file.
4. Click OK.
5. A message at the bottom of the window confirms that the request was successfully exported to a file.

Importing a User Certificate to the Wallet

After a certificate request has been successfully generated, you need to send the request via email to a certificate authority informing it formally that you are requesting a certificate. Once the CA has generated your certificate, you will receive an email informing you that your request was fulfilled. Import the certificate into your wallet either by copying the certificate from the email and pasting it into the wallet or by importing the certificate from a file. If you have already had a certificate provisioned in the browser through other means and you need to be able to use that certificate to authenticate to Oracle, you can use the PKCS#12 format of the certificate and then import it into your wallet

Managing Trusted Certificates

Authentication in active production systems involves verification of the certificate with the issuing CA. This requires that the root certificate of the CA and all of its sub-CAs, if necessary, be imported into the wallet.

The following sections deal with importing and exporting trusted certificates with Wallet Manager.

Importing and Exporting Trusted Certificates

OWM automatically installs trusted certificates from the most common CAs when you create a new wallet. These common certificate authorities include VeriSign, RSA, Entrust, and GTE Cyber Trust.

You can import other trusted certificates into a wallet in the same way that you would import a user certificate, either by pasting the information from the email into the OWM interface or by importing the trusted certificate from a file.

If you need to use a trusted certificate in another file system location, you will need to export it. To accomplish this, you need to follow these steps (these should be starting to look familiar):

1. In Wallet Manager, select Operations ➢ Export Trusted Certificate.
2. When the Export Trusted Certificate dialog box appears, select the directory into which you want to save the trusted certificate.
3. Enter the name that you want the file to have.
4. Click Save.

You can export all of your trusted certificates to another file system location as well:

1. In Wallet Manager, select Operations ➢ Export All Trusted Certificates.
2. When the Export Trusted Certificate dialog box appears, select the directory into which you want to save the trusted certificates.
3. Enter the name that you want the file to have.
4. Click Save.

Exporting a Wallet

Not only can you export and import certificates, you can export entire wallets to text-based PKI formats. The same wallet is often useful in more than one environment (for example, test, development, production, system integration testing, and user acceptance testing), so Wallet Manager provides you with a means to use each wallet in multiple environments. By exporting the wallet from one environment and importing it into another, you can make sure that any and all scenarios are fully testable in every environment. When you export a wallet, the certificate chains and trusted certificates will be formatted in the X.509v3 standard and private keys will be formatted in the PKCS#8 standard.

Follow these steps to export a wallet:

1. In Wallet Manager, select Operations ➢ Export Wallet.
2. When the Export Wallet dialog box appears, select the file system to which you want the wallet saved.
3. Enter a name for the file.
4. Click Save.

You can upload wallets to an LDAP directory. If the wallet specified contains an SSL certificate, OWM uses SSL; otherwise, the directory password is necessary. OWM errs on the side of caution in that it does not allow you to upload unless the target wallet is currently open and it contains at least one user certificate.

Here's how to upload a wallet (be careful, this one is different):

Real World Scenario

Importing Trusted Certificates

It is definitely possible to manage certificates effectively in Wallet Manager. However, sometimes when you put the certificate in the wallet, you can get error messages that lead you in an entirely incorrect direction.

We learned the hard way (after considerable stress and hair pulling) that if you get an error that tells you that you have an incorrect password, it may not always be the whole truth. Heck, it may not be the truth at all.

We downloaded a CA certificate from the certificate provider and converted it to Privacy Enhanced Mail (PEM) format.

```
openssl x509 -inform der -in ~/servercert.crt -outform pem -out thawte.crt.pem
```

When we tried to import the wallet, Wallet Manager complained about an incorrect password, even after several of us tried the password that we all knew was correct. We figured that maybe one of us was just mistyping it consistently and maybe someone else should try. Well, maybe two of us just couldn't type that well. Maybe three? That wasn't it. Wallet Manager just couldn't figure out how to tell us that it couldn't load the wallet because it didn't include the CA certificate. We neglected to put the CA certificate in the wallet with the site certificate, so Wallet Manager, and in turn the browser, didn't know how to reference a parent that wasn't there. This was only an issue with a non–Internet Explorer browser because IE ships with reference to every possible certificate predetermined.

Remember, it is important to make sure that the parent trusted certificate is in the wallet before trying to load subordinate certificates or you could spend needless time trying to figure out what you are doing wrong and chasing the wrong trail.

1. In Wallet Manager, choose Wallet ➢ Upload into the Directory Service. (If the currently open wallet has not yet been saved, you will get a dialog box alerting you that "wallet needs to be saved before uploading.")
2. Choose Yes to proceed. Wallet certificates are checked for SSL key usage. Depending on the results of that test, one of the following will occur:
    1. If at least one certificate in the wallet has SSL key usage, when prompted, enter the name of the LDAP directory server host and the port information and click OK. OWM will attempt to connect to the LDAP directory server using SSL. A message will appear indicating whether the wallet was successfully uploaded.
    2. If all certificates have SSL key usage, when prompted, enter the user's distinguished name (DN), the name of the LDAP server host, and the port information. Click OK and OWM will attempt to connect to the LDAP directory server using simple password authentication (assuming the wallet password is the same as the directory password).

Downloading a Wallet

If you need to download a wallet from an LDAP directory, you will need to follow these steps:

1. In Wallet Manager, select Wallet ➤ Download from the Directory Service.
2. You will see a dialog box that prompts you for the user's DN and the LDAP directory password, hostname, and port information. Again, OWM uses simple password authentication in an attempt to connect to the LDAP directory.
    1. If the download operation fails, check whether you have correctly entered the DN and LDAP information.
    2. If the download operation succeeds, click OK to open the downloaded wallet. OWM will attempt to open the wallet using the LDAP directory password. If this fails, a dialog box opens to prompt you for the wallet password.
    3. If OWM cannot open the target wallet using the wallet password, check whether you have entered the correct password. Otherwise, a message will display at the bottom of the window indicating that you successfully downloaded the wallet.

Requesting a Server Certificate

After you have generated a server certificate request using OWM, you can request the server certificate using the OCA user home page. These are the same OracleAS Certificate Authority user pages we talked about earlier in the chapter (see Figure 8.9). To do this, follow these steps:

1. Open the OCA user pages.
2. Click the Server/SubCA Certificates tab.
3. Click Request a Certificate on the tabbed page that appears.
4. On the Certificate Request form that appears, enter the following details:
    1. PKCS#10 Request: The PKCS#10 result you generated in OWM
    2. Name: Your name
    3. Email or Phone Number: Your contact information
    4. Additional Comments: Any special information or instructions for the OCA administrator
    5. Certificate Usage: The purpose for which you intend to use the certificate
    6. Validity Period: The duration for which you require the certificate
5. Click Submit.

   The certificate can be used only after it is approved by the OCA administrator.

Requesting Subordinate CA Certificates

With the increased size of today's organizations, and given the fact that many companies have thousands, or tens of thousands, of employees as well as partners, many security administrators are choosing to manage certificate issuance by using multiple CAs. This use of multiple CAs creates a hierarchical PKI structure where the root CA is at the top and all subordinate

CAs are located below. Each subordinate CA can in turn issue certificates to lower-level CAs, creating what is known as a certificate chain. Any certificate that is signed by one of the subordinate CAs needs to present the certificates of all of the higher-level CAs up to the root. If they aren't, end users may (depending on the browser they are using) be presented with a screen alerting them to the fact that an unverified CA has signed the certificate and asking them to verify that they are willing to chance continuing. Because each authority's certificate is signed by a higher CA, the user can verify the validity of a particular certificate by tracing the authority path back to the CA root.

You can get subordinate certificates by using the OCA user pages:

1. Open the OCA user pages.
2. Click the Server/SubCA Certificates tab.
3. Click Request a Certificate on this tabbed page.
4. When the request form appears, enter the following information:
   a. PKCS#10 Request: Paste the PKCS#10 result you generated in OWM.
   b. Name: Your name.
   c. Email or Phone Number: Your contact information.
   d. Additional Comments: Any special information or instructions for the OCA administrator.
   e. Certificate Usage: Purpose for which you intend to use the certificate. For the CA certificate, select CA Signing.
   f. Validity Period: Duration for which you require the certificate.
5. Click Submit for the SubCA certificate.

Importing and Downloading a CRL

You can either import or download the latest CRL to enable your browser and other programs to detect revoked and expired certificates. You should avoid the use of such certificates because they can allow your apparently secured applications to be used in inappropriate ways by unauthorized users and applications.

To detect revoked or expired certificates, follow these steps:

1. Launch OCA.
2. Navigate to the user pages.
3. Click the User Certificates tab.
4. When the Authentication page appears (shown earlier in Figure 8.9), select the appropriate method with which to identify yourself to the OCA server.
5. Click Submit.
6. When the User Certificates - SSL Authentication page appears, click the Download CRL button.

7. When the CRL page appears displaying the list of revoked certificates with their serial numbers and revocation dates, you can click the Download button and download the CRL. You can use one of three buttons at this point—Import CRL into Browser, Download CRL in Binary, or Download CRL in BASE64 format. The first button stores the CRL in the browser, and the other two store it in a directory in the operating system.

Configuring Browsers to Trust OCA

Whenever you import a certificate into your browser, the browser imports both the certificate that you requested and the certificate representing the CA that signed and issued your certificate. Because OCA is not trusted by default, you will have to configure your browser for activities for which you need to be able to trust the CA.

This configuration varies based on the browser that you are using.

For Mozilla-based browsers to trust CAs, you have to perform the following steps:

1. From the Edit menu of the browser, select Preferences.
2. Navigate to Privacy and Security.
3. Expand Security and select Certificates. All of the different options surrounding management of certificates are displayed.
4. Click Manage Certificates.
5. When the Manage Certificates dialog box launches, click the Authorities tab.
6. When the list of CAs from which you have received certificates launches, scroll down and find the OCA certificate.
7. Select the certificate and click Edit.
8. When the Edit CA Certificate Trust Settings dialog box appears, select the options listed to allow you to trust the OCA CA certificate.

Configuring Oracle HTTP Server for SSL Certificates

Recall that SSL is the encryption communication protocol designed to securely send messages across the Internet. It sits between the Oracle HTTP server on the application tier and the TCP/IP Transport layer, transparently handling encryption and decryption whenever a client needs a secure connection.

To help support SSL v3.0, `mod_osso` (a Procedural Language/Structured Query Language, PL/SQL, package that Oracle provides to assist you with connecting to the Single Sign-On using encrypted cookies, all without you having to write a line of code) provides encrypted communication between the client and the server using either RSA or DES encryption standards. Further, it allows for integrity checking of the client/server communication using MD5 or SHA checksum algorithms and certificate management using wallets.

Authorization of clients and multiple access checks are performed by mod_ossl.

So, how do we configure this, if it is a stored procedure? The following sections provide you with more detail on just how this is accomplished.

SSL Configuration Tool

The SSL Configuration Tool is an automation tool designed to assist the administrator with automation of the manual steps necessary for securing HTTP. If your architecture is such that both the infrastructure and the middle tier are present, you will need to run the SSL Configuration Tool on the infrastructure first and then on the middle tier. If you installed OracleAS and configure some changes, you should use SSL Configuration Tool and then carefully examine the log files to verify the changes that were made. This tool creates log files in the directory from which the tool was launched. In addition, new log files are created each time it is run. The SSLConfigTool executable can be found in the %ORACLE_HOME%\bin directory. The syntax needed to run it is as follows:

```
SSLConfigTool (-config_w_prompt
 | -config_w_file <input_file>
 | -config_w_default
 | -rollback)
 | [-dry_run]
 | [-wc_for_infra]
 | [-secure_admin]
 | [-opwd <orcladmin_password>]
 | [-ptl_dad <dad_name>]
 | [-ptl_inv_pwd <ptl_inv_password>]
```

When you include valid parameters in the httpd.conf file, you can enable Oracle HTTP server for SSL. Here are the necessary parameters:

ServerName Name of the server on which you are enabling SSL.

SSLEngine [on/off] Off is default. Setting it on enables SSL on the server.

SSLWallet File The location or path of the server wallet.

SSLVerifyClient The verification type for client certificates. (None provides for SSL without certificates, Optional is for server certificates only, and Require provides for server certificates as well as client certificates.)

After you have configured SSL in the httpd.conf file, you can access Oracle HTTP Server with the HTTPS protocol using the URL https://your.domain:443 (the default SSL port). The server displays a certificate and you need to reply as to whether you accept or reject the certificate.

Adding User Certificates to OID

After you have enabled SSL certificates on the SSO server, the user certificates need to be stored in the OID server. You can upload user certificates to the OID server by using an ldif file. The ldapmodify command is used to upload certificates to the OID server.

The command used to upload the certificates looks like this:

```
ldapmodify -h ldaphost -p ldapport -D "cn=orcladmin"
➥ -w password -f filename.ldif
```

And the ldif file looks like this:

```
Dn: cn=ken, o=oracle, dc=com
changetype: modify
replace: usercertificate
usercertificate: :UHOP3UIPHklliuo4nhgaoiBHOIHYOIY5alskjdfoaiuypta...
```

Adding the user certificate to the OID server enables the SSO server to maintain a secure authentication on behalf of the partner applications.

This will be covered in more detail in Chapter 9.

Configuring OracleAS Web Cache to Use SSL

To provide even more security for your website, you can configure Web Cache to receive HTTPS protocol browser requests and send HTTPS requests on the originating server. HTTPS uses SSL to encrypt and decrypt user page requests as well as the pages returned by both Web Cache and the origin servers.

To accomplish this support, you need to follow these steps:

1. Create a wallet.
2. Configure HTTPS ports and the wallet location.
3. Request Client Side Certificates (optional).
4. Permit HTTPS requestor to only view a URL or set of URLs (optional).

Configuring OracleAS Portal to Use SSL

OracleAS Portal communicates with a number of other components, each of which is able to act as a client or a server in the HTTP communication channel. This means that user interactions with Portal, in order to be secure, require that each of these components be configured individually to support HTTPS. After each component is secured, you need to perform the following to secure Portal:

1. Secure the Parallel Page Engine (PPE). PPE is a multithreaded Java servlet that runs on the middle tier and assembles the portal pages whenever a user request comes in. The PPE is called by Oracle HTTP Server and loops back to the Web Cache. *Both* connections need to be secured.
2. Add Portal to SSO as a secured partner application. In doing this, you reassociate a portal instance with SSO by running the Oracle Portal Configuration Assistant (OPCA).
3. Secure the calls that are made from OracleAS Portal to the Delegated Administration Services. This ensures that the calls to the infrastructure tier from user and group information from the OID are secure.

The first two of these topics are discussed in the following sections. Securing the calls is discussed further in Chapter 6.

Securing the PPE

The PPE uses the protocol that is assigned to it by Apache via `mod_oc4j`. This means that if the site is using a protocol different from one at the Apache level, PPE must be instructed to use the protocol of the site to generate URL and loopback requests. If Web Cache is implemented with HTTPS, then connections to the PPE are automatically secured by SSL.

Because PPE creates URLs, it is necessary to specify which ports use HTTPS. To accomplish this, use the following steps:

1. Open the `web.xml` file for the `OC4J_Portal` instance on the middle tier. The file is located in the `$ORACLE_HOME/j2ee/OC4J_Portal/applications/portal/portal/WEB-INF` directory.
2. Add an `<init-param>` block to the `web.xml` file to indicate the ports that are using HTTPS. This should point to the Web Cache listening port. If multiple ports implement SSL-based connections, indicate the separation of ports using a colon:

```
<init-param>
<param-name>httpsports</paramname>
<param-value>4443:4446</param-value>
</init-param>
```

Associating OracleAS Portal with SSO in SSL Mode

Because you have not reconfigured SSO to support HTTPS, you will now have to reassociate the portal instance to the SSO to allow it to use SSL. Portal is a partner application for SSO, and the SSO server stores registration information about partner applications in its repository. The information that is included concerning the partner applications is the application's ID, the home URL, the success URL, the logout URL, and other parameters.

Portal stores information about the SSO server in the form of enabler configuration information. It stores the application ID, listener token (consisting of hostname and port used in the URL for the current request), encryption keys used to encrypt the login cookie, the SSO server login URL, and some auxiliary data.

To associate the portal instance and the SSO server, `ptlconfig` (found on the Portal middle tier's `%ORACLE_HOME%\portal\conf` directory) is used:

```
ptlconfig -dad portal -sso -host <host_name> -port <port> -ssl
```

-dad The Portal's DAD name.

-sso Creates the partner application entries in the SSO server. When run without any additional partner application details, the details are updated using the `iasconfig.xml` file.

-host The name of the host you are registering as a partner application.

-port The port used for registration.

-ssl Indicates that the port in the `-port` parameter is HTTPS.

In contrast to `ptlconfig`, `otlconfig` is a stand-alone utility that is run from the command line; it is not runnable from any other utility.

After you run OPCA successfully, you should be able to access the welcome page of your portal with HTTPS by using the following format:

```
https://<server.name>:<port>/pls/portal
```

Summary

OracleAS has a very complex and robust security architecture with components at every tier and in every piece of the puzzle. In the first part of the chapter we discussed the components of the security architecture and how necessary security is in the Internet and intranet environment.

You can view the security architecture from two general perspectives, authorization and authentication. Authentication can be gained through Single Sign-On and authorization can be gained through SSL and certificates.

After we got a handle on the different pieces, we discussed the intimacies of SSL and how certificates can be implemented in the environment.

Exam Essentials

Understand the OracleAS security terminology. Be able to define the key terms that you use to describe the function of the security components in an OracleAS environment, such as an OracleAS SSL, SSO, OID, and PKI.

Describe the components that make up the security architecture. Understand how the security components can work together to allow OracleAS deployment to be as secure as possible. Be able to explain the dependencies between the security components.

Describe the components that a middle-tier instance installation comprises. Understand the functionality of each middle-tier component. Be able to identify the tools used to develop middle-tier applications.

List the primary tools that provide you with the ability to administer the OracleAS security infrastructure. Describe the function of each tool and when you should use it.

Identify the OracleAS installation types. Understand the dependencies between different OracleAS security components. Identify the components that make up each level in the security chain.

Be able to place OracleAS components into a logical topology. Understand how the security on each tier functions in an n-tier environment and be able to place each OracleAS security component into the appropriate environment.

Review Questions

1. Which of the following components are not part of the OracleAS security infrastructure? (Choose all that apply.)
   - A. Authentication
   - B. OracleAS SSO
   - C. OracleAS Cryptography
   - D. OracleAS Certificate Authority
   - E. Wallets
2. Which is not a component of OracleAS's implementation of PKI?
   - A. SSL
   - B. SSO
   - C. OID
   - D. LDAP
3. What component primarily provides security features to Java programmers?
   - A. JavaBeans
   - B. JVM
   - C. J2EE
   - D. JAAS
   - E. OC4J
4. What is a user? (Choose all that apply.)
   - A. Someone sitting at a computer accessing an application
   - B. A program attempting to access an application
   - C. A file system that an application accesses
   - D. Any human who has been authenticated to the system correctly
5. What does OCA use as its internal repository?
   - A. An Oracle database
   - B. OID
   - C. SSL
   - D. The OID Metadata Repository alone
   - E. All of the above

6. Which of the following components is not a part of Oracle Identity Management?
   - A. Oracle Internet Directory
   - B. Oracle Database
   - C. OracleAS Certificate Authority
   - D. OracleAS Delegated Administration Service
   - E. OracleAS Single Sign-On

7. What is the primary function of Oracle Internet Directory as it applies to security?
   - A. Stores published certificates
   - B. Validates a user's credentials against the database
   - C. Stores metadata for most components of OracleAS
   - D. Assigns administrative duties to non-administrators

8. What is the primary function of OracleAS Single Sign-On?
   - A. Generates and publishes PKI certificates
   - B. Validates a user's credentials against OID
   - C. Stores metadata for most components of OracleAS
   - D. Maintains authentication and authorization information in an LDAP 3 directory
   - E. Assigns administrative duties to non-administrators

9. Which of the following components are not connected in any way to the security infrastructure components of OracleAS? (Choose all that apply.)
   - A. Web Cache
   - B. Oracle HTTP Server
   - C. BI Forms
   - D. Oracle Internet Directory
   - E. Single Sign-On

10. Which of the following is not a security module supported by the HTTP server?
    - A. `mod_plsql`
    - B. `mod_osso`
    - C. `mod_ossl`
    - D. `mod_security`
    - E. `mod_access`

11. Identify the HTTP module that provides for authentication based on username and password.
    - A. `mod_auth`
    - B. `mod_pwd`
    - C. `mod_uid`
    - D. `mod_upass`

12. OracleAS JAAS provides what to the application server?
    A. Enterprise JavaBeans (EJB)
    B. Java Server Pages (JSPs)
    C. Security features to the Java programmer
    D. Portlets
    E. JDBC database connections
13. Of what is Oracle Identity Management composed?
    A. All of the security necessary for running a Portal website
    B. Tools used to authenticate and authorize users
    C. Oracle PL/SQL server pages
    D. LDAP
    E. Single Sign-On
14. Oracle's HTTP server can be configured to use which component of the security infrastructure to ensure secure communication?
    A. Oracle Identity Management (OIM)
    B. Secure Sockets Layer (SSL)
    C. Oracle Internet Directory (OID)
    D. LDAP
15. Identify the two Oracle-provided utilities that can be used to manage security in an OracleAS environment.
    A. SSL and LDAP
    B. OIM and LMNP
    C. OAM and OID
    D. OCA and OWM
16. Using what interface allows an administrator to approve certificate requests, update certificate revocation lists, and configure a certificate authority all in one location?
    A. Wallet Manager
    B. Certificate Authority Interface
    C. Portal Authority
    D. Oracle Internet Directory
17. What technology supports encryption methods through cipher suites?
    A. SSL
    B. OWM
    C. OID
    D. OCA

18. What Oracle-provided database package helps support SSL v3.0-encrypted communication?
    A. `mod_ssl`
    B. `mod_sso`
    C. `mod_plsql`
    D. `mod_osso`
19. What tool do administrators use to assist with the automation of manual steps necessary for securing HTTP?
    A. Certificate Authority Interface
    B. Oracle Interface Directory
    C. SSL Configuration Tool
    D. Wallet Manager
20. What SSL Configuration Tool parameter enables SSL on a server?
    A. `SSLServer`
    B. `SSLEngine`
    C. `SSLWallet`
    D. `SSLVerifyClient`

Answers to Review Questions

1. A, C. Authentication is what some of the components are responsible for. Cryptography is not something unique to OracleAS.

2. D. ODI, SSL, and SSO all work together to provide Oracle's implementation of public key infrastructure.

3. D. JAAS provides Java programmers with key security services by allowing them to use authentication to identify users, authorization as a way to limit what those users can do, and delegation to enable code to run securely.

4. A, B. For the purpose of security discussions, users have to be considered to be not only people accessing a system, but also programs or other systems attempting to access a system.

5. D. OCA uses the OracleAS Infrastructure Metadata Repository as its internal repository for storing not only issued certificates, but also certificate requests and auxiliary information surrounding requested, issued, and revoked certificates.

6. B. Although Oracle Database stores the metadata for many components of OracleAS, including OID, it is not considered a part of Oracle Identity Management.

7. A. Oracle Internet Directory's responsibility in the security framework is to hold published certificates.

8. B. One of several components of OID, Single Sign-On validates a user's credentials against OID and allows transparent access to other applications without reauthenticating.

9. C. The only component in the list that is not connected to the security infrastructure of OracleAS is BI Forms, which is part of a middleware installation.

10. A. `mod_plsql` provides the ability to create dynamic HTML pages based on stored procedures; it is not a security module.

11. A. `mod_auth` provides a module to be used for authentication based on username and password.

12. C. Oracle's Application Server Java Authentication and Authorization Service (JAAS) provides key security services to the Java programmer by allowing them to use authentication to identify users, authorization as a way to limit what those users can do, and delegation to enable code to run securely.

13. B. The OIM suite is a set of tools that are used to provide security administration ability to administrators.

14. B. Secure Sockets Layer, along with public key infrastructure, can be used to allow HTTP to assure communication between users' browsers and OracleAS.

15. D. Oracle Certificate Authority and Oracle Wallet Manager can be used to manage security in an OracleAS environment.

16. B. Certificate Authority Interface is where you can perform all of the tasks in one location.

17. A. SSL technology supports a variety of encryption protocols. Each choice is called a cipher suite, and each type specifies the type of signature-capable certificate that can be used, the type of symmetric encryption, and the type of signature algorithm (secure hash) that should be used.

18. D. `mod_osso` facilitates encrypted communication between the client and the server.

19. C. SSL Configuration Tool assists administrators with the automation of the manual steps necessary for securing HTTP.

20. B. The `SSLEngine` parameter set to `on` enables SSL on the server.

Managing Authentication Using Oracle Internet Directory

ORACLE APPLICATION SERVER 10*g* ADMINISTRATION I EXAM OBJECTIVES COVERED IN THIS CHAPTER:

✓ **Configuring Oracle Application Server Components in OID**

- Describe identity management
- Explain the default Identity Realm
- Describe the OracleAS administration model
- Explain application-specific access control
- Manage users and groups
- Describe the relationship between OracleAS Portal and Oracle Internet Directory
- Identify OracleAS Portal entries in the directory
- Configure OID settings in OracleAS Portal

✓ **Managing the Oracle Internet Directory**

- Explain the Directory and LDAP concepts
- Describe Oracle Internet Directory (OID)
- Explain Oracle Internet Directory architecture
- Start and stop Oracle Internet Directory processes
- Identify various OID command-line tools
- Connect to and disconnect from the OID by using Oracle Directory Manager

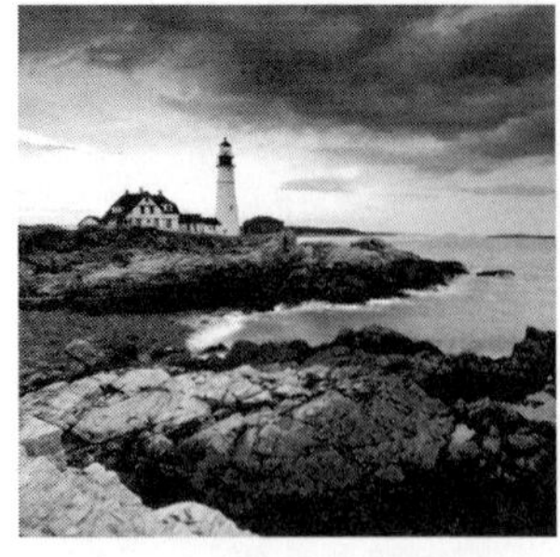

Identity management is the process of centralizing the control, management, and administration of authorization, auditing, and of compliance as well as passwords, provisioning, mobile access, and self-service computing.

As it relates more directly to Oracle, identity management encompasses not only access management, user administration, and self-service application management, but also federation support, user provisioning, Lightweight Directory Access Protocol (LDAP) v3 directory services, directory synchronization, web services management, and an X.509 v3 certificate authority. One of the primary benefits of Oracle Identity Management is the close integration that it allows with other Oracle products; other key benefits include its robustness and scalability, its simple off-the-shelf, out-of-the-box deployment support for Oracle products, and its heterogeneous application support through open, standards-based implementation.

Using Oracle's Identity Management, you can provision not only all of your enterprise application users, but also other users, including computers, Web Services, and "real" users like customers and trading partners. Once they are provisioned, you can manage these users and roles and their associated permissions in the application, store a user's profile information (preferences, user IDs, passwords, and PINs), and provide a facility to allow for personalized application interfaces for individuals by using portals.

Centralized identity management provides any size organization with many benefits. It can help an already overtaxed administration department reduce the time it takes to administer the users and their applications, thereby reducing the administration costs associated with the management and administration of application deployments. At the same time, this centralized interface provides improved overall security for the data and the application. More and more, this security feature is a selling point for an organization.

But even more than security features, centralized identity management can mean more elegant user management. For most organizations, user administration has become one of the most expensive, laborious processes, and, because of its complexity, it can be error prone. Errors can introduce security holes (more security issues!) and always introduce more cost. The selling point for most organizations is the bottom line, the cost. Security is just a side benefit.

Because Identity Management centralizes and automates many of the tasks necessary for the management and administration of users and the security associated with the users and the applications, it can reduce administration costs while improving accuracy. (This means a task can be done once with the assurance that it was likely done correctly.) Because of this, the organization may be able to avoid even more monetary impact by avoiding or plugging any of the holes that may be in its system.

Identity Management also means happier users (something not even on the radar as a selling point for an administration interface). This is because the Oracle Internet Directory allows new users to gain access to applications more quickly than might be accomplished with different tools.

This user self-administration can limit or even eliminate a lot of wasted time for the employee (and for the administrator), reduces costs for the organization, and allows for the customization of administration and security (there is that word again) to an individual user or to a group of users.

What's more, you can allow users to manage their passwords and credentials, also centrally. This can help you to improve usability while reducing the temptation for them to maintain this information in a hard copy in a handy but insecure location (like on a sticky note on their monitor or under their keyboard). This is one of the common ways in which an organization's security is breached.

This chapter is dedicated to how Oracle handles identity management and how you, as the administrator, handle Oracle's utilities.

Understanding Oracle Identity Management

Oracle's Identity Management infrastructure enables administrators to deploy enterprise identities and manage their access to the diverse applications in the enterprise centrally and securely. Oracle Internet Directory (OID) is an LDAPv3 directory that brings with it proxy capabilities, a directory implementation based on the Oracle10*g* database, and quick, millisecond response times to LDAP entries. OID supports server-side entry caching and multimaster and fan-out LDAP replication and leverages Oracle's fine-grained access control. It supports multiple authentication mechanisms and fully integrates with Enterprise Manager. You can create and manage enterprise identities as well as the unique properties of those identities through a single interface. One interface, one price.

Recall that an identity can be human or hardware. Administrators can create groups of identities (groups of users, groups of servers, groups of applications), provision events (account creation, suspension, and deletion, for example), and manage policies that are associated with identities (such as authorization policies, authentication policies, and delegation of privileges).

Oracle Identity Management Overview

The Identity Management functionalities and the corresponding Oracle component that implements each particular functionality can be found in Table 9.1. Many of these components were discussed in Chapter 8.

TABLE 9.1 Identity Management Functionality

Functionality	Component
Lightweight Directory Access Protocol (LDAP)	Oracle Internet Directory (OID)
Directory integration	OID Integration Services

TABLE 9.1 Identity Management Functionality *(continued)*

Functionality	Component
Application user provisioning	OID Provisioning Integration Service
Delegated administration	Oracle Delegated Administration Services
Web single sign-on	OracleAS Single Sign-On
Certificate authority	OracleAS Certificate Authority

As you can see, OID is one of the central components of Oracle Identity Management. It is designed to support not only the Oracle 10*g* database, but also Oracle Application Server 10*g* (OracleAS), Oracle Collaboration Suite, and Oracle E-Business Suite, seamlessly and effectively. It also allows you to extend its functionality to other applications and services in your organization.

As web and other thin client applications become more popular, organizations need to rely on products such as the OID server to store rarely updated data centrally so that they can be accessed by any LDAP-enabled application instantly. OID is not necessarily a security product, but it can be a key component in your organization's security plans. This enterprise data management tool includes the ability to manage security data such as user IDs and passwords for an OracleAS application.

OID is a highly scalable product that can support a large number of entries and a large number of concurrent users out of the box from a central location. Because OID is implemented on top of an OracleAS database (the infrastructure database), it has the ability to take additional advantage of the database's scalability and availability features. This scalability can be even more extensive if OID is riding on top of Oracle's Real Application Cluster (RAC) database. Running on a RAC database can also leverage Oracle's high-availability features and offer Oracle's functionality in a disaster recovery situation or simply provide its functionality in a 24/7 environment.

OID has three levels of directory user authentication:

Anonymous The user does not have to go the extra distance to authenticate.

Password-based The user has a password that gains them access to the application.

Certificate-based via SSL The user is connected via a set of encrypted certificates.

These authentication types were covered in Chapter 8, so you can return there to examine them in more detail.

Despite the fact that OID is not inherently a security component, it does provide many security benefits. OID helps to assure data integrity through the use of Secure Sockets Layer (SSL) to ensure that data received at the client site have not been modified, deleted, compromised, or even accessed and replayed while they were being transmitted. It does this by generating a cryptographically secure message with the level of encryption required by the given organization. OID also helps to ensure data confidentiality (protecting against inadvertent, accidental, or deliberate interception of information while the data are being transmitted between source and destination), again by using encryption available through SSL.

By default, OID uses the MD4 algorithm to check the integrity of the encrypted message digest though the use of 128-bit hashes. MD4, designed by Professor Ron Rivset of MIT, was only one in a line of similar algorithms (later versions included MD5, SHA, and RIPEMD). It is typically represented by 32-digit hexadecimal numbers, and the hash is designed so that even a small, often unnoticeable change in the message will result in an entirely different message digest. Although this hash is not completely unbreakable, it does provide the level of security often necessary for many organizations, and it is customizable to allow further flexibility and even stronger security.

OID supports both read and write access control, not just at the application layer, but on down to the tuple, row, and attribute level in the database. This can be further refined by coupling OID with the security features already resident in the OracleAS database.

OracleAS Components and OID

OracleAS brings together all of the web-based application development tools, including Oracle Developer, Oracle Business Intelligence Discoverer, and Oracle JDeveloper. This one-stop shopping and central administration feature can be a powerful tool in your implementation. All of the necessary components are in one place and can be administered with one set of tools, so you can more easily and elegantly manage and administer access not only to the ultimate end applications, but also to the tools necessary to create these applications. You simply deploy applications built using these components on OracleAS and allow your users to access them. OracleAS provides users with the appropriate level of access through the use of Single Sign-On (SSO). Once they have logged in to OracleAS, they are logged in to all of their personally relevant applications—no need to mess with additional passwords, and no need for the application to request additional authentication from the user to navigate to other applications. Given that many of these applications are deployed, using Portal, through a common front end, it can also mean that a casual hacker will not be able to quickly determine where each individual application resides. It will appear as though they all reside in one central location, even if they are spread throughout the organization, the country, or the world.

SSO stores all of a user's information and credentials in a single storehouse preventing them from having to store them multiple times in multiple applications. Authentication is transparent to the user at the application/application server/OID interface; this means the developer or designer doesn't need to code each individual interface to prompt for a user ID and password, thereby preventing yet another gap in security.

Whenever you install OID, Oracle Universal Installer (OUI) installs a default schema and a default directory information tree (DIT) so you can start using Oracle components in that OID directory. Although this directory and schema are typically sufficient for most organizations, it is possible that, due to business requirements you may need to customize them. OID provides flexibility so you can customize the schema and DIT to meet the business's needs today and as they change. During installation, OUI installs the following:

Base Schema Elements The Base Schema Elements are the basic attributes and object classes that are required by OID for it to function. Some of these elements are defined by the Internet

Engineering Task Force (IETF) and are standard across applications, across platforms, and across product lines; others are specific to Oracle components.

Root Oracle Context Root Oracle Context is an entry in OID that contains a pointer to the default Identity Management Realm in the infrastructure as well as information about how to find the Identity Management Realm with a simple name. This is typically set to OracleContext, which you can usually leave alone.

Default Identity Management Realm Although this always makes us think of knights and dragons, lords and ladies, realm (as it applies to an OID installation) is nothing more than a directory in which all users and group account contexts reside. When you install OracleAS, you create a default realm, which is configured and ready to use. This realm is based on the infrastructure domain that you set during installation.

If your domain is `mydomain.com` then your domain will resemble default identity management realm. Your users will be located in `dc=mydomain,dc=com` and groups would be found in `dc=groups,dc=mydomain,dc=com`. It is important to realize that this default realm is sufficient for most organizations' infrastructure and user/group management needs. Exceptions include one of the following: You require separate password policies for different user communities. You have internal as well as external user communities for the same application and the same management structure. You require different naming attributes, provisioned services, or user schema definitions.

Identity Management Realm-Specific Oracle Context This is the container that maintains the common information about the components, including authentication attributes, privilege assignments, and application-specific data.

Default Password Policy This is a password policy that is used for each subscriber and that applies to all of the users. It can include rules stipulating that passwords should be at least a certain size, such as eight characters in length, or that they should contain uppercase letters or special characters.

Common, Realm-Specific Entries

The common entry in the Identity Management Realm-Specific Oracle Context contains information for locating users and groups. It makes use of the following parameters to accomplish this:

User Search Base (`orclCommonUserSearchBase`) Specifies the node in the subscriber DIT under which all of the users for a given realm or a given application are placed. This value is what is used while searching for a user in the Identity Management Realm.

Group Search Base (`orclCommonGroupSearchBase`) Specifies the node under which you can find all of the groups.

User Object Class (`orclUserObjectClass`) Lists all of the object classes that are to be used to create a user entry under the subscriber tree (person, organizationalPerson, orclUser).

In many hosted environments, each Identity Management Realm typically has its own instance of the application. This means that the instance information and other data that are required by the individual realm are stored in the Identity Management Realm-Specific Oracle Context, as is all of the other information needed for a local installation. General information that is to be accessible by all realms is stored in the default (or root) Identity Management Realm-Specific Oracle Context. Specialized information is in the organization-specific realm.

Although you can create the Identity Management Realm's user under the Identity Management Realm node, you also can create and store users and their individual data outside the Identity Management Realm node. You do this by setting the `orclCommonUserSearchBase` attribute, which points to the value of the node that contains the user and user data and allows OID to follow the trail of bread crumbs to the user information. This can provide you with the flexibility of having new Identity Management Realms without migrating the old user distinguished names (DNs).

Starting and Stopping the OID Interface

There is a simple command, located in the application server infrastructure's `ORACLE_HOME`, that you can use to start and stop `oidmon` (OracleAS's OID component, OID Monitor). Oracle Process Manager and Notification Server (OPMN) enables you to manage components in an integrated way. If you use OPMN to start and stop OID, you don't need to start either OID Monitor or the directory-designated database separately.

The `opmnctl` command starts and stops OID Monitor and also starts and stops the default directory server instance and, on a specific node, stops and restarts all running OID servers and directory servers, directory replication servers, and directory integration and provisioning servers. The format for `opmnctl` is either

```
opmnctl startproc ias -component=OID
```

or

```
opmnctl stopproc ias -component=OID
```

Oracle Internet Directory issues an `oidmon` start command with the appropriate arguments and then issues `oidctl` start commands.

OPMN, consisting of Oracle Notification Server (ONS), Oracle Process Manager (OPM), and Oracle Process Manager Modules, is responsible for monitoring OID and OracleAS components. It knows only about `oidmon` and is blissfully unaware of OID server instances. `oidmon` initiates, monitors, and terminates LDAP server processes and continues to be responsible for starting, stopping, monitoring, and restarting OID server instances.

The command used to start OPMN is `opmnctl startall`. `You can use OPMN to start individual components:`

```
opmnctl startproc ias-component=OID
```

Once opmnctl runs, it accesses the opmn.xml file. When you run the startall command, the contents of the opmn.xml file are reloaded. When you run opmnctl with the startproc parameter, it does not reload the XML file but instead uses the parameters that are already loaded in the environment.

The command

```
opmnctl stopall
```

or

```
opmnctl stopproc ias-component=OID
```

can be used to stop the processes in the same manner.

You can start the OID server if and only if the OID server instance is already up and functional.

To provide load balancing and high availability, you can start more than one OID server instance at a time in order to accommodate the increasing number of users accessing the directory server; however, the newly added instances must be started on different ports.

Once you start oidmon through the OPMN utility, OPMN makes sure that OID Monitor is up and running; if it isn't, OPMN will bring it back up.

Interestingly, if you have started OID Monitor with OPMN and you deliberately stop OID Monitor with the oidmon stop command, the monitor will shut down but OPMN will see that it is no longer there and will restart it.

Starting the *oidmon* Utility

Naturally, before you can start the oidmon process, it has to be down. Although this may be brutally apparent, it is important to remember this and check to see if the process is already running before you try to start it up again. This precaution is often overlooked, but it is a good practice not only for OID, but also for any service. Although most services simply won't start if they are already running with the same name and/or port on the server, the precaution may save you at least some time, but potentially it may save you from corrupting your system. Not corrupting your system will save you even more time because you won't have to recover it (although recovery practice is also a valuable tool to keep in your toolbox).

To shut down the OID server, first stop the OID server instance and then stop the oidmon process. Order is important in this case because oidmon must be running in order to process the commands that are necessary to start and stop OID using the oidctl utility. The oidmon process is responsible for monitoring all of the OID server instances that are running on the various nodes and tries to recover any that it finds have failed.

It is important, to avoid the chance of corruption and to make your management simpler by ensuring that you shut down the services in the correct order—and start them in the right order for that matter. You should shut down the server instance first, and then the oidmon process.

`opmnctl` can be used to start OID as a component.

To start `oidmon`, set `NLS_LANG` to an appropriate UTF8 language set, such as `AMERICAN_AMERICA.UTF8`, and set the TNS connection string appropriately. Then run the following command:

```
oidmon connect=<net_service_name> sleep=20 start
```

`connect=` An optional argument; the connection is assumed to be the system identifier (SID) of the instance that you are running the statement against if the command-line parameter is omitted.

`<net_service_name>` The parameter that specifies the net service name of the database to which you want to connect. This is the infrastructure database or the database where the OracleAS infrastructure is installed and is the network service name that is set in the `tnsnames.ora` file.

`sleep` The number of seconds after which `oidmon` should check for new requests from `oidctl` and request to restart any services that may have been stopped. The default is 10 seconds. The `sleep` argument is optional.

`start` The command that starts the `oidmon` process; naturally, it is required.

If you want to see any error messages that might be written, you can check the `oidmon.log` file, which is typically located in the infrastructure `$ORACLE_HOME/ldap/log` directory.

There are other optional parameters for the `oidmon` command:

`SERVER` This parameter passes the command the server type that should be started. Valid values include `oidldap` for the LDAP server and `odisvr` for the DIP server.

`INSTANCE` This parameter can be passed when there are OID instances of the same process. For example, if you choose to run more than one `oidldap` server, each server process must have a different instance number.

If you don't specify the parameters, the defaults for the arguments will apply. This means that `ORACLE_SID` will be used for the connection string, the current host will be used as the hostname, and 10 seconds will be used for the `sleep` parameter.

Stopping the *oidmon* Utility

You stop the OID Monitor process using the `oidmon` utility:

```
oidmon connect=<net_service_name> stop
```

Again, `connect=<net_service_name>` specifies the net service name, as found in the `tnsnames.ora` file. The net service name is the instance to which you want to be connected.

`stop` is the mandatory command that stops the OID Monitor process.

Do *not* stop the OID Monitor if you are just ending one or more directory server or replication server instances. These services can be started and stopped independently. Shut down the OID Monitor process *only* if you are shutting down the LDAP server altogether.

For more information, please refer to the *Oracle Internet Directory Administrator's Guide.*

Starting and Stopping the OID Server Instance

Remember, you can start and stop OID server instances only if the `oidmon` process is already running so it is available to process the commands. You use the `oidctl` utility to start and stop the OID server instance.

The following is the syntax for starting the OID server process:

```
oidctl connect=<net_service_name>
server=<server_name> instance=
<server_instance_number>
   [configset=<configset_number>]
[flags= '-p <port_number>']   start
   http://download-west.oracle.com/docs/cd/B14099_18/core.1012/b13995/
   chginfra.htm#ASADM902
   http://download-west.oracle.com/docs/cd/B14099_18/idmanage.1012/b14082/
   replic_admin.htm#sthref3039 ajw
```

`connect=<net_service_name>` The `tnsnames.ora` net service name that points to the OracleAS Infrastrucutre database.

`server=<server_name>` The type of server to start. (Valid values are `oidldap`, `oidrepld`, and `oidsrv`.) This parameter is not case sensitive.

`instance=<server_instance_number>` The instance number of the server that you want to start. Valid values are from 1 to 1000. This is particularly important when you are running multiple instances of a given service.

`configset=<configset_number>` The number used to start the server. This should be a number from 0 to 1000. The default, `configset0`, provides a single server instance with one default server process and two database connections preconfigured. If this is inadequate to handle the LDAP load for your implementation, you may need to increase the number of server processes or database connections. To make these changes, you change the values associated with the `orclserverprocs` and `orclmaxcc` attributes.

`flags=` Provides the facility for passing command-line parameters to the utility.

`-p <port_number>` Specifies the port number during server instance startup. The default port number is 389.

`start` Starts the server specified in the server argument.

To start the directory server, type the following command on the new node:

```
oidctl connect=<db_connect_string_of_new_node> server=oidldapd \
   instance=1 flags='-p <port_number>' start
```

The syntax for stopping the OID server instance is as follows:

```
oidctl connect=<net_service_name> server=<server_name> instance=<server_
instance_number> stop
```

`connect=<net_service_name>` The net service name associated with the OID instance.

`server=<server_name>` The type of server that you want to stop. (Valid values are `oidldapd`, `oidrepld`, and `oidsrv`.) The values are not case sensitive.

`instance=<server_instance_number>` The instance number of the server that you want to stop. It should be the number of an existing running instance of the type specified. Again, this is particularly important if more than one of any given service is running on the node.

`stop` The mandatory command that stops the server specified in the server argument.

You can use the `oidctl` command to stop a running instance of the OID server. You need to specify the number of the server instance you want to stop.

Before you stop the instance, ensure that the OID Monitor process is running. Although stopping a server that isn't running won't actually hurt anything, it is a waste of time and computer resources and not a good practice.

Bulk Tools

Oracle, in its infinite wisdom, provides many bulk tools that you can use to manipulate data associated with your LDAP server. You can use these tools to perform bulk data operations on the OID server. They are useful as a means to maintain a large number of directory entries; these entries typically come from other applications or directories or other LDAP servers. Using these tools on a Unix server is simple and straightforward. To use them in a Windows environment, you need to be running a Unix emulation program (like Cygwin or MKS Toolkit) so you can run the Unix shell utilities as natively as is possible.

The following bulk tools available for your use are located in the application server infrastructure in either the `$ORACLE_HOME/bin` directory or the `$ORACLE_HOME/ldap/bin` directory:

`bulkload.sh` Loads a large number of entries into the OID server using an LDIF as input. Lightweight Directory Interchange Format (LDIF) files can be generated or extracted from third-party applications using RFC 2849 as a guide (see `www.ietf.org/rfc/rfc2849.txt`). The syntax for `bulkload.sh` is as follows:

```
bulkload.sh -connect <connect descriptor>
➥<[-check] [-generate] [-restore] [-numThread]
```

```
    [-parallel] [-encode] [-append] [-load] | [-index] |
    [-recover]>
<absolute path to LDIF data file>
```

-connect Specifies the Oracle Net connect descriptor that can be used to connect to the infrastructure database. To use the utility to load data into a single node, simply specify its connect string (e.g., `orclinf`). If you are going to load data into multiple nodes, specify the connect strings of all nodes (e.g., `orclinf1 orclinf2 orclinf3`).

-check Indicates that schema and duplicate DN checks should be performed on the LDAP schema data file.

-generate Creates the Internet Directory Bulk Loader data files for loading.

-restore Used when the LDIF file contains operational attributes that are generated by `ldifwrite`. (This is required when adding a new node to an existing replication group.)

-numThread Specifies the number of threads to be created. The valid range for this parameter is from 1 to 999. This option should be specified with the `-generate` option.

-parallel Specifies whether loading should be done in parallel mode.

-encode Specifies the native character set that should be used.

-append Specifies that incremental mode should be used and that `append` should be the method used. (The default is `bulkmode append`.)

-load Specifies that the data generated during the `-generate` phase should be loaded into the specified database.

-index Specifies that indexes should be re-created on all catalog tables.

-recover Specifies that, if `bulkload.sh` fails, the directory will be recovered with the original data.

At least one of the parameters (`-check`, `-generate`, `-load`, `-recover`, or `-index`) must be specified.

The `-restore` flag should be used only when the LDIF file contains operational attributes such as `orclguid`, `creatorsname`, or the like.

The pathname to the LDIF data file should be fully qualified, and the data file must be specified for the `-check` or `-generate` actions.

`-recover` or `-index` should not be specified with any other option.

ldifwrite/ldifwrite.exe Copies the data from the OID information base into an LDIF file that can then be read by any LDAP-compliant directory server. You can use this resulting LDIF file to transfer data between directory servers. You can use `ldifwrite` (or `ldifwrite.exe` on Windows) in connection with `bulkload.sh`, or you can simply use `ldifwrite` to back up information from a whole or part of a directory. It can be used as a way to prepare for a disaster recovery.

The ldifwrite tool output does not include operational data for the directory itself—for example, cn=subschemasubentry, cn=catalogs, and cn=changelog entries. To export these entries into LDIF format, use ldapsearch with the -L flag.

bulkmodify/bulkmodify.exe Can be used to modify a large number of existing entries efficiently. You can use this tool to change attributes that are common to multiple entries simultaneously. You also can use it to add new attribute values or to replace existing values across a set of entries that you specify with a simple filter.

The bulkmodify tool (bulkmodify.exe on Windows) supports subtree-based modification, a single attribute filter, and attribute value addition and replacement (modifying all matched entries in bulk).

The bulkmodify tool also can perform schema checking on the specified attribute name and value pair during initialization. All entries that are under the specified subtree, meet the single filter condition, and contain the attribute to be modified as either mandatory or optional are modified.

bulkdelete.sh Deletes subtrees for the root node efficiently. The format for bulkdelete.sh is as follows:

```
bulkdelete.sh -connect <connect descriptor>
➥-base "DN" [ -size <commit size> ] -encode
```

-connect Specifies the Oracle Net connect descriptor used to connect to the infrastructure database.

-base Specifies the DN of the root whose subtree is to be deleted. The DN should always be enclosed in double quotes.

-size Specifies the number of entries to be committed as a part of each transaction.

-encode Specifies the native character set.

Using LDAP Command-Line Tools

You can use command-line tools (always a benefit in our opinion) as a means to manipulate entries and attributes in OID servers. This means that anyone can administer the LDAP services by using Oracle Directory Manager or by using command-line tools, allowing anyone to manage users in the manner that they are most comfortable with. These commands operate directly on the directory objects specified on standard I/O or by using a text file written in LDIF as input. Table 9.2 shows the commands and the actions that they perform.

These commands can be found in the OracleAS infrastructure $ORACLE_HOME (%ORACLE_HOME%) in the bin subdirectory.

TABLE 9.2 Table 9.2 LDAP Command-Line Tools

Command	Event
`ldapadd [arguments] -f <filename>`	Use to add one or more entries, object classes, attributes, or values to the directory.
`Ldapaddmt -T <number_of_threads> -h <host> -p <port> -f <file_name>`	Adds entries, their object classes, attributes, and values to the directory. Unlike `ldapadd`, it supports multiple threads for adding entries concurrently. As long as it is processing LDIF entries, `ldapaddmt` logs errors in the `add.log` file in the current directory.
`ldapbind [arguments]`	Authenticates a user to the directory server, or helps you to determine if you can authenticate a client to a server.
`ldapcompare [arguments]`	Use to determine whether an entry contains specific attributes. You can match values that you specify with the attribute values in the directory entry.
`Ldapdelete [arguments]`	Use to delete entire entries that you pass in from the command line.
`ldapmoddn [arguments]`	Use to modify the DN and RDN of an entry, to rename an entry or a subtree, or to move an entry or subtree to a new parent.
`ldapmodify [arguments] -f <file_name>`	Allows you to act upon attributes. Use to create, update, and delete data in an entry; default is `modify`.
`ldapmodifymt -T <number_of_threads> [arguments] -f <file_name>`	Use to modify multiple entries at one time using multithreading.
`ldapsearch [arguments] filter [attributes]`	Use to search for and retrieve a specific entry in the directory.
`ldapUploadAgentFile.sh`	Script used to load mapping and configuration information when you need to synchronize directories.
`ldapcreateConn.sh`	Used to create an integration profile. This script is located in the `/ldap/oid/admin` directory of the infrastructure `$ORACLE_HOME`.
`StopOidServer.sh`	In a client-only installation, where you haven't installed the monitoring and `oidcl` tools, this script can be used to stop the directory integration server. It is located in `$ORACLE_HOME/sysman/admin/scripts`.

Using Oracle Directory Manager

Oracle Directory Manager is a Java-based GUI tool that an administrator can use to maintain and administer OID data. Through Oracle Directory Manager, you can search, view, and maintain object classes; search and maintain attributes; create and drop indexes on an attribute; search, view, and maintain entries; control access to OID entries; and manage a replicated node.

Oracle Directory Manager cannot be used to start or stop directory monitor processes, directory server instances, or directory replication server instances.

Oracle Directory Manager is one of the tools that can be used to administer only Oracle products. It cannot be used to administer LDAP directories other than Oracle Internet Directory.

Before you can start the Oracle Directory Manager, you need to have the directory server instance running.

To start Oracle Directory Manager in Windows, from the Start Menu, select Programs ➢ Oracle-Oracle Internet Directory_Home ➢ Integrated Management Tools ➢ Oracle Directory Manager.

To start Oracle Directory Manager in Linux/Unix, change to the application server infrastructure `$ORACLE_HOME/bin` directory and enter `oidadmin` at the command prompt.

The first time you start the Oracle Directory Manager, an alert tells you that you must connect to a server. Clicking OK will present you with the Directory Server Connection dialog box.

Connecting to the OID Server

When you start the Oracle Directory Manager for the first time, you will be presented with a splash screen alerting you that you need to select a server and port where the OID server instance is running. Once you have made this connection, you will be able to connect to the Oracle Directory Manager. When you click OK on the alert screen, you will see a dialog box into which you need to enter the new server (either by hostname or IP address) and port. (Unless the port has been changed, it will be running in the default port—389 for Windows and 3060 on Unix.) Figure 9.1 shows the OID instance already running.

The Oracle Directory Manager Connect dialog box has two tabs, Credentials and SSL. Fields required on the Credentials tab are as follows:

User The first time you log in, you can log in as either superuser or an anonymous user. To log in as the superuser, specify `orcladmin` as the username and welcome1 (for example) as the password. It is important to understand that the password will vary from installation to installation. Leaving both fields blank logs you in as an anonymous user. If you have already set up user entries, you can log in the following ways:

Browse through entries and select the appropriate one by clicking the button to the right of the User field.

Enter the DN for the user's entry.

Password Enter the password corresponding to the user entered in the User field. For the orcladmin superuser, you enter the password that you specified during the installation of the OracleAS Infrastructure for ias_admin. For anyone else, you just use their password.

FIGURE 9.1 Logging in to Oracle Manager

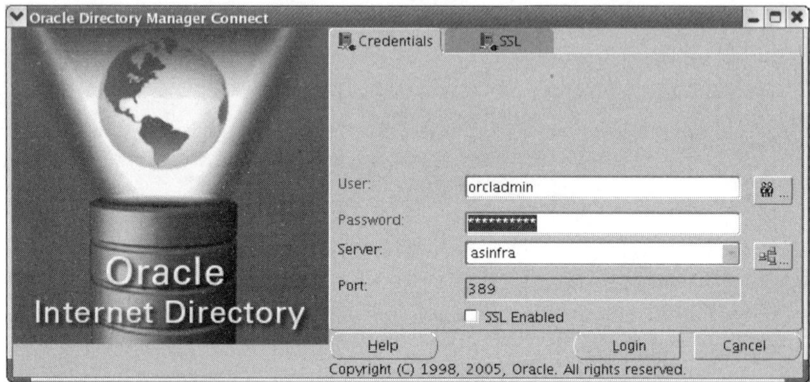

Server From the drop-down list, select the name of the server on which the OID server instance is running. Click the button to the right of the Server field to see whether the OID instance is currently running on the server you selected. Click Add to add a server that isn't already on the list and is running an OID server instance.

Port The default port is typically 389 on Windows or 3060 on Unix. The value is set automatically when you select the server because the port is picked up from the configuration of the server.

SSL Enabled Select this check box if you want the communication between the client and the server to be accomplished over the Secure Sockets Layer. To connect with SSL, the server that you are connecting to needs to be listening on an SSL-enabled port; otherwise, your request will not be authenticated and an error is likely to be raised. At the very least, it will ignore you. If you select the SSL Enabled check box, you will then have to enter additional information in the SSL tabbed page.

SSL Tabbed Page

On the SSL tabbed page (the SSL tab is located next to the Credentials tab), you enter your installation's SSL-specific information. You will need to enter all of the information that is necessary to connect to the OID server through a secure connection using SSL. Recall that in SSL connections, data are transmitted in encrypted format between the client and the server; this means additional overhead and can cause performance issues.

Disconnecting from the OID Server

To disconnect from the directory server and Oracle Directory Manager, follow these steps:

1. Select Exit from the File menu.
2. Click Disconnect from the toolbar.
3. Right-click the OID server and then select Disconnect.

Whenever you exit Oracle Directory Manager, all connections between all directory servers and the directory are automatically disconnected. When you restart Oracle Directory Manager, all previously connected server connections appear in the Directory Server Login window. All connection information is stored in the user's home directory in a file called `osdadmin.ini` and is read into the application when that user next logs in.

OracleAS Bootstrap Model

Because synchronization of data is handled automatically, directory bootstrapping is usually not a necessary maintenance task. However, because this synchronization can be a very time-consuming process the first time it is run, it should be done manually when you first deploy Oracle Directory Integration and Provisioning.

To help facilitate the bootstrap method (the initial migration of data between a connected directory and your Oracle Internet Directory) of an OracleAS deployment, OID installations create the following users:

- The OID superuser (`orcladmin`) can perform all operations in the directory, as any administrator needs to do. No access control lists (ACLs) policy can restrict access to the directory for this user. Although ACLs are implemented as a means to ensure that access to sensitive information is limited to only those who need it, because administrators need to be able to maintain and administer the information, it would be counterproductive to keep them away from the information they are attempting to administer.
- A superuser for the enterprise is identified as `cn=oracleadmin, cn=users, <Subscriber DN>`. When the default ACL is set up during your installation of the OID, this user is given the authority to perform all administrative operations within the enterprise subtree. This user also can create new users by using Delegated Administration Services (DAS) and can delegate privilege assignment to them by virtue of this authority. It is important that anyone with this user level be a trusted individual. Although this level is not a prerequisite to actually administering the applications, it is a good idea to set this user level for anyone administering the applications from a security perspective for the organization.
- The OID superuser, in turn, creates the default DIT as a part of the OID installation. This default DIT creation includes the creation of the Root Oracle Context, a node for the enterprise, and an Oracle Context that is associated with the enterprise node. When the default DIT is created, so is the subscriber superuser associated with the DIT.
- The subscriber superuser delegates the administration of the Oracle Context to the Oracle Context administrators. These administrators administer the users' Security Administrator's group.

- Oracle Context Administrators then delegate the administration of the OracleAS and its components to the OracleAS administrators.
- OracleAS administrators have all of the necessary privileges needed to install and bootstrap all of the OracleAS components. These administrators, in turn, delegate the responsibility of user and group administration to appropriate users.
- User administrators and group administrators are responsible for managing users and groups.

For additional information, refer to the *Oracle Internet Directory Administrator's Guide.*

Delegated OID Administration

OID stores the information necessary to control access to the different applications that are accessed via the OID services. This information is stored as LDAP attributes or entries. To give any user administrative access to any given application, access policies are defined on the entries associated with the applications and the users. In a hosted environment, you can further enable access control to a given subscriber by providing access to that user on the subscriber root node.

You, as administrator, can also provide access to departmental administrators so they can administer access for users in their departments. This is often opted for in a nonhosted environment because department managers know who should have access to what applications and information better than any third-party administrator could.

You can implement this access control either by authorization of users or by authorization of administrators. The choices of how this authorization should be made are based on the business rules and security rules of the organization. Smaller organizations often authorize at the user level, whereas larger and more complex organizations authorize at the administrator level. Much of this depends on how confident the organization is in the ability of the administrators to work as a team.

If you choose to implement access control by using user authorization, you can store in the OID the individual access control policies that will be needed to allow these users to access the external applications. Although there may be increasing numbers of these entries, it is important to note that OID will handle most of the maintenance of these users and will provide you with one-stop shopping for alterations and administration. When users perform operations on application data, the application in question checks with the LDAP server to determine from the access policies stored in the OID whether the user is authorized to do such operations. Each user has to be sought, the correct one found, and then a search on the list of approved applications completed so that the answer can be returned. This is one reason access speed from application to LDAP server and back is so critical. Minimizing the latency that the user notices goes far in maintaining a happy user.

If you choose to implement access control through authorization of administrators, you can set up OID to serve as a single trusted point of administration for all access control policies for the application. You set up access controls and access control policies for each specific application rather than for each particular user, and then you decide who can administer these policies. This option is often chosen because the number of applications and administrators needed is often far fewer than the number of users. Once the access policies are set up for each application, the application requests that the OID check its list of applications, find the one that is relevant, and search the list of users who are allowed to make the requested change to determine whether the user, based on the list of users, is authorized to make such a change.

Roles

One or more OID server domains can be managed by multiple administrators. One or more administrators can administer a given domain. For every domain, there can be different directory roles that are responsible for the administration of the domain. Many-to-many relationships are always interesting to manage, and the more of each component in the set, the more interesting the management dilemma can be. The OID global administrator is the primary role that has all of the privileges over all of the OID servers.

The subscriber-specific role or domain administrator role has privileges over only the specific domain to which they have been assigned and only those privileges delegated to the role by the global administrator.

Application-specific roles are assigned to an application administrator so they can administer application data that fall under the subscriber node; this role is responsible for delegating rights to users on the application data.

The OracleAS Administration Model

The user who is assigned to be an OracleAS administrator not only should have a general idea of the platform and infrastructure that they will be administering but also should be a member of the `iASAdmins` group in the OID. This is an important distinction because unless they are members of this group, they will not be able to configure the OracleAS component entries in the OID server. The user should also be a member of the `iASAdmins` group so they can administer the different OracleAS components individually as well as collectively.

When running OID in stand-alone mode, where OID is used only by OracleAS, the administrator can bootstrap the OracleAS environment using the seed accounts (logged in as the `orcladmin` user) that were set up as a part of the OID installation.

Having installed the various products, an administrator can then create additional users and administrators and delegate administration of OracleAS to others by assigning them to the `iASAdmins` group. This is often difficult if the primary administrator likes to remain in control, but it can add a measure of redundancy for the organization because the administrator does not become the single point of failure.

When running OID in shared mode, where OID is to be used not only for the application server but also for other applications in the environment, requirements for administration may be quite different. When it comes time to perform installations for this kind of environment, it is important to know ahead of time that there will be multiple disparate applications—some OracleAS-based applications and some not—in the mix to be administered through the OID. In this case, the OracleAS administrator should seek those privileges that are roughly equivalent to `iASAdmins` and that are relevant to each application that will be administered via OID. The `iASAdmins` group should then be created under the groups container in Oracle Context.

User Administration

OracleAS users are represented in the OID as user object entries. The default OID gets configured to allow easy administration of users in the Oracle Internet Directory. Figure 9.2 shows the OID configuration details screen. Notice that the details on this screen are informational and are not editable. Figure 9.3 shows the screen where you can make changes to the settings.

User configuration details can be seen in Figures 9.4 and 9.5. Figure 9.4 shows an example of details that can be assigned to all users at the global user level. Figure 9.5 shows the specific user detail (in this case, the administrator). The administrator can alter everything that is not grayed out.

FIGURE 9.2 OID configuration settings

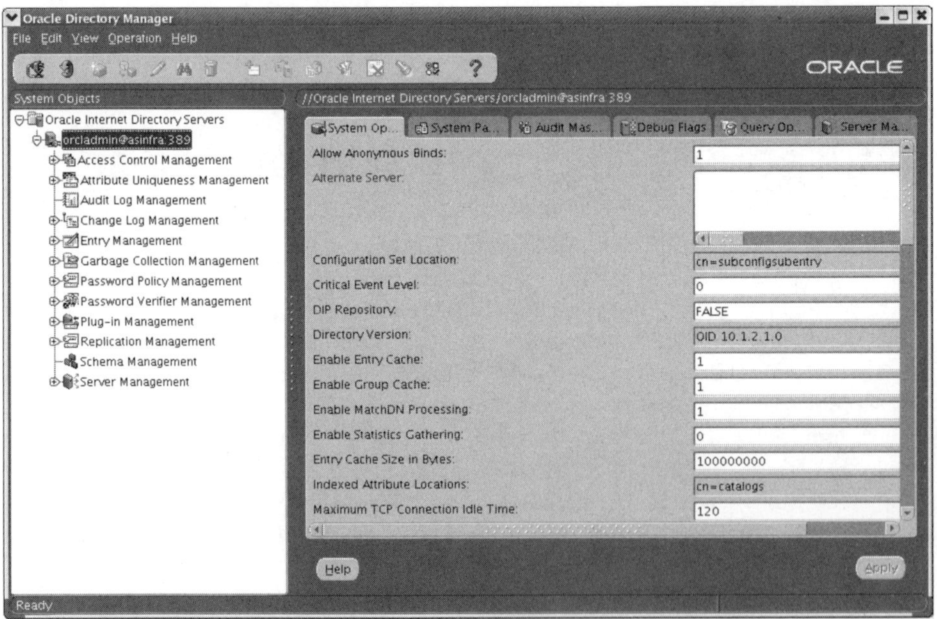

FIGURE 9.3 OID configuration

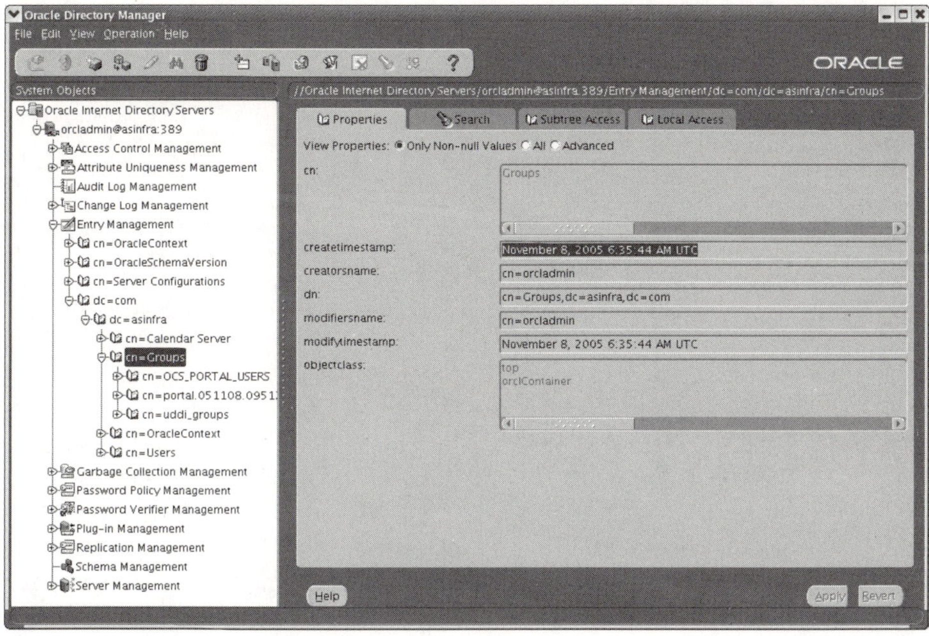

FIGURE 9.4 Global user settings

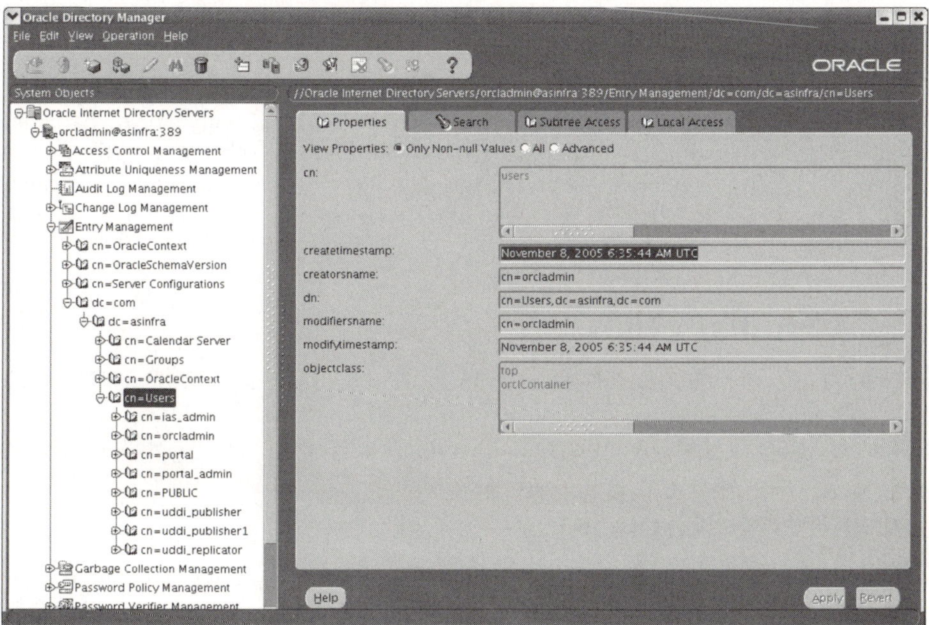

FIGURE 9.5 Individual user settings

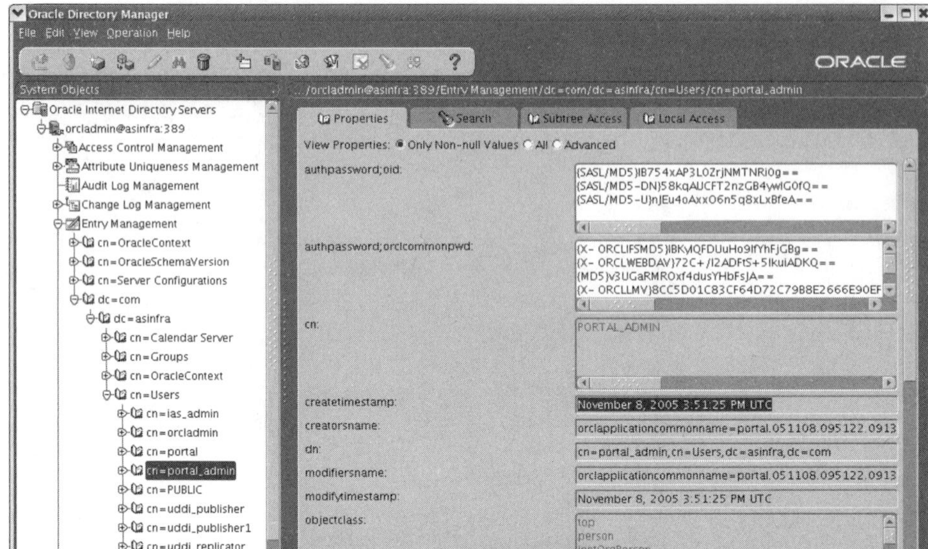

When OID is running in stand-alone mode, the OracleAS administrator uses the seeded users (`cn=orcladmin` or the superuser) to create other users in the OID. You, as the OracleAS administrator, may choose to add some of these new users as user administrators by adding them to the User Create group. This will allow you to delegate the ability to create users to these junior administrator users.

You can also delegate other privileges, like the privilege necessary to edit a user's properties. As the OracleAS administrator, you simply add the user to the User Edit group and you have created a user who can take over some of your duties, freeing yourself to do other administrative tasks.

Likewise, the ability to delete users can be delegated to a user by adding them to the User Delete group. However, it is less dangerous to allow users to create users than to allow them to delete users.

Group Administration

Now you have seen how you can delegate administration of users to other users, but OracleAS administrators also can delegate the right to manage groups to other users. Group management rights are delegated through the Create Group, Edit Group, and Delete Group groups.

Administrative Groups

Some of the other OracleAS components read the user- and group- related information from OID. The default ACL configuration in the OID allows this by granting privileges to various administrative groups. If you think about it, you are granting access to perform maintenance, so the internal use of access control lists is only logical.

Some applications authenticate their end users by comparing the password that is passed to them by the end users to the ones that are stored in OID. To facilitate this comparison authentication, the individual application adds itself as a member of the Authentication Service group, the group that has the "compare permission on password attribute of a user" permissions. The User Security Admin group has permissions to read, compare, and reset the user password of any user in the OID, including ones that access only external applications but not OracleAS applications.

Most of the Oracle products proxy to OID on behalf of their end users (those users whose identities are stored in OID). To be able to do this, the applications add their identity and entities as members of the User Proxy Privilege group. This group has permissions to proxy on behalf of the OID user.

Storing User Credentials

An organization of any size contains many applications, each of which likely has its own authentication mechanism. When this is the case, it becomes increasingly difficult to manage all of the user information, let alone manage it in any central location. This is particularly true for disparate passwords and hard-coded privileges.

To make matters more complicated, if the given user leaves the company or changes jobs, all of the different authentication privileges in each application have to be removed or changed (depending on what the user did) and new ones have to be added to reflect the user's change in status. If anything gets missed, the old access can continue and the user can get into information that they are no longer supposed to be able to access, or they will be unable to do their new job because their access has not caught up to the new responsibilities. This can add significantly to the overall administrative costs of applications, and the cost of lost productivity can be prohibitive. To overcome this additional cost, you can use the OID server as a centralized storage facility for all user authentication credentials.

Once implemented, it is simple to change authentication information for the user if the user leaves the company or changes job descriptions. The OID server can store the user authentication information in either of the following ways:

User Authentication to OID via Password Stores the username and password in the OID server.

Users Authenticate to Oracle Components via Password Stores the username and password of individual Oracle components, and when the user logs into the component, verifies them against the ones stored in the OID.

You can store the credentials of users of LDAP-enabled applications that are not Oracle Components as well, but in order to do this, you need to create containers under the product entry.

Modifying Password Policies Using ODM

Passwords that are stored in OID servers must follow a specific set of rules. These rules are defined in entries known as password policies, which ensure that the passwords of users fulfill certain criteria:

- They have a minimum number of characters.
- They have a minimum number of numeric characters.
- They remain valid for a specific period of time.

The Oracle Universal Installer (OUI) creates the password policy entry for each default subscriber at the time of installation. The individual entries are created below the common entry, which itself resides under the product entry, and the product entry is below the Identity Management Realm entry.

The password policy is applicable to all of the users in the Identity Management Realm and is attached to the `userPassword` attribute of the user. You must set the appropriate value of `orclcommonusersearchbase` in the common entry of the subscriber in order to enforce the password policy.

Figure 9.6 shows the screen on which password policies can be altered. Notice that many of these settings are similar to the settings of policies that can be stored within the database, but these should not be confused with one another.

To create a password policy, you use the `pwdpolicy` auxiliary object class; the password policy entry is created by using this object class.

FIGURE 9.6 Password policy parameters

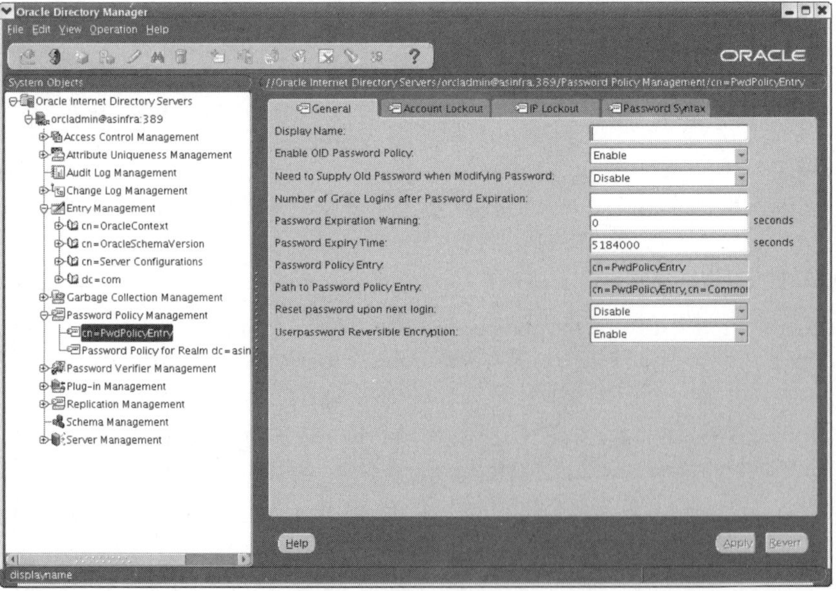

You can view or modify the password policies in the following way:

1. In the navigation pane, expand Oracle Internet Directory Servers/directory_server_instance/Password Policy Management. At this point, the password policy entries are displayed under the node.
2. Select the password policy that you want to view and, in the right-hand pane, the attributes of that policy are displayed.

Modifying the OID Administrator Password

Changing the `orcladmin` password for the Oracle Internet Directory administrator is accomplished using ODM:

1. Log in to the OID using ODM.
2. Expand the Oracle Internet Directory Servers node.
3. Select the OID server node. In the right-hand pane, various properties of the server are displayed on the tabbed pages.
4. Click on the System Passwords tab. (Various usernames and passwords are displayed.)
5. In the Super User Password field, change the password to the desired value.
6. Click Apply to save the new password.

Figure 9.7 shows the screen on which you can alter the administrator's password. Notice that it also shows the ID of the person modifying the password and the time stamp of when the password was altered.

You can change the OID administrator password using the OID Self-Service Console as well.

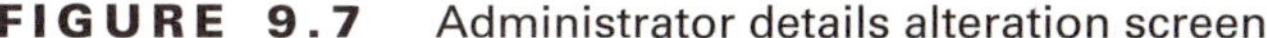

FIGURE 9.7 Administrator details alteration screen

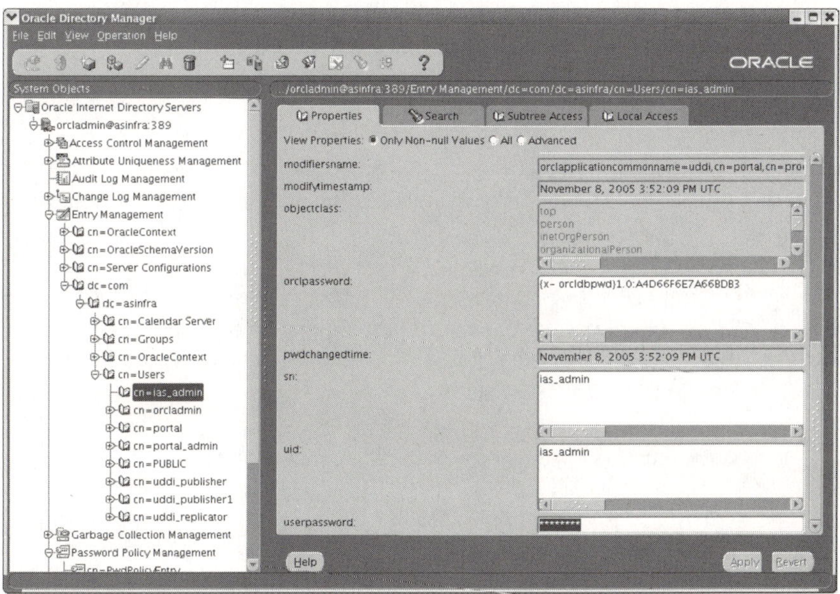

Modifying the Realm-Specific Administrator Password

You can use ODM to change the OracleAS administrator password as well. Both OID administrators and OracleAS administrators are known as `orcladmin`. However, each is located in a different hierarchy tree. The OID administrator is located in the starting node of the OID server and is responsible for managing the entire Oracle Internet Directory server and all included realms. The OID administrator delegates administrative rights to the various subscriber administrators. The OracleAS administrator is the superuser for the specific realm or subscriber.

To change the `ias_admin` password, which is the Application Server Administration password, follow these steps:

1. Stop the Application Server Control.
2. On Unix, in the infrastructure Oracle Home, run the following command:

   ```
   ORACLE_HOME/bin/emctl stop iasconsole
   ```

   To accomplish the same thing on Windows, use the Services control panel to stop the Application Server Control service.
3. Locate and open the following file in a text editor (again, in the infrastructure Oracle Home):

   ```
   ORACLE_HOME/sysman/j2ee/config/jazn-data.xml
   ```

4. Locate the line that defines the credentials property for the `ias_admin` user. The following example shows the section of `jazn-data.xml` with the encrypted `credentials` entry between the `<credentials>` and `</credentials>` parameters:

   ```
   <realm>
     <name>enterprise-manager</name>
       <users>
         <user>
           <name>ias_admin</name>
          <credentials>{903}buG01UsQqTq0nQjdaKQRECL1kbs192Mp
          </credentials>
         </user>
   ```

5. Replace the existing, encrypted password (between `<credentials>` and `</credentials>`) with your new unencrypted password, adding a leading exclamation point to the unencrypted version.

Be sure to prefix the password with an exclamation point (!). For example, this tells the server that you are not passing an encrypted password but a password you are changing:

```
<credentials>!y0urnewpassw0rd</credentials>
```

The password that you use for the `ias_admin` user should be as follows: Have a minimum length of five alphanumeric characters. Have at least one numeric character. Be shorter than 30 characters. Contain only alphanumeric characters from your database character set, the underscore (_), the dollar sign ($), and the number sign (#). Begin with an alphabetic character. As with all passwords, it cannot begin with a number, the underscore (_), the dollar sign ($), or the number sign (#).

1. Start the Application Server Control.

After the restart, the Application Server Control will use your new administrator (`ias_admin`) password, which will now be stored in encrypted format within the `jazn-data.xml` file.

OID Troubleshooting

There are times that the application server crashes and when everything is restarted, you can't seem to restart OID using OIDCTL. This can happen when the server is cycled without the application server being shut down cleanly (such as when you have a new Windows administrator in the department doing their first full server backup). When you reboot the PC and use DCMCTL to check the status of the OC4J instances prior to starting them, you get the following error message:

```
ADMN-202026
    A problem has occurred accessing the Oracle9iAS infrastructure database.
    Base Exception:
    oracle.ias.repository.schema.SchemaException:Unable to connect to
    Directory Server:javax.naming.CommunicationException: ajwr.homeserver.com.
    uk:4032 [Root exception is java.net.ConnectException: Connection
    refused: connect]
    Please, refer to the base exception for resolution, or call Oracle support.
```

Anyone who has had much experience administering OracleAS servers likely recognizes this error. It is caused by OID being down and the DCMCTL utility not being able to function. The assumption is that the infrastructure database is up (a fact that can be proven by logging on to the database). Given that the database is in fact up, this can be resolved by the following command:

```
C:\ajw_home\infra\bin>oidctl server=oidldapd configset=0 instance=1 start
```

This should start an OID instance.

Sometimes it doesn't, however. Sometimes it fails with the following kind of error:

```
C:\ajw_home\infra\bin>oidctl server=oidldapd configset=0 instance=1 start
    *** Instance Number already in use. ***
    *** Please try a different Instance number. ***
```

Huh? Already in use?

This error should be telling you that there's already an OID process running (in this case with an instance number of 1). You will therefore have to start up another OID process using a different number. You can, of course, run OIDCTL again using a different instance number. This is likely to work.

However, you know there is no OID process running instance 1 and there is an errant OID process hanging around (the instance number 1). What you really should do to get by this error is get rid of that errant process. The errant process was caused by the database not seeing the instance shut down cleanly and cleaning itself up.

Using OIDCTL really inserts a row (or updates an already inserted row) in the ODS.ODS_PROCESS table containing the instance number (instance 1 in this case). The instance number has to be unique. The table also contains the process ID associated with the instance, and a flag called state. State can take on four distinct values (0 = stop, 1 = start, 2 = running, and 3 = restart). The OIDMON process pulls this table to find out when a row has a state of 0, reads the process ID (PID), and stops the process. When OIDMON finds state = 1, it starts a new process and updates the process ID column with a new process ID. When it finds a process with state = 2, it reads the PID and checks whether the process with the same PID is in fact running. If it's not, OIDMON starts a new process and updates the PID. Finally, when it finds a process with state = 3, it reads the PID, stops the process, and starts a new process, updating the PID accordingly.

If for any reason OIDMON can't start the server process, it will retry up to 10 times. If it still fails, it deletes the row from the ODS.ODS_PROCESS table.

This all works fine, except when OracleAS crashes. If OIDMON exits but the processes are not killed off, orphan rows are left in the ODS.ODS_PROCESS table; whenever you try to restart the instance after a reboot, it gets confused and can't start.

The way to properly deal with this is to kill off any running server processes in question (for example, OIDMON). (If there aren't any, don't worry about it.) Once that is done, delete any rows that exist in the ODS.ODS_PROCESS table.

```
delete form ODS.ODS_PROCESS;
```

Now you can restart the instance again.

Relationship between OracleAS Portal and OID

Recall that security is integrated into every component of OracleAS. As a means to provide an even more comprehensive security solution, OracleAS Portal makes use of a variety of components in the Oracle Identity Management infrastructure.

OID stores information about OracleAS Portal users and groups, as well as the group membership and privileges that have been granted to portal users and groups, just as it does with other groups and users. That said, OracleAS Portal requires the following interaction with OID:

- Portal-specific entries are stored in the directory.
- Group attributes are stored in the directory.
- User attributes are stored in the directory.
- User and group information is cached from the directory.
- User and group lists of values (LOVs) are populated from the directory through Delegated Administration Services.
- OracleAS Portal Directory Entries are located in OID.

For security to function properly, the OracleAS Portal requires the following entries in the directory's DIT structure:

- OracleAS Portal default user accounts are created in the Default Identity Management Realm's user container.
- The OracleAS Portal group container is created in the directory Identity Management Realm's group container.
- The name of the OracleAS Portal group container is derived from the Portal schema name and the date and time of association with the infrastructure. (The format of the name is <portal_schema_name.yymmdd.hh.mi>.)
- The Portal default groups (`AUTHENTICATED_USERS`, `DBA`, `PORTAL_ADMINISTRATORS`, `PORTAL_DEVELOPERS`, `PORTLET_PUBLISHER`, `RW_ADMNISTRATOR`, `RW_DEVELOPER`, `RW_POWER_USER`, `RW_BASIC_USER`) are created in the Portal group container.
- Portal application entity (`orclApplicationCommonName=`<*portal_schema_name.yymmdd.hh.mi*>) is created in the Root Oracle Context. Portal uses this entity to bind to the directory when it needs to query it or to perform action on it on behalf of the user. This method ensures that the user's authorization restrictions are properly enforced by the directory. The Portal application entity obtains the privileges to initiate proxy connections by its membership in the user proxy privileges group.
- The Portal directory synchronization subscription, a provisioning profile entry, is created in the provisioning profile of the directory. This entry indicates that the directory must notify Portal when user or group privilege information changes. It enables Portal to keep its authorizations synchronized with the information stored in the directory.
- Registration is performed from the directory provisioning subscription tool.

Configuring OID Settings in OracleAS Portal

OID settings in Portal can be accessed and configured in the SSO/OID tab when you click the Global Settings link in the Services portlet. Group Creation Base DN can be configured in this manner. When portal groups are created in the Group portlet, they are created under a node in the DIT that is defined by the DN specified in the Group Creation Base DN global setting. When you need to create groups, you must define the node in which you want Portal to search for the existing group. This is configured through the Local Group Search Base DN. Both OID settings are particularly useful if you adapt Portal to interact with an existing DIT.

Caching the OID Information within Portal

To improve performance, Portal caches some directory information locally:

- Directory connection information for OracleAS Portal
- URLs for Delegated Administration Services
- orclguids of certain privilege groups for authorized checks on directory portlets (User Portlets and Group Portlets)
- Group memberships and default groups for each user

You can refresh this cache with updated information from the OID by selecting the Refresh Cache for OID Parameters check box on the SSO/OID tabbed page and clicking Apply or OK.

The majority of the information that is cached by Portal is static. For those items that are more dynamic, such as group membership and default groups, Portal relies on the Oracle Directory Provisioning Integration Service of the Oracle Directory Integration Platform (DIP) for updates. The Integration service notifies Portal whenever a change is made in the directory that must be reflected in Portal and updated information is pushed to the Portal, which in turn updates the cached OID Information Store.

Summary

This chapter provides you with the background necessary to be able to understand Oracle's identity management interface, Oracle Internet Directory. Oracle Internet Directory provides a common set of utilities and interfaces through which you can provide identity management to your integrated systems. This means centralized management of not only users, but also devices, processes, and applications.

Using OID, you can leverage centralized management, thereby allowing the organization to reduce administration costs associated with the application development cycle.

Hopefully, you have a better understanding of identity management and how important it is to an organization. As more and more organizations move to a centralized application serving model, this will become even more critical.

You now have the tools necessary to manage not only users and groups of users, but also administrators and the utilities themselves. You should be better able to identify and manipulate the different utilities that are necessary to run your system in an efficient and effective manner.

Exam Essentials

Describe the services that can be used in connection with OID. Be able to describe the support services that you can use as an administrator to manage the Oracle Internet Directory. Understand the difference in these services and how to start and stop each.

Describe the functions of the Oracle Internet Directory. Be able to describe the different functions of OID and how you can use them to provide additional security features to your implementation. Be able to describe how you can use OID in a robust environment.

Explain how to start and stop OID. Explain what commands are used to start and stop OID and its components; if order is important, understand in what order things should be started and stopped.

Describe the different command-line utilities and how and when to use them. Describe the different command-line utilities used to administer the OID server and its components. Know the differences between the commands, which are used for each component, and the syntax necessary to use them.

Review Questions

1. Which of the following is not one of the portal default groups? (Choose all that apply.)

   A. authenticated_users

   B. dba

   C. sysadmin

   D. portal_developers

   E. rw_power_users

   F. portal_administrators

2. What is the name of the administrator for OID and for Oracle Application Server?

   A. ODM, orcladmin

   B. oiadmin, orcladmin

   C. oidadmin, iasadmin

   D. oidadmin, oidadmin

   E. orcladmin, orcladmin

3. What auxiliary object class in ODM do you use to create a password policy?

   A. password

   B. passpolicy

   C. pwdpolicy

   D. pwdplcy

   E. pwd

4. The OID server can store the user authentication information in which of the following types? (Choose all that apply.)

   A. Passwords to authenticate users to OID

   B. Passwords to authenticate users to OracleAS components

   C. Passwords to authenticate users to the database

   D. Passwords to authenticate users to the network

   E. Passwords to authenticate users to other users

5. If you choose to implement access control through authorization of administrators, what can be used as a single trusted point of administration for all access control policies for your applications?

   A. OracleAS

   B. OID

   C. ODM

   D. Oracle Database

   E. All of the above

6. What actions can the `orcladmin` user *not* perform? (Choose all that apply.)
   - **A.** All administrative operations within the enterprise subtree
   - **B.** Creating the default DIT
   - **C.** Creating the subscriber superuser
   - **D.** Anything that the ACL restricts it from doing
   - **E.** All of the above
   - **F.** None of the above

7. Which of the following are valid ways of disconnecting from the OID Server? (Choose all that apply.)
   - **A.** Select Disconnect from the File menu.
   - **B.** Select Disconnect from the toolbar.
   - **C.** Right-click the OID server and then select Disconnect.
   - **D.** Type **restart** at the command prompt.
   - **E.** Type "**shutdown abort**" at the command prompt.

8. Whenever you exit ODM, what happens to all of the connections to the directory servers and the directory?
   - **A.** They are automatically disconnected.
   - **B.** You have to manually disconnect them.
   - **C.** All users are logged out of all applications.
   - **D.** The directory server reboots.

9. Which of the following fields are not necessary when connecting to the OID server?
   - **A.** Password
   - **B.** Server
   - **C.** Port
   - **D.** SSL Enabled

10. If you select SSL Enabled on the OID server connection screen, what information do you enter on the SSL tabbed page? (Choose all that apply.)
    - **A.** Password
    - **B.** Server
    - **C.** Port
    - **D.** SSL-specific information

11. What is the default port for the OID server on Windows?

A. 443

B. 80

C. 8080

D. 389

E. 1521

12. The first time you log in to the OID server, what two user options are available to you?

A. superuser, orcladmin

B. sys, system

C. superuser, anonymous

D. superuser, guest

13. When using ODM to start and stop the directory monitor process, directory server instances, and directory replication, what navigation steps are involved? (Choose all that apply.)

A. Navigate to the Start menu.

B. Select Programs.

C. Oracle Internet Directory_home.

D. Integrated Management Tools.

E. You cannot use ODM to start and top these services.

14. Referencing LDAP command line-tools, `ldapmodify` allows you to perform what functions on the LDAP entry?

A. Modify multiple entries at one time

B. Insert, update, and delete

C. Create, update, and delete

D. Search for an entry

E. Add multiple new entries

15. Which of the following is not one of the bulk tools available to manipulate LDAP data?

A. `bulkmodify`

B. `bulkload`

C. `ldiwrite`

D. `bulkdelete`

E. `ldiread`

F. All are available tools.

16. What facility enables administrators to deploy enterprise identities and manage the access of those identities to the various diverse applications in the enterprise centrally and securely?

    A. Database schemas

    B. Oracle's Identity Management infrastructure

    C. Oracle Administrator portal

    D. Wallet Manager

17. Which component of OID provides LDAP functionality?

    A. OID

    B. Oracle Single Sign-On

    C. OID provisioning integration service

    D. OID LDAP service

18. Which component of OID provides application user provisioning?

    A. OID

    B. Oracle Single Sign-On

    C. OID provisioning integration service

    D. OID LDAP service

19. What level of authentication allows a user to provide a simple string of characters as a means of authentication?

    A. Anonymous

    B. Password

    C. Certificate

    D. All of the above

    E. None of the above

20. What command is used to start the Oracle Process Manager and Notification server?

    A. `OID start`

    B. `OPM start`

    C. `opmnctl start`

    D. `opmnctl startall`

Answers to Review Questions

1. C. `sysadmin` is not one of the default portal groups; all of the others are.
2. E. `orcladmin` is the administrator name for both OID and the application server.
3. C. You use `pwdpolicy` to set the new password policy.
4. A, B. OID stores passwords to authenticate users to OID and passwords to authenticate users to the OracleAS components.
5. B. OID can be used to serve as your single trusted point of administration.
6. F. None of the above. This user can perform all operations in the directory. No access control lists can restrict access to this user.
7. A, B, C. Selecting Disconnect from the File menu, selecting Disconnect from the toolbar, and right-clicking the OID server and then selecting Disconnect are all valid ways to disconnect.
8. A. They are automatically disconnected and will reappear in the Directory Server Login window when you restart ODM.
9. D. SSL Enabled is not necessary to connect to the OID server, but it is an option.
10. D. SSL-specific information needs to be added to the information entered on the initial screen.
11. D. The default port for the OID server on Windows is 389. On Unix the default port is 3060.
12. C. The first time you log in to OID server, you can log in as either anonymous or superuser.
13. E. You cannot use ODM to start and stop any of these services.
14. C. `ldapmodify` allows you to create a new entry or update or delete an existing entry.
15. E. `ldiread` is not a tool that you can use; it does not exist.
16. B. Oracle's Identity Management infrastructure is the administrative facility that allows you as the administrator to manage secure access to your applications.
17. A. OID is Oracle's solution to LDAP functionality.
18. C. OID's OID Provisioning Integration Service provides the ability for administrators to provision application users.
19. B. Password authentication requires a user to provide a string of characters in a password as a means to authenticate to the system.
20. D. `opmnctl startall` is the command used to start OPMN.

Configuring and Using Single Sign-On Server and Delegated Administration Services

ORACLE APPLICATION SERVER 10*g* ADMINISTRATION I EXAM OBJECTIVES COVERED IN THIS CHAPTER:

✓ **Administering the OracleAS Single Sign-On Server**

- Describe OracleAS Single Sign-On server components
- Explain OracleAS Sign-On server authentication flow
- Manage and configure OracleAS Single Sign-On server
- Administer partner and external applications
- Monitor OracleAS Single Sign-On Server
- Access OracleAS Single Sign-On server from OracleAS Portal

✓ **Managing Access using Delegated Administration Service**

- Explain the DAS Architecture
- Describe how DAS works
- Start and stop DAS
- Access DAS home page
- Use OID Self Service Console
- Manage user entries using DAS
- Manage group entries using DAS
- Create Identity Management Realm
- Access DAS from OracleAS Portal

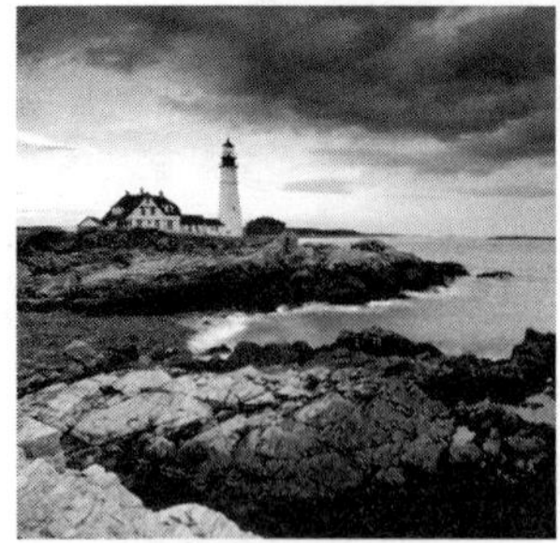

Oracle Application Server Single Sign-On (SSO) server is a key component of Oracle Application Server 10*g* (OracleAS) that allows a user to authenticate explicitly one time and transparently on successive connections to other data or applications. SSO server leverages strong authentication with a single password to authenticate with other applications. These applications can integrate tightly with OracleAS, delegating the authentication process to the SSO server; for other applications, the SSO server stores only the authentication data. In either case, the user connects transparently to all registered applications with a single username and password.

In the first half of this chapter, we'll show you the components of the SSO architecture and how a client request for authentication flows through the various components of OracleAS and back to the client. We'll also show you how the SSO server uses the module `mod_osso` to provide authentication services to other OracleAS applications.

Next, we'll cover many of the same topics we've covered for other OracleAS components in this book: how to administer the SSO server itself as well as two types of applications that leverage the SSO server: partner applications and external applications. Also, we'll show you the GUI tools you use to monitor the status of the SSO server.

In the second part of the chapter, we'll present Oracle Delegated Administration Services (DAS). It complements the SSO server as part of the Oracle Identity Management infrastructure. It is tightly coupled with SSO server as a partner application to centrally store data for users, groups, and services while at the same time delegating the administration and maintenance of that data to other administrators and even the users themselves.

We'll also cover the architectural elements of DAS, how to access it, and how to manage user and group entries. Additionally, we'll show you how to create and maintain an Identity Management realm in DAS to assign identical administrative policies to a specific set of users, groups, and services.

Finally, we'll show you how you can use Oracle Portal to access the DAS administration screens to manage users, groups, and services, depending on your privileges.

Administering the OracleAS Single Sign-On Server

Oracle SSO provides many benefits for your environment. It reduces administrative costs because each user needs only one username and password. This provides similar benefits for an end user because the end user needs to remember only one username and password to access all resources, leaving them less likely to use easily exposed passwords or write them down, thus improving the security of your environment.

In the following sections, we'll present the SSO components, the flow of the authentication request through these components, and how to start and stop the SSO server. In addition, we'll provide the basic configuration steps and administrative tasks you use in an SSO server environment.

We'll also tell you how to distinguish a partner application from an external application and how to configure one or more of each in your environment.

Single Sign-On Components

The *SSO server*, as part of the OracleAS Identity Management infrastructure, consists of several components: the SSO server itself, partner applications, external applications, and the module `mod_osso`. These components work together to manage the life cycle of user accounts and other network entities in a centralized and efficient manner.

SSO Server

The Single Sign-On server consists of a set of programs stored in an OracleAS metadata repository installed with an instance of Oracle HTTP Server and Oracle Containers for J2EE (OC4J) Server; you use the `orasso` database access descriptor (DAD) created in the infrastructure. A *database access descriptor* is a set of values that specify how an application connects to an Oracle database to satisfy an HTTP request. The DAD includes the username, password, database connection information, and National Language Support (NLS) parameters.

Partner Applications

If one of the applications a user accesses is part of an OracleAS installation, the application authenticates the user using SSO. Any OracleAS application that uses SSO for authentication is a *partner application*.

Remember the important difference between authentication and authorization: Authentication determines who you are; authorization determines whether you are permitted to access an application.

SSO authenticates the user on behalf of the application. Once the user is authenticated, the application is responsible for determining what level of authorization the user has within the application.

External Applications

In contrast, an *external application* is an application that is not deployed within an OracleAS instance and does not delegate authentication duties to SSO. Typically, an external application uses its own HTML login forms for user authentication; you can store the username and password on this HTML form in SSO. When a user authenticates with SSO, SSO automatically authenticates any connection requests to the external application using the stored username and password. The username and password are stored in encrypted form in the OracleAS metadata repository. As a result, the user only has to authenticate once with SSO regardless of how many external applications they register with SSO.

mod_osso

The Oracle HTTP Server (OHS) module mod_osso provides the authentication services for all partner applications. mod_osso is a partner application itself—for the SSO server. Once the authentication information is stored in the Oracle Internet Directory (OID) repository, mod_osso retrieves Oracle HTTP Server's cookie to prevent client reauthorization.

After mod_osso authenticates the user, it transmits the following header values to the partner applications for validation purposes:

- Username
- User distinguished name (DN)
- User globally unique identifier (GUID)
- Language and territory information (NLS)

mod_osso replaces the SSO System Development Kit (SDK) used in previous versions of OracleAS to integrate partner applications with the SSO server.

Authentication Flow for OracleAS Single Sign-On

The authentication flow for a user's access to a web resource differs significantly depending on whether the resource is a partner application or an external application. In both cases, however, the SSO server manages the user's credentials and the OID database repository stores the application usernames and passwords in encrypted form.

Partner Application Authentication

Authenticating with a partner application leverages the module mod_osso in Oracle HTTP Server (OHS); the OHS listener is actually another partner application for the SSO server. Figure 10.1 shows the authentication flow starting at the client browser for a client that has not previously authenticated with the partner application.

Here are the authentication steps corresponding to Figure 10.1:

1. A client accesses a partner application using the application's URL. Because the client has not previously authenticated with this application, there is no cookie stored in the client's browser with authentication information for this application.
2. The partner application redirects the client to the SSO server via mod_osso.
3. The SSO server provides a username and password page to the client.
4. The SSO server validates the password in a two-step process. The SSO server first receives the request (step 4a) and then must access the authentication information in an Oracle database (step 4b). Then the SSO server sets a cookie on the client browser for the SSO server.
5. The SSO server redirects the client back to the partner application via mod_osso and passes credentials on to the partner application using an encrypted token.
6. The partner application sets a cookie in the client browser to authenticate the client on subsequent accesses to the application. From this point on, all communication occurs between the client and the partner application.

FIGURE 10.1 Authentication flow for SSO partner applications

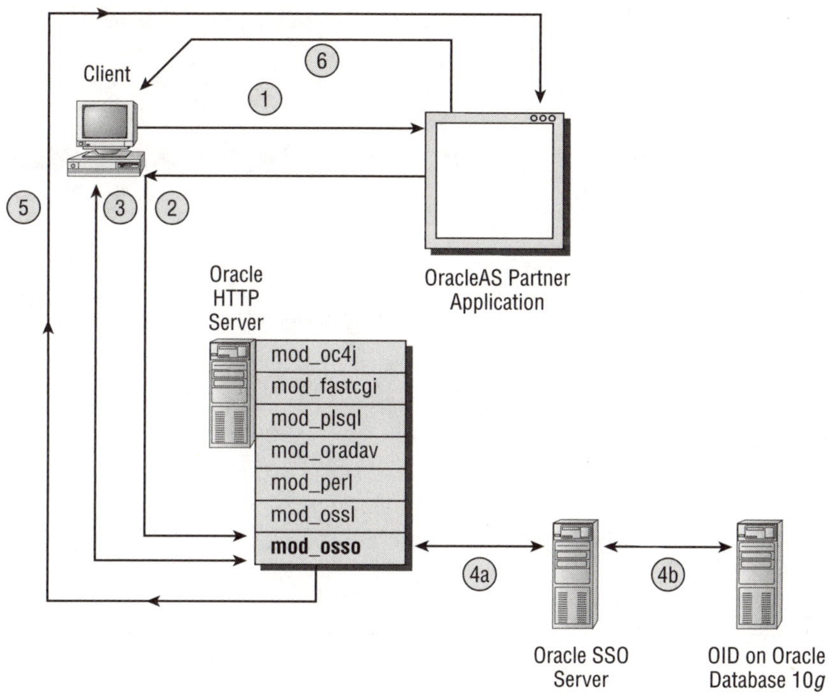

To terminate an SSO session and all active partner applications at the same time, you log out of one of the partner applications. After the logout occurs, you return to the SSO sign-off page shown in Figure 10.2, where you can confirm that SSO has logged you out of all active partner applications.

External Application Authentication

External applications are available on the OracleAS Portal page; OracleAS Portal is an SSO partner application. You use the External Applications portlet to initiate the external application login procedure. Here are the steps you use to authenticate with an external application:

1. The external application login procedure checks to see if your username and password are in the OID database; if not, SSO prompts you for them.
2. Enter the username and password in the web form SSO provides. If you want to save the credentials, click Remember My Login Information.
3. If you saved your credentials, the SSO server constructs a login form to submit to the login processing logic in the external application; this form is essentially a stripped-down version of the external application's own login page with the bare minimum amount of content necessary to log in to the site.

FIGURE 10.2 SSO partner application logout confirmation page

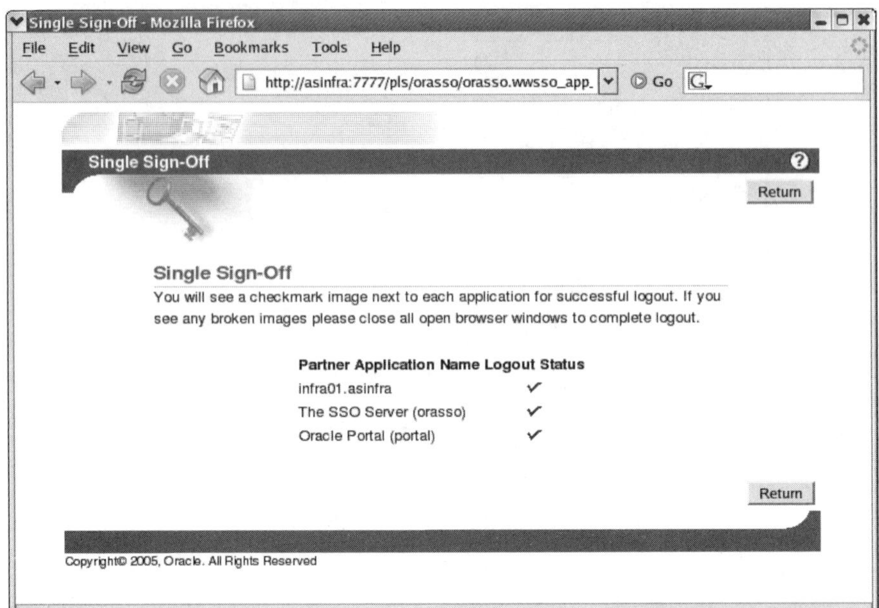

4. The SSO server sends the form to the client browser.
5. The client browser sends this form as a `POST` command to the external application.

If you do not save your login credentials in the SSO repository, you must reenter your username and password every time you access the external application, which more or less defeats the purpose of using the External Applications portlet!

When you log out of an external application, you do not automatically log out of other external applications or any active partner applications. You must log out of each external application manually. Later in this chapter we'll show you an example of creating, editing, and using an external application.

Starting and Stopping OracleAS Single Sign-On

The easiest way to start, stop, or restart the SSO server is via AS Control. First, connect to your OracleAS infrastructure installation. In the System Components section of the Home tab on the AS Control home page, you'll see the list of installed and configured components similar to the ones shown in Figure 10.3.

Since the SSO server is an application that runs on Oracle HTTP Server (OHS), starting or stopping OHS on this page also starts or stops the SSO server. In addition, the SSO server requires an OC4J instance; therefore, starting or stopping OC4J starts or stops the SSO server. In general, to restart the SSO server, you can select HTTP Server, `OC4J_SECURITY`, or Single Sign-On:orasso, shown in Figure 10.3.

FIGURE 10.3 AS Control infrastructure components page

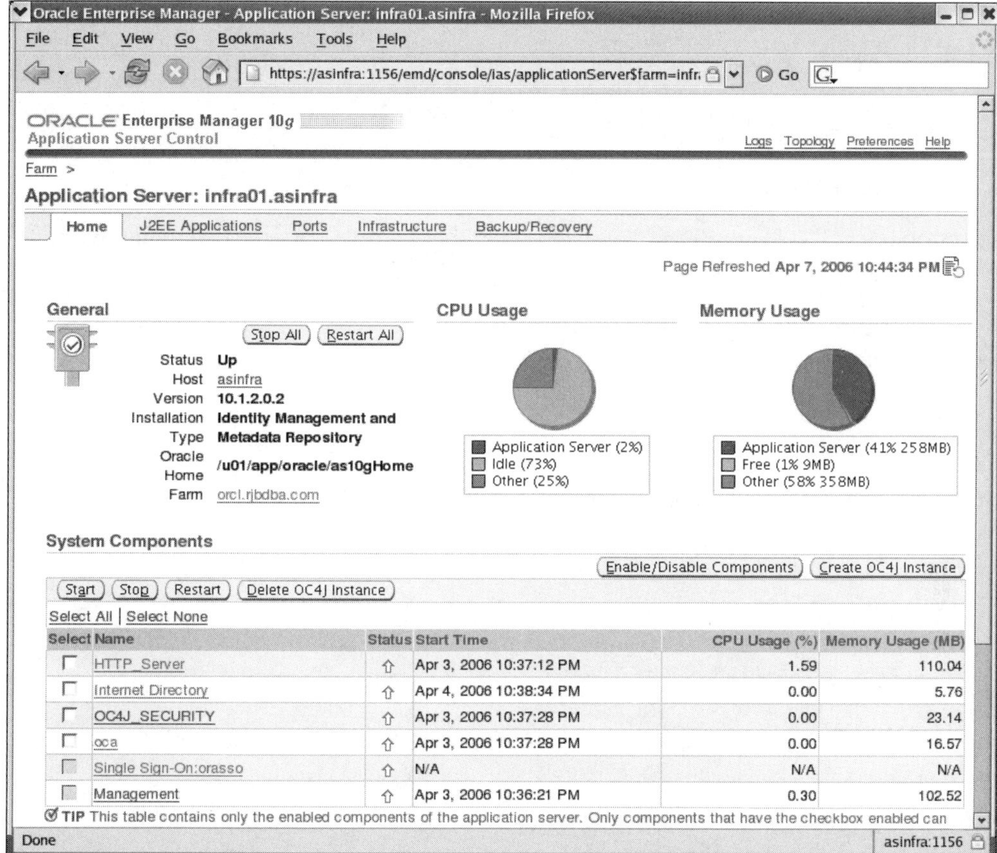

As you might expect, you can also start, stop, or restart any of these components with the `opmnctl` command. To start, stop, or restart the `OC4J_SECURITY` process (and therefore the SSO process), you first need to know the name of the process; you can get the list by using the `opmnctl status` command. Here are the results of that command on the instance `infra01.asinfra`:

```
[oracle@asinfra oracle]$ opmnctl status

Processes in Instance: infra01.asinfra
-------------------+--------------------+---------+---------
ias-component      | process-type       |     pid | status
-------------------+--------------------+---------+---------
DSA                | DSA                |     N/A | Down
```

```
LogLoader          | logloaderd           |      N/A | Down
dcm-daemon         | dcm-daemon           |     3925 | Alive
OC4J               | oca                  |     2724 | Alive
OC4J               | OC4J_SECURITY        |    14309 | Alive
HTTP_Server        | HTTP_Server          |    13825 | Alive
OID                | OID                  |    18136 | Alive

[oracle@asinfra oracle]$
```

To stop the OC4J_SECURITY component, use the `opmnctl stopproc` command with the applicable `process-type` as follows:

```
[oracle@asinfra oracle]$ opmnctl stopproc process-type=OC4J_SECURITY
opmnctl: stopping opmn managed processes...
[oracle@asinfra oracle]$
```

Checking the status of the OC4J_SECURITY component, you see that it stopped:

```
[oracle@asinfra oracle]$ opmnctl status

Processes in Instance: infra01.asinfra
-------------------+--------------------+---------+---------
ias-component      | process-type       |     pid | status
-------------------+--------------------+---------+---------
DSA                | DSA                |     N/A | Down
LogLoader          | logloaderd         |     N/A | Down
dcm-daemon         | dcm-daemon         |    3925 | Alive
OC4J               | oca                |    2724 | Alive
OC4J               | OC4J_SECURITY      |     N/A | Down
HTTP_Server        | HTTP_Server        |   13825 | Alive
OID                | OID                |   18136 | Alive

[oracle@asinfra oracle]$
```

If you refresh the AS Control home page, you see in Figure 10.4 that SSO is also now unavailable.

To start the process again, use the `opmnctl startproc` command:

```
[oracle@asinfra oracle]$ opmnctl startproc process-type=OC4J_SECURITY
opmnctl: starting opmn managed processes...
[oracle@asinfra oracle]$
```

FIGURE 10.4 AS Control infrastructure components status change

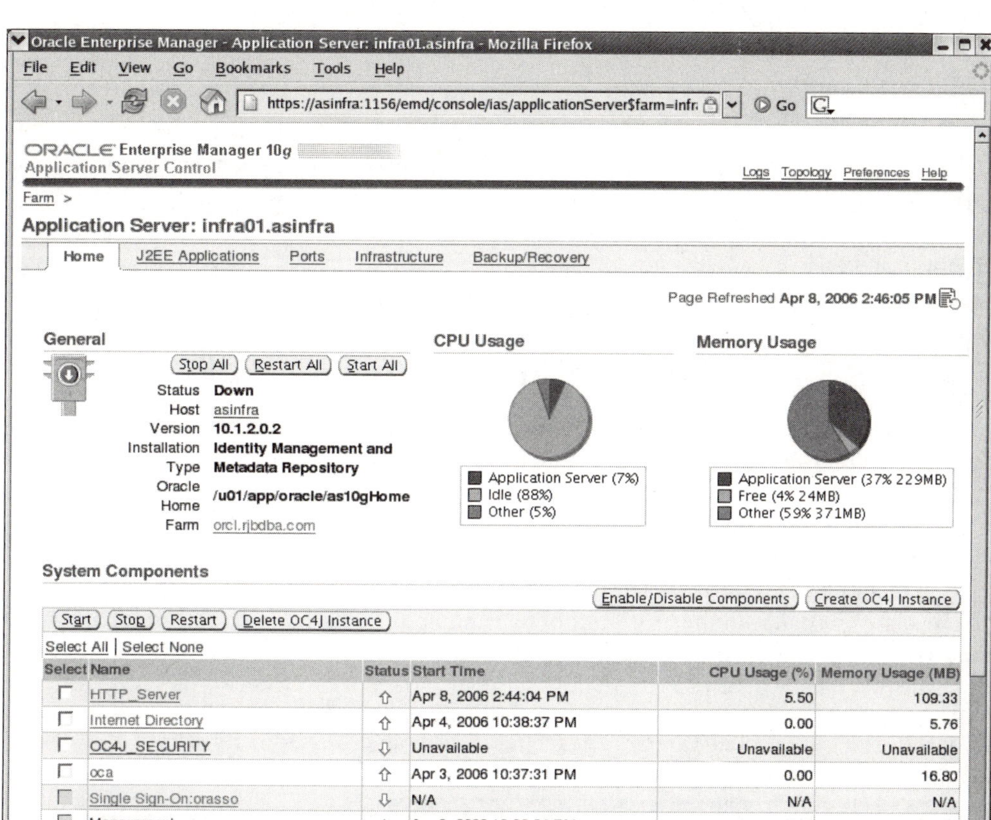

Finally, you check the status one more time:

```
[oracle@asinfra oracle]$ opmnctl status

Processes in Instance: infra01.asinfra
-------------------+--------------------+---------+---------
ias-component      | process-type       |     pid | status
-------------------+--------------------+---------+---------
DSA                | DSA                |     N/A | Down
LogLoader          | logloaderd         |     N/A | Down
dcm-daemon         | dcm-daemon         |    3925 | Alive
OC4J               | oca                |    2724 | Alive
OC4J               | OC4J_SECURITY      |   14530 | Alive
```

```
HTTP_Server          | HTTP_Server          |   13825 | Alive
OID                  | OID                  |   18136 | Alive

[oracle@asinfra oracle]$
```

You can start and stop all OracleAS Web Cache components by using `ias-component` instead of `process-type` in the `opmnctl` command. To do this, you could use `ias-component=OC4J`; however, using this form of the command will also stop the `oca` process (Oracle Certificate Authority), and this may not be the intended result. Notice that the `OC4J_SECURITY` process is up and running with a new process ID (PID); restarting the component starts a new Unix process.

OracleAS Single Sign-On Administrator's Role

After an OracleAS infrastructure is installed, there is one SSO administrator account: `orcladmin`. You use this account to create other administrator accounts using either the OracleAS Self-Service Console or Oracle Directory Manager (ODM). In addition, you can make an existing user an administrator by adding them to the `iASAdmins` group in ODM. OracleAS Self-Service Console is a web-based interface and ODM is a Java-based tool included in an OracleAS infrastructure installation.

You start the ODM administration tool by running the command `oidadmin`; make sure your `PATH` environment variable includes `$ORACLE_HOME/bin`. Figure 10.5 shows the ODM administration page where you can maintain the members of the `iASAdmins` group.

FIGURE 10.5 Oracle Directory Manager iASAdmin group administration

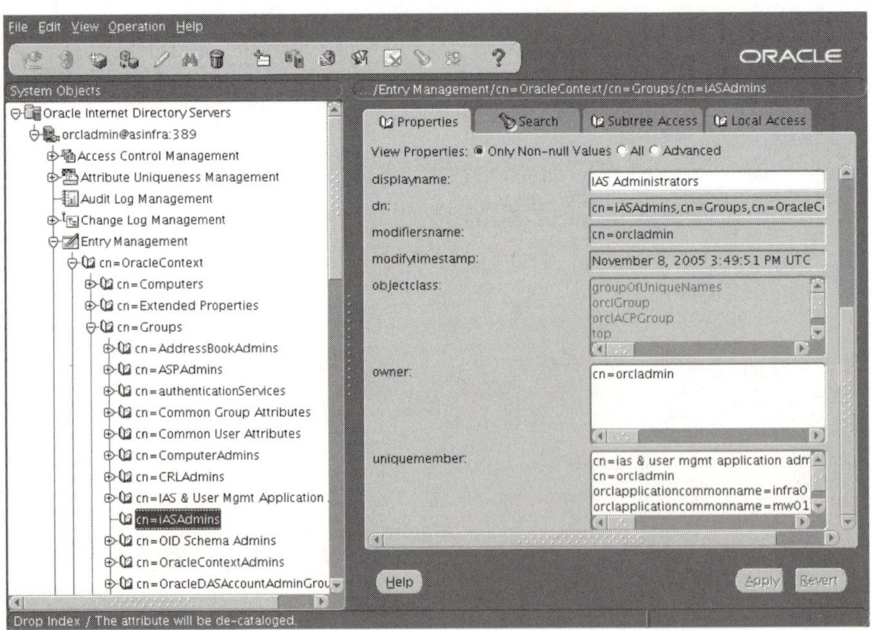

To add a user to the `iASAdmins` group, navigate to `Entry Management`, `cn=OracleContext`, `cn=Groups` and select `cn=iASAdmins`. Add an existing SSO user to the list of users in the `uniquemember` area on the right side of this page. Click Apply to save the settings.

As an SSO administrator, you can also perform the following tasks:

- Edit the SSO server configuration
- Administer partner applications
- Administer external applications

You access the SSO server home page at the following URL:

```
http://<servername>:<portnumber>/pls/orasso
```

In the example in Figure 10.6, the SSO server home page is at `http://asinfra:7777/pls/orasso`.

Configuring the OracleAS Single Sign-On Server

To configure some of the options in the SSO server, click `SSO Server Administration` on the page in Figure 10.6. The next page you will see is the SSO Server Administration page shown in Figure 10.7, where you can launch the SSO server configuration or administer applications.

FIGURE 10.6 The SSO server home page

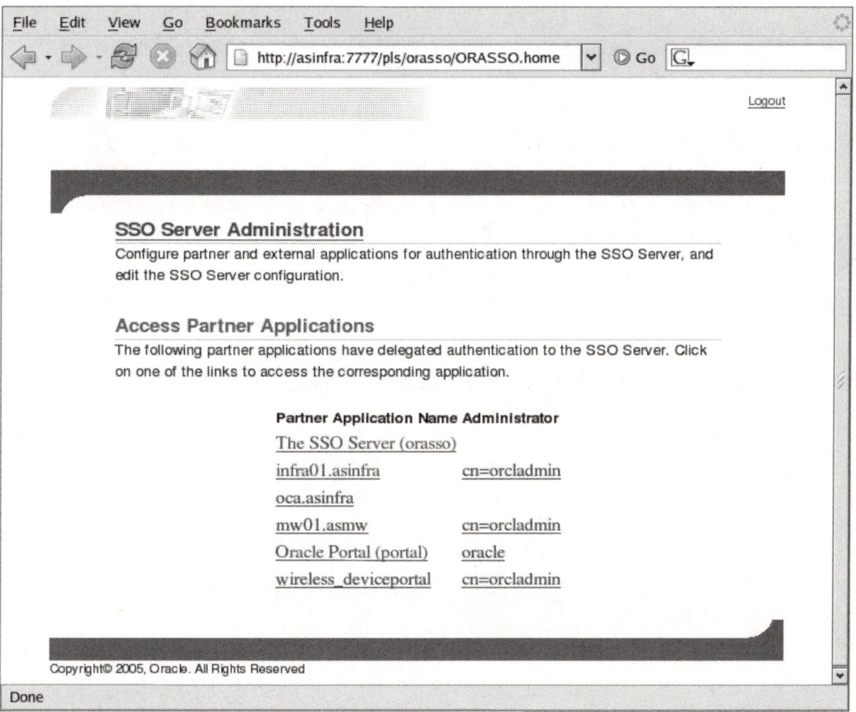

FIGURE 10.7 SSO administration home page

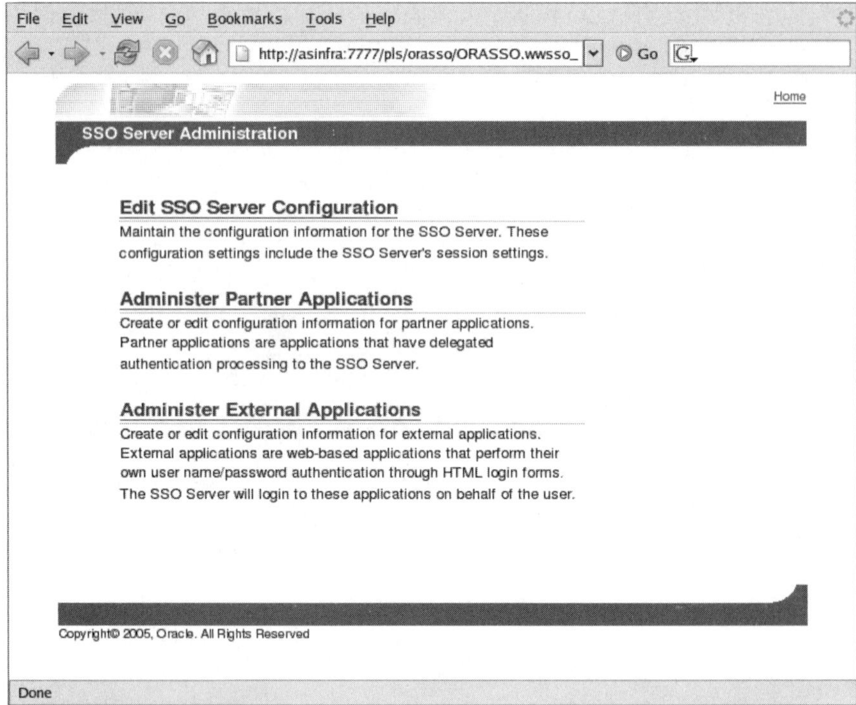

When you click the `Edit SSO Server Configuration` link shown in Figure 10.7, you'll see the Edit SSO Server page shown in Figure 10.8.

On this page, you can adjust the maximum number of hours for an SSO session before it expires, causing a user to have to log back in again. As an additional security feature, you can click the check box to verify that the IP address in any client authentication request matches the IP address of the browser making the authentication request.

Click the Apply button to activate the changes.

Creating and Editing a Partner Application

As part of an OracleAS infrastructure installation, several applications are automatically registered as partner applications, as you can see in Figure 10.6. For applications that are not registered with the OHS module `mod_osso`, you use the `ssoreg.sh` script on Unix and the `ssoreg.bat` script on Windows platforms.

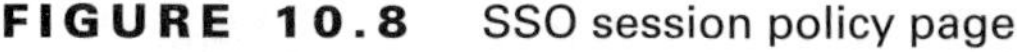

FIGURE 10.8 SSO session policy page

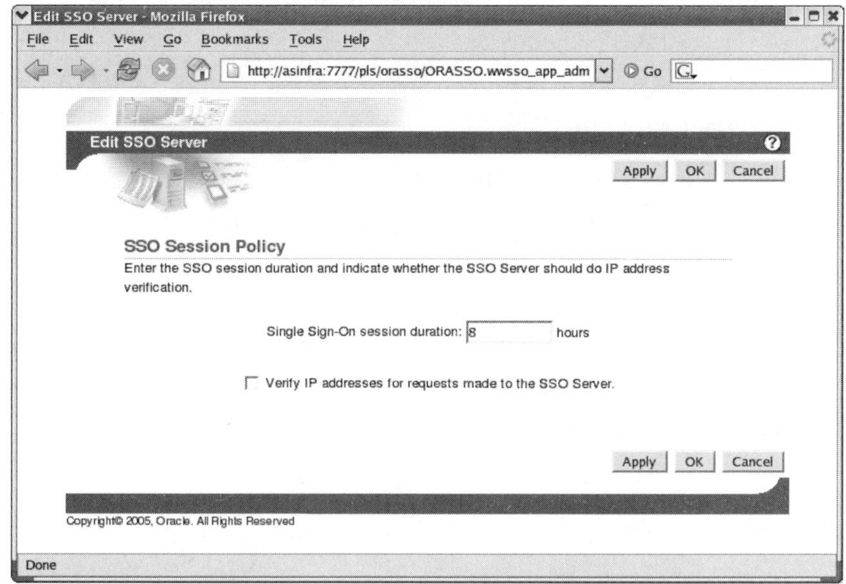

As we mentioned earlier in this chapter, the SSO server treats mod_osso as a partner application itself; therefore, mod_osso must be registered as a partner application. At installation time, mod_osso is automatically registered; however, there are situations where you must reregister mod_osso:

- The OHS hostname or port number are changed after installation.
- The file osso.conf is deleted or corrupted.
- SSL is enabled on the SSO server after installation.

To reregister mod_osso, you use the ssoreg.sh command. This script is located in $ORACLE_HOME/sso/bin, so be sure to include this directory in your PATH command. Here is the syntax of the ssoreg.sh command:

```
ssoreg.sh
   -oracle_home_path orcl_home_path
   -site_name site_name
   -config_mod_osso TRUE
   -mod_osso_url mod_osso_url
   [-virtualhost]
   [-update_mode {CREATE | DELETE | MODIFY} ]
   [-config_file config_file_path]
   [-admin_info admin_info]
   [-admin_id adminid]
```

The parameters to `ssoreg.sh` are as follows:

`-oracle_home_path` The full path for the Oracle home.

`-site_name` A single string containing the hostname and port number.

`-config_mod_osso` If `TRUE`, `mod_osso` is being registered; this creates a new `osso.conf` file.

`-mod_osso_url` The URL (including port number) of the HTTP server.

`-virtualhost` This host is an OHS virtual host.

`-update_mode` Creates, deletes, or modifies a registration record in `osso.conf`.

`-config_file` Specifies the location of `osso.conf`; the default is `$ORACLE_HOME/Apache/Apache/conf/osso`.

`-admin_info` The username of the `mod_osso` administrator.

`-admin_id` Additional administrator information such as the email address of the administrator.

You can also create or edit a partner application using AS Control pages. On the page shown in Figure 10.7, click the `Administer Partner Applications` link. You will see the page shown in Figure 10.9, which allows you to add a new partner application or edit existing partner applications such as the SSO server or Oracle Portal.

FIGURE 10.9 Administer Partner Applications page

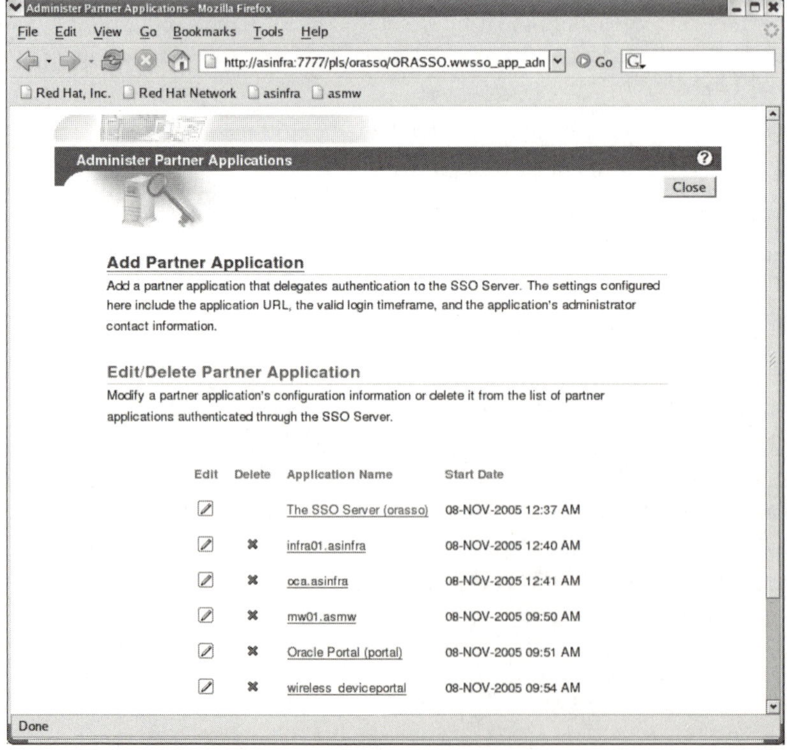

To create a new partner application, click the `Add Partner Application` link shown in Figure 10.9. You will see the Create Partner Application page shown in Figure 10.10.

The required fields for creating a partner application on this page are as follows:

Name A unique name for the partner application; it must be unique within this instance of the SSO server.

Home URL The URL for the application home page.

Success URL The URL for the application responsible for creating and managing the session for the partner application, including the session cookies. This application will redirect the user to the originally requested home page. This application must also access the user's credentials from the SSO server.

FIGURE 10.10 Create Partner Application page

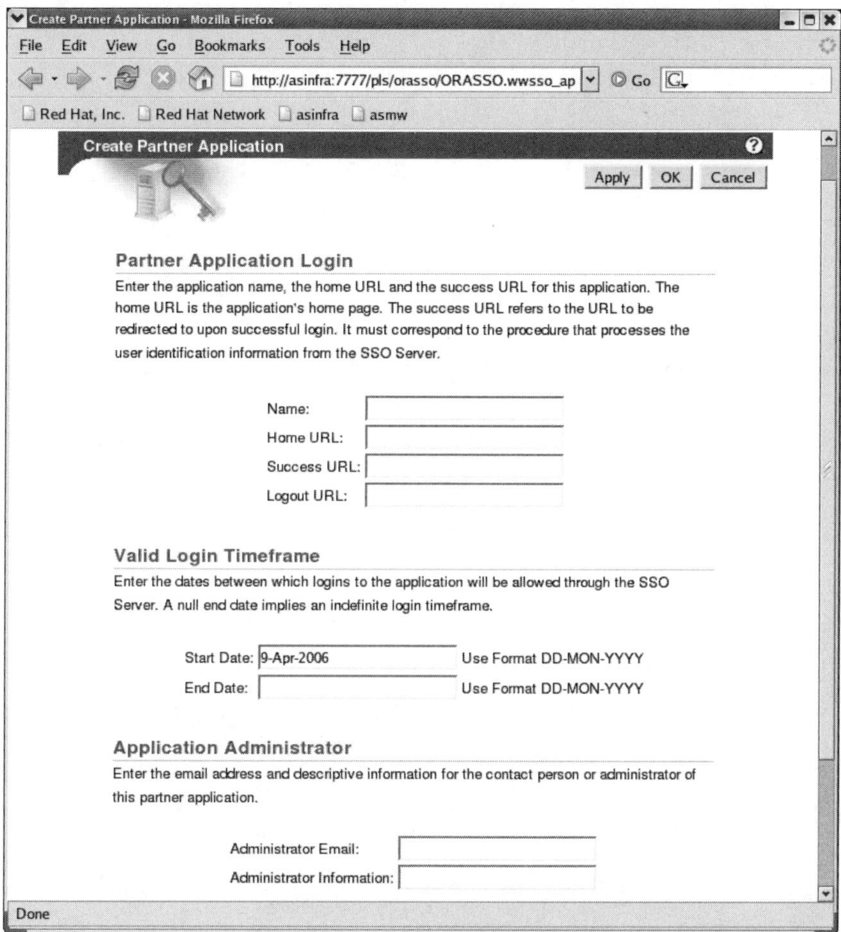

Logout URL The URL for the application's logout routine.

Start Date The first date that the partner application is available through the SSO server.

End Date The last date the partner application is available through the SSO server. If this field is blank, the application is available indefinitely until this field contains a nonblank date or the Start Date field is set to a time in the future.

Administrator Email The email address of the partner application's administrator.

Administrator Information Other information about the partner application's administrator, such as name, location, and so on.

To edit an existing partner application, on the Administer Partner Applications page shown in Figure 10.9, click the Edit button next to the partner application you want to edit. When you click the Edit button next to the Oracle Portal application, you will see the page shown in Figure 10.11.

In addition to the fields you see when you add a partner application, you see these fields when you edit a partner application:

ID The SSO server automatically assigns the ID field when you create the partner application. This field is not editable; the only way to change this field is to delete the partner application and add it again.

FIGURE 10.11 Edit Partner Application page

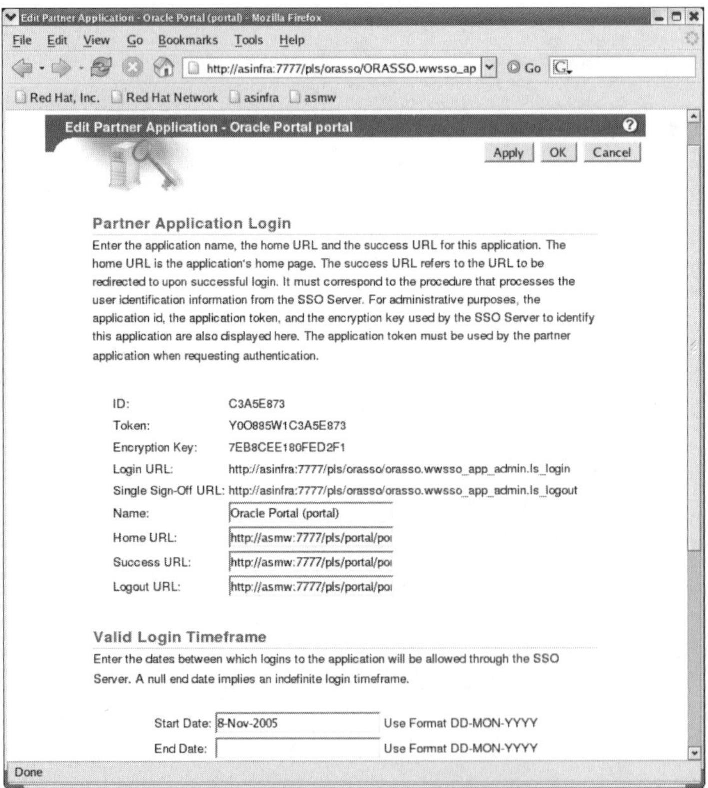

Token When you create a partner application, the SSO server automatically creates the token value. The SSO server uses the token value to identify the partner application when the partner application requests authentication.

Encryption Key The SSO server uses the encryption key to encrypt the client's login cookie.

All the other fields on this page are editable and appear on the Create Partner Application page.

Administering External Applications

You use the OracleAS SSO administration pages to add, edit, or delete external applications. It is optional, but strongly recommended, that you store the external application credentials within the SSO database repository. Once you configure the external application, you can access it from the External Application portlets within OracleAS Portal. A *portal* is a customized and centralized web page location that summarizes or provides access to corporate or external information. A *portlet* is a subcomponent of an OracleAS Portal page; typically, a portlet will summarize information from an information source or provide access to an information source, such as a sales summary graph, a stock ticker, or a weather forecast.

To create an external application, log in as an SSO administrator and click the `Administer External Applications` link shown in Figure 10.7. On the next page, click the `Add External Application` link and you will see the Create External Application page; the top part of the page is in Figure 10.12 and the bottom part is in Figure 10.13.

FIGURE 10.12 Create External Application page, top half

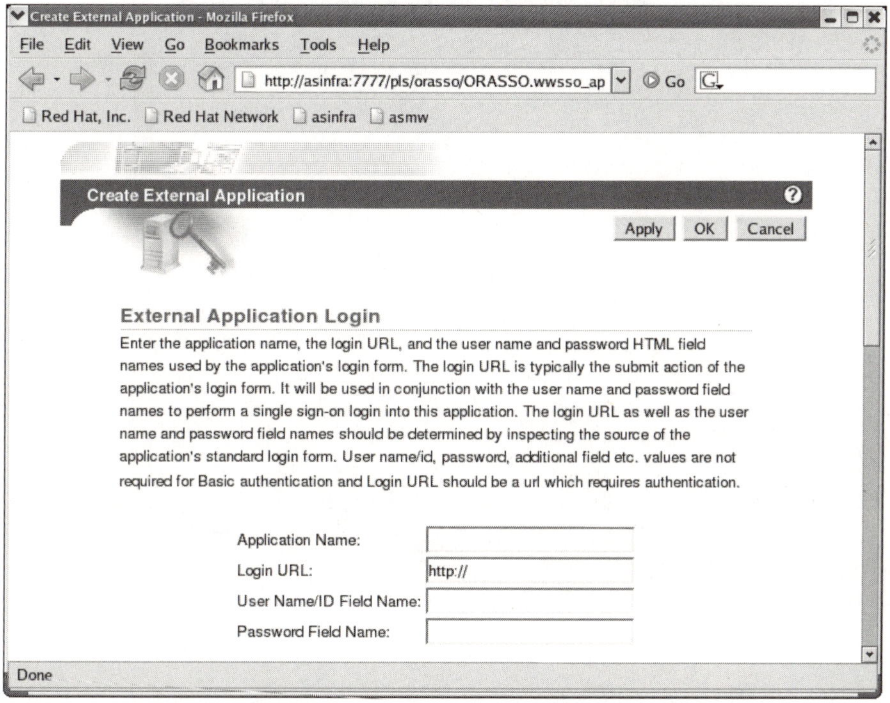

In the External Application Login section in Figure 10.12, enter the following values:

Application Name A unique name that identifies this application.

Login URL The URL of the remote resource to which the HTML login page for the application is submitted for authentication. This is the URL that the client sees after the username and password are submitted.

User Name/ID Field Name The name of the field on the external application's login form where you enter the username. You can find the name of this field by viewing the HTML source for the page.

Password Field Name The name of the field on the external application's login form where you enter the password. You can find the name of this field by viewing the HTML source for the page.

In the Authentication Method section, shown in Figure 10.13, choose one of the following values from the Type of Authentication Used drop-down box:

POST Posts data to the SSO server and submits the user's credentials within the body of the form.

FIGURE 10.13 Create External Application page, bottom half

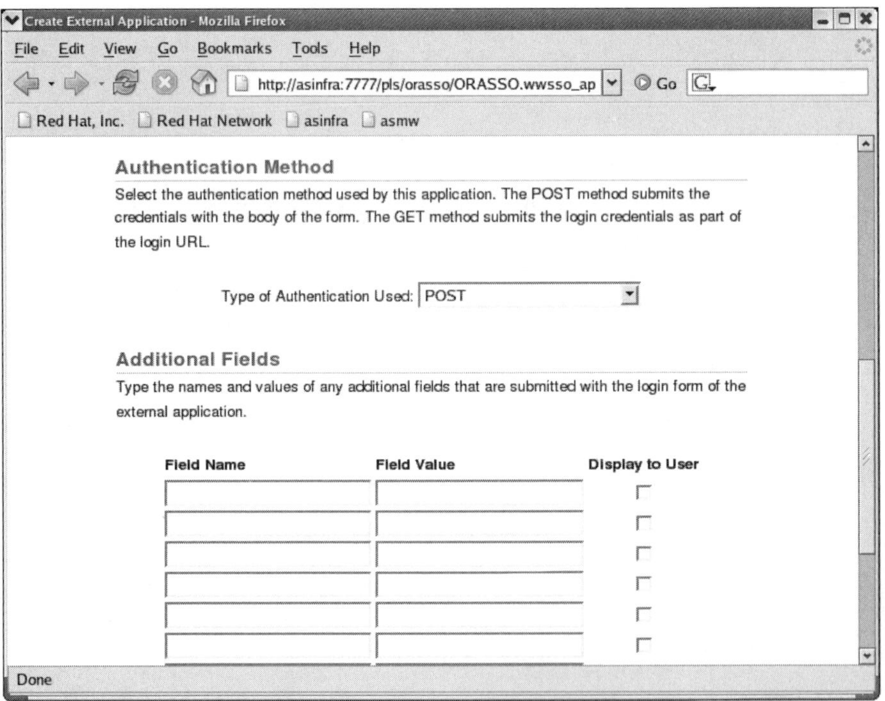

GET Sends a page request to the external server, submitting the login credentials as part of the login URL.

BASIC AUTHENTICATION Submits the login credentials in the application URL. This method is a potential security risk because the username and password are transmitted unencrypted.

In the Additional Fields section, you can enter any additional field names and values required by the external application before authentication is complete.

Creating an External Application

One of your users, Dawn, wants to use Oracle Portal to conveniently access all of her applications, both partner applications and external applications, from one web page. The first step you must perform is to create an entry for her in the Oracle Internet Directory (OID). To accomplish this, navigate to the OID provisioning console.

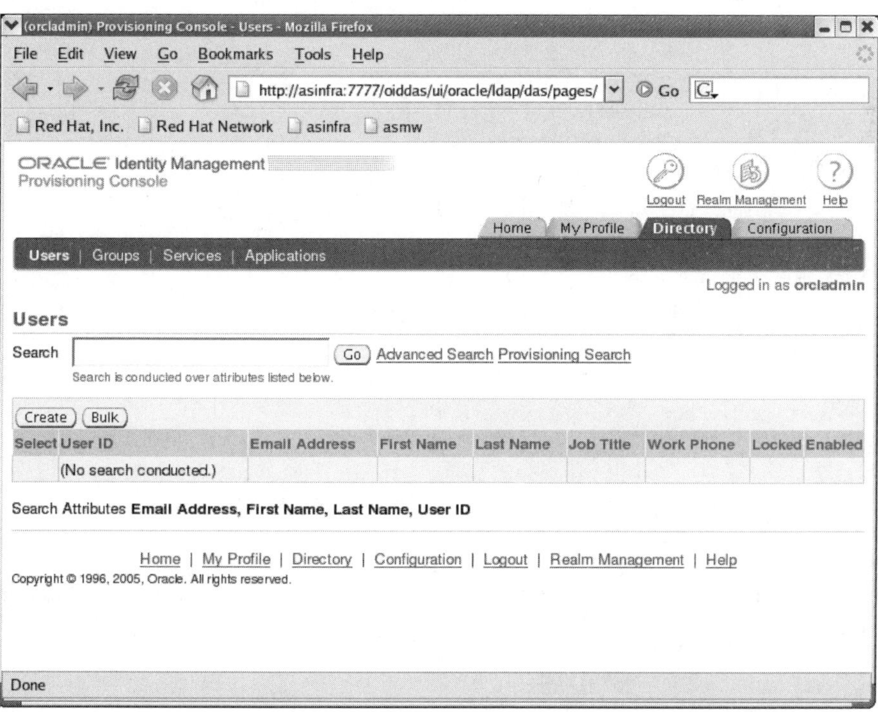

Next, click the Create button to create a new entry in the directory (which in this case is a user object); you will see the page shown here. At a minimum, you fill in the required fields in the form. Notice that at the top of the form you can specify a number of different items on this page, including a photograph, telephone numbers, home and office addresses, and so forth.

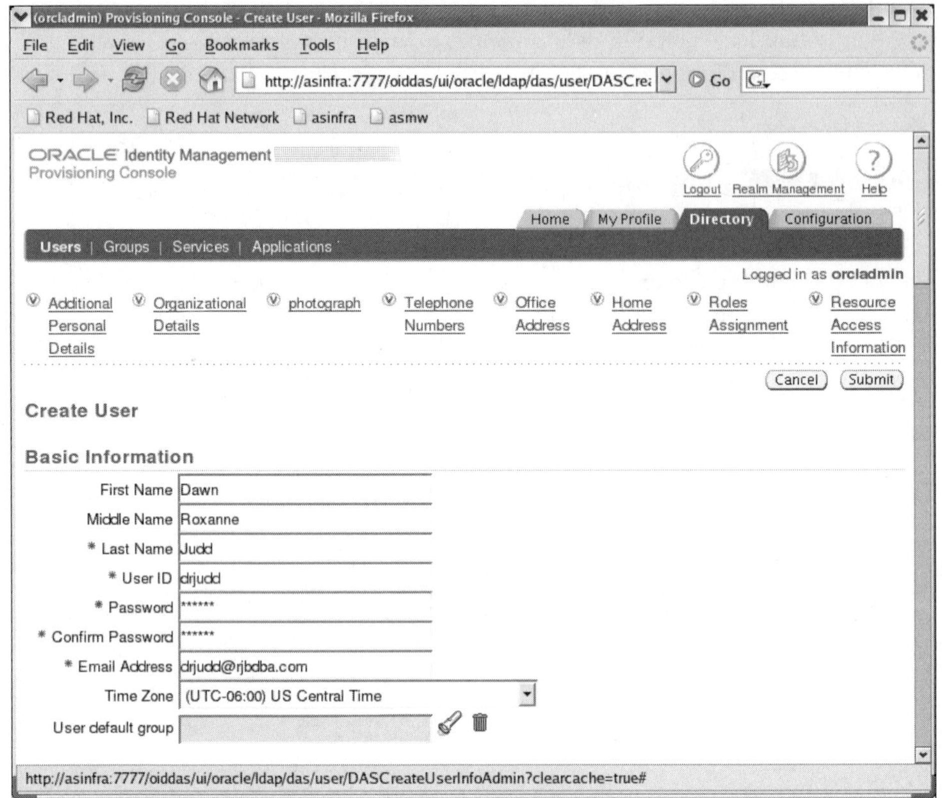

Click Submit to register Dawn's information into the OID repository.

The next step is to add the first external application. Using the page shown in Figure 10.12, enter the following values for one of Dawn's favorite shopping sites, Lands' End Casual Clothing Merchants:

Application Name Lands' End Clothes

Login URL `https://www.landsend.com/cgi-bin/Login.cgi?redirect=cgi-bin/AccountPortal.cgi&type=GenLogin`

User Name/ID Field Name emailAddress

Password Field Name password

Click OK to save the external application settings.

The next time Dawn connects to the SSO server, she sees the new external application; when she clicks the link for the external application, the SSO server prompts for the username and password.

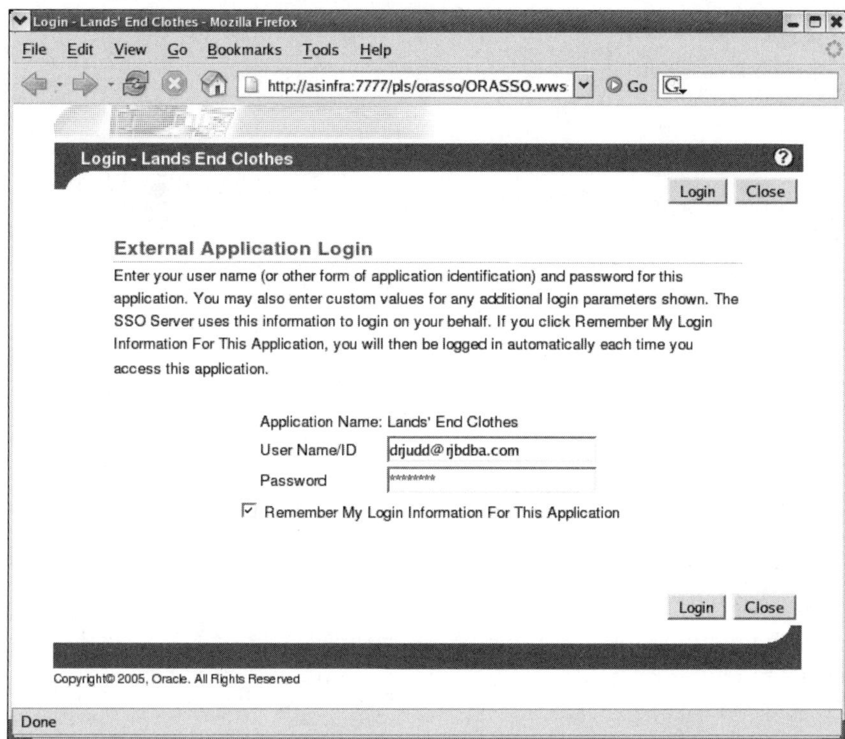

The next time Dawn clicks on this external application from an administration screen or from an external applications portlet within Oracle Portal, she will be automatically logged into the Lands' End website using the stored credentials.

Monitoring OracleAS Single Sign-On Server

You can monitor the health and status of the SSO server in the same way you monitor every other component of OracleAS—by using AS Control. To access the SSO server home page, click the `Single Sign-On:orasso` link shown earlier in Figure 10.3 and you will see the page shown in Figure 10.14.

FIGURE 10.14 External application authentication page

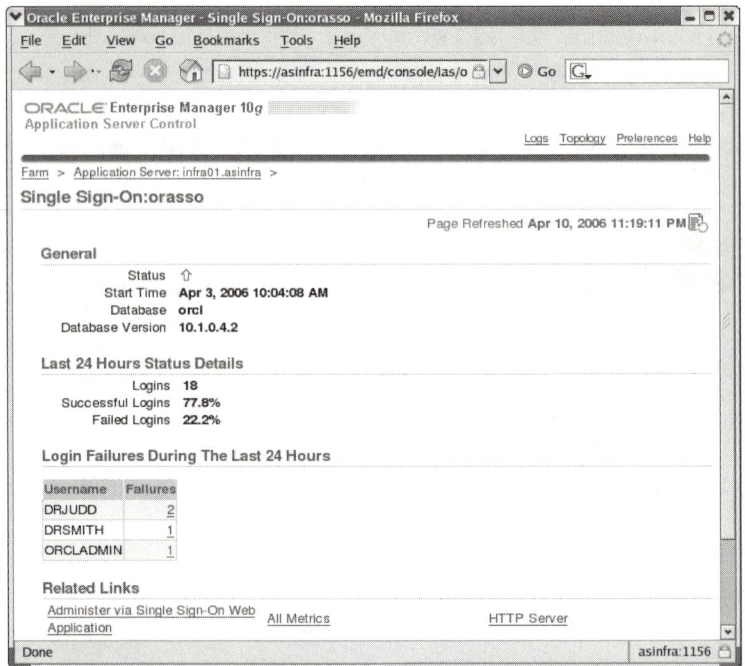

The page in Figure 10.14 is divided into four sections:

General The status of the SSO server (up or down), the last time you started the SSO server, and the metadata repository database name and version

Last 24 Hours Status Details The total number of logins and the percentage of successful and unsuccessful logins

Login Failures During The Last 24 Hours Detailed list of failed login usernames and how many failures for each in the last 24 hours

Related Links SSO server–related links, such as SSO server administration, metrics, and HTTP Server

Accessing the SSO Server and External Applications from OracleAS Portal

You can access many of the administration functions we've presented in this chapter through the portal automatically installed with an OracleAS middle-tier instance. The middle-tier installation process registers OracleAS Portal as a partner application for the SSO server; as a result, when you log in to the SSO server, you can access OracleAS Portal from the SSO server home page shown earlier in Figure 10.6. When you log in as `orcladmin` and click the `Oracle Portal` link, you will see the page shown in Figure 10.15.

FIGURE 10.15 Administration portal page

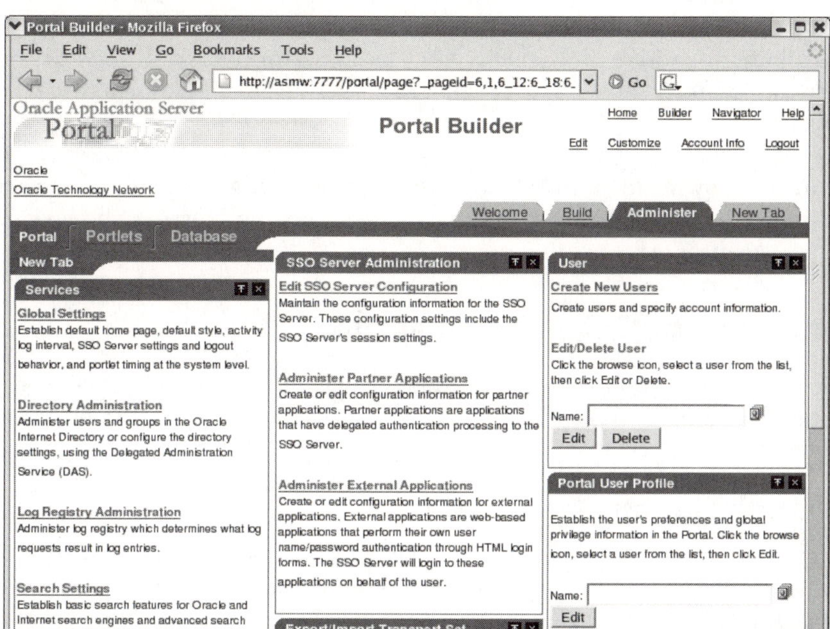

The installation procedure creates the portal page for SSO administration at the same time that it defines OracleAS Portal as a partner application. This page shows you the convenience of centralizing various administration and monitoring tasks. By clicking the `Customize` link in the upper-right portion of the page, you can easily add other portlets to this page, such as an external applications portlet.

Managing Access Using Delegated Administration Services

Briefly, *Delegated Administration Services* (DAS) enables you to centrally store all metadata for users, groups, applications, and services in your environment and at the same time allows you to distribute administration of the data to other administrators and end users. You may have several diverse groups of users, data, and services in your environment; for example, let's say your three biggest user groups are human resources, accounting, and information services. The human resources group manages the employee data, accounting manages the financial data, and information services manages the email service and its associated data. These three disparate data types can exist within the same repository while remaining partitioned within three separate administrator hierarchies.

DAS performs user and group maintenance operations on behalf of an application and provides a user interface that shows the result of the operation; this interface is called the Oracle Internet Directory Self-Service Console.

The delegated administrative tasks you or your users perform using the Self-Service Console is very fine-grained: You can easily delegate user metadata maintenance to the users themselves.

In the following sections, we'll delve more deeply into DAS by providing an overview of the DAS architecture and how to administer DAS by creating Identity Management realms. In addition, we'll show you in detail how to manage users, groups, and services and how to delegate these management tasks to other users.

Understanding the DAS Architecture

To understand how to manage and configure DAS, you need to understand the flow of requests from the client to OID in an SSO environment as well as how the DAS proxy user improves the security in your environment.

DAS Installation Options

Although a single instance of DAS is included in an OID installation, you can also install DAS by itself; therefore, you can install DAS on several different servers and connect with a single instance of OracleAS OID. This helps to increase the availability and scalability of DAS.

DAS Management Flow

DAS is a J2EE application deployed in an OracleAS OC4J instance. In a nutshell, it receives requests from clients; performs OID retrieval, insert, update, and delete operations; compiles the Lightweight Directory Access Protocol (LDAP) results into an HTML page; and sends the HTML page back to the client. In addition, DAS integrates easily with an SSO server. Here is a more detailed request flow using DAS with SSO:

1. The client accesses DAS using the `mod_osso` module with OHS.
2. If the client has never accessed DAS, `mod_osso` transparently redirects the client to the SSO server for authentication.
3. The SSO server prompts the user for a username and password if the user has not yet authenticated with the SSO server or the session has timed out.
4. The SSO server verifies the credentials with those in OID.
5. If the credentials are valid, `mod_osso` redirects the client to DAS.
6. The DAS service logs in with OID as a proxy user with the privileges to switch identities and connects to OID again with the distinguished name (DN) of the user making the request.
7. DAS combines the LDAP results into an HTML page and returns the results to the client.

DAS Proxy User

DAS uses the OID proxy feature to perform administrative tasks on behalf of the user; because the proxy access is a single point of access for all operations, your directory environment is much more secure. The proxy user allows any component (in this case, DAS) to switch its identity to that of the user at the client.

In addition to centralizing the point of access, a proxy account is typically used in an environment with a firewall in the middle tier. Various clients authenticate in the middle tier; the middle tier process logs into OID on behalf of the user and then switches to the client's identity. All subsequent operations on the directory occur using the client's privileges.

Using this method, a user or administrator logs into DAS and then only DAS logs into OID as a proxy user. Connections to DAS originate from the OID Self-Service Console, other OracleAS component consoles, or even third-party application consoles using the appropriate OracleAS application programming interfaces (APIs).

Administering DAS

The easiest way to start, stop, or restart the DAS is via AS Control. First, connect to your OracleAS infrastructure installation. In the System Components section of the Home tab on the AS Control home page, you'll see a list of installed and configured components similar to the ones shown in Figure 10.3 earlier in this chapter.

Since DAS is a J2EE application within OracleAS, you can restart DAS by selecting `OC4J_SECURITY` and clicking Start, Stop, or Restart, depending on the current state of `OC4J_SECURITY`.

As you might expect, you can also start, stop, or restart any of these components with the `opmnctl` command. As we presented earlier in this chapter with the SSO server, stop the `OC4J_SECURITY` process as follows:

```
opmnctl stopproc process-type=OC4J_SECURITY
```

To start the process again, use the `opmnctl startproc` command:

```
opmnctl startproc process-type=OC4J_SECURITY
```

You can start and stop all OracleAS Web Cache components by using `ias-component` instead of `process-type` in the `opmnctl` command; to do this, you could use `ias-component=OC4J`; however, using this form of the command will also stop the `oca` process (Oracle Certificate Authority), and this may not be the intended result.

You can also verify the status of DAS using the Unix command line. Use the `ps` command on the server running the infrastructure instance, as in the following example:

```
[oracle@asinfra oracle]$ ps -ef | egrep "http|java" |
➥    awk '{print $1, $2, $8}'
oracle 2323 /u01/app/oracle/as10gHome/jdk/bin/java
oracle 2691 /u01/app/oracle/as10gHome/jdk/bin/java
```

```
oracle 2724 /u01/app/oracle/as10gHome/jdk/bin/java
oracle 3866 /u01/app/oracle/as10gHome/jdk/bin/java
oracle 3925 /u01/app/oracle/as10gHome/jdk/bin/java
oracle 18146 /u01/app/oracle/as10gHome/jdk/bin/java
oracle 13825 /u01/app/oracle/as10gHome/Apache/Apache/bin/httpd
oracle 20894 /u01/app/oracle/as10gHome/Apache/Apache/bin/httpd
oracle 20896 /u01/app/oracle/as10gHome/Apache/Apache/bin/httpd
oracle 20899 /u01/app/oracle/as10gHome/Apache/Apache/bin/httpd
oracle 20902 /u01/app/oracle/as10gHome/Apache/Apache/bin/httpd
oracle 20904 /u01/app/oracle/as10gHome/Apache/Apache/bin/httpd
oracle 20907 /u01/app/oracle/as10gHome/Apache/Apache/bin/httpd
oracle 20940 /u01/app/oracle/as10gHome/Apache/Apache/bin/httpd
oracle 20970 /u01/app/oracle/as10gHome/jdk/bin/java
oracle 21139 /u01/app/oracle/as10gHome/Apache/Apache/bin/httpd
oracle 21217 /u01/app/oracle/as10gHome/Apache/Apache/bin/httpd
oracle 21768 /u01/app/oracle/as10gHome/Apache/Apache/bin/httpd
oracle 32736 egrep
[oracle@asinfra oracle]$
```

The `egrep` command searches for occurrences of `http` or `java`; the `awk` command returns only the process owner, process ID, and command from the `ps` command output. If you see processes with the `java` command or `httpd` command that were started from `$ORACLE_HOME`, then DAS is running. To verify that the DAS web services are active, navigate to the Self-Service Console using this URL:

```
http://asinfra:7777/oiddas
```

If your HTTP server is using a different port, substitute that port number for 7777 in the preceding example and substitute your infrastructure server name for `asinfra`. You can see the DAS Self-Service Console in Figure 10.16. Both administrators and end users can use this page as a starting point for maintenance tasks.

Creating Identity Management Realms

An Identity Management *realm* is a subtree within OID; it includes subtrees for users and groups along with access control lists to provide fine-grained control of the subtrees' administration. An OID realm also includes an *Oracle Context*: an LDAP-compliant entry in OID containing all information related to the Oracle software within an installation.

Creating realms helps you to centralize the directory information while at the same time permit the delegation of each realm to different administrators. In addition, each realm within OID can store different types of structured data; for example, the accounting realm will store general ledger, accounts receivable, and accounts payable information whereas the human resources realm will store employee and customer information. You also may want to use multiple realms to provision different services to particular user groups. Figure 10.17 shows an OID with three realms.

FIGURE 10.16 DAS Self-Service Console page

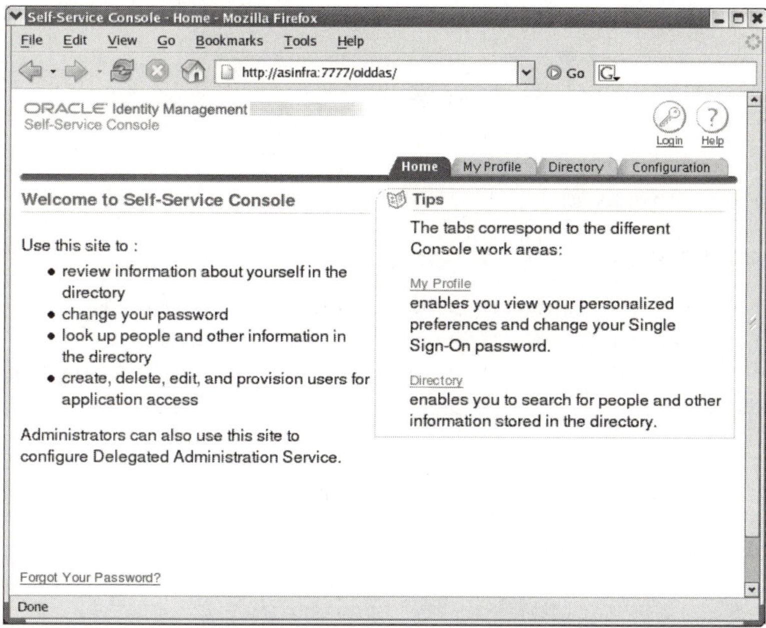

FIGURE 10.17 An OID environment with three realms

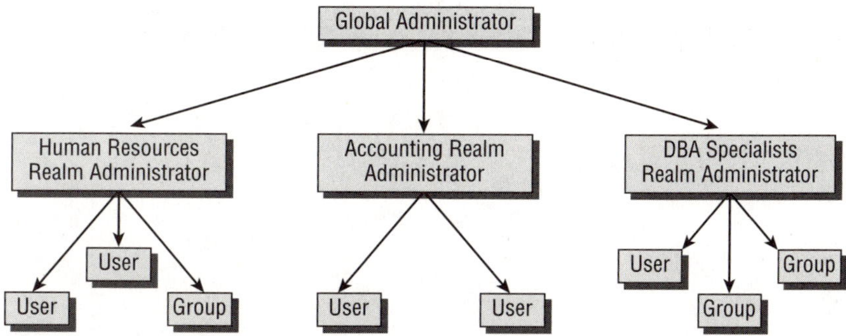

Creating or Editing the Default Realm

After you install DAS, you must set up a default realm to contain entries for a default subscriber; if you install DAS as part of an infrastructure installation, the default realm is automatically created. On the Self-Service Console page shown in Figure 10.16, click the `Login` link and log in with the `orcladmin` account. Next, click the Configuration tab; you will see the page shown in Figure 10.18.

In the examples throughout this book, the infrastructure installation is on the server `asinfra`; therefore, the default domain for this server is as follows:

```
dc=asinfra, dc=com
```

The default users you create in OID are located in

```
cn=users, dc=asinfra, dc=com
```

and the default groups are located in

```
cn=groups, dc=asinfra, dc=com
```

In the Login Name field, `uid` (user ID) is the attribute that users use to log in. Alternatively, you can specify other attributes, such as `cn` (common name), employee number, or any other uniquely identifiable user attribute. Here is a list of the required entries on the page:

Attribute for Login Name Attribute used for login.

Attribute for RDN A relative distinguished name (RDN) used to identify the user component of the complete distinguished name. This should not be the same attribute used for login.

FIGURE 10.18 Identity Management Realm Configuration tab

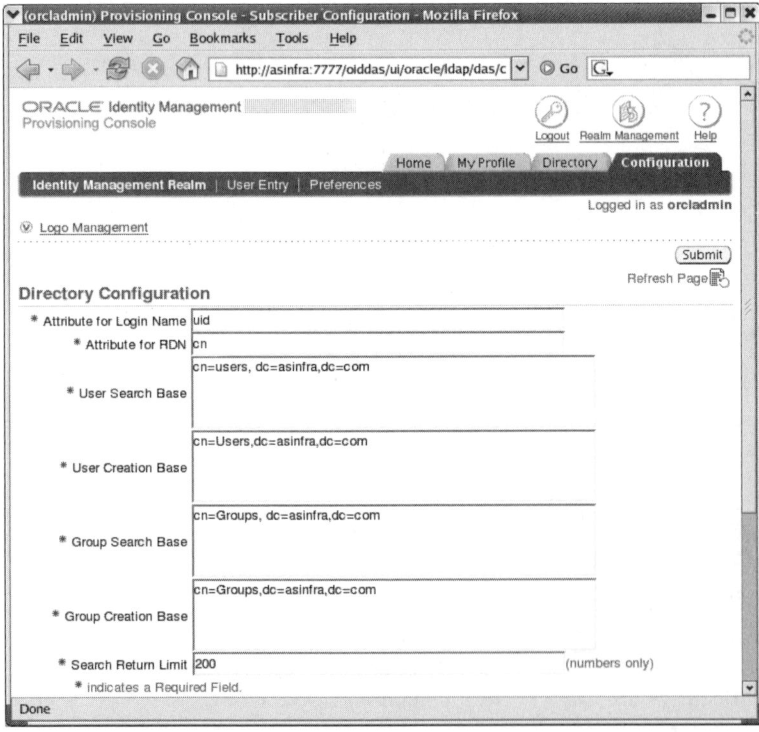

User Search Base The DN used as the starting point in the directory for user search.

User Creation Base The DN used as the base for creating new users.

Group Search Base The DN used as the starting point in the directory for group search.

Group Creation Base The DN used as the base for creating new groups within the realm.

Search Return Limit The maximum number of entries returned when searching the directory.

At the bottom of the page (but not visible in Figure 10.18) is the Logo Management section. You can define a realm logo or product name to include on each page containing attributes for an entry in the directory.

Creating a New Realm

To create a new realm, start at the page shown in Figure 10.18 and click the `Realm Management` link. The next page you see is the Identity Management Realms page; click the Create button. On the screen shown in Figure 10.19, you specify the following attributes:

Realm Name A relatively short version of the realm name. This name is a component of the DN for this realm entry.

Realm Contact Contact information for questions about this realm.

FIGURE 10.19 Create Identity Management Realm page

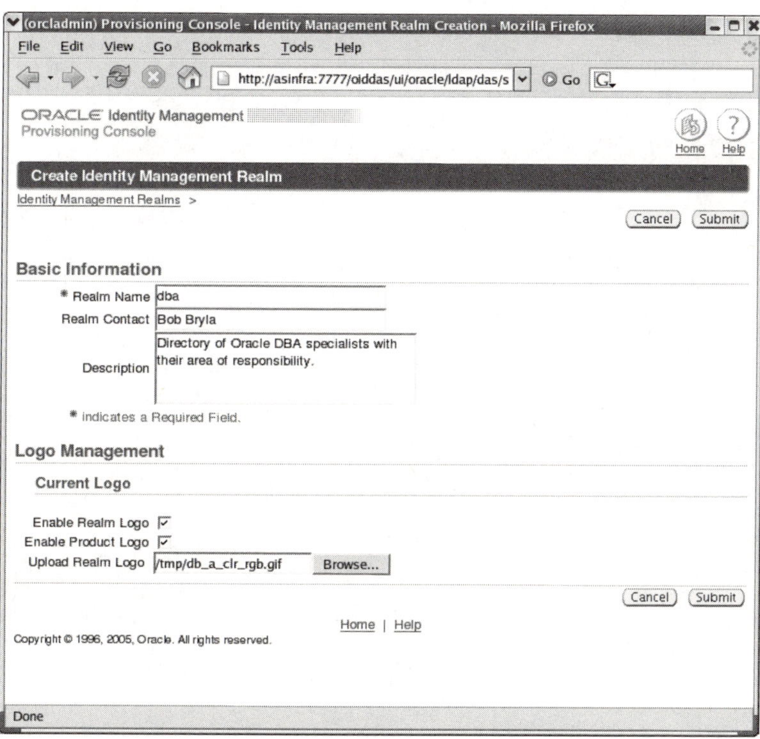

Description An optional field containing any other relevant information about the realm.

Upload Realm Logo An optional field specifying the name of an image to display on the page for each entry in this realm.

When you click the Submit button, you get a confirmation page. The next time you click the `Realm Management` link shown in Figure 10.18, you will see the new realm along with the default realm `asinfra`, as shown in Figure 10.20.

When you select the new realm and click the View button, you will see the page shown in Figure 10.21 with the attributes assigned to each entry in this realm.

Using the Java-based `oidadmin` tool we introduced earlier in this chapter, you can see the new realm in context with the default realm `asinfra` in OID. Figure 10.22 shows the new realm highlighted in the left-hand pane of Oracle Directory Manager.
The default domain for users created in this realm is therefore

```
dc=dba, dc=com
```

The default users you create in this realm are located in

```
cn=users, dc=dba, dc=com
```

And the default groups are located in

```
cn=groups, dc=dba, dc=com
```

FIGURE 10.20 Identity Management Realms page

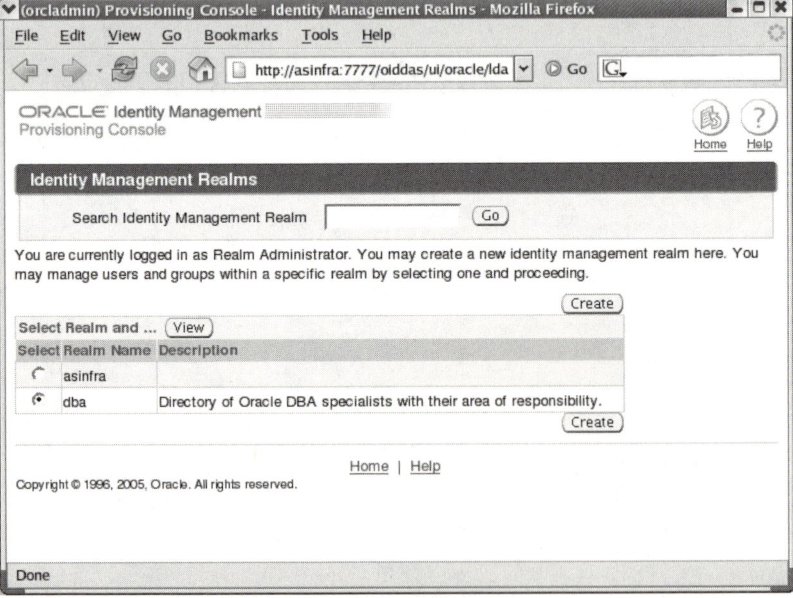

FIGURE 10.21 Realm information page

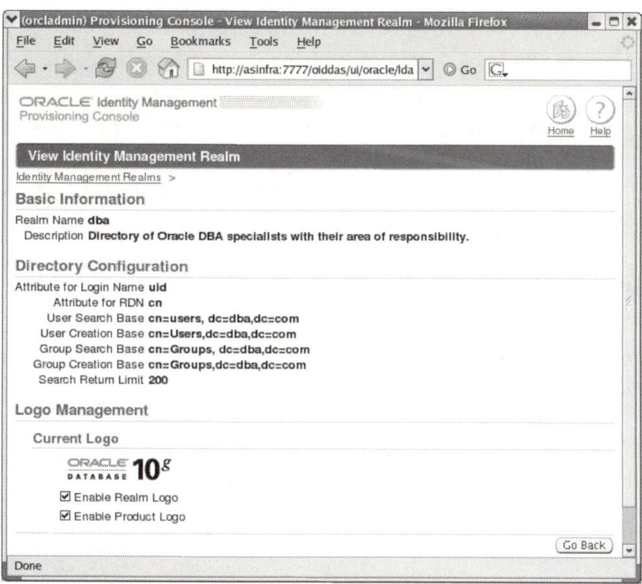

FIGURE 10.22 Browsing Oracle Directory Manager realms

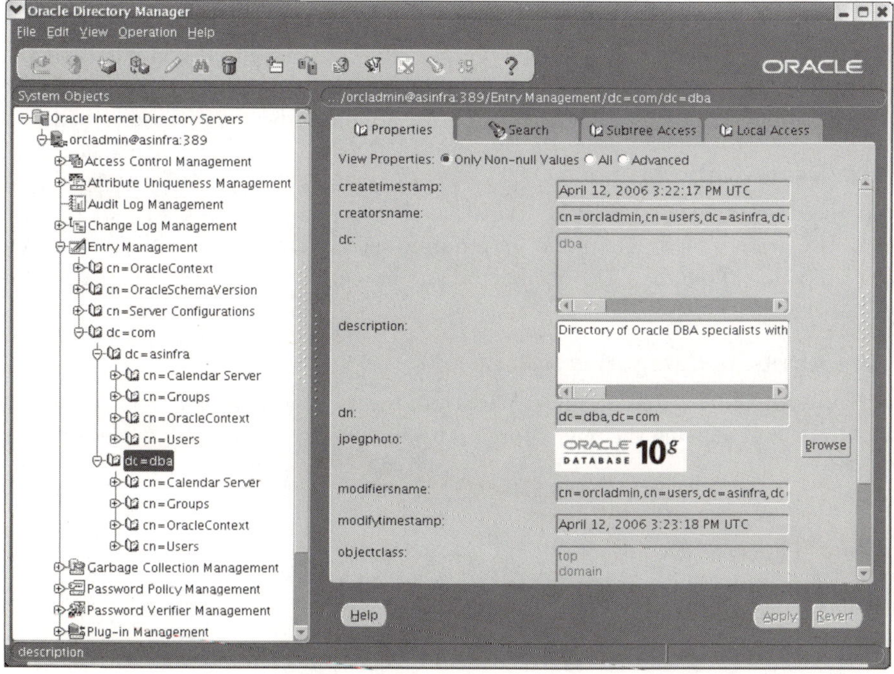

Managing Users and Groups

When you create a user or group using the Self-Service Console, you fill out a form. Because of the flexibility of the data structure in OID, the fields you can enter for a user or group will vary tremendously depending on the type of group and the data retrieval needs of the organization. As a result, the data entry forms for the Self-Service Console must reflect these needs and be highly flexible and customizable. In the following sections, we'll show you how to customize your Self-Service Console user entry template.

In addition, we'll show you how to maintain users and groups, search the users and groups, and maintain users' passwords.

Configuring the User Entry Template

To customize the user entry interface in the Self-Service Console, log in as the administrator (`orcladmin`), click the Configuration tab, and then click the `User` link on the tab's navigation bar. You will see five general steps you need to perform to fully configure the user entry interface:

1. Configure user object classes.
2. Configure user attributes.
3. Configure attribute categories.
4. Configure search table columns.
5. Configure roles.

Each of these steps gives you the opportunity to not only edit elements of the interface, but also add new attributes.

Configure User Object Classes

The Object Class page contains the defined *object classes*: entities you use to classify and group information, such as an Oracle user, a person, or an organization. Each directory entry belongs to one or more object classes, and one object class can inherit the characteristics of another.

Configure User Attributes

The Configure User Attributes page contains each attribute name along with its GUI description and information such as whether it's a required field, viewable, editable, and searchable. You can also control how the GUI formats the attribute on the page. Figure 10.23 shows the currently defined attributes.

Configure Attribute Categories

The Configure Attribute Categories page partitions the user management page into categories to make editing and viewing the page more manageable. The default categories on this page are as follows:

- Basic Information
- Additional Personal Details
- Organizational Details

FIGURE 10.23 Configure User Attributes page

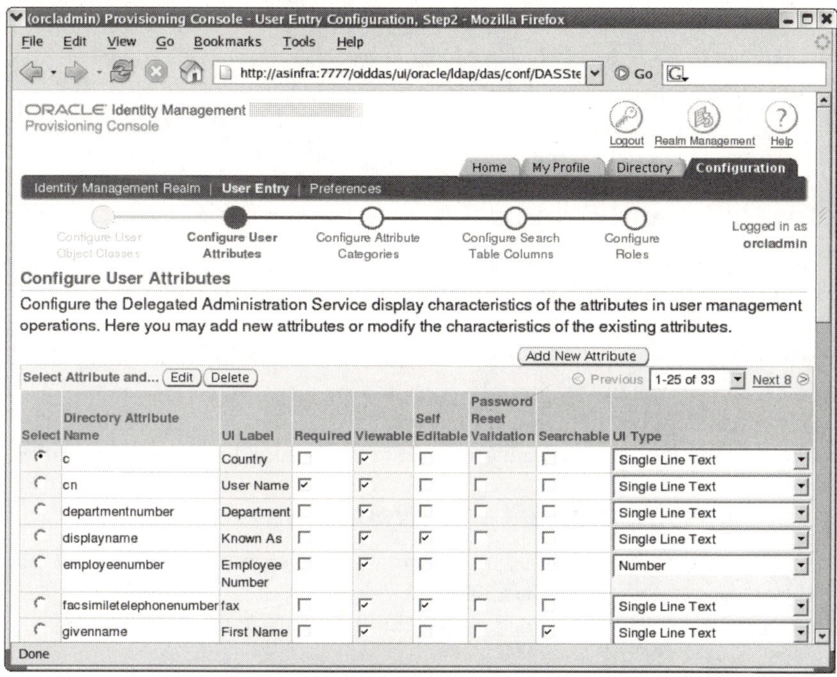

- Photograph
- Telephone Numbers
- Office Address
- Home Address

In addition, you can easily change the display order of these categories on the user management page.

Configure Search Table Columns

You use the Configure Search Table Columns page to specify which of the user attributes are searchable. By default, the following attributes are searchable attributes:

- uid (user ID)
- mail (email address)
- givenname (first name)
- sn (last name)
- title (job title)
- telephonenumber (telephone number)

Configure Roles

The Configure Roles page contains a check box to enable and disable role assignments in the user interface; using roles is a convenient way to define and assign a group of permissions to one or more users. It saves time and reduces errors because you can assign the role to individual users instead of assigning each permission separately to each user.

You can delete existing roles or add a new one on this page. When you click the Finish button, your User Entry changes are saved.

Searching for Users and Groups

To search for a user, start on the page shown in Figure 10.16. Click the Directory tab, and then click the `Users` link on the tab's navigation bar. This is the same page you would use to add a user. To perform a search, enter the search criterion in the Search box and click the Go button. Clicking the `Advanced Search` link gives you the option to search on specific fields within the directory. When you find the user, you can edit the user's characteristics as well as edit, delete, or change the privileges of the user. If the account is locked, you can unlock it.

This is the same as searching and editing a group using the `Groups` link on the navigation bar.

Creating and Maintaining User and Group Entries

To create a user, start on the same page you use to search for a user, but click the Create button. You will see all the fields you defined on the Configure User Attributes page in Figure 10.23; the page is divided into the categories you defined on the Configure Attribute Categories page.

Changing Passwords

You can change your own password by clicking the My Profile tab on the Provisioning Console page. If you are an administrator, you can manage passwords for other users on the user search page.

Assigning Privileges and Roles

Assigning privileges and roles to other users is the basis for DAS: delegating privileges and roles to other users to ease global administration tasks and put the maintenance tasks for groups of users in the hands of local administrators. You can assign the following privileges to a user:

Create Create user entries.

Edit Change user entries.

Delete Delete user entries.

Privileges Assign access rights to users.

Group Create Create groups.

Group Edit Edit groups.

Group Delete Delete a group.

Group Privileges Assign access rights to groups.

Service Management Manage services.

Account Management Enable and disable user accounts.

Allow DAS configuration Allow configuration of user and realm attributes.

You manage privilege assignment by clicking the `Users` or `Groups` link on the Directory tab on the Self-Service Console.

To create a role, first create a group by clicking the `Groups` link on the Directory tab on the Self-Service Console. Click the radio button next to the group you want to edit, and click the Assign Privileges button. In the example shown in Figure 10.24, the DBA group has been selected and now privileges can be assigned to or removed from it.

When you finish the privilege assignment, click the Submit button. To make this group a role, you can add the group to the role in step 5 of the Configure User Entry Template process under the Configuration tab.

FIGURE 10.24 Group privilege assignment page

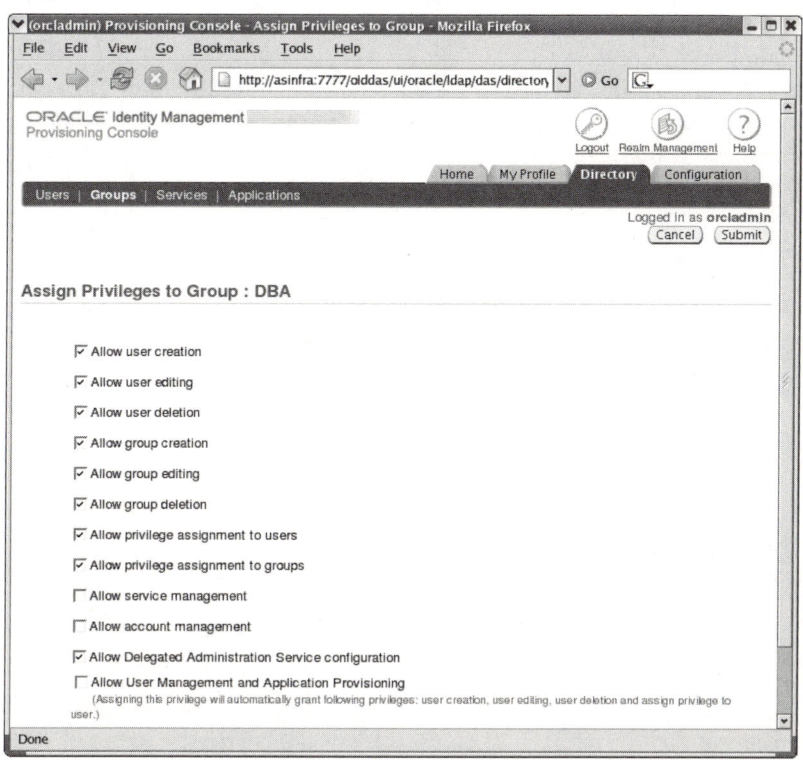

Summary

In the first half of this chapter, we presented an overview of the OracleAS Single Sign-On (SSO) server, starting out with a general description of the SSO architecture and how an OC4J instance manages the core functionality of SSO. You also learned how to use `mod_osso` with HTTP Server to authenticate users via the Web.

As part of the SSO architectural overview, we discussed how client requests for authentication are processed by SSO for both partner applications and external applications and how the logout process differs for these two types of applications.

From an administration point of view, we showed you how to start and stop the SSO server using the command-line interface as well as the familiar AS Control interface. You can start, stop, and restart all components of OracleAS using AS Control; when a web interface is not available, the `opmnctl` command can perform these functions.

Other SSO administrative functions we covered include general SSO configuration, maintaining partner applications, and administering external applications. Finally, we showed you how to monitor the performance of SSO and how to access the SSO server and external applications using OracleAS Portal.

In the second half of the chapter, we introduced Delegated Administration Services (DAS) and explained how this OracleAS component eases your global administrative duties by dividing users into realms and delegating user and group maintenance to local administrators.

First, we presented an overview of the DAS architecture and how DAS uses a proxy feature to improve security in your environment. We showed you some general DAS administrative tasks such as starting and stopping DAS using either AS Control or the `opmnctl` command, which by now should be the most familiar tool in your OracleAS maintenance toolkit!

Next, we introduced the concept of an Identity Management realm and how it helps you to easily categorize user groups for both ease of administration and partitioning of groups with different metadata requirements. We reviewed the details of the default OID realm and showed you how to create and edit a new realm.

Finally, we gave an overview of OID users and groups: how to configure the Self-Service Console web pages for user entries; how to create, edit, and delete users and groups; and how to search for users and groups. We also showed you how roles could make privilege assignments easier and less error prone.

Exam Essentials

Understand the SSO architecture and its components. Be able to identify the core components of SSO and their relationship to Oracle HTTP Server. Describe the relationship between these components and the purpose of the module `mod_osso`.

Describe the authentication flow for SSO. Understand how a client request is processed for both partner applications and external applications. Explain the difference in behavior between a partner application and an external application when a user logs off from each type of application.

Identify and understand the tools you use to administer SSO. Be able to start, stop, and restart SSO using both AS Control and the `opmnctl` command.

Explain the relationship between SSO, partner applications, and external applications. Configure the SSO server, partner applications, and external applications using the AS Control SSO Server Administration page and the URL you use to access these functions. Be able to create, edit, and manage both partner and external applications using other links on the SSO Server Administration page.

Understand the DAS architecture and its components. Explain the different installation options available for DAS. Show the flow of a DAS request from the client to OID and how the proxy feature enhances security.

Be able to create and edit an Identity Management realm. Show how to access the characteristics of the default realm. Add and edit a new realm and be able to access the realm from the Java-based `oidadmin` tool.

Understand the relationship among users, groups, and roles and how to edit each of them. Be able to configure the default template when adding a new user to the directory. Be able to search for a user or group, change the password for a user, and assign privileges and roles to both users and groups.

Review Questions

1. Which of the following is not a Single Sign-On component?
   A. Partner applications
   B. The SSO server
   C. The module `mod_security`
   D. The module `mod_osso`
   E. External applications

2. An application that uses SSO authentication services is known as what kind of application?
   A. An internal application
   B. An authenticated web application
   C. An external application
   D. A partner application

3. An application that does not use SSO authentication services is known as what kind of application?
   A. An internal application
   B. An authenticated web application
   C. An external application
   D. A partner application

4. Which of the following sentences best describes the components that perform authentication and authorization in an OracleAS environment?
   A. SSO authorizes the client, and the external application authenticates the client.
   B. SSO authorizes the client, and the partner application authenticates the client.
   C. `mod_osso` authenticates the client for all external applications.
   D. SSO authenticates the client, and the partner application authorizes the client.

5. After `mod_osso` authenticates a client for a partner application, which of the following values is not transmitted to the partner application for validation purposes? (Choose all that apply.)
   A. The database access descriptor (DAD)
   B. The username
   C. The user distinguished name (DN)
   D. The user globally unique identifier (GUID)
   E. Language and territory information (NLS)
   F. The password

6. To prevent reauthorization with a client every time a client accesses a partner application, `mod_osso` performs which of the following actions the first time it authenticates a client?

   A. `mod_osso` updates every URL request from the client to include authentication information and then redirects to the partner application.

   B. `mod_osso` sends the client's identity to all registered partner applications.

   C. `mod_osso` places the authentication information on the client and places a cookie on the server running SSO.

   D. `mod_osso` places the authentication information into OID and places a cookie on the client.

   E. `mod_osso` sends the client's identity to all registered external applications.

7. Which of the following characteristics is shared by partner applications and external applications?

   A. An external application stores a cookie on the client; the partner application does not.

   B. A partner application stores a cookie on the client; the external application does not.

   C. Authentication information is stored in OID.

   D. Authorization information is stored in OID.

8. Using the `opmnctl` command, which of the following commands will restart the SSO server?

   A. `opmnctl restartproc process-type=OC4J`

   B. `opmnctl restart process-type=OC4J`

   C. `opmnctl restartproc ias-component=OC4J_SECURITY`

   D. `opmnctl restartproc process-type=OC4J`

   E. `opmnctl restartproc process-type=OC4J_SECURITY`

   F. `opmnctl restart ias-component=HTTP_Server`

9. Which of the following is not considered a partner application in the SSO server?

   A. `mod_osso`

   B. DAS

   C. OHS

   D. DAD

10. Place the following six steps in the correct chronological order when authenticating with a partner application:
    1. The SSO server provides a username and password page to the client.
    2. The SSO server redirects the client back to the partner application and passes credentials on to the partner application using an encrypted token.
    3. The SSO server validates the password and sets a cookie on the client browser for the SSO server.
    4. The partner application sets a cookie in the client browser to authenticate the client on subsequent accesses to the application.
    5. A client accesses a partner application using the application's URL.
    6. The partner application redirects the client to the SSO server via `mod_osso`.

    A. 5, 6, 1, 3, 4, 2

    B. 5, 4, 1, 3, 2, 4

    C. 5, 6, 1, 3, 2, 4

    D. 5, 4, 6, 1, 3, 2

11. How do you terminate an SSO session and all partner applications at the same time?

    A. Log out of one of the partner applications.

    B. Log out of all partner applications, and then log out of OracleAS Portal.

    C. Log out of all partner applications and you are automatically logged out of OracleAS Portal as well.

    D. Log out of any partner application or external application.

    E. Log out of all external and partner applications.

12. Which of the following best describes how SSO stores usernames and passwords?

    A. SSO does not store usernames and passwords; it only provides a common interface for all partner applications and external applications.

    B. SSO stores the username and password for external applications only.

    C. SSO stores the username and password for partner applications only; usernames and passwords for external applications must reside in a cookie on the client machine.

    D. SSO stores usernames and passwords for access to partner applications and all external applications in OID.

    E. SSO stores the username and password for partner applications only; usernames and passwords for external applications must reside in a cookie on the SSO server host.

13. Which of the following methods is not used to authenticate with an external application after a user authenticates with the SSO server and connects to the external application?

A. `PUT`

B. `GET`

C. `POST`

D. `BASIC AUTHENTICATION`

14. Which of the following is not available from the SSO Server Administration page?

A. Administer External Applications

B. Edit SSO Server Configuration

C. Administer Partner Applications

D. SSO Session Policy

15. Which of the following values is not valid for the `-update_mode` parameter of the `ssoreg.sh` script?

A. `CREATE`

B. `MODIFY`

C. `DELETE`

D. `VIEW`

16. Place the following seven steps in the order in which they would occur when a client performs an administrative request through DAS:

1. DAS combines the LDAP results into an HTML page and returns the results to the client.
2. If the client has never accessed DAS, `mod_osso` transparently redirects the client to the SSO server for authentication.
3. The DAS service logs in with OID as a proxy user with the privileges to switch identities and connects to OID again with the distinguished name (DN) of the user making the request.
4. The client accesses DAS using the `mod_osso` module with OHS.
5. If the credentials are valid, `mod_osso` redirects the client to DAS.
6. The SSO server verifies the credentials with those in OID.
7. The SSO server prompts the user for a username and password if the user has not yet authenticated with the SSO server or the session has timed out.

   A. 4, 2, 7, 6, 5, 1, 3

   B. 7, 4, 2, 6, 5, 1, 3

   C. 4, 2, 7, 6, 5, 3, 1

   D. 7, 4, 2, 6, 5, 3, 1

17. Using the `opmnctl` command, which of the following commands will restart the DAS server?
    A. `opmnctl restartproc process-type=OC4J`
    B. `opmnctl restart process-type=OC4J`
    C. `opmnctl restartproc ias-component=OC4J_SECURITY`
    D. `opmnctl restartproc process-type=OC4J_SECURITY`
    E. `opmnctl restartproc process-type=OC4J`
    F. `opmnctl restart ias-component=HTTP_Server`

18. To check the status of DAS using the Unix command line, you use the ________ command and pipe it to the ________ command to search for the strings ________ and ________.
    A. `egrep`, `ps`, `http`, `java`
    B. `opmnctl`, `egrep`, `http`, `java`
    C. `ssoreg.sh`, `egrep`, `http`, `java`
    D. `ps`, `egrep`, `http`, `java`
    E. `ps`, `egrep`, `http`, `oc4j`
    F. `ps`, `egrep`, `oc4j`, `java`

19. You create a new realm called `ms_exchange`. What are the default users stored in this realm?
    A. `cn=users, dc=ms_exchange, dc=com`
    B. `cn=groups, dc=ms_exchange, dc=com`
    C. `cn=users, dc=dba, dc=com`
    D. `cn=users, dc=ms_exchange, dc=asinfra, dc=com`
    E. `cn=users, dc=asinfra, dc=com`

20. Which of the following is not one of the default searchable attributes in the Self-Service Console?
    A. First name
    B. Email address
    C. Telephone number
    D. Mailing address
    E. Last name

Answers to Review Questions

1. C. The module `mod_security` is a component available in OracleAS but is not considered a component of SSO.

2. D. A partner application uses SSO to perform authentication before the user can use the application.

3. C. An external application does not delegate authentication duties to SSO; however, SSO can store the username and password required by the external application's HTML login form.

4. D. Authentication determines who the client is, and authorization determines if the client has the appropriate privileges to access the application.

5. A, F. SSO does not send the database access descriptor to the partner application as part of an authentication request; the password is not required because the client is already authenticated by the time SSO sends the username to the partner application.

6. D. The first time the client authenticates with SSO, SSO places a cookie on the client machine to prevent client reauthorization.

7. C. Whether the application is a partner application or an external application, SSO stores the username and password in OID. SSO stores a single username and password for all partner applications and one username and password for each registered external application.

8. E. You use the `restartproc` option to restart a component, and the `process-type` option must be `OC4J_SECURITY`; the `process-type` parameter value is case sensitive.

9. D. DAD, or database access descriptor, is not an application but information required by SSO to connect to a database repository.

10. C. After authenticating with the SSO server, the client is automatically authenticated with all other partner applications that have delegated their validation to the SSO server.

11. A. After you log out of one of the partner applications, SSO automatically logs you out of all partner applications.

12. D. SSO stores a username and password in encrypted form for access to any and all partner applications and a single username and password for each registered external application.

13. A. The SSO server can use `POST`, `GET`, or `BASIC AUTHENTICATION` to validate the user with the external application. `PUT` is a valid HTTP method, but the SSO server does not use it to authenticate with external applications.

14. D. The SSO Server Administration page contains three links: Edit SSO Server Configuration, Administer Partner Applications, and Administer External Applications. The SSO Session Policy page is available after you click the `Edit SSO Server Configuration` link.

15. D. `VIEW` is not a valid value for the `-update_mode` parameter of `ssoreg.sh`.

16. C. DAS performs these steps both for a stand-alone DAS installation and as part of an OracleAS infrastructure installation.

17. D. You use the `restartproc` option to restart the DAS service, and the `process-type` option must be `OC4J_SECURITY`; the `process-type` parameter value is case sensitive.

18. D. You can also use the Unix `grep` or `fgrep` commands; however, this will increase the number of commands you must run to check the status of DAS.

19. A. When you create a new user in this realm, the user entries are stored in the domain with a common name (`cn`) of `users` and domain components (`dc`) `ms_exchange` and `com`.

20. D. The default searchable attributes are user ID, email address, first name, last name, job title, and telephone number.

Configuring the *mod_rewrite* Routine

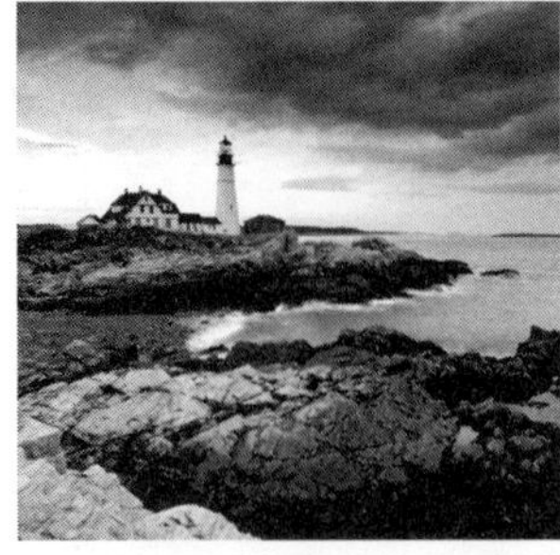

In Chapter 4, "Performing HTTP Server Configuration and Management Tasks," we showed you how to load and configure the OHS module `mod_security` to enhance the security of your application server environment by filtering cross-site scripting and SQL insertion attacks at the point of entry. Another module you will most likely customize for your environment is the module `mod_rewrite`; with this module, you can rewrite any URL request on-the-fly based on several types of conditions and rules.

Think of the advantages to the user: They can use the same URL to request an application server resource while the web server delivers a different result depending on the time of day, inventory levels in a database, or server environment variables. The user needs to remember only one URL.

In the following sections, we'll show you how to enable and configure `mod_rewrite` on your server. Before we dive into `mod_rewrite`, however, we'll give you a brief overview of Unix regular expressions—they are the key to successfully configuring `mod_rewrite`.

Understanding Unix Regular Expressions

In Chapter 4, we used file patterns as part of many different directives, such as `DirectoryMatch` and `FilesMatch`, to specify a group of files to which the directive applies. This file pattern or template is known as a *regular expression*, commonly abbreviated as *regex*. A regular expression matches a set of strings according to a set of syntax rules that we will describe in the following sections. Regular expressions are not just for HTTP Server; they are used throughout the Unix world in text editors, programming languages, and virtually every Unix utility that supports a way to specify a set of strings that matches the regular expression.

Within `mod_rewrite`, you will use regular expressions to specify which URLs requested by the client will be rewritten to request a document or service from a different location. All URLs that do not match the regular expression within a directive will be processed with no modifications.

Matching Characters and Metacharacters

At the lowest level of regular expressions are the characters that make up the regular expression; most characters match themselves. For example, if you specified `Oracle` as your regular expression, it will match any other string as long as it is `Oracle`. In other words, specifying a string without any *metacharacters*, which are characters that match something other than the character itself, doesn't leverage the power of the regular expression engine.

Regular expressions are case sensitive; you must take into account any white space characters, such as spaces, tabs, and newlines, when you want to match a regular expression.

The most commonly used metacharacters are the . (dot), [ ] (brackets), - (dash), ^ (caret), and $ (dollar sign).

. (dot)

The . matches any single character. Therefore, the pattern

```
Sm.th.
```

matches the strings `Smythe`, `Smithe`, and `Smithy` but not `Smith`.

[ ] (brackets) and - (dash)

Specifying one or more characters within a pair of brackets will match any character within the brackets; the list of characters within brackets is called a *class*. If you specify the pattern

```
Srvr[1234789]
```

it matches the strings `Srvr1`, `Srvr8`, and `Srvr3` but not `Srvr0`.

The ^ symbol used inside of the brackets (not to be confused with the use of the ^ with $ discussed in the next section) negates the list of characters within the brackets; in other words, if your pattern is

```
Srvr[^1234789]
```

it matches `Srvr5`, `SrvrX`, `Srvr0`, and `SrvrZ`. In fact, it matches every string that contains `Srvr` plus one character except for `Srvr1`, `Srvr2`, `Srvr3`, `Srvr4`, `Srvr7`, `Srvr8`, and `Srvr9`.

Note that any other metacharacters other than - and ^ within a class are treated as literals instead of metacharacters; for example, the pattern

```
The End[.?!]
```

matches only these three strings:

```
The End.
The End?
The End!
```

If you want to test out your pattern quickly and easily at the Unix command line, just type the command **`grep`** `'<pattern>'`. After you press the Enter key, any strings you type that match the pattern will be echoed and the strings that don't match will not.

The - character makes it easier to specify one or more ranges of values within a class. In the earlier example, instead of specifying

```
Srvr[1234789]
```

you can instead specify

```
Srvr[1-47-9]
```

to save keystrokes and make the pattern more readable. To match the string bkup plus any single character or digit, regardless of case, specify

```
bkup[a-zA-Z0-9]
```

^ (caret) and $ (dollar sign)

The ^ and $ characters are metacharacters that mark the beginning and end of a line, respectively; they are known as regular expression *anchors*. They ensure that the regular expression matches at the beginning of the line, the end of the line, or both. For example, To ensure that a regular expression matches any line that begins with Oracle, you use this:

```
^Oracle
```

To search for Oracle at the end of a line, use this instead:

```
Oracle$
```

If you want to match lines that contain Oracle Rocks and nothing else, you use this regular expression:

```
^Oracle Rocks$
```

To include one of these characters literally, you need to use an escape character; we will explain escape characters later in this appendix.

Alternating Text

Another useful tool available when you construct regular expressions is the *alternating text* construct: parentheses ( ) and the pipe character |. The | gives you the option to specify one or more alternatives in the regular expression. Let's say you want to search for lines that contain Tuesday or Thursday or Friday. Instead of specifying three separate regular expressions, you can use a single regular expression as follows:

```
(Tuesday|Thursday|Friday)
```

Character Quantifiers

In many cases, you want to specify a regular expression that matches zero, one, or more than one occurrence of a single character. You use ?, +, or * for these situations.

The ? character matches zero or one instances of a character. Therefore, the regular expression `Smithe?` matches either `Smith` or `Smithe`.

The + character, on the other hand, matches one or more instances of a character. You use it when you're sure that there is at least one character you're looking for that may repeat in the target string. Using the regular expression

```
Normal+
```

the following lines match

```
Normally, a price-conscious shop will choose open source software.
Normal operating procedures dictate frequent database backups.
```

but not

```
Goodbye Norma Jean is a popular Elton John song.
```

Finally, the * character matches zero or more characters. The characters you are searching for in a string may not appear at all, may appear once, or may appear many times in a row. Given the regular expression

```
Gr*eat
```

both of the following lines match:

```
Tony the Tiger says that Sugar Frosted Flakes are Grrrrrrreat!
Beowulf was a Geat: a Scandinavian people from southern Sweden.
```

Escape Characters

You may be curious by now as to how you can specify in a search string a character that normally operates as a metacharacter. You use an *escape character*. An escape character changes the meaning of the character that follows it, treating it as a single character you are searching for instead of as a metacharacter. The default escape character is the metacharacter \, or backslash.

You use the \ primarily to specify a character in a regular expression that would normally be interpreted as a metacharacter: ^, $, ., +, *, ?, (,), and so forth. In this example, if you want to create a regular expression that matches simple arithmetic expressions with two operands for multiplication and addition, you can use this:

```
[0-9] (\*|\+) [0-9]
```

Without the escape character in front of * and +, the regular expression is invalid because the regular expression tries to match the (character with the *, and therefore the closing) character is unmatched.

You can also use the \ with another character to represent a longer sequence, usually a class. Here are the escaped letters that represent white space in a line or document:

\t Tab character

\n Newline

\r Carriage return

\f Form feed

\v Vertical tab

\e Escape

\b Backspace

Finally, here are the most common escaped characters with the equivalent class; it's an easy way to save a lot of typing:

\d Matches any digit, equivalent to `[0-9]`

\D Matches anything but a digit, equivalent to `[^0-9]`

\s Matches any white space character, equivalent to `[\t\n\r\f\v]`

\S Matches any non-white-space character, equivalent to `[^\t\n\r\f\v]`

\w Matches any alphanumeric character, equivalent to `[a-zA-Z0-9_]`

\W Matches any non-alphanumeric character, equivalent to `[^a-zA-Z0-9_]`

You can place these sequences within a class, effectively nesting a class definition.

Configuring and Using *mod_rewrite*

Now that you have a better grasp of how regular expressions work, you will be able to configure `mod_rewrite` with confidence, because the cornerstone of `mod_rewrite` is to match an incoming URL request and rewrite that URL.

In the following sections, we'll tell you more about how `mod_rewrite` works and the directives used with `mod_rewrite` and give you some usage examples.

Overview of *mod_rewrite*

The Apache server processes HTTP requests in phases; any module built for Apache can hook in and perform some kind of processing for each phase. `mod_rewrite` uses two of these phases:

URL to filename translation Occurs after the HTTP request is received but before authorization has been performed

Fixup hook Occurs after the authorization phase and after any `.htaccess` files are read

`mod_rewrite` reads the rule sets defined at startup and dynamically from each `.htaccess` file. `mod_rewrite` then uses any `RewriteRule` directives found and checks the conditions found in each `RewriteCond` directive after each `RewriteRule` and changes the URL if the requested URL matches the condition. A URL may be changed several times by several different rules before the HTTP server delivers content.

We present the `RewriteRule` and `RewriteCond` directives, along with other related directives, in the next section.

mod_rewrite Directives

The primary directives you use with mod_rewrite are RewriteEngine, RewriteOptions, RewriteLog, RewriteBase, RewriteCond, and RewriteRule. Typically, you specify RewriteEngine, RewriteOptions, RewriteLog, and RewriteBase once in the server configuration file (httpd.conf), directory configuration file (.htaccess), or virtual host section. The RewriteCond and RewriteRule directives appear at least once and often many times in each configuration file depending on the complexity of your site's content structure and security requirements.

RewriteEngine

You use the RewriteEngine directive to turn on or off mod_rewrite processing. You can use RewriteEngine in the main server configuration file, a virtual host section, a directory directive block, or any .htaccess file. By default, RewriteEngine is off. This directive makes it easy to turn on or off all other RewriteCond or RewriteRule directives without commenting out each individually. Here is how you enable RewriteEngine:

```
RewriteEngine on
```

RewriteOptions

The RewriteOptions directive controls mod_rewrite inheritance and the maximum number of redirects. You can specify the RewriteOptions directive in the main server configuration, a virtual host, a directory directive block, or any .htaccess file. The two options to the RewriteOptions directive are inherit and MaxRedirects.

The inherit option, as the name implies, inherits the mod_rewrite options using the directive inheritance rules for any server directive. A virtual server inherits the settings for the main server, and in a per-directory context, the parent directory's settings in .htaccess are inherited. Here is an example of the inherit option:

```
RewriteOptions inherit
```

The MaxRedirects option specifies the number of redirects that occur for a given URL, usually to prevent endless looping when multiple redirects cycle through to the same URL more than once. The default value is 10; this is sufficient in all but the most complex URL rewrite scenarios. In this example, you specify a maximum of 15 redirects:

```
RewriteOptions MaxRedirects=15
```

RewriteLog

The RewriteLog directive specifies where mod_rewrite sends the log entries for rewriting actions. If the specified path does not begin with /, it is relative to the server root. In this example, you send the log entries to /usr/admin/logs/OHS/rw.log:

```
RewriteLog /usr/admin/logs/OHS/rw.log
```

RewriteBase

You use the RewriteBase directive to explicitly set the base URL for per-directory rewrites. As you might expect, this directive is only allowed in a directory directive or a .htaccess file. If the URLs on your web server are not directly related to physical file paths, you must specify RewriteBase with RewriteRule in every .htaccess file.

In this example, you have a .htaccess file in the directory /u09/HumanResources, but the URL the users will use ends with /EmployeeServices. You also want to redirect requests to the document le_emp.html to sh_emp.html instead. Here are the directives you need in .htaccess:

```
RewriteEngine On
RewriteBase /EmployeeServices
RewriteRule ^le_emp\.html$ sh_emp.html
```

As a result, a request to the document /EmployeeServices/le_emp.html will be rewritten as /u09/HumanResources/sh_emp.html.

We will explain how to use RewriteRule shortly.

RewriteCond

The RewriteCond directive defines a condition that must be satisfied before mod_rewrite considers a rewrite rule. (We will explain the RewriteRule directive in the next section.) All conditions that precede a rewrite rule must be true for the rewrite rule to be evaluated; once all conditions are true, the rewrite rule is evaluated and all other rewrite conditions are skipped.

Here is a pair of rewrite conditions that both must evaluate to true before the rewrite rule is evaluated:

```
RewriteCond %{TIME_HOUR}%{TIME_MIN} >0700
RewriteCond %{TIME_HOUR}%{TIME_MIN} <1700
RewriteRule . . .
```

Both of the rewrite conditions use system variables, enclosed with %{ }, that in this case evaluate to the time of day (hour and minute in 24-hour format). In this case, if the URL request occurs after 7:00 AM and before 5:00 PM, the subsequent rewrite rule is evaluated.

RewriteRule

The RewriteRule directive uses a regular expression to perform a URL rewrite if the preceding RewriteCond directives have all evaluated to true. If there are no RewriteCond directives, the RewriteRule directive is always evaluated and mod_rewrite performs the substitution if the URL matches the specified regular expression.

In this example, you have moved the target resources to a different directory (or it could even be a different website!); you don't want to require users to use a different URL, so you rewrite the requested URL to access a different directory:

```
RewriteRule ^/shirt_promo(.*)$ /oxford_promo/$1
```

A bit of explanation is required here; however, you've seen most of these constructs already. The only thing new here is the ( ) construct; whatever the user specifies in this part of the URL is carried over to the substitution string where you see $1; if you have a second ( ) construct, you use $2 in the substitution string, and so on.

To expand on the example in the previous section, we want to send all users who request helpdesk_staff.html to helpdesk_core_staff.html during daytime hours and to helpdesk_notcore_staff.html outside of core business hours.

```
RewriteCond %{TIME_HOUR}%{TIME_MIN} >1700 [OR]
RewriteCond %{TIME_HOUR}%{TIME_MIN} <0700
RewriteRule ^helpdesk_staff\.html$ helpdesk_notcore_staff.html

RewriteRule ^helpdesk_staff\.html$ helpdesk_core_staff.html
```

If, for example, it is 8:30 PM (after 5:00 PM), the first rewrite condition is true, the first rewrite rule is used, and the second rewrite rule is skipped. If it is 4:00 AM, the second rewrite condition is true instead, and again the first rewrite rule is used and the second rewrite rule is skipped. In the third scenario, if it is between 7:00 AM and 5:00 PM, both rewrite conditions are false, the first rewrite rule is skipped, and the second rewrite rule is evaluated instead.

Note the use of the [OR] construct: By default, all of the rewrite conditions preceding a rewrite rule must be true before a rewrite rule is used.

Appendix B

New Features in Release 2

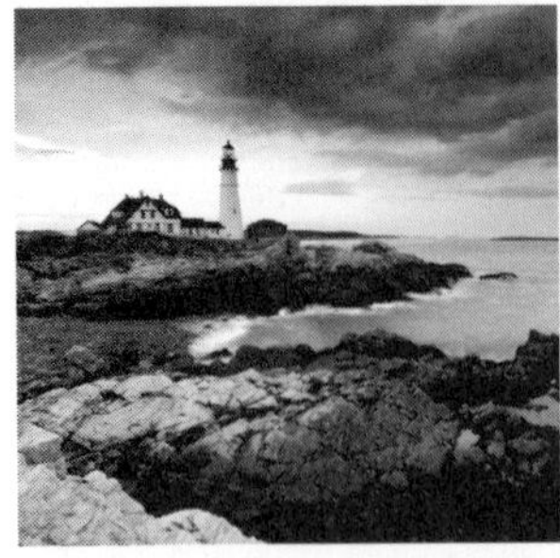

Oracle Application Server 10*g* Release 2 (10.1.2) contains many significant new features over Oracle Application Server 10*g* Release 1 (9.0.4). In the following sections, we'll give an overview of the improvements in Release 2; if you have experience with Release 1 or any previous releases, this appendix will provide you with a good starting point in the main part of the book if you want to focus on the new features.

Two of the biggest improvements are in the areas of database infrastructure and backup and recovery; we'll also cover some improvements in port number assignments, SSL tools, and Application Server Control.

Database Support

If you manage an installation of Oracle Application Server 10*g* Release 1, you were probably surprised that the database version installed with Application Server 10*g* Release 1 is Oracle Database 9*i* Release 1 (9.0.*x*.*x*). This can be disconcerting considering that it is several versions behind the most recent release, Oracle Database 10*g* Release 2. In most environments, you want to ideally support only one database release, usually the latest or most stable. It is rare that you will find an environment that still uses Oracle Database version 9.0.x.x; if you are not yet at 10*g* Release 2, most environments are using version 9*i* Release 2 (9.2.*x*.*x*).

To make matters worse, Oracle only supports Oracle Database 9*i* Release 1 as part of an Oracle Application Server 10*g* Release 1 installation. Even with Oracle support, you still have to maintain another version of Oracle Database in your environment.

Oracle Application Server 10*g* Release 2 remedies these problems to a certain degree; a default installation of Release 2 installs Oracle Database 10*g* Release 1 (10.1). Although it is not the most recent release of Oracle Database 10*g*, it has most of the key features of Oracle Database 10*g* Release 2, such as automatic statistics collection via the Automatic Workload Repository (AWR), flashback features, and Automatic Storage Management (ASM).

Even if you are still using Oracle Application Server 10*g* Release 1, you have the option to migrate your database repository to a later version of Oracle Database; in Appendix C, we'll show you how to migrate your application server's database repository to an Oracle 10*g* Release 2 Real Application Clusters (RAC) database.

Along with Oracle Database 10*g* Release 1, you automatically get an installation of Oracle Enterprise Manager 10*g* Database Control to monitor and manage your infrastructure's database instance. Between Database Control and Application Server Control, you have a complete GUI solution for monitoring and managing your OracleAS environment.

Backup and Recovery

Backup and recovery of your application server instances just got easier with Oracle Application Server 10*g* Release 2. You can use Application Server Control to manage every aspect of instance backup and recovery, including the database repository instance. In previous versions of Oracle Application Server, you had to use a variety of nonintuitive command-line procedures to back up your entire application server environment. We'll present the other improvements to AS Control later in this appendix.

If your installation includes an OracleAS Portal installation, you can optionally use a new utility called the Portal Schema Validation/Cleanup Utility (Portal SVU), which performs additional integrity checks on the Portal database tables when backing up the instance.

Another availability enhancement to Oracle Application Server 10*g* Release 2 is an automatic recovery service: When the instance host fails, the automatic recovery service restores the instance to a new host. We will cover this scenario along with other backup and recovery scenarios in Appendix D.

Application Server Control

In addition to the backup and recovery features mentioned in the previous section, there are quite a few improvements and enhancements to Application Server Control (AS Control). These improvements include a topology viewer, performance metrics, and port management.

Topology Viewer

We covered Topology Viewer in Chapter 3. It's a great way to see a graphical, real-time view of the entire OracleAS environment, complete with drill-down capabilities and statistics for each node. Not only can you view the topology, but you also can click on each node to start, stop, or restart a component or node. The Topology Viewer lets you see the relationships between OracleAS components that would be hard or difficult to imply by looking at text-based configuration files and directory structures.

Configuring a File-Based Repository

If you use a file-based repository instead of a database-based repository, you can view, re-create, or reconfigure the repository using a web-based wizard.

Performance Metrics

Performance metrics are available in a web interface for all components in a Middle-tier or an Infrastructure installation. For each real-time component statistic, you can drill down to see historical component statistics.

Web Cache Administration

In previous versions of OracleAS, you used OracleAS Web Cache Manager to monitor and control the OracleAS Web Cache component; in Release 2, it is now fully integrated and managed with all other components within AS Control. If you have a stand-alone installation of Web Cache with no AS Control installation, you still have the `webcachectl` administrative tool.

Miscellaneous Changes

Here are a few more enhancements that make it easier to use and manage Oracle Application Server 10*g* and to coexist with other applications on both Windows and Linux environments.

Port Number Assignments

If you use a previous version of OracleAS under Windows, temporary port number assignments by the Windows OS may cause a conflict with the default port numbers and ranges for some components of OracleAS. As a result, the default port numbers and ranges have been changed for the AS Control console, OracleAS Web Cache, OracleAS Integration B2B, Oracle Containers for J2EE (OC4J), Oracle Internet Directory (OID), and OracleAS Certificate Authority (OCA).

SSL Configuration

Distributed computing resources and a widely distributed user base require enhanced network security beyond the host system. As a result, you are highly encouraged to use Secure Sockets Layer (SSL) for all communication between components, servers, and users. However, configuring SSL in previous releases of OracleAS was tedious and error prone. In Release 2, you run the new SSL Configuration Tool Wizard after a successful Infrastructure and Middle-tier installation to configure SSL security.

Migrating Applications from Test to Production

After successfully developing an application, most developers dread the process of deploying it (and its associated data) to a production environment. Even after the application is in production, there will be inevitable bugs in the application or changes in requirements that make it necessary to perform another round of time-consuming and error-prone steps to implement the changes from the test environment to the production environment.

For example, to deploy changes in an OracleAS Portal test instance to production, you export the changed objects to a transport set using a wizard-based command-line script, transfer the object set to the production environment with your favorite file transfer utility, and import the changed objects with another easy to use wizard-based command-line script.

Updating a J2EE application in production from a test environment is even easier: You can use the `dcmctl redeployApplication` command or use the Applications tab on an OC4J home page to redeploy the Enterprise Archive (EAR) file.

Cloning Application Server Instances

To make it easier to ensure high availability in your Application Server environment, you can easily clone the following components of an installation to another server:

- Portal and Wireless
- Business Intelligence
- J2EE and Web Cache

Although the cloning process still uses a command-line interface, it generates the scripts that automate most of the tasks required to clone the component.

Creating an OracleAS Repository

Oracle Application Server 10*g* (OracleAS) provides many levels of redundancy to ensure high availability and failover in your environment. It's easy to create and cluster additional instances of Web Cache, Oracle HTTP Server (OHS), and OC4J; however, the Oracle Universal Installer (OUI) installs a single instance of Oracle Database 10*g* Release 1 in a default OracleAS installation. Even with clustered instances of all other components in your OracleAS environment, your high availability is at risk if you do not have redundancy at the database tier.

In this appendix, we will show you the required steps to create the schemas for an OracleAS database infrastructure in a Real Application Clusters (RAC) database using the Repository Creation Assistant (RepCA). You can use the same procedure against any 9*i* or 10*g* single-instance database as well. The repository you create using this tool can be the repository database for a new installation of OracleAS; you can also use this repository to migrate the contents of the repository from an existing OracleAS installation. This appendix will cover the steps required for a new OracleAS installation. Here are the other functions of the Repository Creation Assistant:

- Registering an OracleAS Metadata Repository with Oracle Internet Directory
- Removing the Metadata Repository schemas and tablespaces from a database
- Deregistering a Metadata Repository from Oracle Internet Directory

Follow these steps to create a starter repository in a database before you install OracleAS:

1. Review and confirm preinstallation requirements.
2. Install the Repository Creation Assistant tool from the Oracle Database 10*g* Companion CD.
3. Run the RepCA tool to create the infrastructure in an RAC database.

Confirming Preinstallation Requirements

Your existing database installation must fulfill two general prerequisites before you can create an OracleAS repository. First, you must ensure that you have Oracle Ultra Search installed. Second, you need to ensure that several system parameters and tablespace sizes have been set to the minimum values to support a repository installation.

Oracle Ultra Search and User Accounts

Before installing the Repository Creation Assistant, you must have Ultra Search installed in your database. If you do not have it installed, you can get it from the Oracle Database 10*g* Companion CD for Linux at the following URL:

```
http://www.oracle.com/technology/software/products
➥     /database/oracle10g/htdocs/10201linuxsoft.html
```

An Oracle Ultra Search installation creates two user accounts: WKSYS and WKPROXY. The installer for the Repository Creation Assistant will fail if either of these accounts does not exist.

System Parameters

Your target database must have minimum values for six system parameters. Table C.1 shows the system parameters and their minimum values.

TABLE C.1 System Parameters Minimum Requirements

Parameter Name	Minimum Value
SGA_TARGET	600MB
DB_CACHE_SIZE	144MB
SHARED_POOL_SIZE	175MB
JAVA_POOL_SIZE	120MB
PGA_AGGREGATE_TARGET	96MB
SESSIONS	400

Here is the command you use to change the DB_CACHE_SIZE parameter:

```
SQL> alter system set db_cache_size=144m scope=spfile;

System altered.
```

As of Oracle Database 10*g*, setting SGA_TARGET enables Automatic Shared Memory Management (ASMM) to automatically size DB_CACHE_SIZE, SHARED_POOL_SIZE, and JAVA_POOL_SIZE as needed depending on the current database activity; specifying an explicit value for these three parameters does not invalidate the automatic sizing but it does set minimum values for those parameters.

Tablespace Free Space

The Oracle Universal Installer for the Repository Creation Assistant requires an additional 350MB of free space in the SYSTEM and UNDO tablespaces. If you are using Automatic Storage Management (ASM), you can extend the size of these tablespaces by adding a new data file for each tablespace in the DATA disk group using the following commands:

```
SQL> alter tablespace system add datafile '+DATA' size 350m;

Tablespace altered.

SQL> alter tablespace undotbs1 add datafile '+DATA' size 350m;

Tablespace altered.

SQL>
```

Installing the Repository Creation Assistant

The installation CD for the OracleAS Repository Creation Assistant is available as a separate download from the other OracleAS components at this URL:

`http://www.oracle.com/technology/software/products/ias/htdocs/101202.html`

From the root directory of the CD, run the command `runInstaller` and you will see the typical OUI window shown in Figure C.1.

Click Next, and specify the location for the installation files, the name for the RepCA home directory, and the home directory for the RepCA tool itself in the screen shown in Figure C.2.

The source directory defaults to the location of `runInstaller` on the CD; specify a name and location of the home directory for RepCA that follows the naming convention for other Oracle products on your server. When you click Next on the screen shown in Figure C.2, OUI checks for minimum system requirements, such as operating system version, memory, and minimum package versions. If any of the checks fail, correct the problem, select the corresponding check box, and click the Next button shown in Figure C.3.

FIGURE C.1 The initial OUI window

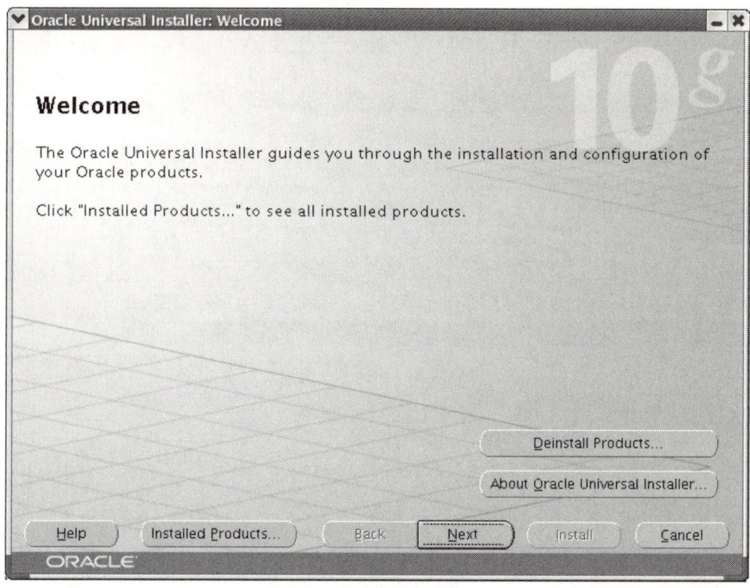

FIGURE C.2 Specifying the RepCA source and destination directories

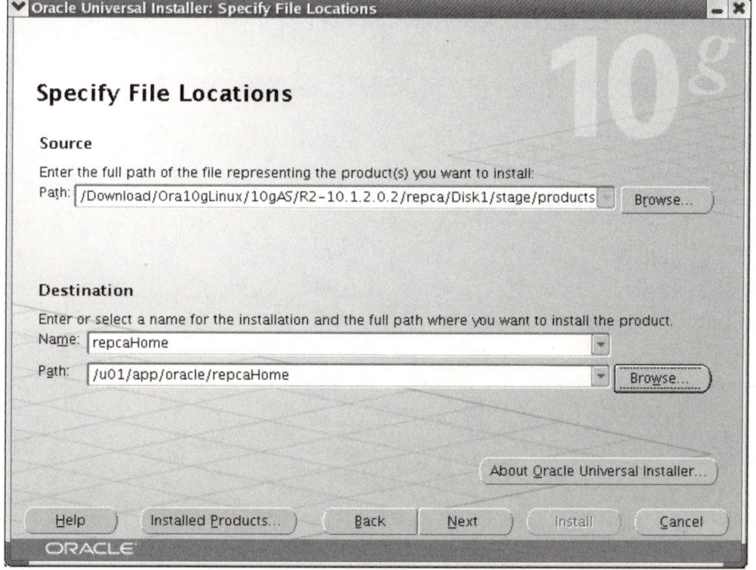

In the screen shown in Figure C.4, you select the additional language support you require; by default, English is selected. Click the Next button to continue.

FIGURE C.3 OUI product-specific prerequisite checks

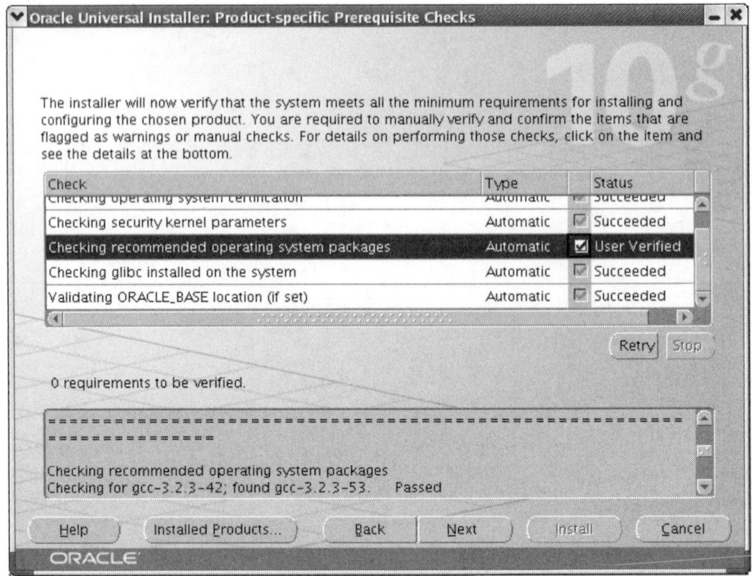

FIGURE C.4 Specifying additional language support

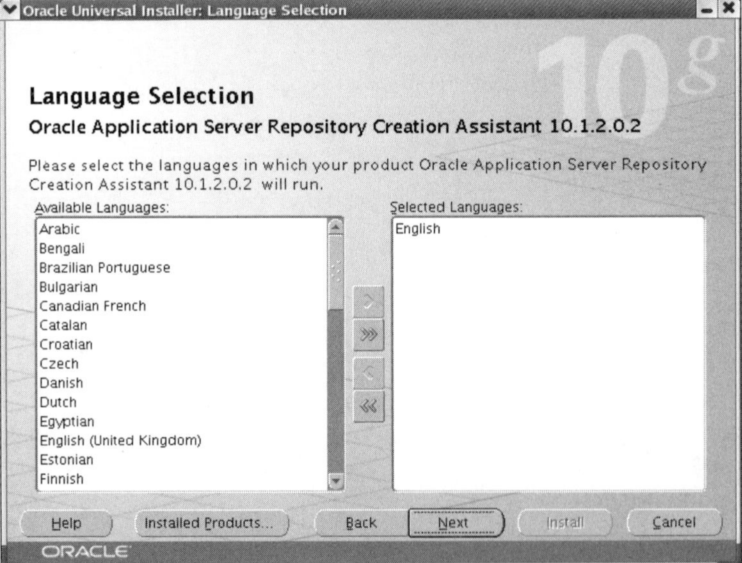

In the screen shown in Figure C.5, you have the option to launch RepCA automatically after installation is complete. To launch it manually, run the script `runRepca` in the Repository Creation Assistant home directory.

After you click Next in the screen in Figure C.5, you will see the installation options summary screen shown in Figure C.6. Click the Install button to proceed with the installation. Figure C.7 shows the installation in progress.

FIGURE C.5 RepCA auto-launch option

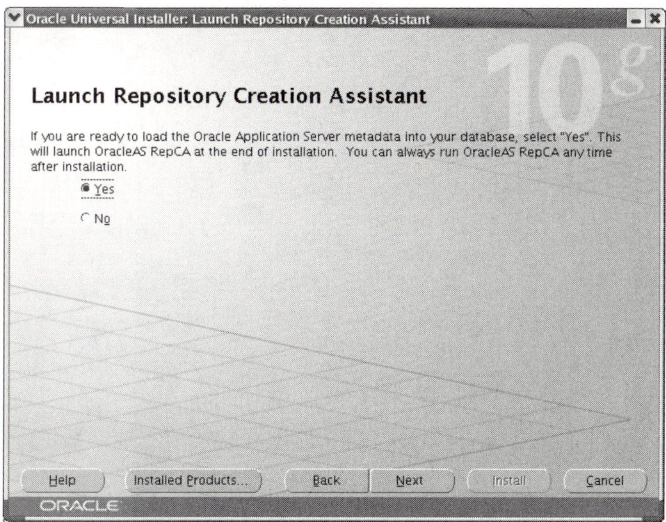

FIGURE C.6 Installation options summary window

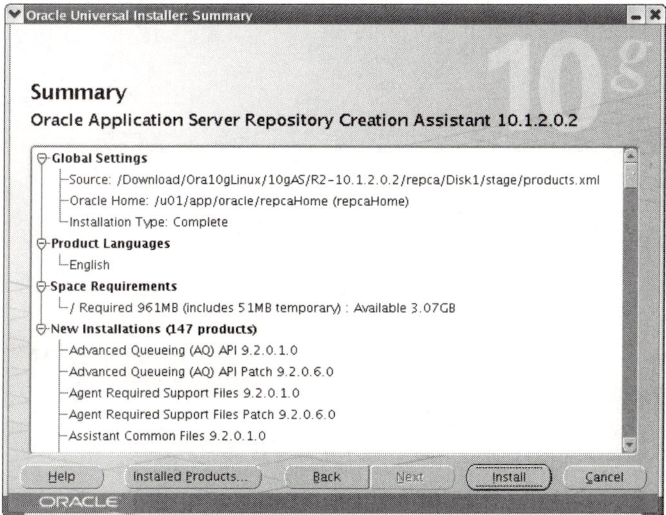

If you specified auto-launch in the installation options summary window, you will see the Configuration Assistants window shown in Figure C.8 and RepCA will launch in a new window.

FIGURE C.7 Installation in progress

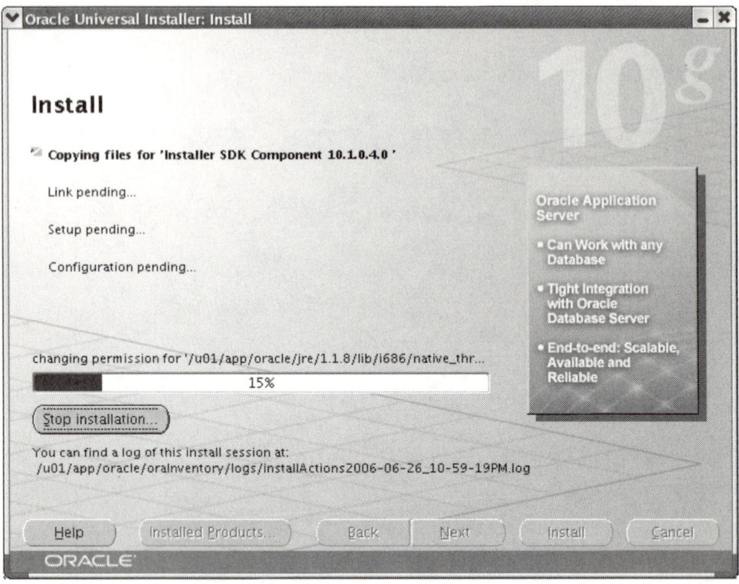

FIGURE C.8 Configuration Assistants window

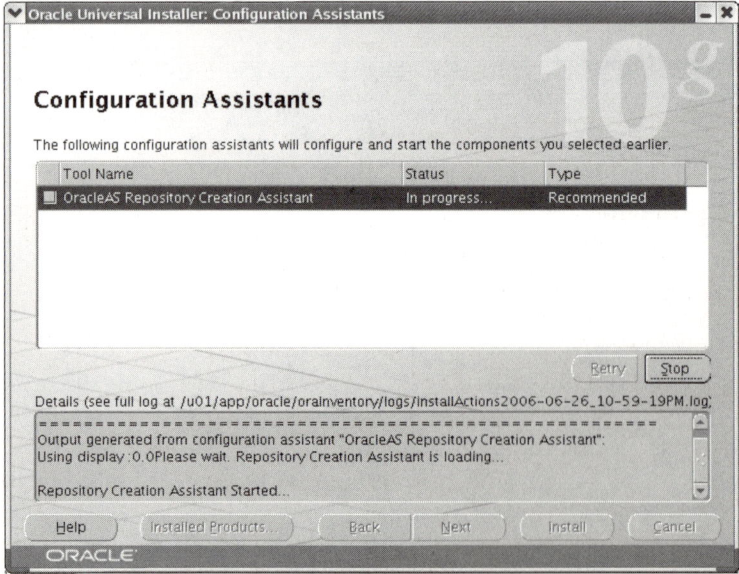

Running RepCA

Whether you launched RepCA automatically after the installation is complete or manually, you will see the window shown in Figure C.9.

Click the Next button to specify the path for your Oracle Database 10*g* home directory (`$ORACLE_HOME`) as well as a directory for log files created during this RepCA session. Figure C.10 shows the Home Path window.

FIGURE C.9 RepCA splash window

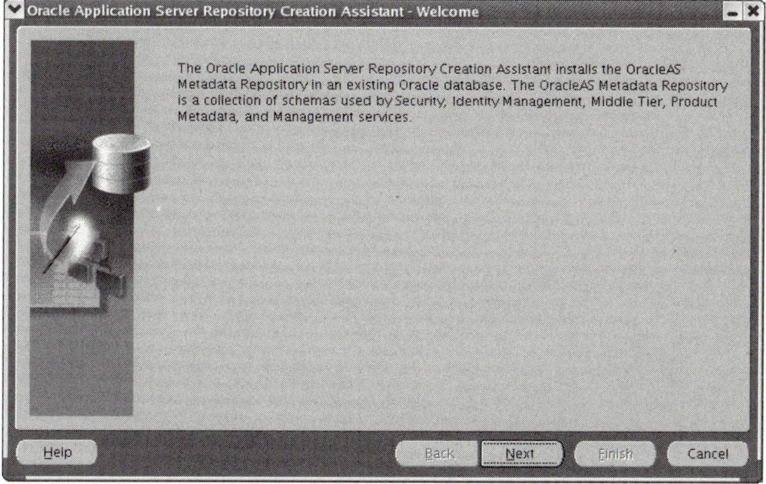

FIGURE C.10 RepCA Home Path window

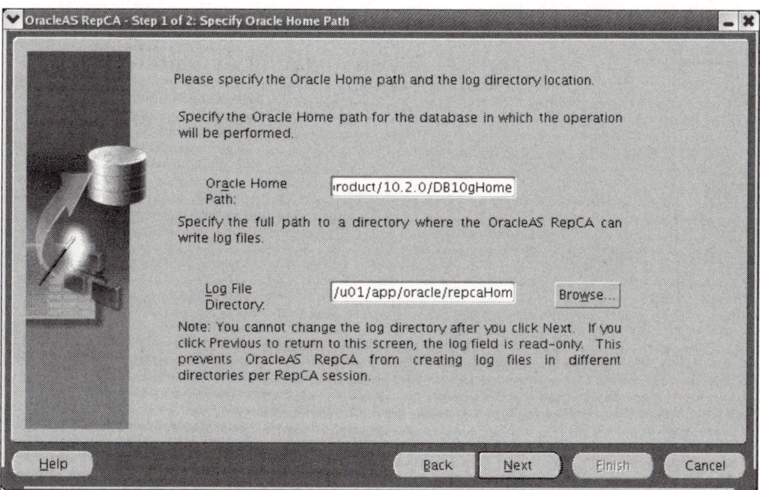

Clicking the Next button shows you the four possible RepCA functions in Figure C.11:

- Load OracleAS Metadata Repository schemas into a database
- Register the OracleAS Metadata Repository with OID
- Load and register an OracleAS Metadata Repository
- Remove and deregister an OracleAS Metadata Repository

FIGURE C.11 RepCA Operation Type window

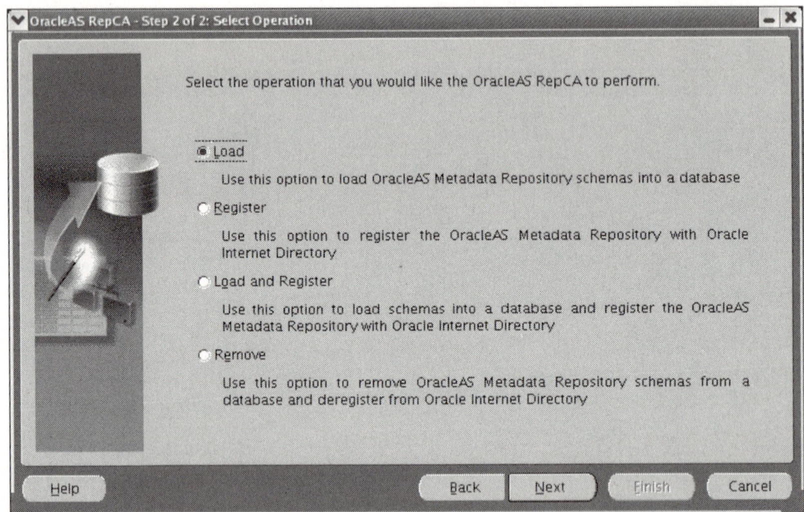

Click the Load radio button and then click the Next button.

In the screen shown in Figure C.12, you specify the connection information for your RAC database. Specify the password for the SYS account, the hostnames and ports for all nodes in the cluster, and the service name you use to connect to the cluster. In this example, you specify the hostnames and port numbers for a three-node RAC database; all three nodes use the default port number. You also specify `racsvc.world` as the service name you would use from SQL*Plus to connect to one of the nodes in the cluster.

After you complete the required information the screen in Figure C.12, click the Next button and you'll see a summary of the RepCA tool installation in the End of Installation screen shown in Figure C.13. It may appear confusing at first, because you have already specified some of the options for creating a new repository even though the installation is not complete. The next time you run RepCA (via the `runRepca` script), the first window you will see is the window in Figure C.9.

FIGURE C.12 RepCA Database Connection Information window

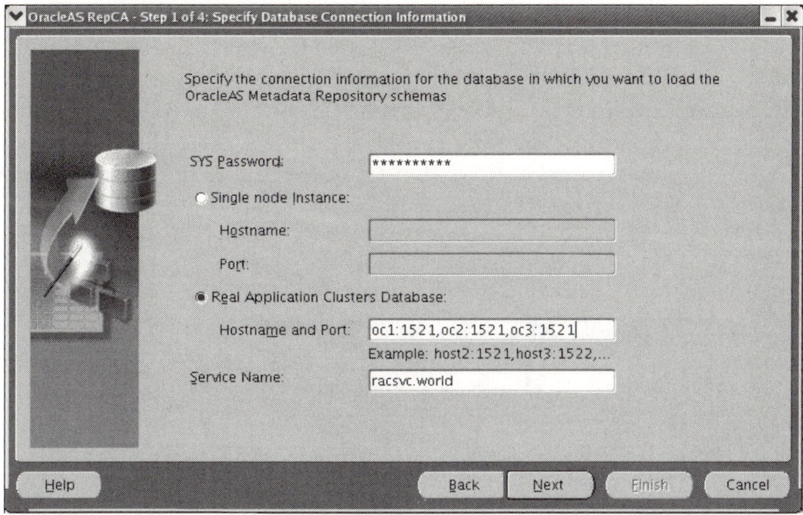

FIGURE C.13 RepCA installation complete window

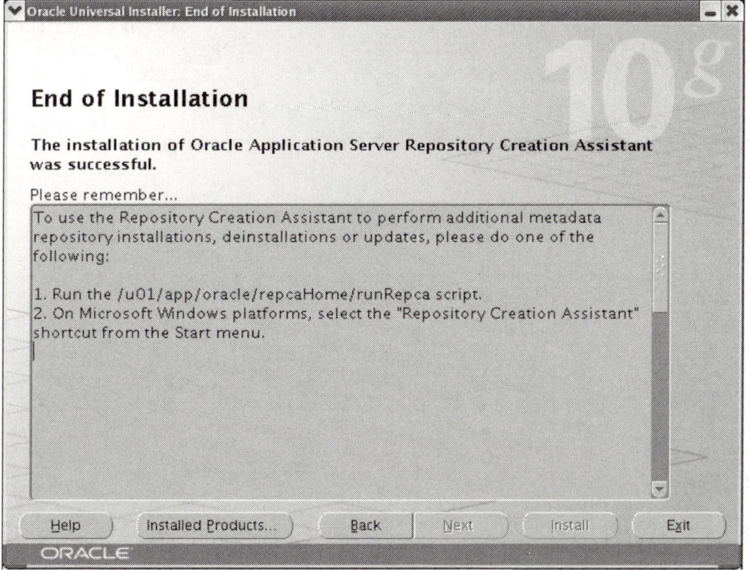

When you click the Next button in the End of Installation screen, you will see the storage options window shown in Figure C.14. The RAC database in this example uses Automatic Storage Management (ASM). Click the Next button to continue to the next window.

In the next screen (Figure C.15), you specify which ASM disk group to use for the Metadata Repository–related tablespaces and schemas. The RAC database in this example has one disk group for all tablespaces, DATA. Click the Next button to continue, and in the next screen (Figure C.16), you will see a summary of the OracleAS components, their tablespaces, and their default sizes. If you have any specific requirements to increase the size of a tablespace, you can do it in this window.

FIGURE C.14 RepCA Specify Storage Option window

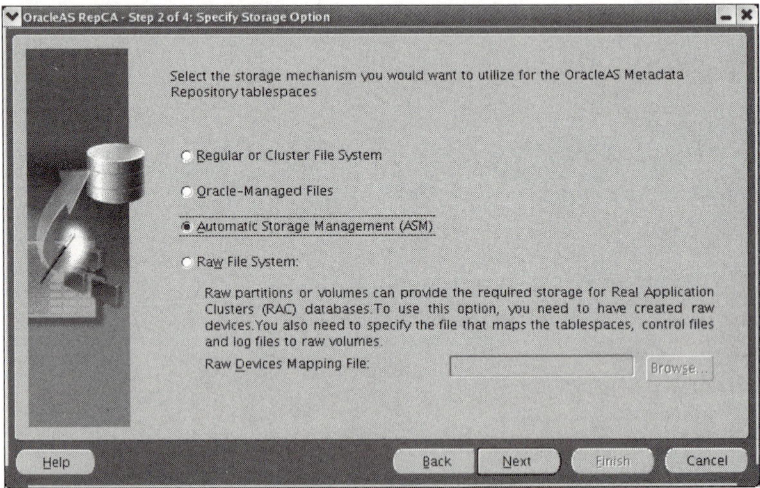

FIGURE C.15 Specify Disk Group window

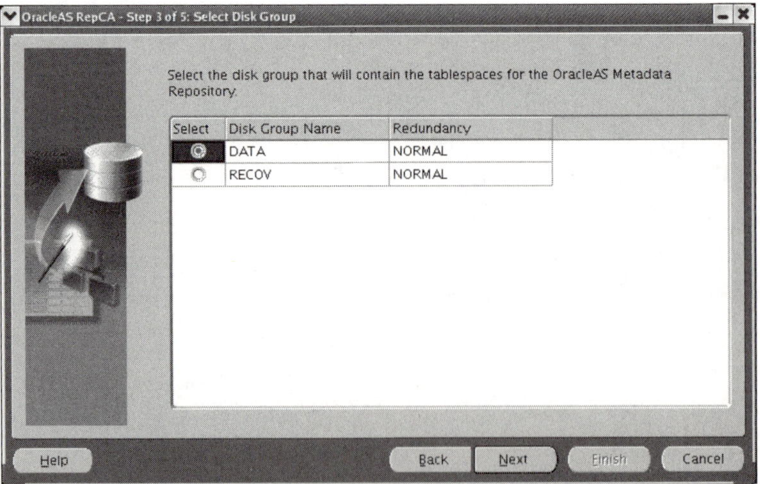

FIGURE C.16 Component and tablespace summary window

OracleAS RepCA - Step 4 of 5: Specify Tablespace Information

The following tablespaces will be created for you. Specify the size for the tablespaces depending on the use of the components.It is recommended that tablespaces for components that will be used heavily should be allocated large sizes.

Selected Disk Group :DATA

Tablespaces:

Component	Tablespace	Size
OracleAS Portal	PORTAL	100M
OracleAS Portal	PORTAL_DOC	40M
OracleAS Portal	PORTAL_IDX	50M
OracleAS Portal	PORTAL_LOG	50M
OracleAS Single Sign-on	IAS_META	300M
OracleAS Discoverer	DISCO_PTM5_META	10M
OracleAS Discoverer	DISCO_PTM5_CACHE	10M
OracleAS Distributed Configuration Man...	DCM	100M

Help Back Next Finish Cancel

When you click the Next button in the screen in Figure C.16, you will see a reminder screen like the one in Figure C.17, reminding you to increase the size of the SYSTEM and UNDO tablespaces if you do not have at least 350MB free in these tablespaces. You can use the following commands to increase the disk space allocated for these tablespaces:

```
SQL> alter tablespace system add datafile '+DATA' size 350m;

Tablespace altered.

SQL> alter tablespace undotbs1 add datafile '+DATA' size 350m;

Tablespace altered.

SQL>
```

FIGURE C.17 Space requirements reminder in SYSTEM and UNDO tablespaces window

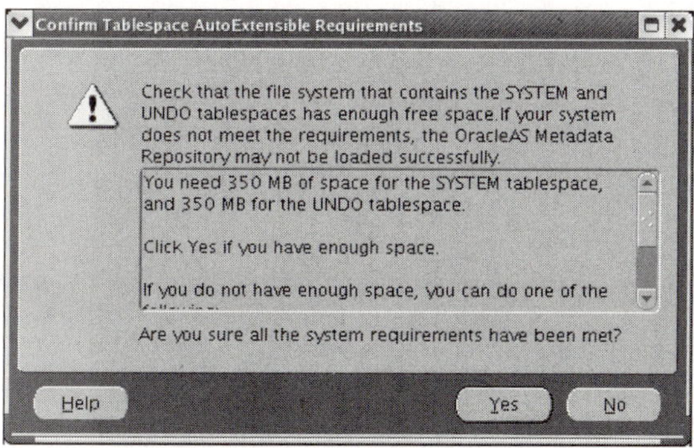

Click the Yes button in the screen in Figure C.17 to confirm that there is enough disk space in the SYSTEM and UNDO tablespaces. On the next window, shown in Figure C.18, you see the progress of the Metadata Repository creation process. As the new required tablespaces are created, you will see messages similar to the following in the alert log file:

```
Tue Jun 27 22:40:59 2006
Completed: create tablespace PORTAL_LOG DATAFILE
➥'+DATA' SIZE 50M REUSE AUTOEXTEND ON NEXT 30M
➥ MAXSIZE UNLIMITED PERMANENT
```

After the process is complete, you will see the window shown in Figure C.19, which confirms that the Metadata Repository now exists in your RAC database.

Your database is now ready for a new OracleAS installation or to register with an existing OracleAS OID installation.

FIGURE C.18 Metadata Repository creation progress window

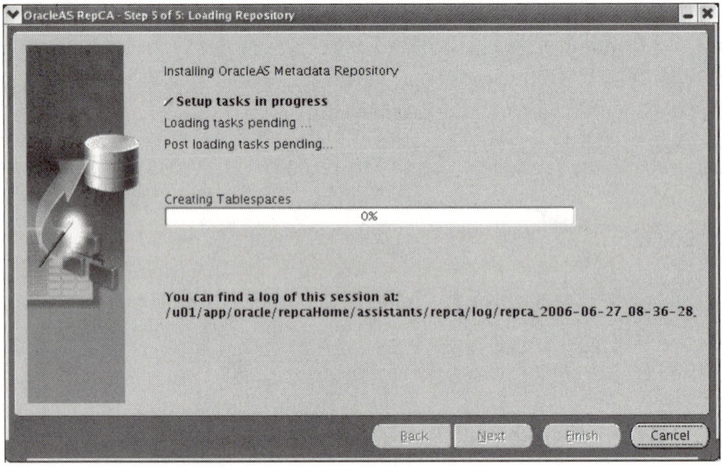

FIGURE C.19 Metadata Repository creation completion window

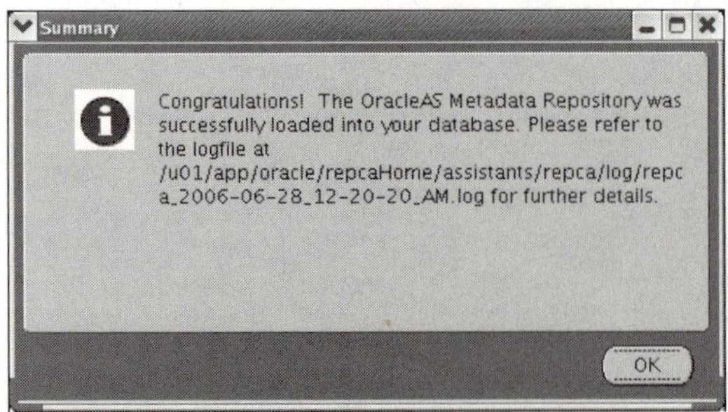

Appendix D

Backing Up and Recovering Oracle Application Server

Even if you have a highly redundant and available application server environment, you must prepare for the possibility that all of the servers in the cluster may fail at the same time. A high level of redundancy in your environment doesn't prevent unintentional data entry errors or viruses from being introduced and corrupting all servers in your redundant environment. Therefore, you must perform backups of your application server environment on a regular basis.

In this appendix, we will show you how to set up your backup and recovery environment, including recording your environment's key metadata. We will then show you the steps, primarily using AS Control, to back up and restore your application server environment. Your backups will consist of occasional full backups and frequent incremental backups. Finally, you can perform your backups either while all application server processes are shut down or while they are still running and available; which type of backup you choose depends on a number of factors, including the availability requirements of your environment.

Performing OracleAS Backup

Before you perform your first backup, you need to configure and optimize your backup environment to ensure maximum recoverability as well as to minimize the amount of time it takes to perform the backup. You meet these two goals primarily by changing some of your infrastructure database settings.

Your next step is to record important settings in your environment in case of a massive failure where you need to reinstall the entire application server environment or even reinstall the operating system software in the event of a disk failure.

Finally, you perform a full backup after the installation is complete or after major changes to your environment and perform incremental backups on a regular basis.

Configuring the Backup Environment

Before you start your first backup, you need to specify some database options as well as a destination file system for the backup itself. Your database must be in `ARCHIVELOG` mode to ensure maximum recoverability, and you should enable Block Change Tracking in your database to minimize the amount of data you need to back up during an incremental backup.

Enabling *ARCHIVELOG* Mode

By enabling ARCHIVELOG in your database, you dramatically improve the recoverability of the database in your infrastructure instance. In ARCHIVELOG mode, you save all copies of your online redo log files before they are reused by new transactions. When (not if) you have a media failure, archived redo log files are essential to recover your database.

To enable ARCHIVELOG mode, be sure to shut down the entire infrastructure instance and any other instances that depend on the OracleAS Metadata Repository of this infrastructure instance. Next, connect to the database using SQL*Plus, shut down the database, and restart the database in MOUNT mode:

```
[oracle@asinfra oracle]$ sqlplus / as sysdba

SQL*Plus: Release 10.1.0.4.2 - Production on Sat Jul 1 23:57:24 2006

Copyright (c) 1982, 2005, Oracle.  All rights reserved.


Connected to:
Oracle Database 10g Enterprise Edition Release 10.1.0.4.2 - Production
With the Partitioning, OLAP and Data Mining options

SQL> shutdown immediate
Database closed.
Database dismounted.
ORACLE instance shut down.
SQL> startup mount
ORACLE instance started.

Total System Global Area  281018368 bytes
Fixed Size                   778968 bytes
Variable Size             229645608 bytes
Database Buffers           50331648 bytes
Redo Buffers                 262144 bytes
Database mounted.
SQL>
```

Next, you enable ARCHIVELOG mode and then confirm that the database is in ARCHIVELOG mode:

```
SQL> alter database archivelog;

Database altered.
```

```
SQL> alter database open;

Database altered.

SQL> archive log list;
Database log mode              Archive Mode
Automatic archival             Enabled
Archive destination            USE_DB_RECOVERY_FILE_DEST
Oldest online log sequence     5275
Next log sequence to archive   5277
Current log sequence           5277
SQL>
```

In this example, the database uses a flash recovery area for the default log file destination. If you are not using a flash recovery area, you will have to set one of the LOG_ARCHIVE_DEST_*n* parameters for your archived log files. For a default installation of Oracle Application Server 10g Release 2, the Oracle Universal Installer (OUI) creates a flash recovery area, as you can see when you query the DB_RECOVERY_FILE_DEST system parameter:

```
SQL> show parameter db_recovery

NAME                         TYPE         VALUE
---------------------------  -----------  ----------------------
db_recovery_file_dest        string       /u01/app/oracle/flash_
                                          recovery_area
db_recovery_file_dest_size   big integer  2G

SQL>
```

The flash recovery feature is new as of Oracle Database 10*g* Release 1. If you are still running Oracle Database 9*i*, you must ensure that at least one LOG_ARCHIVE_DEST_*n* parameter is set.

Enabling Block Change Tracking

Starting with Oracle Database 10g Release 1, you can use *block change tracking* to improve the efficiency of your incremental backups. When you enable block change tracking, Oracle maintains a list of all data blocks changed since the last incremental backup in an operating system file. Without this mechanism, every block within a data file is read to determine if it has been changed. Using the block change tracking file, only the changed blocks within each data file are read, dramatically reducing the amount of time it takes to perform an incremental backup for a database with low insert, update, or delete activity against the database tables.

To enable block change tracking, use the following ALTER DATABASE command:

```
SQL> alter database enable block change tracking
➥      using file '/u01/app/oracle/bct.dbf';

Database altered.

SQL>
```

If you are using Oracle Managed Files (OMF) and the system parameter DB_CREATE_FILE_DEST is set, you can omit the USING FILE clause and a block change tracking file is named automatically.

Specifying a Backup Destination

Finally, you need to specify a place for the backup itself to reside. It can reside on the same server as the database or on a file system that resides on a different server; preferably it is not on the same disk as the other files in the Infrastructure installation.

To specify the backup destination using AS Control, start at the instance home page and select the Backup/Recovery tab. You can see the Backup/Recovery page in Figure D.1.

FIGURE D.1 The Backup/Recovery home page

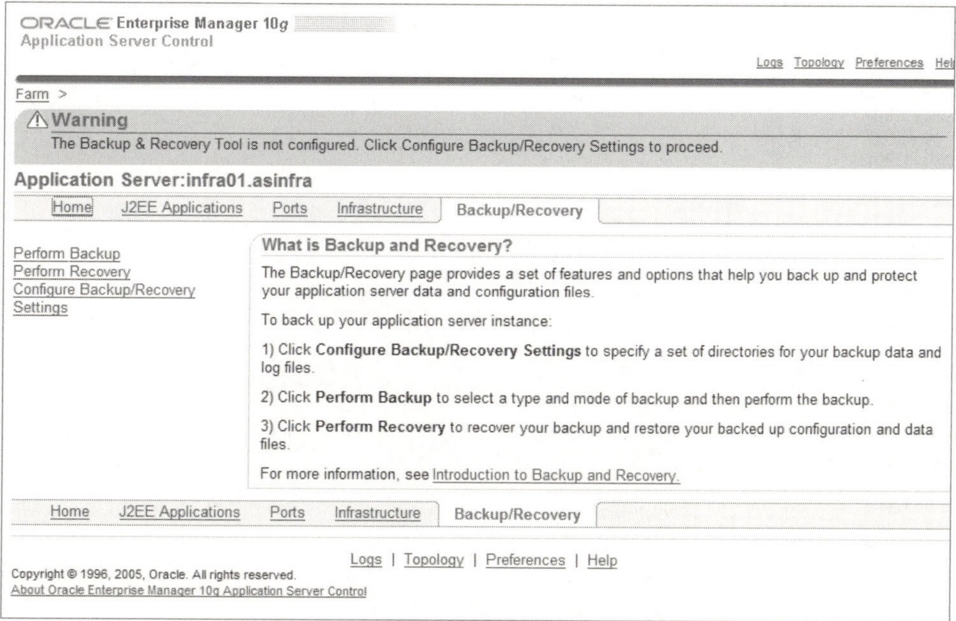

When you click the Configure Backup/Recovery link, you will see the page shown in Figure D.2, where you can specify the following information for your backup environment:

- Log file location
- Configuration files backup location
- Database backup location
- System identifier (SID) of the database instance

You cannot perform a backup through AS Control until you fill out this page completely.

The log file location defaults to the `backup_restore/logs` directory in your `ORACLE_HOME` for the OracleAS installation; the database SID defaults to `orcl`, which is the SID that OUI uses when you install an OracleAS infrastructure. You should specify a different file system (and preferably on a different server) for both the configuration files backup location (`/u02/oracle/infra_backup/config`) and the database backup location (`/u02/oracle/infra_backup/database`). To save your settings, click the OK button. AS Control prompts you to create the directories if they do not already exist; click the OK button to confirm.

FIGURE D.2 Backup and recovery settings

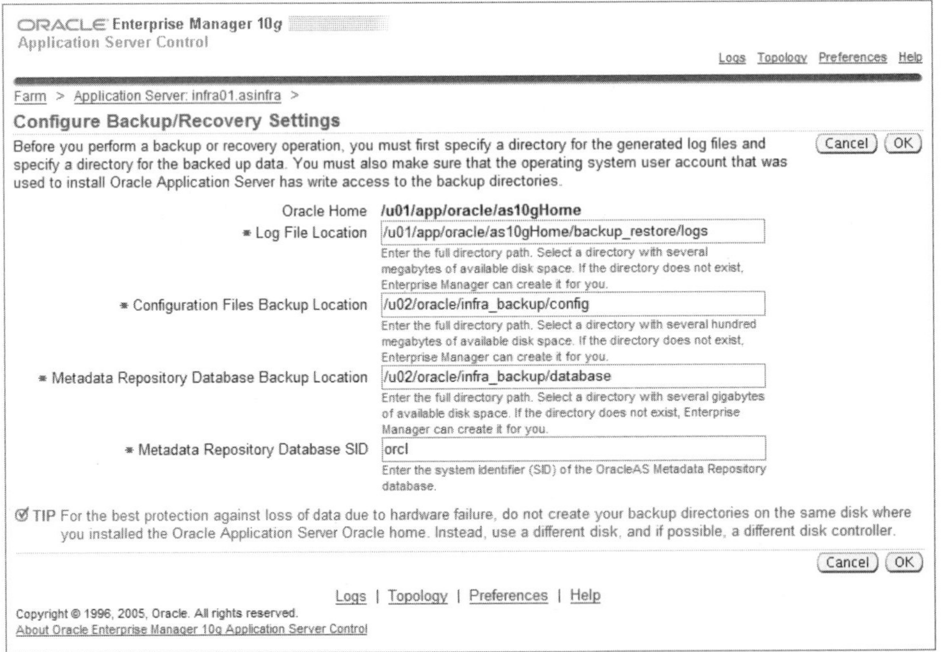

Recording Environment Characteristics

In the case of a catastrophic disaster in your data center, you should have on hand in a remote location not only the backup files themselves, but also the hardware and software configuration settings for your operating system and every OracleAS installation.

For each host in your environment, you need to record the following:

- Hostname and domain name
- Virtual hostnames (if any)
- IP address
- Hardware platform
- Operating system release and patch levels

For each OracleAS installation, you need to record the following:

- Installation type: Infrastructure or Middle-tier
- Hostname for each installation
- Entries in `/etc/passwd` and `/etc/group` (username, user ID number, group name, group ID number, environment profile, and default shell for the `oracle` user)
- Directory structure, mount points, and full path name for the Oracle home directory (`$ORACLE_HOME`)
- Disk space requirements for the installation
- Port numbers used by the components of the installation

Finally, for each metadata repository (one per farm), you will need the following information:

- Oracle database version and patches
- Base language and installed character sets
- Global database name and SID

Performing a Full Backup

Whether you perform a full backup (all files) or an incremental backup (changed files since the last backup), you must decide whether to do the backup when the AS repository instance is completely shut down (a *cold backup*) or when the instance is running and serving content (*online backup*, also known as a *hot backup*). Cold backups are easier, but your application server is unavailable when the backup is running. In contrast, online backups may take longer and affect response time for your users, but the application server is available during the entire backup.

Oracle best practices dictate a full backup right after you perform an installation or make a major change to your environment, such as adding a new OC4J application; you should perform frequent incremental backups to minimize the amount of rework required to restore an installation from a backup. Assuming no changes to your application server installation's configuration and your metadata in an Oracle database with `ARCHIVELOG` enabled, you should be able to restore your environment up to the point in time of the failure with no data loss.

Ideally, you will perform full backups of all application server installations within your environment at the same time, especially when one or more Middle-tier installations depend on an Infrastructure installation. You can perform both cold backups and online backups using AS Control.

Full Online Backup

To start a full online backup, start at the instance home page, and select the Backup/Recovery tab shown earlier in Figure D.1. Click the `Perform Backup` link and you will see the available backup options in the screen shown in Figure D.3.

To start a full online backup, select the Full Online Backup radio button. At the top of the page, you will see the installation type you are backing up plus the locations for the configuration files, log files, and database backup. If you are backing up a middle-tier instance, you will not see the Database Backup Location listed (because a middle-tier instance does not include a database repository); otherwise, the options for this backup apply to middle-tier backups as well.

FIGURE D.3 Selecting a backup mode

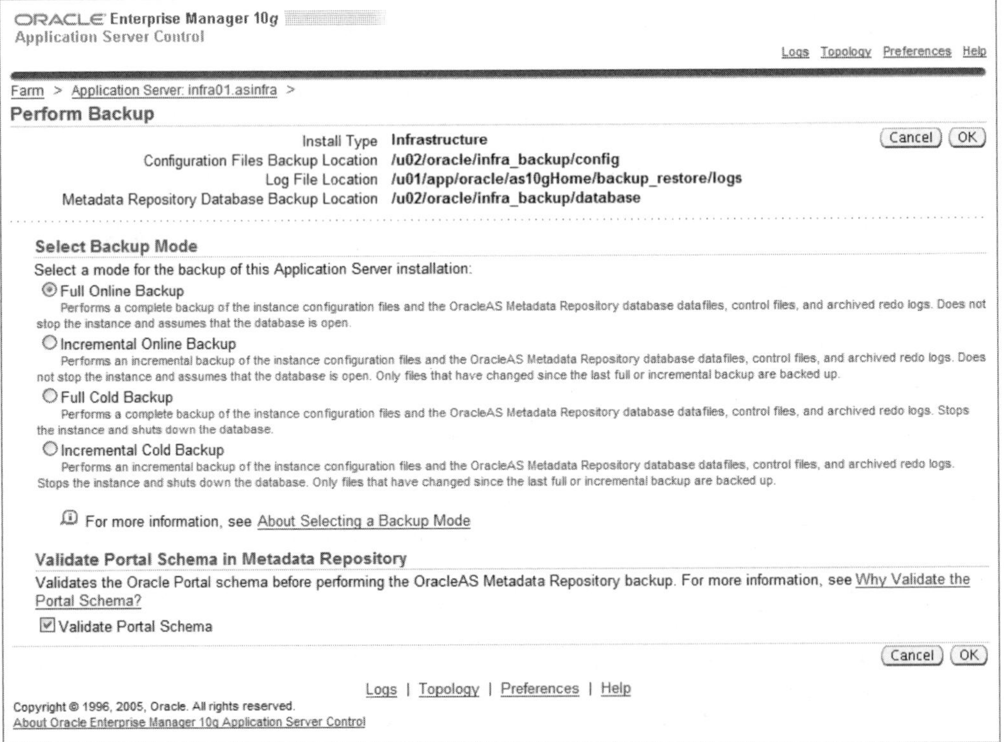

At the bottom of this page, you have the option to validate the portal schema by checking for any inconsistencies among your portal definitions. This is a good check to perform occasionally to ensure that all portlets in a portal have the proper permissions, are not orphaned, and so forth.

Click the OK button to start the backup. While the backup is in progress, you do not see much more than the OracleAS ticking clock shown in Figure D.4.

When the backup completes, you will see a confirmation page similar to the page in Figure D.5. In this example, the backup completed successfully—but with warning messages.

FIGURE D.4 Full online backup in progress

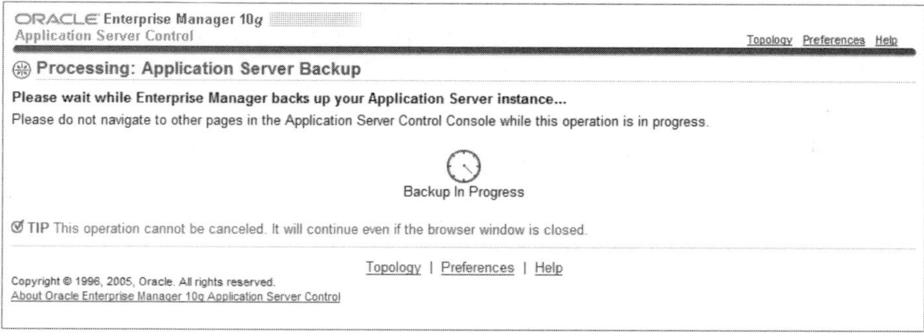

FIGURE D.5 Full online backup completion page

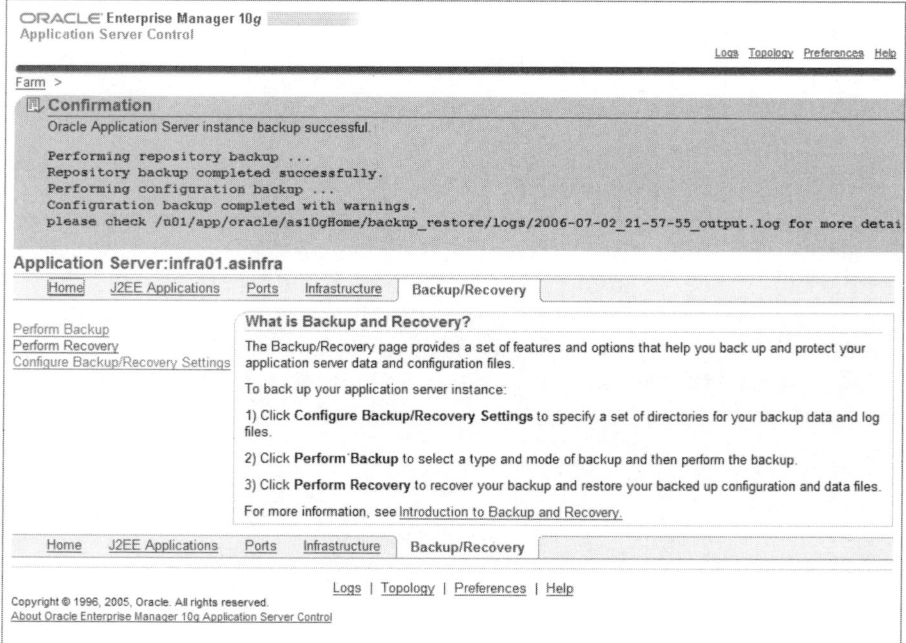

Checking the log file in the confirmation message, you see why the backup completed with a warning:

```
==================== Sun Jul  2 22:11:22 2006 ====================
/u01/app/oracle/as10gHome/bin/sqlplus -l -s "/ as sysdba"
   @/u01/app/oracle/as10gHome/backup_restore/svurpt.sql
   /u01/app/oracle/as10gHome/backup_restore/logs/2006-07-02_21-57-
   55_portal_validation.log
Running the Portal Schema Validation Utility in report mode ...
Inconsistencies found in portal schema!
Check /u01/app/oracle/as10gHome/backup_restore/logs/
➥   2006-07-02_21-57-55_portal_validation.log for
➥   any inconsistency.
Portal validation completed!
```

When you configured the backup, you selected the option to validate the entries in the portal schema. At the bottom of the portal validation log, you see this message:

```
|  Validate Security ACLs
|   . Inconsistency: Number of Security ACLs that
➥    need to be deleted = 168
|   . List of security ACLs that need to be deleted
|   .. Owner: PORTAL , Object Type: DOCUMENT , Name: 1.JPG ,
➥    Grantee Type: USER ,
 Grantee Name: PORTAL , Privilege: OWN
|   .. Owner: PORTAL , Object Type: DOCUMENT , Name: 10.JPG ,
➥    Grantee Type: USER
, Grantee Name: PORTAL , Privilege: OWN
. . .
```

Although these warnings do not prevent the portal application from serving content, they may be indicative of missing content. Typically, these messages mean that access control list (ACL) entries still exist but point to a nonexistent object (for example, `1.JPG`).

Checking the backup destinations you specified on the page in Figure D.2, which are both under `/u02/oracle/infra_backup`, you see that a single full online backup requires approximately 35MB for an infrastructure configuration backup and 1.75GB for an infrastructure metadata repository backup:

```
[root@asinfra infra_backup]# ls
config  database
[root@asinfra infra_backup]# du -s config database
34928   config
1750648 database
[root@asinfra infra_backup]#
```

Full Cold Backup

To perform a full cold backup, start on the page in Figure D.3 and select the Full Cold Backup radio button. Since the cold backup shuts down the AS repository instance, Oracle strongly recommends that you shut down all other AS instances that depend on this repository instance for two reasons. First, if you are using the cold backup option on an infrastructure instance, the metadata repository is unavailable during the backup and any other instances that use the metadata repository will fail. Second, to maintain consistency among instances within the same farm, you should shut down all other instances. While the other instances are down, you can perform a cold backup on those as well.

When you click the OK button, AS Control reminds you that the backup operation will shut down the entire instance, including the metadata repository, for the duration of the backup. Click the Yes button to continue.

The cold backup proceeds in the same manner as the online backup, with a ticking clock and a summary page similar to the one you see in Figure D.5. After the backup completes, the instance restarts and is once again available to users.

The log file for the backup shows that Recovery Manager (RMAN) shuts down the database, then opens it in `MOUNT` mode so that the database is not available to users while RMAN performs the backup:

```
using target database controlfile instead of recovery catalog
database closed
database dismounted
Oracle instance shut down

connected to target database (not started)
Oracle instance started
database mounted

Total System Global Area     281018368 bytes

Fixed Size                      778968 bytes
Variable Size                229645608 bytes
Database Buffers              50331648 bytes
Redo Buffers                    262144 bytes
```

Performing Incremental Backups

Because a full backup takes a lot of disk space, you can use incremental backups to back up only the parts of your installation that have changed since the last backup. When you need to restore from a backup, the backup process will restore from the full backup and apply each incremental backup since the last full backup; thus, you still want to perform a full backup on a regular basis to minimize the recovery time.

You can perform online or cold incremental backups in much the same way as full backups using AS Control.

Incremental Online Backup

To perform an incremental online backup, start on the page shown in Figure D.3 and select the Incremental Online Backup radio button. Click the OK button and you will see the AS Control ticking clock while the incremental backup is in progress. When the incremental backup completes, you will see the summary of the backup on a page similar to what you saw for a full backup in Figure D.5.

Reviewing the database backup log in `$ORACLE_HOME/backup_restore/logs`, you see that RMAN performs an incremental backup that includes only changed data blocks:

```
4> run {
5> allocate channel dev1 device type disk format
   '/u02/oracle/infra_backup/database/%U';
6> backup incremental level=1 database plus archivelog not backed up;
7> release channel dev1;
8> }
```

Incremental Cold Backup

Performing an incremental cold backup is identical to performing an incremental online backup except that the database is shut down during the incremental backup. Select the Incremental Cold Backup radio button shown in Figure D.3 and click the OK button to start the backup.

Performing OracleAS Recovery

Although you hope that you never have to perform a recovery operation, you know you're prepared for it if you've followed the steps outlined so far in this appendix to back up your OracleAS instances with full and incremental backups. However, because of eventual disk hardware failures and user errors, you will most likely eventually need to recover part or all of one of your OracleAS instances from backup files.

In the following scenario, you lose this database data file due to media failure:

```
/u01/app/oracle/oradata/orcl/b2b_idx.dbf
```

Your AS repository database instance fails, and your infrastructure instance fails as well. Your AS Control management interface is still up and running, however, allowing you to navigate to the infrastructure instance home page shown in Figure D.1 and click the `Perform Recovery` link.

In Figure D.6, you can see a drop-down box with the available backup files. Select the most recent incremental backup; because this backup will not have the dropped data file in its entirety, the recovery operation will first recover from the last full backup and then apply all incremental backups including the one you selected.

Since you did not lose a control file, be sure to uncheck the box next to Recover Control Files; although you will still have a successful recovery, you will invalidate all previous database backups if you recover the control file.

To perform the recovery, the instance and database will be shut down—although in many situations, they both already will be down! Click the Yes button on the next page to confirm that the instance will be shut down.

During the recovery operation, you will see the familiar ticking clock until the recovery operation is complete. You will then see a summary of the recovery operation, as in Figure D.7.

AS Control automatically restarts the instance after recovery is complete, and you can once again serve content to your users.

FIGURE D.6 Perform Recovery page

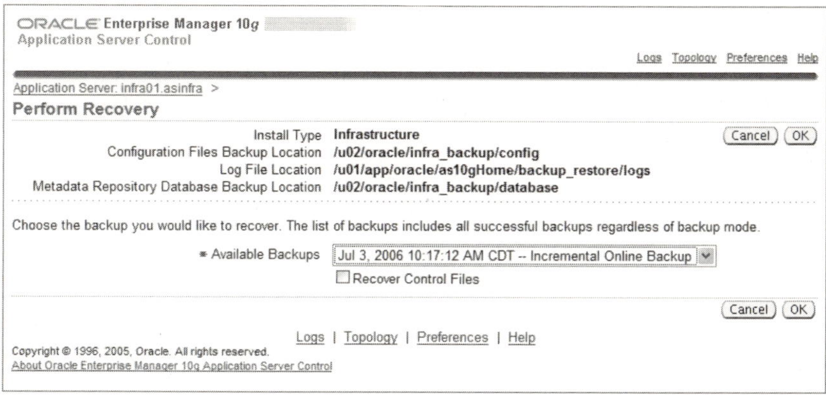

FIGURE D.7 Recovery operation complete page

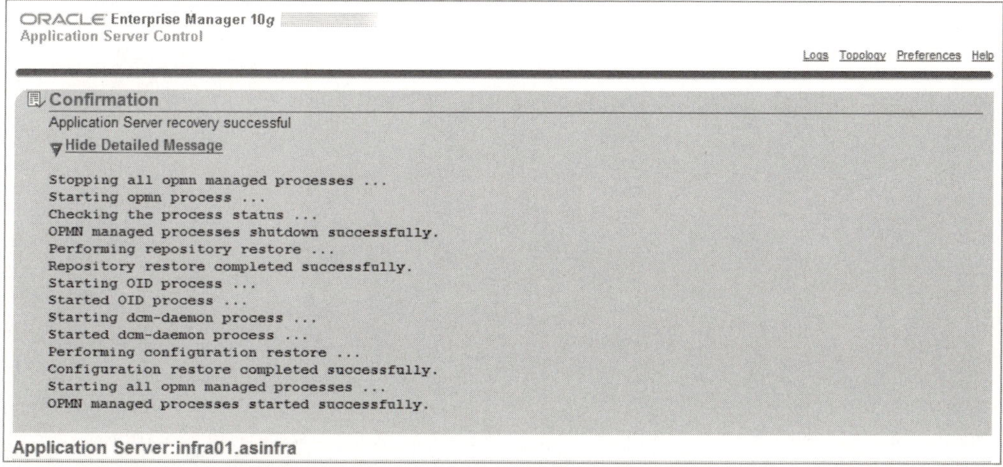

Glossary

access log A Web Cache log file that contains entries for all HTTP requests sent to Web Cache.

applet A Java program that runs from an applet viewer or is embedded in a Web page.

Application Server Control console A web application that provides an administrator with a web-based user interface to monitor and administer every component within an Oracle Application Server installation.

authentication Process that enables the target system to verify the identity of the user or the system that is requesting access.

authorization Process used to determine the privileges that users and other systems have for accessing resources.

bash One of many command-line shells available in a Linux environment. Other shells include csh, ksh, and sh.

block directive A directive that is enclosed by `<DirectiveName>` and `</DirectiveName>` and does not restrict the scope of the enclosed configuration directives.

`bulkdelete` Bulk tool used to delete OID subtrees.

`bulkload` Bulk tool used to load a large number of entries into the OID server.

`bulkmodify` Bulk tool used to modify a large number of entries in the OID server.

cluster A collection of application server instances within a farm that have identical configuration and application deployment.

Common Log Format The default log entry format for OHS. Also known as CLF.

configuration directive A command that resides within a server configuration file, consists of a single line, and defines OHS features within the defined context.

container directive A block of configuration directives that restricts the scope of those directives based on criteria defined in the block header, such as location, filename, or virtual host.

content streaming A feature of Web Cache that begins to send the first part of an uncompressed or compressed document before receiving the entire document from the origin server.

database access descriptor A set of values that specify how an application connects to an Oracle database to satisfy an HTTP request.

DCM See Distributed Configuration Management.

Delegated Administration Services (DAS) A component of OracleAS that enables you to centrally store all metadata for users, groups, applications, and services in your environment and at the same time allows you to distribute administration of the data to other administrators and end users.

diagnostic message database repository A database schema that stores the diagnostic and informational messages from components in one or more Oracle Application Server instances.

directive An OHS configuration instruction or a block of instructions with a header and a footer placed in OHS configuration files to determine the behavior of the server.

directory information tree (DIT) Simple hierarchical tree organization of an LDAP directory.

directory server An OracleAS component that defines a hierarchical view of organizational data such as employees, resources, and applications.

Distributed Configuration Management An application within Oracle Application Server that enables you to create and manage multiple Oracle Application Server instances as a single instance. DCM synchronizes the configuration across all instances and maintains this information in either a file-based repository or a database repository.

DIT See *directory information tree.*

DMS See *Dynamic Monitoring Service.*

Dynamic Monitoring Service A component of Oracle Application Server that collects performance data from application server components.

Edge Side Includes Also known as ESI; a markup language similar to XML that enables dynamic content assembly of individual content fragments.

encryption Method used to scramble or unscramble data.

Enterprise Archive (EAR) Enterprise Archives (EARs) are simply standard Java archive files that have a `.ear` extension. EAR files can contain one or more web modules, one or more EJB modules, one or more application client modules, or JAR files that might be required in any combination.

Enterprise JavaBeans (EJB) Enterprise JavaBeans are the server-side components of the Java architecture. EJB also describes how these components are used in a J2EE environment.

environment variables A variable assigned either during a user's login or during the session containing values that you reference by the environment variable name later in the session. In a Linux or Unix environment, environment variables are typically all uppercase, such as `TMP` and `ORACLE_HOME`.

/etc/oratab A regular file created by OUI that contains the location of all OUI installation locations and history.

event log The Web Cache log file that contains startup errors such as port conflicts or any other errors that occur while Web Cache is running.

expiration rule A rule that defines when a cached version of a document is expected to become stale and should be refreshed.

external application An application that is not deployed within an OracleAS instance and does not delegate authentication duties to SSO.

farm A collection of OracleAS instances that share the same configuration data.

Identity Management OracleAS's distributed security solution, which includes OID, SSO, and OCA.

infrastructure A reference to a combination of applications such as the Metadata Repository, Oracle Internet Directory, and Single Sign-On. The OracleAS Infrastructure supports other middle-tier applications.

installation The set of executables and configuration files you create when you install one or more OracleAS components.

instance An operational OracleAS installation that runs one or more of the OracleAS components at any tier.

invalidation messages A message that can be sent by several different methods to Web Cache to immediately mark a cached page or group of pages as stale.

Java Archive (JAR) Java Archive is a type of compressed file that contains a set of Java classes, compiled Java programs, and associated metadata that make up a program.

Java Platform Enterprise Edition (J2EE) Java Platform Enterprise Edition is a programming platform that is used for developing and running multitier Java applications.

`ldapadd` LDAP command-line tool used to add one or more entries.

`ldapaddmt` LDAP command-line tool used to add entries concurrently using multiple threads.

`ldapbind` LDAP command-line tool used to authenticate a user to the directory server.

`ldapcompare` LDAP command-line tool used to determine whether an entry contains specific attributes.

`ldapdelete` LDAP command-line tool used to delete an entry.

`ldapmoddn` LDAP command-line tool used to modify the DN and RDN of an entry, rename an entry or a subtree, or move an entry or subtree to a new parent.

`ldapmodify` LDAP command-line tool used to create, update, and delete data in an entry.

`ldapmodifymt` LDAP command-line tool used to modify multiple entries at one time using multithreading.

`ldapsearch` LDAP command-line tool used to search for an entry in the directory.

`ldfwrite` Bulk tool used to load copy data from OID information base to LDIF.

LDIF See *Lightweight Directory Interchange Format.*

Lightweight Directory Interchange Format (LDIF) An ASCII file format used to exchange data and enable the synchronization of that data between LDAP servers.

Log Loader process A process that monitors Oracle Application Server instance components and updates a log repository with the instance components' diagnostic messages.

log repository See *diagnostic message database repository.*

managed target An Oracle Application Server installation controlled by an OEM 10*g* Grid Control installation.

metadata repository An Oracle database, created during the infrastructure installation that contains the persistent metadata required by various OracleAS instances.

metrics Units of measurement used to report the health and performance level of an instance or its components.

mod_access Module that provides for server access control on request.

mod_auth Module that provides for authentication based on username and password.

mod_ossl Module that provides the facility for authentication and encryption with X.509 client certificates over SSL.

mod_osso Module that enables Single Sign-On authentication for web applications.

mod_security A noninvasive method to define filters that is used to detect anomalies such as SQL injections and to prescribe appropriate actions when such anomalies are detected.

mods See *modules.*

modules Plug-ins for Apache HTTP Server providing additional functionality available to the HTTP server. mod_php and mod_perl are examples of modules.

namespace A hierarchically structured set of management policies, authorization, and authentication metadata used to enforce security and control resources for a set of Oracle Application Server applications.

nickname A tag assigned to a log format defined with a LogFormat directive to make it easy to reuse the log format in subsequent directives.

object classes An entity within OID that you use to classify and group information, such as an Oracle user, a person, or an organization. Each directory entry belongs to one or more object classes, and one object class can inherit the characteristics of another.

oidctl Command-line utility used to start and stop the OID server instance.

oidmon Oracle Internet Directory Monitor.

OMA See *Oracle Management Agent.*

OMR See *Oracle Management Repository.*

OMS See *Oracle Management Service.*

OPMN See *Oracle Process Manager and Notification Server.*

opmnctr Command-line utility used to start and stop OID Monitor.

Oracle Containers for J2EE (OC4J) Oracle Containers for J2EE are the core J2EE runtime components of the Oracle Application Server.

Oracle Context An LDAP-compliant entry in OID containing all information related to the Oracle software within an installation.

Oracle Directory Manager Java-based GUI tool that administrators can use to maintain and administer OID data.

Oracle Management Agent A process within an Oracle Application Server instance that collects information about performance, configuration, and availability for all targets on the host and passes that information to an Oracle Management Service.

Oracle Management Repository A schema in a new or existing database that stores the availability, configuration, and performance information from one or more OMS instances for later retrieval and analysis.

Oracle Management Service A process within an Oracle Application Server instance that collects the information from one or more OMAs and makes that information available to one or more administrators via a web interface or, in the case of an alert, a pager message or email message.

Oracle Management Watchdog A process within the Oracle Application Server instance that monitors the local OMA and the Application Server console itself to make sure that both of these components are up and running continuously. If these components fail unexpectedly, the watchdog process automatically restarts OMA.

Oracle Process Manager and Notification Server An Oracle Application Server process that is responsible for starting and stopping components within an application server instance.

Oracle Universal Installer The common application framework used by all Oracle products to install, uninstall, and configure Oracle application files.

OUI See Oracle Universal Installer.

partner application An application that delegates authentication to an Oracle Application Server SSO server.

partner application Any OracleAS application that uses SSO for authentication.

performance assurance A Web Cache option to serve slightly stale content instead of no content at all during a spike in website usage that prevents the delivery of timely and expected refreshed content from the origin server.

pipe A Linux/Unix construct that redirects output from an application to another process instead of the default standard output location.

portal A customized and centralized web page location that summarizes or provides access to corporate or external information.

portlet A subcomponent of an OracleAS Portal page; typically, a portlet will summarize information from an information source or provide access to an information source such as a sales summary graph, a stock ticker, or a weather forecast.

realm A subtree within Oracle Internet Directory (OID); it includes subtrees for users and groups along with access control lists to provide fine-grained control of the subtrees' administration. See also *namespace*.

secondary key An alternate method of specifying which content to invalidate when the exact URL or a regular expression that matches a URL is not available.

servlet A small Java program that runs on the web server and take client requests from the browser, generates dynamic content, and sends the response back to the browser.

Single Sign-On A component of Oracle Identity Management that validates a user's credentials against Oracle Internet Directory.

SSO server A part of the OracleAS Identity Management infrastructure. It consists of several components: the SSO server itself, partner applications, external applications, and the module `mod_osso`. These components work together to manage the life cycle of user accounts and other network entities in a centralized and efficient manner.

subtree One or more URLs, documents, or complete directories that result from evaluating a regular expression or a wildcard expression.

superuser account On a host, a user account that has all possible privileges and has full access to all resources on the host.

surge protection A Web Cache automatic tuning feature that queues simultaneous requests beyond a specified threshold to prevent an overload of request traffic on the origin server.

target A physical server that hosts an Oracle Application Server installation and other user applications.

tier A hardware layer consisting of one or more servers that implement a particular class of OracleAS components.

Topology Viewer An Oracle Application Server component that contains a graphical viewer. Available as either an HTML-based or a Java-based application, the viewer shows the relationships between installations and components along with statistics for each installation or component.

virtual host A website that responds to IP addresses or hostnames other than the main server's IP address or hostname. Also, an additional host or website defined alongside the main server.

virtual path A reference to content within a URL that may not necessarily reside within the server's file system.

Web Archive (WAR) Web Archive files are packaged web applications that can be used to import an entire application into a web server. WAR files contain the project resources and a web deployment descriptor file.

Web Cache log format Also known as WCLF; a log format that is optimized for analyzing end-user performance of Web Cache.

Index

Note to the Reader: Throughout this index **boldfaced** page numbers indicate primary discussions of a topic. *Italicized* page numbers indicate illustrations.

A

B

C

D

E

F

I

J

K

L

M

N

O

P

Q

R

S

T

U

V

W

Wiley Publishing, Inc. End-User License Agreement

READ THIS. You should carefully read these terms and conditions before opening the software packet(s) included with this book "Book". This is a license agreement "Agreement" between you and Wiley Publishing, Inc. "WPI". By opening the accompanying software packet(s), you acknowledge that you have read and accept the following terms and conditions. If you do not agree and do not want to be bound by such terms and conditions, promptly return the Book and the unopened software packet(s) to the place you obtained them for a full refund.

1. License Grant. WPI grants to you (either an individual or entity) a nonexclusive license to use one copy of the enclosed software program(s) (collectively, the "Software," solely for your own personal or business purposes on a single computer (whether a standard computer or a workstation component of a multi-user network). The Software is in use on a computer when it is loaded into temporary memory (RAM) or installed into permanent memory (hard disk, CD-ROM, or other storage device). WPI reserves all rights not expressly granted herein.

2. Ownership. WPI is the owner of all right, title, and interest, including copyright, in and to the compilation of the Software recorded on the physical packet included with this Book "Software Media". Copyright to the individual programs recorded on the Software Media is owned by the author or other authorized copyright owner of each program. Ownership of the Software and all proprietary rights relating thereto remain with WPI and its licensers.

3. Restrictions On Use and Transfer.

(a) You may only (i) make one copy of the Software for backup or archival purposes, or (ii) transfer the Software to a single hard disk, provided that you keep the original for backup or archival purposes. You may not (i) rent or lease the Software, (ii) copy or reproduce the Software through a LAN or other network system or through any computer subscriber system or bulletin-board system, or (iii) modify, adapt, or create derivative works based on the Software.

(b) You may not reverse engineer, decompile, or disassemble the Software. You may transfer the Software and user documentation on a permanent basis, provided that the transferee agrees to accept the terms and conditions of this Agreement and you retain no copies. If the Software is an update or has been updated, any transfer must include the most recent update and all prior versions.

4. Restrictions on Use of Individual Programs. You must follow the individual requirements and restrictions detailed for each individual program in the About the CD-ROM appendix of this Book or on the Software Media. These limitations are also contained in the individual license agreements recorded on the Software Media. These limitations may include a requirement that after using the program for a specified period of time, the user must pay a registration fee or discontinue use. By opening the Software packet(s), you will be agreeing to abide by the licenses and restrictions for these individual programs that are detailed in the About the CD-ROM appendix and/or on the Software Media. None of the material on this Software Media or listed in this Book may ever be redistributed, in original or modified form, for commercial purposes.

5. Limited Warranty.

(a) WPI warrants that the Software and Software Media are free from defects in materials and workmanship under normal use for a period of sixty (60) days from the date of purchase of this Book. If WPI receives notification within the warranty period of defects in materials or workmanship, WPI will replace the defective Software Media.

(b) WPI AND THE AUTHOR(S) OF THE BOOK DISCLAIM ALL OTHER WARRANTIES, EXPRESS OR IMPLIED, INCLUDING WITHOUT LIMITATION IMPLIED WARRANTIES OF MERCHANTABILITY AND FITNESS FOR A PARTICULAR PURPOSE, WITH RESPECT TO THE SOFTWARE, THE PROGRAMS, THE SOURCE CODE CONTAINED THEREIN, AND/OR THE TECHNIQUES DESCRIBED IN THIS BOOK. WPI DOES NOT WARRANT THAT THE FUNCTIONS CONTAINED IN THE SOFTWARE WILL MEET YOUR REQUIREMENTS OR THAT THE OPERATION OF THE SOFTWARE WILL BE ERROR FREE.

(c) This limited warranty gives you specific legal rights, and you may have other rights that vary from jurisdiction to jurisdiction.

6. Remedies.

(a) WPI's entire liability and your exclusive remedy for defects in materials and workmanship shall be limited to replacement of the Software Media, which may be returned to WPI with a copy of your receipt at the following address: Software Media Fulfillment Department, Attn.: OCA: Oracle Application Server 10*g* Administration I Study Guide, Wiley Publishing, Inc., 10475 Crosspoint Blvd., Indianapolis, IN 46256, or call 1-800-762-2974. Please allow four to six weeks for delivery. This Limited Warranty is void if failure of the Software Media has resulted from accident, abuse, or misapplication. Any replacement Software Media will be warranted for the remainder of the original warranty period or thirty (30) days, whichever is longer.

(b) In no event shall WPI or the author be liable for any damages whatsoever (including without limitation damages for loss of business profits, business interruption, loss of business information, or any other pecuniary loss) arising from the use of or inability to use the Book or the Software, even if WPI has been advised of the possibility of such damages.

(c) Because some jurisdictions do not allow the exclusion or limitation of liability for consequential or incidental damages, the above limitation or exclusion may not apply to you.

7. U.S. Government Restricted Rights. Use, duplication, or disclosure of the Software for or on behalf of the United States of America, its agencies and/or instrumentalities "U.S. Government" is subject to restrictions as stated in paragraph (c)(1)(ii) of the Rights in Technical Data and Computer Software clause of DFARS 252.227-7013, or subparagraphs (c) (1) and (2) of the Commercial Computer Software - Restricted Rights clause at FAR 52.227-19, and in similar clauses in the NASA FAR supplement, as applicable.

8. General. This Agreement constitutes the entire understanding of the parties and revokes and supersedes all prior agreements, oral or written, between them and may not be modified or amended except in a writing signed by both parties hereto that specifically refers to this Agreement. This Agreement shall take precedence over any other documents that may be in conflict herewith. If any one or more provisions contained in this Agreement are held by any court or tribunal to be invalid, illegal, or otherwise unenforceable, each and every other provision shall remain in full force and effect.

The Absolute Best Oracle Application Server 10*g* Administrator Book/CD Package on the Market!

Get Ready for Oracle's Oracle Application Server 10g Administration I Exam with the most comprehensive and challenging sample tests anywhere!

The Sybex Test Engine features:

- All the review questions, as covered in each chapter of the book.
- Challenging questions representative of those you'll find on the real exam.
- Two full length bonus exams available only on the CD.
- An Assessment Test to narrow your focus to certain objective groups.

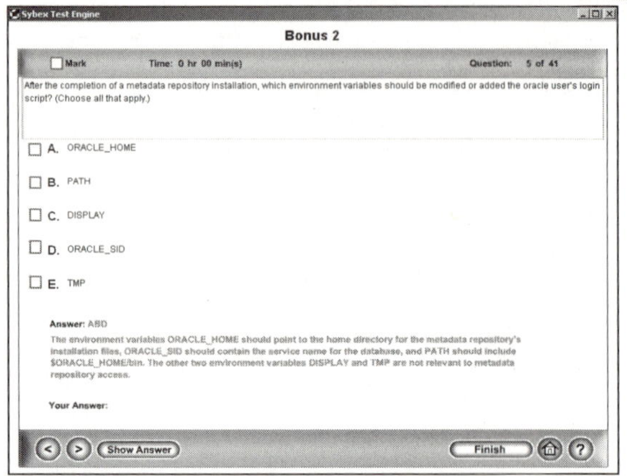

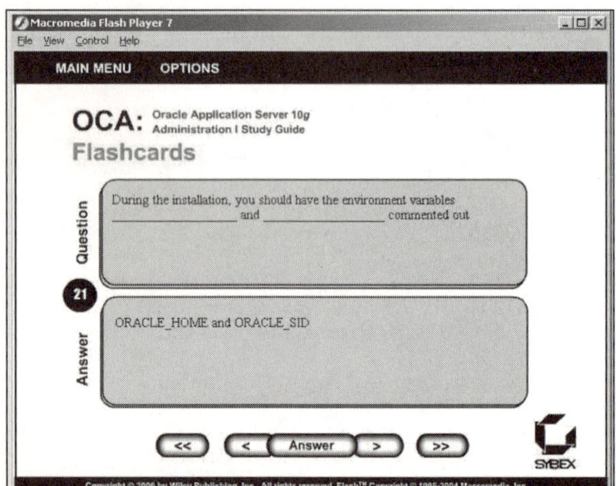

Use the Electronic Flashcards for PCs or Palm devices to jog your memory and prep last-minute for the exam!

- Reinforce your understanding of key concepts with these hardcore flashcard-style questions.
- Download the Flashcards to your Palm device and go on the road. Now you can study for the Oracle Application Server 10*g* Administration I exam any time, anywhere.

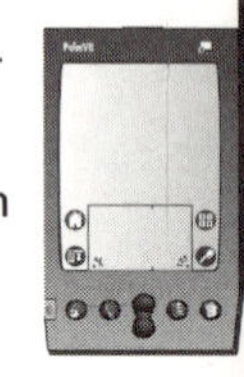

Search through the complete book in PDF!

- Access the entire *Oracle Application Server 10g Administration I Study Guide*, complete with figures and tables, in electronic format.
- Search the *Oracle Application Server 10g Administration I Study Guide* chapters to find information on any topic in seconds.

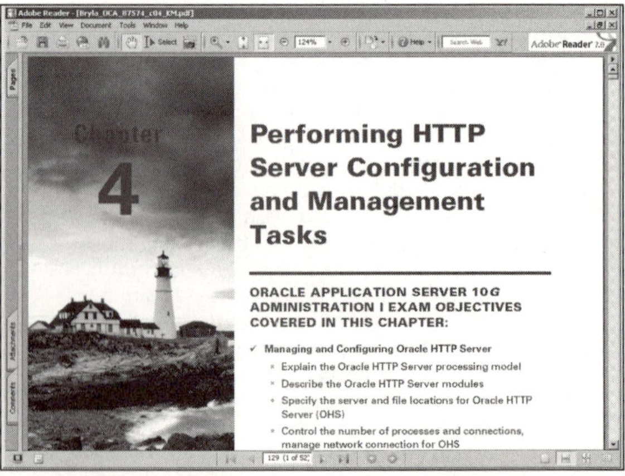